MAD
ABOUT TV

MW00611426

Also available from MAD Books:
MAD About the Movies

MAD ABOUT TV

By "The Usual Gang of Idiots"

Edited by Nick Meglin & John Ficarra

Introduction by "Weird Al" Yankovic

New York

MAD BOOKS

MAD BOOKS

William Gaines Founder

Jenette Kahn President & Editor-in-Chief

Paul Levitz Executive Vice President & Publisher

Nick Meglin & John Ficarra Editors (*MAD*)

Dorothy Crouch VP–Licensed Publishing & Associate Publisher

Sam Viviano Art Director

Charles Kochman Editor (Licensed Publishing)

Elisabeth Vincentelli Associate Editor

Trent Duffy Managing Editor

Dan Brown Director–Business Development & Mass Market Sales

Patrick Caldon VP–Finance & Operations

Alison Gill Executive Director–Manufacturing

Lillian Laserson VP & General Counsel

Compilation and new material (cover and introduction) © 1999 by E.C. Publications, Inc. All Rights Reserved.

MAD, boy's head device, and all related indicia are trademarks of E.C. Publications, Inc.

Published by MAD Books. An imprint of DC Comics, 1700 Broadway, New York, NY 10019. A division of Warner Bros. — A Time Warner Entertainment Company.

No part of this book may be reproduced in any form or by any electronic or mechanical means, including information storage and retrieval systems, without permission in writing from the publisher, except in the case of brief quotations embodied in critical articles and reviews.

The names and characters used in *MAD* fiction and semi-fiction are fictitious. A similarity without satiric purpose to a living person is a coincidence.

ISBN 1-56389-569-2

Printed in Canada

First edition
10 9 8 7 6 5 4 3 2 1

Visit *MAD* online at www.madmag.com

Though Alfred E. Neuman wasn't the first to say "A fool and his money are soon parted," here's your chance to prove the old adage right—subscribe to MAD! Simply call 1-800-4-MADMAG and mention code 9CZ97. Operators are standing by (the water cooler).

CONTENTS

MAD Magazine changed my life. Oh sure, I could have been "Normal Al." I could have gone through my pitiful existence on this planet completely oblivious to the joys of this time-honored satirical publication. But once I was exposed to *MAD*, there was no turning back. I had no choice but to look at the world in a new way. I learned to be cynical about the media … distrusting of authority figures … and skeptical of just about everything. Yes, *MAD* Magazine made me into a bitter, paranoid freak. Thanks, guys. Thanks a lot.

My first *MAD* experience? Why, I remember that day as if it were just thirty years ago—which, I'm horrified to say, it actually *was*. I was just an impressionable young lad, and a friend of mine with whom I was taking accordion lessons lent me the first copy of *MAD* Magazine that I had ever seen (#130, October 1969). I was instantly hooked. I immediately got a subscription so that I wouldn't have to camp out by the newsstand waiting for the next issue to arrive. I coerced my poor parents into driving me all around town so that I could scour funky old used magazine stores for back issues. I made a total nuisance of myself asking relatives and neighbors for any old *MAD*s that they might happen to have lying around in their attics. I became completely and utterly obsessed.

By the time I was twelve years old, I had already decided what I wanted to do with my life. I proudly walked into the office of my school guidance counselor and told him that I wanted to be a writer for *MAD* Magazine. He was less than encouraging. "Sure, that's fine *now*," he told me, "But what about when you're an adult? That's no job for a *grown man*! Think about your *future*!" He went on to suggest that perhaps I should be an architect, since I was pretty good in math and rather handy with a T square. Not wanting to upset him or cause a scene, I quickly agreed and signed up for four years of architecture school.

The most important thing I learned in college was that I absolutely, positively, did *not* want to be an architect. My classmates wanted to design and build things—I just wanted to *make fun of them*. Apparently, *MAD* had left a permanent scar on my psyche.

Anyway, to make a long, pointless story slightly less long and pointless, I graduated, paid my dues, got a record deal, sold a gazillion albums, and now I'm finally at the pinnacle of my career—writing an introduction to *MAD*'s latest collection of recycled garbage … let's see, what is it? Oh yes, *MAD About TV*.

And believe me, I should know about recycled garbage. My old record label was quite fond of trying to make a quick buck by re-releasing my old songs on a series of cheesy compilation albums. One of these was a collection of my TV-themed songs called, ironically enough, *The TV Album*. The cover artist? *MAD* Magazine's own Jack Davis. Coincidence? I think not.

But I digress.

MAD supplied me with my first real jolt of irreverent humor—but in a bizarre way, it was also quite educational. I'm convinced that I learned more about American history and politics from reading back issues of *MAD* than I ever learned in school. And at the same time I got to revel in the pop culture of the 1950s, '60s, and '70s, learning about movies that I wasn't old enough to see and TV shows that were canceled before I was born.

Shortly after my *MAD*-mania had reached its peak, I discovered the Doctor Demento Radio Show and was exposed for the first time to the likes of Spike Jones, Allan Sherman, Stan

Freberg, and Tom Lehrer. To me, their music was the audio equivalent of *MAD* Magazine, and it was here that I found my true calling.

From my early adolescence up through this very moment, *MAD* has always been a big part of my life. In high school I competed in a number of statewide speech tournaments, acting out Dick DeBartolo's TV spoof "The Straights of San Francisco" and scenes from the hilarious off-Broadway musical *The MAD Show*. In 1989 I did a feature film called *UHF*, in which I played a guy who has to come up with bizarre programming ideas for a tiny TV station (one of those shows was "Uncle Nutzy's Playhouse," an obvious rip-off of — uh, I mean *homage to* one of my favorite *MAD* pieces). And Alfred E. Neuman's glorious countenance has graced everything from my first album cover to the tattooed arm of one of the cheerleaders in my video for "Smells Like Nirvana." By the way, have I mentioned that my first name is short for *Alfred*? Coincidence? I think not.

MAD's impact on our current cultural landscape, and the world of television comedy in particular, is unmistakable. This is no doubt because the last few generations of TV writers have been profoundly influenced by the *MAD* zeitgeist. I know that I personally owe a huge debt of gratitude to *MAD*. The magazine prepared me for my adult life (and certainly my current livelihood) more than four years of college ever did. And I'm proud to carry on in the great *MAD* tradition by warping a whole new generation of impressionable young minds in my own twisted way.

Let's see … they told me I had to write at least 1000 words … let me count here … 938… 939… hmm …

Perhaps I should tell you a little about the pancreas.

The pancreas is a long, thin organ that has both endocrine and digestive functions. It is nestled within the curve of the duodenum and stretches transversely across the posterior abdomen behind the stomach, in front of the spine and aorta, terminating near the spleen under the left diaphragm.

Okay, almost there … 996 … 997 … 998 … and … *done.*

—"Weird Al" Yankovic

Drew Friedman

AIDE-DE-"CAMP" DEPT.

Everybody's going wild over that new TV show featuring "The Caped Crusader" and his teenage side-kick. But has anyone ever wondered what it would really be like as the side-kick of a "Caped Crusader"? Would a typical red-blooded teenage boy really be happy dressing in some far-out costume and spending all of his free time chasing crooks? Or would he much prefer dressing in chinos and go-go boots and spending all of his free time chasing chicks? We at MAD think the latter! In fact, we're ready to prove it! Let's take a MAD look at "Boy Wonderful" as he is slowly being driven

BATS-MAN

ARTIST: MORT DRUCKER WRITER: LOU SILVERSTONE

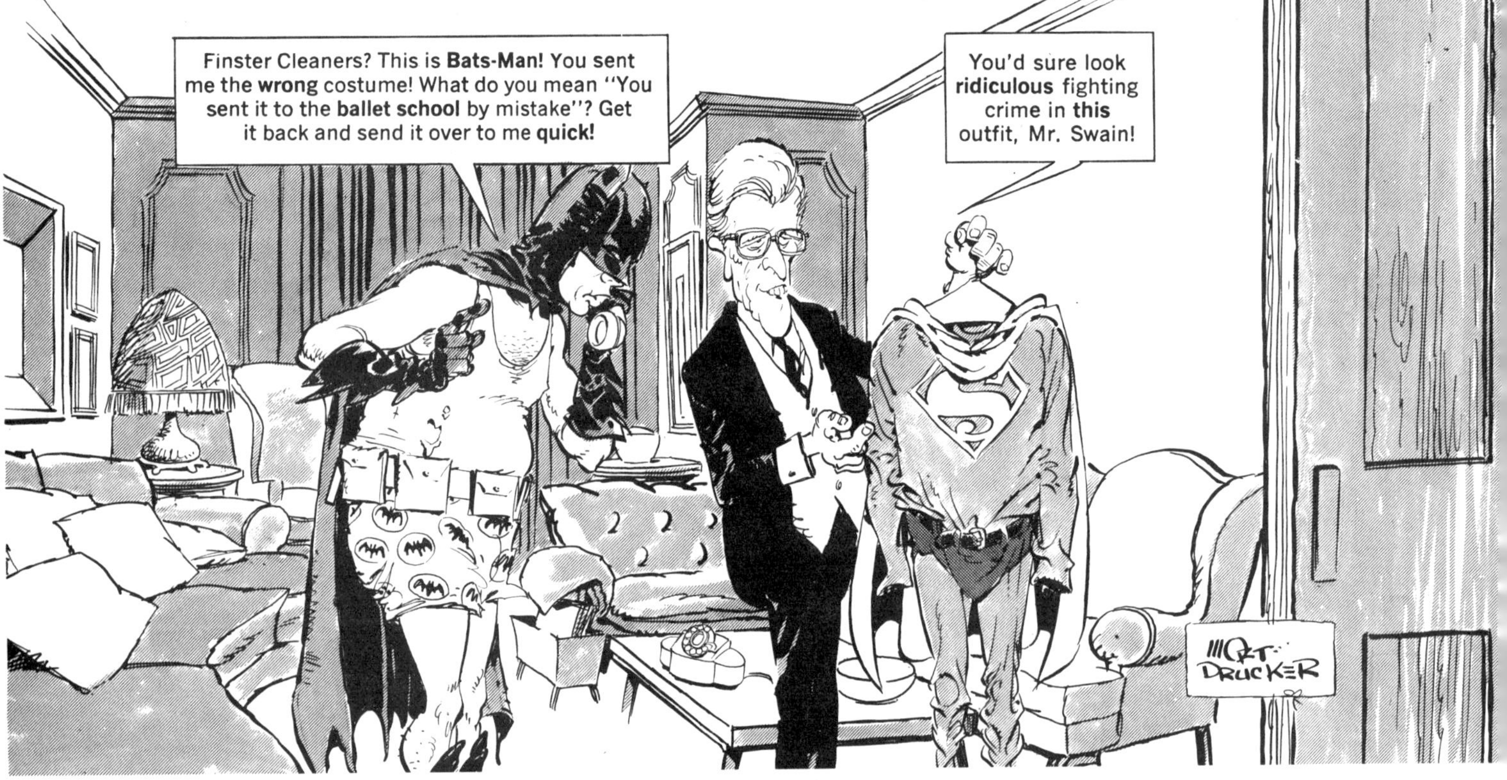
Finster Cleaners? This is **Bats-Man!** You sent me the **wrong** costume! What do you mean "You sent it to the **ballet school** by mistake"? Get it back and send it over to me **quick!**
You'd sure look **ridiculous** fighting crime in **this** outfit, Mr. Swain!
MORT DRUCKER

Meanwhile, at Franklin D. Wilson High School . . .

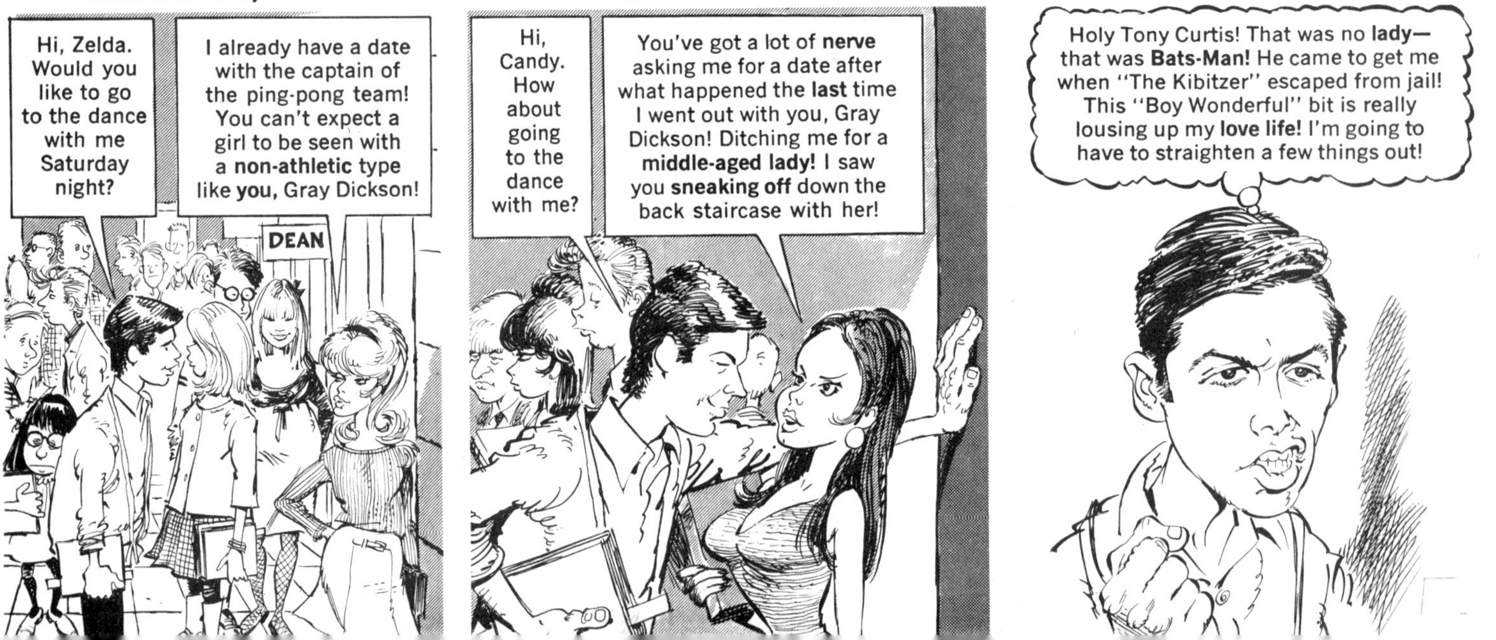
Hi, Zelda. Would you like to go to the dance with me Saturday night?
I already have a date with the captain of the ping-pong team! You can't expect a girl to be seen with a **non-athletic** type like **you**, Gray Dickson!
DEAN
Hi, Candy. How about going to the dance with me?
You've got a lot of **nerve** asking me for a date after what happened the **last** time I went out with you, Gray Dickson! Ditching me for a **middle-aged lady!** I saw you **sneaking off** down the back staircase with her!
Holy Tony Curtis! That was no **lady**—that was **Bats-Man!** He came to get me when "The Kibitzer" escaped from jail! This "Boy Wonderful" bit is really lousing up my **love life!** I'm going to have to straighten a few things out!

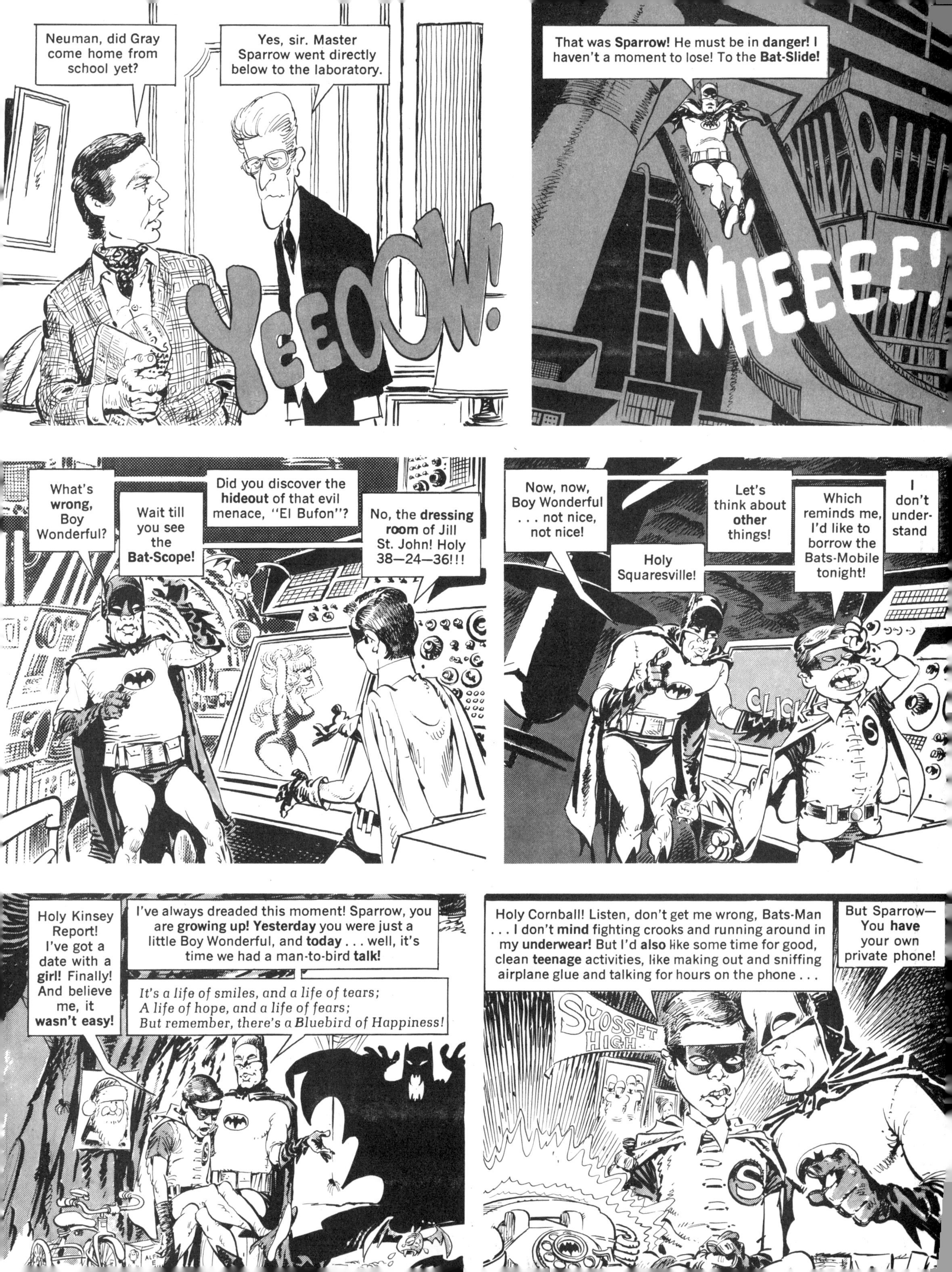
Neuman, did Gray come home from school yet?
Yes, sir. Master Sparrow went directly below to the laboratory.
YEEOOW!
That was Sparrow! He must be in danger! I haven't a moment to lose! To the Bat-Slide!
WHEEEE!
What's wrong, Boy Wonderful?
Wait till you see the Bat-Scope!
Did you discover the hideout of that evil menace, "El Bufon"?
No, the dressing room of Jill St. John! Holy 38—24—36!!!
Now, now, Boy Wonderful . . . not nice, not nice!
Holy Squaresville!
Let's think about other things!
Which reminds me, I'd like to borrow the Bats-Mobile tonight!
I don't under-stand
CLICK
Holy Kinsey Report! I've got a date with a girl! Finally! And believe me, it wasn't easy!
I've always dreaded this moment! Sparrow, you are growing up! Yesterday you were just a little Boy Wonderful, and today . . . well, it's time we had a man-to-bird talk!
It's a life of smiles, and a life of tears;
A life of hope, and a life of fears;
But remember, there's a Bluebird of Happiness!
Holy Cornball! Listen, don't get me wrong, Bats-Man . . . I don't mind fighting crooks and running around in my underwear! But I'd also like some time for good, clean teenage activities, like making out and sniffing airplane glue and talking for hours on the phone . . .
But Sparrow— You have your own private phone!
SYOSSET HIGH

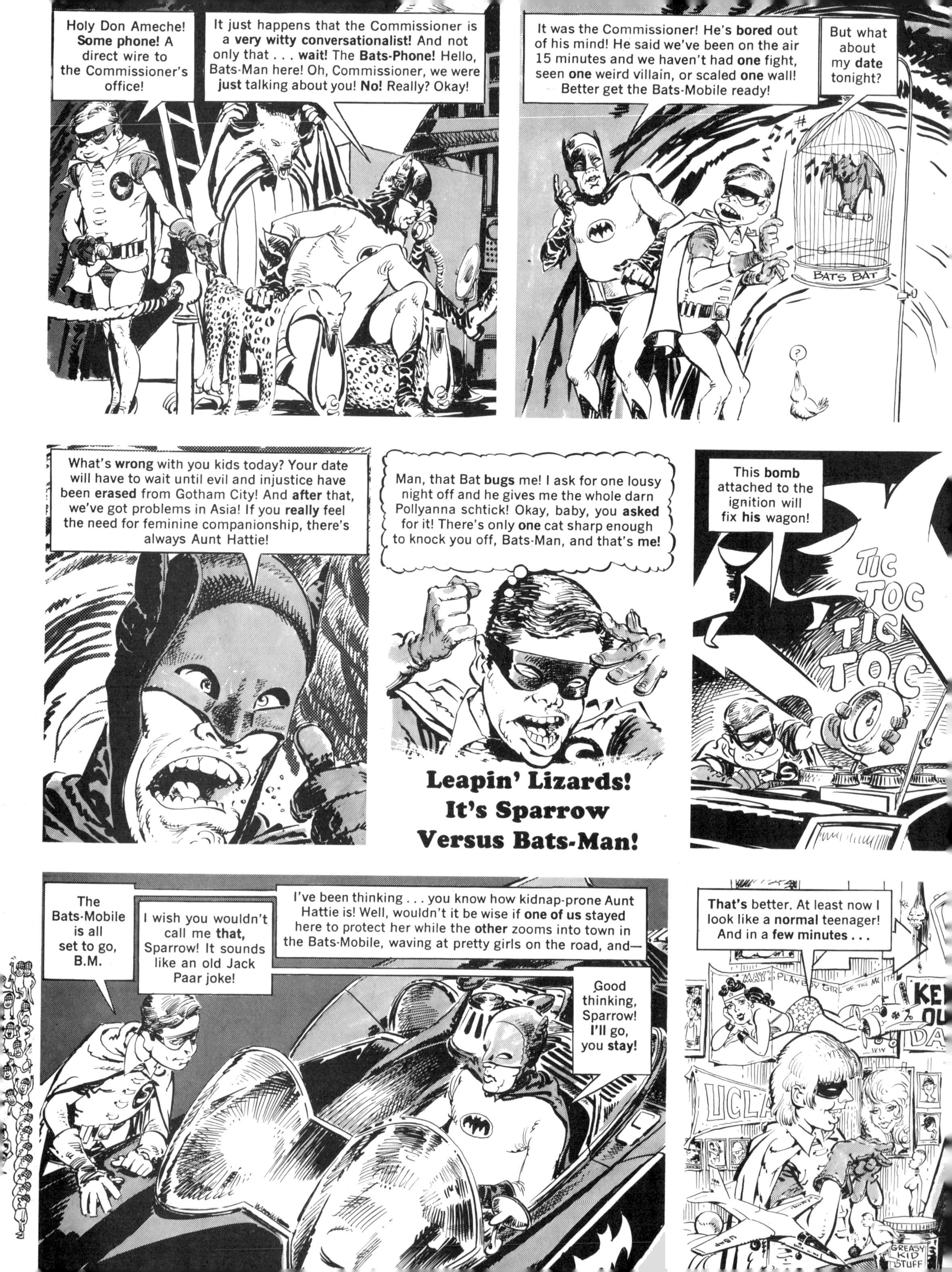
Holy Don Ameche! Some phone! A direct wire to the Commissioner's office!
It just happens that the Commissioner is a very witty conversationalist! And not only that . . . wait! The Bats-Phone! Hello, Bats-Man here! Oh, Commissioner, we were just talking about you! No! Really? Okay!
It was the Commissioner! He's bored out of his mind! He said we've been on the air 15 minutes and we haven't had one fight, seen one weird villain, or scaled one wall! Better get the Bats-Mobile ready!
But what about my date tonight?
BATS BAT
What's wrong with you kids today? Your date will have to wait until evil and injustice have been erased from Gotham City! And after that, we've got problems in Asia! If you really feel the need for feminine companionship, there's always Aunt Hattie!
Man, that Bat bugs me! I ask for one lousy night off and he gives me the whole darn Pollyanna schtick! Okay, baby, you asked for it! There's only one cat sharp enough to knock you off, Bats-Man, and that's me!
Leapin' Lizards! It's Sparrow Versus Bats-Man!
This bomb attached to the ignition will fix his wagon!
TIC TOC TIC TOC
The Bats-Mobile is all set to go, B.M.
I wish you wouldn't call me that, Sparrow! It sounds like an old Jack Paar joke!
I've been thinking . . . you know how kidnap-prone Aunt Hattie is! Well, wouldn't it be wise if one of us stayed here to protect her while the other zooms into town in the Bats-Mobile, waving at pretty girls on the road, and—
Good thinking, Sparrow! I'll go, you stay!
That's better. At least now I look like a normal teenager! And in a few minutes . . .
UCLA
GREASY KID STUFF

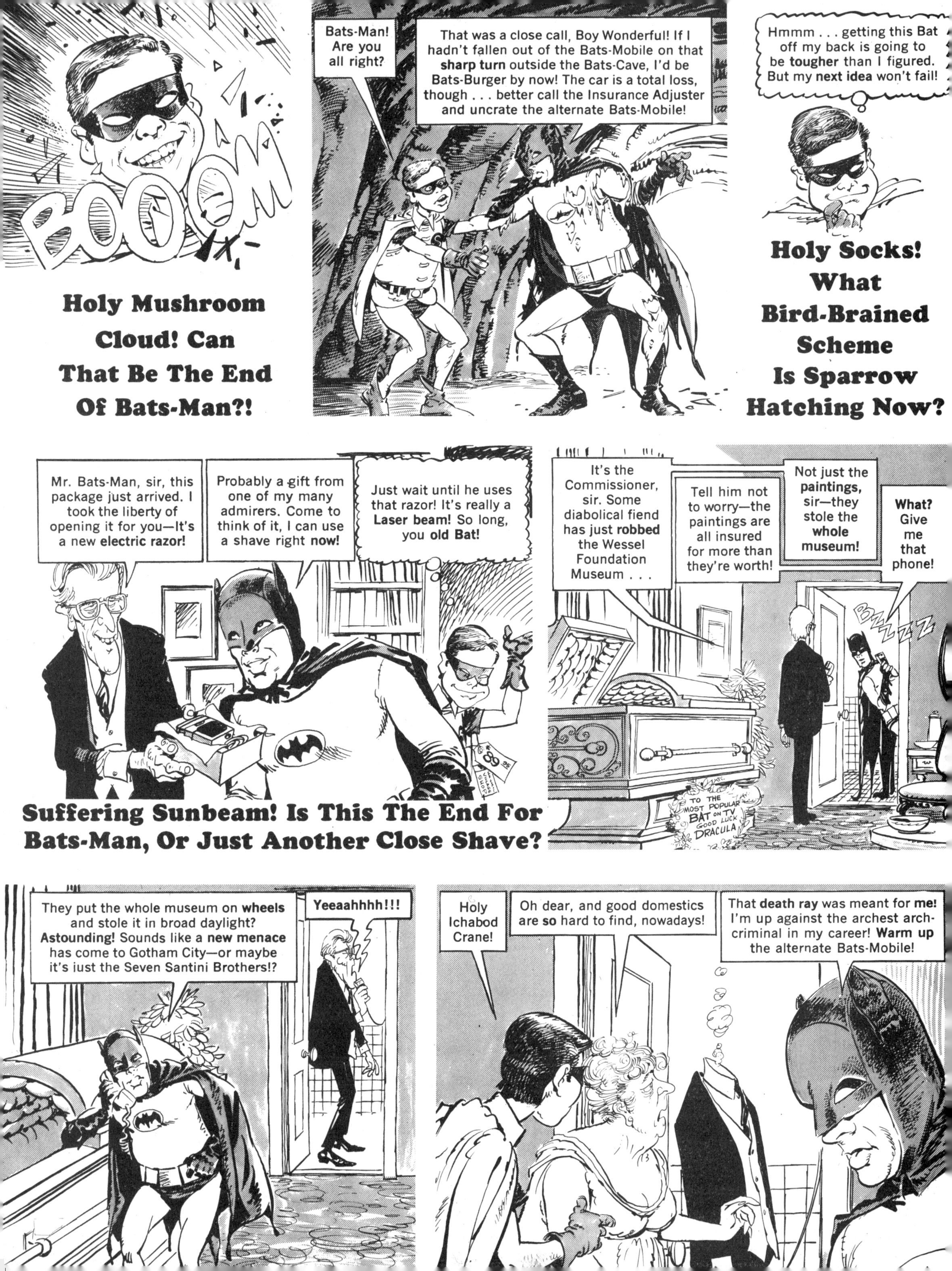

BOOOM
Holy Mushroom Cloud! Can That Be The End Of Bats-Man?!
Bats-Man! Are you all right?
That was a close call, Boy Wonderful! If I hadn't fallen out of the Bats-Mobile on that **sharp turn** outside the Bats-Cave, I'd be Bats-Burger by now! The car is a total loss, though . . . better call the Insurance Adjuster and uncrate the alternate Bats-Mobile!
Hmmm . . . getting this Bat off my back is going to be **tougher** than I figured. But my **next idea** won't fail!
Holy Socks! What Bird-Brained Scheme Is Sparrow Hatching Now?
Mr. Bats-Man, sir, this package just arrived. I took the liberty of opening it for you—It's a new **electric razor!**
Probably a gift from one of my many admirers. Come to think of it, I can use a shave right **now!**
Just wait until he uses that razor! It's really a **Laser beam!** So long, you **old Bat!**
Suffering Sunbeam! Is This The End For Bats-Man, Or Just Another Close Shave?
It's the Commissioner, sir. Some diabolical fiend has just **robbed** the Wessel Foundation Museum . . .
Tell him not to worry—the paintings are all insured for more than they're worth!
Not just the **paintings,** sir—they stole the **whole museum!**
What? Give me that phone!
BZZZZ
TO THE MOST POPULAR BAT ON TV GOOD LUCK DRACULA
They put the whole museum on **wheels** and stole it in broad daylight? **Astounding!** Sounds like a **new menace** has come to Gotham City—or maybe it's just the Seven Santini Brothers!?
Yeeaahhhh!!!
Holy Ichabod Crane!
Oh dear, and good domestics are **so** hard to find, nowadays!
That **death ray** was meant for **me!** I'm up against the archest arch-criminal in my career! **Warm up** the alternate Bats-Mobile!

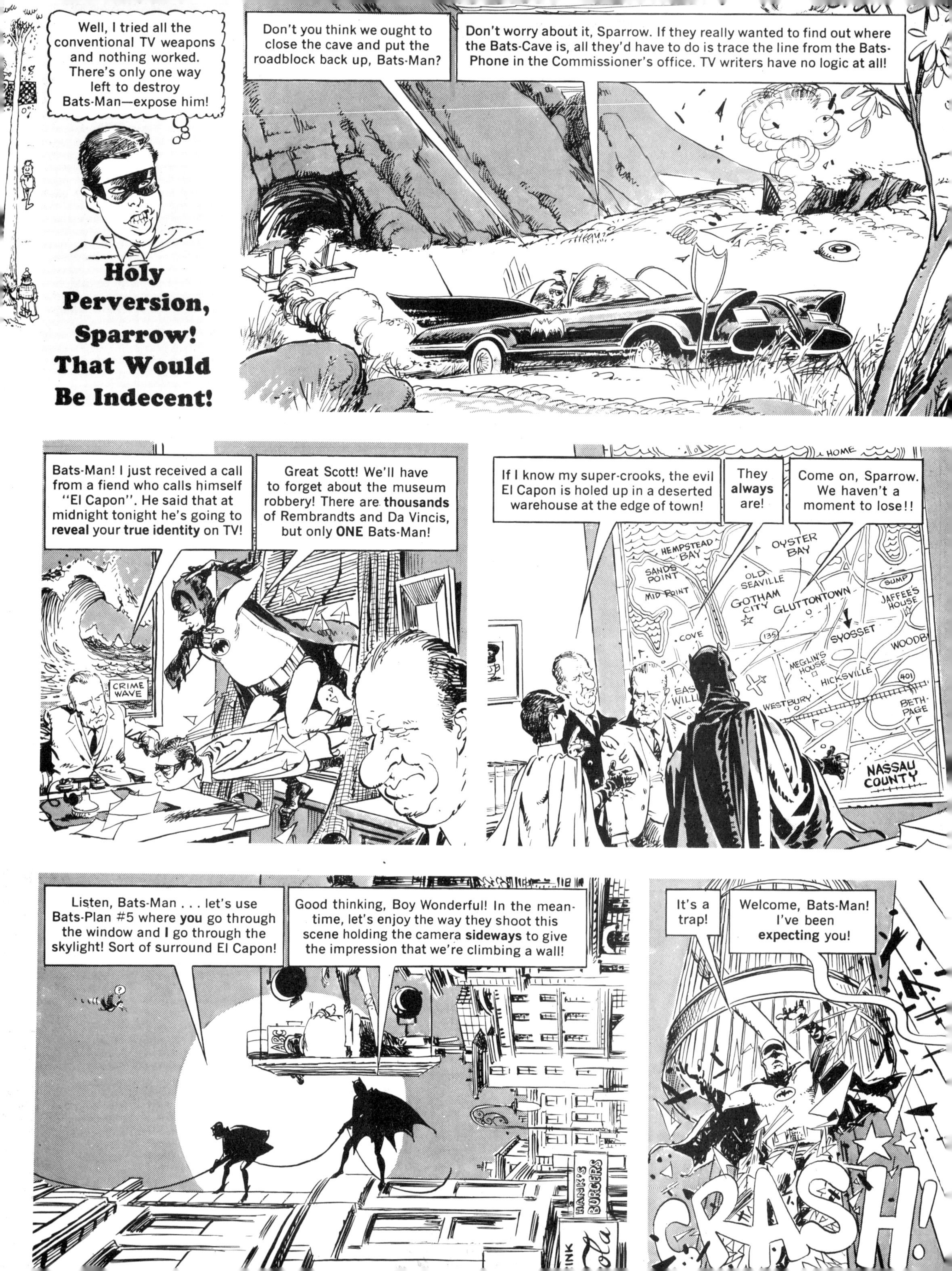
Well, I tried all the conventional TV weapons and nothing worked. There's only one way left to destroy Bats-Man—expose him!
Holy Perversion, Sparrow! That Would Be Indecent!
Don't you think we ought to close the cave and put the roadblock back up, Bats-Man?
Don't worry about it, Sparrow. If they really wanted to find out where the Bats-Cave is, all they'd have to do is trace the line from the Bats-Phone in the Commissioner's office. TV writers have no logic at all!
Bats-Man! I just received a call from a fiend who calls himself "El Capon". He said that at midnight tonight he's going to **reveal** your **true identity** on TV!
Great Scott! We'll have to forget about the museum robbery! There are **thousands** of Rembrandts and Da Vincis, but only **ONE** Bats-Man!
CRIME WAVE
If I know my super-crooks, the evil El Capon is holed up in a deserted warehouse at the edge of town!
They **always** are!
Come on, Sparrow. We haven't a moment to lose!!
HOME
HEMPSTEAD BAY
OYSTER BAY
SANDS POINT
MID POINT
OLD SEAVILLE
GOTHAM CITY
GLUTTONTOWN
SUMP
JAFFEE'S HOUSE
COVE
135
SYOSSET
MEGLIN'S HOUSE
HICKSVILLE
401
WESTBURY
BETH-PAGE
NASSAU COUNTY
Listen, Bats-Man . . . let's use Bats-Plan #5 where **you** go through the window and **I** go through the skylight! Sort of surround El Capon!
Good thinking, Boy Wonderful! In the meantime, let's enjoy the way they shoot this scene holding the camera **sideways** to give the impression that we're climbing a wall!
?
ABC
HANK'S BURGERS
It's a trap!
Welcome, Bats-Man! I've been **expecting** you!
CRASH!

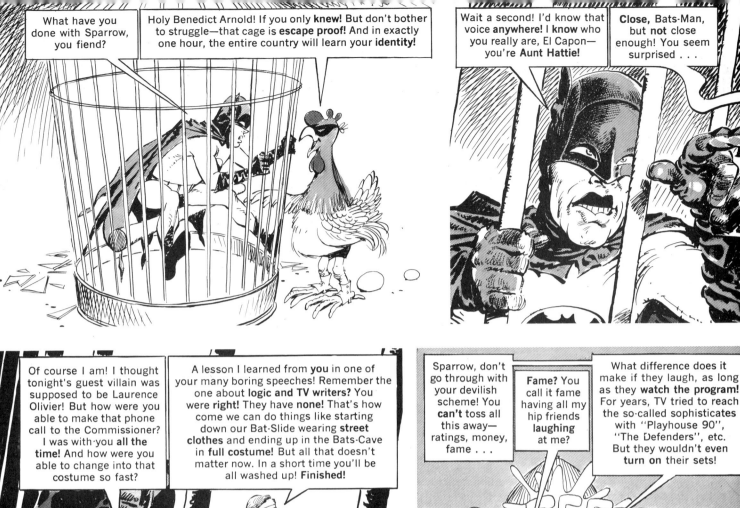

What have you done with Sparrow, you fiend?
Holy Benedict Arnold! If you only **knew!** But don't bother to struggle—that cage is **escape proof!** And in exactly one hour, the entire country will learn your **identity!**
Wait a second! I'd know that voice **anywhere!** I **know** who you really are, El Capon—you're **Aunt Hattie!**
Close, Bats-Man, but **not** close enough! You seem surprised . . .
Of course I am! I thought tonight's guest villain was supposed to be Laurence Olivier! But how were you able to make that phone call to the Commissioner? I was with you **all the time!** And how were you able to change into that costume so fast?
A lesson I learned from **you** in one of your many boring speeches! Remember the one about **logic and TV writers?** You were **right!** They have **none!** That's how come we can do things like starting down our Bat-Slide wearing **street clothes** and ending up in the Bats-Cave in **full costume!** But all that doesn't matter now. In a short time you'll be all washed up! **Finished!**
Sparrow, don't go through with your devilish scheme! You **can't** toss all this away—ratings, money, fame . . .
Fame? You call it fame having all my hip friends **laughing** at me?
What difference **does it** make if they laugh, as long as they **watch the program!** For years, TV tried to reach the so-called **sophisticates** with "Playhouse 90", "The Defenders", etc. But they wouldn't **even turn on** their sets!
P-FFFFFT!!!...
Then along came **"Bats-Man"** and the industry made a revolutionary **discovery.** Give the **"in"** group **garbage**—make the show **bad** enough and they'll call it **"camp"** and stay **glued** to their sets!
Holy Nielsen! You mean the swingers are really squarer than the squares?
Exactly! So let them laugh! Because we **laugh** too—all the way to the **bank!** And about your little **problems,** Boy Wonderful . . . remember, I promised you a **Bluebird of Happiness?** Now that you're . . . shall we say "old enough" . . . you can start sharing the show's **fringe benefits!** Like, why do you think we have these gorgeous-doll guest stars?
I dig, Bats-Man, I dig! Yeah! Yeah! YEAH!
DON'T WALK FLY
BAT vs MAN NOW PLAYING
BAT COSTUMS AND TUXEDOS
BAT CAVE
כשר BAT MEAT
BAT WAY
BAT BAR AND GRILL
BAT BLOOD BANK
SAM FLAX BAT SUPPLIES
STUFFED BATS
CHEAP
BAT TIRES
BAT CUT $2.25
BAT TOYS
SPARROW SHIRTS

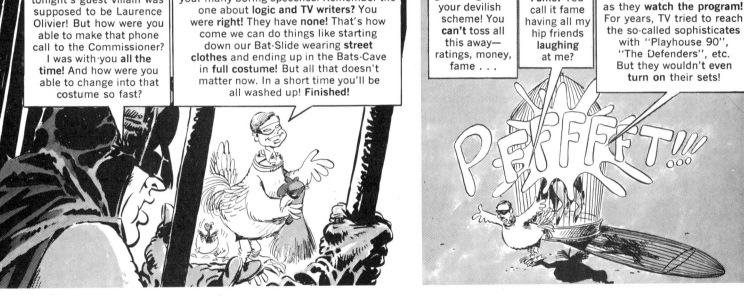

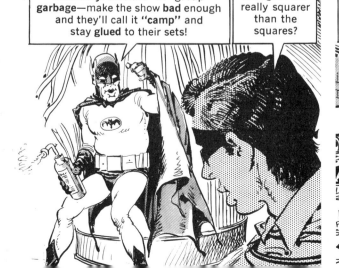

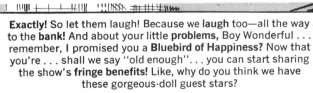

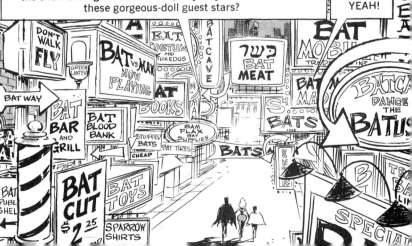

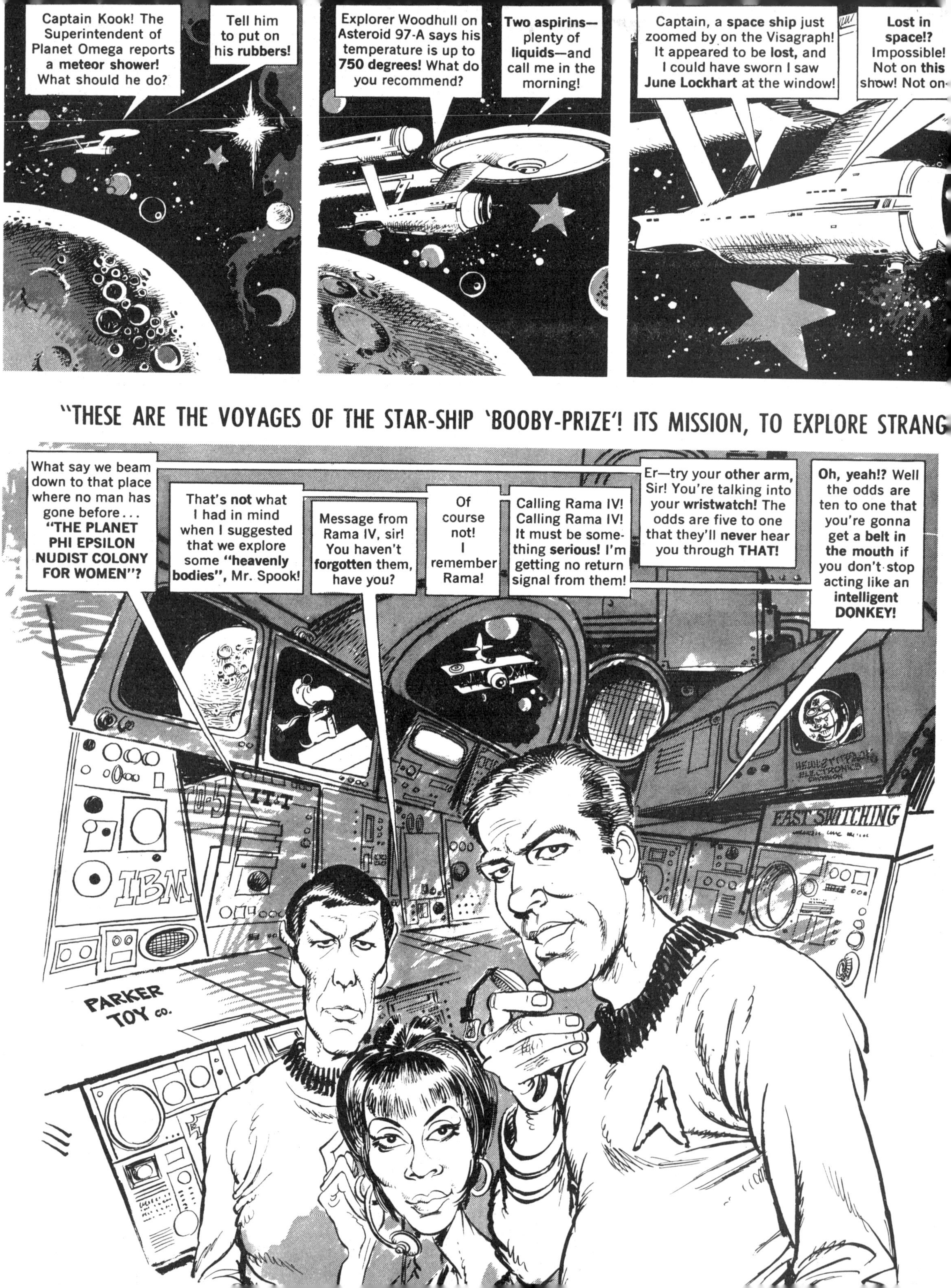

Captain Kook! The Superintendent of Planet Omega reports a **meteor shower!** What should he do?
Tell him to put on his **rubbers!**
Explorer Woodhull on Asteroid 97-A says his temperature is up to **750 degrees!** What do you recommend?
Two aspirins—plenty of **liquids**—and call me in the morning!
Captain, a **space ship** just zoomed by on the Visagraph! It appeared to be **lost,** and I could have sworn I saw **June Lockhart** at the window!
Lost in space!? Impossible! Not on **this** show! Not on-
"THESE ARE THE VOYAGES OF THE STAR-SHIP 'BOOBY-PRIZE'! ITS MISSION, TO EXPLORE STRANG
What say we beam down to that place where no man has gone before . . . **"THE PLANET PHI EPSILON NUDIST COLONY FOR WOMEN"?**
That's **not** what I had in mind when I suggested that we explore some **"heavenly bodies",** Mr. Spook!
Message from Rama IV, sir! You haven't **forgotten** them, have you?
Of course not! I remember Rama!
Calling Rama IV! Calling Rama IV! It must be something **serious!** I'm getting no return signal from them!
Er—try your **other arm,** Sir! You're talking into your **wristwatch!** The odds are five to one that they'll **never** hear you through **THAT!**
Oh, yeah!? Well the odds are ten to one that you're gonna get a **belt in the mouth** if you don't stop acting like an **intelligent DONKEY!**
ITT
IBM
PARKER TOY co.
FAST SWITCHING

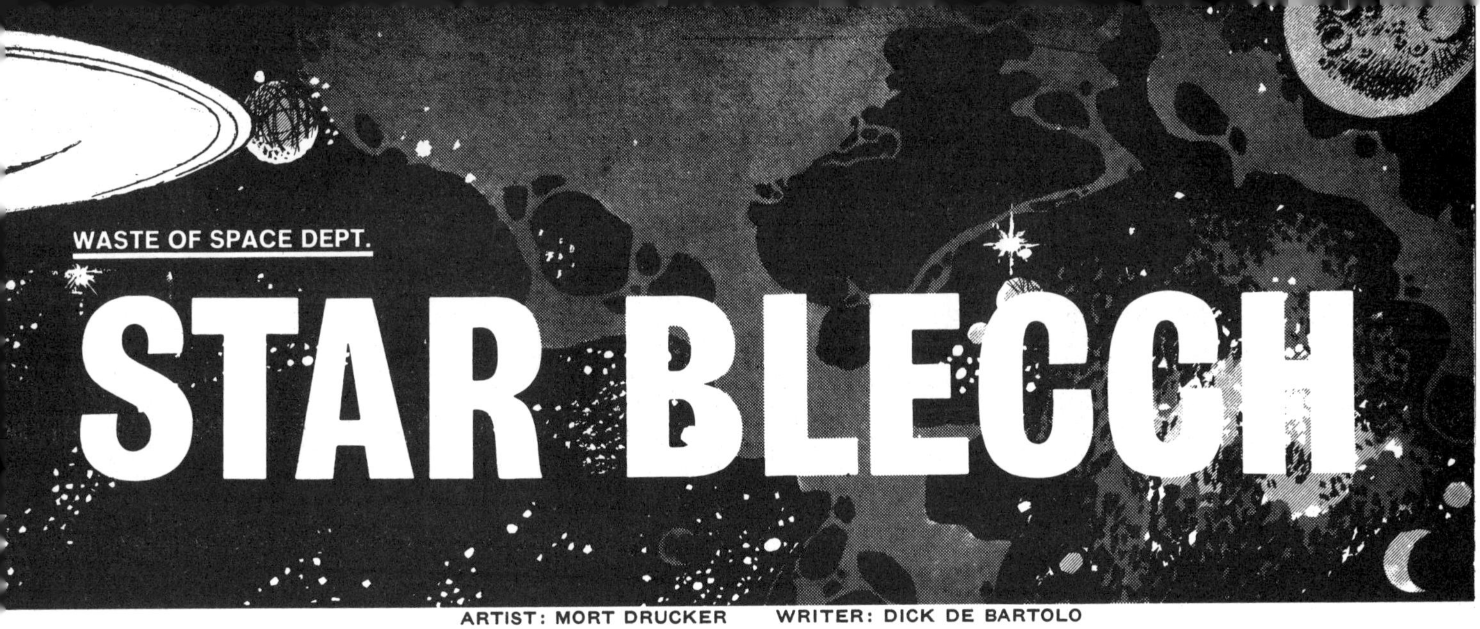
WASTE OF SPACE DEPT.
STAR BLECCH

ARTIST: MORT DRUCKER WRITER: DICK DE BARTOLO

EW WORLDS, TO SEEK OUT NEW LIFE, AND TO BOLDLY GO WHERE NO MAN HAS EVER GONE BEFORE!"

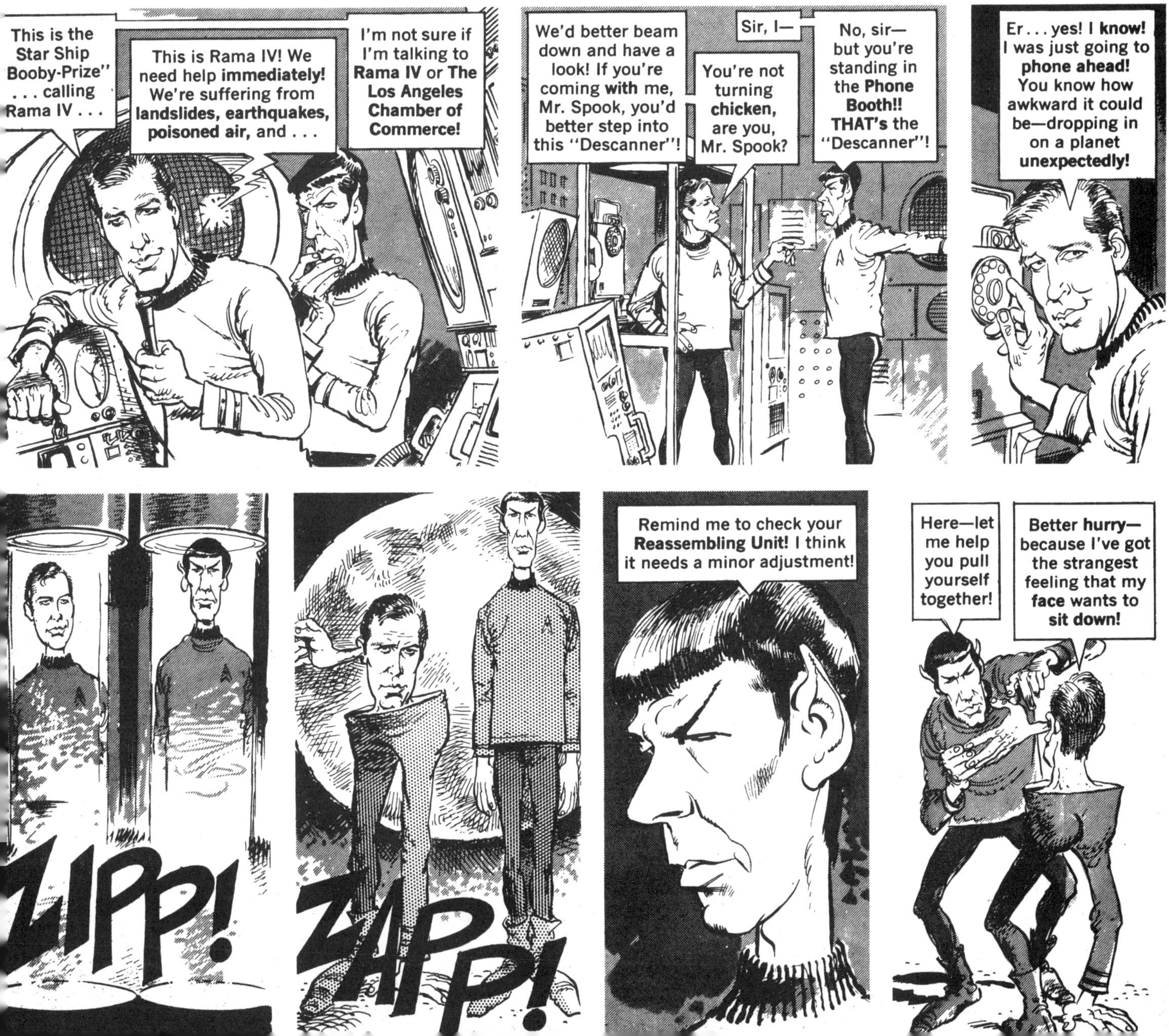
This is the Star Ship "Booby-Prize" . . . calling Rama IV . . .
This is Rama IV! We need help **immediately!** We're suffering from **landslides, earthquakes, poisoned air,** and . . .
I'm not sure if I'm talking to **Rama IV** or **The Los Angeles Chamber of Commerce!**
We'd better beam down and have a look! If you're coming **with** me, Mr. Spook, you'd better step into this "Descanner"!
Sir, I—
You're not turning **chicken,** are you, Mr. Spook?
No, sir—but you're standing in the **Phone Booth!! THAT's** the "Descanner"!
Er . . . yes! I **know!** I was just going to **phone ahead!** You know how awkward it could be—dropping in on a planet **unexpectedly!**
ZIPP!
ZAPP!
Remind me to check your **Reassembling Unit!** I think it needs a minor adjustment!
Here—let me help you pull yourself together!
Better **hurry**—because I've got the strangest feeling that my **face** wants to **sit down!**

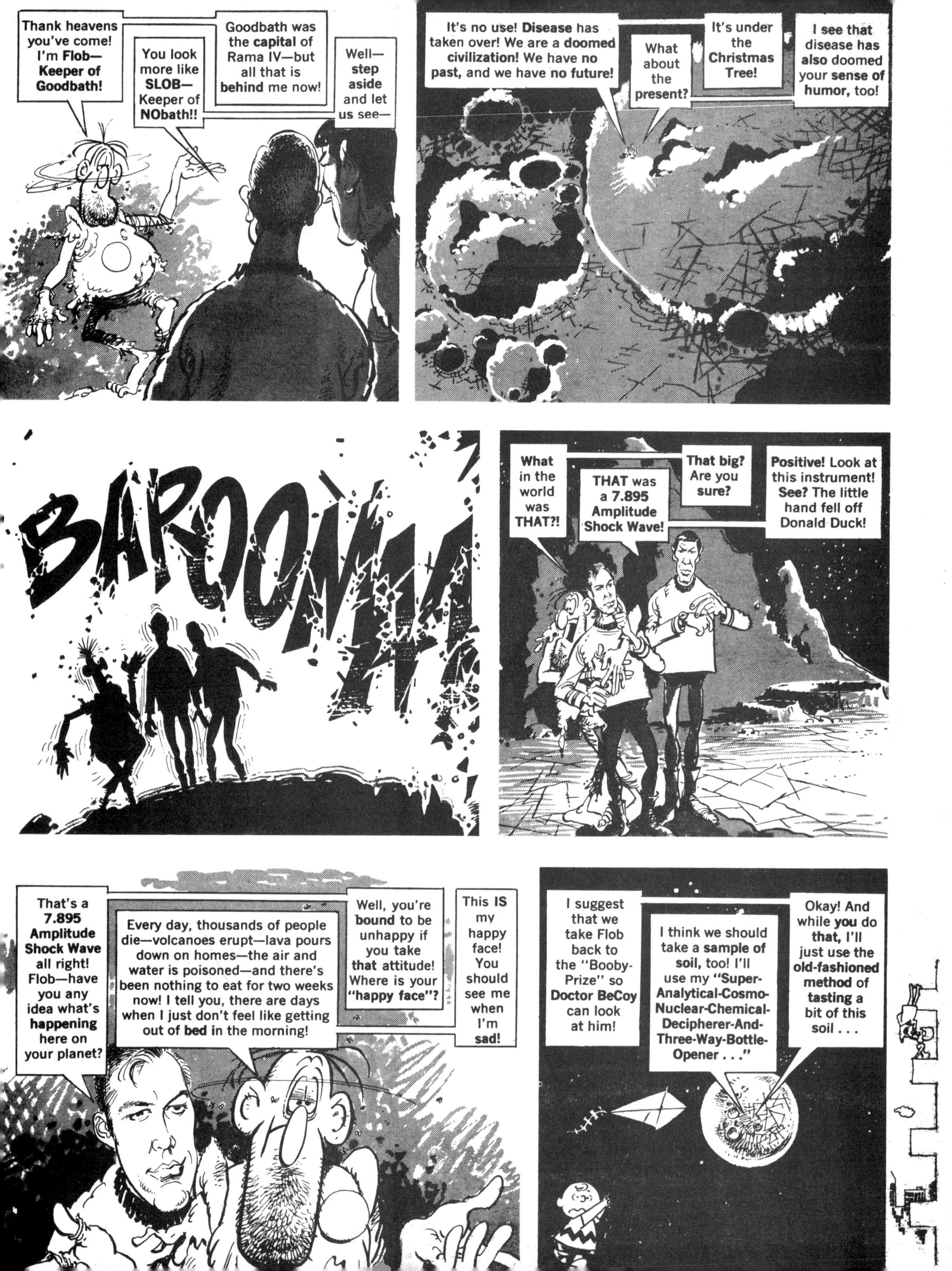
Thank heavens you've come! I'm Flob—Keeper of Goodbath!
You look more like SLOB—Keeper of NObath!!
Goodbath was the capital of Rama IV—but all that is behind me now!
Well—step aside and let us see—
It's no use! Disease has taken over! We are a doomed civilization! We have no past, and we have no future!
What about the present?
It's under the Christmas Tree!
I see that disease has also doomed your sense of humor, too!
BAROOMM
What in the world was THAT?!
THAT was a 7.895 Amplitude Shock Wave!
That big? Are you sure?
Positive! Look at this instrument! See? The little hand fell off Donald Duck!
That's a 7.895 Amplitude Shock Wave all right! Flob—have you any idea what's happening here on your planet?
Every day, thousands of people die—volcanoes erupt—lava pours down on homes—the air and water is poisoned—and there's been nothing to eat for two weeks now! I tell you, there are days when I just don't feel like getting out of bed in the morning!
Well, you're bound to be unhappy if you take that attitude! Where is your "happy face"?
This IS my happy face! You should see me when I'm sad!
I suggest that we take Flob back to the "Booby-Prize" so Doctor BeCoy can look at him!
I think we should take a sample of soil, too! I'll use my "Super-Analytical-Cosmo-Nuclear-Chemical-Decipherer-And-Three-Way-Bottle-Opener . . ."
Okay! And while you do that, I'll just use the old-fashioned method of tasting a bit of this soil . . .

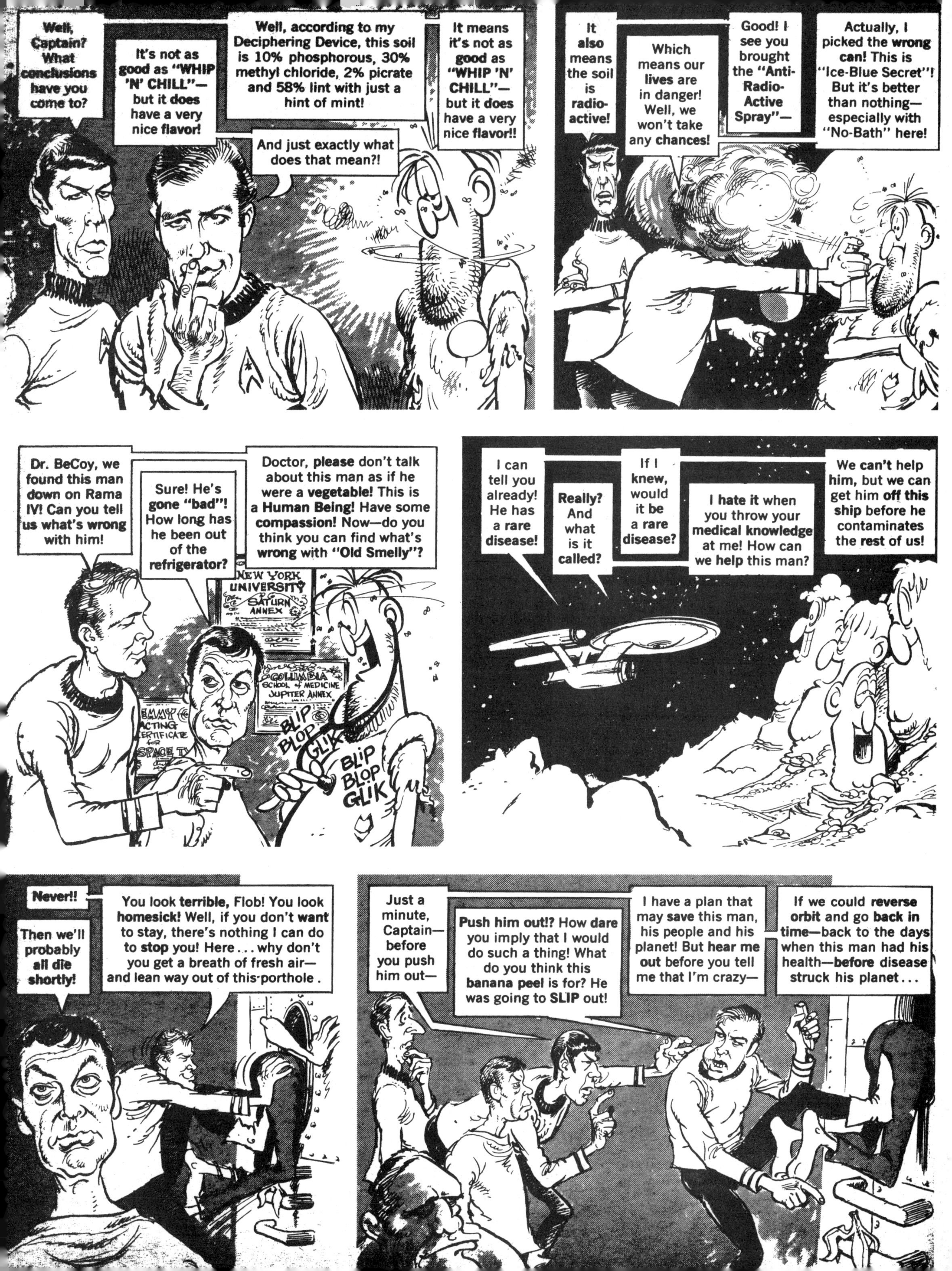
Well, Captain? What conclusions have you come to?
It's not as good as "WHIP 'N' CHILL"—but it does have a very nice flavor!
Well, according to my Deciphering Device, this soil is 10% phosphorous, 30% methyl chloride, 2% picrate and 58% lint with just a hint of mint!
And just exactly what does that mean?!
It means it's not as good as "WHIP 'N' CHILL"—but it does have a very nice flavor!!
It also means the soil is radio-active!
Which means our lives are in danger! Well, we won't take any chances!
Good! I see you brought the "Anti-Radio-Active Spray"—
Actually, I picked the wrong can! This is "Ice-Blue Secret"! But it's better than nothing—especially with "No-Bath" here!
Dr. BeCoy, we found this man down on Rama IV! Can you tell us what's wrong with him!
Sure! He's gone "bad"! How long has he been out of the refrigerator?
Doctor, please don't talk about this man as if he were a vegetable! This is a Human Being! Have some compassion! Now—do you think you can find what's wrong with "Old Smelly"?
NEW YORK UNIVERSITY SATURN ANNEX
COLUMBIA SCHOOL of MEDICINE JUPITER ANNEX
EMMY ACTING CERTIFICATE for SPACE T
BLIP BLOP GLIK
BLIP BLOP GLIK
I can tell you already! He has a rare disease!
Really? And what is it called?
If I knew, would it be a rare disease?
I hate it when you throw your medical knowledge at me! How can we help this man?
We can't help him, but we can get him off this ship before he contaminates the rest of us!
Never!!
Then we'll probably all die shortly!
You look terrible, Flob! You look homesick! Well, if you don't want to stay, there's nothing I can do to stop you! Here . . . why don't you get a breath of fresh air—and lean way out of this porthole .
Just a minute, Captain—before you push him out—
Push him out!? How dare you imply that I would do such a thing! What do you think this banana peel is for? He was going to SLIP out!
I have a plan that may save this man, his people and his planet! But hear me out before you tell me that I'm crazy—
If we could reverse orbit and go back in time—back to the days when this man had his health—before disease struck his planet . . .

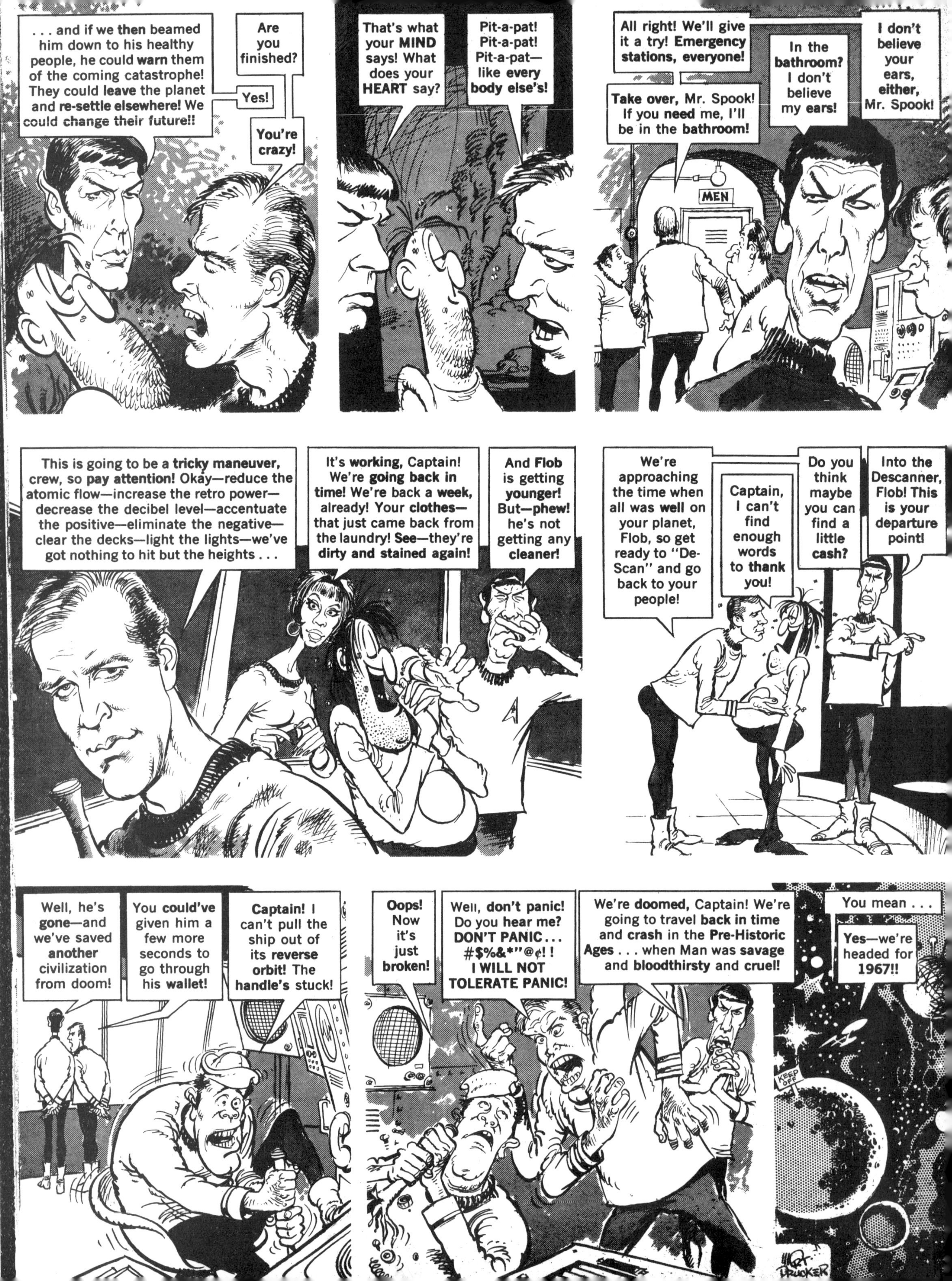
. . . and if we then beamed him down to his healthy people, he could warn them of the coming catastrophe! They could leave the planet and re-settle elsewhere! We could change their future!!
Are you finished?
Yes!
You're crazy!
That's what your MIND says! What does your HEART say?
Pit-a-pat! Pit-a-pat! Pit-a-pat—like every body else's!
All right! We'll give it a try! Emergency stations, everyone!
Take over, Mr. Spook! If you need me, I'll be in the bathroom!
MEN
In the bathroom? I don't believe my ears!
I don't believe your ears, either, Mr. Spook!
This is going to be a tricky maneuver, crew, so pay attention! Okay—reduce the atomic flow—increase the retro power—decrease the decibel level—accentuate the positive—eliminate the negative—clear the decks—light the lights—we've got nothing to hit but the heights . . .
It's working, Captain! We're going back in time! We're back a week, already! Your clothes—that just came back from the laundry! See—they're dirty and stained again!
And Flob is getting younger! But—phew! he's not getting any cleaner!
We're approaching the time when all was well on your planet, Flob, so get ready to "De-Scan" and go back to your people!
Captain, I can't find enough words to thank you!
Do you think maybe you can find a little cash?
Into the Descanner, Flob! This is your departure point!
Well, he's gone—and we've saved another civilization from doom!
You could've given him a few more seconds to go through his wallet!
Captain! I can't pull the ship out of its reverse orbit! The handle's stuck!
Oops! Now it's just broken!
Well, don't panic! Do you hear me? DON'T PANIC . . . #$%&*"@¢! ! I WILL NOT TOLERATE PANIC!
We're doomed, Captain! We're going to travel back in time and crash in the Pre-Historic Ages . . . when Man was savage and bloodthirsty and cruel!
You mean . . .
Yes—we're headed for 1967!!
KEEP OFF
MORT DRUCKER

LITTLE BIGOT MAN DEPT.

Ever since Television began, situation comedies have been, more or less, the same. Now, all of a sudden, a new situation comedy has come along . . . and it's entirely different from the old-fashioned family fare. It doesn't deal with the same old stupid subjects involving idiotic, unbelievable characters. Instead, it concerns itself with relevant "now" subjects, involving even more idiotic unbelievable characters! Here, then, is MAD's version of . . .

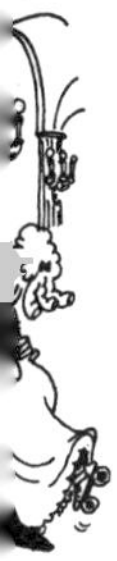

GALL IN THE FAMILY FARE

This Week's Episode: "A Visit From A World War II Buddy"

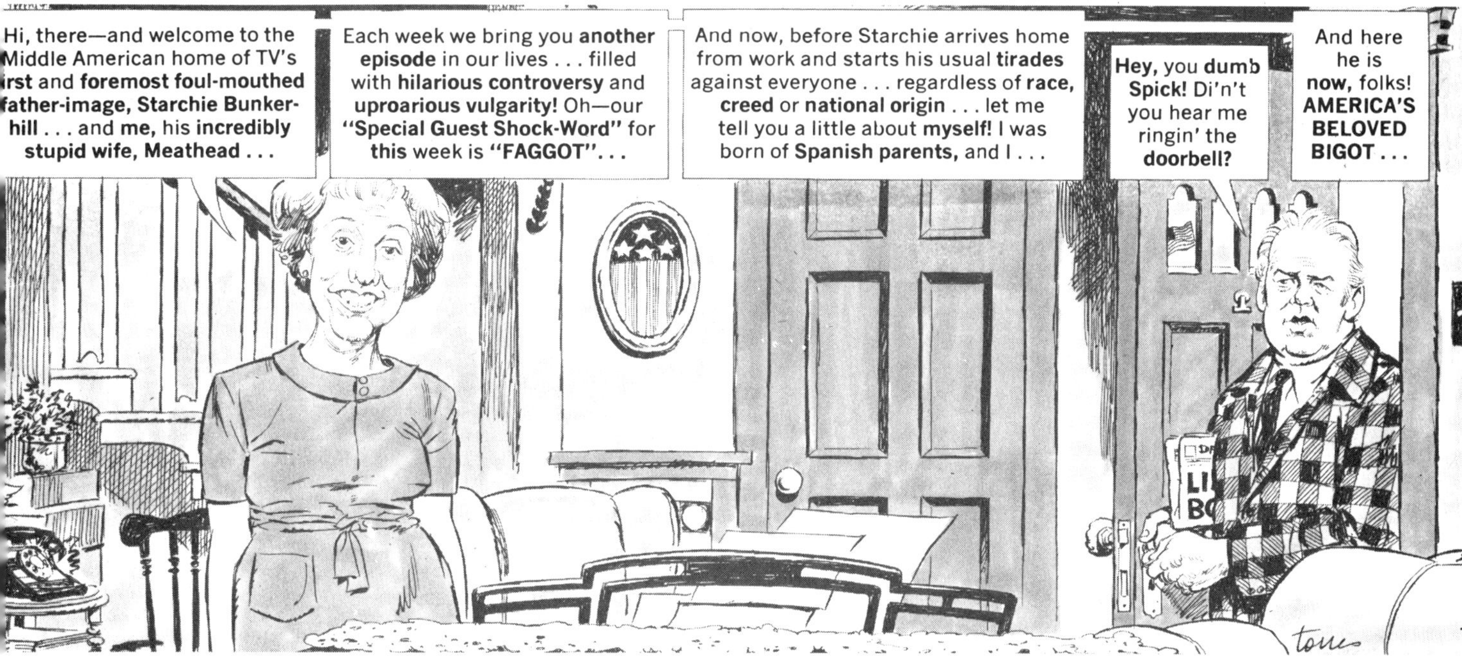

Hi, there—and welcome to the Middle American home of TV's irst and foremost foul-mouthed ather-image, Starchie Bunker-hill . . . and me, his incredibly stupid wife, Meathead . . .
Each week we bring you another episode in our lives . . . filled with hilarious controversy and uproarious vulgarity! Oh—our "Special Guest Shock-Word" for this week is "FAGGOT" . . .
And now, before Starchie arrives home from work and starts his usual tirades against everyone . . . regardless of race, creed or national origin . . . let me tell you a little about myself! I was born of Spanish parents, and I . . .
Hey, you dumb Spick! Di'n't you hear me ringin' the doorbell?
And here he is now, folks! AMERICA'S BELOVED BIGOT . . .

ARTIST: ANGELO TORRES WRITER: LARRY SIEGEL

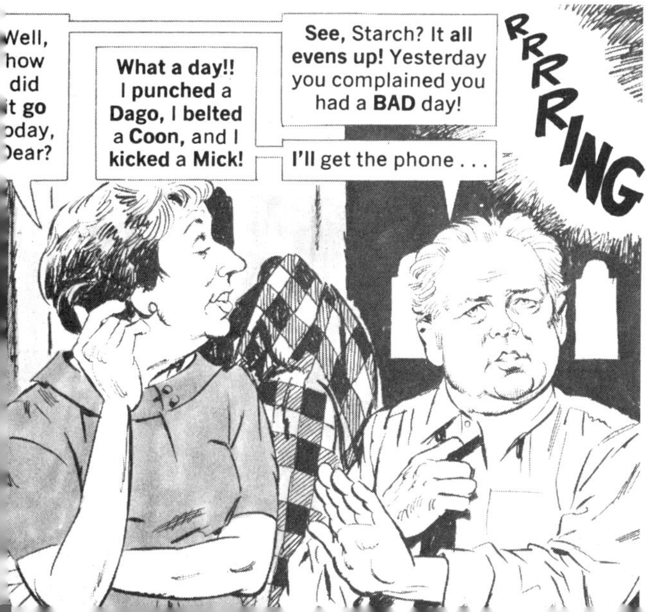

Well, how did t go oday, Dear?
What a day!! I punched a Dago, I belted a Coon, and I kicked a Mick!
See, Starch? It all evens up! Yesterday you complained you had a BAD day!
I'll get the phone . . .
RRRRING

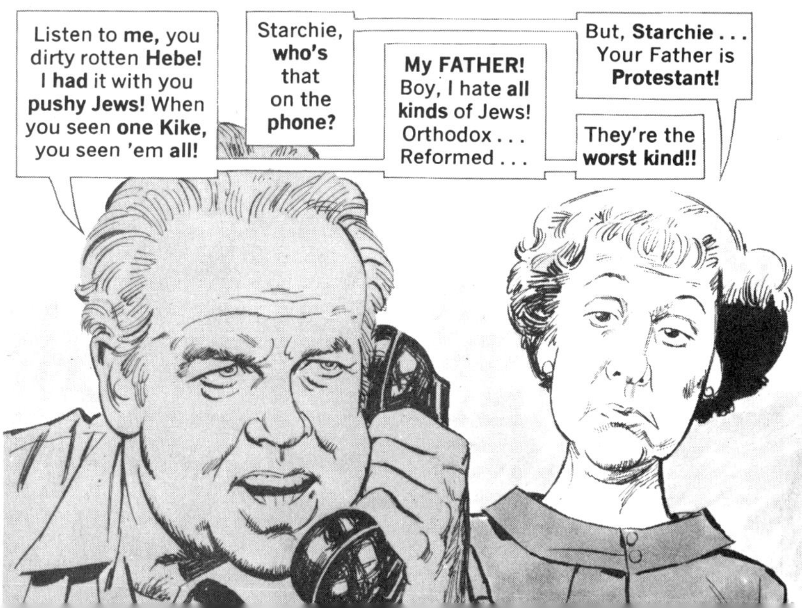

Listen to me, you dirty rotten Hebe! I had it with you pushy Jews! When you seen one Kike, you seen 'em all!
Starchie, who's that on the phone?
My FATHER! Boy, I hate all kinds of Jews! Orthodox . . . Reformed . . .
But, Starchie . . . Your Father is Protestant!
They're the worst kind!!

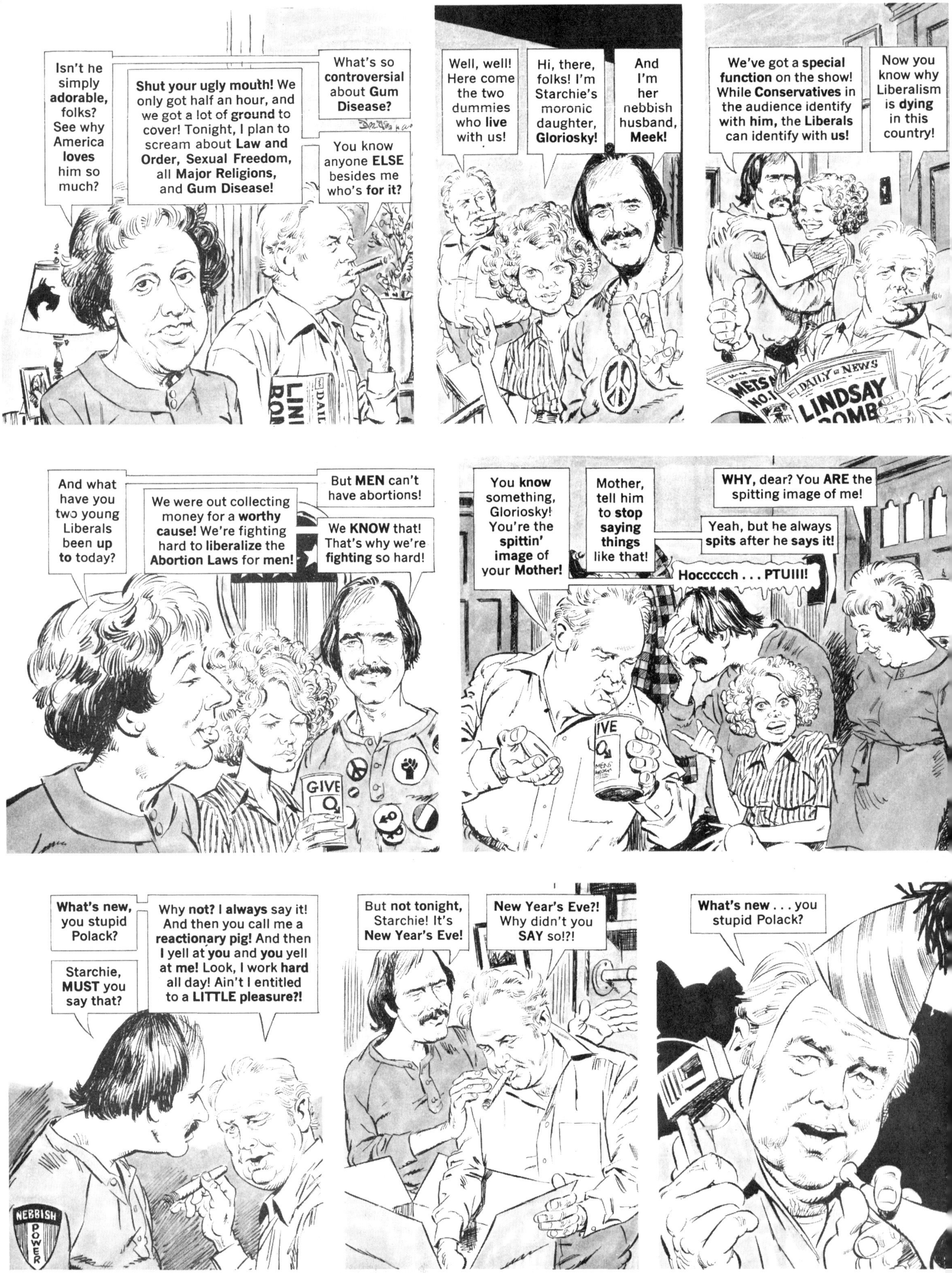

Isn't he simply **adorable,** folks? See why America **loves** him so much?
Shut your ugly mouth! We only got half an hour, and we got a lot of **ground** to cover! Tonight, I plan to scream about **Law and Order, Sexual Freedom,** all **Major Religions,** and **Gum Disease!**
What's so **controversial** about **Gum Disease?**
You know anyone **ELSE** besides me who's **for it?**
Well, well! Here come the two dummies who **live** with us!
Hi, there, folks! I'm Starchie's moronic daughter, **Gloriosky!**
And I'm her nebbish husband, **Meek!**
We've got a **special function** on the show! While **Conservatives** in the audience identify with **him,** the **Liberals** can identify with **us!**
Now you know why Liberalism is **dying** in this country!
DAILY NEWS
LINDSAY
And what have you two young Liberals been **up to** today?
We were out collecting money for a **worthy cause!** We're fighting hard to **liberalize** the **Abortion Laws** for **men!**
But **MEN** can't have abortions!
We **KNOW** that! That's why we're **fighting** so hard!
GIVE
You **know** something, Gloriosky! You're the **spittin' image** of your **Mother!**
Mother, tell him to **stop saying things** like that!
WHY, dear? You **ARE** the spitting image of me!
Yeah, but he always **spits** after he **says it!**
Hoccccch . . . PTUIII!
What's new, you stupid Polack?
Starchie, **MUST** you say that?
Why **not? I always** say it! And then you call me a **reactionary pig!** And then **I** yell at **you** and **you** yell **at me!** Look, I work **hard** all day! Ain't I entitled to a **LITTLE pleasure?!**
NEBBISH POWER
But **not tonight,** Starchie! It's **New Year's Eve!**
New Year's Eve?! Why didn't you **SAY** so!?!
What's new . . . you stupid Polack?

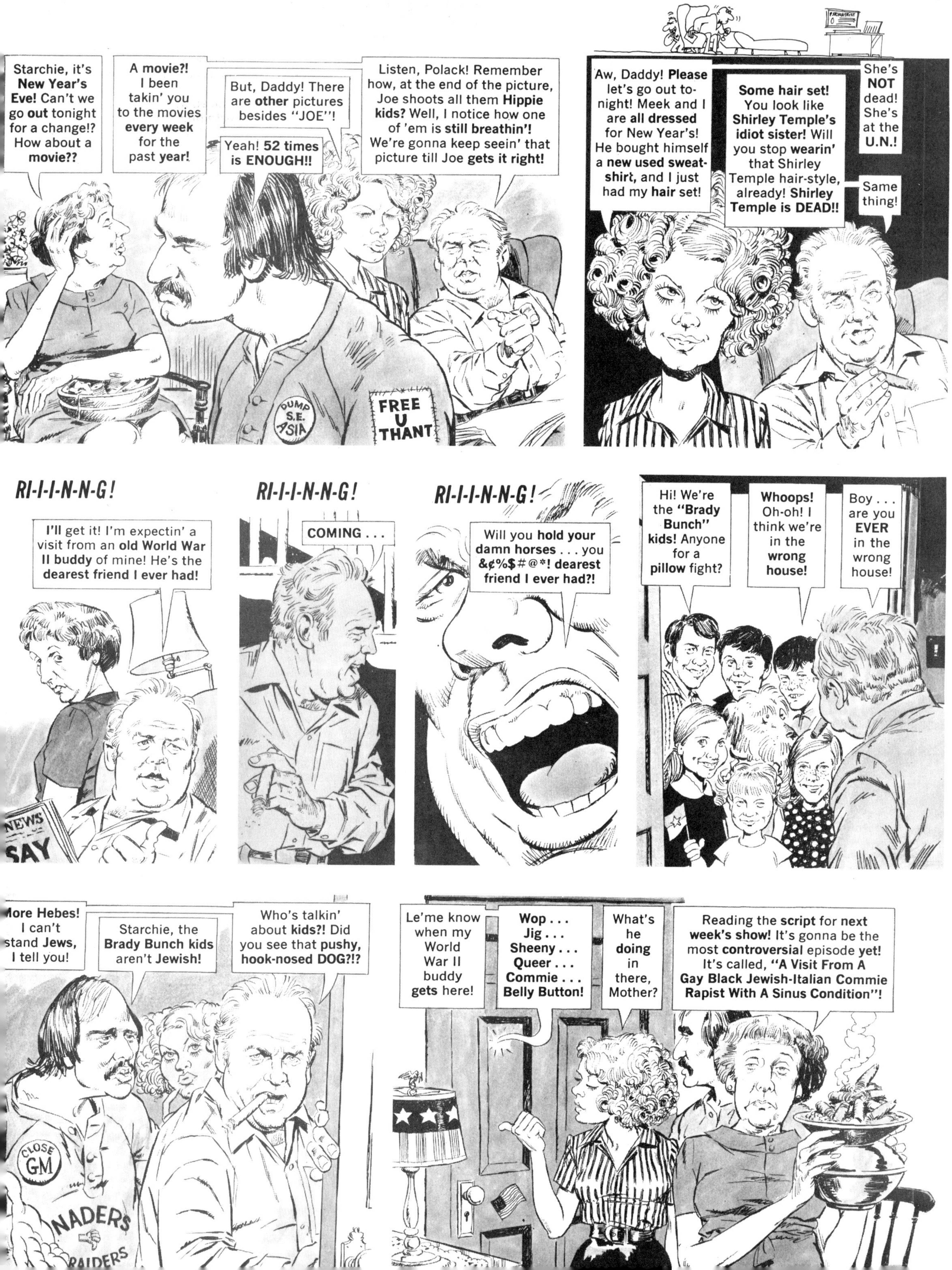
Starchie, it's New Year's Eve! Can't we go out tonight for a change!? How about a movie??
A movie?! I been takin' you to the movies every week for the past year!
But, Daddy! There are other pictures besides "JOE"!
Yeah! 52 times is ENOUGH!!
Listen, Polack! Remember how, at the end of the picture, Joe shoots all them Hippie kids? Well, I notice how one of 'em is still breathin'! We're gonna keep seein' that picture till Joe gets it right!
DUMP S.E. ASIA
FREE U THANT
Aw, Daddy! Please let's go out tonight! Meek and I are all dressed for New Year's! He bought himself a new used sweatshirt, and I just had my hair set!
Some hair set! You look like Shirley Temple's idiot sister! Will you stop wearin' that Shirley Temple hair-style, already! Shirley Temple is DEAD!!
She's NOT dead! She's at the U.N.!
Same thing!
RI-I-I-N-N-G!
I'll get it! I'm expectin' a visit from an old World War II buddy of mine! He's the dearest friend I ever had!
NEWS
SAY
RI-I-I-N-N-G!
COMING . . .
RI-I-I-N-N-G!
Will you hold your damn horses . . . you &¢%$#@*! dearest friend I ever had?!
Hi! We're the "Brady Bunch" kids! Anyone for a pillow fight?
Whoops! Oh-oh! I think we're in the wrong house!
Boy . . . are you EVER in the wrong house!
More Hebes! I can't stand Jews, I tell you!
Starchie, the Brady Bunch kids aren't Jewish!
Who's talkin' about kids?! Did you see that pushy, hook-nosed DOG?!?
CLOSE GM
NADERS RAIDERS
Le'me know when my World War II buddy gets here!
Wop . . . Jig . . . Sheeny . . . Queer . . . Commie . . . Belly Button!
What's he doing in there, Mother?
Reading the script for next week's show! It's gonna be the most controversial episode yet! It's called, "A Visit From A Gay Black Jewish-Italian Commie Rapist With A Sinus Condition"!

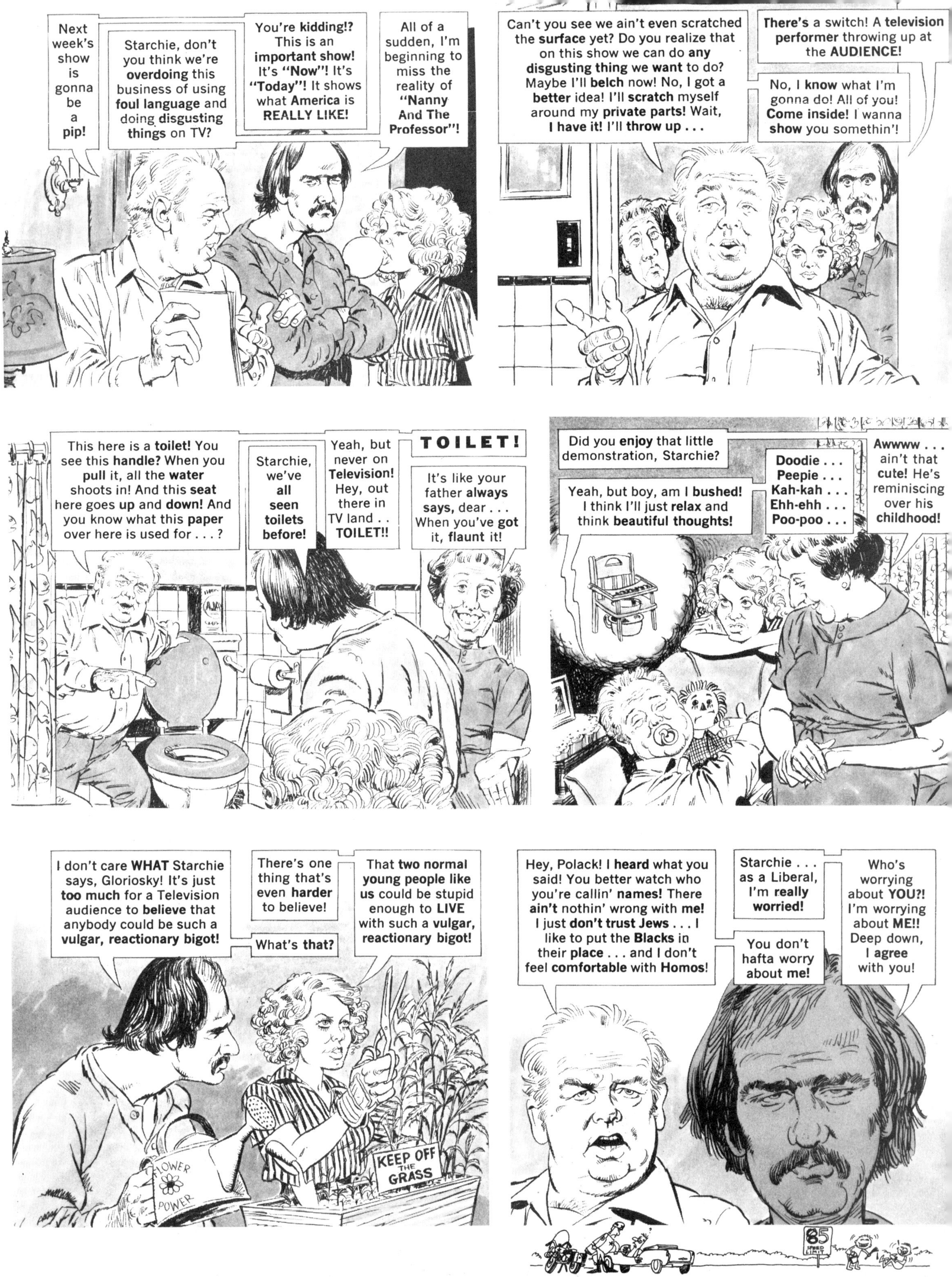

Next week's show is gonna be a pip!
Starchie, don't you think we're overdoing this business of using foul language and doing disgusting things on TV?
You're kidding!? This is an important show! It's "Now"! It's "Today"! It shows what America is REALLY LIKE!
All of a sudden, I'm beginning to miss the reality of "Nanny And The Professor"!
Can't you see we ain't even scratched the surface yet? Do you realize that on this show we can do any disgusting thing we want to do? Maybe I'll belch now! No, I got a better idea! I'll scratch myself around my private parts! Wait, I have it! I'll throw up . . .
There's a switch! A television performer throwing up at the AUDIENCE!
No, I know what I'm gonna do! All of you! Come inside! I wanna show you somethin'!
This here is a toilet! You see this handle? When you pull it, all the water shoots in! And this seat here goes up and down! And you know what this paper over here is used for . . . ?
Starchie, we've all seen toilets before!
Yeah, but never on Television! Hey, out there in TV land . . TOILET!!
TOILET!
It's like your father always says, dear . . . When you've got it, flaunt it!
Did you enjoy that little demonstration, Starchie?
Yeah, but boy, am I bushed! I think I'll just relax and think beautiful thoughts!
Doodie . . . Peepie . . . Kah-kah . . . Ehh-ehh . . . Poo-poo . . .
Awwww . . . ain't that cute! He's reminiscing over his childhood!
I don't care WHAT Starchie says, Gloriosky! It's just too much for a Television audience to believe that anybody could be such a vulgar, reactionary bigot!
There's one thing that's even harder to believe!
What's that?
That two normal young people like us could be stupid enough to LIVE with such a vulgar, reactionary bigot!
FLOWER POWER
KEEP OFF THE GRASS
Hey, Polack! I heard what you said! You better watch who you're callin' names! There ain't nothin' wrong with me! I just don't trust Jews . . . I like to put the Blacks in their place . . . and I don't feel comfortable with Homos!
Starchie . . . as a Liberal, I'm really worried!
You don't hafta worry about me!
Who's worrying about YOU?! I'm worrying about ME!! Deep down, I agree with you!
85

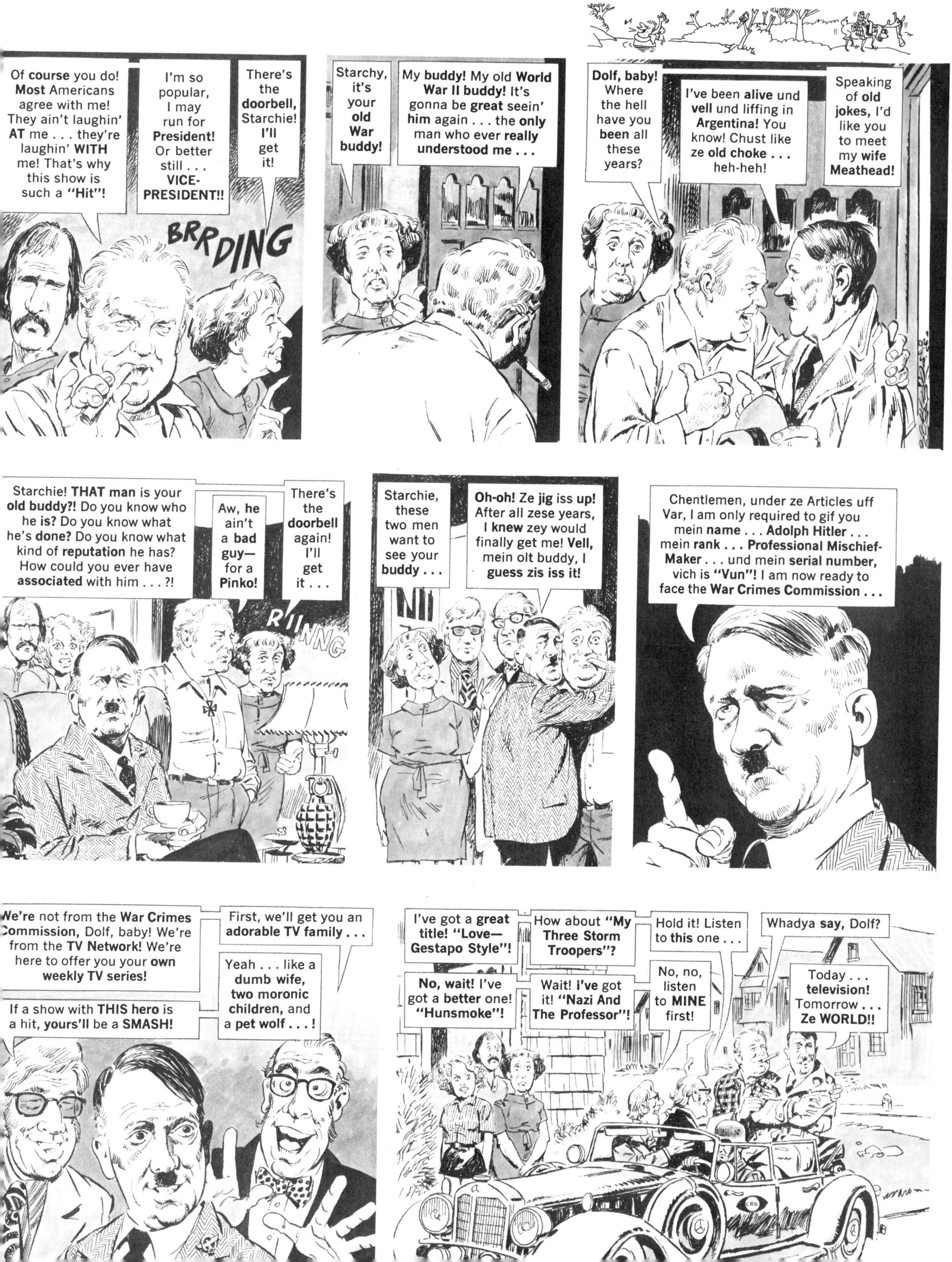
Of course you do! Most Americans agree with me! They ain't laughin' AT me . . . they're laughin' WITH me! That's why this show is such a "Hit"!
I'm so popular, I may run for President! Or better still . . . VICE-PRESIDENT!!
There's the doorbell, Starchie! I'll get it!
BRRDING
Starchy, it's your old War buddy!
My buddy! My old World War II buddy! It's gonna be great seein' him again . . . the only man who ever really understood me . . .
Dolf, baby! Where the hell have you been all these years?
I've been alive und vell und liffing in Argentina! You know! Chust like ze old choke . . . heh-heh!
Speaking of old jokes, I'd like you to meet my wife Meathead!
Starchie! THAT man is your old buddy?! Do you know who he is? Do you know what he's done? Do you know what kind of reputation he has? How could you ever have associated with him . . .?!
Aw, he ain't a bad guy— for a Pinko!
There's the doorbell again! I'll get it . . .
RIINNG
Starchie, these two men want to see your buddy . . .
Oh-oh! Ze jig iss up! After all zese years, I knew zey would finally get me! Vell, mein olt buddy, I guess zis iss it!
Chentlemen, under ze Articles uff Var, I am only required to gif you mein name . . . Adolph Hitler . . . mein rank . . . Professional Mischief-Maker . . . und mein serial number, vich is "Vun"! I am now ready to face the War Crimes Commission . . .
We're not from the War Crimes Commission, Dolf, baby! We're from the TV Network! We're here to offer you your own weekly TV series!
If a show with THIS hero is a hit, yours'll be a SMASH!
First, we'll get you an adorable TV family . . .
Yeah . . . like a dumb wife, two moronic children, and a pet wolf . . . !
I've got a great title! "Love— Gestapo Style"!
No, wait! I've got a better one! "Hunsmoke"!
How about "My Three Storm Troopers"?
Wait! I've got it! "Nazi And The Professor"!
Hold it! Listen to this one . . .
No, no, listen to MINE first!
Whadya say, Dolf?
Today . . . television! Tomorrow . . . Ze WORLD!!
CBS

TROUBLE IS A-BRUIN DEPT.

They've got Humane Societies to protect animals from being tortured and abused by people . . . but there's nothing to protect people from being tortured and abused by animals! Mainly, TV animals—like "Lassie" and "Flipper" and "Clarence", The Cross-Eyed Lion and "Judy, The Chimp" and that worst torture and abuse of all . . .

GENTEEL BEN

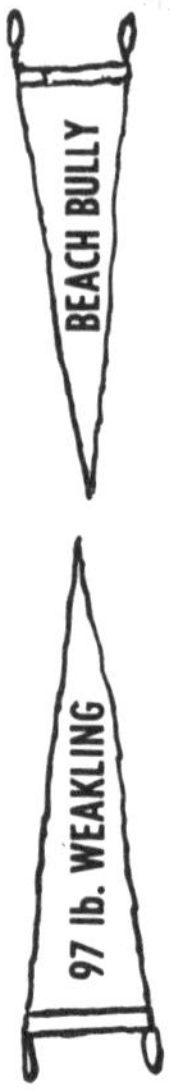
BEACH BULLY
97 lb. WEAKLING

Starring . . .

DENNIS WEAVING as **Warden Tame**

BETH BRICKWALL as his **Wife, Helpem**

CLINT HOWLER as their **Son, Marsh**

&

SOME FURRY IDIOT as **Genteel Ben**

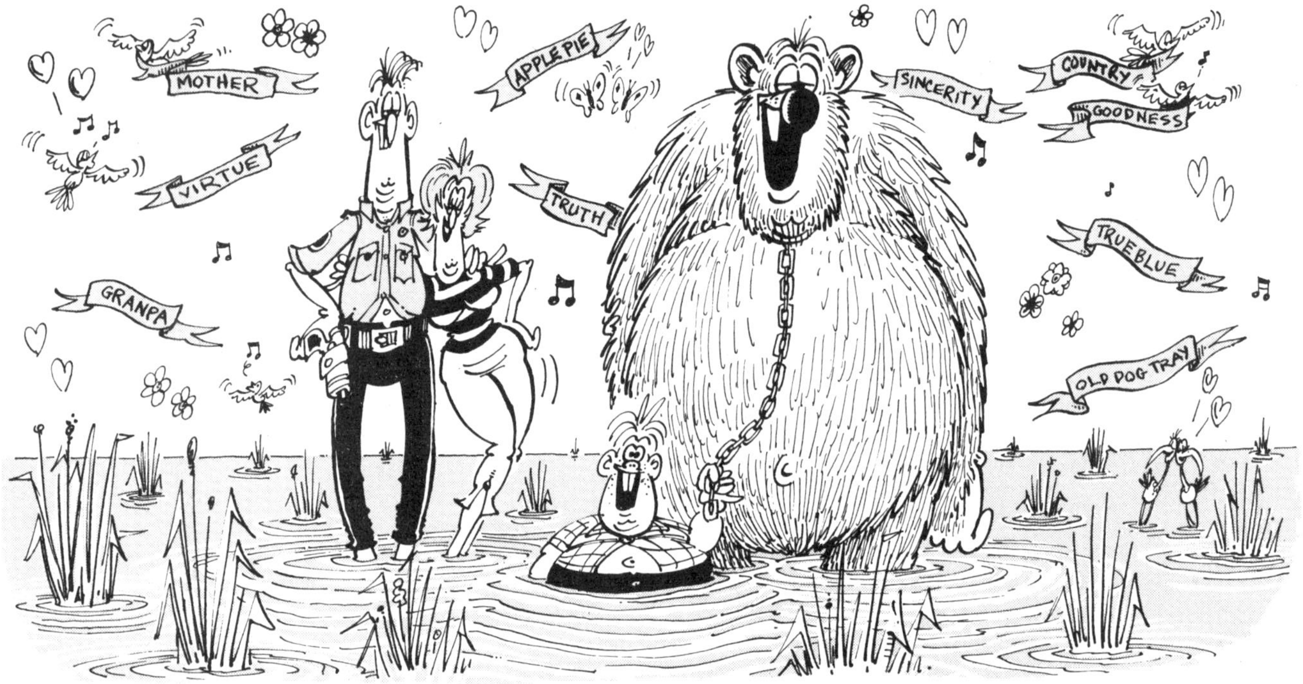
MOTHER
APPLE PIE
SINCERITY
COUNTRY
GOODNESS
VIRTUE
TRUTH
TRUEBLUE
GRANPA
OLD DOG TRAY

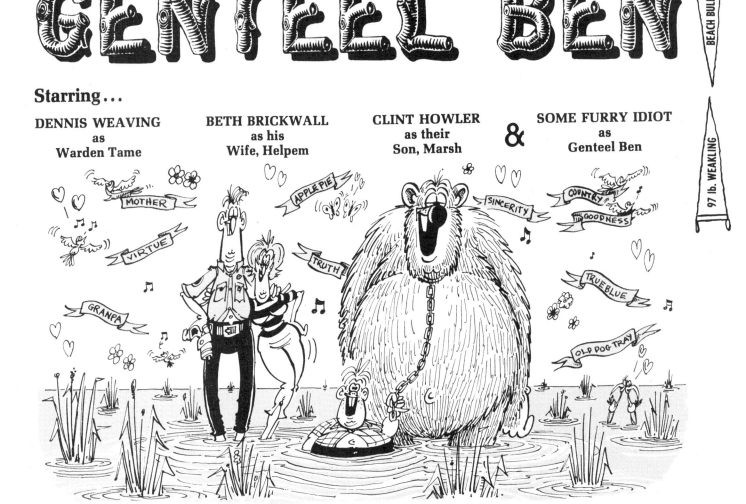

ARTIST: DON MARTIN WRITER: DICK DE BARTOLO

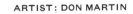

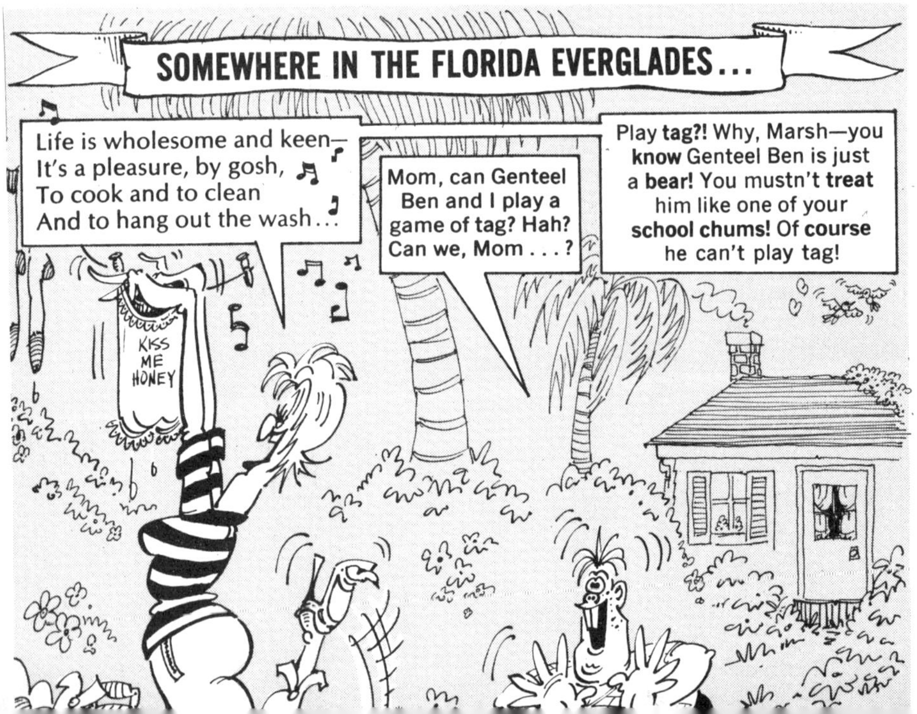
SOMEWHERE IN THE FLORIDA EVERGLADES . . .
Life is wholesome and keen—
It's a pleasure, by gosh,
To cook and to clean
And to hang out the wash . . .
Mom, can Genteel Ben and I play a game of tag? Hah? Can we, Mom . . . ?
Play tag?! Why, Marsh—you know Genteel Ben is just a bear! You mustn't treat him like one of your school chums! Of course he can't play tag!
KISS ME HONEY

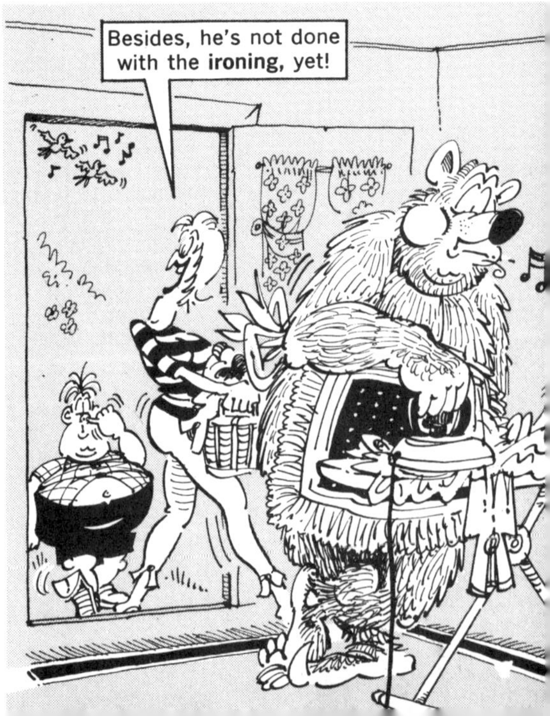
Besides, he's not done with the ironing, yet!

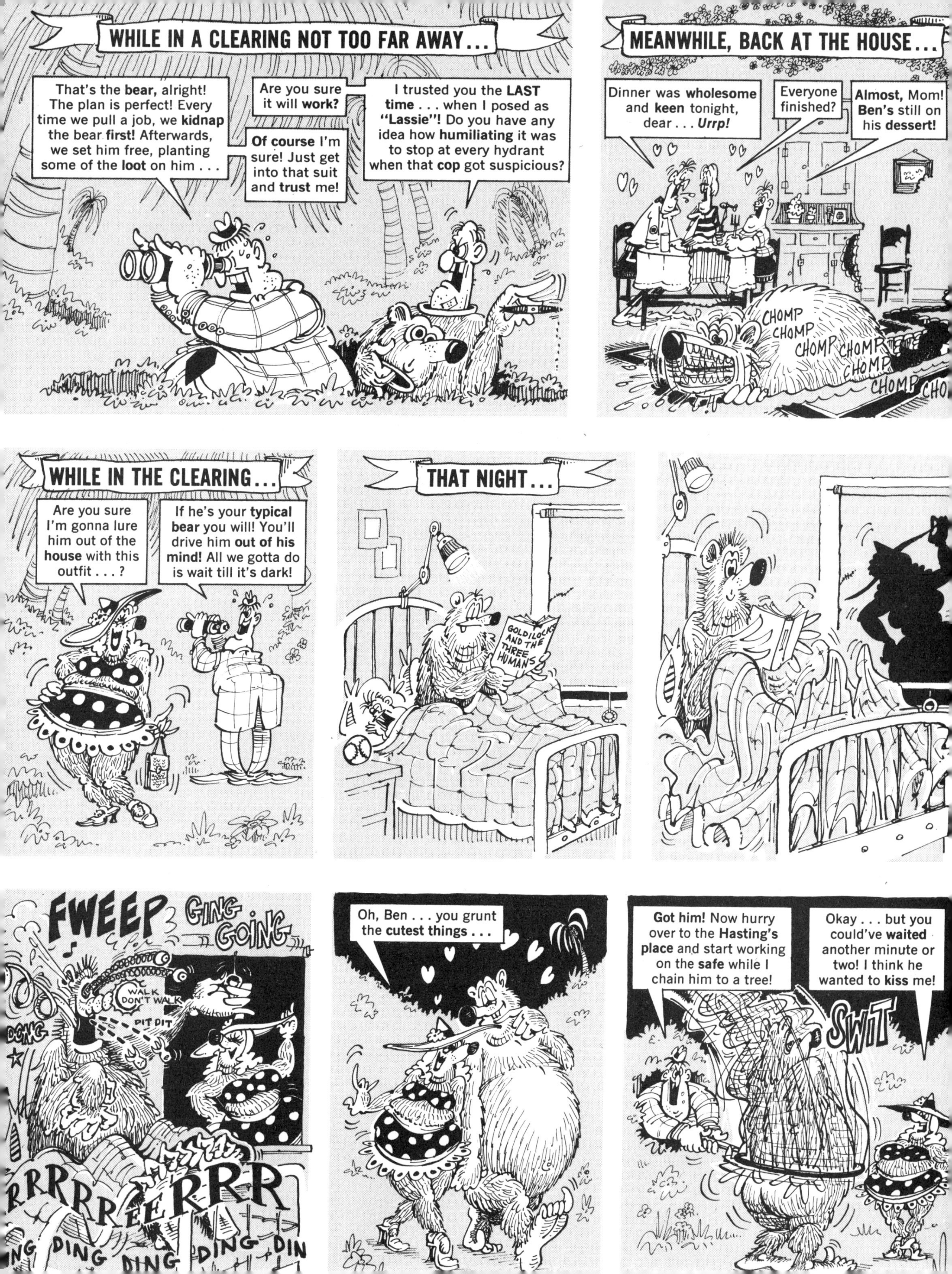
WHILE IN A CLEARING NOT TOO FAR AWAY...
That's the bear, alright! The plan is perfect! Every time we pull a job, we kidnap the bear first! Afterwards, we set him free, planting some of the loot on him . . .
Are you sure it will work?
Of course I'm sure! Just get into that suit and trust me!
I trusted you the LAST time . . . when I posed as "Lassie"! Do you have any idea how humiliating it was to stop at every hydrant when that cop got suspicious?
MEANWHILE, BACK AT THE HOUSE...
Dinner was wholesome and keen tonight, dear . . . Urrp!
Everyone finished?
Almost, Mom! Ben's still on his dessert!
CHOMP CHOMP CHOMP CHOMP CHOMP CHOMP
WHILE IN THE CLEARING...
Are you sure I'm gonna lure him out of the house with this outfit . . . ?
If he's your typical bear you will! You'll drive him out of his mind! All we gotta do is wait till it's dark!
THAT NIGHT...
GOLDILOCKS AND THE THREE HUMANS
FWEEP
GING GOING
WALK DON'T WALK
PIT DIT
DONG
RRRRRREEERRR
DING DING DING DIN
Oh, Ben . . . you grunt the cutest things . . .
Got him! Now hurry over to the Hasting's place and start working on the safe while I chain him to a tree!
Okay . . . but you could've waited another minute or two! I think he wanted to kiss me!
SWIT

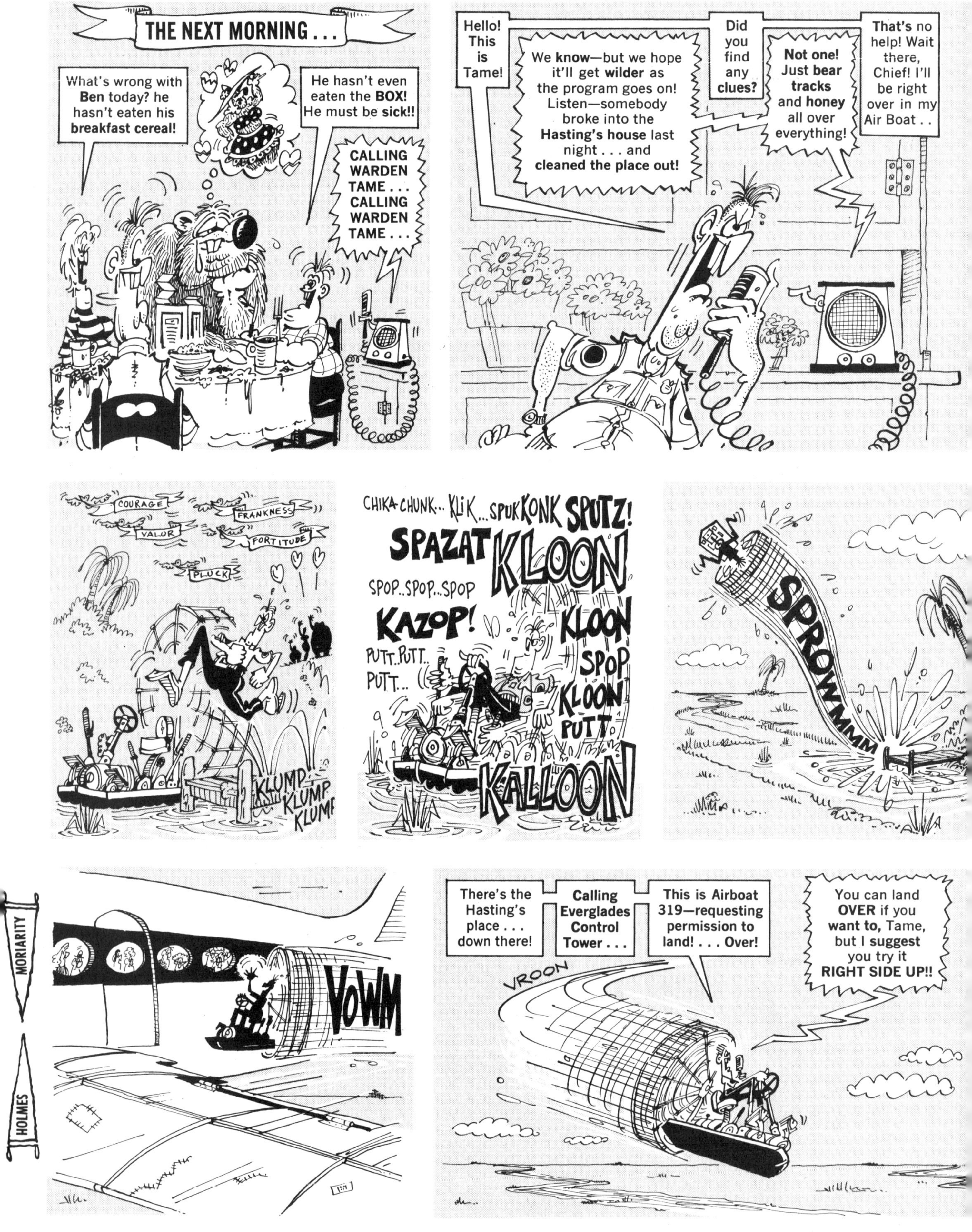
THE NEXT MORNING . . .
What's wrong with Ben today? he hasn't eaten his breakfast cereal!
He hasn't even eaten the BOX! He must be sick!!
CALLING WARDEN TAME . . . CALLING WARDEN TAME . . .
Hello! This is Tame!
We know—but we hope it'll get wilder as the program goes on! Listen—somebody broke into the Hasting's house last night . . . and cleaned the place out!
Did you find any clues?
Not one! Just bear tracks and honey all over everything!
That's no help! Wait there, Chief! I'll be right over in my Air Boat . .
COURAGE
FRANKNESS
VALOR
FORTITUDE
PLUCK
KLUMP KLUMP KLUMP
CHIKA CHUNK.. KLIK... SPUK KONK SPUTZ!
SPAZAT KLOON
SPOP..SPOP..SPOP
KAZOP!
PUTT..PUTT.. PUTT...
KLOON
SPOP
KLOON
PUTT
KALLOON
SPROWMMM
MORIARITY
HOLMES
VOWM
VROON
There's the Hasting's place . . . down there!
Calling Everglades Control Tower . . .
This is Airboat 319—requesting permission to land! . . . Over!
You can land OVER if you want to, Tame, but I suggest you try it RIGHT SIDE UP!!

Did you dig up any more **clues**, Chief?

Just this handkerchief with the initials **"G.B."**! I don't know any **"G.B."**—unless it was the entire **Green Bay** football team!

"G.B." Hmmmm! I wonder! **"Genteel Ben"**...

Genteel Ben!? You think **HE** might know some **"G.B.'s"**?

Doesn't hurt to **ask!** I'll see you later...

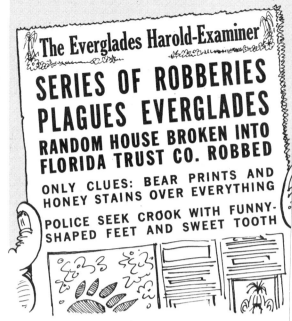

The Everglades Harold-Examiner

SERIES OF ROBBERIES PLAGUES EVERGLADES

RANDOM HOUSE BROKEN INTO
FLORIDA TRUST CO. ROBBED

ONLY CLUES: BEAR PRINTS AND HONEY STAINS OVER EVERYTHING

POLICE SEEK CROOK WITH FUNNY-SHAPED FEET AND SWEET TOOTH

There's something **funny** going on, Marsh!

You can't mean in **this** story!

No—with **Ben!** He goes out **every night!** Do you know **where?**

Sure! Let's look at his **appointment book:** Monday—Bowling with **Smokey The Bear** ... Tuesday—Poker with **Yogi Bear** ... Wednesday—Dinner with the **Three Bears** ... Thursday—Watch Fight Films with **Max Bear** ...

Quite frankly, Marsh ... there have been several **robberies** in the area recently, and ... well, what with the **bear tracks** and the **honey**—

Dad!! Are you suggesting that **Genteel Ben** had something to do with them? How could you **say** that? How could you even **THINK** that ... especially when he's standing right there **behind you!**

Look! You **hurt** his **feelings!** Poor Ben ...

And you a **Game Warden** ... a **protector** of our helpless furry friends!

SNIFFLE SKNIFFLE

You're **right,** Marsh! I'm—I'm **sorry,** Ben! I—I guess I **lost my head** when I heard that the **Everglades Jewelry Store** was robbed a few hours ago ...

SNIFFLE SNIF... SKNIKLE SKLUK SKLUKLE SKNOSH

SNUFFLE SHNORKLE SLOBBLE SOB

Shake hands with me, Ben ... so I'll know you **forgive me** for even **suspecting** you ...

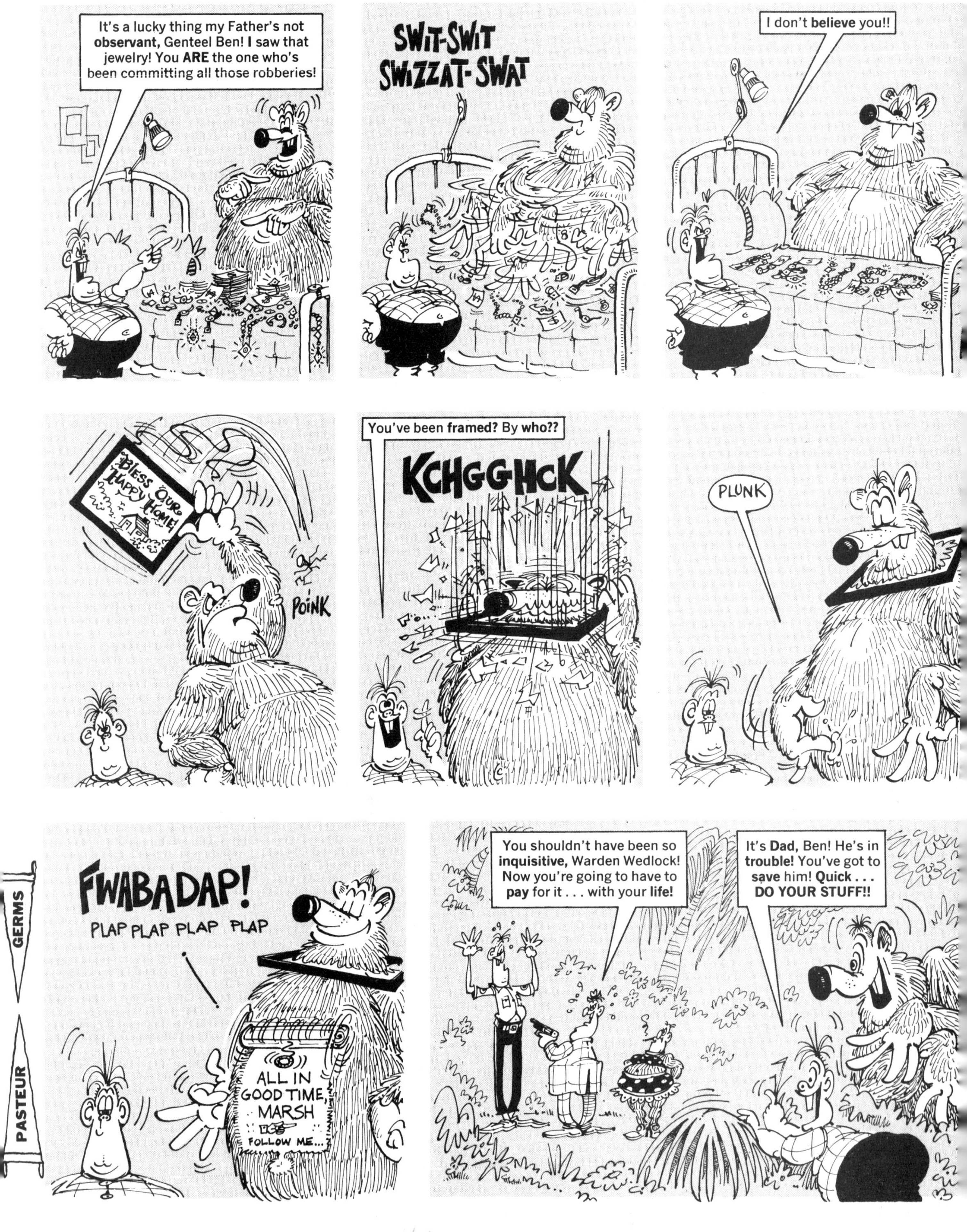
It's a lucky thing my Father's not **observant,** Genteel Ben! **I** saw that jewelry! You **ARE** the one who's been committing all those robberies!
SWIT-SWIT
SWIZZAT-SWAT
I don't **believe** you!!
BLESS OUR HAPPY HOME
POINK
You've been **framed?** By **who??**
KCHGGHCK
PLUNK
FWABADAP!
PLAP PLAP PLAP PLAP
ALL IN GOOD TIME, MARSH
FOLLOW ME...
You shouldn't have been so **inquisitive,** Warden Wedlock! Now you're going to have to **pay** for it . . . with your **life!**
It's **Dad,** Ben! He's in **trouble!** You've got to **save** him! **Quick . . . DO YOUR STUFF!!**
GERMS
PASTEUR

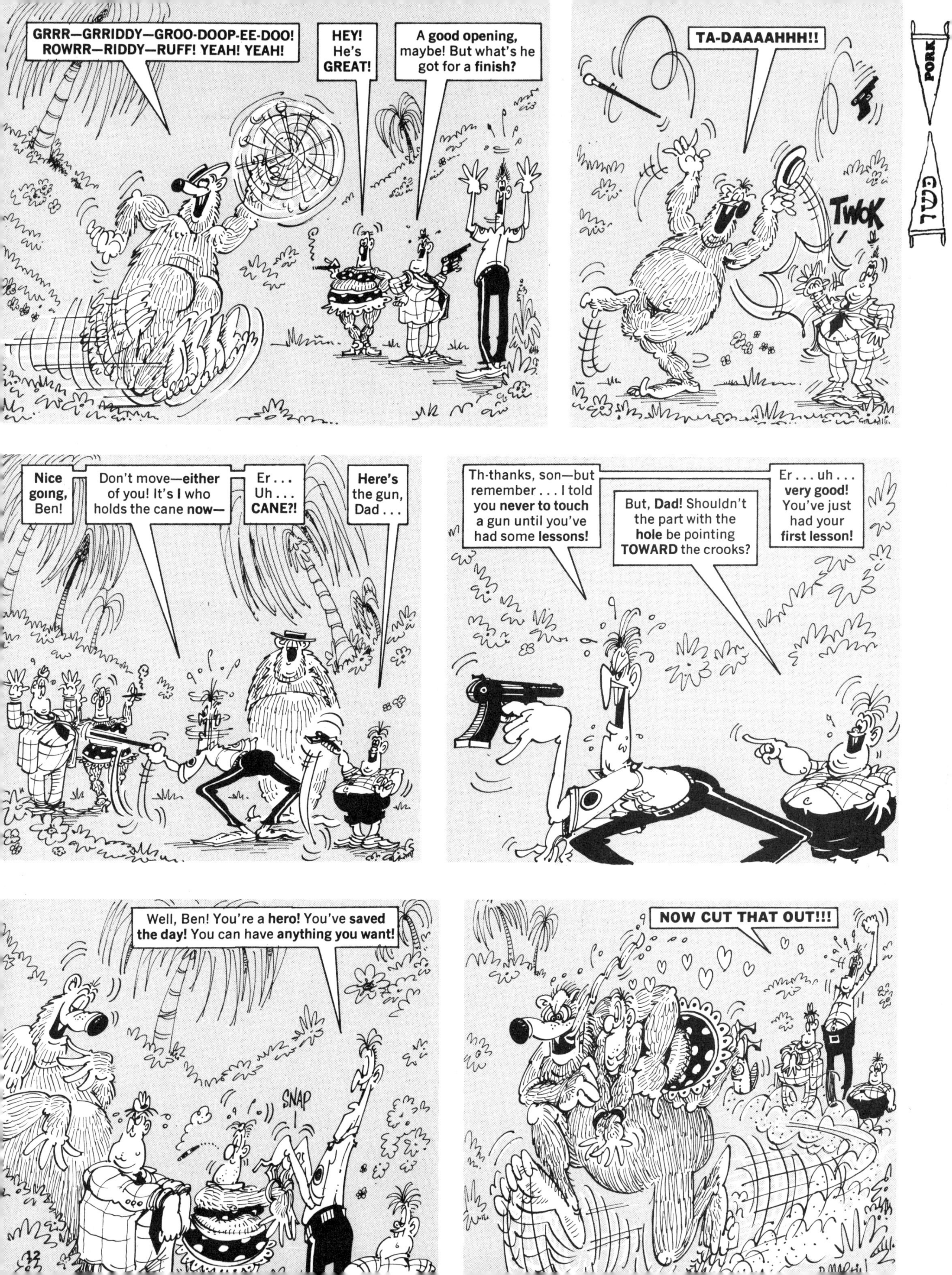
GRRR—GRRIDDY—GROO-DOOP-EE-DOO! ROWRR—RIDDY—RUFF! YEAH! YEAH!
HEY! He's GREAT!
A good opening, maybe! But what's he got for a finish?
TA-DAAAAHHH!!
TWOK
PORK
Nice going, Ben!
Don't move—either of you! It's I who holds the cane now—
Er . . . Uh . . . CANE?!
Here's the gun, Dad . . .
Th-thanks, son—but remember . . . I told you never to touch a gun until you've had some lessons!
Er . . . uh . . . very good! You've just had your first lesson!
But, Dad! Shouldn't the part with the hole be pointing TOWARD the crooks?
Well, Ben! You're a hero! You've saved the day! You can have anything you want!
SNAP
NOW CUT THAT OUT!!!

KNIFIN' FALK DEPT.

There have been many famous fictional Detectives through the years, and each has had his own special technique for solving a crime.

F'rinstance, there was Sherlock Holmes who relied on cold logic and British common sense . . .

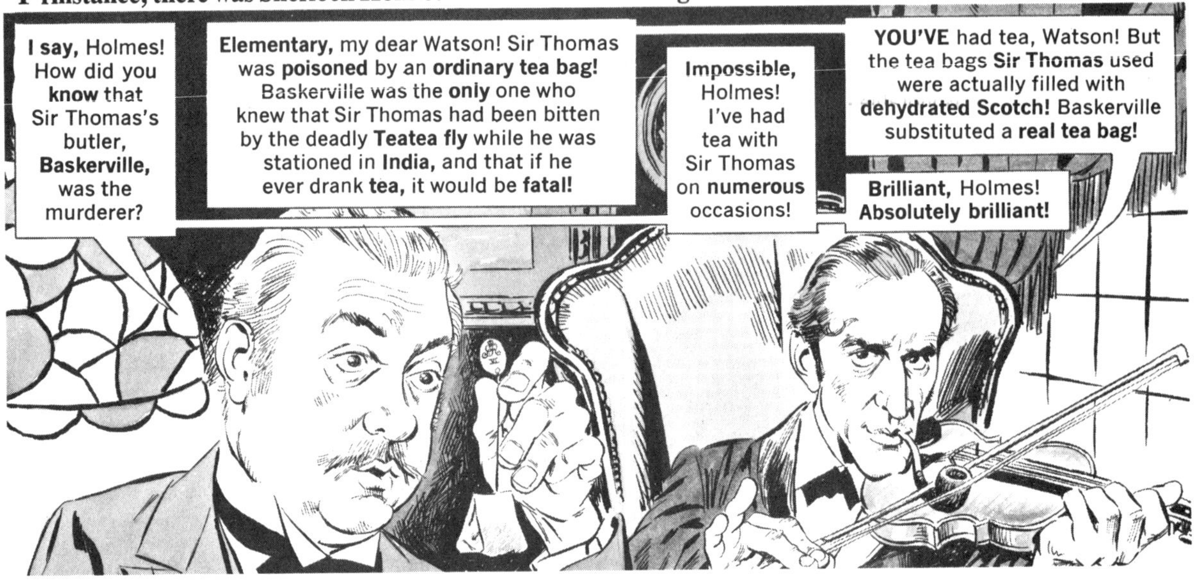

I say, Holmes! How did you know that Sir Thomas's butler, Baskerville, was the murderer?
Elementary, my dear Watson! Sir Thomas was poisoned by an ordinary tea bag! Baskerville was the only one who knew that Sir Thomas had been bitten by the deadly Teatea fly while he was stationed in India, and that if he ever drank tea, it would be fatal!
Impossible, Holmes! I've had tea with Sir Thomas on numerous occasions!
YOU'VE had tea, Watson! But the tea bags Sir Thomas used were actually filled with dehydrated Scotch! Baskerville substituted a real tea bag!
Brilliant, Holmes! Absolutely brilliant!

But enough of the crime-fighters of the past! Today, we have a new style TV Detective wit

CLOD

ARTIST: ANGELO TORRE

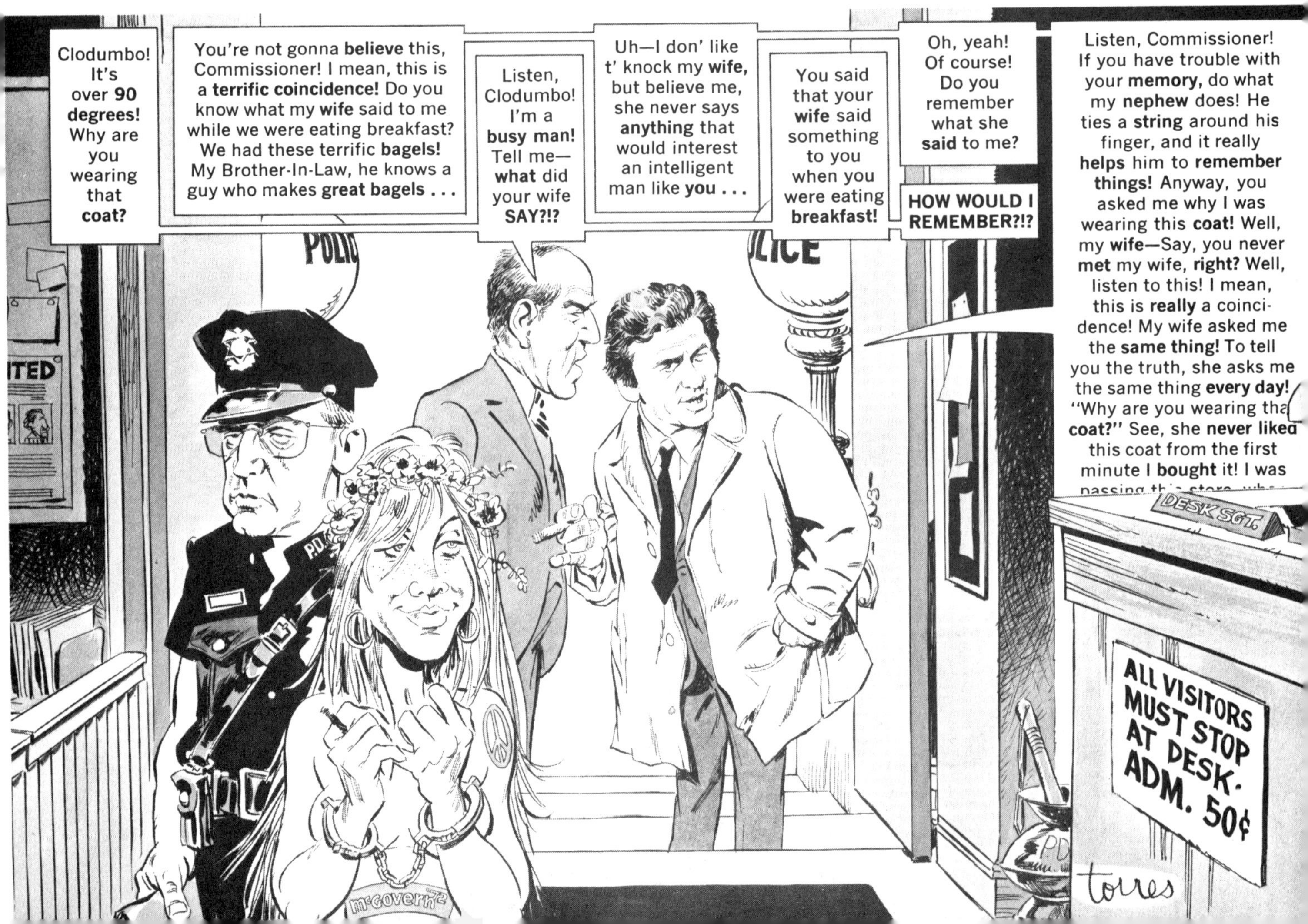

Clodumbo! It's over 90 degrees! Why are you wearing that coat?
You're not gonna believe this, Commissioner! I mean, this is a terrific coincidence! Do you know what my wife said to me while we were eating breakfast? We had these terrific bagels! My Brother-In-Law, he knows a guy who makes great bagels . . .
Listen, Clodumbo! I'm a busy man! Tell me—what did your wife SAY?!?
Uh—I don' like t' knock my wife, but believe me, she never says anything that would interest an intelligent man like you . . .
You said that your wife said something to you when you were eating breakfast!
Oh, yeah! Of course! Do you remember what she said to me?
HOW WOULD I REMEMBER?!?
Listen, Commissioner! If you have trouble with your memory, do what my nephew does! He ties a string around his finger, and it really helps him to remember things! Anyway, you asked me why I was wearing this coat! Well, my wife—Say, you never met my wife, right? Well, listen to this! I mean, this is really a coincidence! My wife asked me the same thing! To tell you the truth, she asks me the same thing every day! "Why are you wearing tha coat?" See, she never liked this coat from the first minute I bought it! I was
POLICE
DESK SGT.
ALL VISITORS MUST STOP AT DESK. ADM. 50¢
McGovern '72
torres

There was Charlie Chan with his inscrutable reasoning . . .

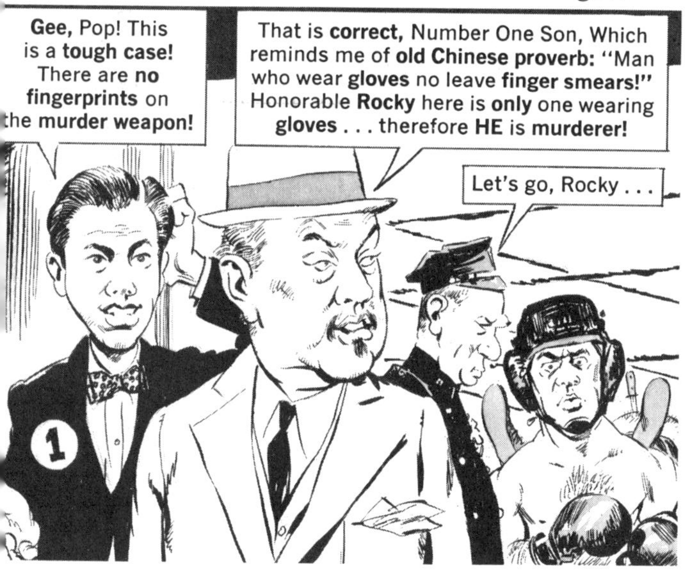
Gee, Pop! This is a tough case! There are no fingerprints on the murder weapon!
That is correct, Number One Son, Which reminds me of old Chinese proverb: "Man who wear gloves no leave finger smears!" Honorable Rocky here is only one wearing gloves . . . therefore HE is murderer!
Let's go, Rocky . . .
1

And there was Mike Hammer with his American approach . . .

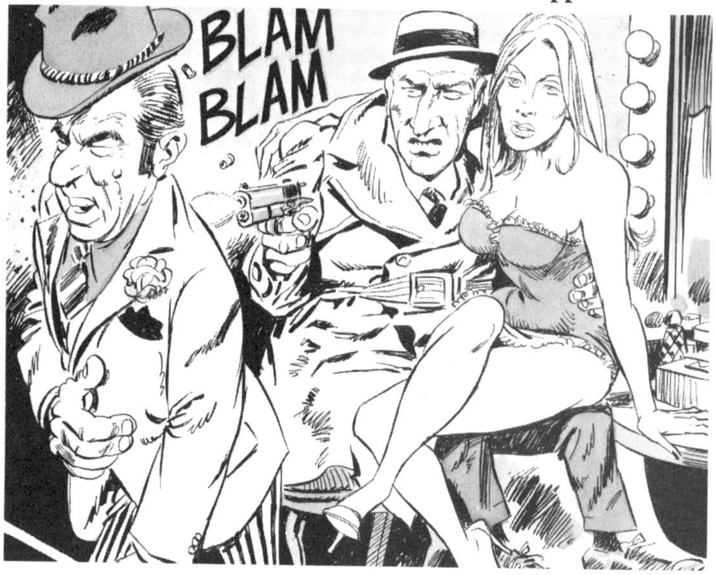
BLAM
BLAM

is own unique method of solving cases. You'll see what we mean as we take a MAD look at . . .

UMBO

VRITE: LOU SILVERSTONE

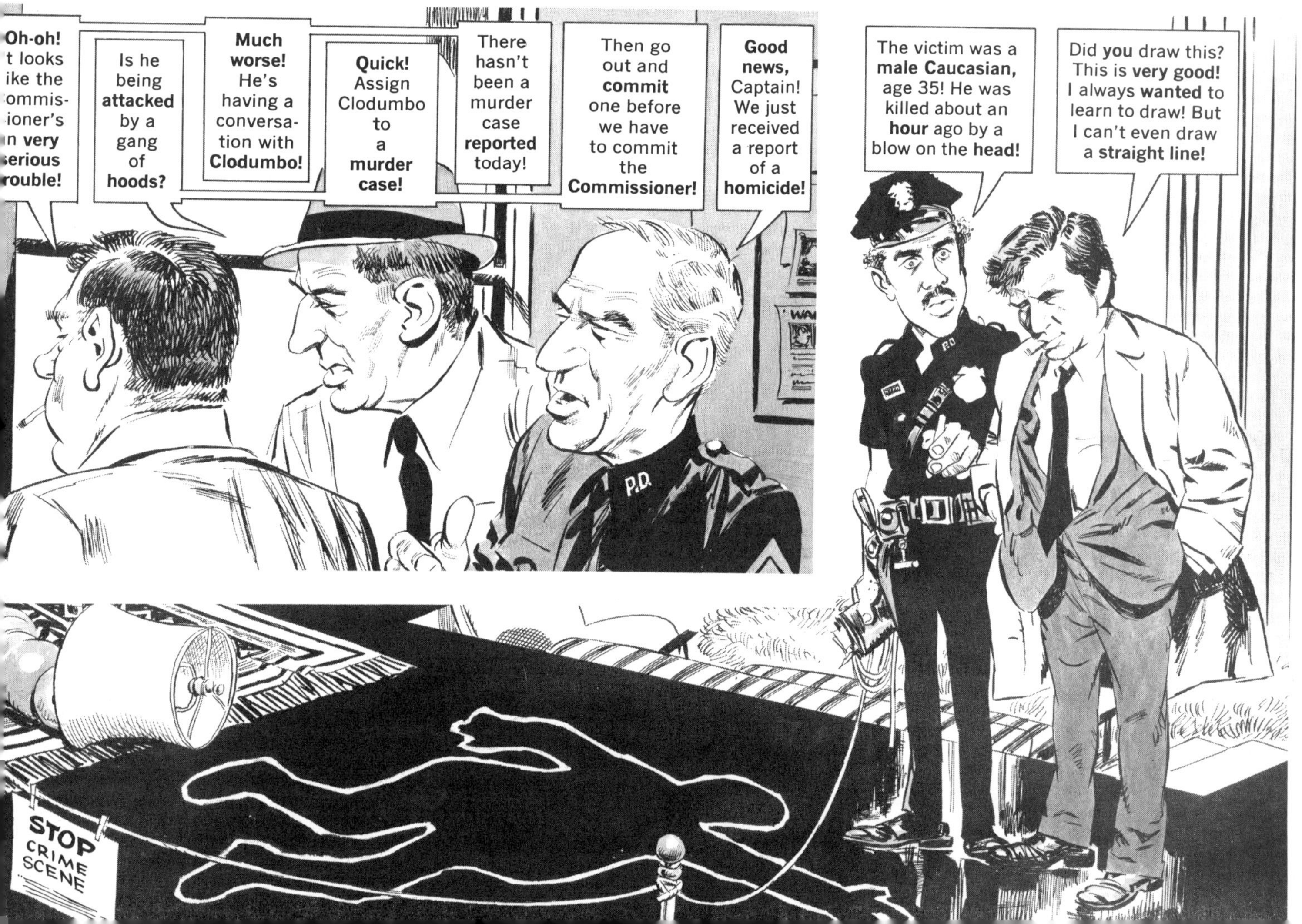
Oh-oh! t looks ike the ommis- ioner's n very erious rouble!
Is he being attacked by a gang of hoods?
Much worse! He's having a conversa- tion with Clodumbo!
Quick! Assign Clodumbo to a murder case!
There hasn't been a murder case reported today!
Then go out and commit one before we have to commit the Commissioner!
Good news, Captain! We just received a report of a homicide!
The victim was a male Caucasian, age 35! He was killed about an hour ago by a blow on the head!
Did you draw this? This is very good! I always wanted to learn to draw! But I can't even draw a straight line!
P.D.
STOP CRIME SCENE

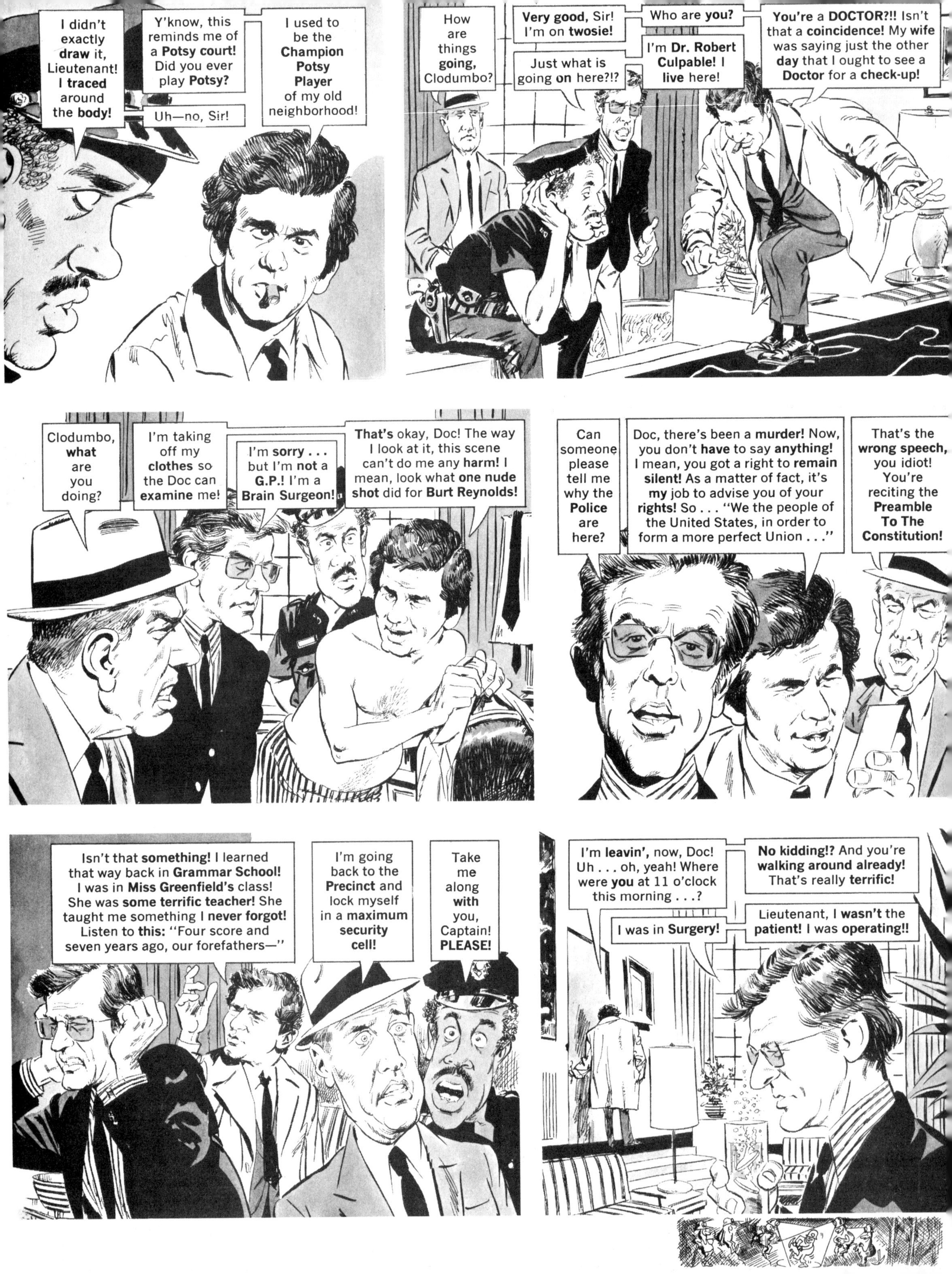

I didn't exactly draw it, Lieutenant! I traced around the body!
Y'know, this reminds me of a Potsy court! Did you ever play Potsy?
Uh—no, Sir!
I used to be the Champion Potsy Player of my old neighborhood!
How are things going, Clodumbo?
Very good, Sir! I'm on twosie!
Just what is going on here?!?
Who are you?
I'm Dr. Robert Culpable! I live here!
You're a DOCTOR?!! Isn't that a coincidence! My wife was saying just the other day that I ought to see a Doctor for a check-up!
Clodumbo, what are you doing?
I'm taking off my clothes so the Doc can examine me!
I'm sorry . . . but I'm not a G.P.! I'm a Brain Surgeon!
That's okay, Doc! The way I look at it, this scene can't do me any harm! I mean, look what one nude shot did for Burt Reynolds!
Can someone please tell me why the Police are here?
Doc, there's been a murder! Now, you don't have to say anything! I mean, you got a right to remain silent! As a matter of fact, it's my job to advise you of your rights! So . . . "We the people of the United States, in order to form a more perfect Union . . ."
That's the wrong speech, you idiot! You're reciting the Preamble To The Constitution!
Isn't that something! I learned that way back in Grammar School! I was in Miss Greenfield's class! She was some terrific teacher! She taught me something I never forgot! Listen to this: "Four score and seven years ago, our forefathers—"
I'm going back to the Precinct and lock myself in a maximum security cell!
Take me along with you, Captain! PLEASE!
I'm leavin', now, Doc! Uh . . . oh, yeah! Where were you at 11 o'clock this morning . . . ?
I was in Surgery!
No kidding!? And you're walking around already! That's really terrific!
Lieutenant, I wasn't the patient! I was operating!!

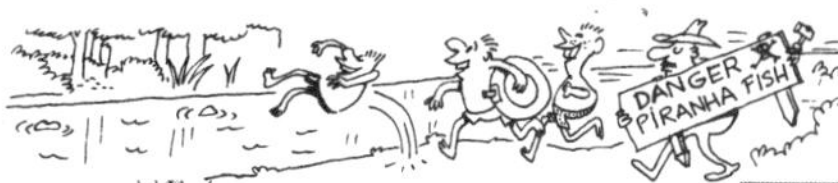
DANGER PIRANHA FISH

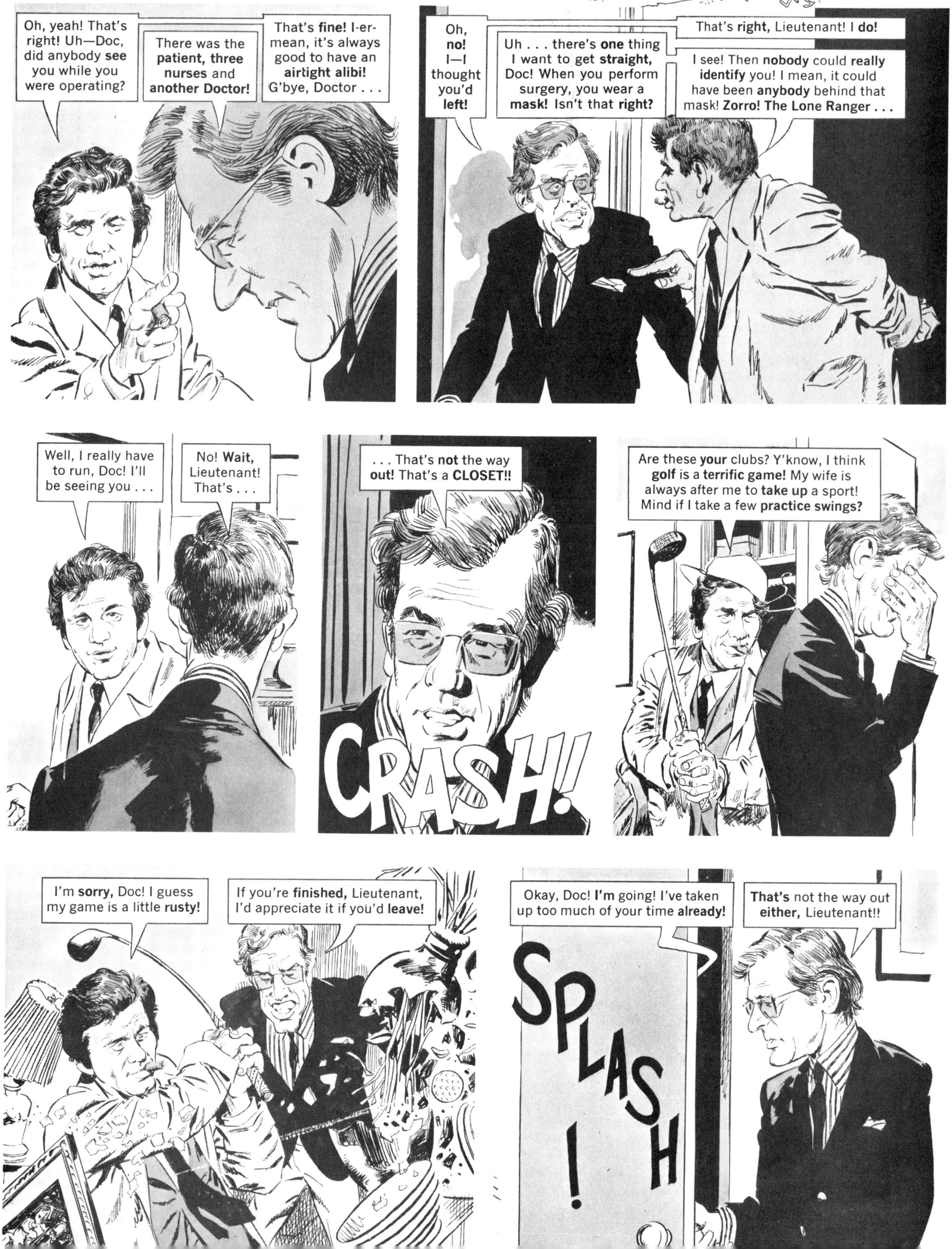
Oh, yeah! That's right! Uh—Doc, did anybody **see** you while you were operating?
There was the **patient, three nurses** and **another Doctor!**
That's **fine!** I-er-mean, it's always good to have an **airtight alibi!** G'bye, Doctor . . .
Oh, **no!** I—I thought you'd **left!**
Uh . . . there's **one** thing I want to get **straight,** Doc! When you perform surgery, you wear a **mask!** Isn't that **right?**
That's **right,** Lieutenant! I **do!**
I see! Then **nobody** could **really identify** you! I mean, it could have been **anybody** behind that mask! **Zorro! The Lone Ranger . . .**
Well, I really have to run, Doc! I'll be seeing you . . .
No! **Wait,** Lieutenant! That's . . .
. . . That's **not** the way **out!** That's a **CLOSET!!**
CRASH!!
Are these **your** clubs? Y'know, I think **golf** is a **terrific game!** My wife is always after me to **take up** a sport! Mind if I take a few **practice swings?**
I'm **sorry,** Doc! I guess my game is a little **rusty!**
If you're **finished,** Lieutenant, I'd appreciate it if you'd **leave!**
Okay, Doc! **I'm** going! I've taken up too much of your time **already!**
SPLASH!
That's not the way out **either,** Lieutenant!!

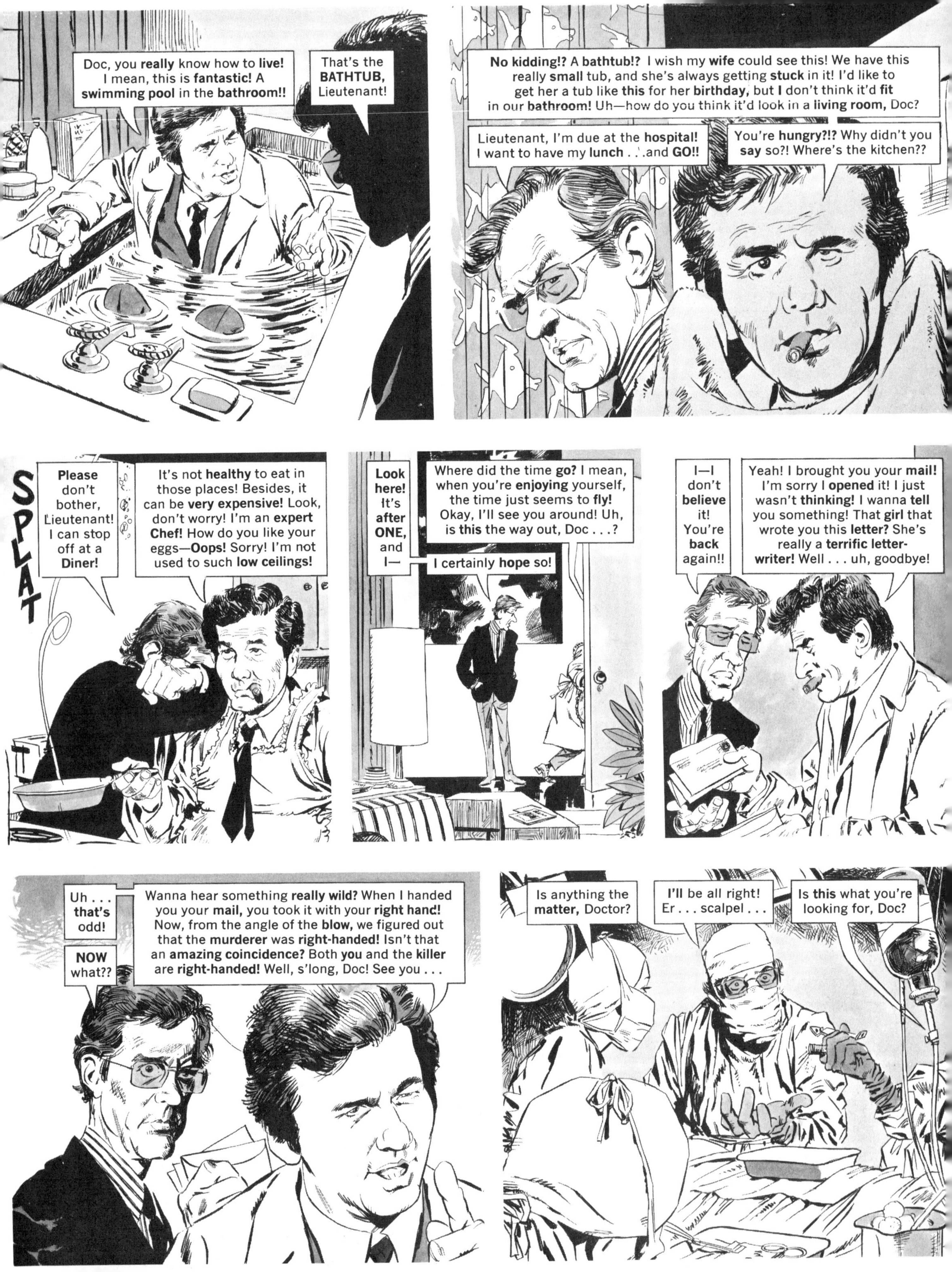
Doc, you really know how to live! I mean, this is fantastic! A swimming pool in the bathroom!!
That's the BATHTUB, Lieutenant!
No kidding!? A bathtub!? I wish my wife could see this! We have this really small tub, and she's always getting stuck in it! I'd like to get her a tub like this for her birthday, but I don't think it'd fit in our bathroom! Uh—how do you think it'd look in a living room, Doc?
Lieutenant, I'm due at the hospital! I want to have my lunch . . .and GO!!
You're hungry?!? Why didn't you say so?! Where's the kitchen??
Please don't bother, Lieutenant! I can stop off at a Diner!
It's not healthy to eat in those places! Besides, it can be very expensive! Look, don't worry! I'm an expert Chef! How do you like your eggs—Oops! Sorry! I'm not used to such low ceilings!
SPLAT
Look here! It's after ONE, and I—
Where did the time go? I mean, when you're enjoying yourself, the time just seems to fly! Okay, I'll see you around! Uh, is this the way out, Doc . . .?
I certainly hope so!
I—I don't believe it! You're back again!!
Yeah! I brought you your mail! I'm sorry I opened it! I just wasn't thinking! I wanna tell you something! That girl that wrote you this letter? She's really a terrific letter-writer! Well . . . uh, goodbye!
Uh . . . that's odd!
NOW what??
Wanna hear something really wild? When I handed you your mail, you took it with your right hand! Now, from the angle of the blow, we figured out that the murderer was right-handed! Isn't that an amazing coincidence? Both you and the killer are right-handed! Well, s'long, Doc! See you . . .
Is anything the matter, Doctor?
I'll be all right! Er . . . scalpel . . .
Is this what you're looking for, Doc?

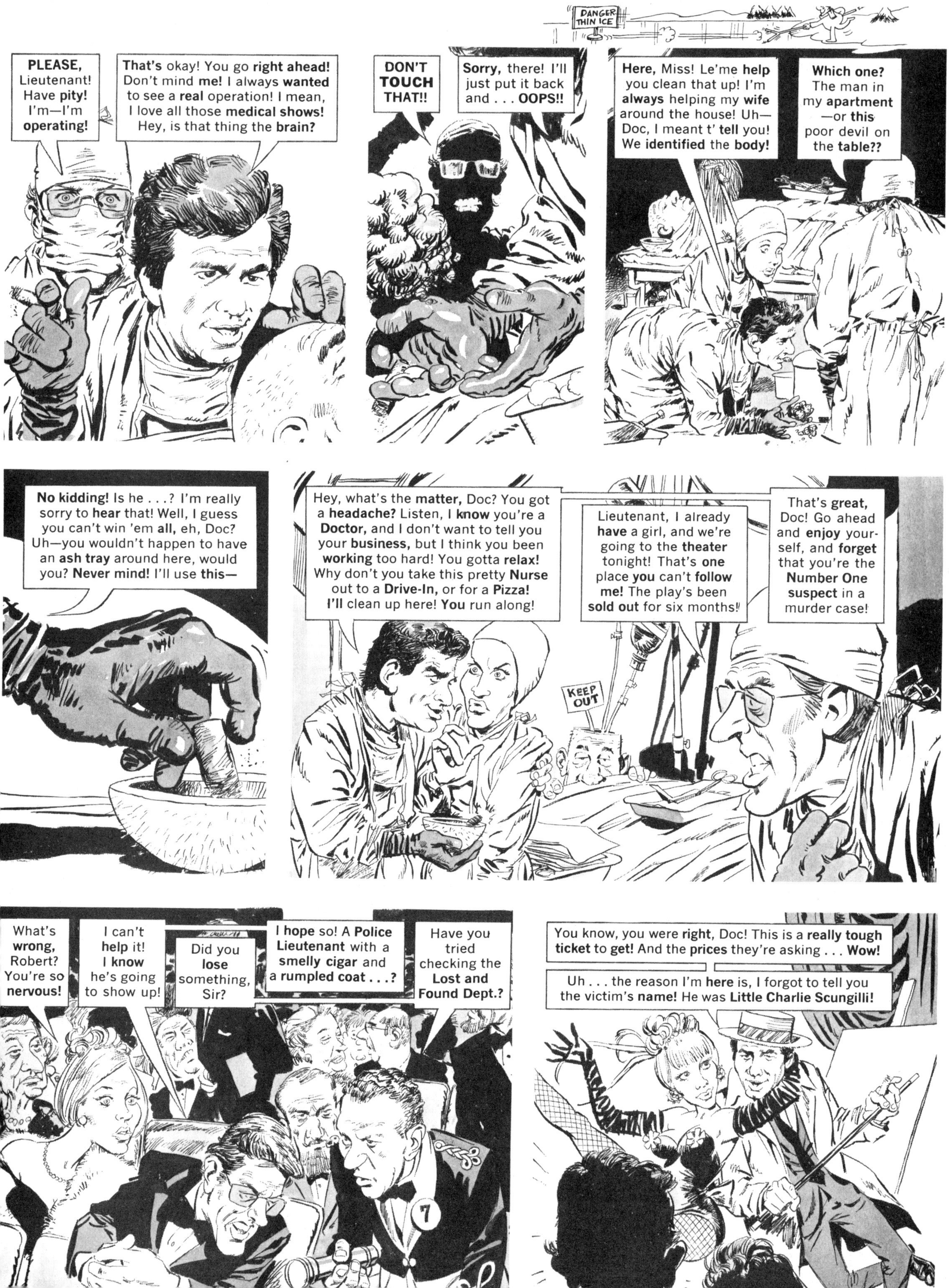
DANGER THIN ICE
PLEASE, Lieutenant! Have pity! I'm—I'm operating!
That's okay! You go right ahead! Don't mind me! I always wanted to see a real operation! I mean, I love all those medical shows! Hey, is that thing the brain?
DON'T TOUCH THAT!!
Sorry, there! I'll just put it back and . . . OOPS!!
Here, Miss! Le'me help you clean that up! I'm always helping my wife around the house! Uh—Doc, I meant t' tell you! We identified the body!
Which one? The man in my apartment —or this poor devil on the table??
No kidding! Is he . . .? I'm really sorry to hear that! Well, I guess you can't win 'em all, eh, Doc? Uh—you wouldn't happen to have an ash tray around here, would you? Never mind! I'll use this—
Hey, what's the matter, Doc? You got a headache? Listen, I know you're a Doctor, and I don't want to tell you your business, but I think you been working too hard! You gotta relax! Why don't you take this pretty Nurse out to a Drive-In, or for a Pizza! I'll clean up here! You run along!
Lieutenant, I already have a girl, and we're going to the theater tonight! That's one place you can't follow me! The play's been sold out for six months!
That's great, Doc! Go ahead and enjoy yourself, and forget that you're the Number One suspect in a murder case!
KEEP OUT
What's wrong, Robert? You're so nervous!
I can't help it! I know he's going to show up!
Did you lose something, Sir?
I hope so! A Police Lieutenant with a smelly cigar and a rumpled coat . . .?
Have you tried checking the Lost and Found Dept.?
7
You know, you were right, Doc! This is a really tough ticket to get! And the prices they're asking . . . Wow!
Uh . . . the reason I'm here is, I forgot to tell you the victim's name! He was Little Charlie Scungilli!

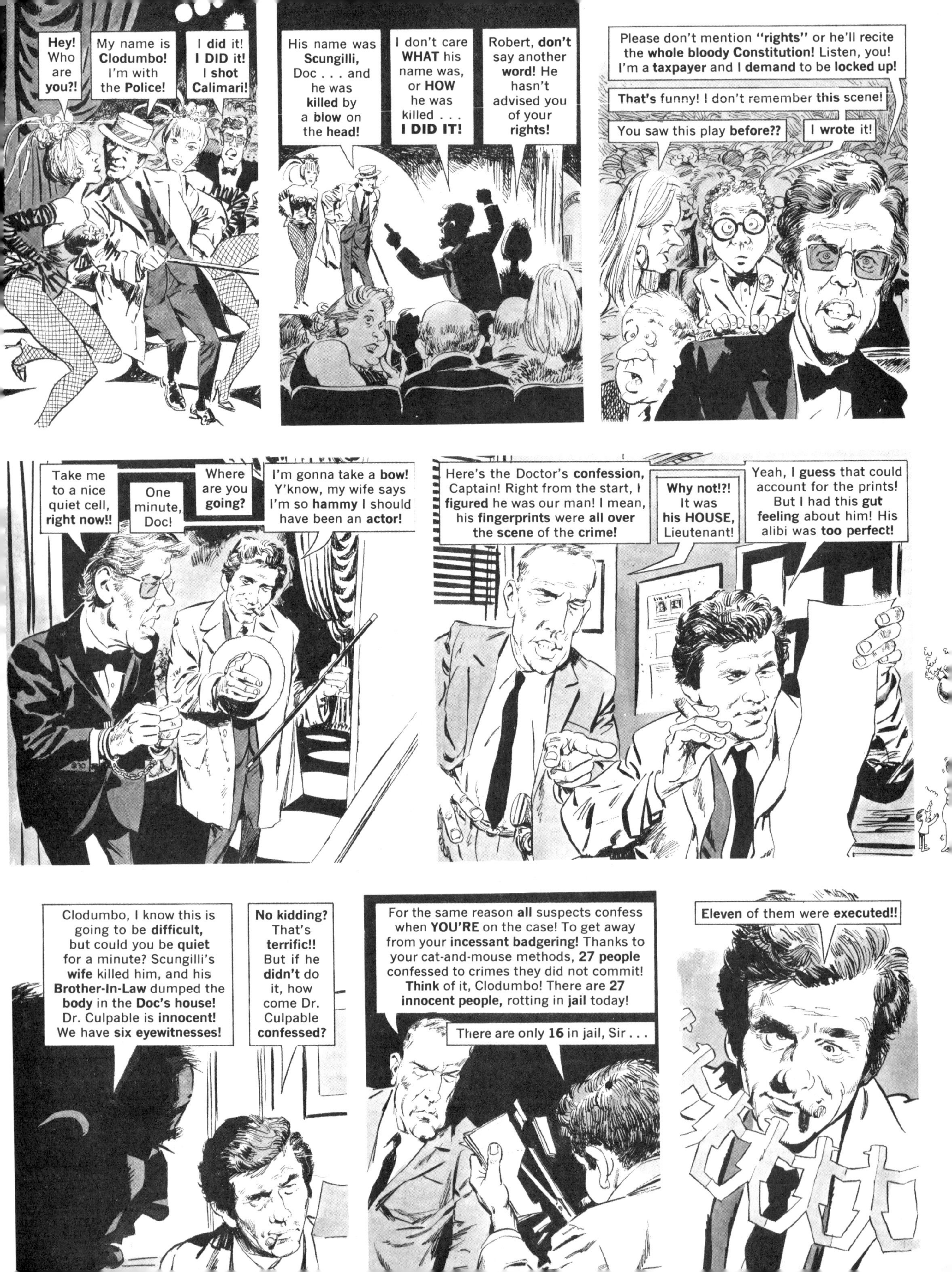
Hey! Who are you?!
My name is Clodumbo! I'm with the Police!
I did it! I DID it! I shot Calimari!
His name was Scungilli, Doc . . . and he was killed by a blow on the head!
I don't care WHAT his name was, or HOW he was killed . . . I DID IT!
Robert, don't say another word! He hasn't advised you of your rights!
Please don't mention "rights" or he'll recite the whole bloody Constitution! Listen, you! I'm a taxpayer and I demand to be locked up!
That's funny! I don't remember this scene!
You saw this play before??
I wrote it!
Take me to a nice quiet cell, right now!!
One minute, Doc!
Where are you going?
I'm gonna take a bow! Y'know, my wife says I'm so hammy I should have been an actor!
Here's the Doctor's confession, Captain! Right from the start, I figured he was our man! I mean, his fingerprints were all over the scene of the crime!
Why not!?! It was his HOUSE, Lieutenant!
Yeah, I guess that could account for the prints! But I had this gut feeling about him! His alibi was too perfect!
Clodumbo, I know this is going to be difficult, but could you be quiet for a minute? Scungilli's wife killed him, and his Brother-In-Law dumped the body in the Doc's house! Dr. Culpable is innocent! We have six eyewitnesses!
No kidding? That's terrific!! But if he didn't do it, how come Dr. Culpable confessed?
For the same reason all suspects confess when YOU'RE on the case! To get away from your incessant badgering! Thanks to your cat-and-mouse methods, 27 people confessed to crimes they did not commit! Think of it, Clodumbo! There are 27 innocent people, rotting in jail today!
There are only 16 in jail, Sir . . .
Eleven of them were executed!!

MOORE OF THE SAME DEPT.

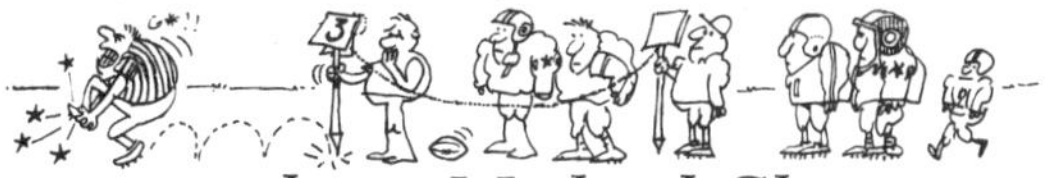

Television may have an excuse for putting on all those unrealistic Medical Shows and unrealistic Police Shows and unrealistic Lawyer Shows and unrealistic Western Shows. After all, Television writers don't have any first-hand experience at being Doctors or Cops or Lawyers or Cowboys. But what's the alibi when Television puts on an unrealistic Comedy about Television? We're talking about the show that took that down-to-earth gal from the old "Dick Van Dyke Show," put her into an idiotic Television situation, and came up with the same old garbage...even though it was

THE MARY TAILOR-MADE SHOW

ARTIST: ANGELO TORRES — WRITER: TOM KOCH

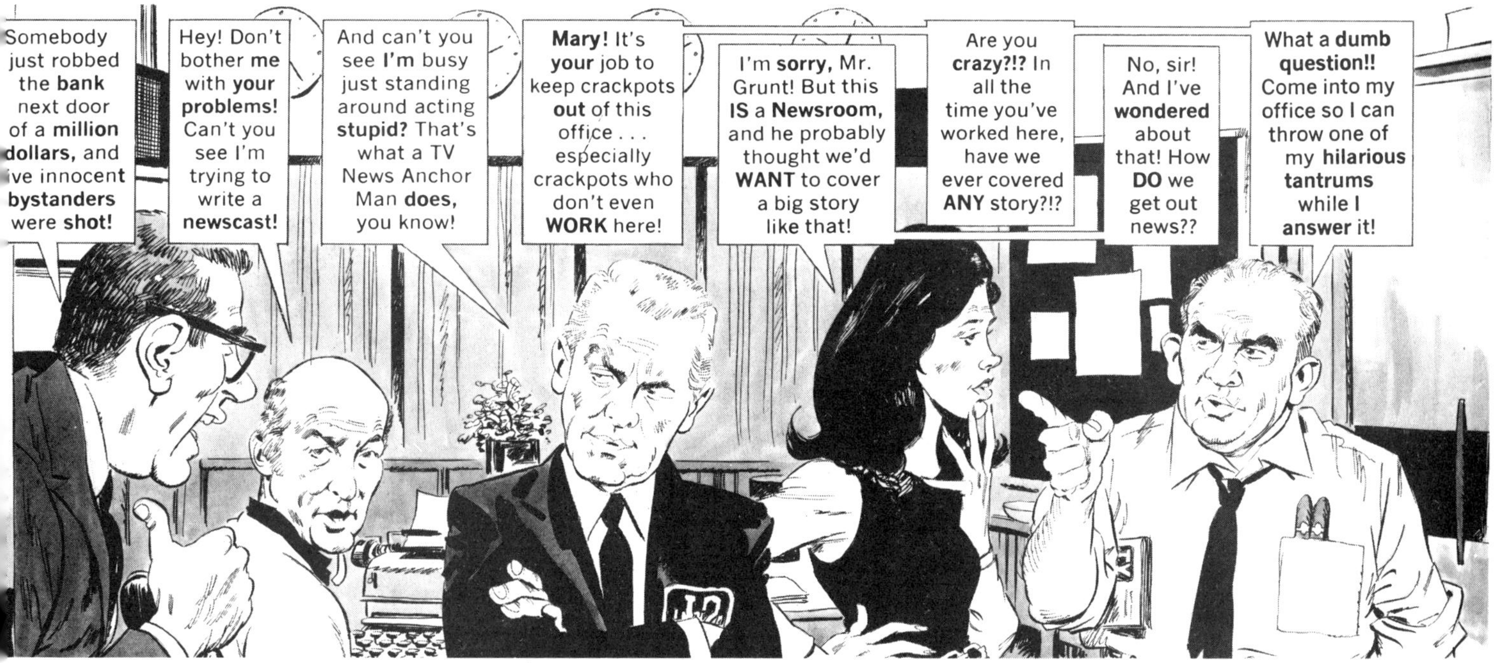

Somebody just robbed the bank next door of a million dollars, and ive innocent bystanders were shot!
Hey! Don't bother me with your problems! Can't you see I'm trying to write a newscast!
And can't you see I'm busy just standing around acting stupid? That's what a TV News Anchor Man does, you know!
Mary! It's your job to keep crackpots out of this office . . . especially crackpots who don't even WORK here!
I'm sorry, Mr. Grunt! But this IS a Newsroom, and he probably thought we'd WANT to cover a big story like that!
Are you crazy?!? In all the time you've worked here, have we ever covered ANY story?!?
No, sir! And I've wondered about that! How DO we get out news??
What a dumb question!! Come into my office so I can throw one of my hilarious tantrums while I answer it!

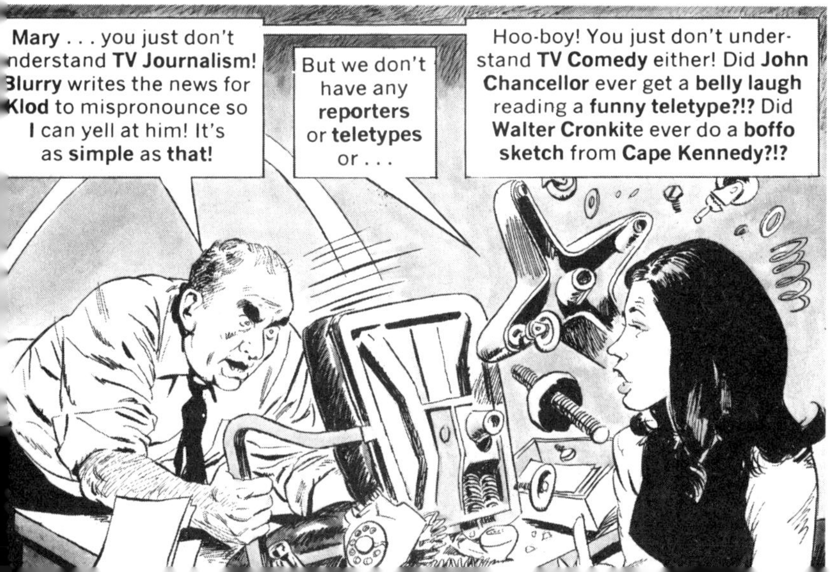

Mary . . . you just don't nderstand TV Journalism! Blurry writes the news for Klod to mispronounce so I can yell at him! It's as simple as that!
But we don't have any reporters or teletypes or . . .
Hoo-boy! You just don't understand TV Comedy either! Did John Chancellor ever get a belly laugh reading a funny teletype?!? Did Walter Cronkite ever do a boffo sketch from Cape Kennedy?!?

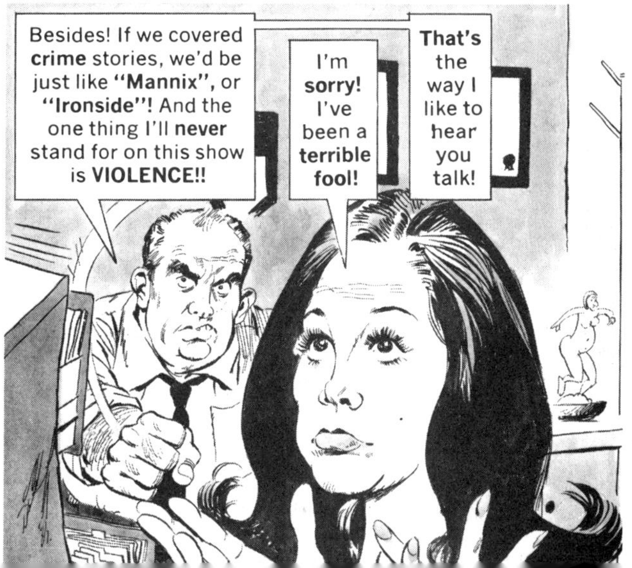

Besides! If we covered crime stories, we'd be just like "Mannix", or "Ironside"! And the one thing I'll never stand for on this show is VIOLENCE!!
I'm sorry! I've been a terrible fool!
That's the way I like to hear you talk!

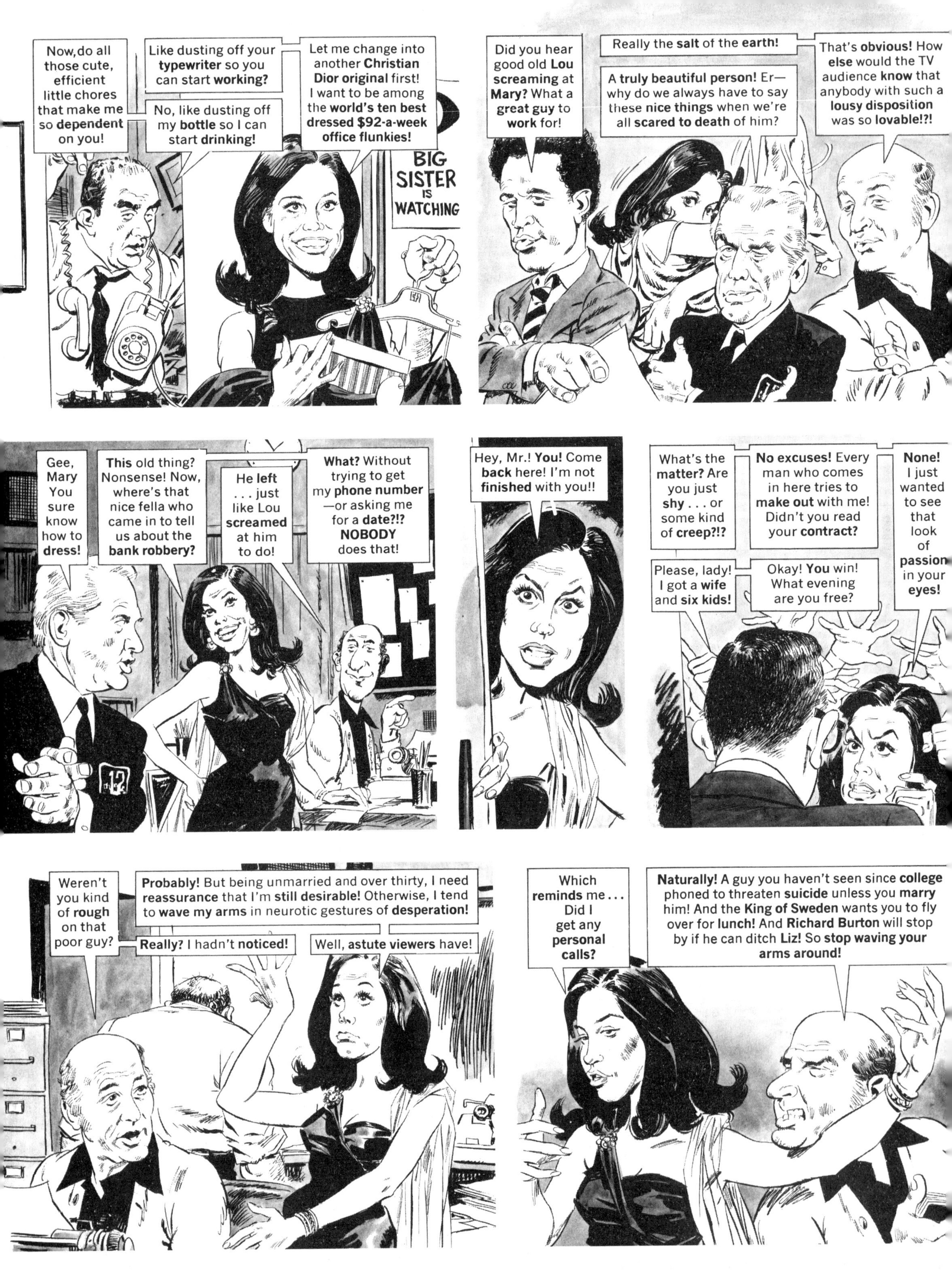

Now, do all those cute, efficient little chores that make me so dependent on you!
Like dusting off your typewriter so you can start working?
No, like dusting off my bottle so I can start drinking!
Let me change into another Christian Dior original first! I want to be among the world's ten best dressed $92-a-week office flunkies!
BIG SISTER IS WATCHING
Did you hear good old Lou screaming at Mary? What a great guy to work for!
Really the salt of the earth!
A truly beautiful person! Er— why do we always have to say these nice things when we're all scared to death of him?
That's obvious! How else would the TV audience know that anybody with such a lousy disposition was so lovable!?!
Gee, Mary You sure know how to dress!
This old thing? Nonsense! Now, where's that nice fella who came in to tell us about the bank robbery?
He left . . . just like Lou screamed at him to do!
What? Without trying to get my phone number —or asking me for a date?!? NOBODY does that!
Hey, Mr.! You! Come back here! I'm not finished with you!!
What's the matter? Are you just shy . . . or some kind of creep?!?
Please, lady! I got a wife and six kids!
No excuses! Every man who comes in here tries to make out with me! Didn't you read your contract?
Okay! You win! What evening are you free?
None! I just wanted to see that look of passion in your eyes!
Weren't you kind of rough on that poor guy?
Probably! But being unmarried and over thirty, I need reassurance that I'm still desirable! Otherwise, I tend to wave my arms in neurotic gestures of desperation!
Really? I hadn't noticed!
Well, astute viewers have!
Which reminds me . . . Did I get any personal calls?
Naturally! A guy you haven't seen since college phoned to threaten suicide unless you marry him! And the King of Sweden wants you to fly over for lunch! And Richard Burton will stop by if he can ditch Liz! So stop waving your arms around!

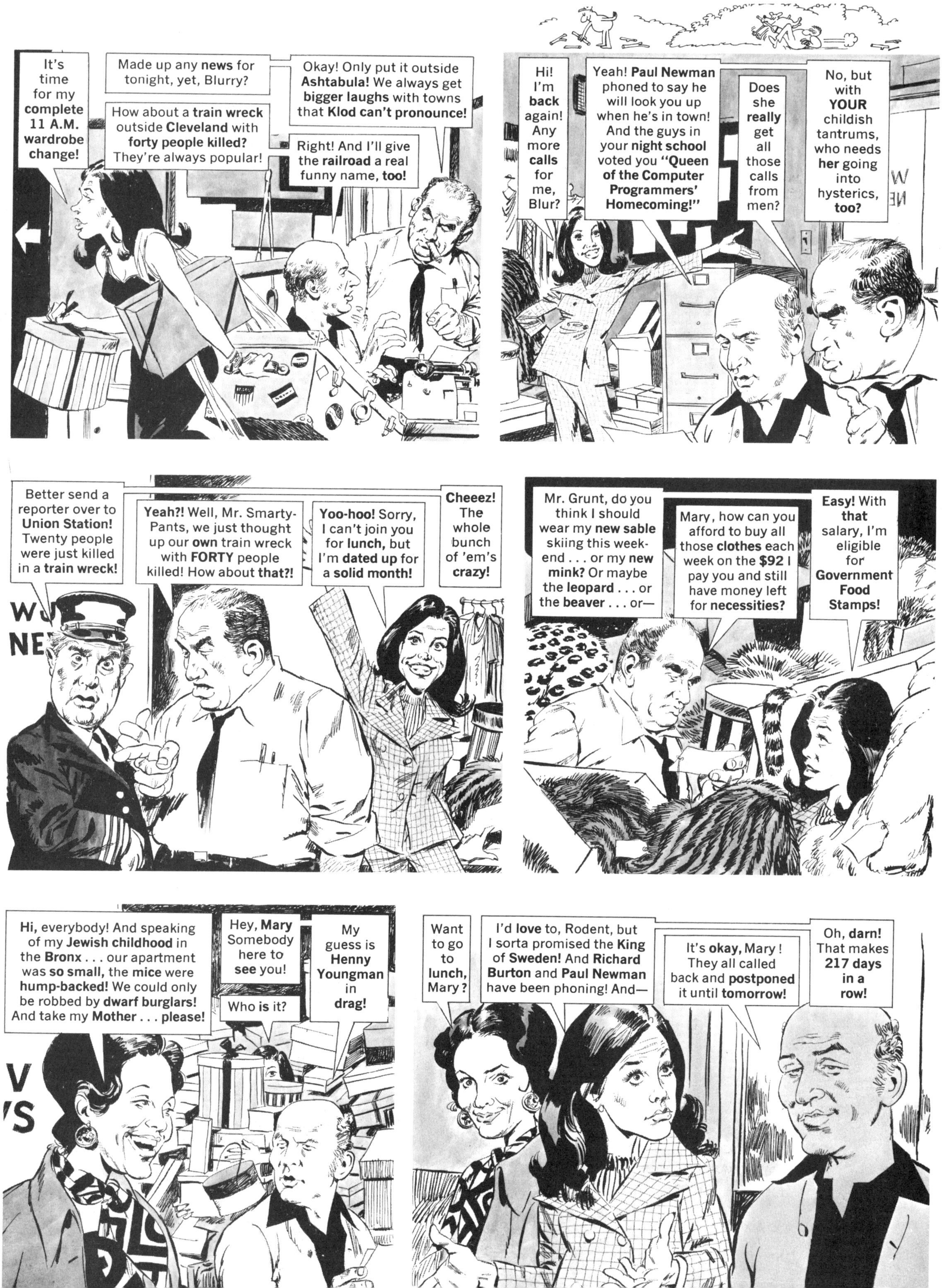

It's time for my complete 11 A.M. wardrobe change!
Made up any news for tonight, yet, Blurry?
How about a train wreck outside Cleveland with forty people killed? They're always popular!
Okay! Only put it outside Ashtabula! We always get bigger laughs with towns that Klod can't pronounce!
Right! And I'll give the railroad a real funny name, too!
Hi! I'm back again! Any more calls for me, Blur?
Yeah! Paul Newman phoned to say he will look you up when he's in town! And the guys in your night school voted you "Queen of the Computer Programmers' Homecoming!"
Does she really get all those calls from men?
No, but with YOUR childish tantrums, who needs her going into hysterics, too?
Better send a reporter over to Union Station! Twenty people were just killed in a train wreck!
Yeah?! Well, Mr. Smarty-Pants, we just thought up our own train wreck with FORTY people killed! How about that?!
Yoo-hoo! Sorry, I can't join you for lunch, but I'm dated up for a solid month!
Cheeez! The whole bunch of 'em's crazy!
Mr. Grunt, do you think I should wear my new sable skiing this week-end . . . or my new mink? Or maybe the leopard . . . or the beaver . . . or—
Mary, how can you afford to buy all those clothes each week on the $92 I pay you and still have money left for necessities?
Easy! With that salary, I'm eligible for Government Food Stamps!
Hi, everybody! And speaking of my Jewish childhood in the Bronx . . . our apartment was so small, the mice were hump-backed! We could only be robbed by dwarf burglars! And take my Mother . . . please!
Hey, Mary Somebody here to see you!
Who is it?
My guess is Henny Youngman in drag!
Want to go to lunch, Mary?
I'd love to, Rodent, but I sorta promised the King of Sweden! And Richard Burton and Paul Newman have been phoning! And—
It's okay, Mary! They all called back and postponed it until tomorrow!
Oh, darn! That makes 217 days in a row!

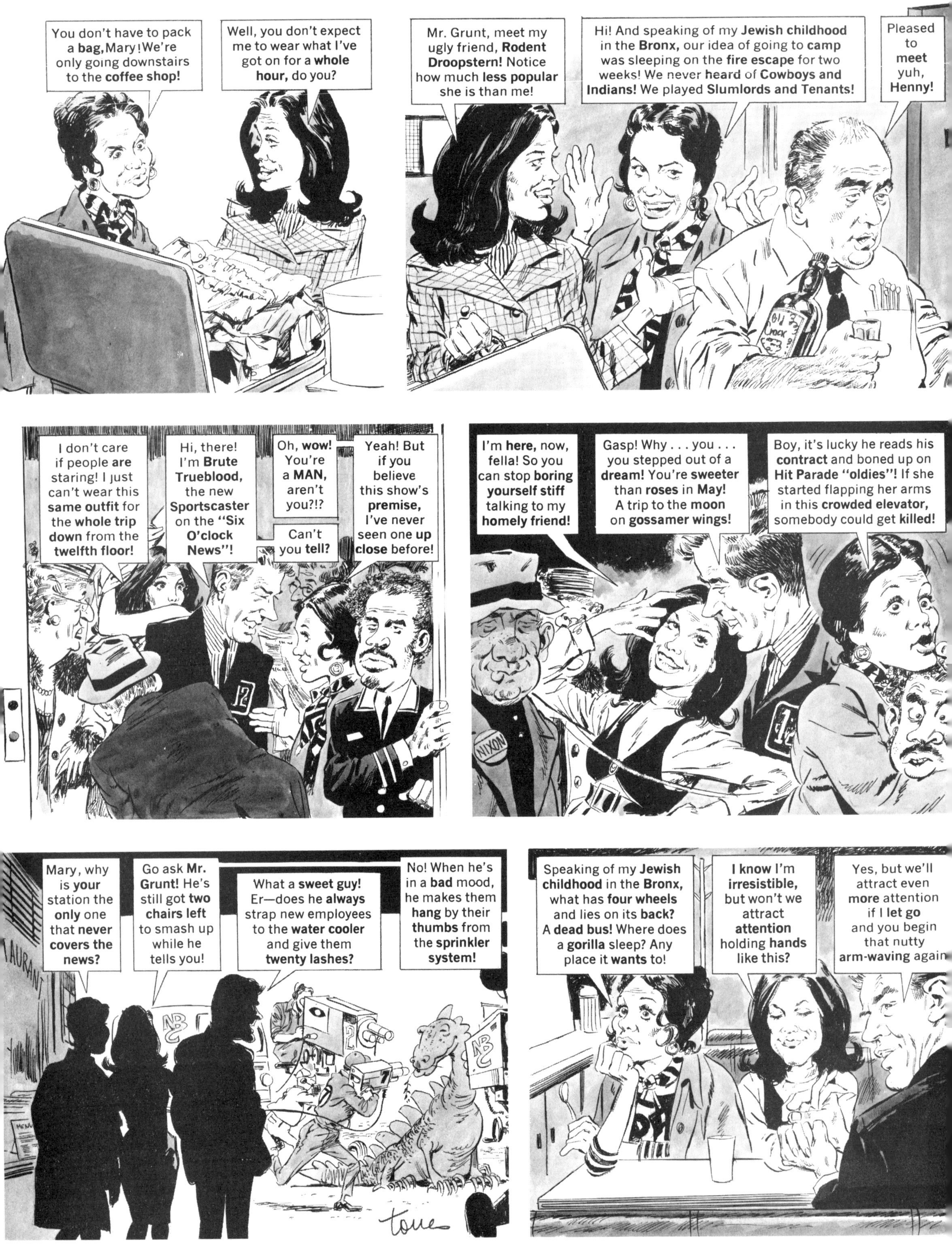
You don't have to pack a bag, Mary! We're only going downstairs to the coffee shop!
Well, you don't expect me to wear what I've got on for a whole hour, do you?
Mr. Grunt, meet my ugly friend, Rodent Droopstern! Notice how much less popular she is than me!
Hi! And speaking of my Jewish childhood in the Bronx, our idea of going to camp was sleeping on the fire escape for two weeks! We never heard of Cowboys and Indians! We played Slumlords and Tenants!
Pleased to meet yuh, Henny!
I don't care if people are staring! I just can't wear this same outfit for the whole trip down from the twelfth floor!
Hi, there! I'm Brute Trueblood, the new Sportscaster on the "Six O'clock News"!
Oh, wow! You're a MAN, aren't you?!?
Can't you tell?
Yeah! But if you believe this show's premise, I've never seen one up close before!
I'm here, now, fella! So you can stop boring yourself stiff talking to my homely friend!
Gasp! Why . . . you . . . you stepped out of a dream! You're sweeter than roses in May! A trip to the moon on gossamer wings!
Boy, it's lucky he reads his contract and boned up on Hit Parade "oldies"! If she started flapping her arms in this crowded elevator, somebody could get killed!
NIXON
Mary, why is your station the only one that never covers the news?
Go ask Mr. Grunt! He's still got two chairs left to smash up while he tells you!
What a sweet guy! Er—does he always strap new employees to the water cooler and give them twenty lashes?
No! When he's in a bad mood, he makes them hang by their thumbs from the sprinkler system!
Speaking of my Jewish childhood in the Bronx, what has four wheels and lies on its back? A dead bus! Where does a gorilla sleep? Any place it wants to!
I know I'm irresistible, but won't we attract attention holding hands like this?
Yes, but we'll attract even more attention if I let go and you begin that nutty arm-waving again

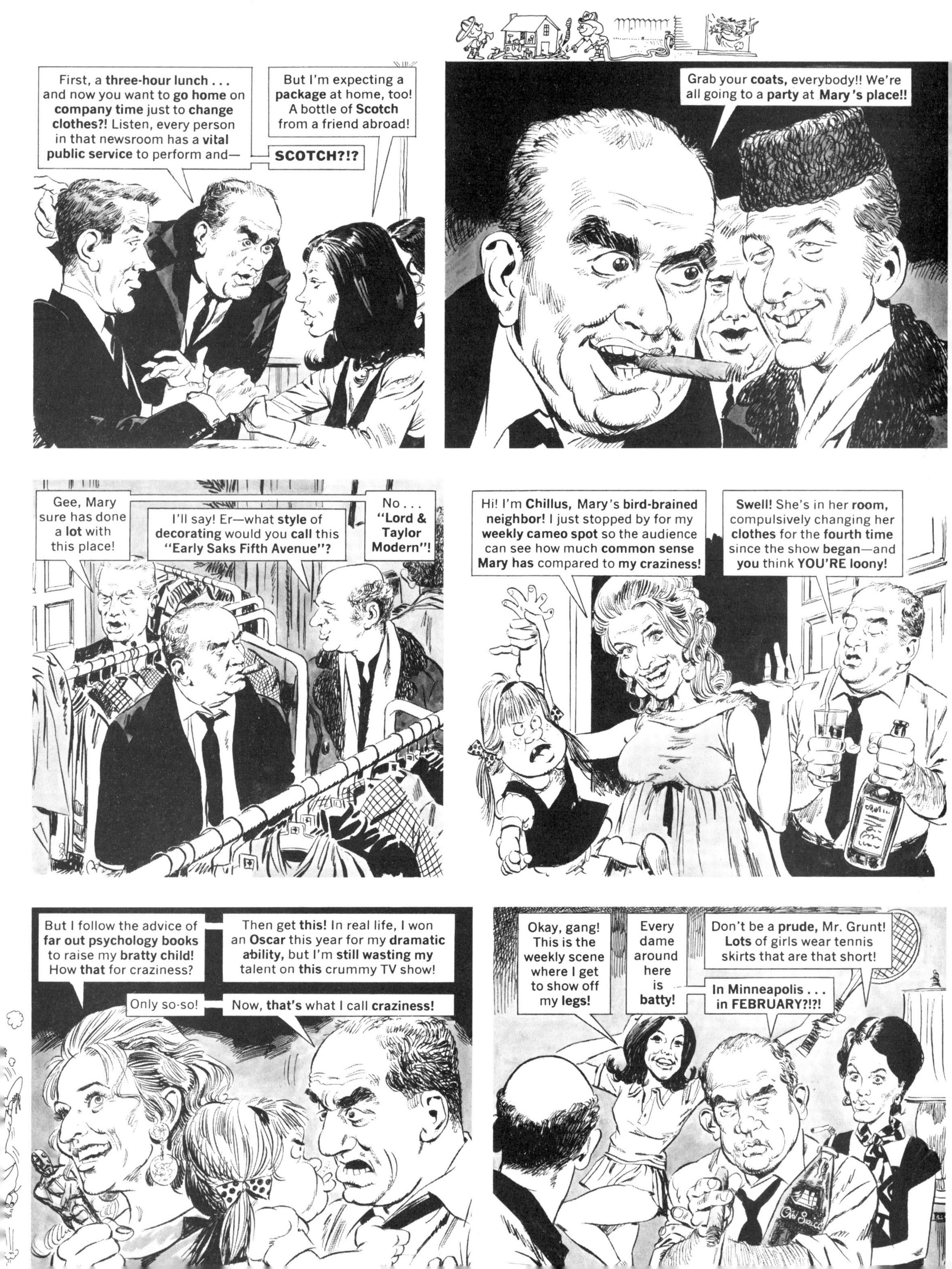

First, a three-hour lunch . . . and now you want to go home on company time just to change clothes?! Listen, every person in that newsroom has a vital public service to perform and—
But I'm expecting a package at home, too! A bottle of Scotch from a friend abroad!
SCOTCH?!?
Grab your coats, everybody!! We're all going to a party at Mary's place!!
Gee, Mary sure has done a lot with this place!
I'll say! Er—what style of decorating would you call this "Early Saks Fifth Avenue"?
No . . . "Lord & Taylor Modern"!
Hi! I'm Chillus, Mary's bird-brained neighbor! I just stopped by for my weekly cameo spot so the audience can see how much common sense Mary has compared to my craziness!
Swell! She's in her room, compulsively changing her clothes for the fourth time since the show began—and you think YOU'RE loony!
But I follow the advice of far out psychology books to raise my bratty child! How that for craziness?
Then get this! In real life, I won an Oscar this year for my dramatic ability, but I'm still wasting my talent on this crummy TV show!
Only so-so!
Now, that's what I call craziness!
Okay, gang! This is the weekly scene where I get to show off my legs!
Every dame around here is batty!
Don't be a prude, Mr. Grunt! Lots of girls wear tennis skirts that are that short!
In Minneapolis . . . in FEBRUARY?!?!

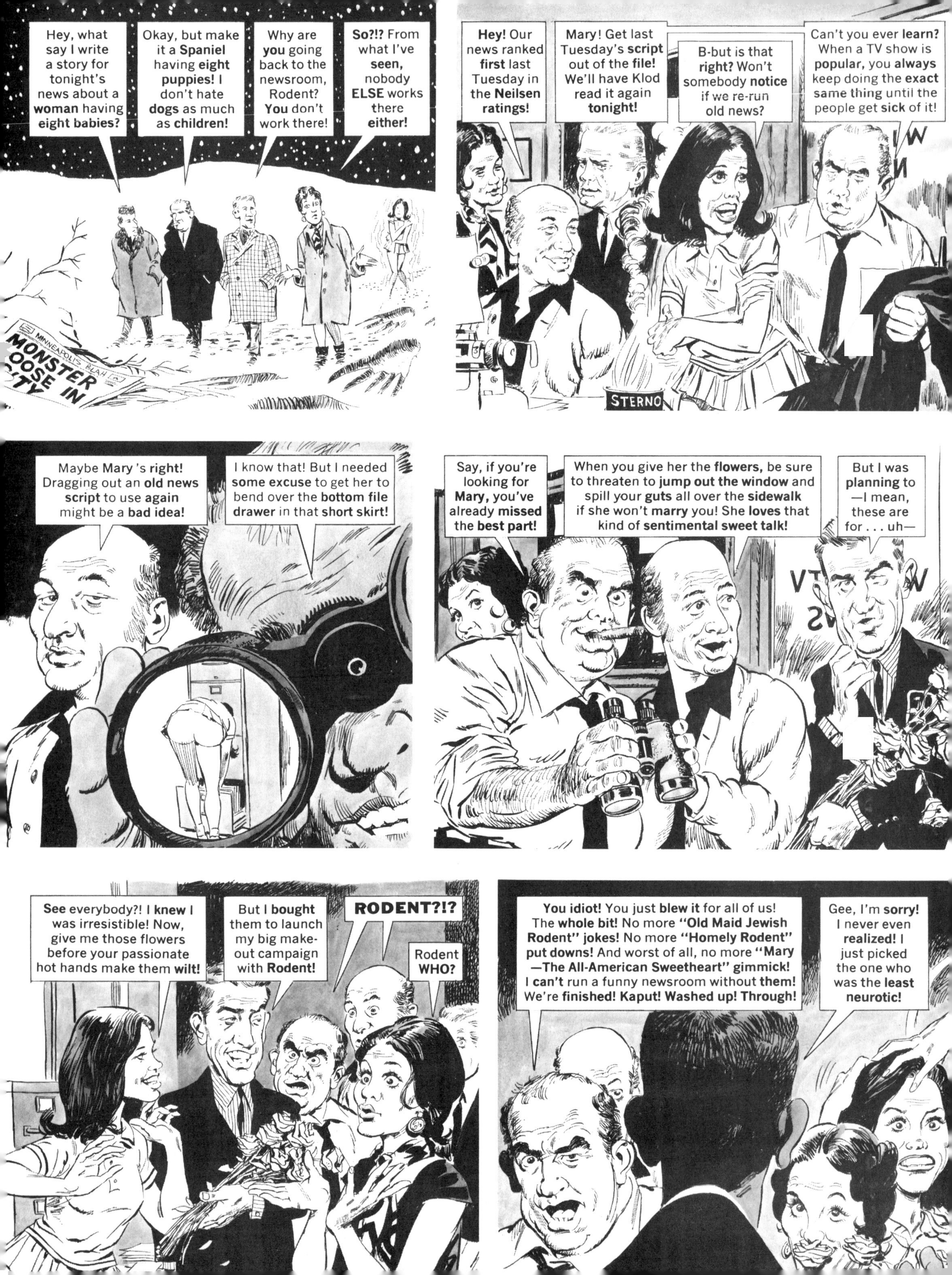

Hey, what say I write a story for tonight's news about a **woman** having **eight babies?**
Okay, but make it a **Spaniel** having **eight puppies!** I don't hate **dogs** as much as **children!**
Why are **you** going back to the newsroom, Rodent? **You** don't work there!
So?!? From what I've **seen,** nobody **ELSE** works there **either!**
MINNEAPOLIS BLAH
MONSTER
Hey! Our news ranked **first** last Tuesday in the **Neilsen ratings!**
Mary! Get last Tuesday's **script** out of the **file!** We'll have Klod read it again **tonight!**
B-but is that **right?** Won't somebody **notice** if we re-run old news?
Can't you ever **learn?** When a TV show is **popular,** you **always** keep doing the **exact same thing** until the people get **sick** of it!
STERNO
Maybe Mary 's **right!** Dragging out an **old news script** to use **again** might be a **bad idea!**
I know that! But I needed **some excuse** to get her to bend over the **bottom file drawer** in that **short skirt!**
Say, if you're looking for **Mary, you've** already **missed** the **best part!**
When you give her the **flowers,** be sure to threaten to **jump out the window** and spill your **guts** all over the **sidewalk** if she won't **marry** you! She **loves** that kind of **sentimental sweet talk!**
But I was **planning** to —I mean, these are for . . . uh—
See everybody?! I **knew** I was irresistible! Now, give me those flowers before your passionate hot hands make them **wilt!**
But I **bought** them to launch my big make-out campaign with **Rodent!**
RODENT?!?
Rodent **WHO?**
You idiot! You just **blew it** for all of us! The **whole bit!** No more **"Old Maid Jewish Rodent"** jokes! No more **"Homely Rodent" put downs!** And worst of all, no more **"Mary —The All-American Sweetheart" gimmick!** I **can't** run a funny newsroom without **them!** We're **finished! Kaput! Washed up! Through!**
Gee, I'm **sorry!** I never even **realized!** I just picked the one who was the **least neurotic!**

SPORTS-BLASTER DEPT.

This ode to his favorite Monday night commentator is a good example of the type of idiocy MAD sports freak, Frank Jacobs, is offering in his all-new paperback, "MAD About Sports." So consider yourself warned about this "Humor In A Jock-ular Vein."

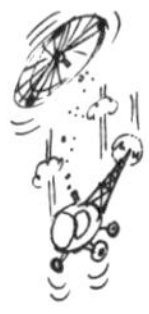

HOWARD AT THE MIKE

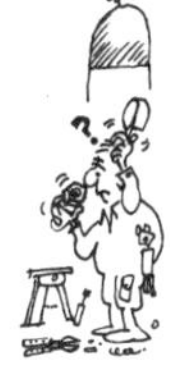

(with apologies to Ernest Lawrence Thayer)

ARTIST: JACK DAVIS WRITER: FRANK JACOBS

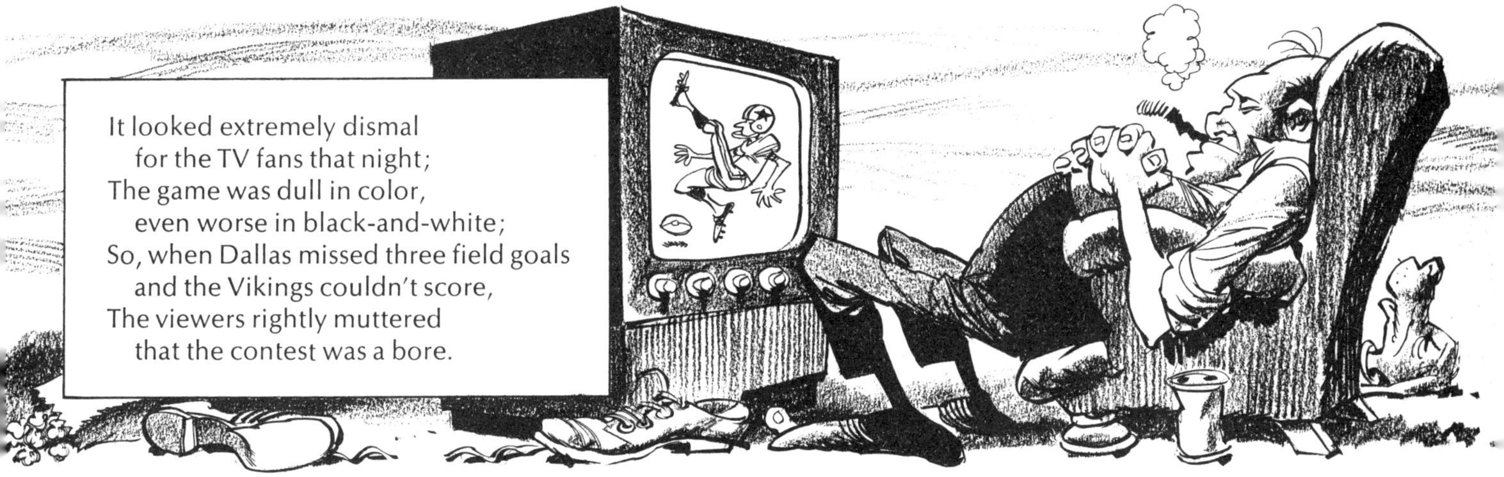

It looked extremely dismal
for the TV fans that night;
The game was dull in color,
even worse in black-and-white;
So, when Dallas missed three field goals
and the Vikings couldn't score,
The viewers rightly muttered
that the contest was a bore.

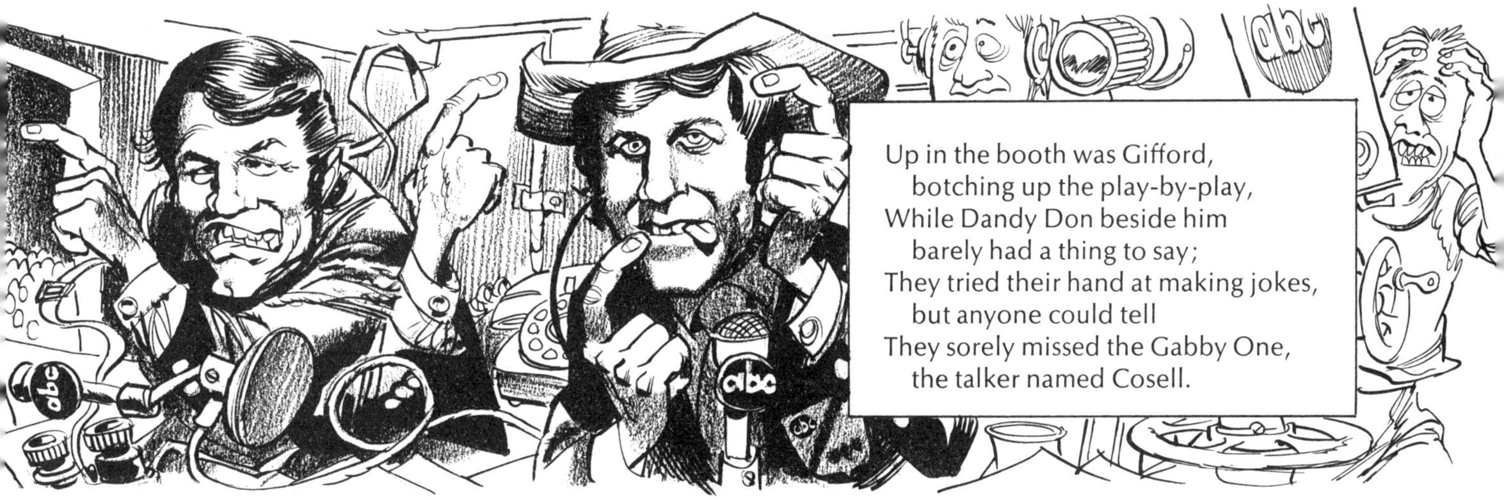

abc
abc

Up in the booth was Gifford,
botching up the play-by-play,
While Dandy Don beside him
barely had a thing to say;
They tried their hand at making jokes,
but anyone could tell
They sorely missed the Gabby One,
the talker named Cosell.

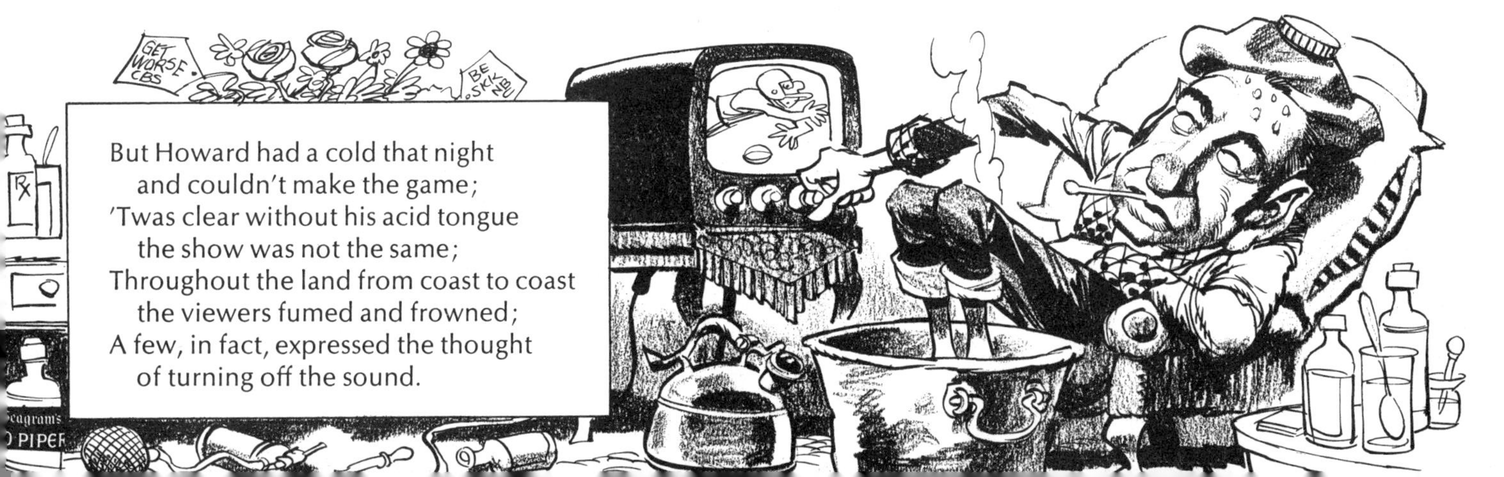

GET WORSE CBS

But Howard had a cold that night
and couldn't make the game;
'Twas clear without his acid tongue
the show was not the same;
Throughout the land from coast to coast
the viewers fumed and frowned;
A few, in fact, expressed the thought
of turning off the sound.

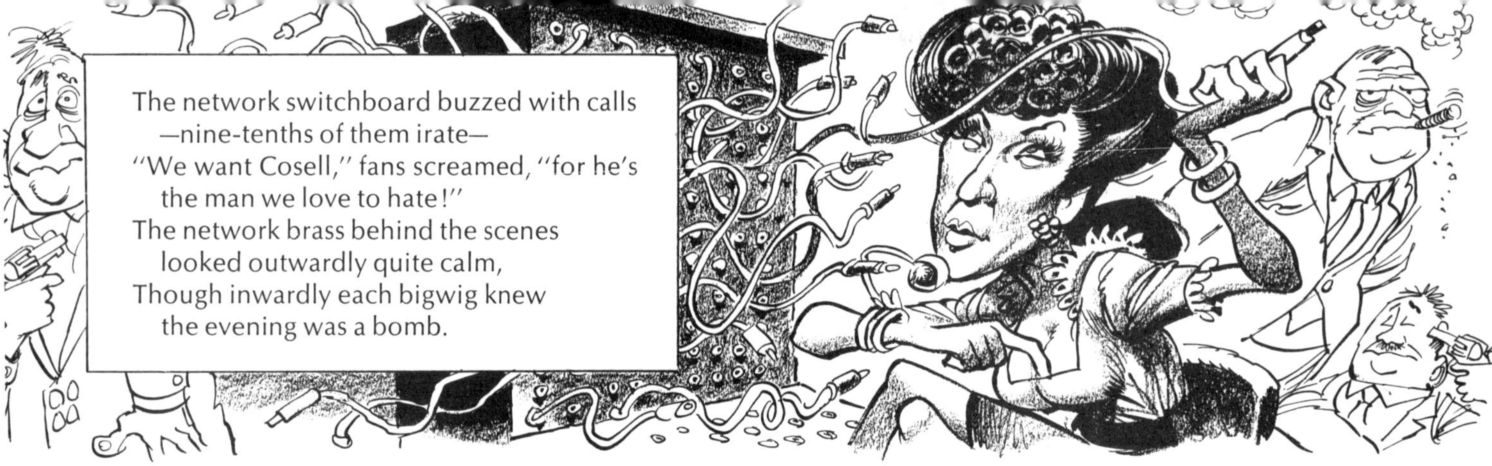

The network switchboard buzzed with calls
—nine-tenths of them irate—
"We want Cosell," fans screamed, "for he's
the man we love to hate!"
The network brass behind the scenes
looked outwardly quite calm,
Though inwardly each bigwig knew
the evening was a bomb.

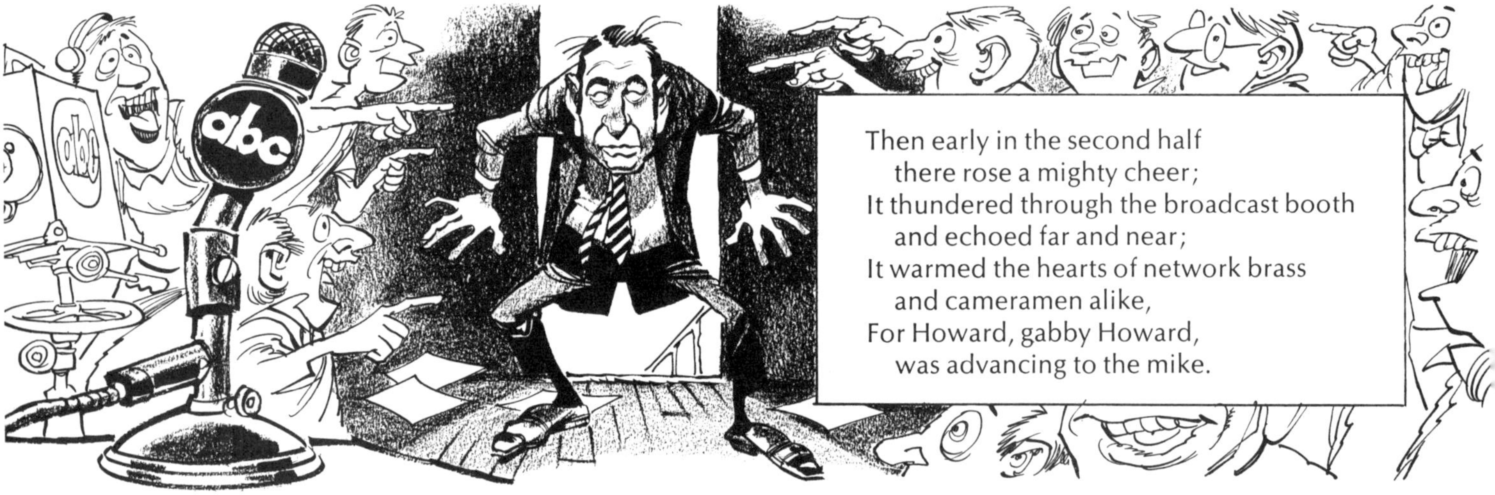

Then early in the second half
there rose a mighty cheer;
It thundered through the broadcast booth
and echoed far and near;
It warmed the hearts of network brass
and cameramen alike,
For Howard, gabby Howard,
was advancing to the mike.

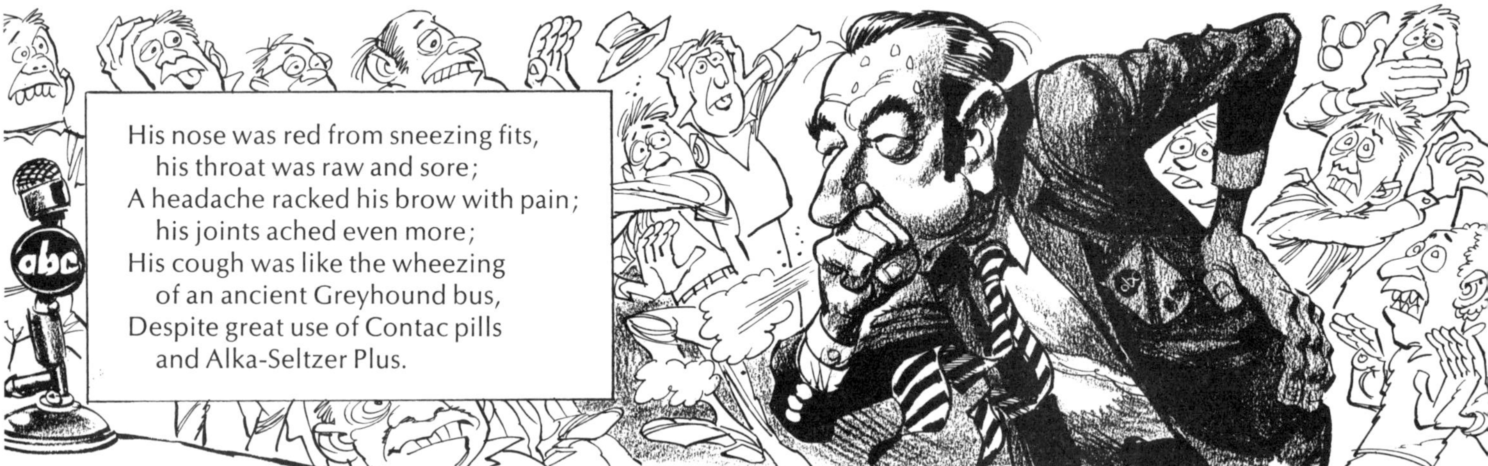

His nose was red from sneezing fits,
his throat was raw and sore;
A headache racked his brow with pain;
his joints ached even more;
His cough was like the wheezing
of an ancient Greyhound bus,
Despite great use of Contac pills
and Alka-Seltzer Plus.

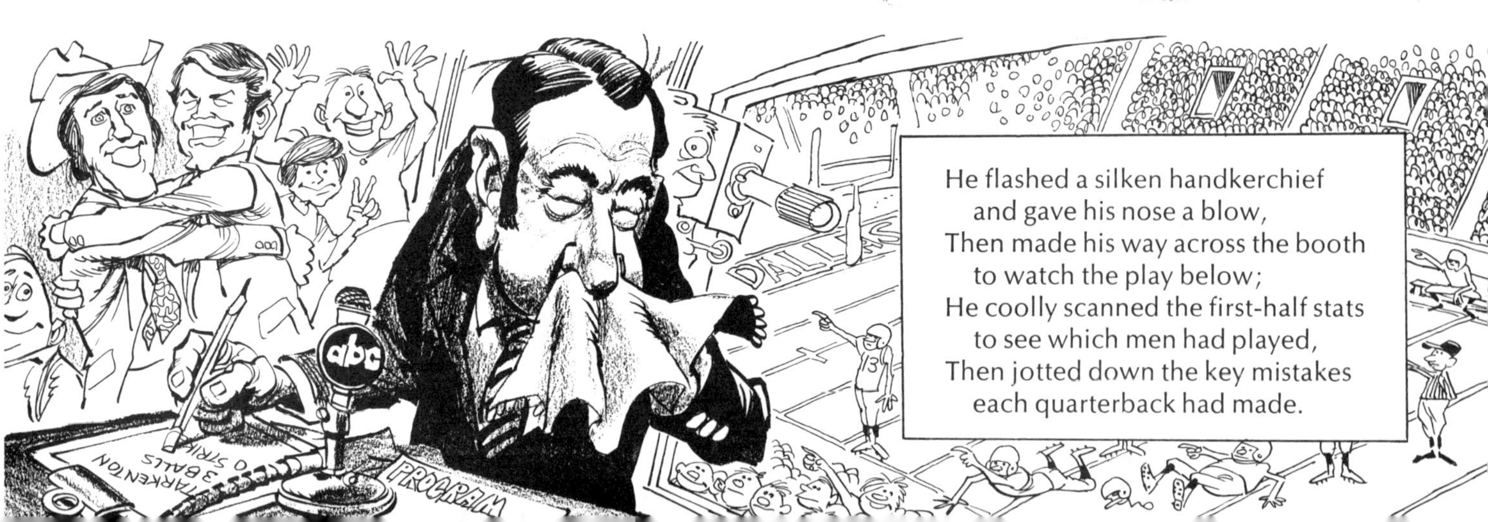

He flashed a silken handkerchief
and gave his nose a blow,
Then made his way across the booth
to watch the play below;
He coolly scanned the first-half stats
to see which men had played,
Then jotted down the key mistakes
each quarterback had made.

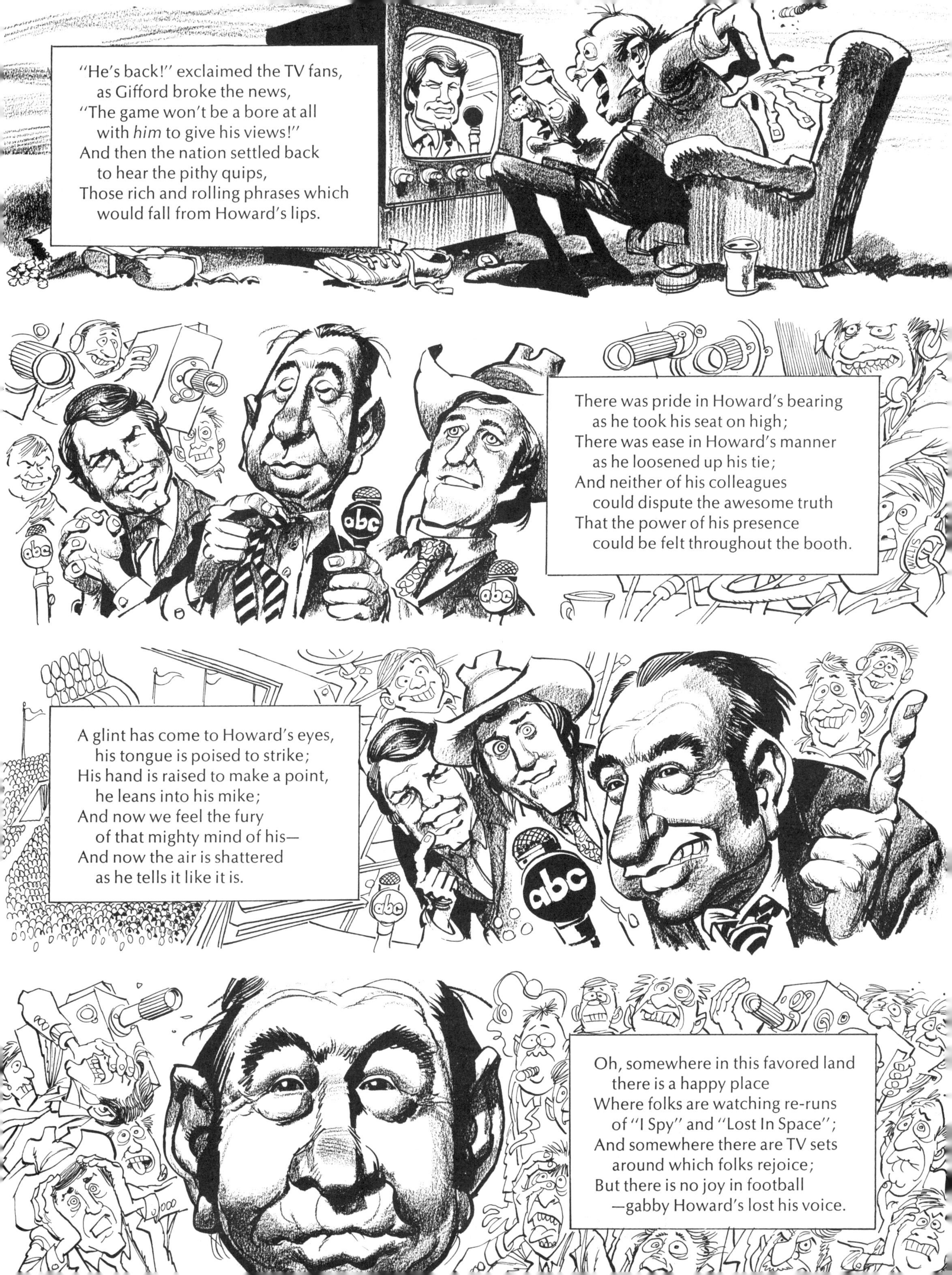
"He's back!" exclaimed the TV fans,
as Gifford broke the news,
"The game won't be a bore at all
with *him* to give his views!"
And then the nation settled back
to hear the pithy quips,
Those rich and rolling phrases which
would fall from Howard's lips.

There was pride in Howard's bearing
as he took his seat on high;
There was ease in Howard's manner
as he loosened up his tie;
And neither of his colleagues
could dispute the awesome truth
That the power of his presence
could be felt throughout the booth.

A glint has come to Howard's eyes,
his tongue is poised to strike;
His hand is raised to make a point,
he leans into his mike;
And now we feel the fury
of that mighty mind of his—
And now the air is shattered
as he tells it like it is.

Oh, somewhere in this favored land
there is a happy place
Where folks are watching re-runs
of "I Spy" and "Lost In Space";
And somewhere there are TV sets
around which folks rejoice;
But there is no joy in football
—gabby Howard's lost his voice.

THERE'S A VERY STRANGE SHOW ON TELEVISION THIS SEASON, AND IT BEGINS LIKE THIS . .

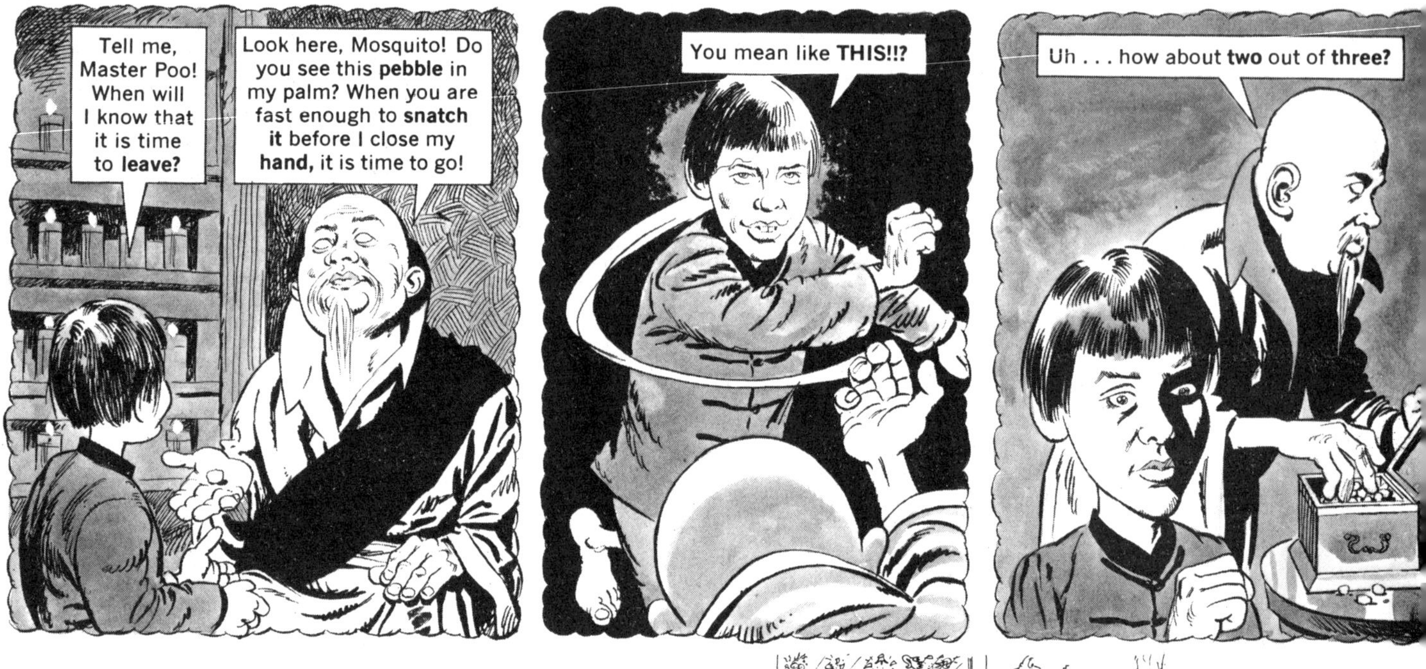

Tell me, Master Poo! When will I know that it is time to **leave?**
Look here, Mosquito! Do you see this **pebble** in my palm? When you are fast enough to **snatch it** before I close my **hand,** it is time to go!
You mean like **THIS!!?**
Uh . . . how about **two** out of **three?**

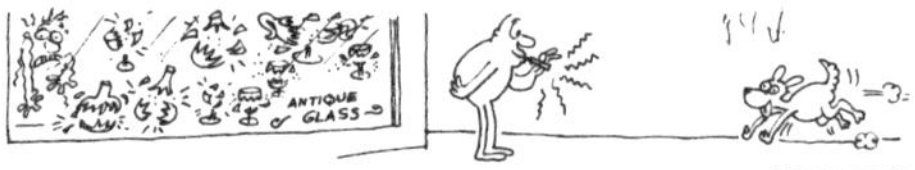

ANTIQUE GLASS

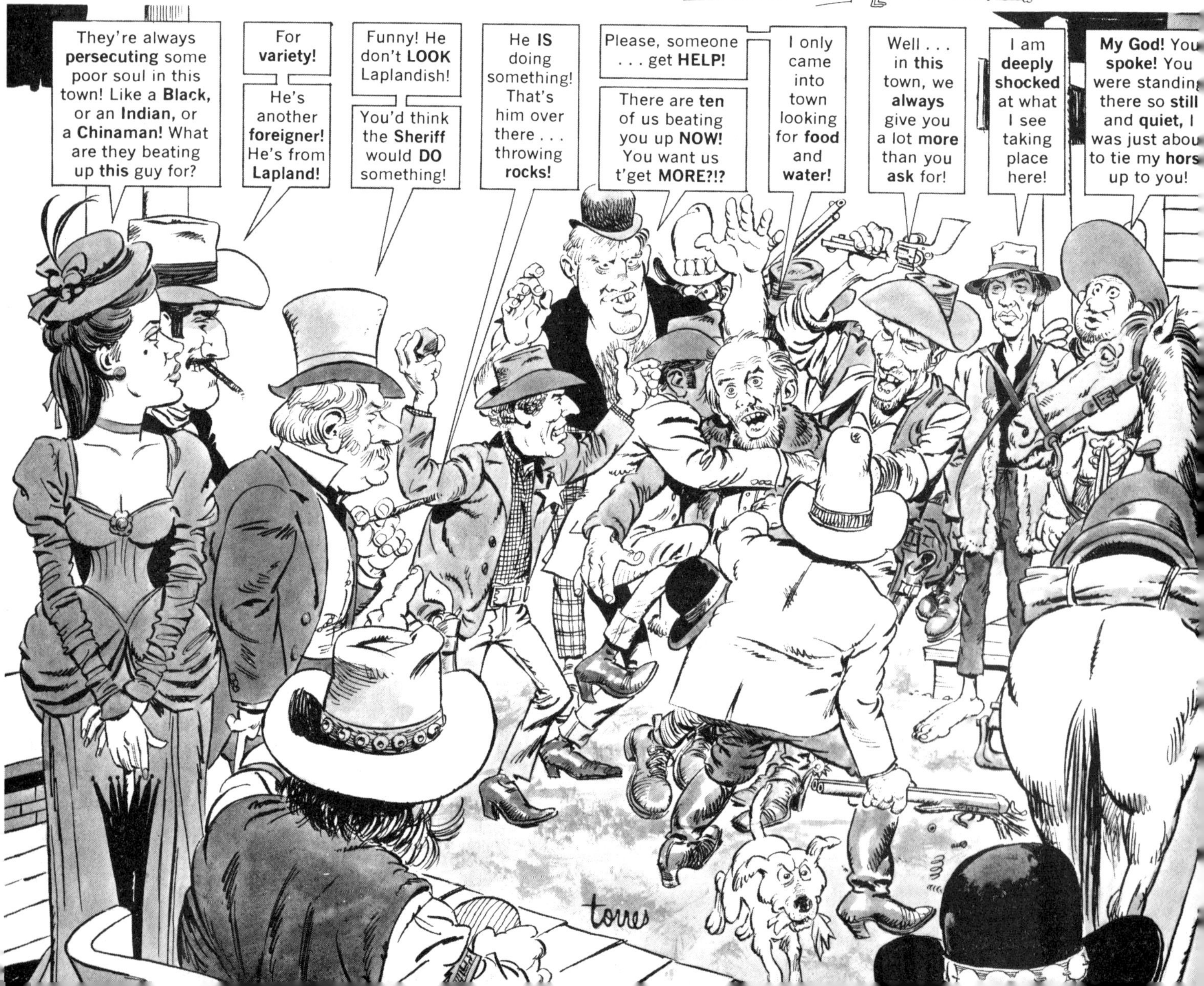

They're always **persecuting** some poor soul in this town! Like a **Black,** or an **Indian,** or a **Chinaman!** What are they beating up **this** guy for?
For **variety!**
He's another **foreigner!** He's from **Lapland!**
Funny! He don't **LOOK** Laplandish!
You'd think the **Sheriff** would **DO** something!
He **IS** doing something! That's him over there . . . throwing **rocks!**
Please, someone . . . get **HELP!**
There are **ten** of us beating you up **NOW!** You want us t'get **MORE?!?**
I only came into town looking for **food** and **water!**
Well . . . in **this** town, we **always** give you a lot **more** than you **ask** for!
I am **deeply shocked** at what I see taking place here!
My God! You **spoke!** You were standin there so **still** and **quiet,** I was just abou to tie my **hors** up to you!
torres

THE REASON THIS SHOW IS STRANGE IS BECAUSE THE LEADING CHARACTER DOES NOT BELIEVE IN KILLING ANY LIVING THING. HE BELIEVES IN TRUST AND THE ULTIMATE GOOD OF MANKIND. HE OFTEN SPEAKS IN PARABLES FROM WHICH WE LEARN. AND HE PREACHES NON-VIOLENCE! IF THAT'S NOT A STRANGE CONCEPT FOR TELEVISION, YOU HAVEN'T SEEN THE OTHER SHOWS COMPETING WITH–

CHOP SHTICK DEPT.

KUNG FOOL

ARTIST: ANGELO TORRES WRITER: DICK DE BARTOLO

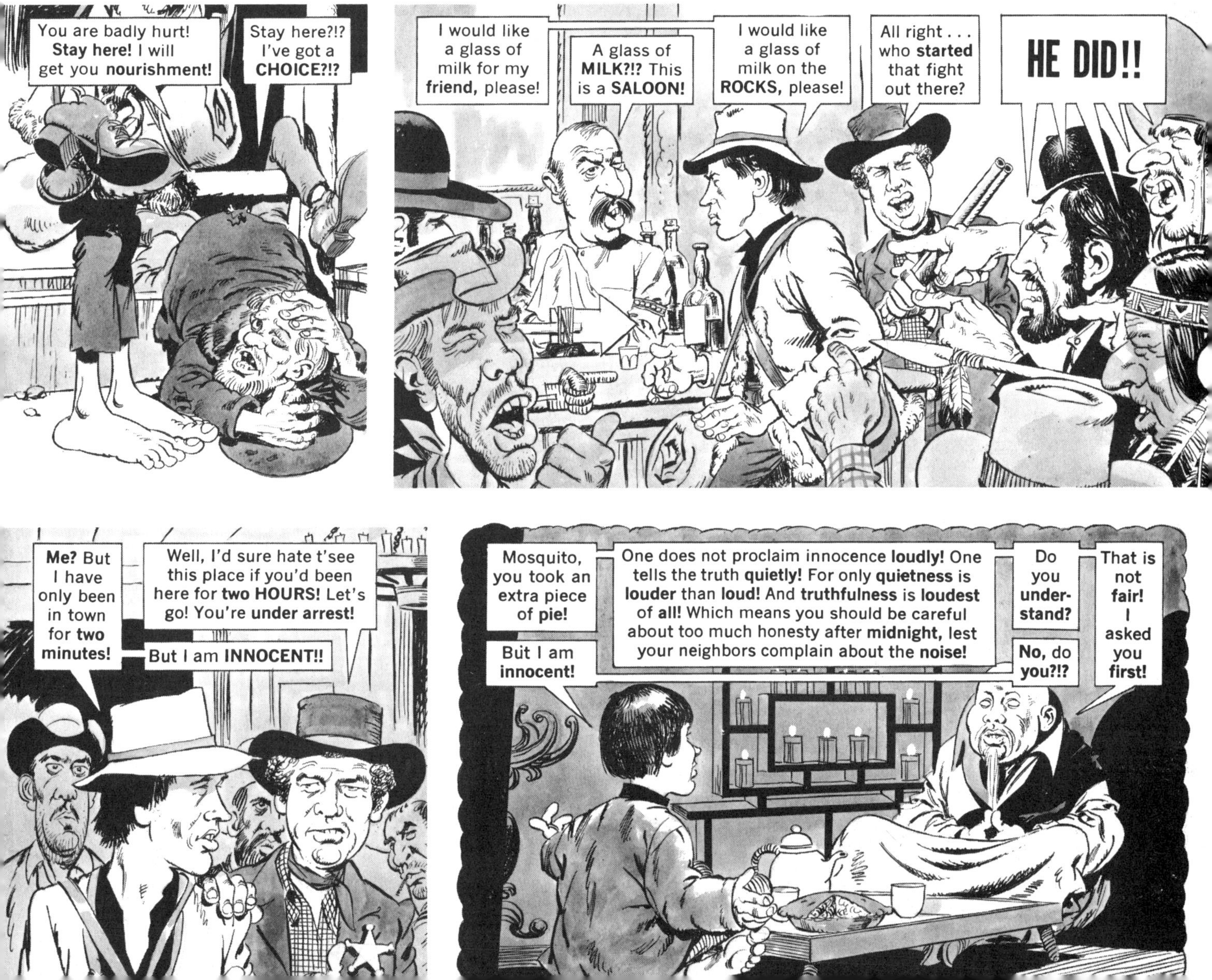
You are badly hurt! Stay here! I will get you nourishment!
Stay here?!? I've got a CHOICE?!?
I would like a glass of milk for my friend, please!
A glass of MILK?!? This is a SALOON!
I would like a glass of milk on the ROCKS, please!
All right . . . who started that fight out there?
HE DID!!
Me? But I have only been in town for two minutes!
Well, I'd sure hate t'see this place if you'd been here for two HOURS! Let's go! You're under arrest!
But I am INNOCENT!!
Mosquito, you took an extra piece of pie!
But I am innocent!
One does not proclaim innocence loudly! One tells the truth quietly! For only quietness is louder than loud! And truthfulness is loudest of all! Which means you should be careful about too much honesty after midnight, lest your neighbors complain about the noise!
Do you under-stand?
No, do you?!?
That is not fair! I asked you first!

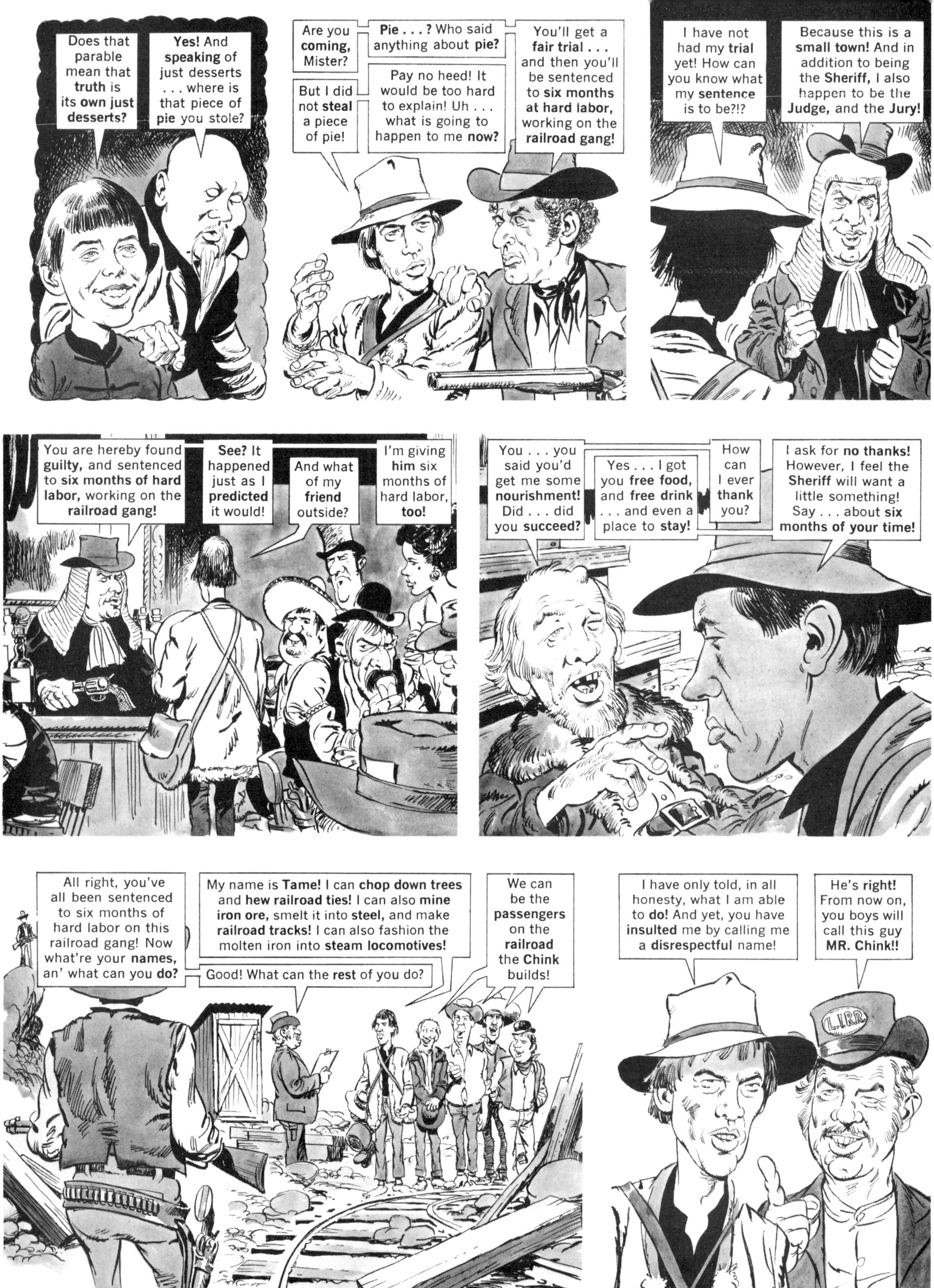

Does that parable mean that **truth** is its **own just desserts?**
Yes! And **speaking** of just desserts . . . where is that piece of **pie** you stole?
Are you **coming,** Mister?
Pie . . . ? Who said anything about **pie?**
But I did not **steal** a piece of pie!
Pay no heed! It would be too hard to explain! Uh . . . what is going to happen to me **now?**
You'll get a **fair trial . . .** and then you'll be sentenced to **six months at hard labor,** working on the **railroad gang!**
I have not had my **trial** yet! How can you know what my **sentence** is to be?!?
Because this is a **small town!** And in addition to being the **Sheriff,** I also happen to be the **Judge,** and the **Jury!**
You are hereby found **guilty,** and sentenced to **six months of hard labor,** working on the **railroad gang!**
See? It happened just as I **predicted** it would!
And what of my **friend** outside?
I'm giving **him** six months of hard labor, **too!**
You . . . you said you'd get me some **nourishment!** Did . . . did you **succeed?**
Yes . . . I got you **free food,** and **free drink** . . . and even a place to **stay!**
How can I ever **thank** you?
I ask for **no thanks!** However, I feel the **Sheriff** will want a little something! Say . . . about **six months of your time!**
All right, you've all been sentenced to six months of hard labor on this railroad gang! Now what're your **names,** an' what can you **do?**
My name is **Tame!** I can **chop down trees** and **hew railroad ties!** I can also **mine iron ore,** smelt it into **steel,** and make **railroad tracks!** I can also fashion the molten iron into **steam locomotives!**
Good! What can the **rest** of you do?
We can be the **passengers** on the **railroad** the **Chink** builds!
I have only told, in all honesty, what I am able to **do!** And yet, you have **insulted** me by calling me a **disrespectful** name!
He's **right!** From now on, you boys will call this guy **MR. Chink!!**
L.I.RR.

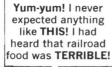
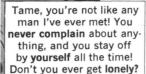

Okay! Before you begin to work, we give you a **healthy breakfast** . . .

Y-you call **this** a "healthy breakfast"?! A cup of **hot water**, a piece of **stale bread**, and a strip of **bacon** covered with—u/p—**maggots!?**

Yum-yum! I never expected anything like **THIS!** I had heard that railroad food was **TERRIBLE!**

Tame, you're not like any man I've ever met! You **never complain** about anything, and you stay off by **yourself** all the time! Don't you ever get **lonely?**

Is a **tree** lonely? Does a **flower** crave companionship? Does a **butterfly** need a night out, bowling with the boys? No!

And mainly, I am never in one town **long enough** to **MAKE OUT** with anybody!

Okay! Breakfast is over! Now . . . here's your schedule! You'll work **six straight hours** until your 10-minute **Lunch** break! Then, you'll work **nine straight hours** until your 10-minute **Dinner** break! Then, you'll work **five more hours,** get a full **four hours sleep,** and start all over!

Hey! We won't **stand** for that!

It's—it's **inhuman!**

Cruel!!

Why aren't **you** complaining?!?

A little **vacation** never hurt **anyone!**

I see that you men are all set to go to **work,** so I will move out of your way . . .

That'd **spoil everything! You're** the one we want to go to **work** on! **We'll** teach you to do **more** work than the **rest of us put together,** and make us look **bad** . . .

Master . . . how can one **defend** one's self when there are a **GROUP** of adversaries?

Here, Mosquito! Take this **stick** . . . and the **rest** of you **each** take a stick! Now . . . all of you, **attack me!**

SOCK
CRACK
CRUNCH
WHACK!

That is how!

But, **Master!** We have **beaten** you!

That is **correct!** Not only did you **assault** me, but you assaulted me with **weapons!** And even though you far **outnumbered** me, you did not **care!** But . . . notice now how your **consciences** are beginning to **bother** you! Boy, I'd **hate** to be in **YOUR** sandals now!

You are **right, Master!** I will never forget this **terrible, awful feeling!**

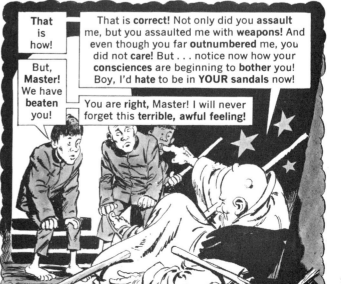

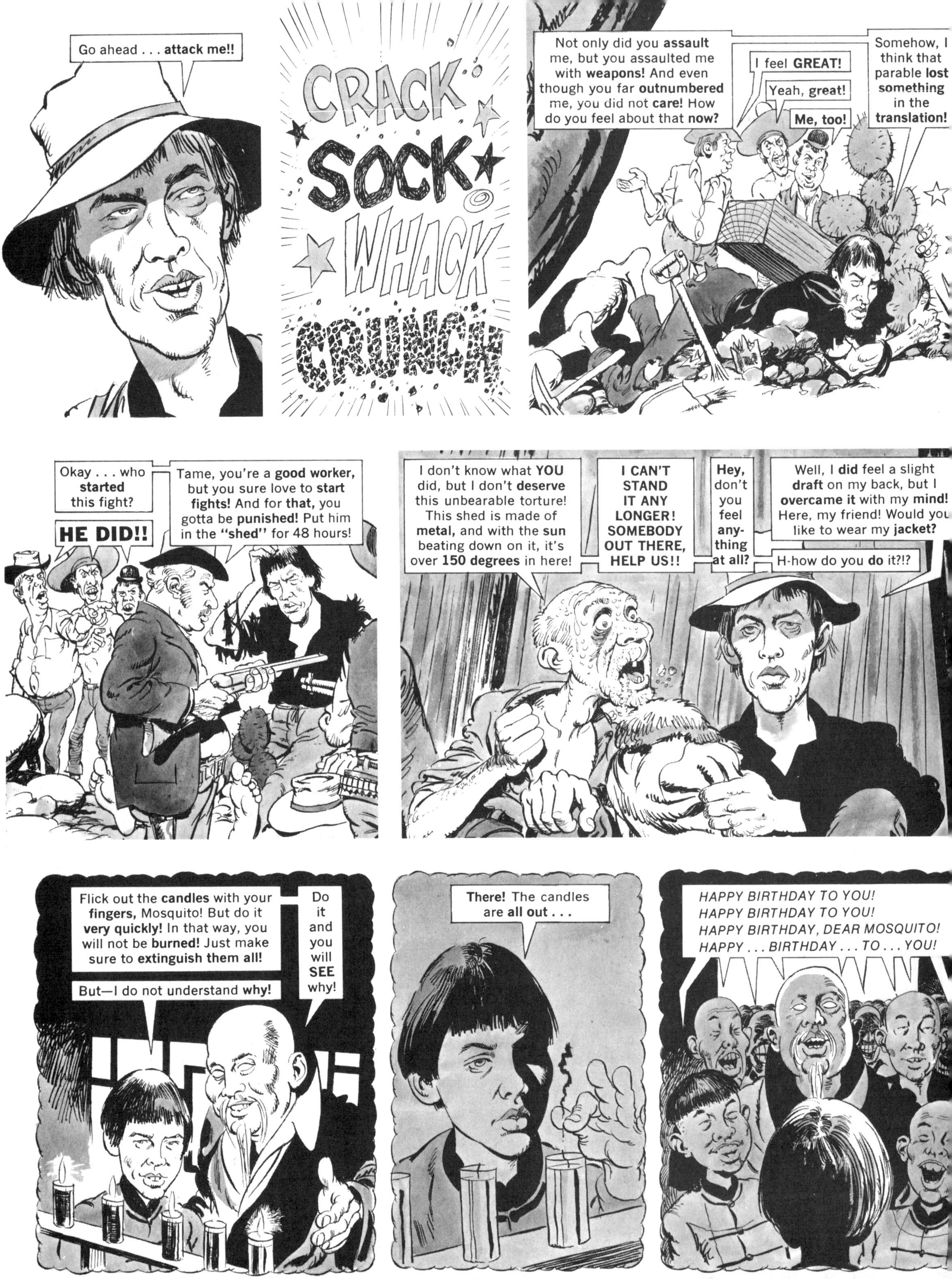
Go ahead . . . attack me!!
CRACK
SOCK
WHACK
CRUNCH
Not only did you assault me, but you assaulted me with weapons! And even though you far outnumbered me, you did not care! How do you feel about that now?
I feel GREAT!
Yeah, great!
Me, too!
Somehow, I think that parable lost something in the translation!
Okay . . . who started this fight?
HE DID!!
Tame, you're a good worker, but you sure love to start fights! And for that, you gotta be punished! Put him in the "shed" for 48 hours!
I don't know what YOU did, but I don't deserve this unbearable torture! This shed is made of metal, and with the sun beating down on it, it's over 150 degrees in here!
I CAN'T STAND IT ANY LONGER! SOMEBODY OUT THERE, HELP US!!
Hey, don't you feel any-thing at all?
Well, I did feel a slight draft on my back, but I overcame it with my mind! Here, my friend! Would you like to wear my jacket?
H-how do you do it?!?
Flick out the candles with your fingers, Mosquito! But do it very quickly! In that way, you will not be burned! Just make sure to extinguish them all!
But—I do not understand why!
Do it and you will SEE why!
There! The candles are all out . . .
HAPPY BIRTHDAY TO YOU!
HAPPY BIRTHDAY TO YOU!
HAPPY BIRTHDAY, DEAR MOSQUITO!
HAPPY . . . BIRTHDAY . . . TO . . . YOU!

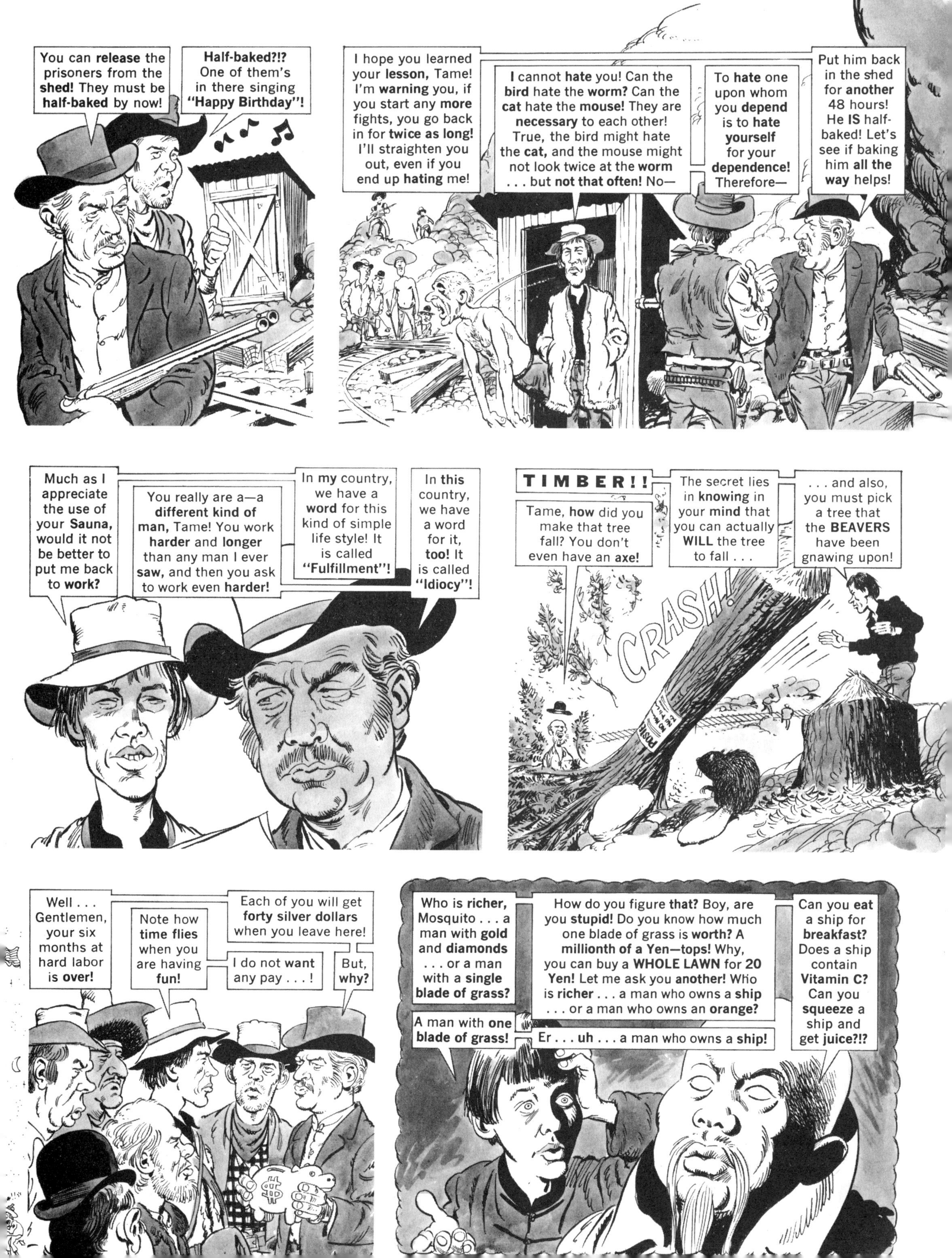

You can **release** the prisoners from the **shed!** They must be **half-baked** by now!
Half-baked?!? One of them's in there singing **"Happy Birthday"!**
I hope you learned your **lesson,** Tame! I'm **warning** you, if you start any **more** fights, you go back in for **twice as long!** I'll straighten you out, even if you end up **hating** me!
I cannot **hate** you! Can the **bird** hate the **worm?** Can the **cat** hate the **mouse!** They are **necessary** to each other! True, the bird might hate the **cat,** and the mouse might not look twice at the **worm** . . . but **not that often!** No—
To **hate** one upon whom you **depend** is to **hate yourself** for your **dependence!** Therefore—
Put him back in the shed for **another** 48 hours! He **IS** half-baked! Let's see if baking him **all the way** helps!
Much as I appreciate the use of your **Sauna,** would it not be better to put me back to **work?**
You really are a—a **different kind of man,** Tame! You work **harder** and **longer** than any man I ever **saw,** and then you ask to work even **harder!**
In **my** country, we have a **word** for this kind of simple life style! It is called **"Fulfillment"!**
In **this** country, we have a word for it, **too!** It is called **"Idiocy"!**
TIMBER!!
Tame, **how** did you make that tree fall? You don't even have an **axe!**
The secret lies in **knowing** in your **mind** that you can actually **WILL** the tree to fall . . .
. . . and also, you must pick a tree that the **BEAVERS** have been gnawing upon!
CRASH!
PUSH
Well . . . Gentlemen, your six months at hard labor is **over!**
Note how **time flies** when you are having **fun!**
Each of you will get **forty silver dollars** when you leave here!
I do not **want** any pay . . . !
But, **why?**
Who is **richer,** Mosquito . . . a man with **gold** and **diamonds** . . . or a man with a **single blade of grass?**
How do you figure **that?** Boy, are you **stupid!** Do you know how much one blade of grass is **worth?** A **millionth of a Yen—tops!** Why, you can buy a **WHOLE LAWN** for **20** Yen! Let me ask you **another!** Who is **richer** . . . a man who owns a **ship** . . . or a man who owns an **orange?**
Can you **eat** a ship for **breakfast?** Does a ship contain **Vitamin C?** Can you **squeeze** a ship and **get juice?!?**
A man with **one blade of grass!**
Er . . . **uh** . . . a man who owns a **ship!**

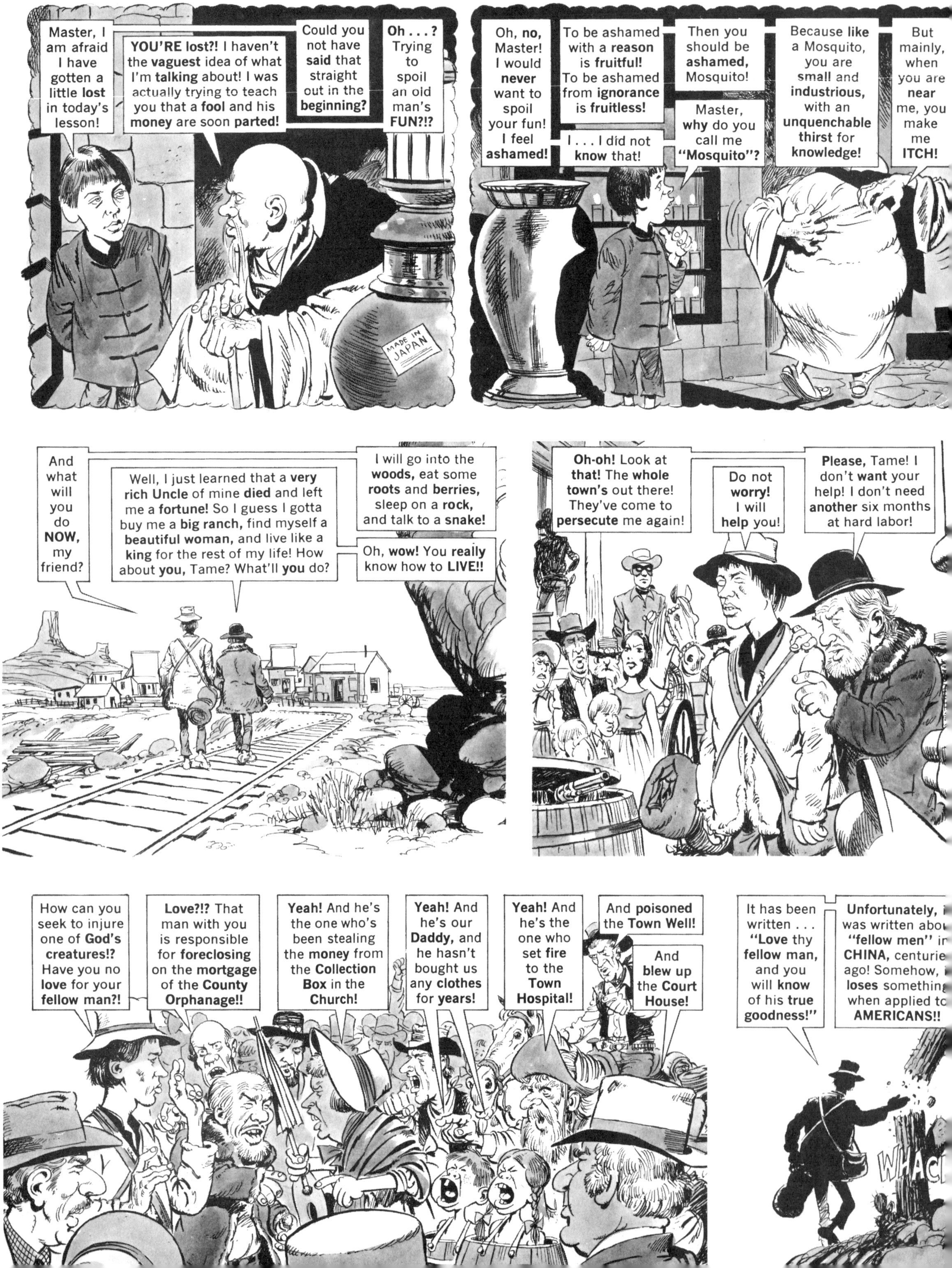

Master, I am afraid I have gotten a little lost in today's lesson!
YOU'RE lost?! I haven't the vaguest idea of what I'm talking about! I was actually trying to teach you that a fool and his money are soon parted!
Could you not have said that straight out in the beginning?
Oh . . .? Trying to spoil an old man's FUN?!?
MADE IN JAPAN
Oh, no, Master! I would never want to spoil your fun! I feel ashamed!
To be ashamed with a reason is fruitful! To be ashamed from ignorance is fruitless!
I . . . I did not know that!
Then you should be ashamed, Mosquito!
Master, why do you call me "Mosquito"?
Because like a Mosquito, you are small and industrious, with an unquenchable thirst for knowledge!
But mainly, when you are near me, you make me ITCH!
And what will you do NOW, my friend?
Well, I just learned that a very rich Uncle of mine died and left me a fortune! So I guess I gotta buy me a big ranch, find myself a beautiful woman, and live like a king for the rest of my life! How about you, Tame? What'll you do?
I will go into the woods, eat some roots and berries, sleep on a rock, and talk to a snake!
Oh, wow! You really know how to LIVE!!
Oh-oh! Look at that! The whole town's out there! They've come to persecute me again!
Do not worry! I will help you!
Please, Tame! I don't want your help! I don't need another six months at hard labor!
How can you seek to injure one of God's creatures!? Have you no love for your fellow man?!
Love?!? That man with you is responsible for foreclosing on the mortgage of the County Orphanage!!
Yeah! And he's the one who's been stealing the money from the Collection Box in the Church!
Yeah! And he's our Daddy, and he hasn't bought us any clothes for years!
Yeah! And he's the one who set fire to the Town Hospital!
And poisoned the Town Well!
And blew up the Court House!
It has been written . . . "Love thy fellow man, and you will know of his true goodness!"
Unfortunately, was written abo "fellow men" i CHINA, centurie ago! Somehow, loses somethin when applied t AMERICANS!!
WHAC

PATRONS OF THE ODDS DEPT.

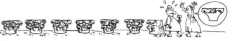

Remember not too long ago, when we were taught that "War is Hell"? Well, maybe we were taught wrong. Because for the second year in a row, there's a show on the tube that seems to prove —not that "War is Hell!"—but that "War is A Hell-Of-A-Lot-Of-Fun!" Which, when you think about it, is a sickeningly idiotic idea, in any language. In French, it's "Fou," in Spanish, it's "Loco," in Italian, it's "Pazzo," in German, it's "Ferrucht" and in Yiddish, it's . . .

M*A*S*H*UGA

ARTIST: ANGELO TORRES WRITER: STAN HART

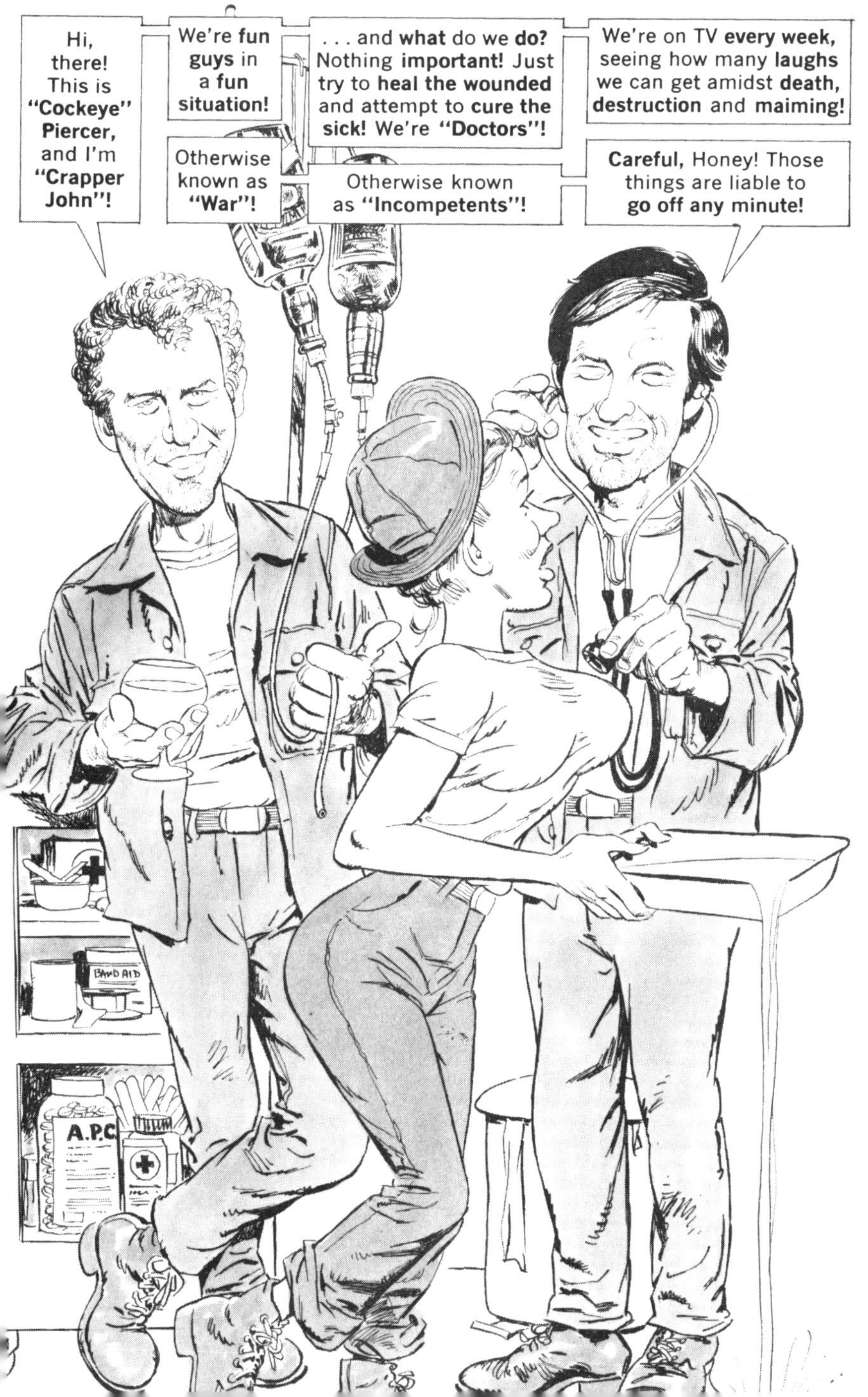

Hi, there! This is "Cockeye" Piercer, and I'm "Crapper John"!
We're fun guys in a fun situation!
Otherwise known as "War"!
. . . and what do we do? Nothing important! Just try to heal the wounded and attempt to cure the sick! We're "Doctors"!
Otherwise known as "Incompetents"!
We're on TV every week, seeing how many laughs we can get amidst death, destruction and maiming!
Careful, Honey! Those things are liable to go off any minute!
BAND AID
A.P.C.

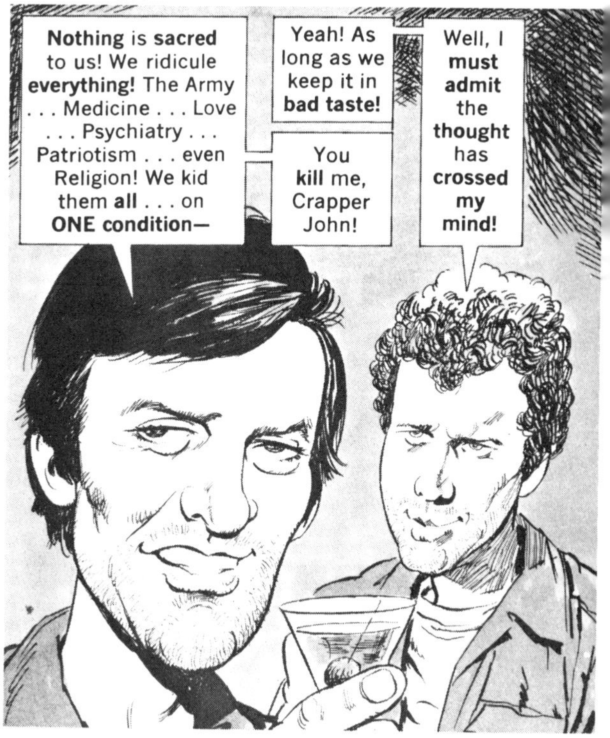

Nothing is sacred to us! We ridicule everything! The Army . . . Medicine . . . Love . . . Psychiatry . . . Patriotism . . . even Religion! We kid them all . . . on ONE condition—
Yeah! As long as we keep it in bad taste!
You kill me, Crapper John!
Well, I must admit the thought has crossed my mind!

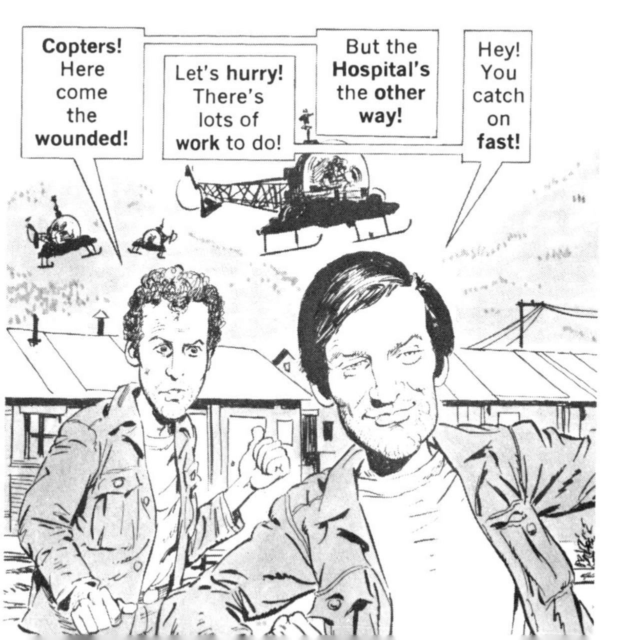

Copters! Here come the wounded!
Let's hurry! There's lots of work to do!
But the Hospital's the other way!
Hey! You catch on fast!

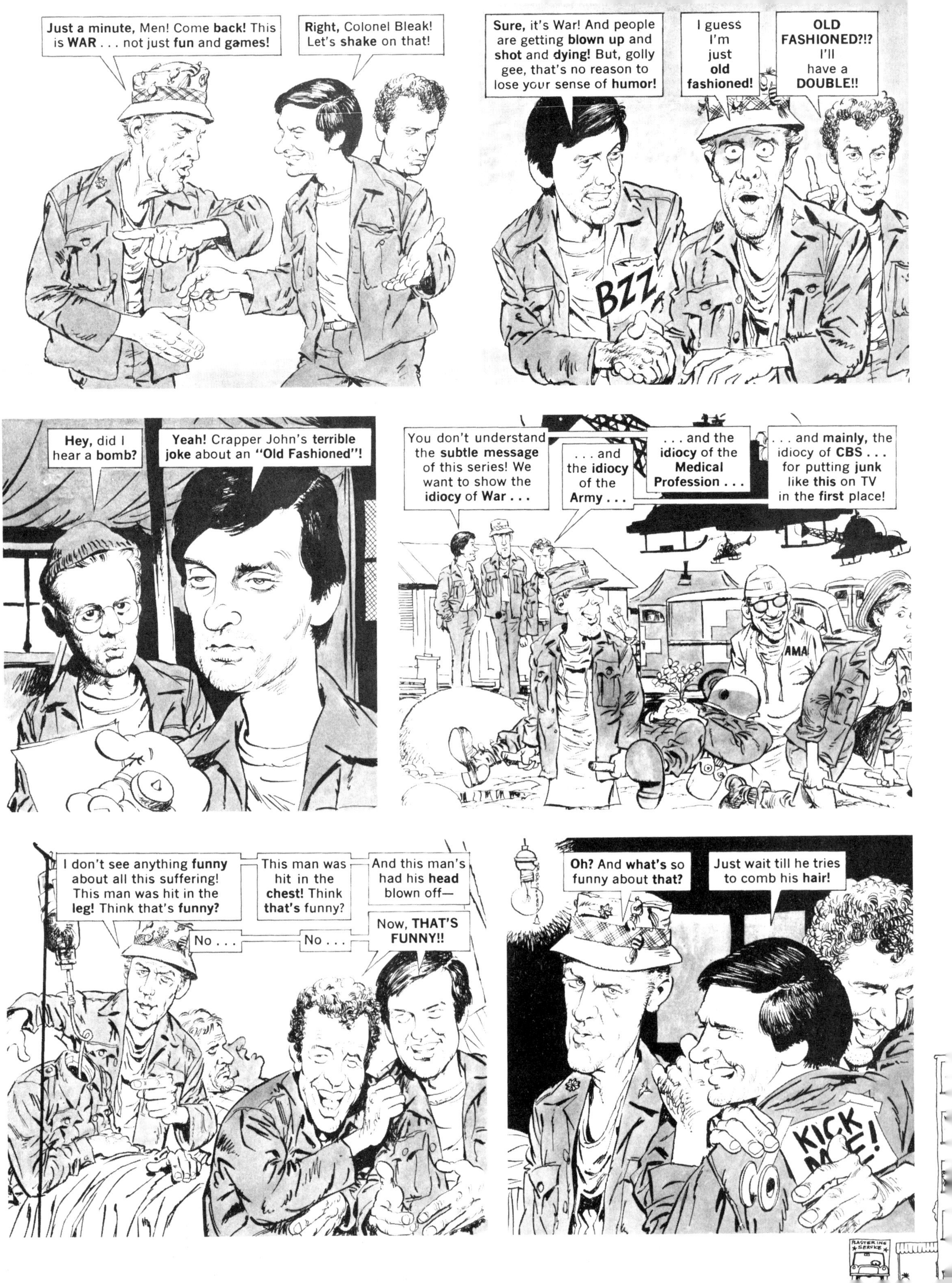

Just a minute, Men! Come back! This is WAR . . . not just fun and games!
Right, Colonel Bleak! Let's shake on that!
Sure, it's War! And people are getting blown up and shot and dying! But, golly gee, that's no reason to lose your sense of humor!
BZZ
I guess I'm just old fashioned!
OLD FASHIONED?!? I'll have a DOUBLE!!
Hey, did I hear a bomb?
Yeah! Crapper John's terrible joke about an "Old Fashioned"!
You don't understand the subtle message of this series! We want to show the idiocy of War . . .
. . . and the idiocy of the Army . . .
. . . and the idiocy of the Medical Profession . . .
. . . and mainly, the idiocy of CBS . . . for putting junk like this on TV in the first place!
AMA
I don't see anything funny about all this suffering! This man was hit in the leg! Think that's funny?
No . . .
This man was hit in the chest! Think that's funny?
No . . .
And this man's had his head blown off—
Now, THAT'S FUNNY!!
Oh? And what's so funny about that?
Just wait till he tries to comb his hair!
KICK ME!
PLASTERING SERVICE

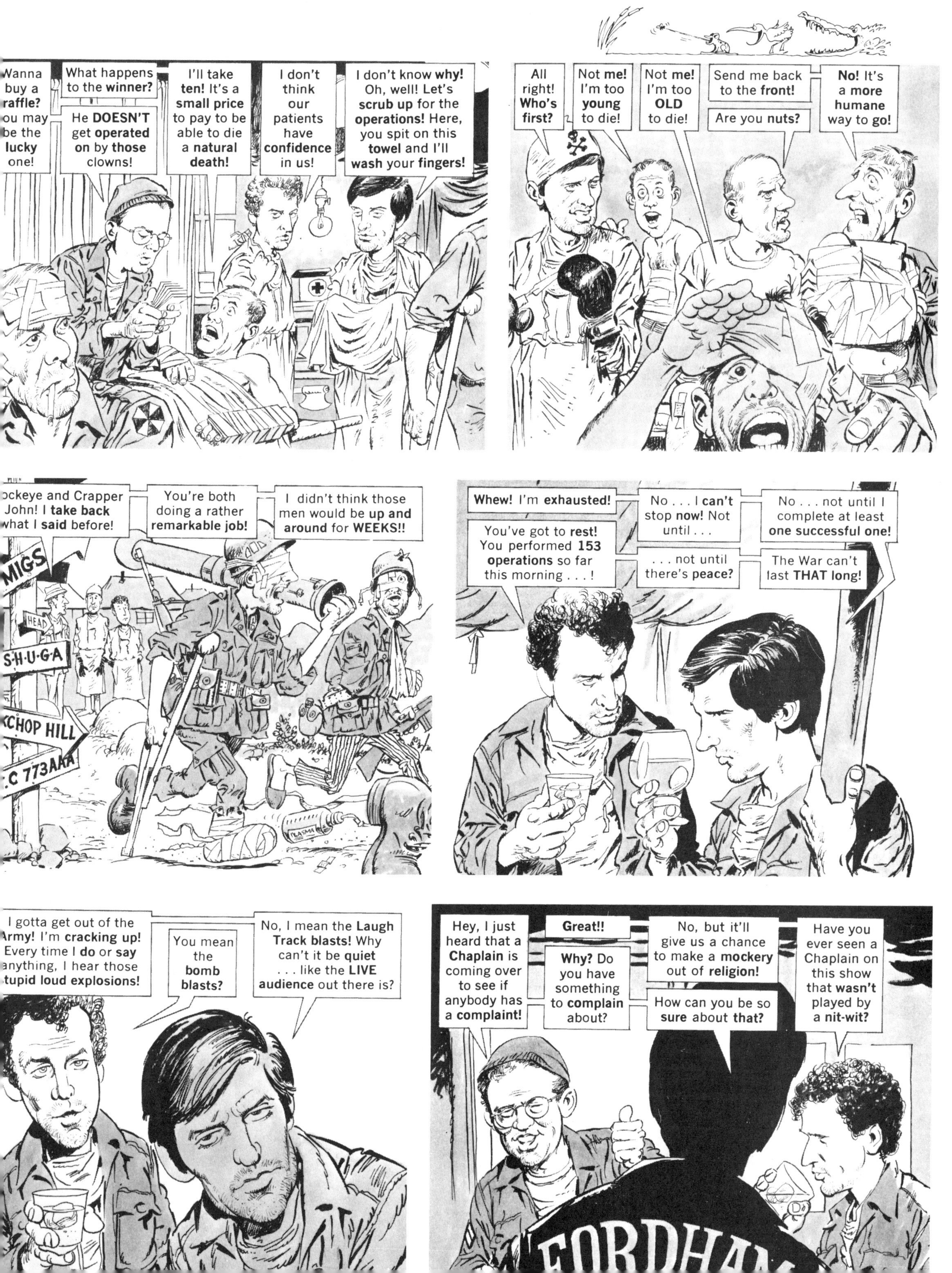

Wanna buy a raffle? ou may be the lucky one!
What happens to the winner?
He DOESN'T get operated on by those clowns!
I'll take ten! It's a small price to pay to be able to die a natural death!
I don't think our patients have confidence in us!
I don't know why! Oh, well! Let's scrub up for the operations! Here, you spit on this towel and I'll wash your fingers!
All right! Who's first?
Not me! I'm too young to die!
Not me! I'm too OLD to die!
Send me back to the front!
Are you nuts?
No! It's a more humane way to go!
ockeye and Crapper John! I take back what I said before!
You're both doing a rather remarkable job!
I didn't think those men would be up and around for WEEKS!!
MIGS
HEAD
S·H·U·G·A
CHOP HILL
C 773AAA
PLASMA
Whew! I'm exhausted!
You've got to rest! You performed 153 operations so far this morning . . . !
No . . . I can't stop now! Not until . . .
. . . not until there's peace?
No . . . not until I complete at least one successful one!
The War can't last THAT long!
I gotta get out of the Army! I'm cracking up! Every time I do or say anything, I hear those tupid loud explosions!
You mean the bomb blasts?
No, I mean the Laugh Track blasts! Why can't it be quiet . . . like the LIVE audience out there is?
Hey, I just heard that a Chaplain is coming over to see if anybody has a complaint!
Great!!
Why? Do you have something to complain about?
No, but it'll give us a chance to make a mockery out of religion!
How can you be so sure about that?
Have you ever seen a Chaplain on this show that wasn't played by a nit-wit?
FORDHAM

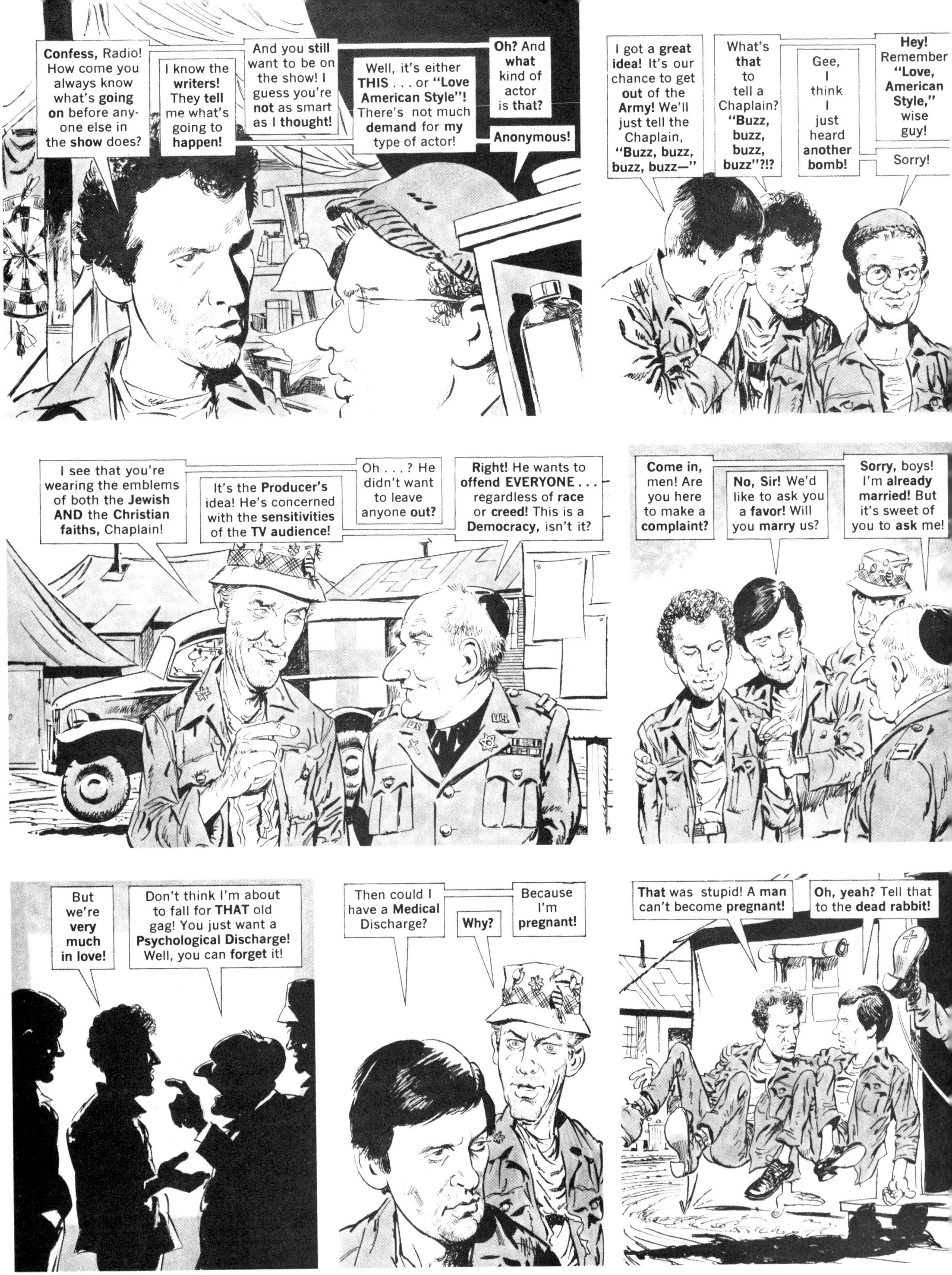

Confess, Radio! How come you always know what's going on before any-one else in the show does?
I know the writers! They tell me what's going to happen!
And you still want to be on the show! I guess you're not as smart as I thought!
Well, it's either THIS . . . or "Love American Style"! There's not much demand for my type of actor!
Oh? And what kind of actor is that?
Anonymous!
I got a great idea! It's our chance to get out of the Army! We'll just tell the Chaplain, "Buzz, buzz, buzz, buzz—"
What's that to tell a Chaplain? "Buzz, buzz, buzz, buzz"?!?
Gee, I think I just heard another bomb!
Hey! Remember "Love, American Style," wise guy!
Sorry!
I see that you're wearing the emblems of both the Jewish AND the Christian faiths, Chaplain!
It's the Producer's idea! He's concerned with the sensitivities of the TV audience!
Oh . . . ? He didn't want to leave anyone out?
Right! He wants to offend EVERYONE . . . regardless of race or creed! This is a Democracy, isn't it?
Come in, men! Are you here to make a complaint?
No, Sir! We'd like to ask you a favor! Will you marry us?
Sorry, boys! I'm already married! But it's sweet of you to ask me!
But we're very much in love!
Don't think I'm about to fall for THAT old gag! You just want a Psychological Discharge! Well, you can forget it!
Then could I have a Medical Discharge?
Why?
Because I'm pregnant!
That was stupid! A man can't become pregnant!
Oh, yeah? Tell that to the dead rabbit!

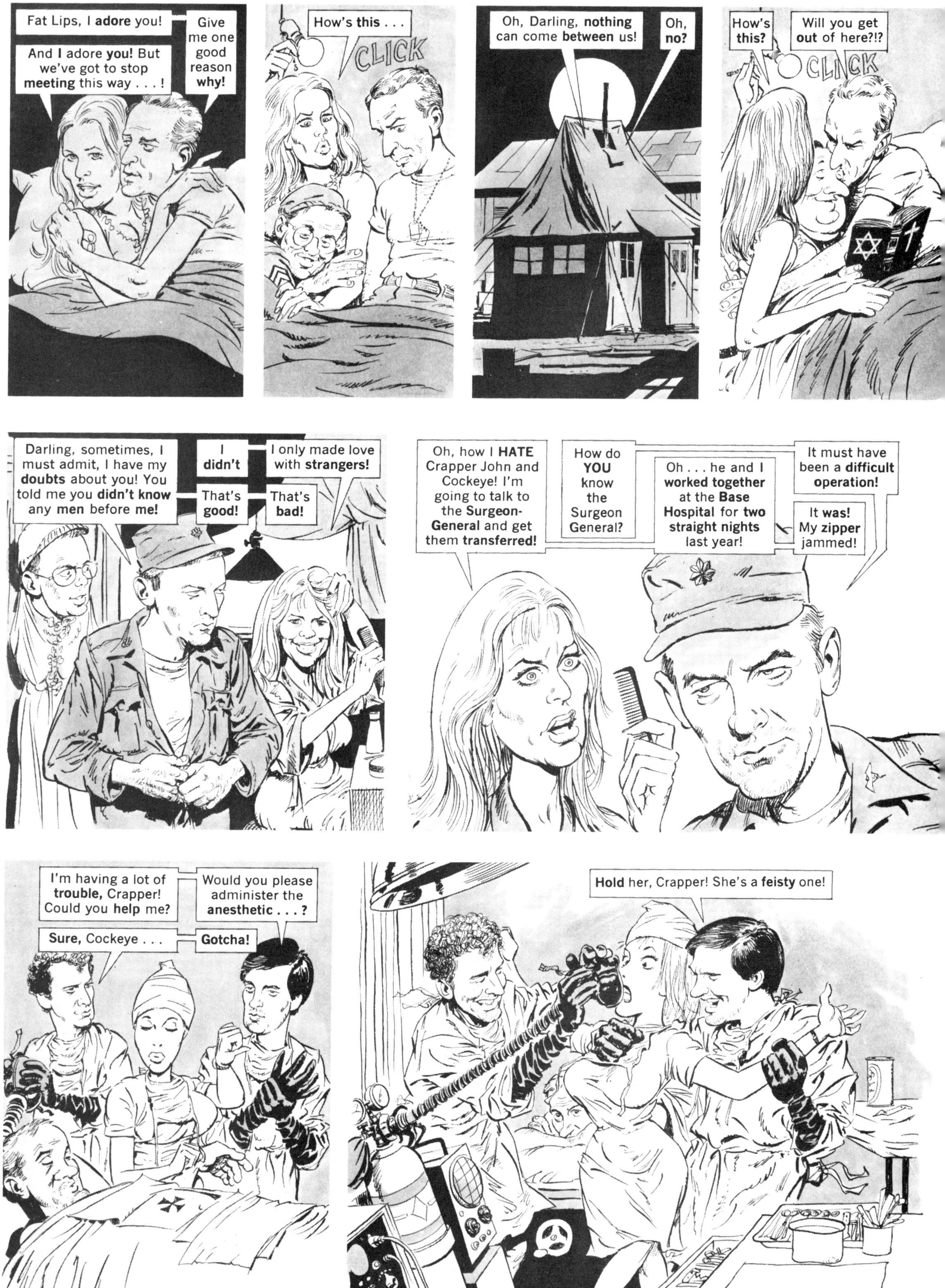
Fat Lips, I adore you!
And I adore you! But we've got to stop meeting this way . . . !
Give me one good reason why!
How's this . . .
CLICK
Oh, Darling, nothing can come between us!
Oh, no?
How's this?
Will you get out of here?!?
CLICK
Darling, sometimes, I must admit, I have my doubts about you! You told me you didn't know any men before me!
I didn't
I only made love with strangers!
That's good!
That's bad!
Oh, how I HATE Crapper John and Cockeye! I'm going to talk to the Surgeon-General and get them transferred!
How do YOU know the Surgeon General?
Oh . . . he and I worked together at the Base Hospital for two straight nights last year!
It must have been a difficult operation!
It was! My zipper jammed!
I'm having a lot of trouble, Crapper! Could you help me?
Would you please administer the anesthetic . . . ?
Sure, Cockeye . . .
Gotcha!
Hold her, Crapper! She's a feisty one!

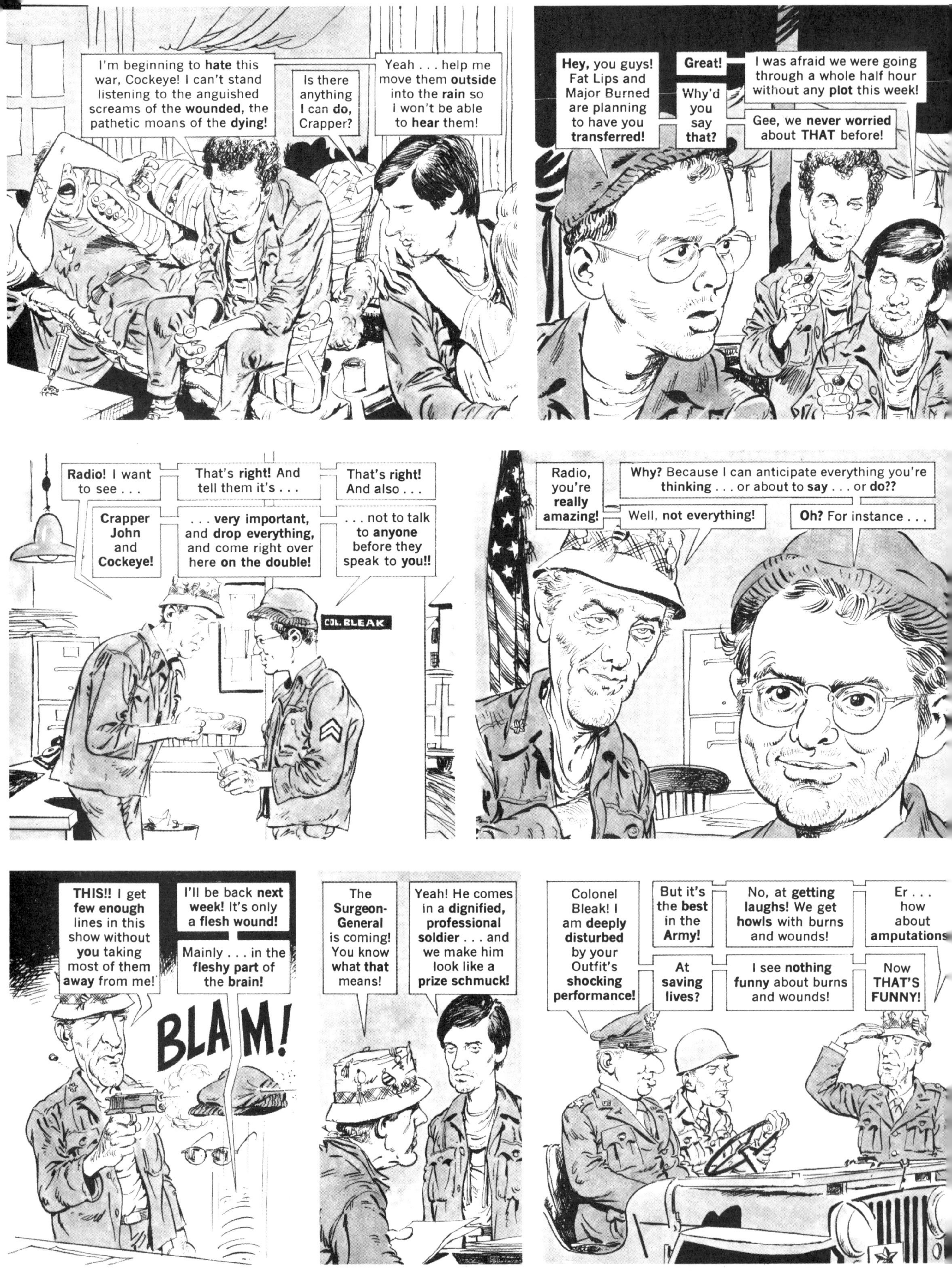
I'm beginning to hate this war, Cockeye! I can't stand listening to the anguished screams of the wounded, the pathetic moans of the dying!
Is there anything I can do, Crapper?
Yeah . . . help me move them outside into the rain so I won't be able to hear them!
Hey, you guys! Fat Lips and Major Burned are planning to have you transferred!
Great!
I was afraid we were going through a whole half hour without any plot this week!
Why'd you say that?
Gee, we never worried about THAT before!
Radio! I want to see . . .
That's right! And tell them it's . . .
That's right! And also . . .
Crapper John and Cockeye!
. . . very important, and drop everything, and come right over here on the double!
. . . not to talk to anyone before they speak to you!!
COL. BLEAK
Radio, you're really amazing!
Why? Because I can anticipate everything you're thinking . . . or about to say . . . or do??
Well, not everything!
Oh? For instance . . .
THIS!! I get few enough lines in this show without you taking most of them away from me!
I'll be back next week! It's only a flesh wound!
Mainly . . . in the fleshy part of the brain!
BLAM!
The Surgeon-General is coming! You know what that means!
Yeah! He comes in a dignified, professional soldier . . . and we make him look like a prize schmuck!
Colonel Bleak! I am deeply disturbed by your Outfit's shocking performance!
But it's the best in the Army!
At saving lives?
No, at getting laughs! We get howls with burns and wounds!
I see nothing funny about burns and wounds!
Er . . . how about amputations
Now THAT'S FUNNY!

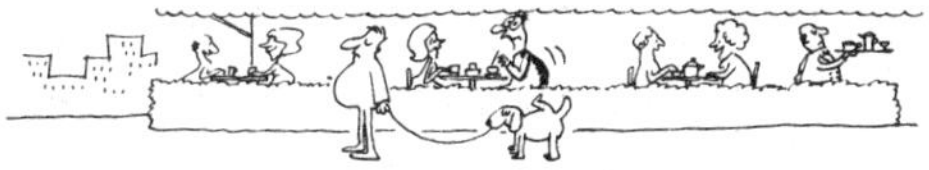

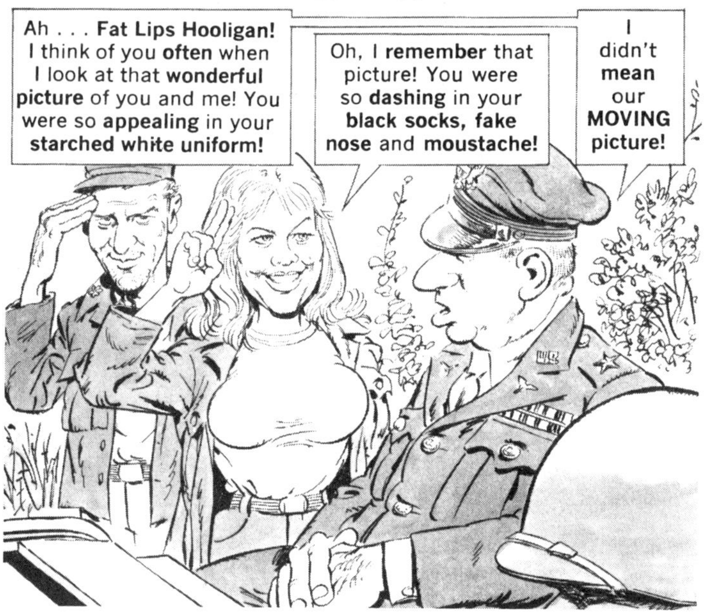

Ah . . . Fat Lips Hooligan! I think of you often when I look at that wonderful picture of you and me! You were so appealing in your starched white uniform!
Oh, I remember that picture! You were so dashing in your black socks, fake nose and moustache!
I didn't mean our MOVING picture!

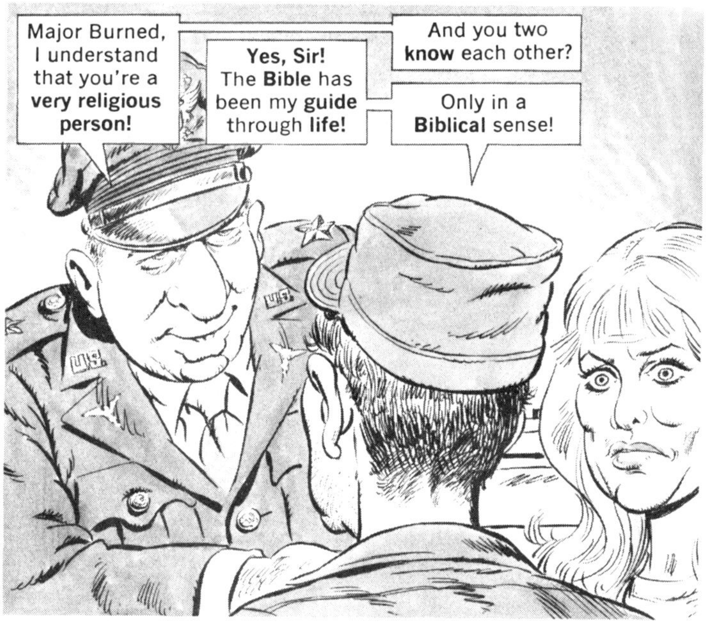

Major Burned, I understand that you're a very religious person!
Yes, Sir! The Bible has been my guide through life!
And you two know each other?
Only in a Biblical sense!

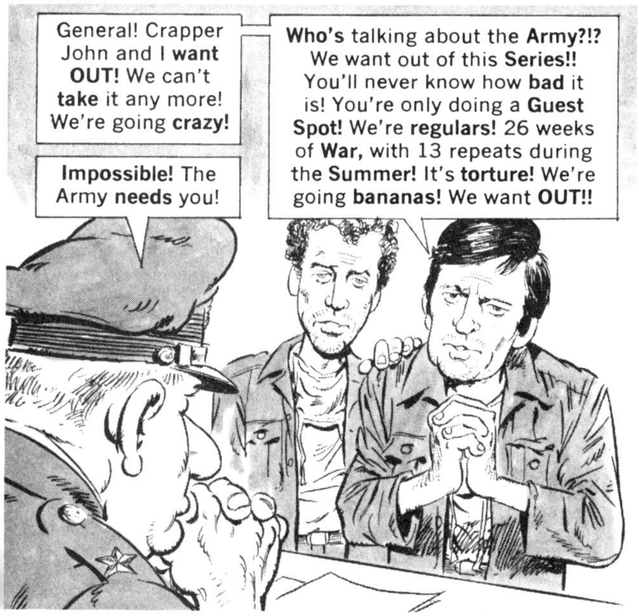

General! Crapper John and I want OUT! We can't take it any more! We're going crazy!
Impossible! The Army needs you!
Who's talking about the Army?!? We want out of this Series!! You'll never know how bad it is! You're only doing a Guest Spot! We're regulars! 26 weeks of War, with 13 repeats during the Summer! It's torture! We're going bananas! We want OUT!!

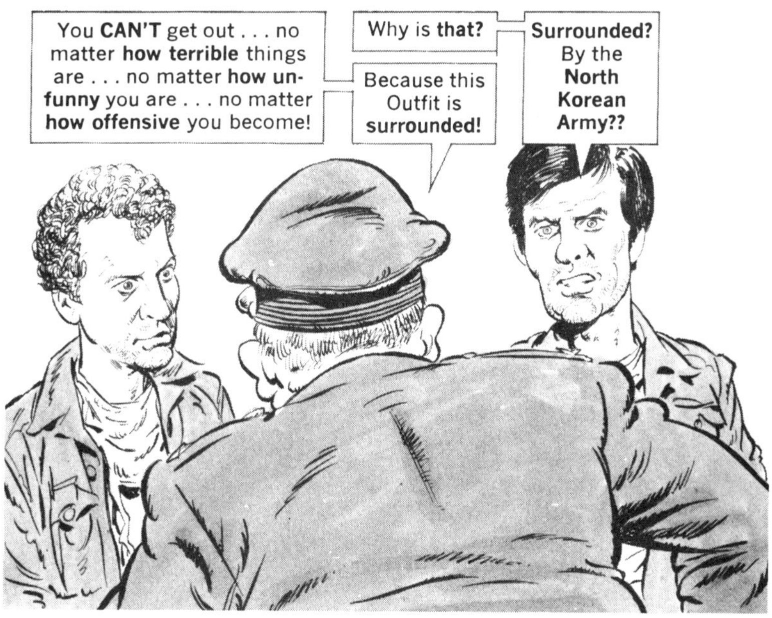

You CAN'T get out . . . no matter how terrible things are . . . no matter how un-funny you are . . . no matter how offensive you become!
Why is that?
Because this Outfit is surrounded!
Surrounded? By the North Korean Army??

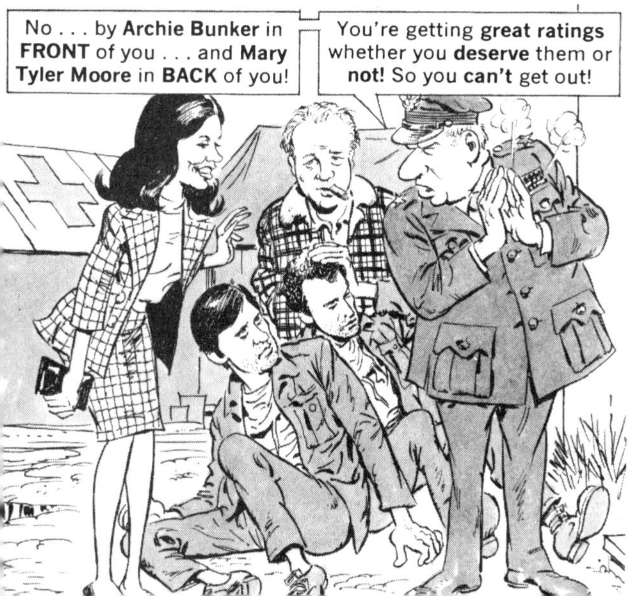

No . . . by Archie Bunker in FRONT of you . . . and Mary Tyler Moore in BACK of you!
You're getting great ratings whether you deserve them or not! So you can't get out!

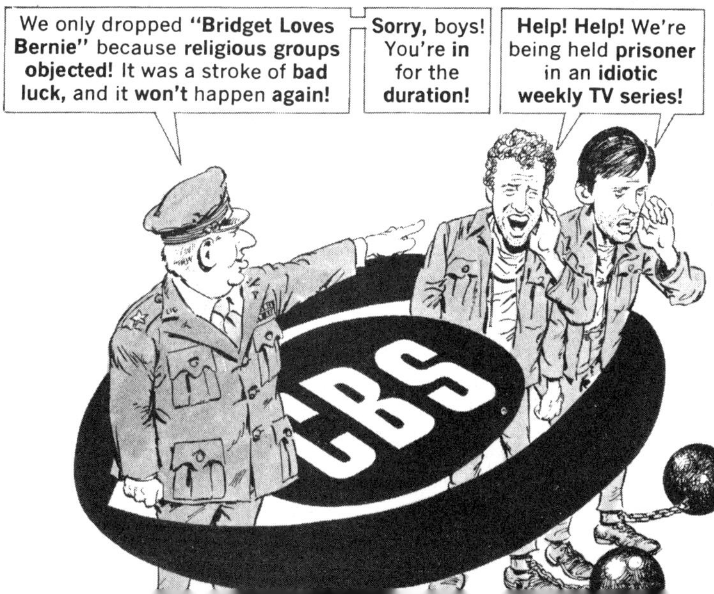

We only dropped "Bridget Loves Bernie" because religious groups objected! It was a stroke of bad luck, and it won't happen again!
Sorry, boys! You're in for the duration!
Help! Help! We're being held prisoner in an idiotic weekly TV series!
CBS

CREEP IN THE HEART OF TEXAS DEPT.

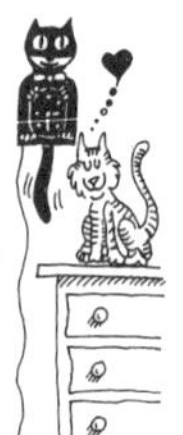

TV programs about families have always been popular! The Nelsons, the Waltons, the Bradfords, the Ingles, the Cunninghams, etc., all these families had certain things in common: they were all happy, they all loved each other, and none of them had very much money! Now, a different type of TV family has emerged to capture the top ratings. These people are more like the Borgias than the Bradfords! These people hate each other, they're miserable, and they're filthy rich! Yep, we're talking about that nighttime "soap" about a typical Texas family, soaking in depravity and sex! Boy, when it comes to remembering that there are finer things in life, all that base immorality on the TV screen tends to numb us, to deaden us, to—

DU

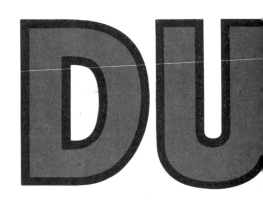

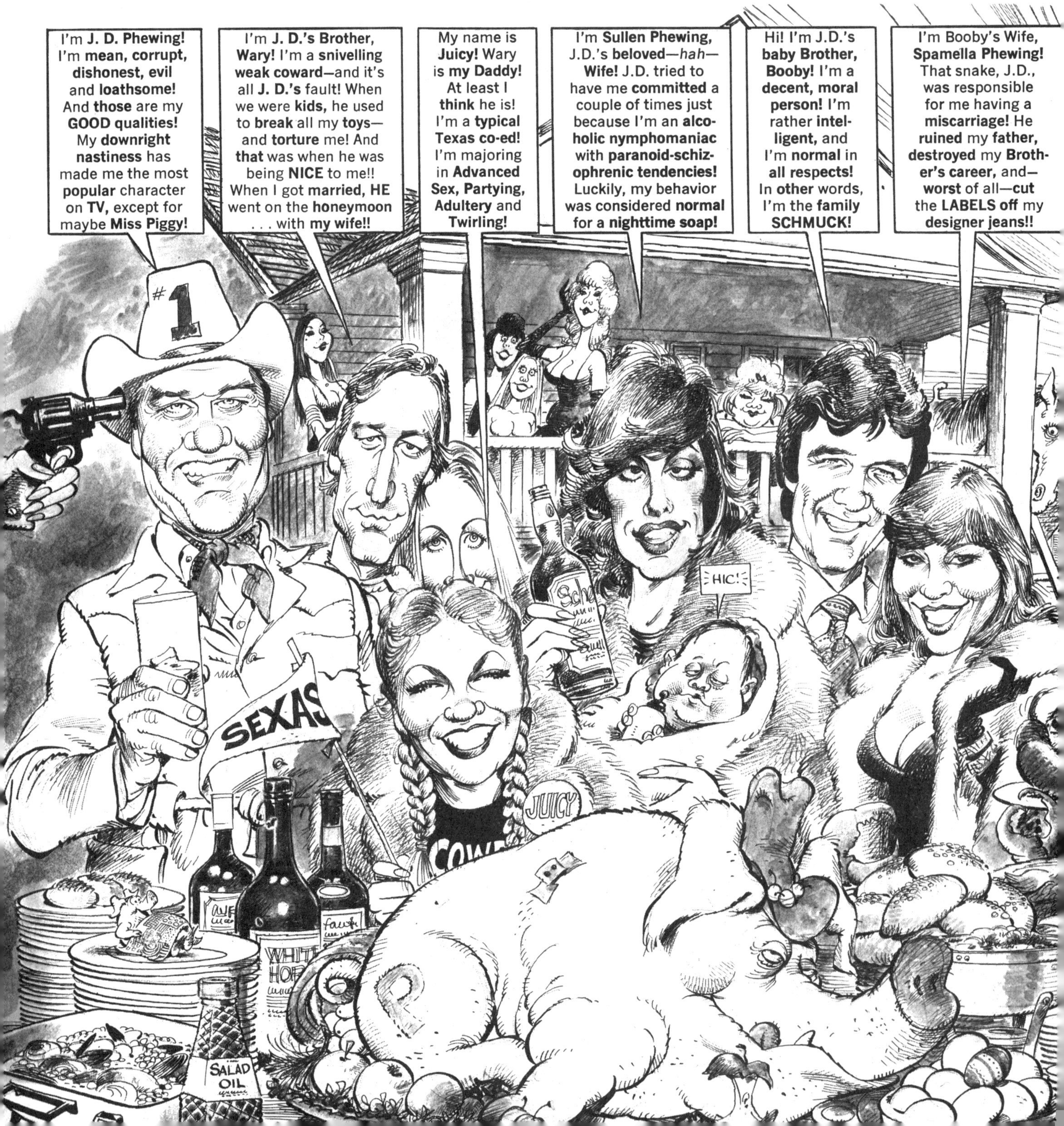
I'm J. D. Phewing! I'm mean, corrupt, dishonest, evil and loathsome! And those are my GOOD qualities! My downright nastiness has made me the most popular character on TV, except for maybe Miss Piggy!
I'm J. D.'s Brother, Wary! I'm a snivelling weak coward—and it's all J. D.'s fault! When we were kids, he used to break all my toys—and torture me! And that was when he was being NICE to me!! When I got married, HE went on the honeymoon . . . with my wife!!
My name is Juicy! Wary is my Daddy! At least I think he is! I'm a typical Texas co-ed! I'm majoring in Advanced Sex, Partying, Adultery and Twirling!
I'm Sullen Phewing, J.D.'s beloved—hah—Wife! J.D. tried to have me committed a couple of times just because I'm an alcoholic nymphomaniac with paranoid-schizophrenic tendencies! Luckily, my behavior was considered normal for a nighttime soap!
Hi! I'm J.D.'s baby Brother, Booby! I'm a decent, moral person! I'm rather intelligent, and I'm normal in all respects! In other words, I'm the family SCHMUCK!
I'm Booby's Wife, Spamella Phewing! That snake, J.D., was responsible for me having a miscarriage! He ruined my father, destroyed my Brother's career, and—worst of all—cut the LABELS off my designer jeans!!
#1
SEXAS
HIC!
JUICY
SALAD OIL

LLUS

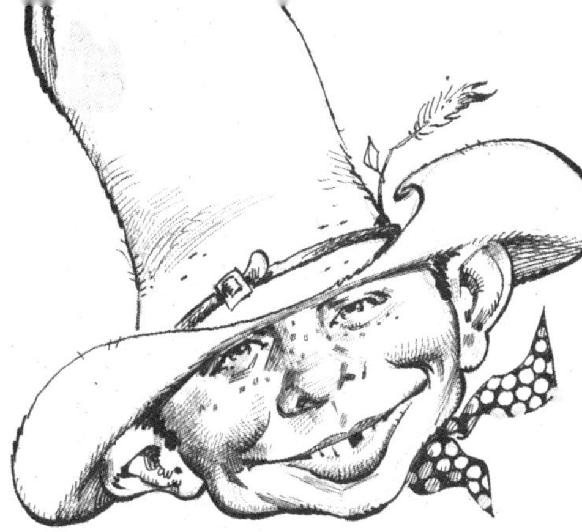

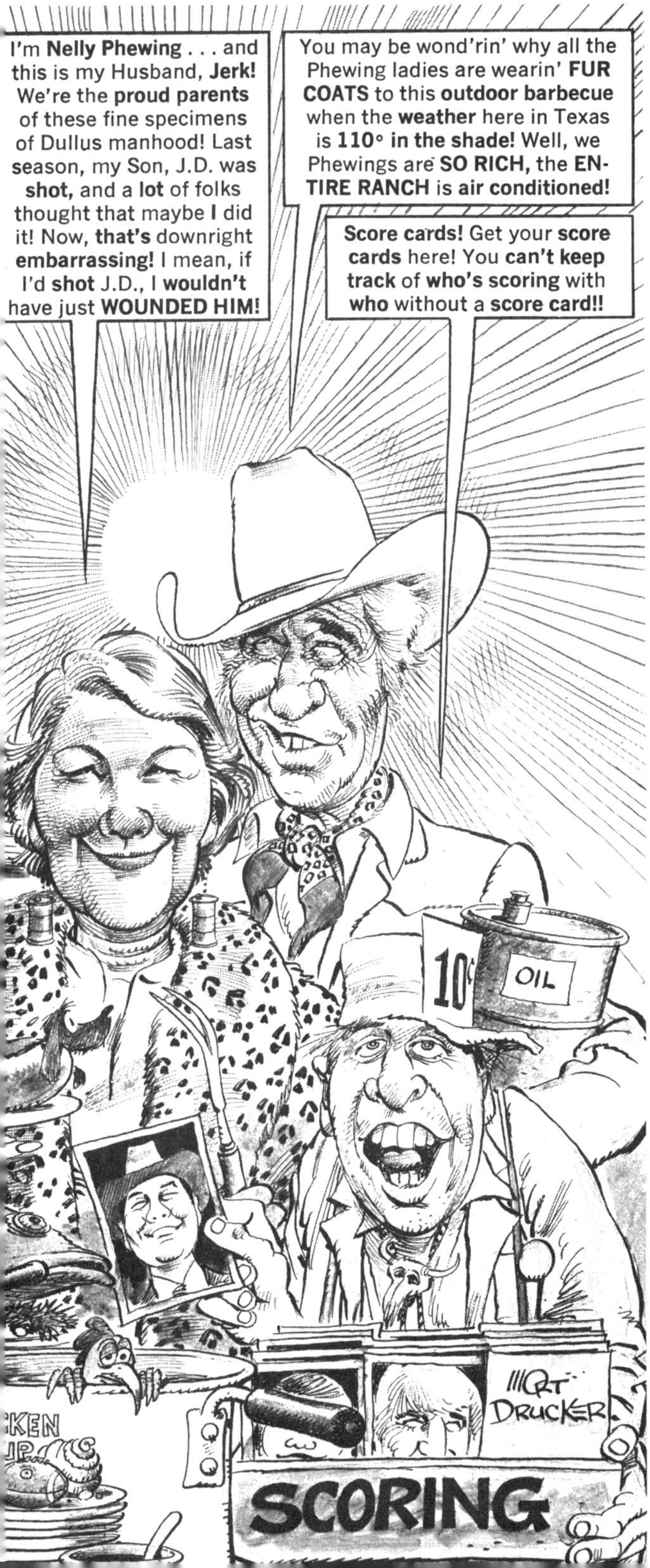
I'm **Nelly Phewing** . . . and this is my Husband, **Jerk!** We're the **proud parents** of these fine specimens of Dullus manhood! Last season, my Son, J.D. was **shot,** and a **lot** of folks thought that maybe **I** did it! Now, **that's** downright **embarrassing!** I mean, if I'd **shot** J.D., I **wouldn't** have just **WOUNDED HIM!**
You may be wond'rin' why all the Phewing ladies are wearin' **FUR COATS** to this **outdoor barbecue** when the **weather** here in Texas is **110° in the shade!** Well, we Phewings are **SO RICH,** the **ENTIRE RANCH is air conditioned!**
Score cards! Get your **score cards** here! You **can't keep track** of **who's scoring** with **who** without a **score card!!**
10¢
OIL
MORT DRUCKER
SCORING

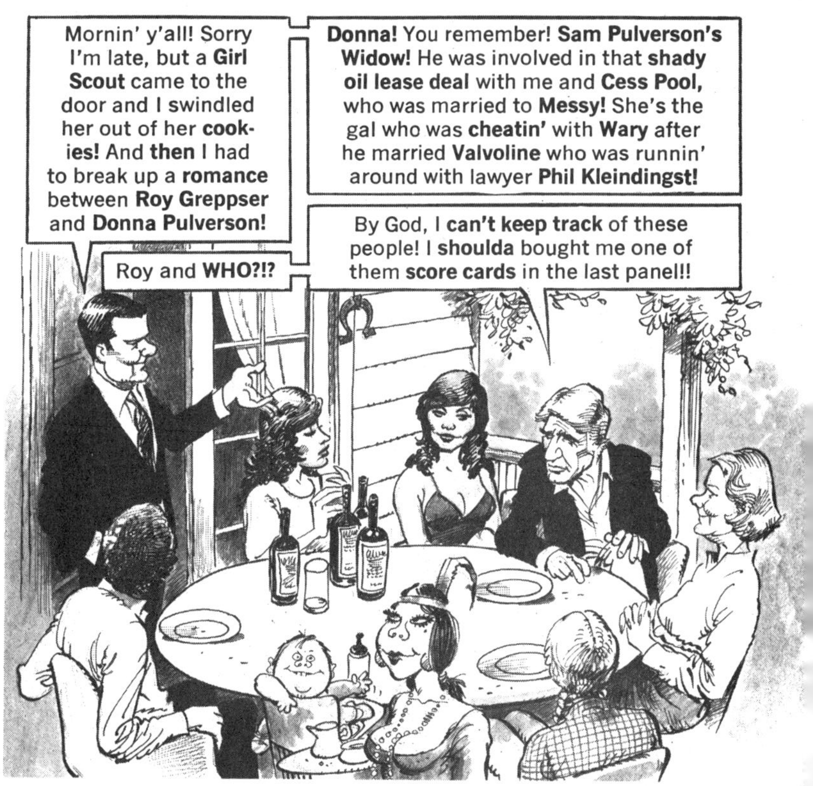
Mornin' y'all! Sorry I'm late, but a **Girl Scout** came to the door and I swindled her out of her **cookies!** And **then** I had to break up a **romance** between **Roy Greppser** and **Donna Pulverson!**
Roy and **WHO?!?**
Donna! You remember! **Sam Pulverson's Widow!** He was involved in that **shady oil lease deal** with me and **Cess Pool,** who was married to **Messy!** She's the gal who was **cheatin'** with **Wary** after he married **Valvoline** who was runnin' around with lawyer **Phil Kleindingst!**
By God, I **can't keep track** of these people! I **shoulda** bought me one of them **score cards** in the last panel!!

ARTIST: MORT DRUCKER WRITER: LOU SILVERSTONE

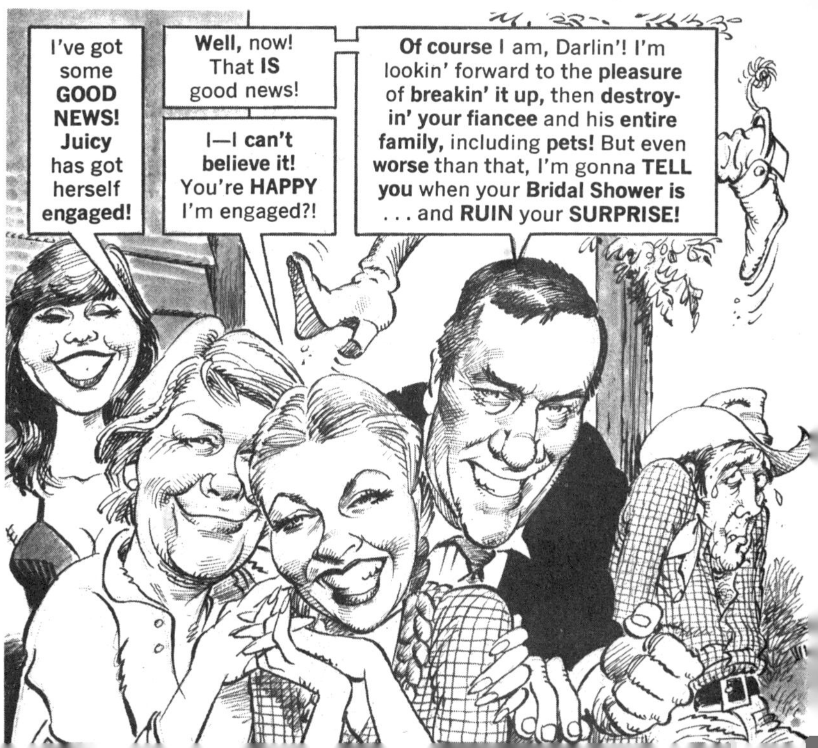
I've got some **GOOD NEWS! Juicy** has got herself **engaged!**
Well, now! That **IS** good news!
I—I **can't believe it!** You're **HAPPY** I'm engaged?!
Of course I am, Darlin'! I'm lookin' forward to the **pleasure** of **breakin' it up,** then **destroyin' your fiancee** and his **entire family,** including **pets!** But even **worse** than that, I'm gonna **TELL you** when your **Bridal Shower is . . .** and **RUIN** your **SURPRISE!**

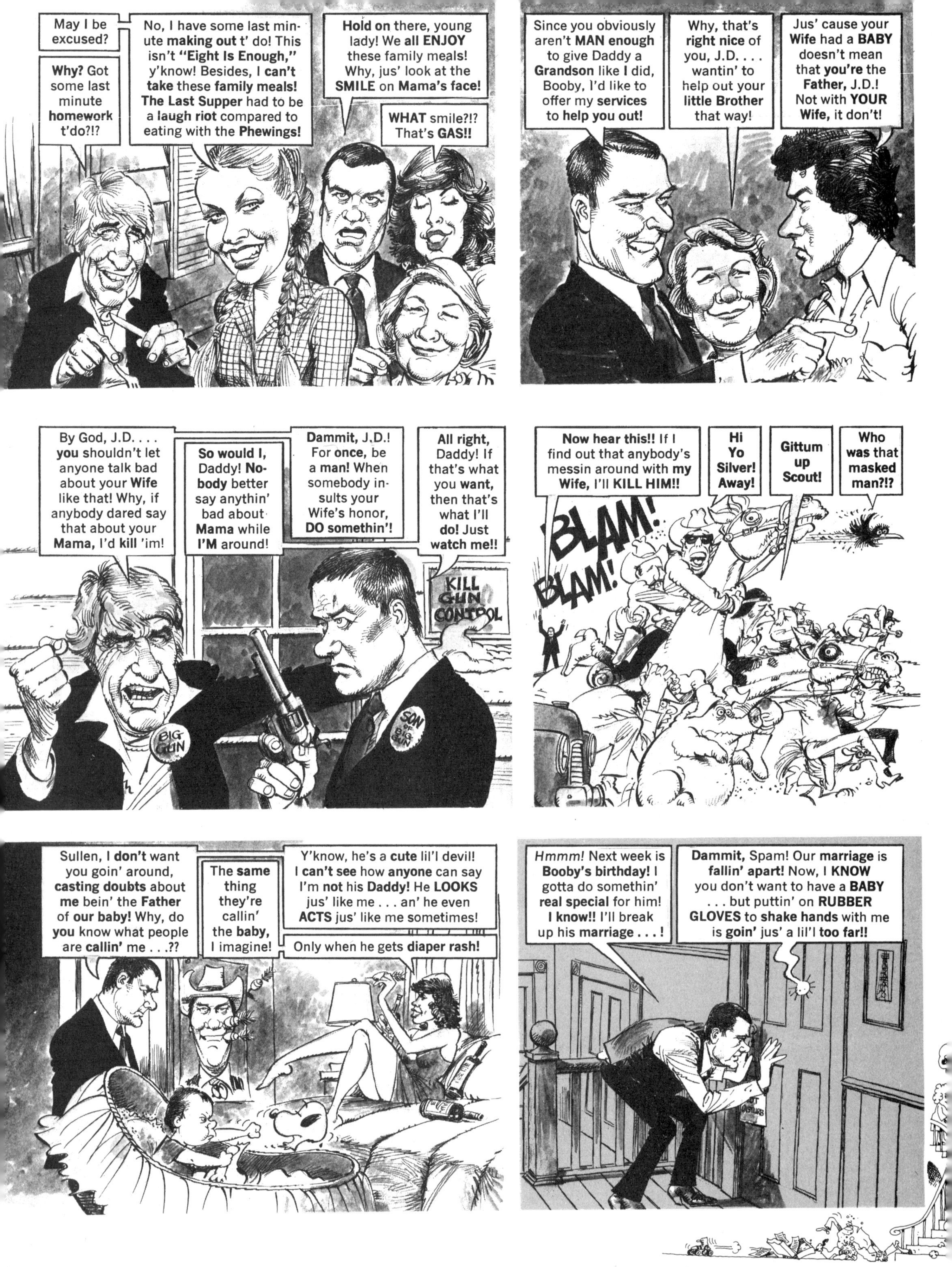
May I be excused?
Why? Got some last minute homework t'do?!?
No, I have some last minute **making out** t' do! This isn't **"Eight Is Enough,"** y'know! Besides, I **can't take** these **family meals! The Last Supper** had to be a **laugh riot** compared to eating with the **Phewings!**
Hold on there, young lady! We **all ENJOY** these family meals! Why, jus' look at the **SMILE** on **Mama's face!**
WHAT smile?!? That's **GAS!!**
Since you obviously aren't **MAN enough** to give Daddy a **Grandson** like **I** did, Booby, I'd like to offer my **services** to **help you out!**
Why, that's **right nice** of you, J.D. . . . wantin' to help out your **little Brother** that way!
Jus' cause your **Wife** had a **BABY** doesn't mean that **you're** the **Father,** J.D.! Not with **YOUR Wife,** it don't!
By God, J.D. . . . **you** shouldn't let anyone talk bad about your **Wife** like that! Why, if anybody dared say that about your **Mama,** I'd **kill** 'im!
So would I, Daddy! **Nobody** better say anythin' bad about **Mama** while **I'M** around!
Dammit, J.D.! For **once,** be a **man!** When somebody insults your Wife's honor, **DO somethin'!**
All right, Daddy! If that's what you **want,** then that's what I'll **do!** Just **watch me!!**
KILL GUN CONTROL
BIG GUN
SON OF BIG GUN
Now hear this!! If I find out that anybody's messin around with **my Wife,** I'll **KILL HIM!!**
BLAM! BLAM!
Hi Yo Silver! Away!
Gittum up Scout!
Who was that masked man?!?
Sullen, I **don't** want you goin' around, **casting doubts** about **me** bein' the **Father** of **our baby!** Why, do **you** know what people are **callin'** me . . .??
The **same** thing they're callin' the **baby,** I imagine!
Y'know, he's a **cute** lil'l devil! I **can't see** how **anyone** can say I'm **not** his **Daddy!** He **LOOKS** jus' like me . . . an' he even **ACTS** jus' like me sometimes!
Only when he gets **diaper rash!**
Hmmm! Next week is **Booby's birthday!** I gotta do somethin' **real special** for him! **I know!!** I'll break up his **marriage . . . !**
Dammit, Spam! Our **marriage** is **fallin' apart!** Now, I **KNOW** you don't want to have a **BABY** . . . but puttin' on **RUBBER GLOVES** to **shake hands** with me is **goin'** jus' a lil'l **too far!!**

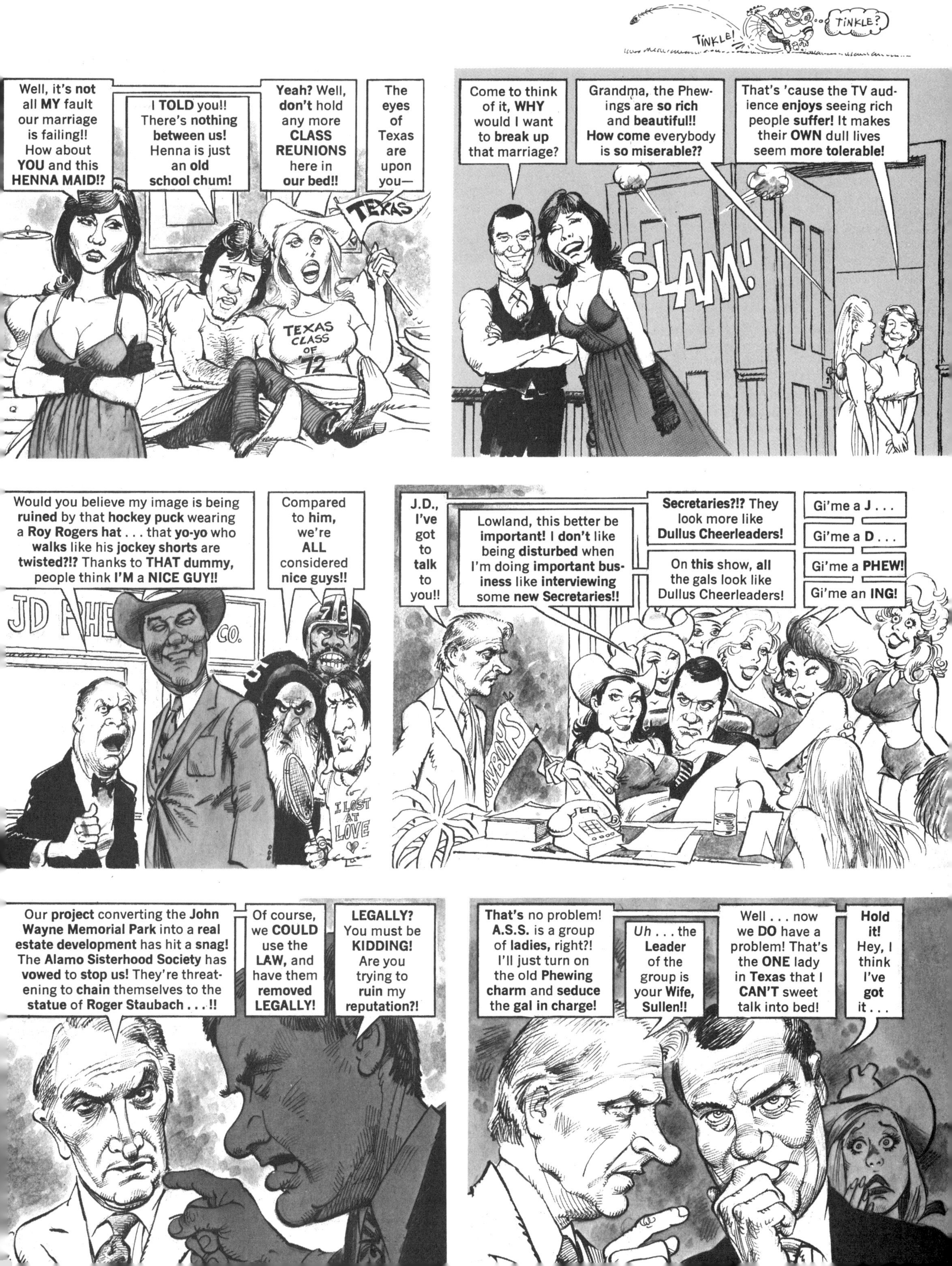

TINKLE!
TINKLE?
Well, it's not all MY fault our marriage is failing!! How about YOU and this HENNA MAID!?
I TOLD you!! There's nothing between us! Henna is just an old school chum!
Yeah? Well, don't hold any more CLASS REUNIONS here in our bed!!
The eyes of Texas are upon you—
TEXAS
TEXAS CLASS OF '72
Come to think of it, WHY would I want to break up that marriage?
Grandma, the Phewings are so rich and beautiful!! How come everybody is so miserable??
That's 'cause the TV audience enjoys seeing rich people suffer! It makes their OWN dull lives seem more tolerable!
SLAM!
Would you believe my image is being ruined by that hockey puck wearing a Roy Rogers hat . . . that yo-yo who walks like his jockey shorts are twisted?!? Thanks to THAT dummy, people think I'M a NICE GUY!!
Compared to him, we're ALL considered nice guys!!
JD PHE
CO.
75
I LOST AT LOVE
J.D., I've got to talk to you!!
Lowland, this better be important! I don't like being disturbed when I'm doing important business like interviewing some new Secretaries!!
Secretaries?!? They look more like Dullus Cheerleaders!
On this show, all the gals look like Dullus Cheerleaders!
Gi'me a J . . .
Gi'me a D . . .
Gi'me a PHEW!
Gi'me an ING!
COWBOYS
Our project converting the John Wayne Memorial Park into a real estate development has hit a snag! The Alamo Sisterhood Society has vowed to stop us! They're threatening to chain themselves to the statue of Roger Staubach . . .!!
Of course, we COULD use the LAW, and have them removed LEGALLY!
LEGALLY? You must be KIDDING! Are you trying to ruin my reputation?!
That's no problem! A.S.S. is a group of ladies, right?! I'll just turn on the old Phewing charm and seduce the gal in charge!
Uh . . . the Leader of the group is your Wife, Sullen!!
Well . . . now we DO have a problem! That's the ONE lady in Texas that I CAN'T sweet talk into bed!
Hold it! Hey, I think I've got it . . .

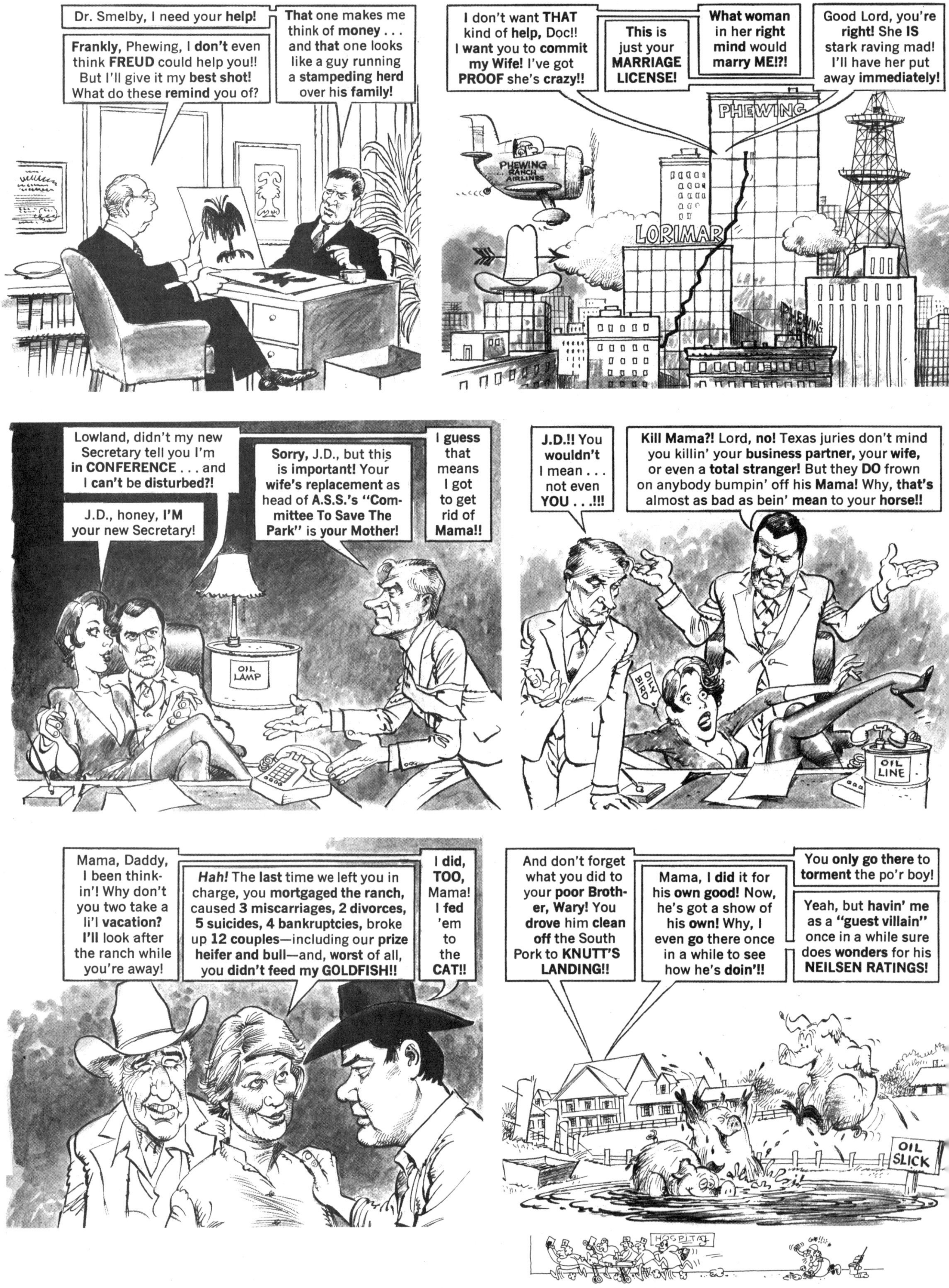
Dr. Smelby, I need your help!
Frankly, Phewing, I don't even think FREUD could help you!! But I'll give it my best shot! What do these remind you of?
That one makes me think of money . . . and that one looks like a guy running a stampeding herd over his family!
I don't want THAT kind of help, Doc!! I want you to commit my Wife! I've got PROOF she's crazy!!
This is just your MARRIAGE LICENSE!
What woman in her right mind would marry ME!?!
Good Lord, you're right! She IS stark raving mad! I'll have her put away immediately!
PHEWING
PHEWING RANCH AIRLINES
LORIMAR
Lowland, didn't my new Secretary tell you I'm in CONFERENCE . . . and I can't be disturbed?!
J.D., honey, I'M your new Secretary!
Sorry, J.D., but this is important! Your wife's replacement as head of A.S.S.'s "Committee To Save The Park" is your Mother!
I guess that means I got to get rid of Mama!!
OIL LAMP
J.D.!! You wouldn't I mean . . . not even YOU . . .!!!
Kill Mama?! Lord, no! Texas juries don't mind you killin' your business partner, your wife, or even a total stranger! But they DO frown on anybody bumpin' off his Mama! Why, that's almost as bad as bein' mean to your horse!!
OILY BIRD
OIL LINE
Mama, Daddy, I been thinkin'! Why don't you two take a li'l vacation? I'll look after the ranch while you're away!
Hah! The last time we left you in charge, you mortgaged the ranch, caused 3 miscarriages, 2 divorces, 5 suicides, 4 bankruptcies, broke up 12 couples—including our prize heifer and bull—and, worst of all, you didn't feed my GOLDFISH!!
I did, TOO, Mama! I fed 'em to the CAT!!
And don't forget what you did to your poor Brother, Wary! You drove him clean off the South Pork to KNUTT'S LANDING!!
Mama, I did it for his own good! Now, he's got a show of his own! Why, I even go there once in a while to see how he's doin'!!
You only go there to torment the po'r boy!
Yeah, but havin' me as a "guest villain" once in a while sure does wonders for his NEILSEN RATINGS!
OIL SLICK

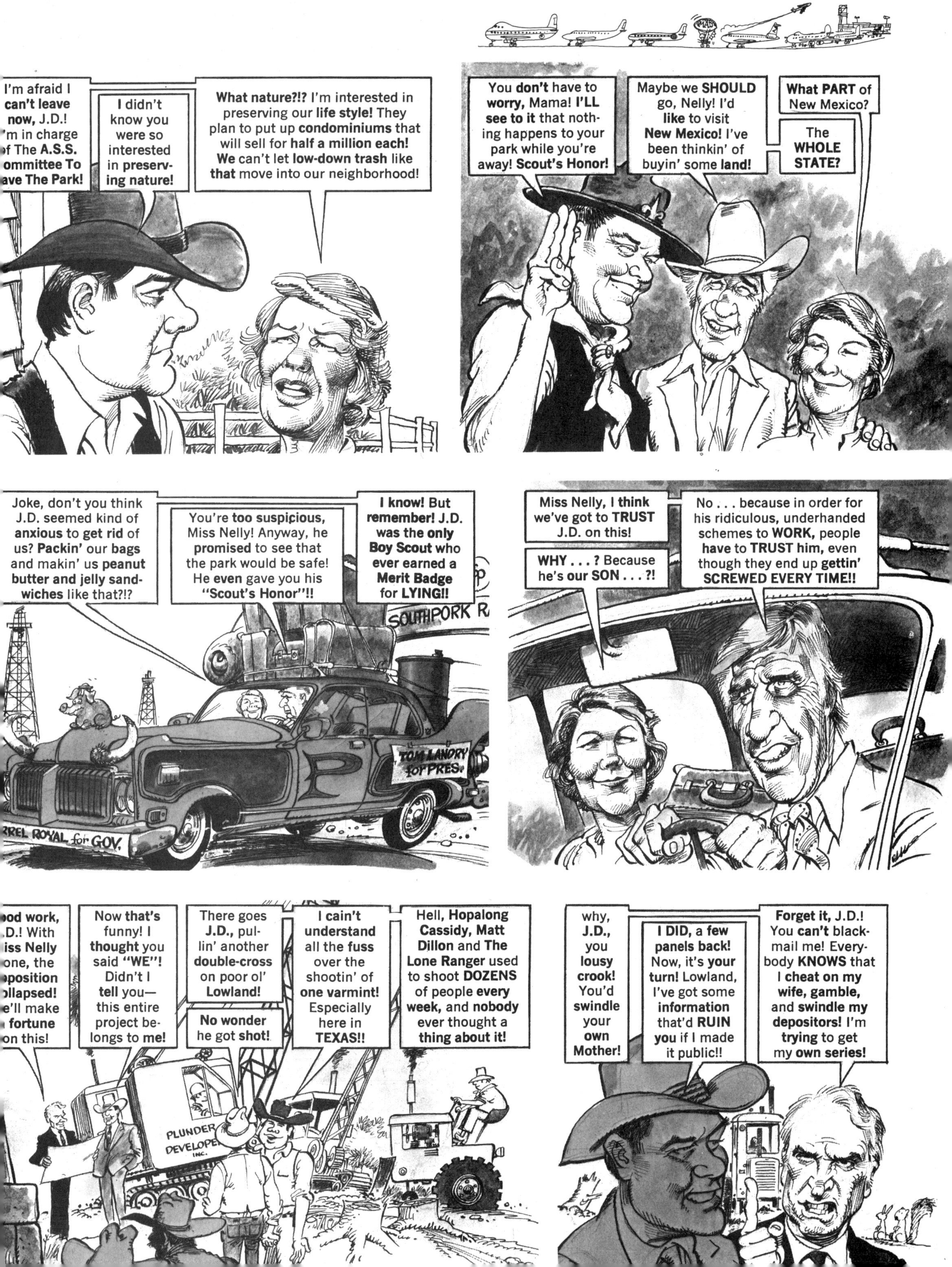

I'm afraid I can't leave now, J.D.! 'm in charge f The A.S.S. ommittee To ave The Park!
I didn't know you were so interested in preserving nature!
What nature?!? I'm interested in preserving our life style! They plan to put up condominiums that will sell for half a million each! We can't let low-down trash like that move into our neighborhood!
You don't have to worry, Mama! I'LL see to it that nothing happens to your park while you're away! Scout's Honor!
Maybe we SHOULD go, Nelly! I'd like to visit New Mexico! I've been thinkin' of buyin' some land!
What PART of New Mexico?
The WHOLE STATE?
Joke, don't you think J.D. seemed kind of anxious to get rid of us? Packin' our bags and makin' us peanut butter and jelly sandwiches like that?!?
You're too suspicious, Miss Nelly! Anyway, he promised to see that the park would be safe! He even gave you his "Scout's Honor"!!
I know! But remember! J.D. was the only Boy Scout who ever earned a Merit Badge for LYING!!
SOUTHPORK R
TOM LANDRY for PRES.
RREL ROYAL for GOV.
Miss Nelly, I think we've got to TRUST J.D. on this!
WHY . . . ? Because he's our SON . . . ?!
No . . . because in order for his ridiculous, underhanded schemes to WORK, people have to TRUST him, even though they end up gettin' SCREWED EVERY TIME!!
ood work, .D.! With iss Nelly one, the pposition ollapsed! e'll make fortune on this!
Now that's funny! I thought you said "WE"! Didn't I tell you—this entire project belongs to me!
There goes J.D., pullin' another double-cross on poor ol' Lowland!
No wonder he got shot!
I cain't understand all the fuss over the shootin' of one varmint! Especially here in TEXAS!!
Hell, Hopalong Cassidy, Matt Dillon and The Lone Ranger used to shoot DOZENS of people every week, and nobody ever thought a thing about it!
PLUNDER DEVELOPE INC.
why, J.D., you lousy crook! You'd swindle your own Mother!
I DID, a few panels back! Now, it's your turn! Lowland, I've got some information that'd RUIN you if I made it public!!
Forget it, J.D.! You can't blackmail me! Everybody KNOWS that I cheat on my wife, gamble, and swindle my depositors! I'm trying to get my own series!

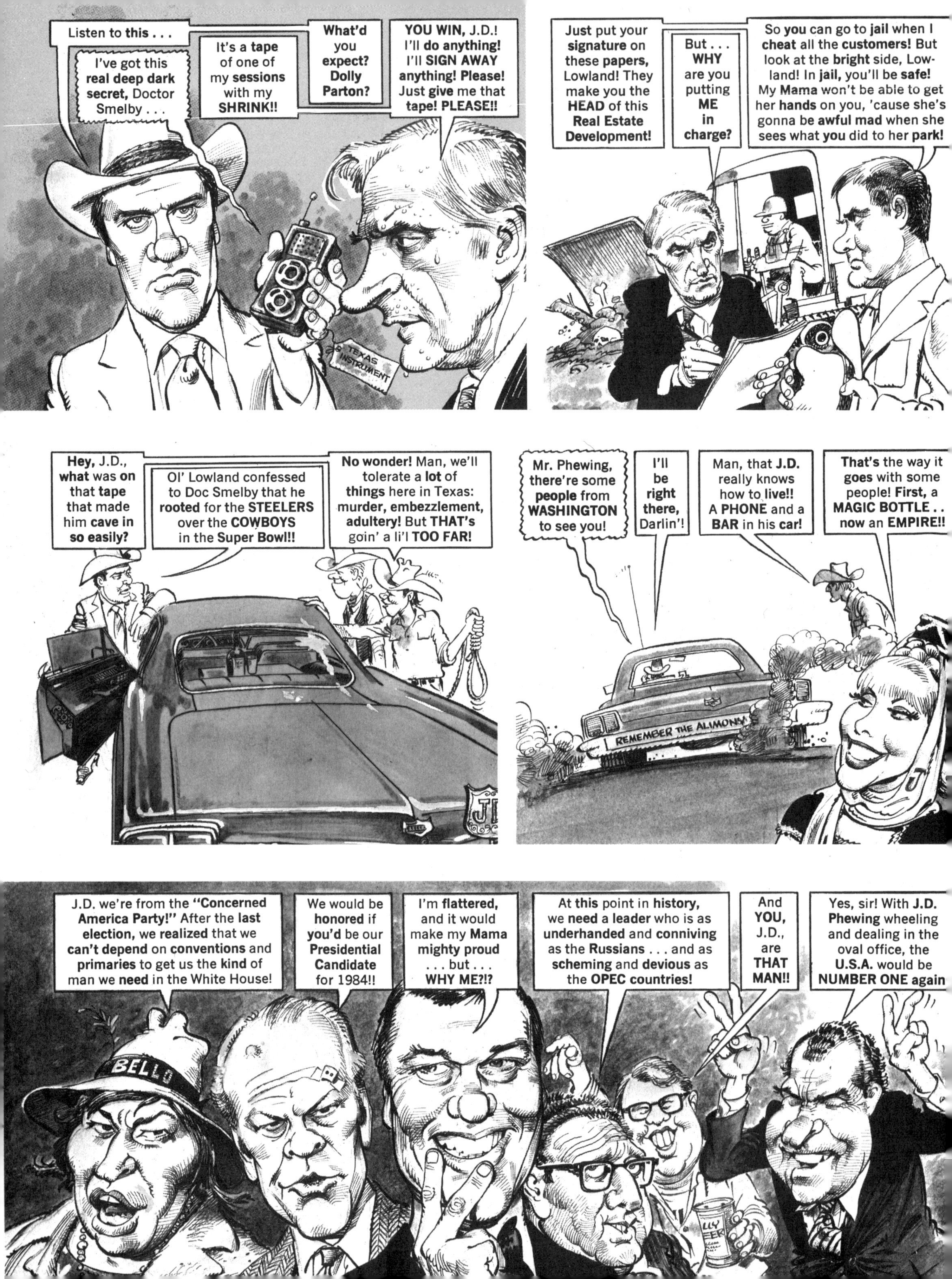
Listen to this . . .
I've got this real deep dark secret, Doctor Smelby . . .
It's a tape of one of my sessions with my SHRINK!!
What'd you expect? Dolly Parton?
YOU WIN, J.D.! I'll do anything! I'll SIGN AWAY anything! Please! Just give me that tape! PLEASE!!
TEXAS INSTRUMENT
Just put your signature on these papers, Lowland! They make you the HEAD of this Real Estate Development!
But . . . WHY are you putting ME in charge?
So you can go to jail when I cheat all the customers! But look at the bright side, Lowland! In jail, you'll be safe! My Mama won't be able to get her hands on you, 'cause she's gonna be awful mad when she sees what you did to her park!
Hey, J.D., what was on that tape that made him cave in so easily?
Ol' Lowland confessed to Doc Smelby that he rooted for the STEELERS over the COWBOYS in the Super Bowl!!
No wonder! Man, we'll tolerate a lot of things here in Texas: murder, embezzlement, adultery! But THAT's goin' a li'l TOO FAR!
Mr. Phewing, there're some people from WASHINGTON to see you!
I'll be right there, Darlin'!
Man, that J.D. really knows how to live!! A PHONE and a BAR in his car!
That's the way it goes with some people! First, a MAGIC BOTTLE . . now an EMPIRE!!
REMEMBER THE ALIMONY
J.D. we're from the "Concerned America Party!" After the last election, we realized that we can't depend on conventions and primaries to get us the kind of man we need in the White House!
We would be honored if you'd be our Presidential Candidate for 1984!!
I'm flattered, and it would make my Mama mighty proud . . . but . . . WHY ME?!?
At this point in history, we need a leader who is as underhanded and conniving as the Russians . . . and as scheming and devious as the OPEC countries!
And YOU, J.D., are THAT MAN!!
Yes, sir! With J.D. Phewing wheeling and dealing in the oval office, the U.S.A. would be NUMBER ONE again
BELLO

THE FATUOUS FIFTIES DEPT.

Have you noticed that people seem to get disgustingly nostalgic about things they weren't really very crazy about in the first place? Like the 50's? We figure that any decade that had the Korean War, the Edsel, Senator Joseph McCarthy, Davy Crockett hats, the Hula-Hoop and Pat Boone wearing fruit boots can't be ALL GOOD! And yet, the hottest show on TV these days is about this very bland, very silly decade where the biggest problem seemed to be *who* was making out with *whom,* and how fast your *face* would clear up. So, okay nerds. Go put on your blue suede shoes, your pedal pushers, your ankle slave bracelets and your leather jackets and get yourselves arrested for committing an idiocy while reading

CRAPPY DAYS

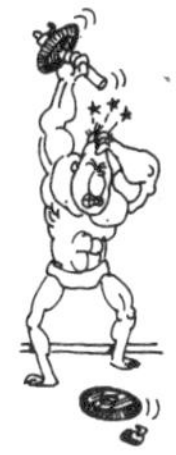

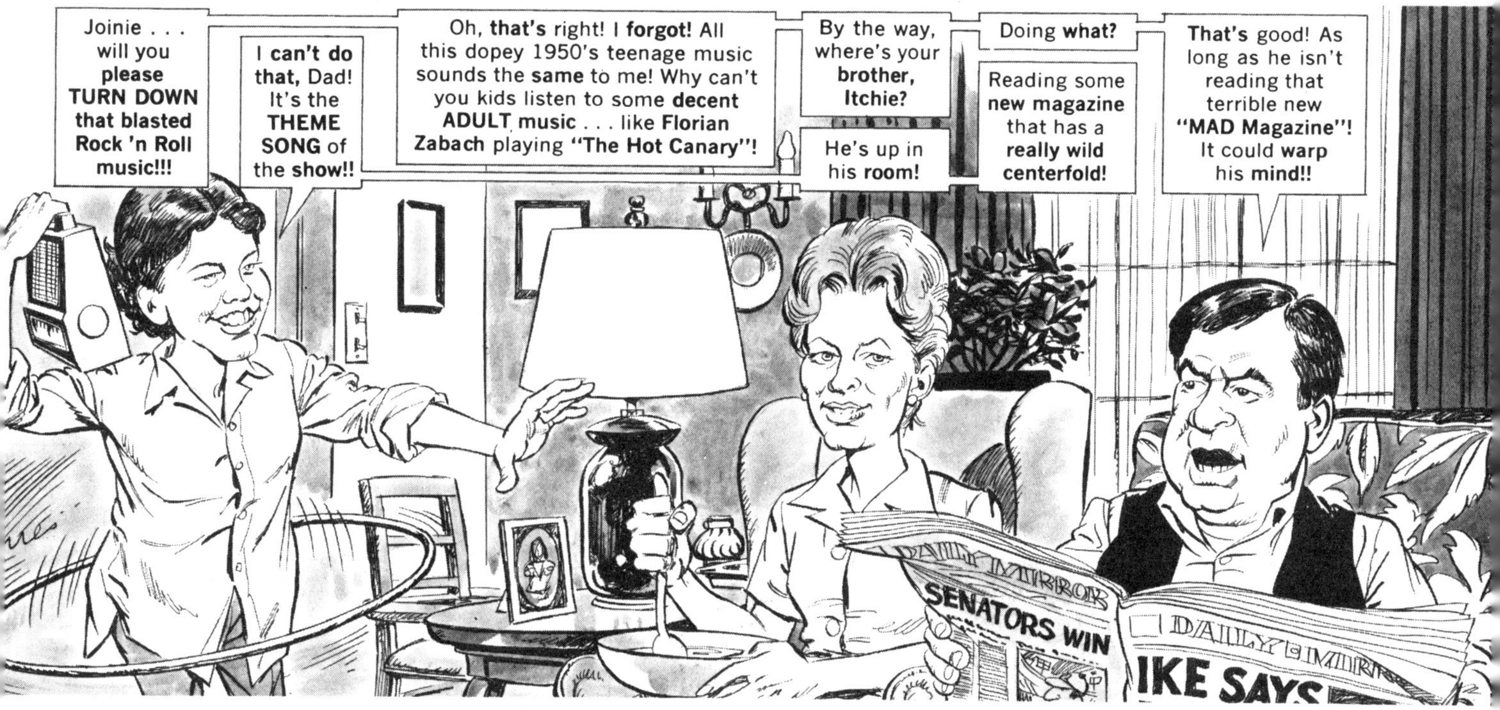
Joinie . . . will you please TURN DOWN that blasted Rock 'n Roll music!!!
I can't do that, Dad! It's the THEME SONG of the show!!
Oh, that's right! I forgot! All this dopey 1950's teenage music sounds the same to me! Why can't you kids listen to some decent ADULT music . . . like Florian Zabach playing "The Hot Canary"!
By the way, where's your brother, Itchie?
He's up in his room!
Doing what?
Reading some new magazine that has a really wild centerfold!
That's good! As long as he isn't reading that terrible new "MAD Magazine"! It could warp his mind!!
DAILY MIRROR
SENATORS WIN
IKE SAYS

ARTIST: ANGELO TORRES WRITER: ARNIE KOGEN

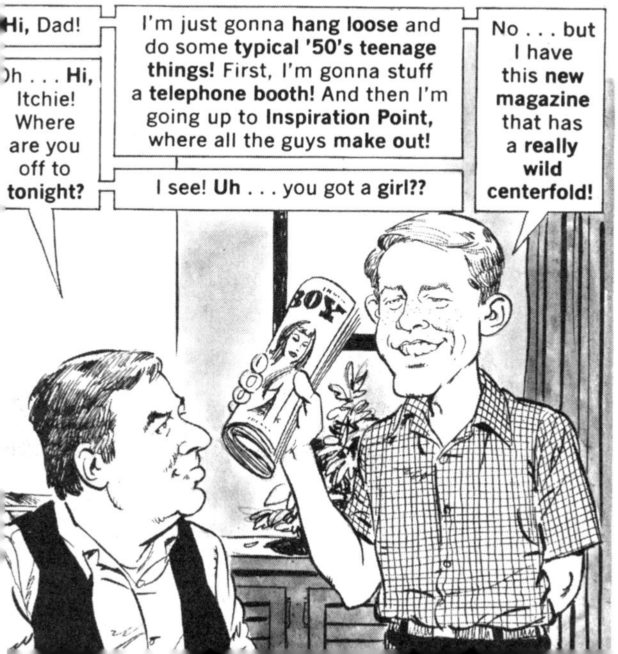
Hi, Dad!
h . . . Hi, Itchie! Where are you off to tonight?
I'm just gonna hang loose and do some typical '50's teenage things! First, I'm gonna stuff a telephone booth! And then I'm going up to Inspiration Point, where all the guys make out!
I see! Uh . . . you got a girl??
No . . . but I have this new magazine that has a really wild centerfold!
BOY

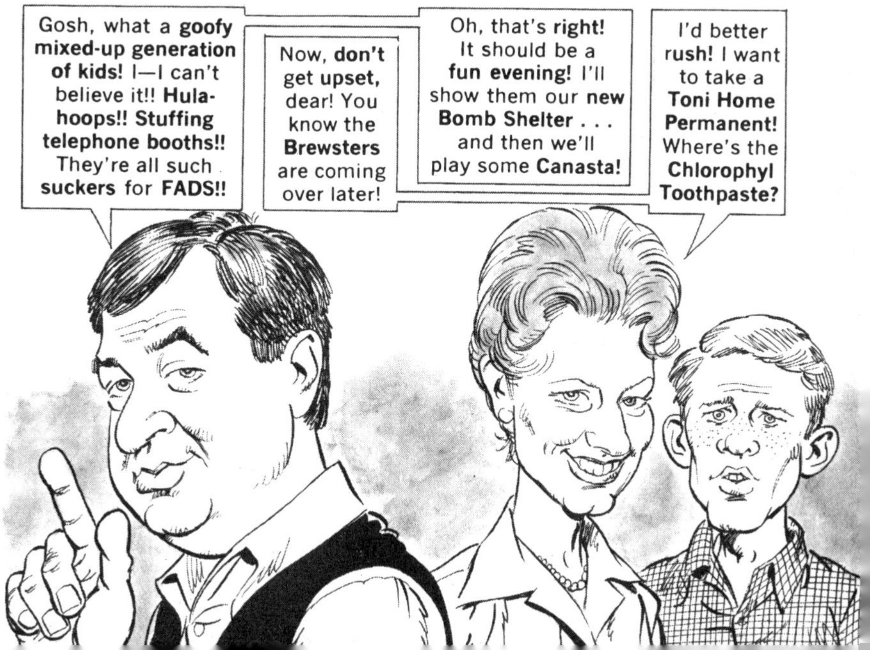
Gosh, what a goofy mixed-up generation of kids! I—I can't believe it!! Hula-hoops!! Stuffing telephone booths!! They're all such suckers for FADS!!
Now, don't get upset, dear! You know the Brewsters are coming over later!
Oh, that's right! It should be a fun evening! I'll show them our new Bomb Shelter . . . and then we'll play some Canasta!
I'd better rush! I want to take a Toni Home Permanent! Where's the Chlorophyl Toothpaste?

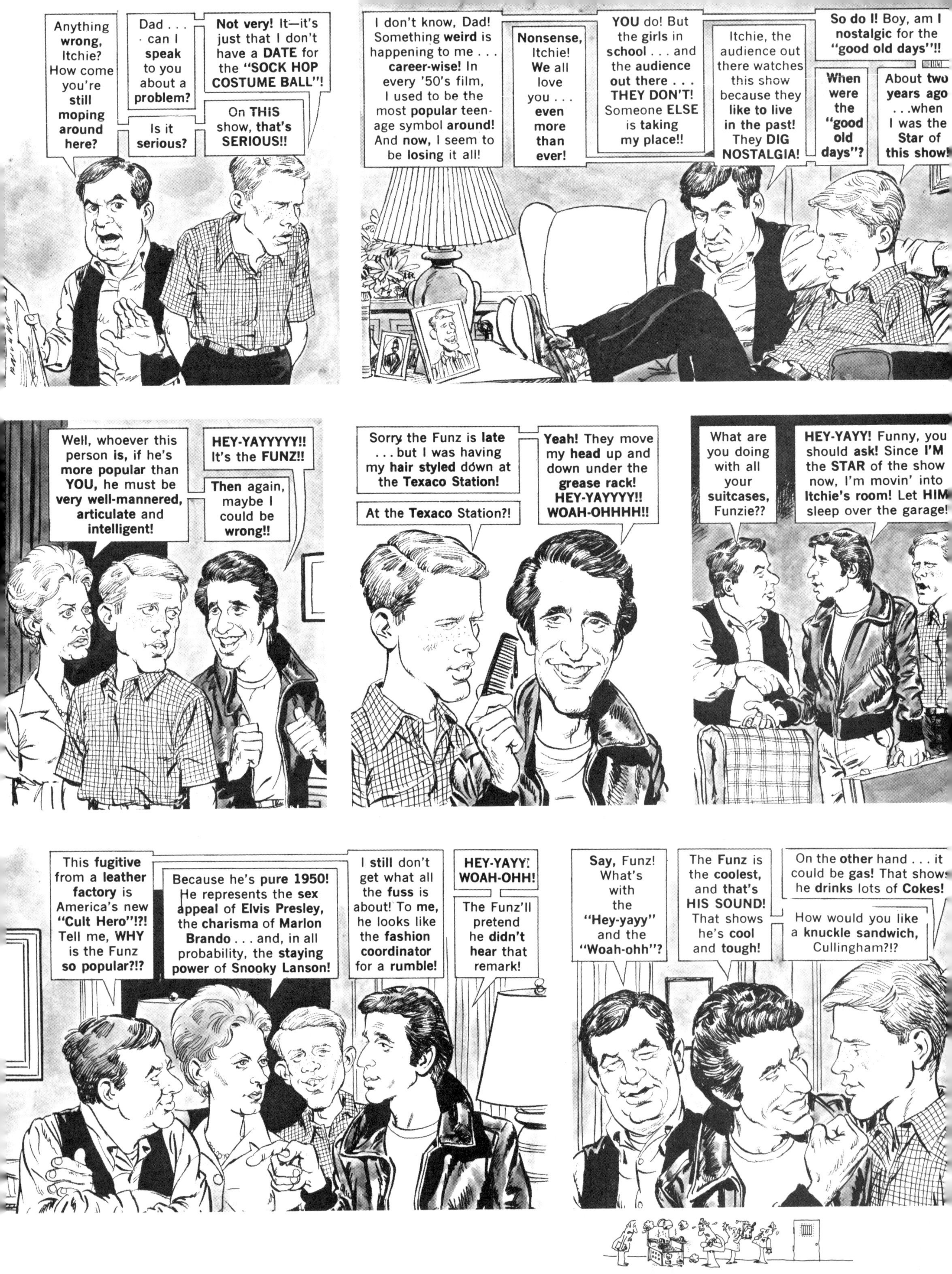

Anything wrong, Itchie? How come you're still moping around here?
Dad . . . can I speak to you about a problem?
Not very! It—it's just that I don't have a DATE for the "SOCK HOP COSTUME BALL"!
Is it serious?
On THIS show, that's SERIOUS!!
I don't know, Dad! Something weird is happening to me . . . career-wise! In every '50's film, I used to be the most popular teen-age symbol around! And now, I seem to be losing it all!
Nonsense, Itchie! We all love you . . . even more than ever!
YOU do! But the girls in school . . . and the audience out there . . . THEY DON'T! Someone ELSE is taking my place!!
Itchie, the audience out there watches this show because they like to live in the past! They DIG NOSTALGIA!
So do I! Boy, am I nostalgic for the "good old days"!!
When were the "good old days"?
About two years ago . . . when I was the Star of this show!
Well, whoever this person is, if he's more popular than YOU, he must be very well-mannered, articulate and intelligent!
HEY-YAYYYYY!! It's the FUNZ!!
Then again, maybe I could be wrong!!
Sorry the Funz is late . . . but I was having my hair styled down at the Texaco Station!
At the Texaco Station?!
Yeah! They move my head up and down under the grease rack! HEY-YAYYYY!! WOAH-OHHHH!!
What are you doing with all your suitcases, Funzie??
HEY-YAYY! Funny, you should ask! Since I'M the STAR of the show now, I'm movin' into Itchie's room! Let HIM sleep over the garage!
This fugitive from a leather factory is America's new "Cult Hero"!?! Tell me, WHY is the Funz so popular?!?
Because he's pure 1950! He represents the sex appeal of Elvis Presley, the charisma of Marlon Brando . . . and, in all probability, the staying power of Snooky Lanson!
I still don't get what all the fuss is about! To me, he looks like the fashion coordinator for a rumble!
HEY-YAYY! WOAH-OHH!
The Funz'll pretend he didn't hear that remark!
Say, Funz! What's with the "Hey-yayy" and the "Woah-ohh"?
The Funz is the coolest, and that's HIS SOUND! That shows he's cool and tough!
On the other hand . . . it could be gas! That shows he drinks lots of Cokes!
How would you like a knuckle sandwich, Cullingham?!?

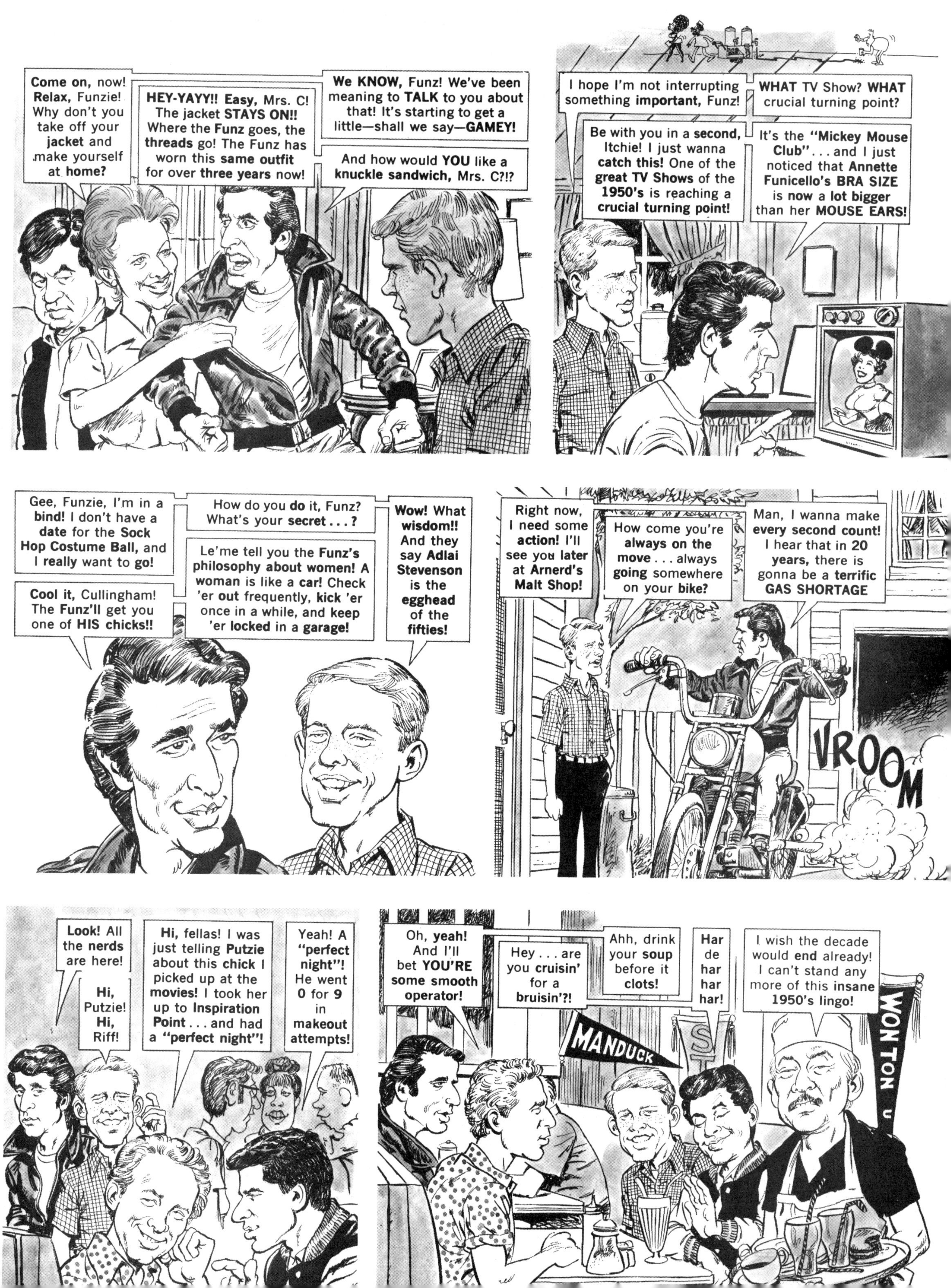

Come on, now! Relax, Funzie! Why don't you take off your jacket and make yourself at home?
HEY-YAYY!! Easy, Mrs. C! The jacket STAYS ON!! Where the Funz goes, the threads go! The Funz has worn this same outfit for over three years now!
We KNOW, Funz! We've been meaning to TALK to you about that! It's starting to get a little—shall we say—GAMEY!
And how would YOU like a knuckle sandwich, Mrs. C?!?
I hope I'm not interrupting something important, Funz!
Be with you in a second, Itchie! I just wanna catch this! One of the great TV Shows of the 1950's is reaching a crucial turning point!
WHAT TV Show? WHAT crucial turning point?
It's the "Mickey Mouse Club" . . . and I just noticed that Annette Funicello's BRA SIZE is now a lot bigger than her MOUSE EARS!
Gee, Funzie, I'm in a bind! I don't have a date for the Sock Hop Costume Ball, and I really want to go!
Cool it, Cullingham! The Funz'll get you one of HIS chicks!!
How do you do it, Funz? What's your secret . . . ?
Le'me tell you the Funz's philosophy about women! A woman is like a car! Check 'er out frequently, kick 'er once in a while, and keep 'er locked in a garage!
Wow! What wisdom!! And they say Adlai Stevenson is the egghead of the fifties!
Right now, I need some action! I'll see you later at Arnerd's Malt Shop!
How come you're always on the move . . . always going somewhere on your bike?
Man, I wanna make every second count! I hear that in 20 years, there is gonna be a terrific GAS SHORTAGE
VROOM
Look! All the nerds are here!
Hi, Putzie! Hi, Riff!
Hi, fellas! I was just telling Putzie about this chick I picked up at the movies! I took her up to Inspiration Point . . . and had a "perfect night"!
Yeah! A "perfect night"! He went 0 for 9 in makeout attempts!
Oh, yeah! And I'll bet YOU'RE some smooth operator!
Hey . . . are you cruisin' for a bruisin'?!
Ahh, drink your soup before it clots!
Har de har har har!
I wish the decade would end already! I can't stand any more of this insane 1950's lingo!
MANDUCK
WON TON U

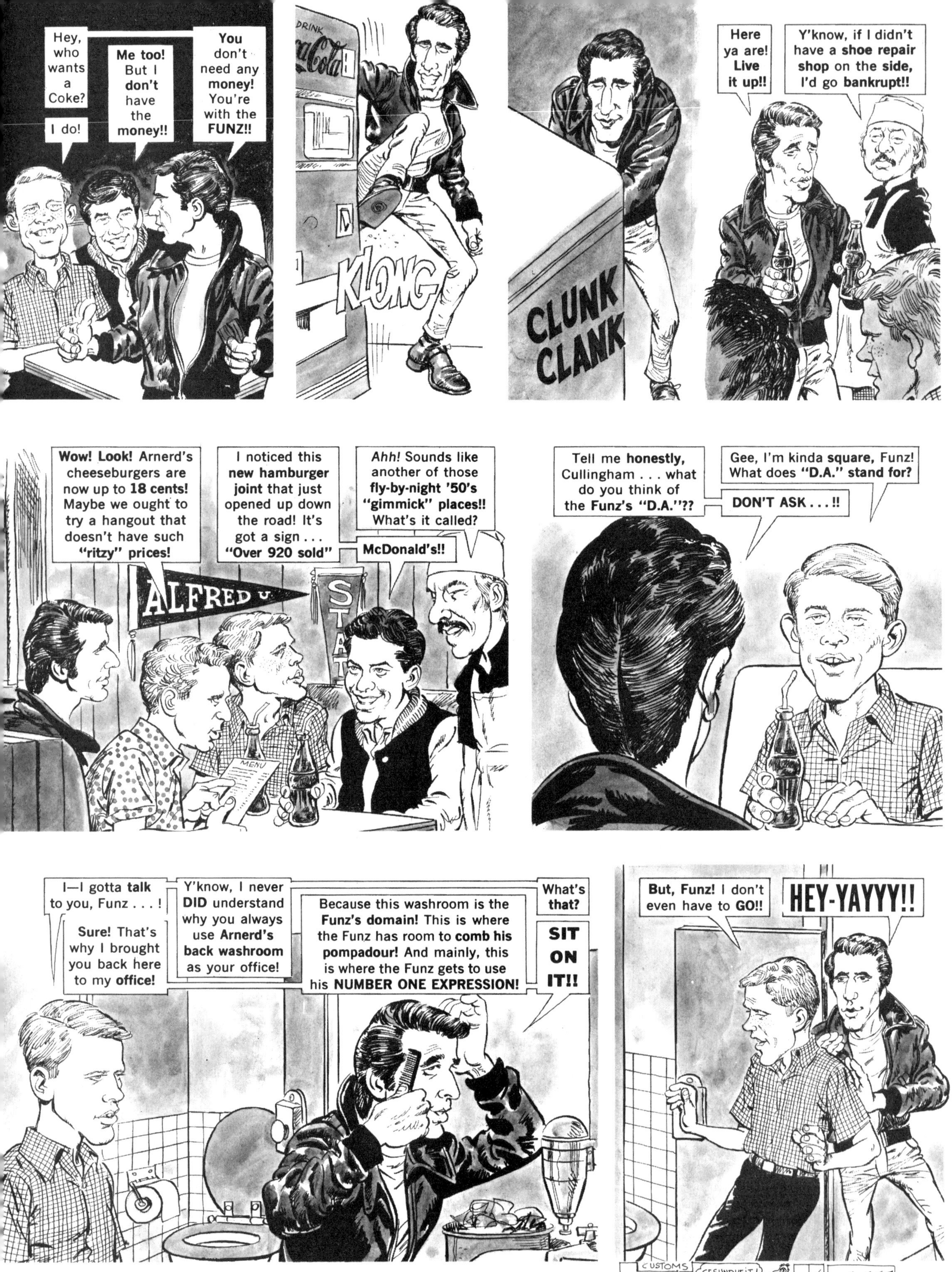
Hey, who wants a Coke?
I do!
Me too! But I don't have the money!!
You don't need any money! You're with the FUNZ!!
DRINK Coca-Cola
KLONG
CLUNK CLANK
Here ya are! Live it up!!
Y'know, if I didn't have a shoe repair shop on the side, I'd go bankrupt!!
Wow! Look! Arnerd's cheeseburgers are now up to 18 cents! Maybe we ought to try a hangout that doesn't have such "ritzy" prices!
I noticed this new hamburger joint that just opened up down the road! It's got a sign . . . "Over 920 sold"
Ahh! Sounds like another of those fly-by-night '50's "gimmick" places!! What's it called?
McDonald's!!
ALFRED U.
STATE
MENU
Tell me honestly, Cullingham . . . what do you think of the Funz's "D.A."??
Gee, I'm kinda square, Funz! What does "D.A." stand for?
DON'T ASK . . . !!
I—I gotta talk to you, Funz . . . !
Sure! That's why I brought you back here to my office!
Y'know, I never DID understand why you always use Arnerd's back washroom as your office!
What's that?
Because this washroom is the Funz's domain! This is where the Funz has room to comb his pompadour! And mainly, this is where the Funz gets to use his NUMBER ONE EXPRESSION!
SIT ON IT!!
But, Funz! I don't even have to GO!!
HEY-YAYYY!!

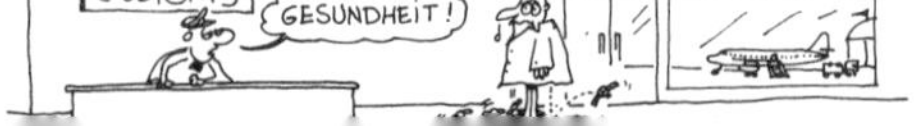
CUSTOMS
GESUNDHEIT!

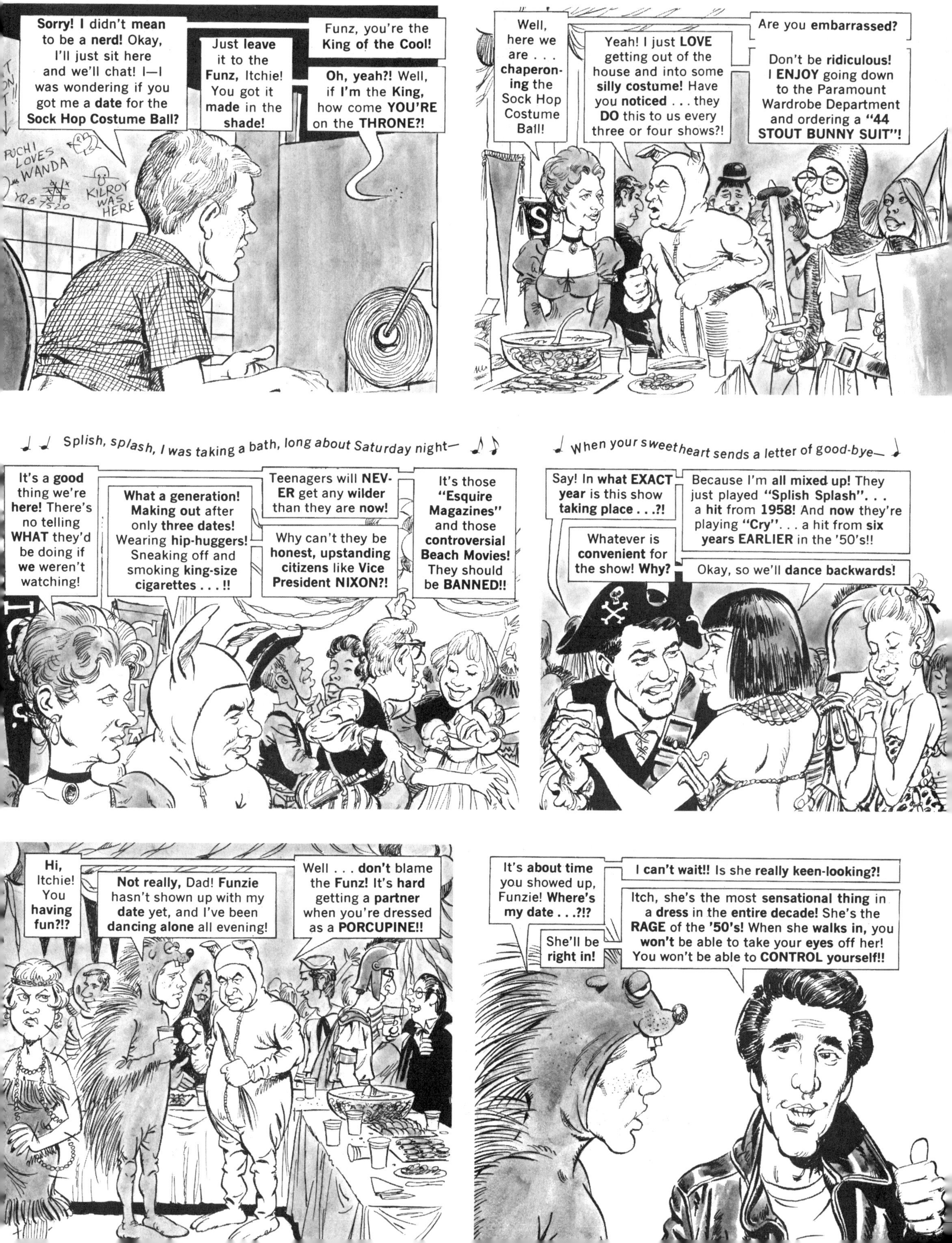
Sorry! I didn't mean to be a nerd! Okay, I'll just sit here and we'll chat! I—I was wondering if you got me a date for the Sock Hop Costume Ball?
Just leave it to the Funz, Itchie! You got it made in the shade!
Funz, you're the King of the Cool!
Oh, yeah?! Well, if I'm the King, how come YOU'RE on the THRONE?!
KILROY WAS HERE
Well, here we are . . . chaperoning the Sock Hop Costume Ball!
Yeah! I just LOVE getting out of the house and into some silly costume! Have you noticed . . . they DO this to us every three or four shows?!
Are you embarrassed?
Don't be ridiculous! I ENJOY going down to the Paramount Wardrobe Department and ordering a "44 STOUT BUNNY SUIT"!
Splish, splash, I was taking a bath, long about Saturday night—
It's a good thing we're here! There's no telling WHAT they'd be doing if we weren't watching!
What a generation! Making out after only three dates! Wearing hip-huggers! Sneaking off and smoking king-size cigarettes . . . !!
Teenagers will NEVER get any wilder than they are now!
Why can't they be honest, upstanding citizens like Vice President NIXON?!
It's those "Esquire Magazines" and those controversial Beach Movies! They should be BANNED!!
When your sweetheart sends a letter of good-bye—
Say! In what EXACT year is this show taking place . . .?!
Because I'm all mixed up! They just played "Splish Splash". . . a hit from 1958! And now they're playing "Cry". . . a hit from six years EARLIER in the '50's!!
Whatever is convenient for the show! Why?
Okay, so we'll dance backwards!
Hi, Itchie! You having fun?!?
Not really, Dad! Funzie hasn't shown up with my date yet, and I've been dancing alone all evening!
Well . . . don't blame the Funz! It's hard getting a partner when you're dressed as a PORCUPINE!!
It's about time you showed up, Funzie! Where's my date . . .?!?
She'll be right in!
I can't wait!! Is she really keen-looking?!
Itch, she's the most sensational thing in a dress in the entire decade! She's the RAGE of the '50's! When she walks in, you won't be able to take your eyes off her! You won't be able to CONTROL yourself!!

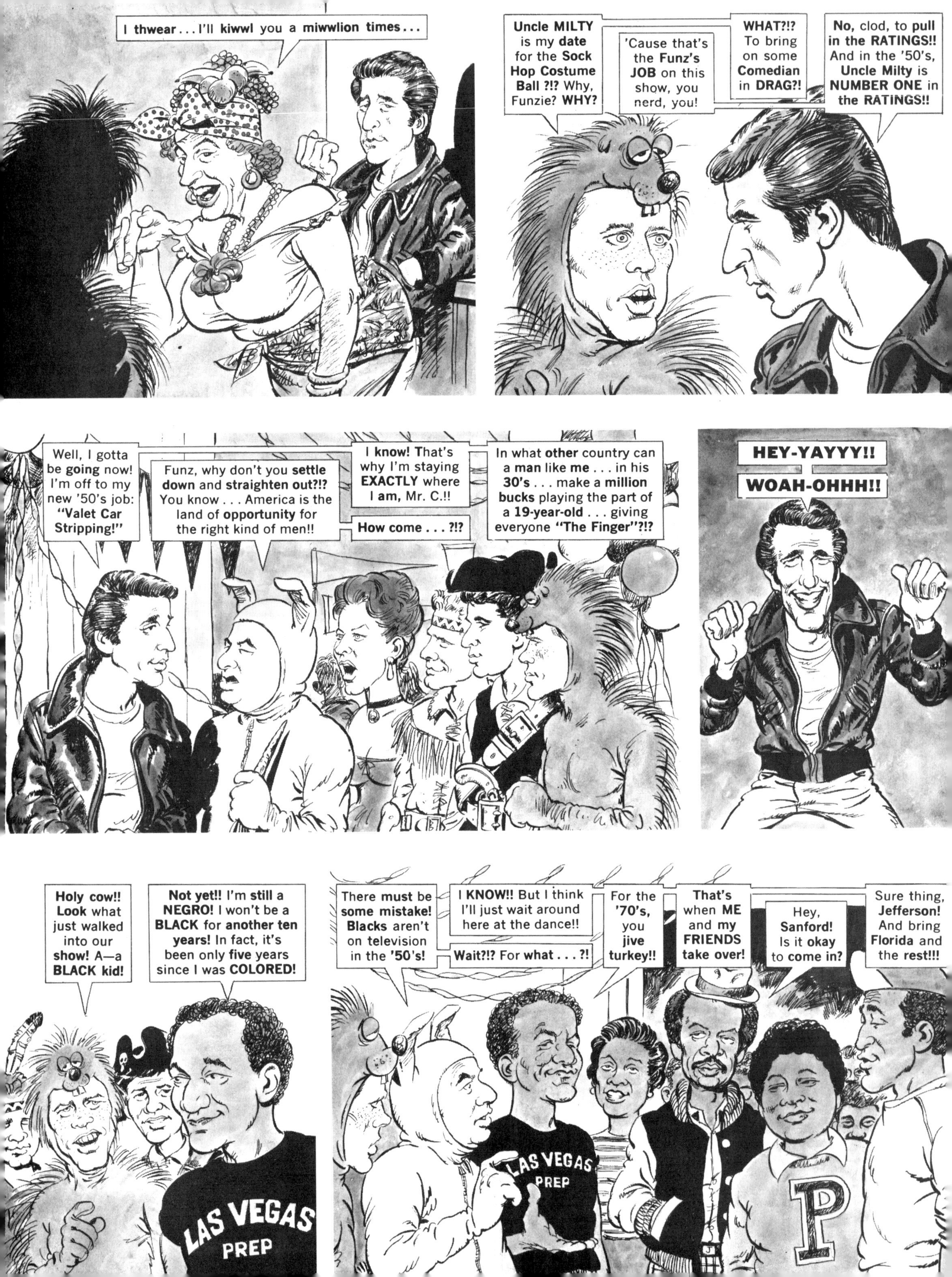

I thwear . . . I'll kiwwl you a miwwlion times . . .
Uncle MILTY is my date for the Sock Hop Costume Ball ?!? Why, Funzie? WHY?
'Cause that's the Funz's JOB on this show, you nerd, you!
WHAT?!? To bring on some Comedian in DRAG?!
No, clod, to pull in the RATINGS!! And in the '50's, Uncle Milty is NUMBER ONE in the RATINGS!!
Well, I gotta be going now! I'm off to my new '50's job: "Valet Car Stripping!"
Funz, why don't you settle down and straighten out?!? You know . . . America is the land of opportunity for the right kind of men!!
I know! That's why I'm staying EXACTLY where I am, Mr. C.!!
How come . . . ?!?
In what other country can a man like me . . . in his 30's . . . make a million bucks playing the part of a 19-year-old . . . giving everyone "The Finger"?!?
HEY-YAYYY!!
WOAH-OHHH!!
Holy cow!! Look what just walked into our show! A—a BLACK kid!
Not yet!! I'm still a NEGRO! I won't be a BLACK for another ten years! In fact, it's been only five years since I was COLORED!
LAS VEGAS PREP
There must be some mistake! Blacks aren't on television in the '50's!
I KNOW!! But I think I'll just wait around here at the dance!!
Wait?!? For what . . . ?!
For the '70's, you jive turkey!!
That's when ME and my FRIENDS take over!
Hey, Sanford! Is it okay to come in?
Sure thing, Jefferson! And bring Florida and the rest!!!
LAS VEGAS PREP
P

CRUISES FOR SCHMOOZERS, BOOZERS AND LOSERS DEPT.

When you think of sea disasters, you think of the "Titanic", the "Lusitania" and the "Andrea Doria." But ABC-TV has added another name to that list of ill-fated launchings. And we call our version of their "see" disaster . . .

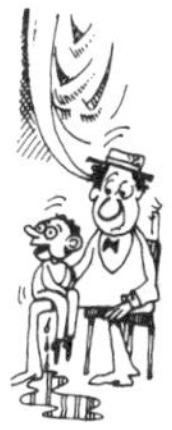

LUST BOAT

ARTIST: ANGELO TORRES WRITER: DICK DE BARTOLO

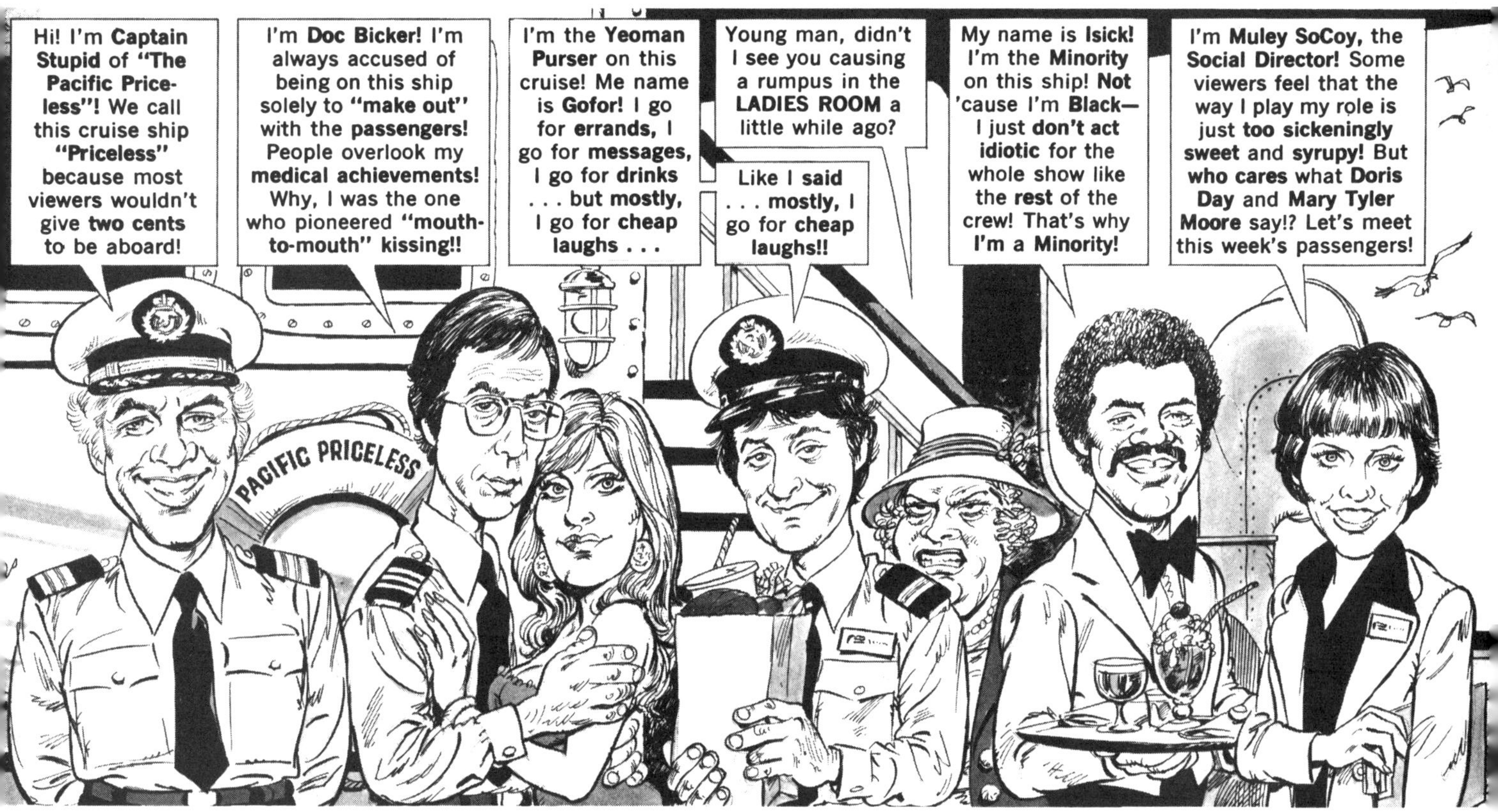

Hi! I'm Captain Stupid of "The Pacific Priceless"! We call this cruise ship "Priceless" because most viewers wouldn't give two cents to be aboard!
I'm Doc Bicker! I'm always accused of being on this ship solely to "make out" with the passengers! People overlook my medical achievements! Why, I was the one who pioneered "mouth-to-mouth" kissing!!
I'm the Yeoman Purser on this cruise! Me name is Gofor! I go for errands, I go for messages, I go for drinks . . . but mostly, I go for cheap laughs . . .
Young man, didn't I see you causing a rumpus in the LADIES ROOM a little while ago?
Like I said . . . mostly, I go for cheap laughs!!
My name is Isick! I'm the Minority on this ship! Not 'cause I'm Black— I just don't act idiotic for the whole show like the rest of the crew! That's why I'm a Minority!
I'm Muley SoCoy, the Social Director! Some viewers feel that the way I play my role is just too sickeningly sweet and syrupy! But who cares what Doris Day and Mary Tyler Moore say!? Let's meet this week's passengers!
PACIFIC PRICELESS

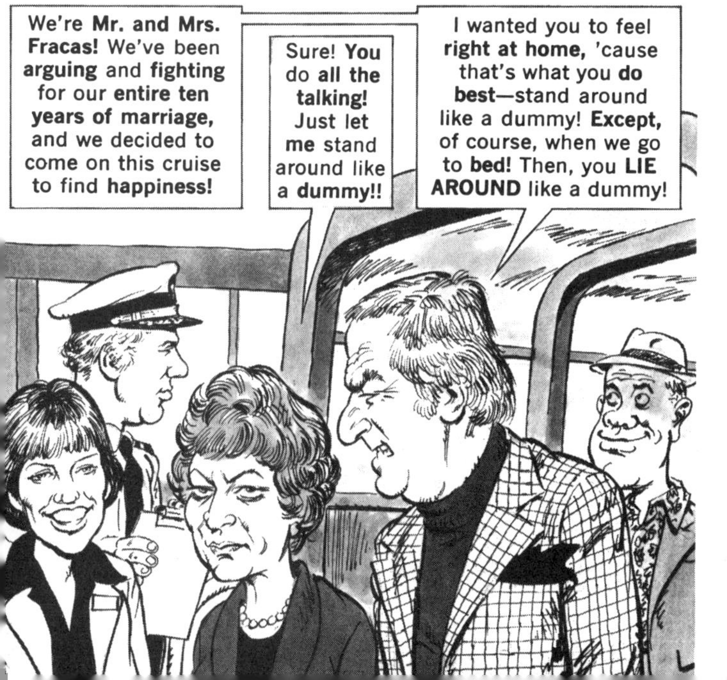

We're Mr. and Mrs. Fracas! We've been arguing and fighting for our entire ten years of marriage, and we decided to come on this cruise to find happiness!
Sure! You do all the talking! Just let me stand around like a dummy!!
I wanted you to feel right at home, 'cause that's what you do best—stand around like a dummy! Except, of course, when we go to bed! Then, you LIE AROUND like a dummy!

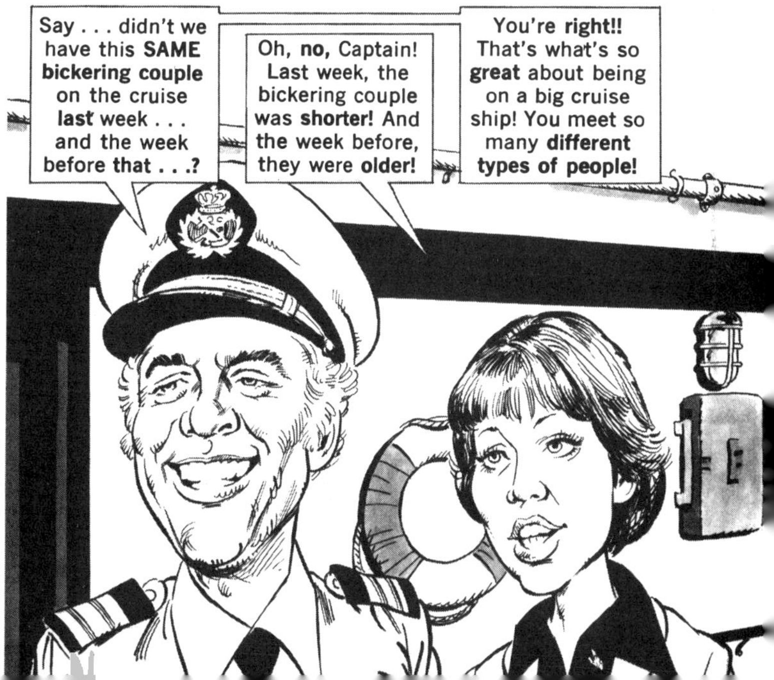

Say . . . didn't we have this SAME bickering couple on the cruise last week . . . and the week before that . . .?
Oh, no, Captain! Last week, the bickering couple was shorter! And the week before, they were older!
You're right!! That's what's so great about being on a big cruise ship! You meet so many different types of people!

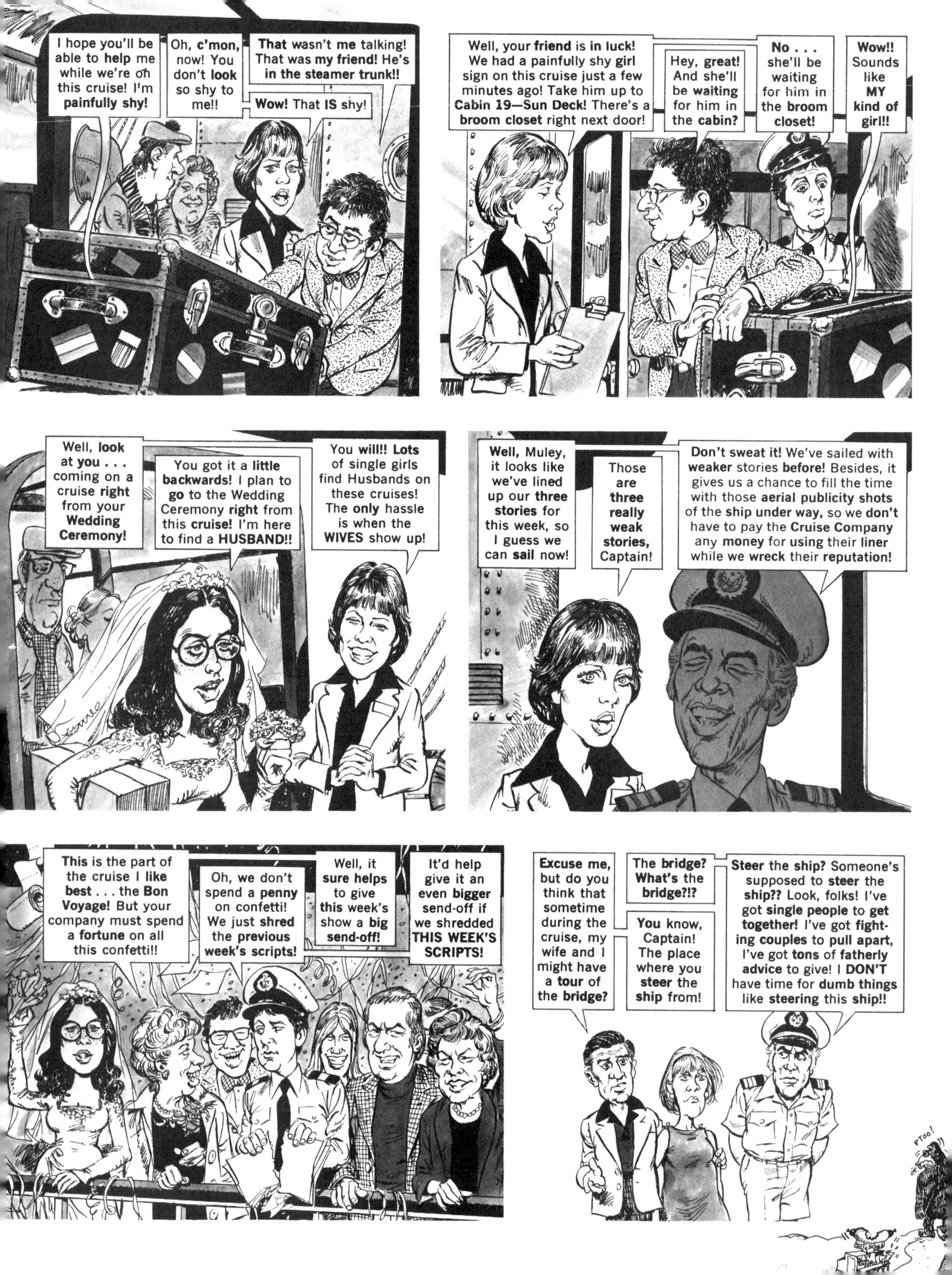

I hope you'll be able to help me while we're on this cruise! I'm painfully shy!
Oh, c'mon, now! You don't look so shy to me!!
That wasn't me talking! That was my friend! He's in the steamer trunk!!
Wow! That IS shy!
Well, your friend is in luck! We had a painfully shy girl sign on this cruise just a few minutes ago! Take him up to Cabin 19—Sun Deck! There's a broom closet right next door!
Hey, great! And she'll be waiting for him in the cabin?
No . . . she'll be waiting for him in the broom closet!
Wow!! Sounds like MY kind of girl!!
Well, look at you . . . coming on a cruise right from your Wedding Ceremony!
You got it a little backwards! I plan to go to the Wedding Ceremony right from this cruise! I'm here to find a HUSBAND!!
You will!! Lots of single girls find Husbands on these cruises! The only hassle is when the WIVES show up!
Well, Muley, it looks like we've lined up our three stories for this week, so I guess we can sail now!
Those are three really weak stories, Captain!
Don't sweat it! We've sailed with weaker stories before! Besides, it gives us a chance to fill the time with those aerial publicity shots of the ship under way, so we don't have to pay the Cruise Company any money for using their liner while we wreck their reputation!
This is the part of the cruise I like best . . . the Bon Voyage! But your company must spend a fortune on all this confetti!!
Oh, we don't spend a penny on confetti! We just shred the previous week's scripts!
Well, it sure helps to give this week's show a big send-off!
It'd help give it an even bigger send-off if we shredded THIS WEEK'S SCRIPTS!
Excuse me, but do you think that sometime during the cruise, my wife and I might have a tour of the bridge?
The bridge? What's the bridge?!?
You know, Captain! The place where you steer the ship from!
Steer the ship? Someone's supposed to steer the ship?? Look, folks! I've got single people to get together! I've got fighting couples to pull apart, I've got tons of fatherly advice to give! I DON'T have time for dumb things like steering this ship!!
PTOO!

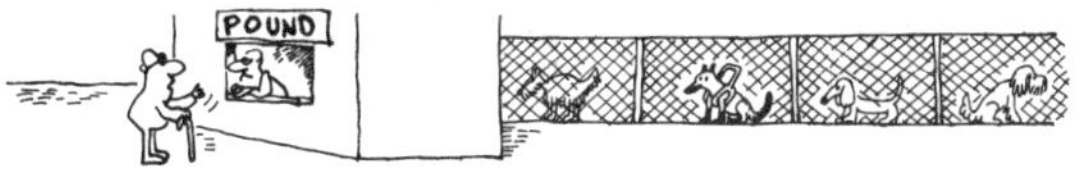

POUND

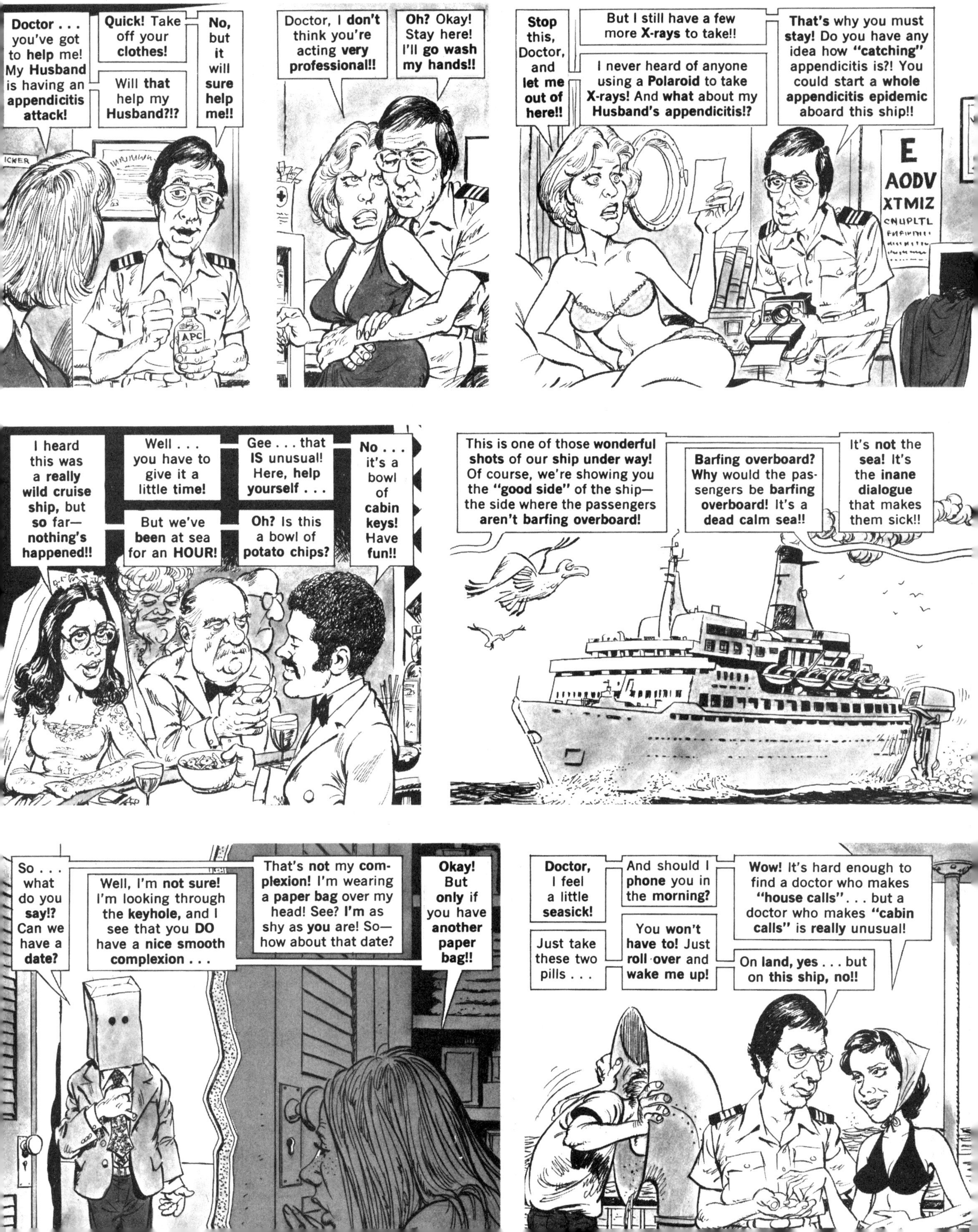

Doctor . . . you've got to help me! My Husband is having an appendicitis attack!
Quick! Take off your clothes!
Will that help my Husband?!?
No, but it will sure help me!!
ICKER
APC
Doctor, I don't think you're acting very professional!!
Oh? Okay! Stay here! I'll go wash my hands!!
Stop this, Doctor, and let me out of here!!
But I still have a few more X-rays to take!!
I never heard of anyone using a Polaroid to take X-rays! And what about my Husband's appendicitis!?
That's why you must stay! Do you have any idea how "catching" appendicitis is?! You could start a whole appendicitis epidemic aboard this ship!!
E
AODV
XTMIZ
I heard this was a really wild cruise ship, but so far—nothing's happened!!
Well . . . you have to give it a little time!
But we've been at sea for an HOUR!
Gee . . . that IS unusual! Here, help yourself . . .
Oh? Is this a bowl of potato chips?
No . . . it's a bowl of cabin keys! Have fun!!
This is one of those wonderful shots of our ship under way! Of course, we're showing you the "good side" of the ship—the side where the passengers aren't barfing overboard!
Barfing overboard? Why would the passengers be barfing overboard! It's a dead calm sea!!
It's not the sea! It's the inane dialogue that makes them sick!!
So . . . what do you say!? Can we have a date?
Well, I'm not sure! I'm looking through the keyhole, and I see that you DO have a nice smooth complexion . . .
That's not my complexion! I'm wearing a paper bag over my head! See? I'm as shy as you are! So—how about that date?
Okay! But only if you have another paper bag!!
Doctor, I feel a little seasick!
Just take these two pills . . .
And should I phone you in the morning?
You won't have to! Just roll over and wake me up!
Wow! It's hard enough to find a doctor who makes "house calls" . . . but a doctor who makes "cabin calls" is really unusual!
On land, yes . . . but on this ship, no!!

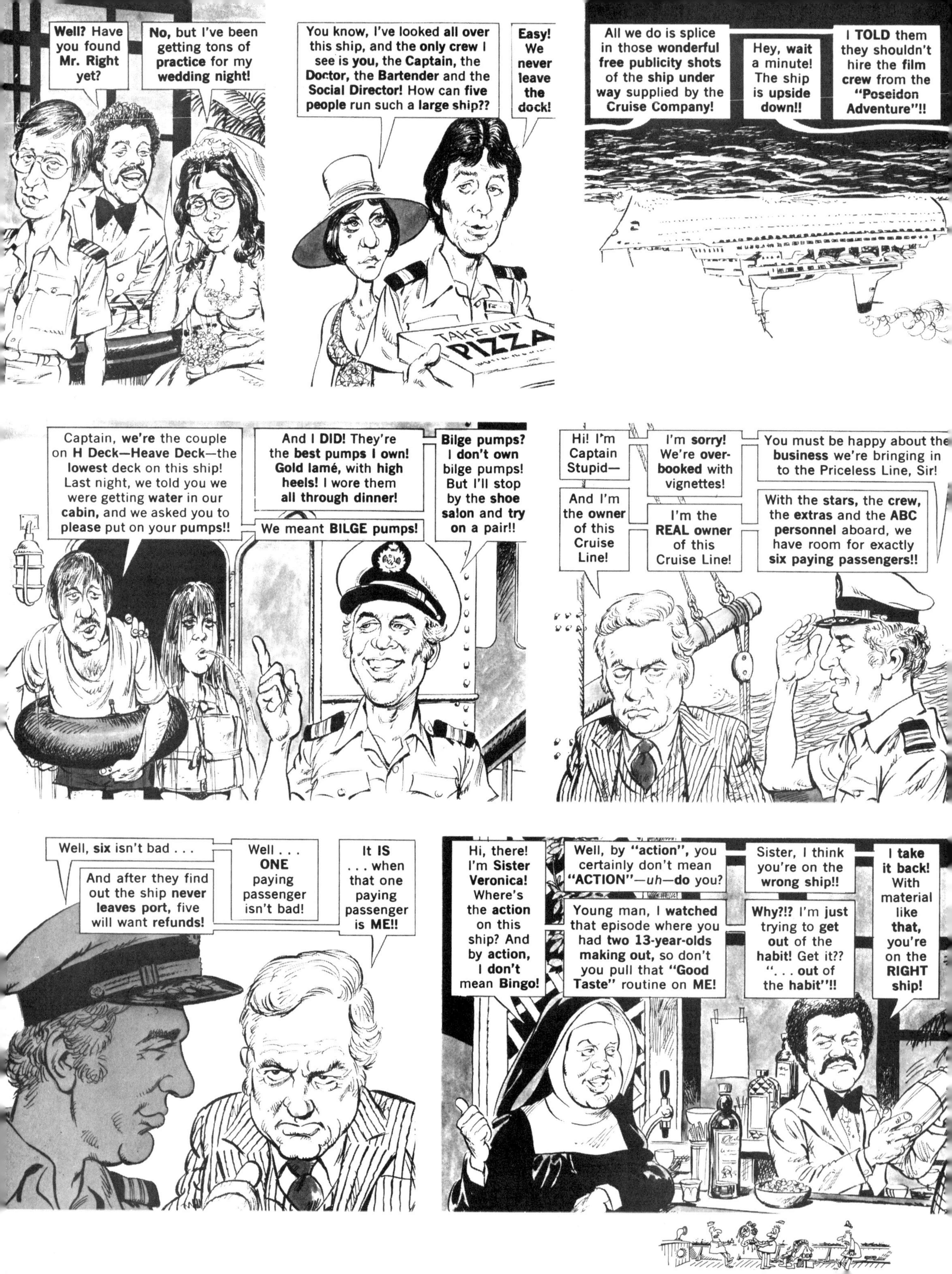

Well? Have you found Mr. Right yet?
No, but I've been getting tons of practice for my wedding night!
You know, I've looked all over this ship, and the only crew I see is you, the Captain, the Doctor, the Bartender and the Social Director! How can five people run such a large ship??
Easy! We never leave the dock!
TAKE OUT PIZZA
All we do is splice in those wonderful free publicity shots of the ship under way supplied by the Cruise Company!
Hey, wait a minute! The ship is upside down!!
I TOLD them they shouldn't hire the film crew from the "Poseidon Adventure"!!
Captain, we're the couple on H Deck—Heave Deck—the lowest deck on this ship! Last night, we told you we were getting water in our cabin, and we asked you to please put on your pumps!!
And I DID! They're the best pumps I own! Gold lamé, with high heels! I wore them all through dinner!
We meant BILGE pumps!
Bilge pumps? I don't own bilge pumps! But I'll stop by the shoe salon and try on a pair!!
Hi! I'm Captain Stupid—
And I'm the owner of this Cruise Line!
I'm sorry! We're overbooked with vignettes!
I'm the REAL owner of this Cruise Line!
You must be happy about the business we're bringing in to the Priceless Line, Sir!
With the stars, the crew, the extras and the ABC personnel aboard, we have room for exactly six paying passengers!!
Well, six isn't bad . . .
And after they find out the ship never leaves port, five will want refunds!
Well . . . ONE paying passenger isn't bad!
It IS . . . when that one paying passenger is ME!!
Hi, there! I'm Sister Veronica! Where's the action on this ship? And by action, I don't mean Bingo!
Well, by "action", you certainly don't mean "ACTION"—uh—do you?
Young man, I watched that episode where you had two 13-year-olds making out, so don't you pull that "Good Taste" routine on ME!
Sister, I think you're on the wrong ship!!
Why?!? I'm just trying to get out of the habit! Get it?? ". . . out of the habit"!!
I take it back! With material like that, you're on the RIGHT ship!

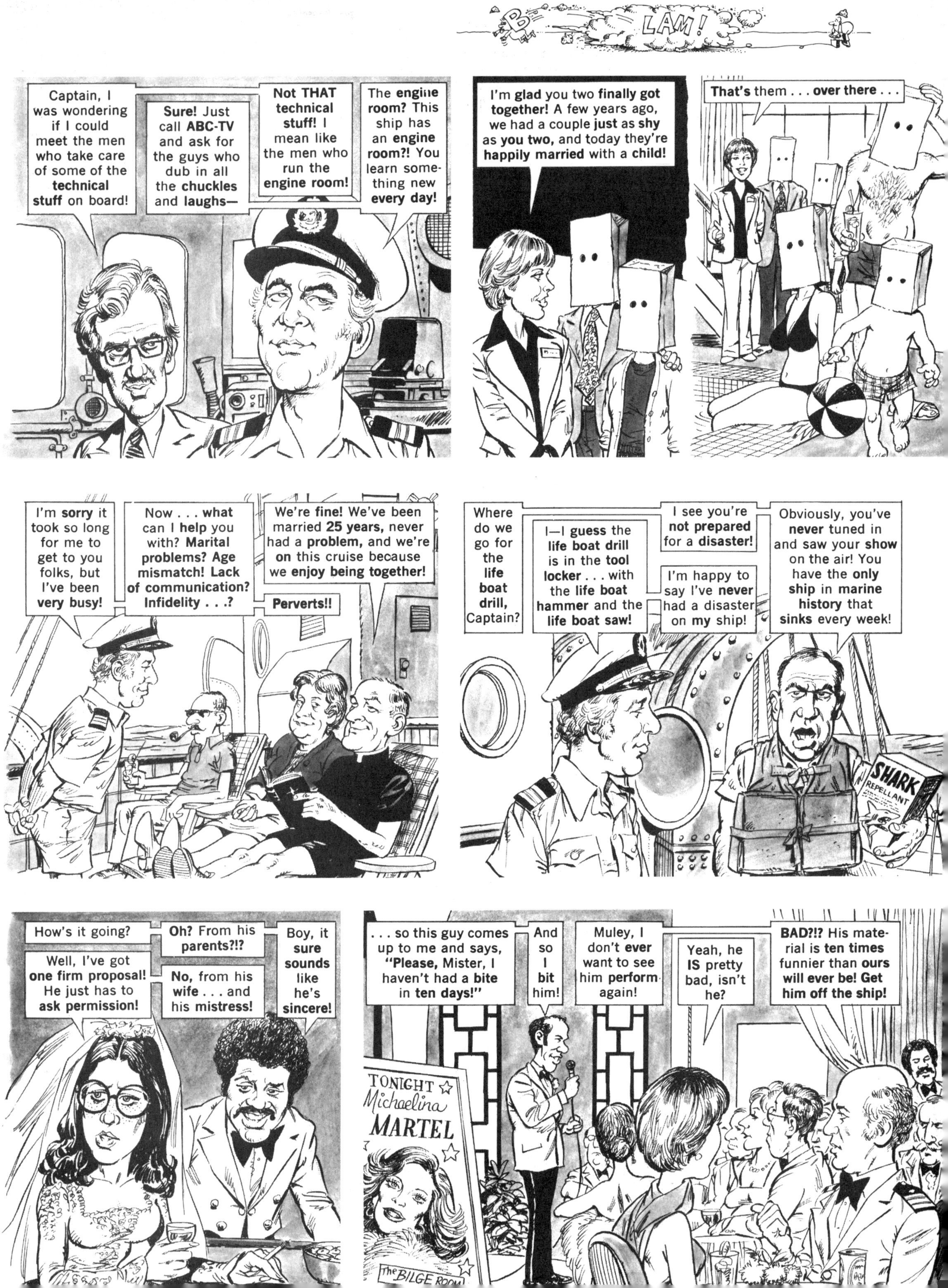

B LAM!
Captain, I was wondering if I could meet the men who take care of some of the **technical stuff** on board!
Sure! Just call **ABC-TV** and ask for the guys who dub in all the **chuckles** and **laughs—**
Not THAT technical stuff! I mean like the men who run the **engine room!**
The **engine room?** This ship has an **engine room?!** You learn something new **every day!**
I'm **glad** you two **finally got together!** A few years ago, we had a couple **just as shy** as **you two,** and today they're **happily married** with a **child!**
That's them . . . **over there . . .**
I'm **sorry** it took so long for me to get to you folks, but I've been **very busy!**
Now . . . **what** can I **help** you with? **Marital problems? Age mismatch! Lack of communication? Infidelity . . .?**
We're **fine!** We've been married **25 years,** never had a **problem,** and we're **on** this cruise because we **enjoy being together!**
Perverts!!
Where do we go for the **life boat drill,** Captain?
I—I **guess** the **life boat drill** is in the **tool locker** . . . with the **life boat hammer** and the **life boat saw!**
I see you're **not prepared** for a **disaster!**
I'm happy to say I've **never** had a disaster on **my** ship!
Obviously, you've **never** tuned in and saw your **show** on the air! You have the **only ship** in **marine history** that **sinks** every week!
SHARK REPELLANT
How's it going?
Well, I've got **one firm proposal!** He just has to **ask permission!**
Oh? From his **parents?!?**
No, from his **wife** . . . and his **mistress!**
Boy, it **sure sounds** like he's **sincere!**
. . . so this guy comes up to me and says, **"Please,** Mister, I haven't had a **bite** in **ten days!"**
And so **I bit** him!
Muley, I don't **ever** want to see him **perform** again!
Yeah, he **IS** pretty bad, isn't he?
BAD?!? His material is **ten times** funnier than **ours will ever be! Get him off the ship!**
TONIGHT Michaelina MARTEL
The BILGE ROOM

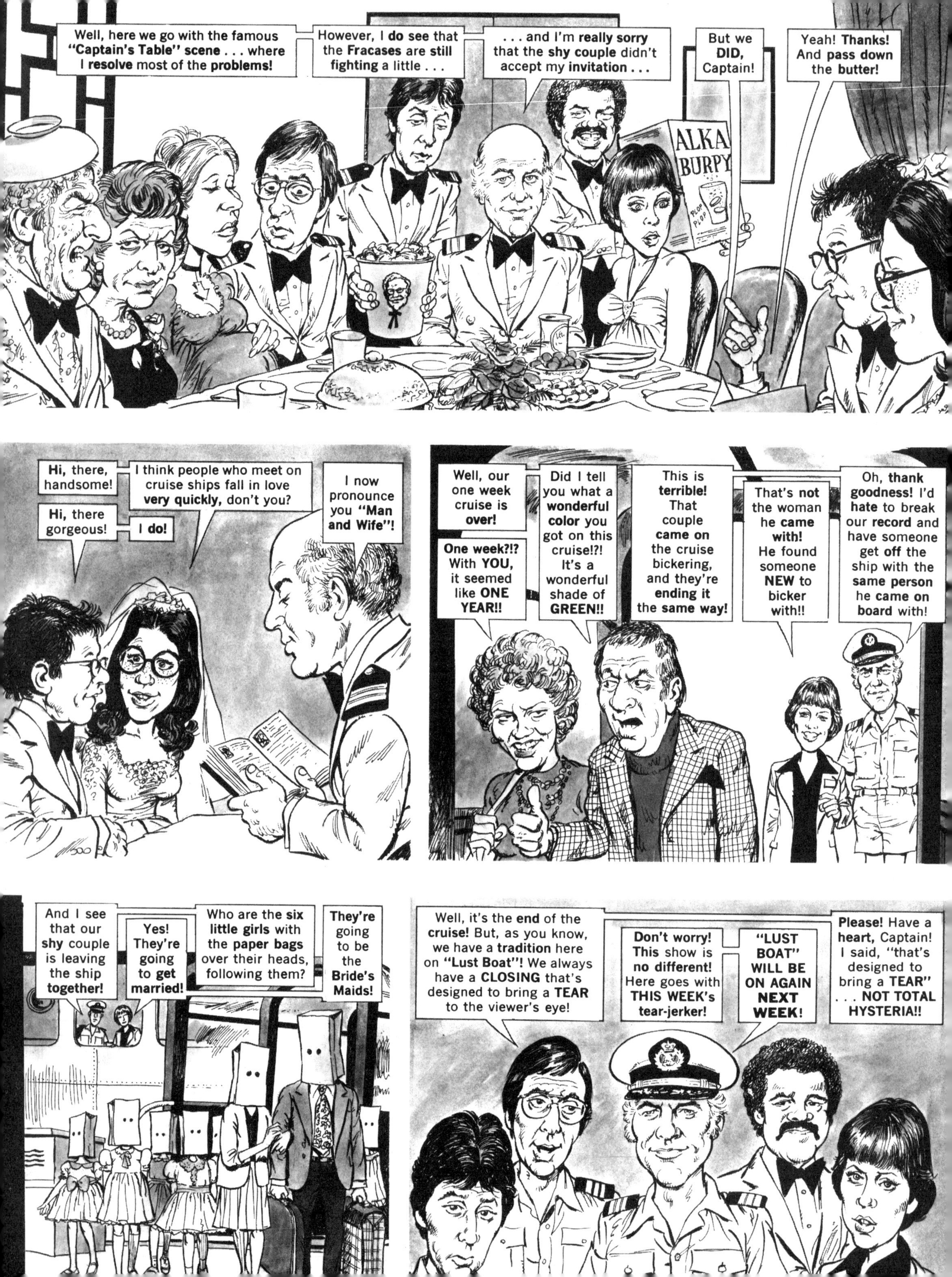

Well, here we go with the famous "Captain's Table" scene . . . where I resolve most of the problems!
However, I do see that the Fracases are still fighting a little . . .
. . . and I'm really sorry that the shy couple didn't accept my invitation . . .
But we DID, Captain!
Yeah! Thanks! And pass down the butter!
ALKA BURPY
PLOP PLOP
Hi, there, handsome!
Hi, there gorgeous!
I think people who meet on cruise ships fall in love very quickly, don't you?
I do!
I now pronounce you "Man and Wife"!
Well, our one week cruise is over!
One week?!? With YOU, it seemed like ONE YEAR!!
Did I tell you what a wonderful color you got on this cruise!?! It's a wonderful shade of GREEN!!
This is terrible! That couple came on the cruise bickering, and they're ending it the same way!
That's not the woman he came with! He found someone NEW to bicker with!!
Oh, thank goodness! I'd hate to break our record and have someone get off the ship with the same person he came on board with!
And I see that our shy couple is leaving the ship together!
Yes! They're going to get married!
Who are the six little girls with the paper bags over their heads, following them?
They're going to be the Bride's Maids!
Well, it's the end of the cruise! But, as you know, we have a tradition here on "Lust Boat"! We always have a CLOSING that's designed to bring a TEAR to the viewer's eye!
Don't worry! This show is no different! Here goes with THIS WEEK's tear-jerker!
"LUST BOAT" WILL BE ON AGAIN NEXT WEEK!
Please! Have a heart, Captain! I said, "that's designed to bring a TEAR" . . . NOT TOTAL HYSTERIA!!

EXPANSE ACCOUNT DEPT.

Have you ever noticed what happens to a TV situation comedy that's lucky enough to stay on the air beyond its opening season? The network "experts" immediately begin to tinker with its characters, its setting and even its basic premise in an effort to make sure the program has "something for everyone." In no time at all, the show becomes a total mish-mosh that includes "nothing for anyone." If you can remember the good old days when Archie Bunker still had a wife and a daughter and worked on a loading dock, or when Laverne and Shirley were brewery employees living in Milwaukee, then you're already familiar with the winding path that must be followed in this ridiculous article that studiously charts:

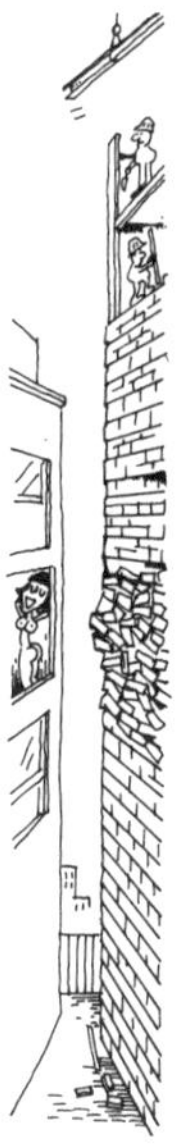

THE EVOLUTION OF A TV SITUATION COMEDY

ARTIST: HARRY NORTH

WRITER: TOM KOCH

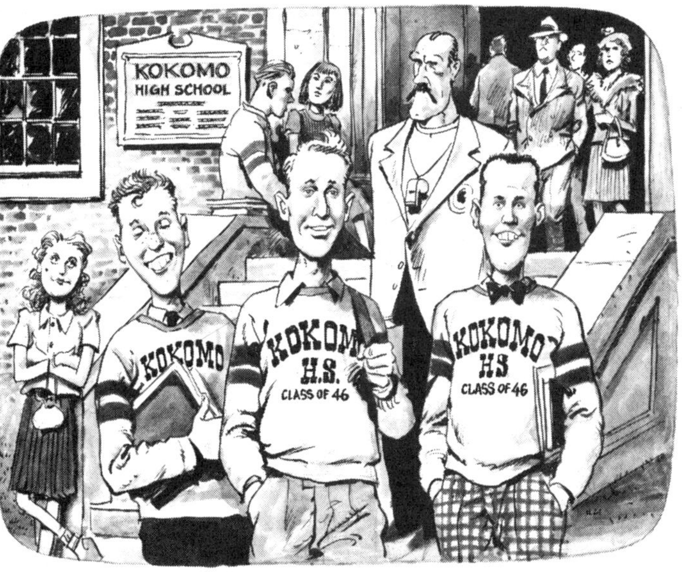
KOKOMO
HIGH SCHOOL
KOKOMO
KOKOMO
H.S.
CLASS OF 46
KOKOMO
H.S
CLASS OF 46

THE FIRST SEASON

To the surprise of the network and the horror of many viewers, "Idle Hours" makes a successful debut. It is a nostalgic comedy about three high school chums (Nipsy, Conrad and The Horse) growing up in Kokomo, Indiana in 1946. Their idle hours are spent working as klutzy pin boys at a bowling alley which is owned by a retired clarinet player named Elsa. Also featured are the boy's gym teacher, Mr. Faunce, and Conrad's little sister, Buffy Lu. Buffy Lu is a typically American 14-year-old sexpot, whose smutty one-liners provide endless mirth.

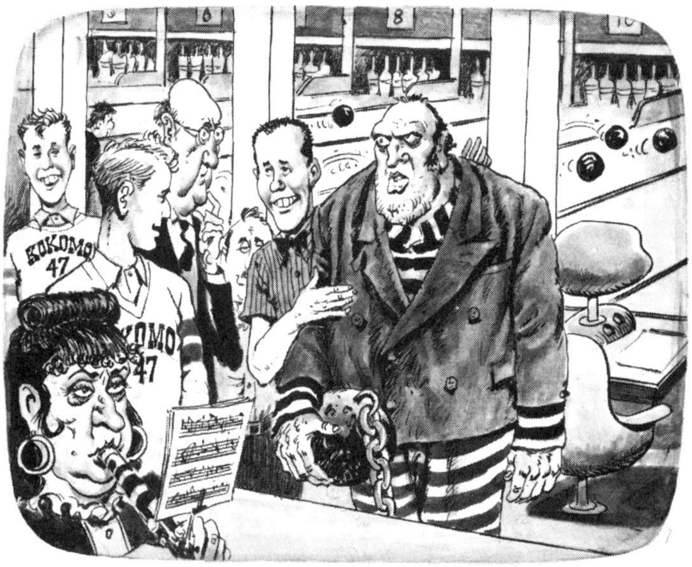
8
KOKOMO
47
KOMO
47

THE SECOND SEASON

To avoid critics' charges that the show is too sugary, the network adds "social significance" by introducing The Horse's cousin, Mangler, as a new member of the cast. Mangler is a certified psychopath (but a funny one) who has chosen to hide in Kokomo following his escape from a southern chain gang. The leading characters try to rehabilitate him to a life of unending dullness by convincing him that he should enroll as an apprentice mortician at Kokomo's funeral home, which is operated by another new series regular, Mr. Ferndipper.

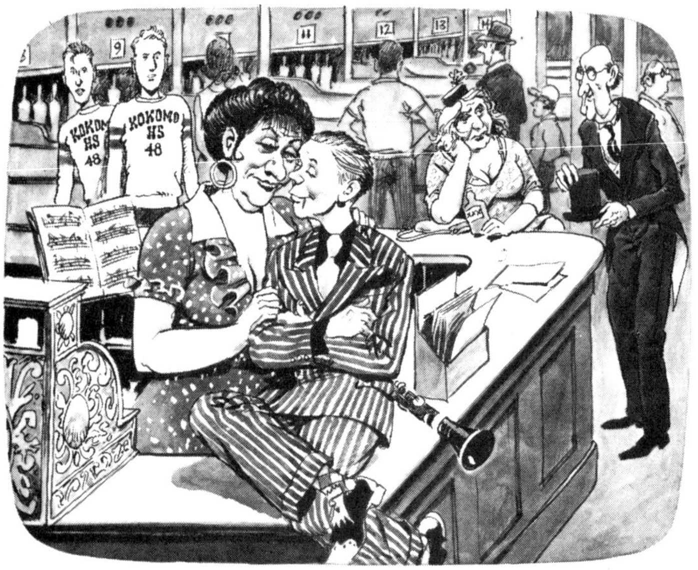
KOKOMO
HS
48

THE THIRD SEASON

The kid who played the role of The Horse quits the show to become a truly awful rock musician. The producers write him out of future scripts by saying he went to live in a leper colony. To take up the slack, Nipsy's little brother, Pooky, joins the cast as Elsa's new boy friend, despite a 35-year difference in their ages. Another element of hilarious romance is added as Mr. Ferndipper takes time out from his duties at the funeral home to begin courting Conrad's mother, a sassy, wisecracking widow who takes in laundry and drinks too much.

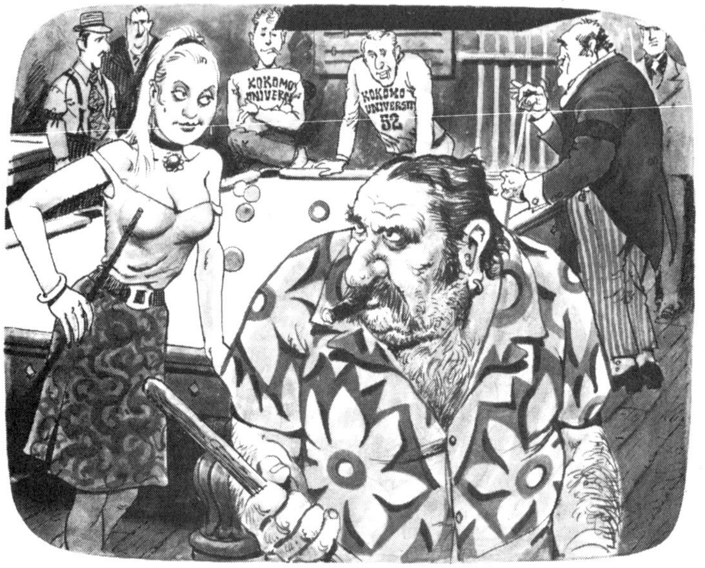

THE FOURTH SEASON

After portraying the high school seniors for three years, Nipsy and Conrad finally enter college, making it unrealistic for them to go on working as pin boys in a bowling alley. Therefore, Elsa trades her bowling alley for half interest in a sleazy poolroom operated by a hysterically funny Puerto Rican bigot named Emilio. This provides Nipsy and Conrad with a more adult hangout. It also provides the producers with a great chance to star the boy's former high school gym teacher, Mr. Faunce, in a new spinoff entitled, "The White Nebbish."

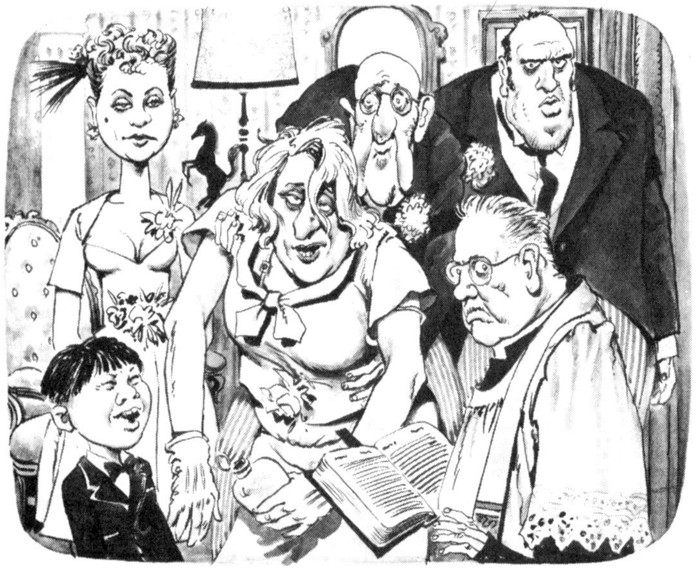

THE SEVENTH SEASON

Elsa, left without a partner at the poolroom following Emilio's departure, is allowed to die of chalk dust inhalation. Pooky thus becomes a widower at 13, and is quietly dumped from the cast after giving the Korean war orphan to Conrad's mother and Mr. Ferndipper to raise. This naturally leads Mr. Ferndipper into asking Conrad's mother to marry him so the orphan won't think he's an illegitimate child. Their wedding is presented as a gala two-part episode that features Buffy Lu as the maid of honor and Mangler as mortician-in-waiting.

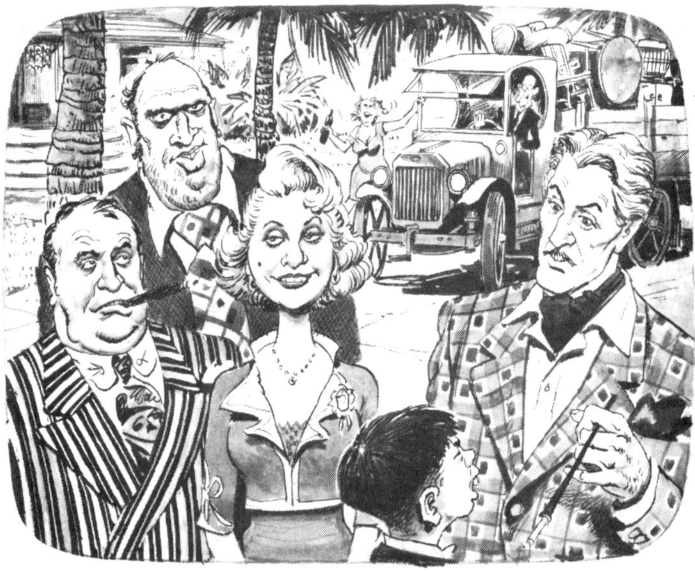

THE EIGHTH SEASON

Faced with the task of keeping a show alive that now stars an embalming teacher, his drunken wife and their Korean war orphan, the producers decide to move the setting from Kokomo, Indiana to Hollywood, California. This is logically explained by having Buffy Lu get a movie screen test offer that includes free lifetime lodging in California for all of her family and friends. The new locale permits the introduction of two wacky new series regulars, an unscrupulous talent agent named Marty and an untalented actor named Lance Surfshimmer.

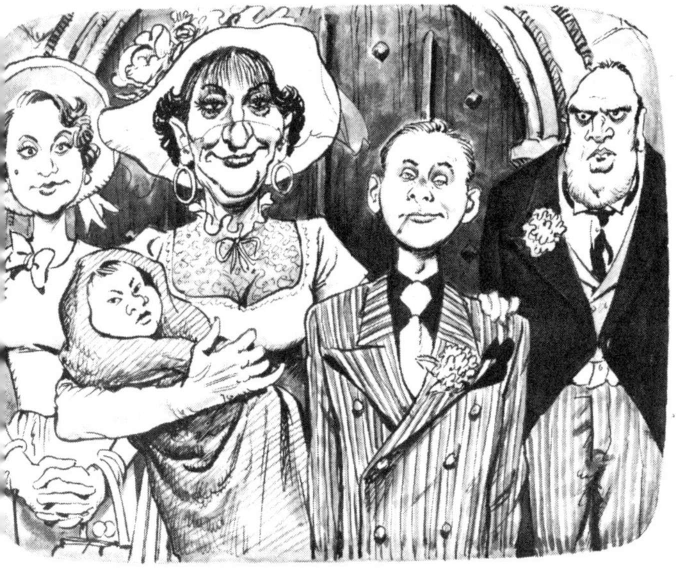

THE FIFTH SEASON

Following a fight in a tavern during the off-season, the actors playing Nipsy and Conrad both quit the show because neither will stoop to working with the other. To distract from their absence, the producers arrange for Pooky and Elsa to marry and adopt a Korean war orphan. Buffy Lu finally makes it to high school at 18, and finds Mr. Ferndipper teaching Freshman Embalming after turning over his funeral home to Mangler. Meantime, in a special Christmas Show, Emilio's 14 younger brothers and sisters arrive unexpectedly from Puerto Rico.

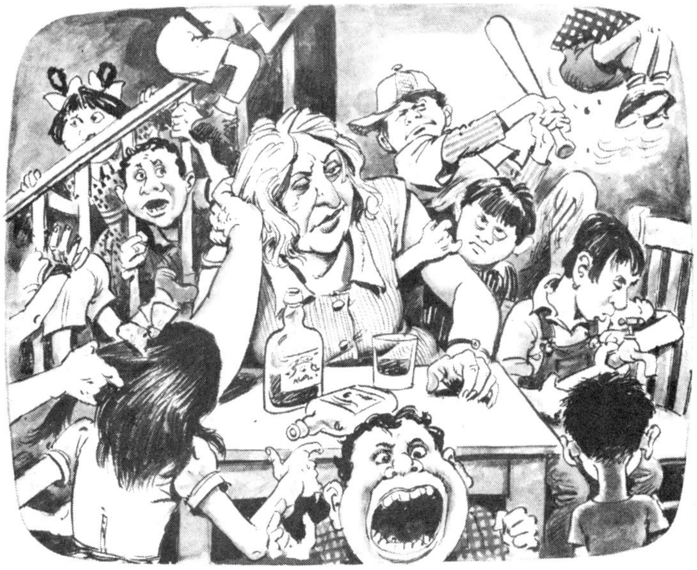

THE SIXTH SEASON

The program's creative planners become convinced that involving a tipsy midwestern widow with a lot of unruly children who don't speak English will make for a sure-fire comedy. Therefore, the new season is launched by having Conrad's mother opening a big rooming house for Emilio's younger brothers and sisters. While this brainstorm proves a total disaster, the network is nevertheless able to reap millions from its mistake by having Emilio and his family leave the show to star in a new spin-off entitled, "Fourteen Puerto Ricans Is Enough!"

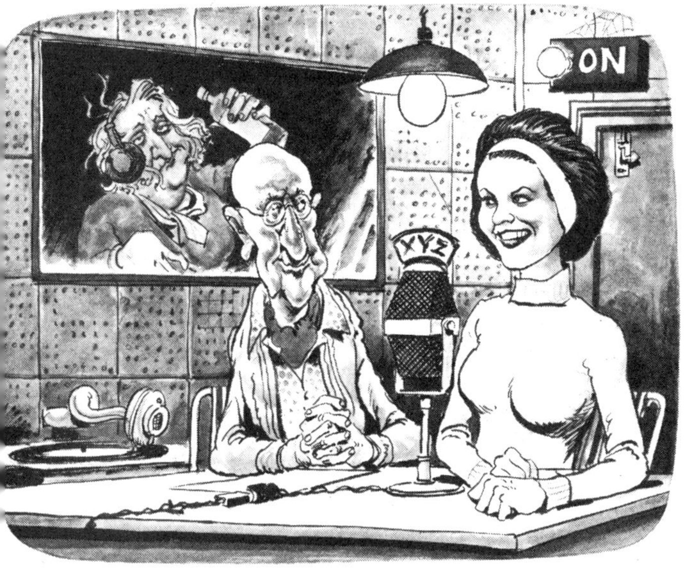
ON
XYZ

THE NINTH SEASON

Seeking to capitalize fully on the new Hollywood setting, the show begins to feature such weekly guest celebrities as Annette Funicello and Conway Twitty. They blend in the shows format by appearing as performers on a small radio station that Mr. Ferndipper has bought by borrowing on his life insurance. Meanwhile, Buffy Lu and Lance Surfshimmer become co-stars of food chopper demonstrations at supermarket openings, while Mangler leaves the show to move into bachelor pad at the beach and launch a new spin-off entitled, "One's Company."

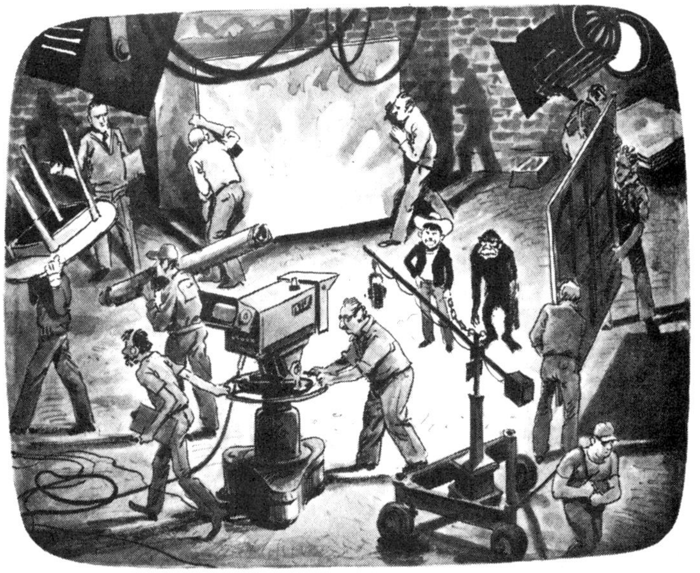

THE TENTH SEASON

With the guest celebrity idea having fizzled; the network tries starring Marty, Mr. Ferndipper and Conrad's mother in a new show about life in a small radio station entitled, "KWRP In Anaheim." Buffy Lu and Lance Surfshimmer also depart to launch their own series about appliance demonstrators called, "One Supermarket Opening At A Time." This leaves no one on the orginal show except the Korean war orphan. When efforts fail to recast him as a 7-year-old truck driver with a pet ape, "Idle Hours" quietly goes off the air after 13 weeks.

SOAP DE JOUR DEPT.

Pressure groups like the Moral Majority have been forcing the TV Networks to cut out sex and violence in their prime time shows. But actually, the evening shows are fun and games compared to what goes on in the afternoon. We figure it won't be long before these self

DeGenerat

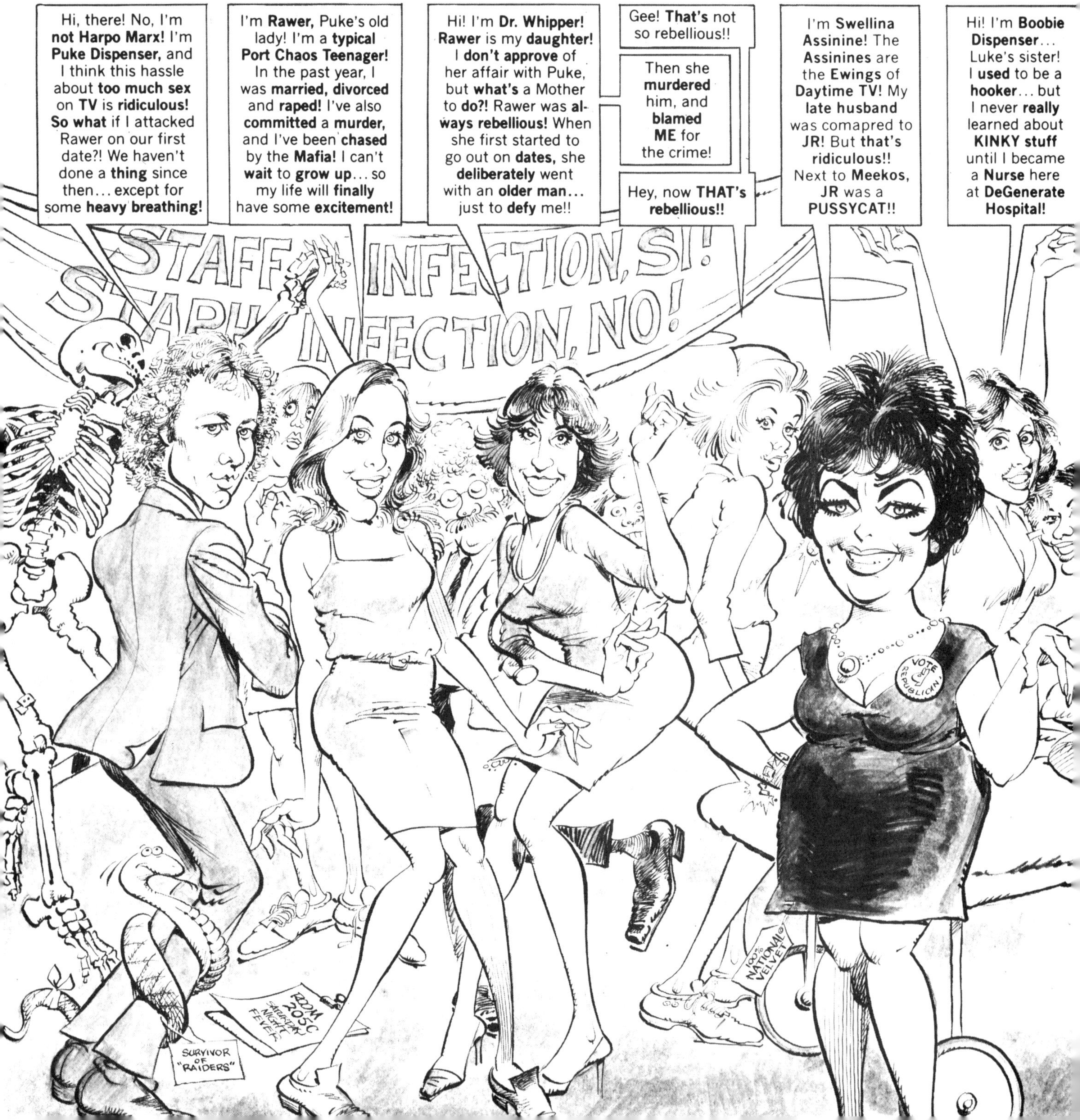

Hi, there! No, I'm not Harpo Marx! I'm Puke Dispenser, and I think this hassle about too much sex on TV is ridiculous! So what if I attacked Rawer on our first date?! We haven't done a thing since then... except for some heavy breathing!
I'm Rawer, Puke's old lady! I'm a typical Port Chaos Teenager! In the past year, I was married, divorced and raped! I've also committed a murder, and I've been chased by the Mafia! I can't wait to grow up... so my life will finally have some excitement!
Hi! I'm Dr. Whipper! Rawer is my daughter! I don't approve of her affair with Puke, but what's a Mother to do?! Rawer was always rebellious! When she first started to go out on dates, she deliberately went with an older man... just to defy me!!
Gee! That's not so rebellious!!
Then she murdered him, and blamed ME for the crime!
Hey, now THAT's rebellious!!
I'm Swellina Assinine! The Assinines are the Ewings of Daytime TV! My late husband was comapred to JR! But that's ridiculous!! Next to Meekos, JR was a PUSSYCAT!!
Hi! I'm Boobie Dispenser... Luke's sister! I used to be a hooker... but I never really learned about KINKY stuff until I became a Nurse here at DeGenerate Hospital!
STAFF INFECTION, SI!
STAPH INFECTION, NO!
VOTE REPUBLICAN
100% NATIONAL VELVET
ROOM 205C
SATURDAY NIGHT FEVER
SURVIVOR OF "RAIDERS"

appointed censors discover the "Soaps." Can the TV Networks from the large metropolises resist, and stand up for their Constitutional Rights...or will they cave in to the groups from small-town mid-America? For our version of what may happen, stay tuned as MAD visits

E HOSPITAL

ARTIST: MORT DRUCKER WRITER: LOU SILVERSTONE

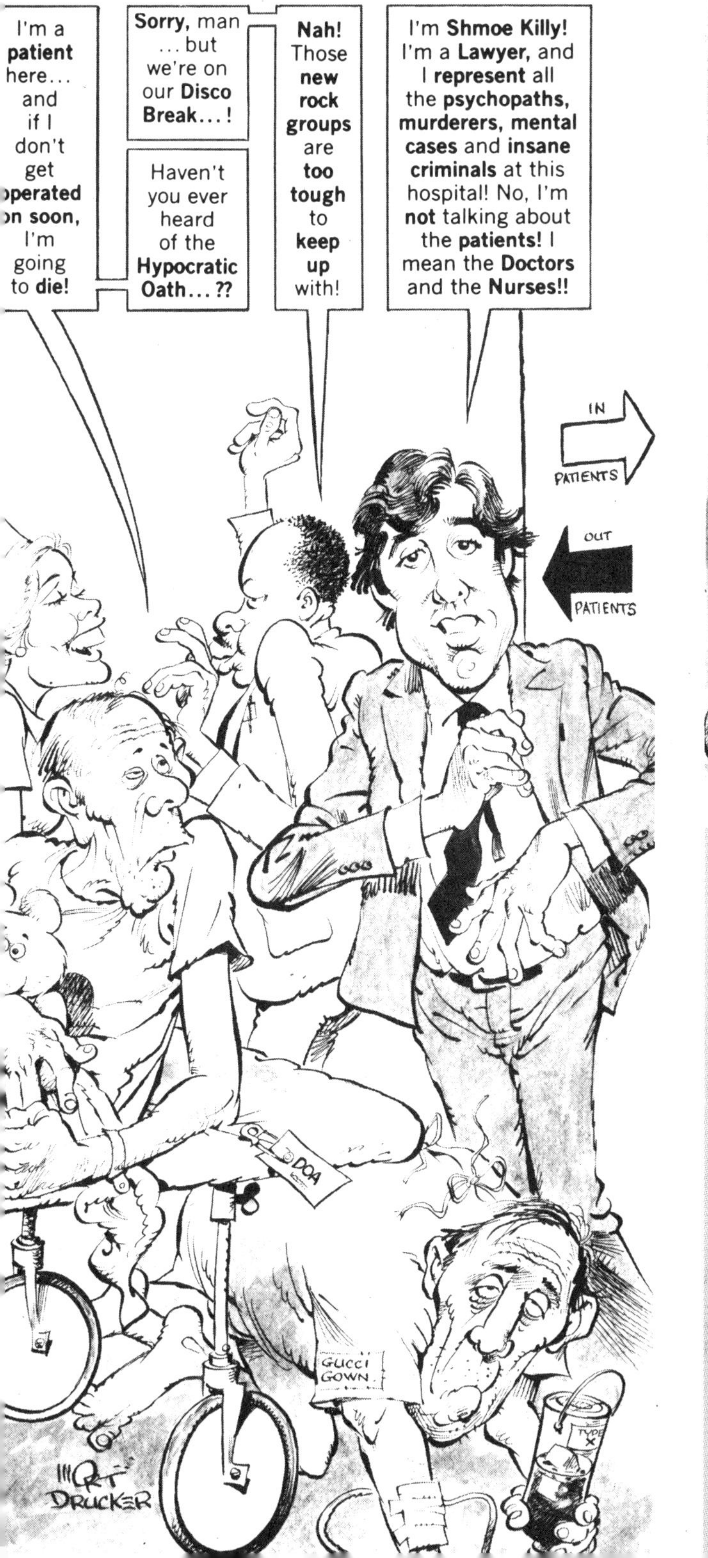
I'm a **patient** here... and if I don't get **perated n soon,** I'm going to **die!**
Sorry, man ... but we're on our **Disco Break...!**
Haven't you ever heard of the **Hypocratic Oath...??**
Nah! Those **new rock groups** are **too tough** to **keep up** with!
I'm **Shmoe Killy!** I'm a **Lawyer,** and I **represent** all the **psychopaths, murderers, mental cases** and **insane criminals** at this hospital! No, I'm **not** talking about the **patients!** I mean the **Doctors** and the **Nurses!!**
IN
PATIENTS
OUT
PATIENTS
DOA
GUCCI GOWN
MORT DRUCKER

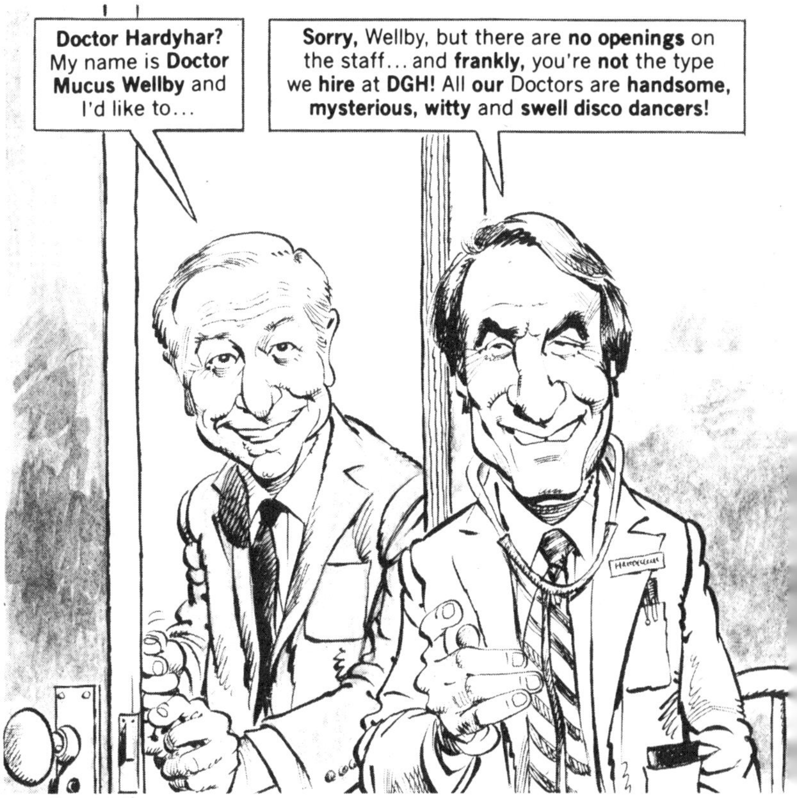
Doctor Hardyhar? My name is **Doctor Mucus Wellby** and I'd like to...
Sorry, Wellby, but there are **no openings** on the staff... and **frankly,** you're **not** the type we **hire** at **DGH!** All **our** Doctors are **handsome, mysterious, witty** and **swell disco dancers!**

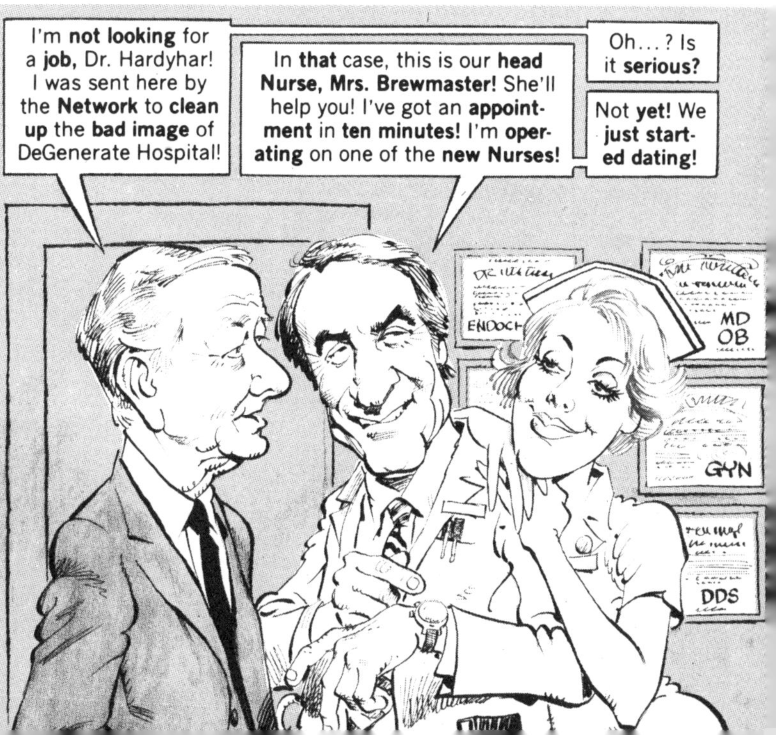
I'm **not looking** for a **job,** Dr. Hardyhar! I was sent here by the **Network** to **clean up** the **bad image** of DeGenerate Hospital!
In **that** case, this is our **head Nurse, Mrs. Brewmaster!** She'll help you! I've got an **appointment** in **ten minutes!** I'm **operating** on one of the **new Nurses!**
Oh...? Is it **serious?**
Not **yet!** We **just started dating!**
ENDOCH
MD OB
GYN
DDS

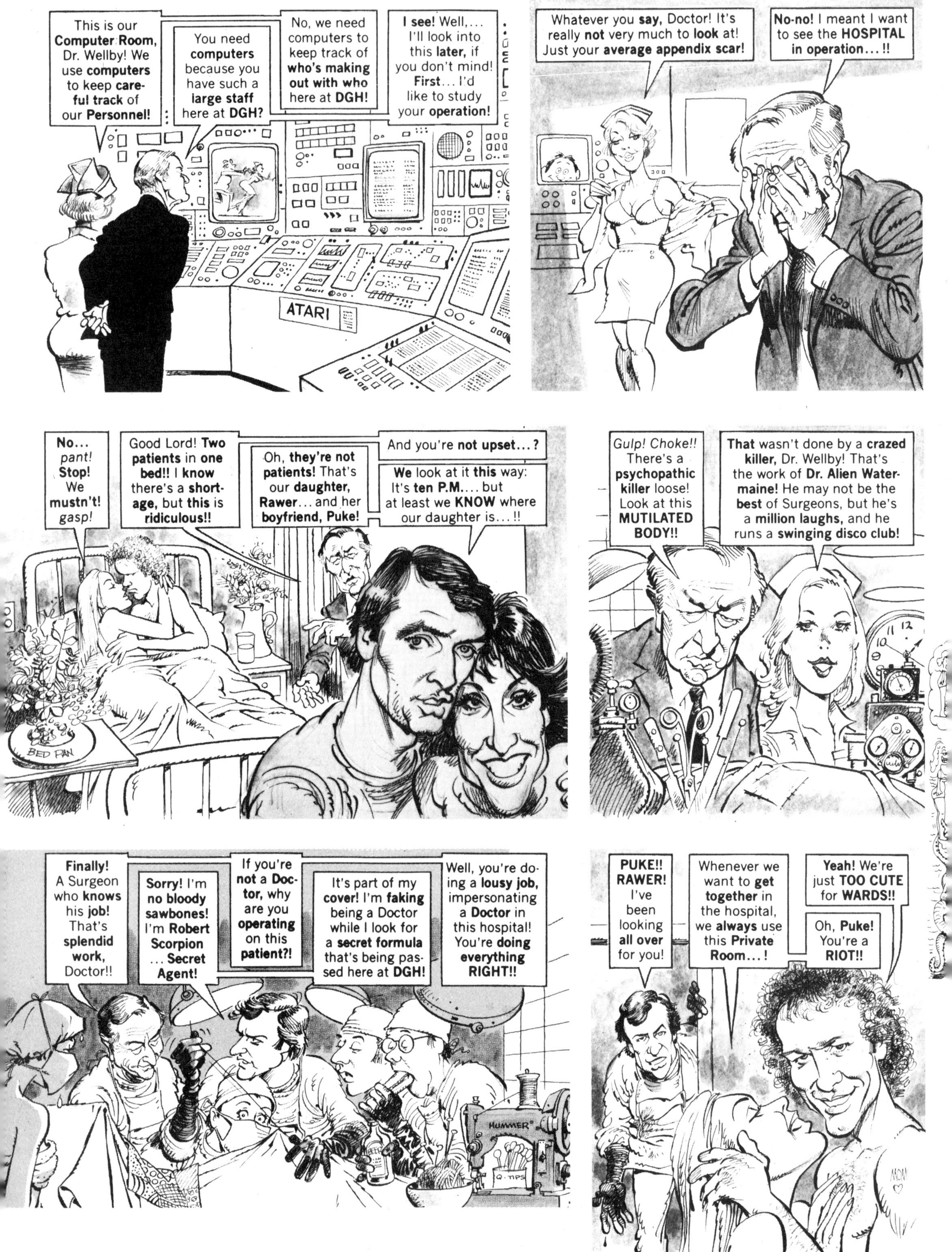
This is our Computer Room, Dr. Wellby! We use computers to keep careful track of our Personnel!
You need computers because you have such a large staff here at DGH?
No, we need computers to keep track of who's making out with who here at DGH!
I see! Well,... I'll look into this later, if you don't mind! First... I'd like to study your operation!
ATARI
Whatever you say, Doctor! It's really not very much to look at! Just your average appendix scar!
No-no! I meant I want to see the HOSPITAL in operation...!!
No... pant! Stop! We mustn't! gasp!
Good Lord! Two patients in one bed!! I know there's a shortage, but this is ridiculous!!
Oh, they're not patients! That's our daughter, Rawer... and her boyfriend, Puke!
And you're not upset...?
We look at it this way: It's ten P.M.... but at least we KNOW where our daughter is...!!
BED PAN
Gulp! Choke!! There's a psychopathic killer loose! Look at this MUTILATED BODY!!
That wasn't done by a crazed killer, Dr. Wellby! That's the work of Dr. Alien Watermaine! He may not be the best of Surgeons, but he's a million laughs, and he runs a swinging disco club!
Finally! A Surgeon who knows his job! That's splendid work, Doctor!!
Sorry! I'm no bloody sawbones! I'm Robert Scorpion ... Secret Agent!
If you're not a Doctor, why are you operating on this patient?!
It's part of my cover! I'm faking being a Doctor while I look for a secret formula that's being passed here at DGH!
Well, you're doing a lousy job, impersonating a Doctor in this hospital! You're doing everything RIGHT!!
HUMMER
Q-TIPS
PUKE!! RAWER! I've been looking all over for you!
Whenever we want to get together in the hospital, we always use this Private Room...!
Yeah! We're just TOO CUTE for WARDS!!
Oh, Puke! You're a RIOT!!
MOM

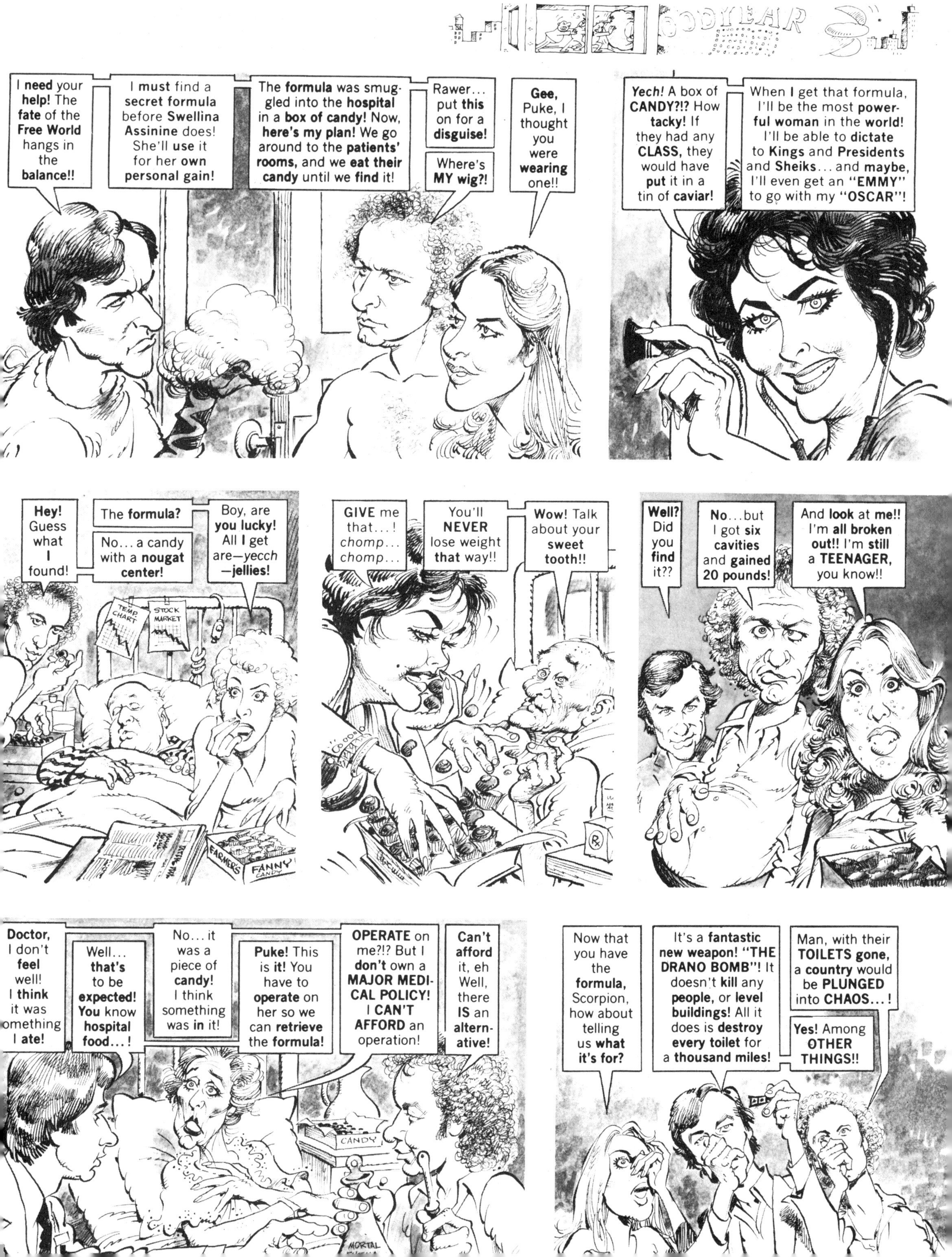

I **need** your **help!** The **fate** of the **Free World** hangs in the **balance!!**
I **must** find a **secret formula** before **Swellina Assinine** does! She'll **use** it for her **own** personal gain!
The **formula** was smuggled into the **hospital** in a **box of candy!** Now, **here's my plan!** We go around to the **patients' rooms,** and we **eat their candy** until we **find** it!
Rawer... put **this** on for a **disguise!**
Where's **MY wig?!**
Gee, Puke, I thought you were **wearing** one!!
Yech! A box of **CANDY?!?** How **tacky!** If they had any **CLASS,** they would have **put** it in a tin of **caviar!**
When **I** get that formula, I'll be the most **powerful woman** in the **world!** I'll be able to **dictate** to **Kings** and **Presidents** and **Sheiks**... and **maybe,** I'll even get an **"EMMY"** to go with my **"OSCAR"!**
Hey! Guess what **I** found!
The **formula?**
No... a candy with a **nougat center!**
Boy, are **you lucky!** All **I** get are—*yecch*—**jellies!**
TEMP CHART
STOCK MARKET
FARMER'S
FANNY CANDY
GIVE me that...! *chomp... chomp...*
You'll **NEVER** lose weight **that** way!!
Wow! Talk about your **sweet tooth!!**
Well? Did you **find** it??
No...but I got **six cavities** and **gained 20 pounds!**
And **look at me!!** I'm **all broken out!!** I'm **still** a **TEENAGER,** you know!!
Doctor, I don't **feel** well! I **think** it was omething I **ate!**
Well... **that's** to be **expected! You** know **hospital food...!**
No... it was a piece of **candy!** I think something was **in** it!
Puke! This is **it!** You have to **operate** on her so we can **retrieve** the **formula!**
OPERATE on me?!? But I **don't** own a **MAJOR MEDICAL POLICY!** I **CAN'T AFFORD** an operation!
Can't afford it, eh Well, there **IS** an **alternative!**
CANDY
Now that you have the **formula,** Scorpion, how about telling us **what it's for?**
It's a **fantastic new weapon! "THE DRANO BOMB"!** It doesn't **kill** any **people,** or **level buildings!** All it does is **destroy every toilet** for a **thousand miles!**
Man, with their **TOILETS gone,** a **country** would be **PLUNGED** into **CHAOS...!**
Yes! Among **OTHER THINGS!!**

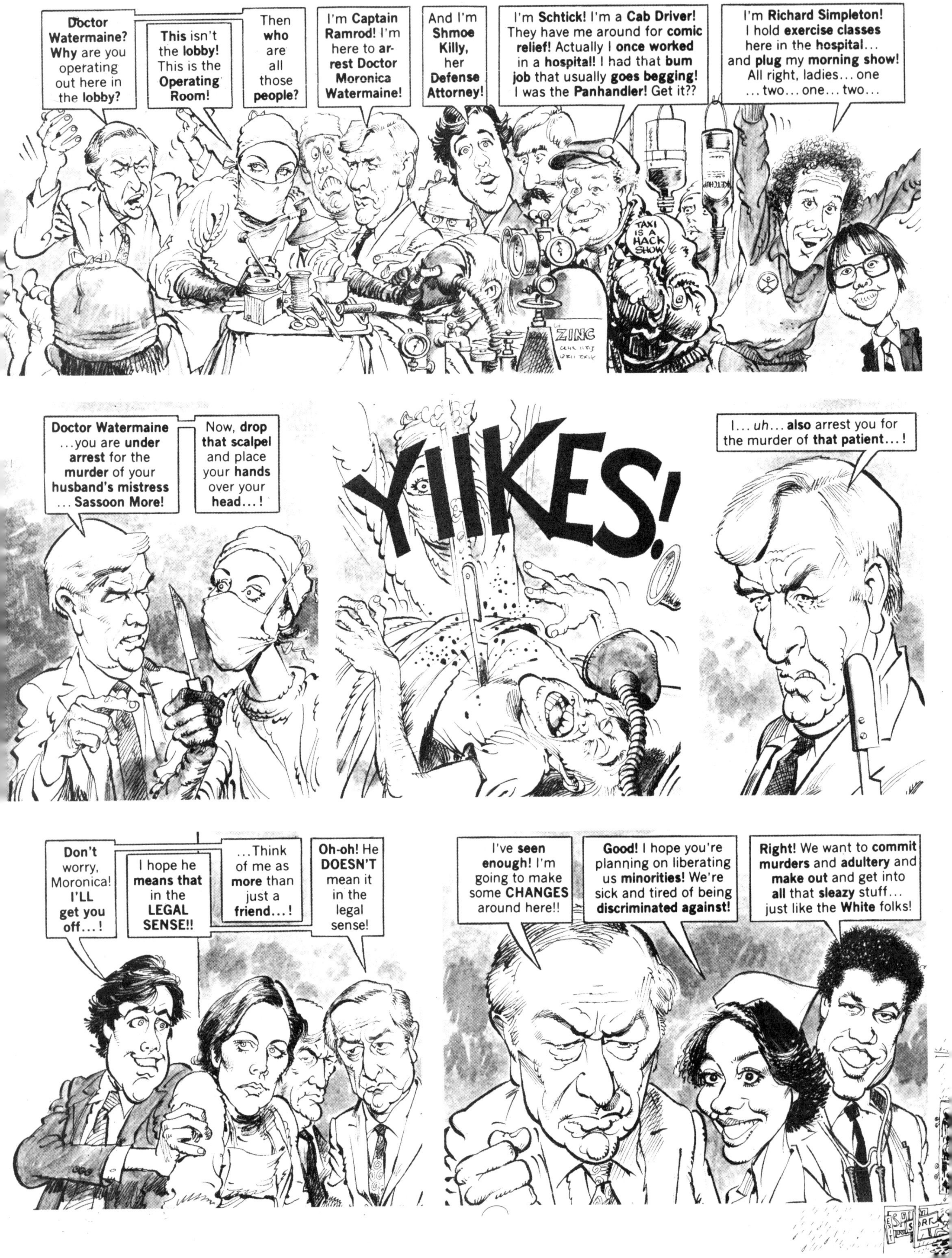

Doctor Watermaine? Why are you operating out here in the lobby?
This isn't the lobby! This is the Operating Room!
Then who are all those people?
I'm Captain Ramrod! I'm here to arrest Doctor Moronica Watermaine!
And I'm Shmoe Killy, her Defense Attorney!
I'm Schtick! I'm a Cab Driver! They have me around for comic relief! Actually I once worked in a hospital! I had that bum job that usually goes begging! I was the Panhandler! Get it??
I'm Richard Simpleton! I hold exercise classes here in the hospital... and plug my morning show! All right, ladies... one ...two...one...two...
TAXI IS A HACK SHOW
ZINC
Doctor Watermaine ...you are under arrest for the murder of your husband's mistress ... Sassoon More!
Now, drop that scalpel and place your hands over your head...!
YIIKES!
I... uh... also arrest you for the murder of that patient...!
Don't worry, Moronica! I'LL get you off...!
I hope he means that in the LEGAL SENSE!!
...Think of me as more than just a friend...!
Oh-oh! He DOESN'T mean it in the legal sense!
I've seen enough! I'm going to make some CHANGES around here!!
Good! I hope you're planning on liberating us minorities! We're sick and tired of being discriminated against!
Right! We want to commit murders and adultery and make out and get into all that sleazy stuff... just like the White folks!

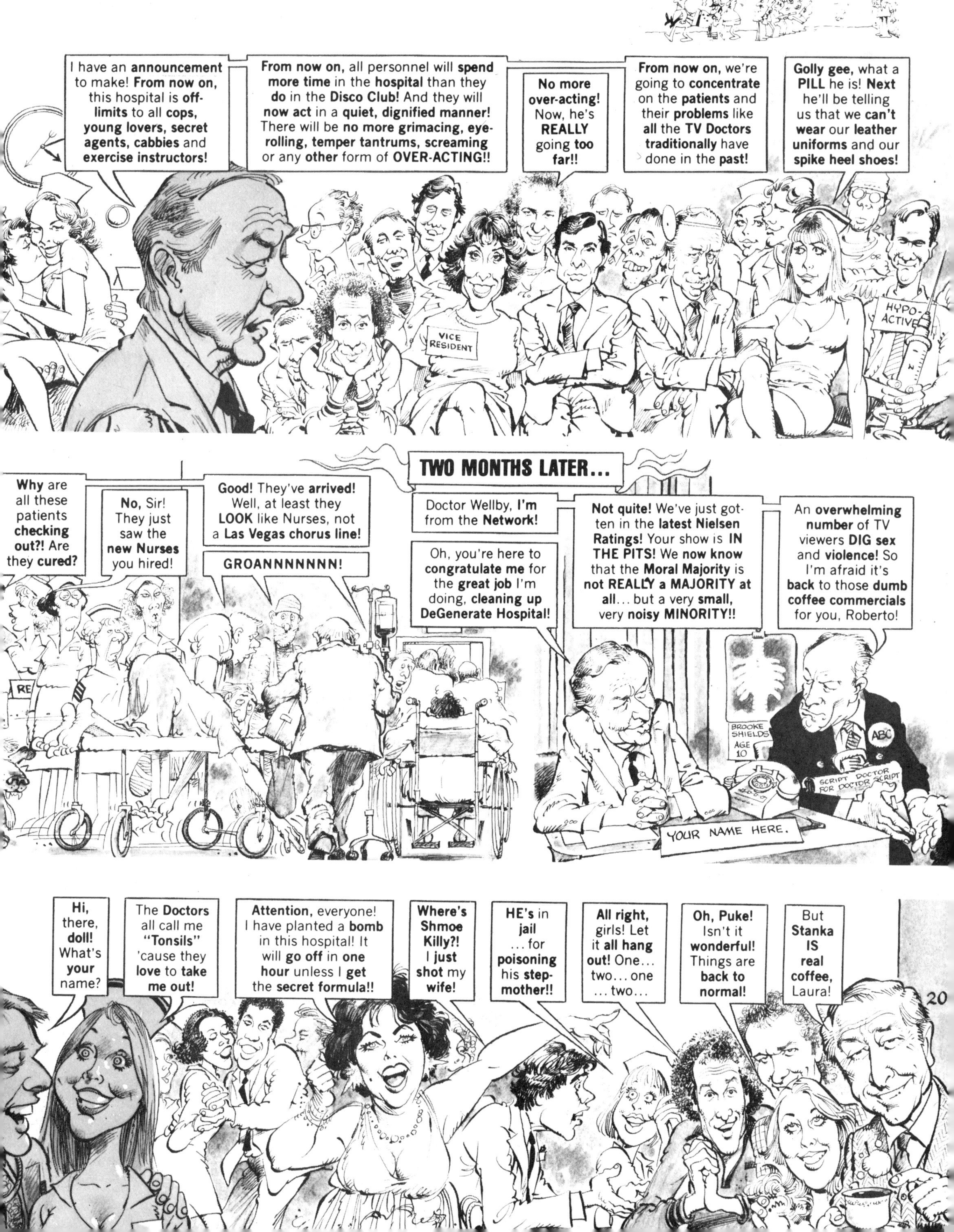

I have an announcement to make! From now on, this hospital is off-limits to all cops, young lovers, secret agents, cabbies and exercise instructors!
From now on, all personnel will spend more time in the hospital than they do in the Disco Club! And they will now act in a quiet, dignified manner! There will be no more grimacing, eye-rolling, temper tantrums, screaming or any other form of OVER-ACTING!!
No more over-acting! Now, he's REALLY going too far!!
From now on, we're going to concentrate on the patients and their problems like all the TV Doctors traditionally have done in the past!
Golly gee, what a PILL he is! Next he'll be telling us that we can't wear our leather uniforms and our spike heel shoes!
VICE RESIDENT
HYPO-ACTIVE
TWO MONTHS LATER...
Why are all these patients checking out?! Are they cured?
No, Sir! They just saw the new Nurses you hired!
Good! They've arrived! Well, at least they LOOK like Nurses, not a Las Vegas chorus line!
GROANNNNNNNN!
Doctor Wellby, I'm from the Network!
Oh, you're here to congratulate me for the great job I'm doing, cleaning up DeGenerate Hospital!
Not quite! We've just gotten in the latest Nielsen Ratings! Your show is IN THE PITS! We now know that the Moral Majority is not REALLY a MAJORITY at all... but a very small, very noisy MINORITY!!
An overwhelming number of TV viewers DIG sex and violence! So I'm afraid it's back to those dumb coffee commercials for you, Roberto!
BROOKE SHIELDS AGE 10
ABC
SCRIPT DOCTOR FOR DOCTOR SCRIPT
YOUR NAME HERE.
Hi, there, doll! What's your name?
The Doctors all call me "Tonsils" 'cause they love to take me out!
Attention, everyone! I have planted a bomb in this hospital! It will go off in one hour unless I get the secret formula!!
Where's Shmoe Killy?! I just shot my wife!
HE's in jail ...for poisoning his step-mother!!
All right, girls! Let it all hang out! One... two... one ... two...
Oh, Puke! Isn't it wonderful! Things are back to normal!
But Stanka IS real coffee, Laura!

LAW AND DISORDER DEPT.

Suppose they produced a TV show where the cast of characters was an entire big cit[y] police force. Then, suppose they gave each character his own separate, complicate[d] story to be dramatized. Then, suppose they tried to dramatize all of these storie[s]

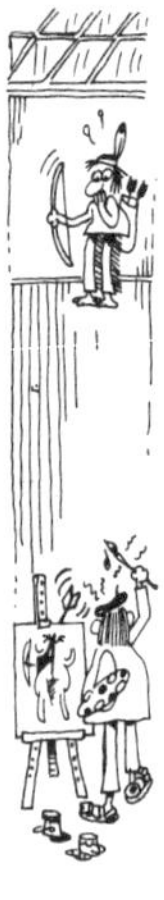

SWILL STR

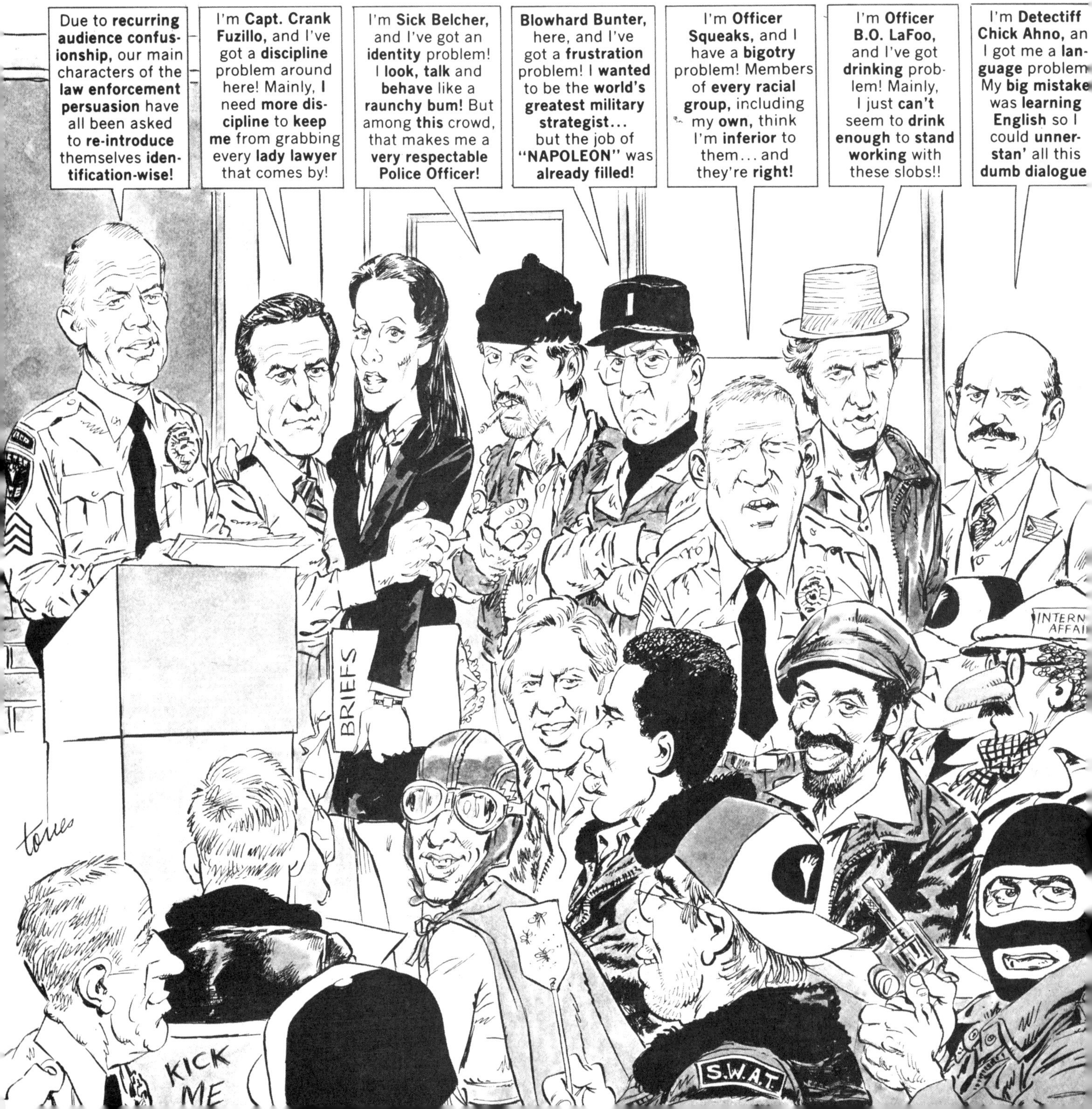
Due to recurring audience confusionship, our main characters of the law enforcement persuasion have all been asked to re-introduce themselves identification-wise!
I'm Capt. Crank Fuzillo, and I've got a discipline problem around here! Mainly, I need more discipline to keep me from grabbing every lady lawyer that comes by!
I'm Sick Belcher, and I've got an identity problem! I look, talk and behave like a raunchy bum! But among this crowd, that makes me a very respectable Police Officer!
Blowhard Bunter, here, and I've got a frustration problem! I wanted to be the world's greatest military strategist... but the job of "NAPOLEON" was already filled!
I'm Officer Squeaks, and I have a bigotry problem! Members of every racial group, including my own, think I'm inferior to them... and they're right!
I'm Officer B.O. LaFoo, and I've got drinking problem! Mainly, I just can't seem to drink enough to stand working with these slobs!!
I'm Detectiff Chick Ahno, an I got me a language problem My big mistake was learning English so I could unnerstan' all this dumb dialogue
BRIEFS
INTERN AFFAI
KICK ME
S.W.A.T.

at the same time. Then, what would they have? Well, frankly, we don't know what they would have, and we're pretty sure that NBC doesn't know what it has either. But we do know what the TV audience has... an incomprehensible, chaotic mess entitled...

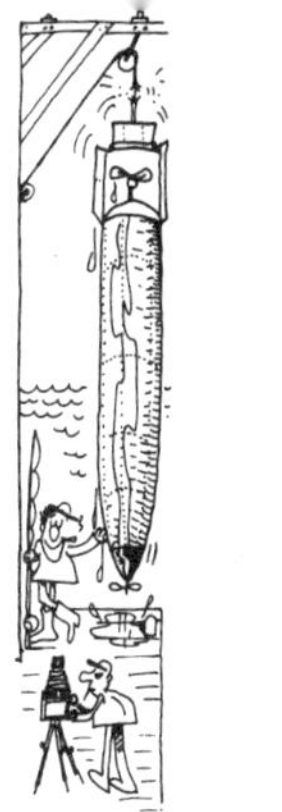

EET BLUES

ARTIST: ANGELO TORRES WRITER: TOM KOCH

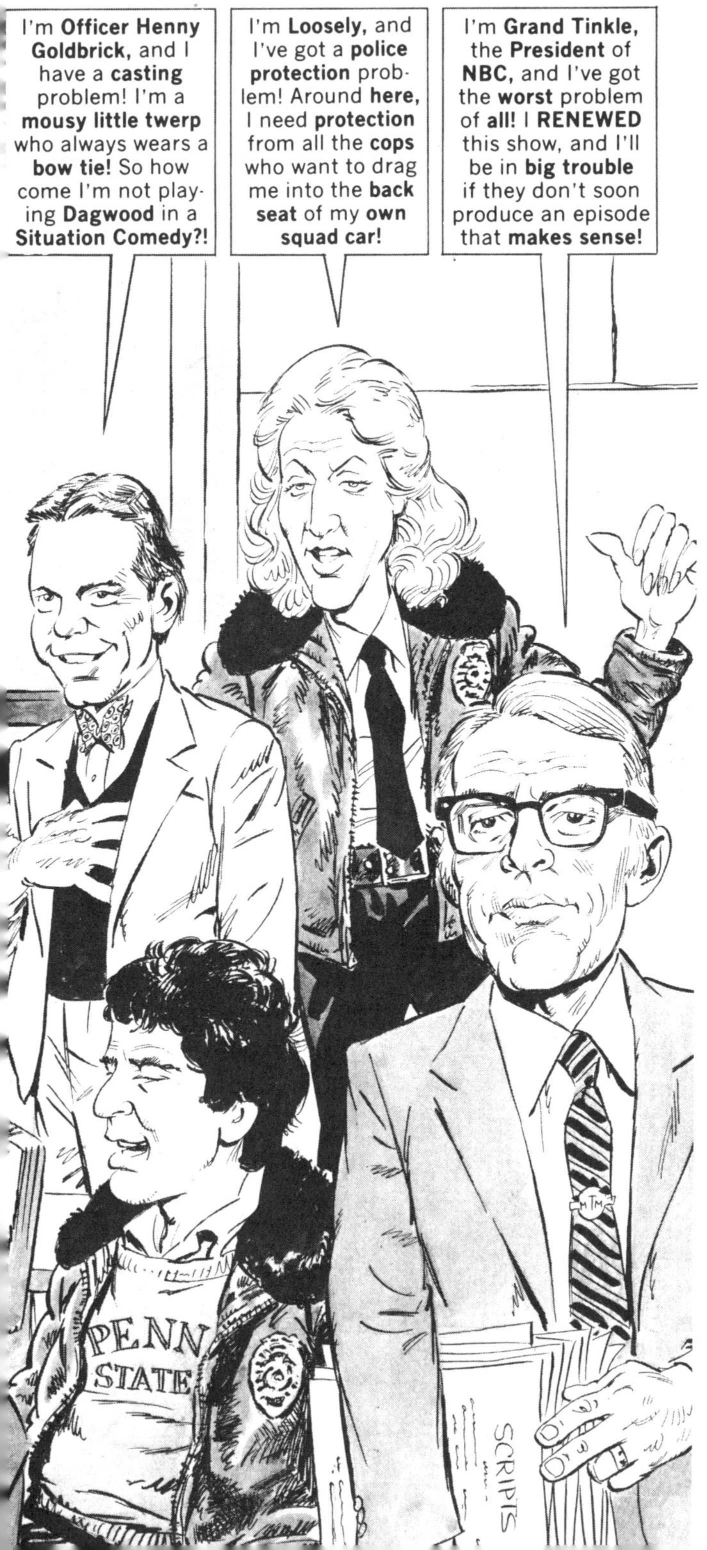

I'm Officer Henny Goldbrick, and I have a casting problem! I'm a mousy little twerp who always wears a bow tie! So how come I'm not playing Dagwood in a Situation Comedy?!
I'm Loosely, and I've got a police protection problem! Around here, I need protection from all the cops who want to drag me into the back seat of my own squad car!
I'm Grand Tinkle, the President of NBC, and I've got the worst problem of all! I RENEWED this show, and I'll be in big trouble if they don't soon produce an episode that makes sense!
PENN STATE
SCRIPTS

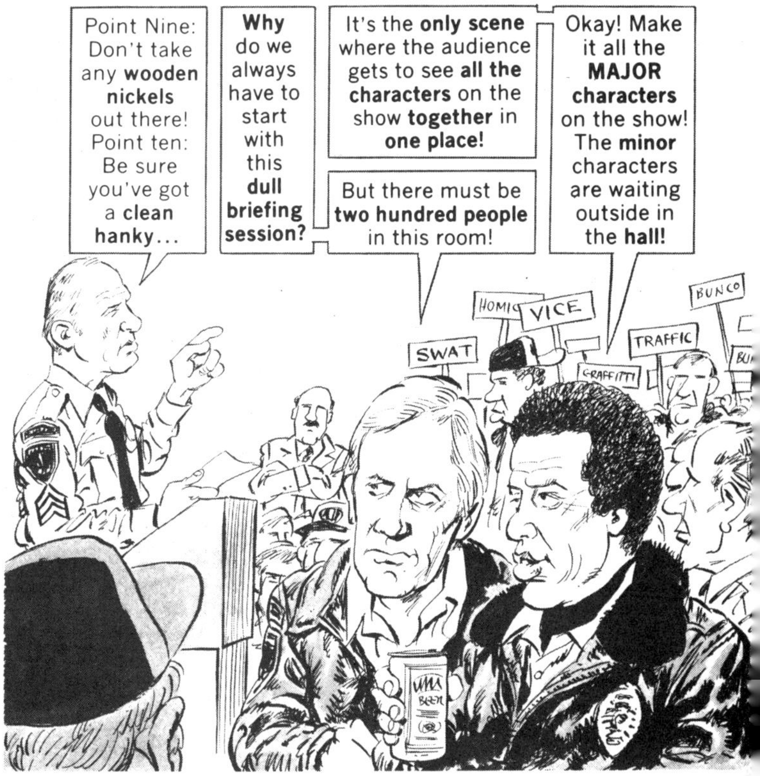

Point Nine: Don't take any wooden nickels out there! Point ten: Be sure you've got a clean hanky...
Why do we always have to start with this dull briefing session?
It's the only scene where the audience gets to see all the characters on the show together in one place!
But there must be two hundred people in this room!
Okay! Make it all the MAJOR characters on the show! The minor characters are waiting outside in the hall!
BUNCO
HOMI
VICE
SWAT
TRAFFIC
GRAFFITTI
BEER

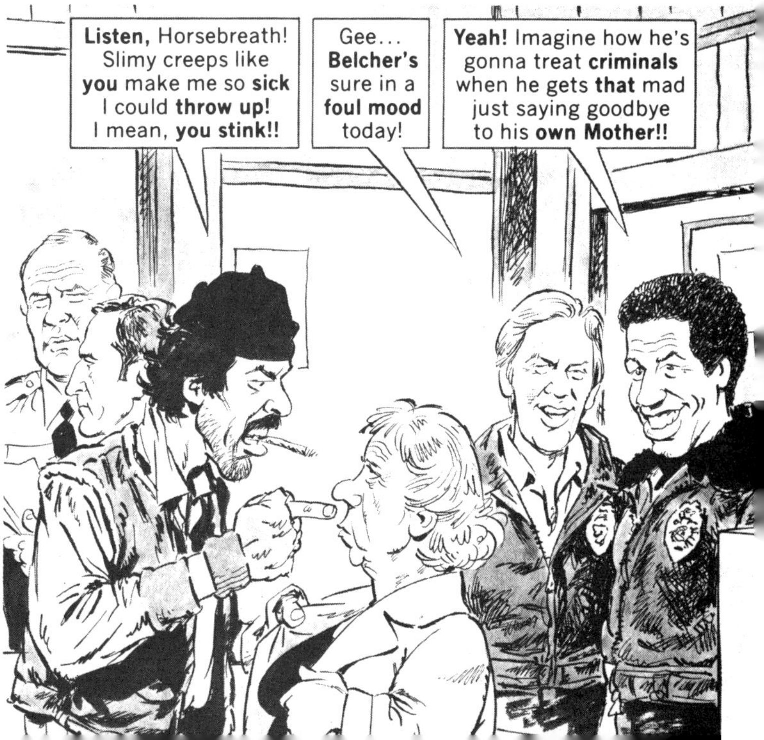

Listen, Horsebreath! Slimy creeps like you make me so sick I could throw up! I mean, you stink!!
Gee... Belcher's sure in a foul mood today!
Yeah! Imagine how he's gonna treat criminals when he gets that mad just saying goodbye to his own Mother!!

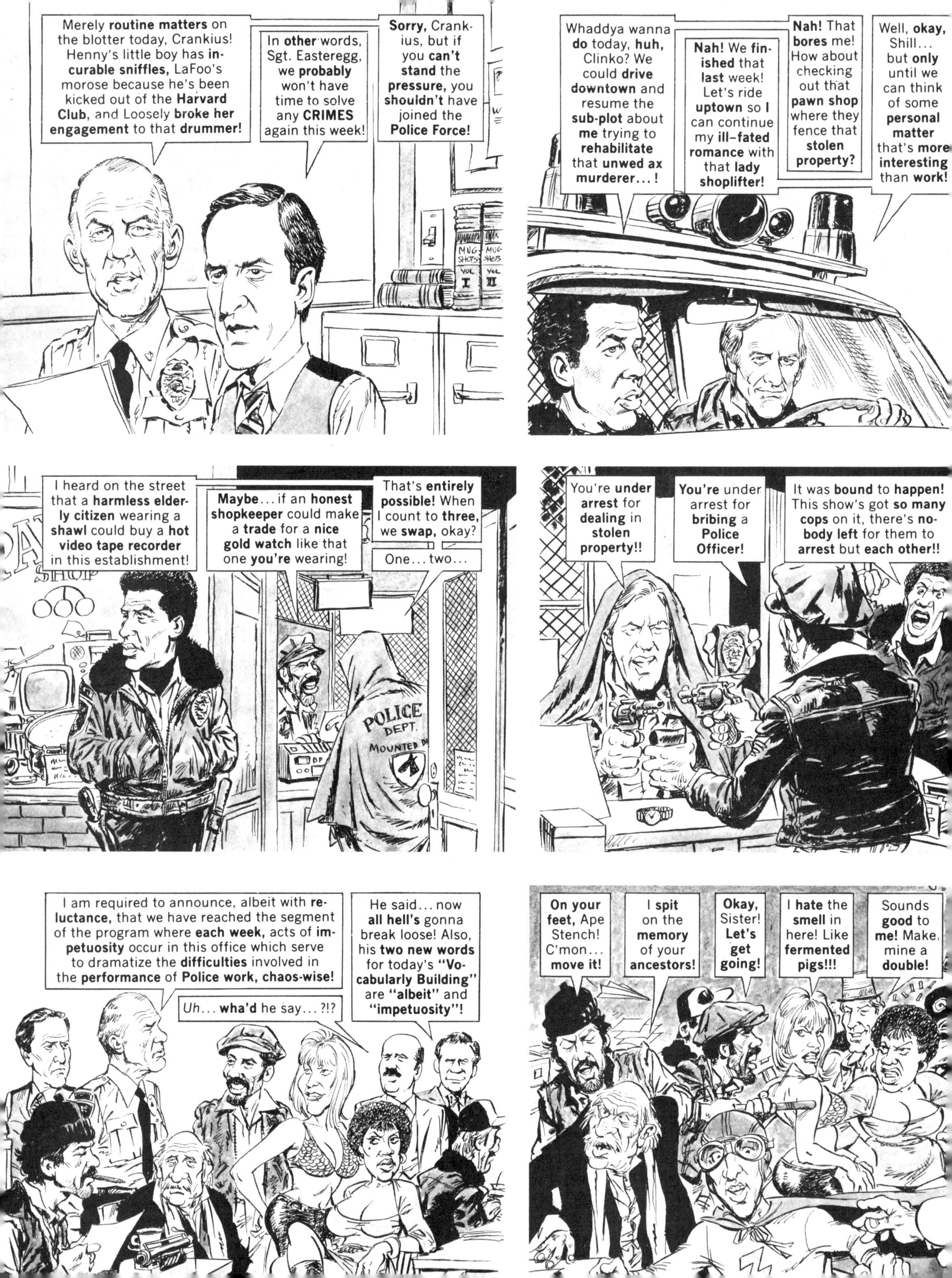

Merely routine matters on the blotter today, Crankius! Henny's little boy has incurable sniffles, LaFoo's morose because he's been kicked out of the Harvard Club, and Loosely broke her engagement to that drummer!
In other words, Sgt. Easteregg, we probably won't have time to solve any CRIMES again this week!
Sorry, Crankius, but if you can't stand the pressure, you shouldn't have joined the Police Force!
MUG SHOTS VOL I
MUG SHOTS VOL II
Whaddya wanna do today, huh, Clinko? We could drive downtown and resume the sub-plot about me trying to rehabilitate that unwed ax murderer...!
Nah! We finished that last week! Let's ride uptown so I can continue my ill-fated romance with that lady shoplifter!
Nah! That bores me! How about checking out that pawn shop where they fence that stolen property?
Well, okay, Shill... but only until we can think of some personal matter that's more interesting than work!
I heard on the street that a harmless elderly citizen wearing a shawl could buy a hot video tape recorder in this establishment!
Maybe... if an honest shopkeeper could make a trade for a nice gold watch like that one you're wearing!
That's entirely possible! When I count to three, we swap, okay?
One... two...
POLICE DEPT. MOUNTED
You're under arrest for dealing in stolen property!!
You're under arrest for bribing a Police Officer!
It was bound to happen! This show's got so many cops on it, there's nobody left for them to arrest but each other!!
I am required to announce, albeit with reluctance, that we have reached the segment of the program where each week, acts of impetuosity occur in this office which serve to dramatize the difficulties involved in the performance of Police work, chaos-wise!
Uh... wha'd he say...?!?
He said... now all hell's gonna break loose! Also, his two new words for today's "Vocabulary Building" are "albeit" and "impetuosity"!
On your feet, Ape Stench! C'mon... move it!
I spit on the memory of your ancestors!
Okay, Sister! Let's get going!
I hate the smell in here! Like fermented pigs!!!
Sounds good to me! Make mine a double!

This place is full of **weirdos!** I can't even turn my **back** to do some **filing** without having some pervert **pinch** me!

Thaz **too bad!** Why doan you get a chob **someplace else...??**

Are you **kidding?!?** **Where else** can a dame **six feet tall** with a figure like a **floor lamp** be the **reigning sex symbol?!**

Hey...! **What happened!?** A minute ago, I was in the **Precinct's Squad Room!** Now, the scene has shifted to this **hospital!**

The **writers** discovered that they only started **four new sub-plots** in this episode! So they decided to have your **Captain's ex-wife** get hit by a **bus!** And now, she's **calling** for you!

But... but I never even **MET** the Captain's ex-wife!

You know that! And I know that! But we have the audience **so confused, THEY** don't know that!!

We always have at least **one touching scene** to demonstrate that cops are **warm, caring people!** So, **Flo...** I just want to say that I don't think I could **go on** if anything **happened** to you... Can you **hear** me??

No, but if he **could,** he'd probably tell you you're in the **wrong room!** **This** is a **stiff** we just brought in for **Quincy** to **disect!!**

Oh...! **Forgive** the **intrusion,** Crankius! I perceive that **you** and the **winsome Public Defender** would prefer a moment of **privacy** at this time!

Nonsense! You **know** I never get involved with **female business associates** at the **office!** I much prefer taking them to their **apartments** and getting involved with them **there!**

You'll be wanting **these,** I daresay, Captain!

Thanks! If anyone **asks,** tell them I'll be back from lunch about **two...** Or maybe **Friday... Week** after **next** at the **least!**

This is **ridiculous!** Why must we keep it a **secret** that we **go out** together!?

Because it would look **bad** if people knew that the **Police Captain** was having an **affair** with the **Public Defender!**

If **that** would look bad, **how** do you think it looks for you to **carry** me out of here every day like a **roll** of **linoleum!**

Shh! Please! These people are all **very highly-trained Police Officers!** They may **KNOW** that **linoleum can't talk!!**

Taking a **long lunch hour** like this every day, aren't you afraid you'll **lose track** of **what's happening** back at the **Precinct?**

No, that's the **great thing** about this show! You can lose track of what's happening **WHEREVER** you are!!

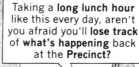

Hanky Panky APTS. — NO VAGRANTS ALLOWED.

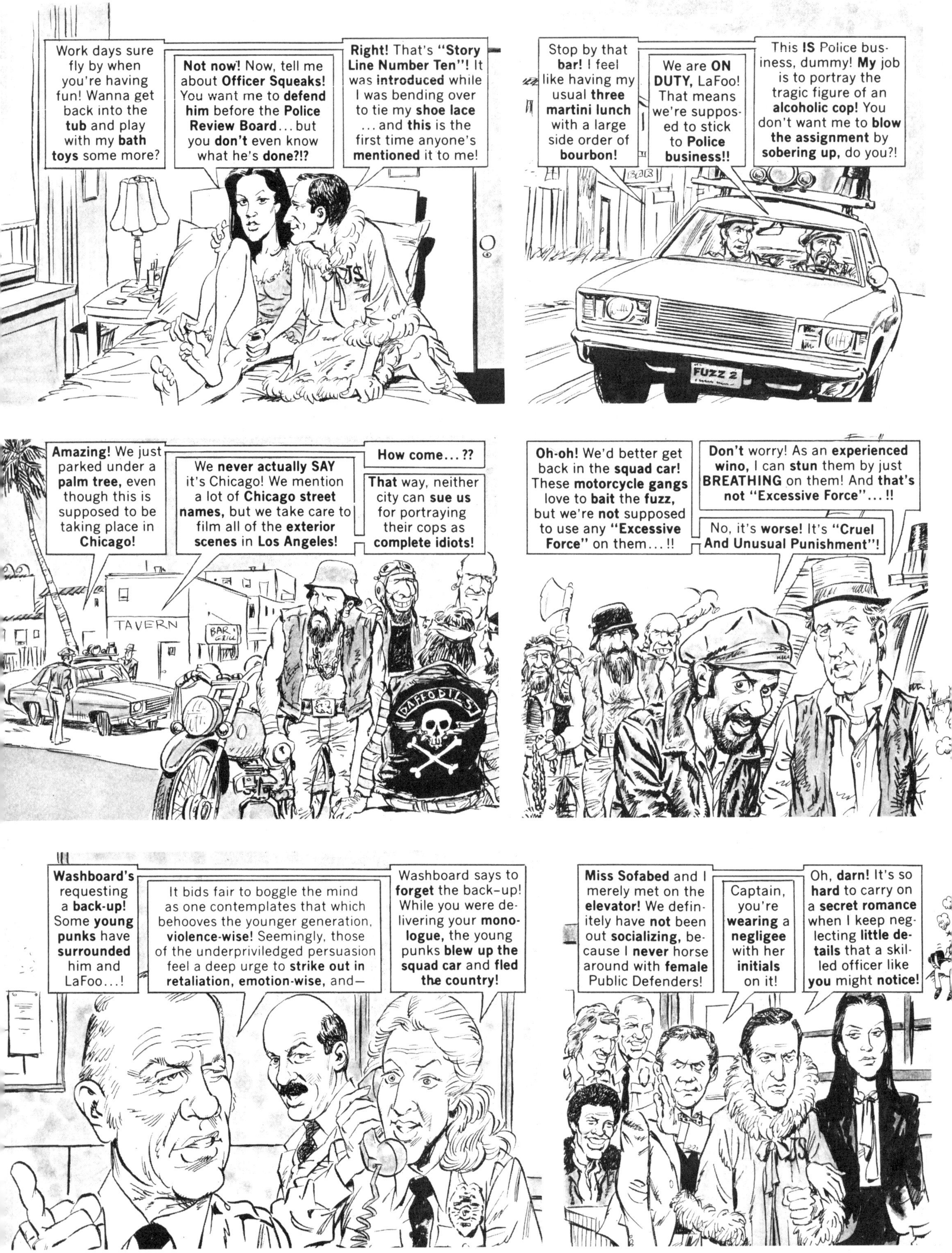

Work days sure fly by when you're having fun! Wanna get back into the tub and play with my bath toys some more?
Not now! Now, tell me about Officer Squeaks! You want me to defend him before the Police Review Board... but you don't even know what he's done?!?
Right! That's "Story Line Number Ten"! It was introduced while I was bending over to tie my shoe lace ...and this is the first time anyone's mentioned it to me!
Stop by that bar! I feel like having my usual three martini lunch with a large side order of bourbon!
We are ON DUTY, LaFoo! That means we're supposed to stick to Police business!!
This IS Police business, dummy! My job is to portray the tragic figure of an alcoholic cop! You don't want me to blow the assignment by sobering up, do you?!
BAR
FUZZ 2
Amazing! We just parked under a palm tree, even though this is supposed to be taking place in Chicago!
How come...??
We never actually SAY it's Chicago! We mention a lot of Chicago street names, but we take care to film all of the exterior scenes in Los Angeles!
That way, neither city can sue us for portraying their cops as complete idiots!
TAVERN
BAR & GRILL
DAFFODILS
Oh-oh! We'd better get back in the squad car! These motorcycle gangs love to bait the fuzz, but we're not supposed to use any "Excessive Force" on them...!!
Don't worry! As an experienced wino, I can stun them by just BREATHING on them! And that's not "Excessive Force"...!!
No, it's worse! It's "Cruel And Unusual Punishment"!
Washboard's requesting a back-up! Some young punks have surrounded him and LaFoo...!
It bids fair to boggle the mind as one contemplates that which behooves the younger generation, violence-wise! Seemingly, those of the underpriviledged persuasion feel a deep urge to strike out in retaliation, emotion-wise, and—
Washboard says to forget the back-up! While you were delivering your monologue, the young punks blew up the squad car and fled the country!
Miss Sofabed and I merely met on the elevator! We definitely have not been out socializing, because I never horse around with female Public Defenders!
Captain, you're wearing a negligee with her initials on it!
Oh, darn! It's so hard to carry on a secret romance when I keep neglecting little details that a skilled officer like you might notice!

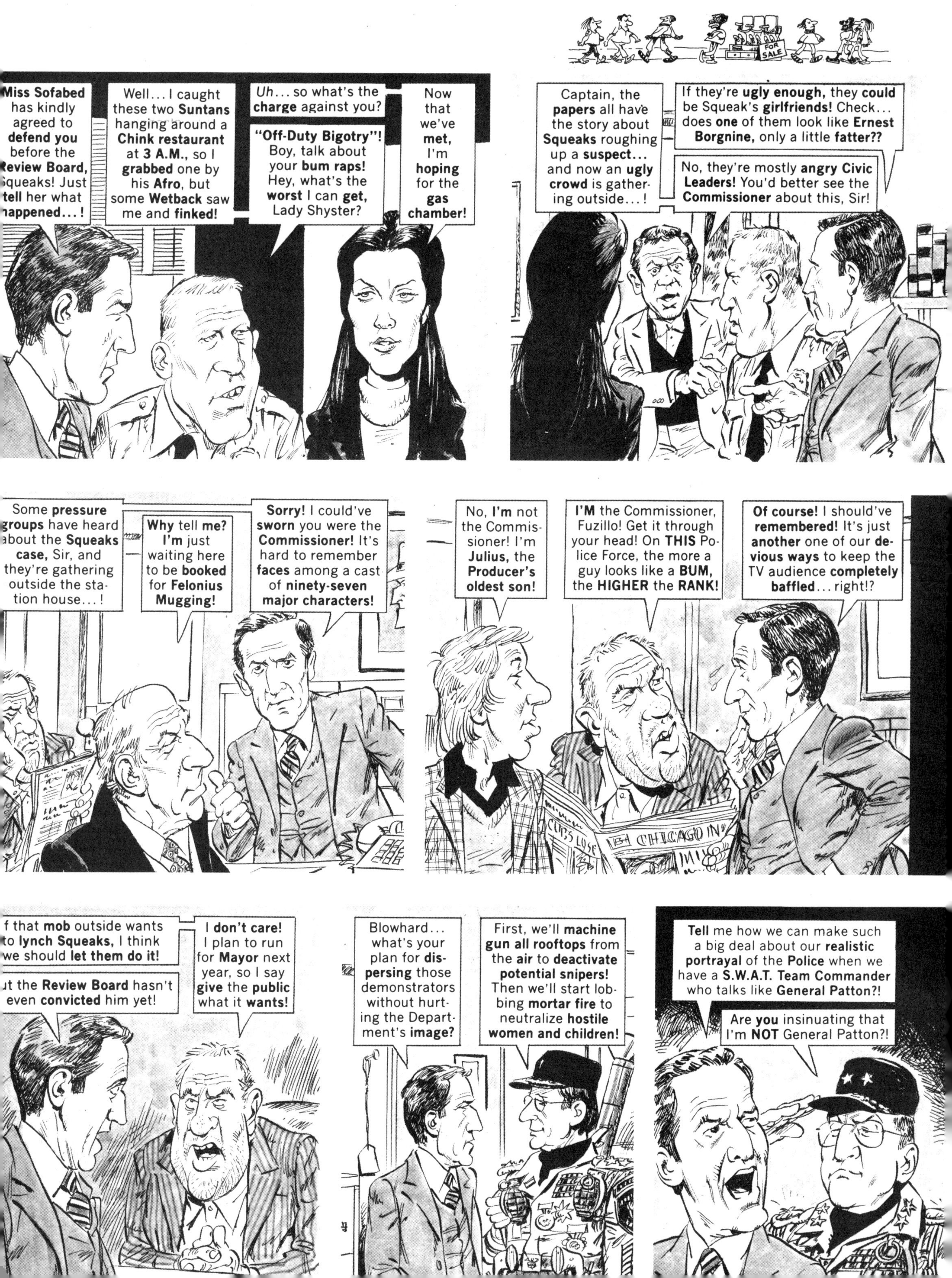
FOR SALE
Miss Sofabed has kindly agreed to defend you before the Review Board, Squeaks! Just tell her what happened...!
Well... I caught these two Suntans hanging around a Chink restaurant at 3 A.M., so I grabbed one by his Afro, but some Wetback saw me and finked!
Uh... so what's the charge against you?
"Off-Duty Bigotry"! Boy, talk about your bum raps! Hey, what's the worst I can get, Lady Shyster?
Now that we've met, I'm hoping for the gas chamber!
Captain, the papers all have the story about Squeaks roughing up a suspect... and now an ugly crowd is gathering outside...!
If they're ugly enough, they could be Squeak's girlfriends! Check... does one of them look like Ernest Borgnine, only a little fatter??
No, they're mostly angry Civic Leaders! You'd better see the Commissioner about this, Sir!
Some pressure groups have heard about the Squeaks case, Sir, and they're gathering outside the station house...!
Why tell me? I'm just waiting here to be booked for Felonius Mugging!
Sorry! I could've sworn you were the Commissioner! It's hard to remember faces among a cast of ninety-seven major characters!
No, I'm not the Commissioner! I'm Julius, the Producer's oldest son!
I'M the Commissioner, Fuzillo! Get it through your head! On THIS Police Force, the more a guy looks like a BUM, the HIGHER the RANK!
Of course! I should've remembered! It's just another one of our devious ways to keep the TV audience completely baffled... right!?
CUBS LOSE
CHICAGO IN
If that mob outside wants to lynch Squeaks, I think we should let them do it!
But the Review Board hasn't even convicted him yet!
I don't care! I plan to run for Mayor next year, so I say give the public what it wants!
Blowhard... what's your plan for dispersing those demonstrators without hurting the Department's image?
First, we'll machine gun all rooftops from the air to deactivate potential snipers! Then we'll start lobbing mortar fire to neutralize hostile women and children!
Tell me how we can make such a big deal about our realistic portrayal of the Police when we have a S.W.A.T. Team Commander who talks like General Patton?!
Are you insinuating that I'm NOT General Patton?!

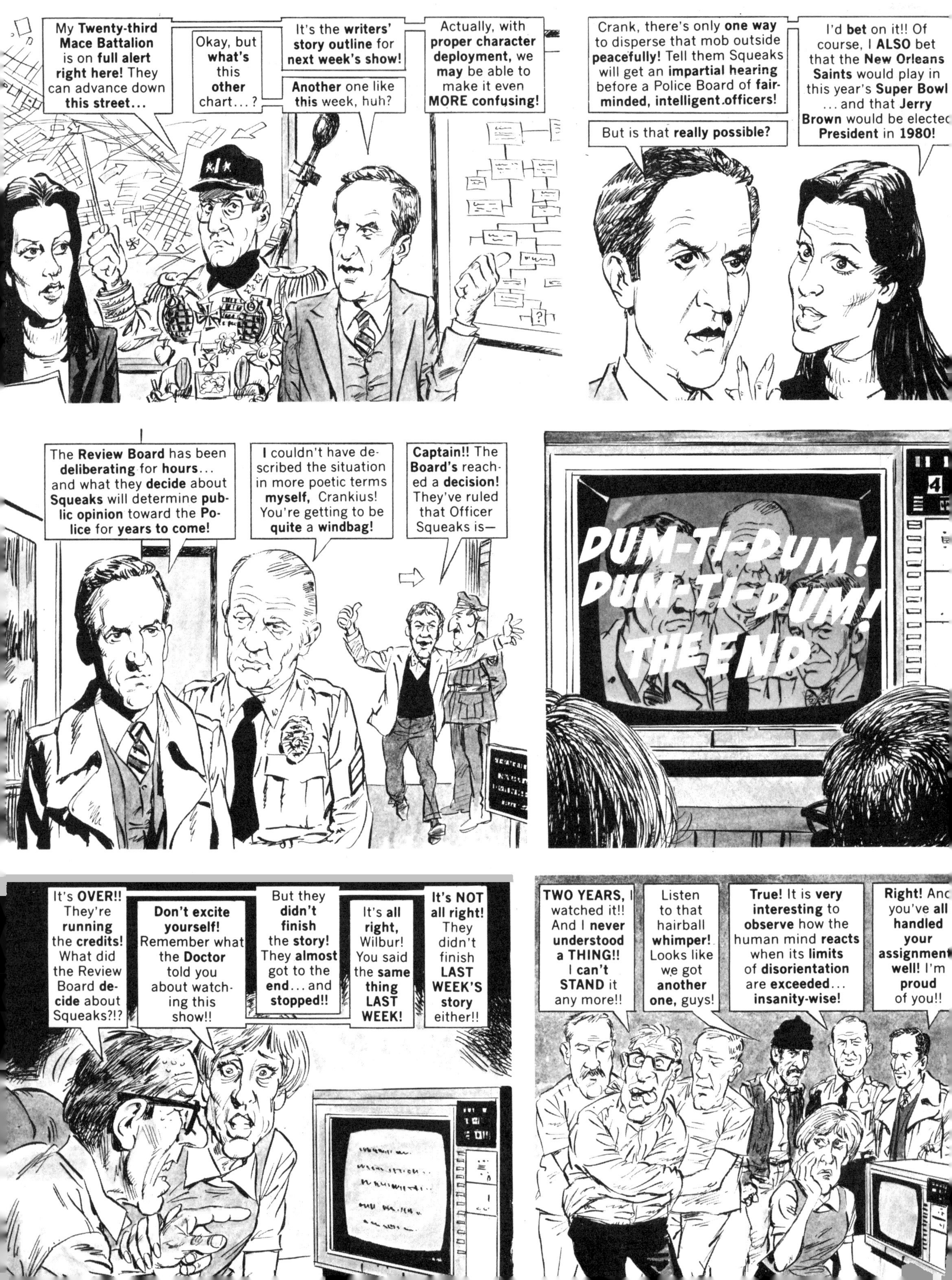
My Twenty-third Mace Battalion is on full alert right here! They can advance down this street...
Okay, but what's this other chart...?
It's the writers' story outline for next week's show!
Another one like this week, huh?
Actually, with proper character deployment, we may be able to make it even MORE confusing!
Crank, there's only one way to disperse that mob outside peacefully! Tell them Squeaks will get an impartial hearing before a Police Board of fair-minded, intelligent officers!
But is that really possible?
I'd bet on it!! Of course, I ALSO bet that the New Orleans Saints would play in this year's Super Bowl ... and that Jerry Brown would be electec President in 1980!
The Review Board has been deliberating for hours... and what they decide about Squeaks will determine public opinion toward the Police for years to come!
I couldn't have described the situation in more poetic terms myself, Crankius! You're getting to be quite a windbag!
Captain!! The Board's reached a decision! They've ruled that Officer Squeaks is—
DUM-TI-DUM! DUM-TI-DUM! THE END
It's OVER!! They're running the credits! What did the Review Board decide about Squeaks?!?
Don't excite yourself! Remember what the Doctor told you about watching this show!!
But they didn't finish the story! They almost got to the end... and stopped!!
It's all right, Wilbur! You said the same thing LAST WEEK!
It's NOT all right! They didn't finish LAST WEEK'S story either!!
TWO YEARS, I watched it!! And I never understood a THING!! I can't STAND it any more!!
Listen to that hairball whimper! Looks like we got another one, guys!
True! It is very interesting to observe how the human mind reacts when its limits of disorientation are exceeded... insanity-wise!
Right! And you've all handled your assignment well! I'm proud of you!!

DON MARTIN DEPT.

ONE FINE EVENING DURING PRIME TIME

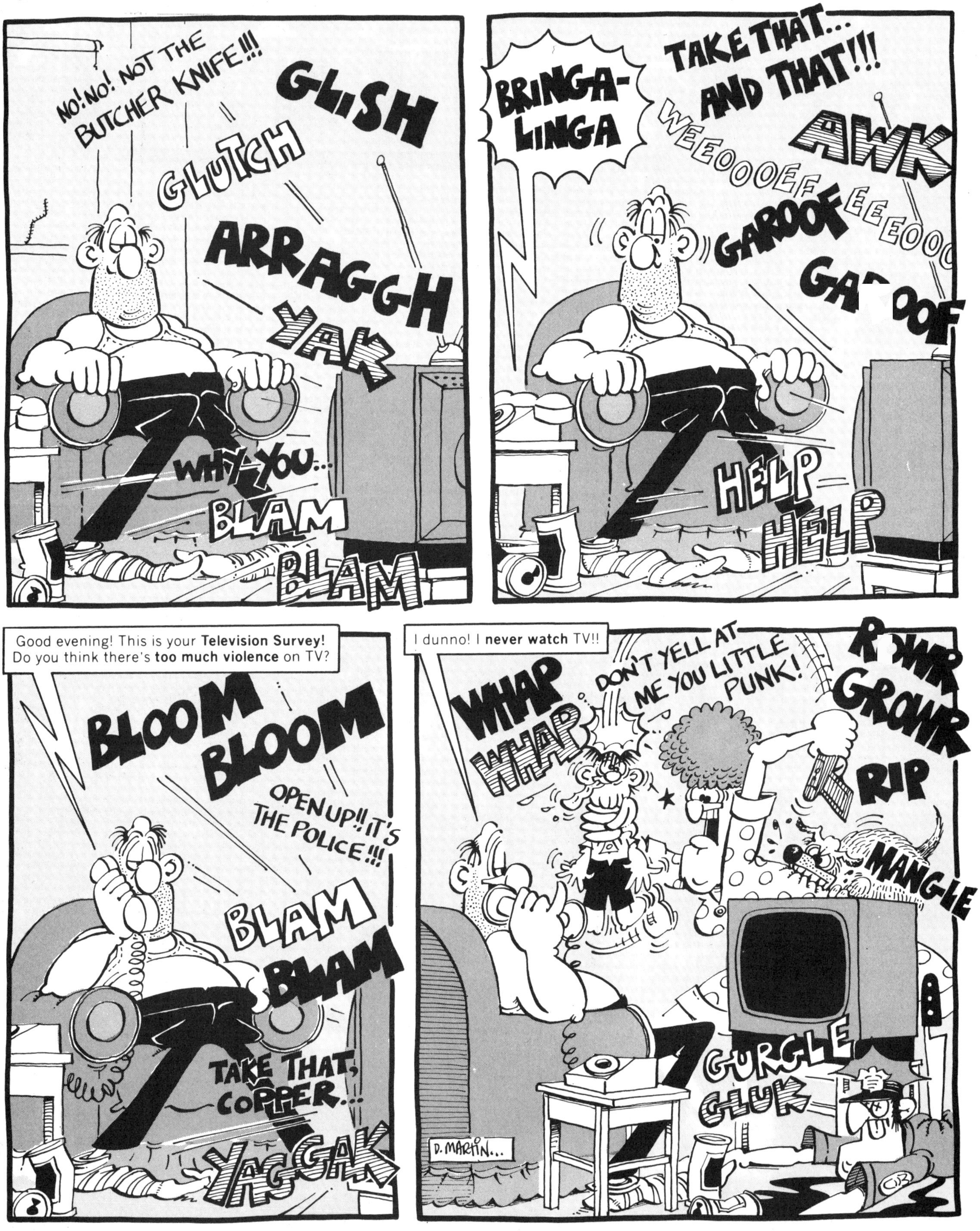

NO! NO! NOT THE BUTCHER KNIFE!!!
GLISH
GLUTCH
ARRAGGH
YAK
WHY YOU...
BLAM
BLAM
BRINGA-LINGA
TAKE THAT... AND THAT!!!
AWK
WEEEOOOOEF
EEEEOOO
GAROOF
HELP
HELP
Good evening! This is your **Television Survey**! Do you think there's **too much violence** on TV?
BLOOM
BLOOM
OPEN UP!! IT'S THE POLICE!!!
BLAM
BLAM
TAKE THAT, COPPER...
YAGGAK
I dunno! I **never watch** TV!!
WHAP
WHAP
DON'T YELL AT ME YOU LITTLE PUNK!
GROWR
RIP
MANGLE
GURGLE
GLUK
D. MARTIN...

"T" AND *A* DEPT.

Do you need a group of highly-paid skilled professionals who can operate withi and around the law to accomplish dangerous specialized assignments? Then hir

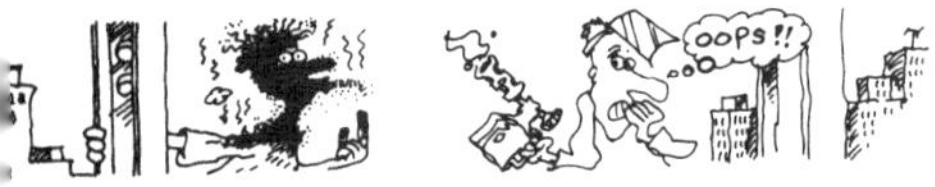
OOPS!!

THE *A

ARTIST: MORT DRUCKER

*ASININE

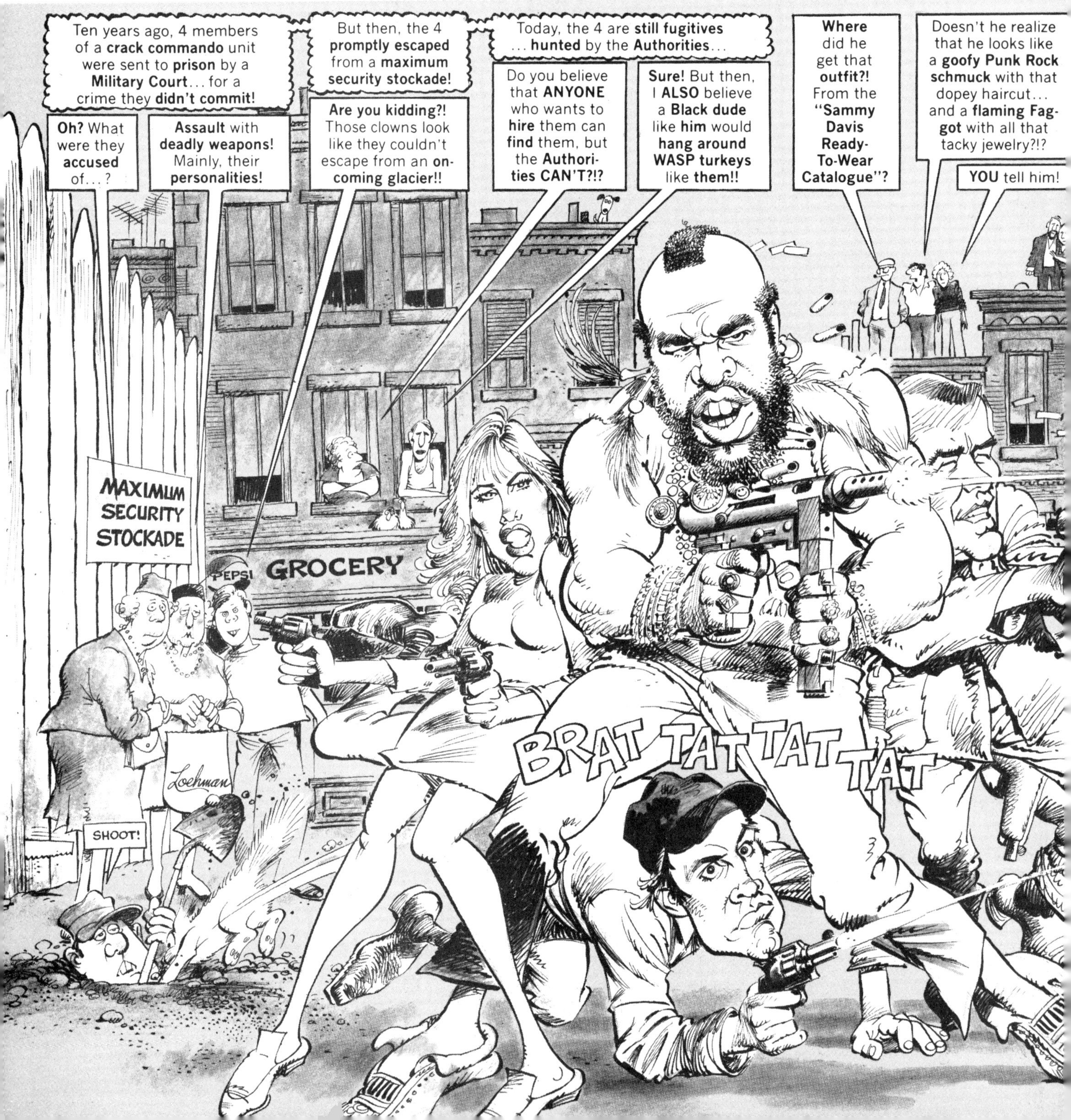
Ten years ago, 4 members of a crack commando unit were sent to prison by a Military Court... for a crime they didn't commit!
Oh? What were they accused of...?
Assault with deadly weapons! Mainly, their personalities!
But then, the 4 promptly escaped from a maximum security stockade!
Are you kidding?! Those clowns look like they couldn't escape from an on-coming glacier!!
Today, the 4 are still fugitives ... hunted by the Authorities...
Do you believe that ANYONE who wants to hire them can find them, but the Authorities CAN'T?!?
Sure! But then, I ALSO believe a Black dude like him would hang around WASP turkeys like them!!
Where did he get that outfit?! From the "Sammy Davis Ready-To-Wear Catalogue"?
Doesn't he realize that he looks like a goofy Punk Rock schmuck with that dopey haircut... and a flaming Fag-got with all that tacky jewelry?!?
YOU tell him!
MAXIMUM SECURITY STOCKADE
PEPSI GROCERY
Loehman
SHOOT!
BRAT TAT TAT TAT

:he old "Mission Impossible" team! But if you want a group of bumbling misfit
nercenaries whose only advantage is: they always forget to get paid, then try

* TEAM

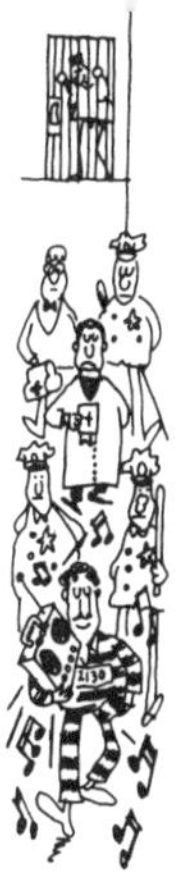

WRITER: STAN HART

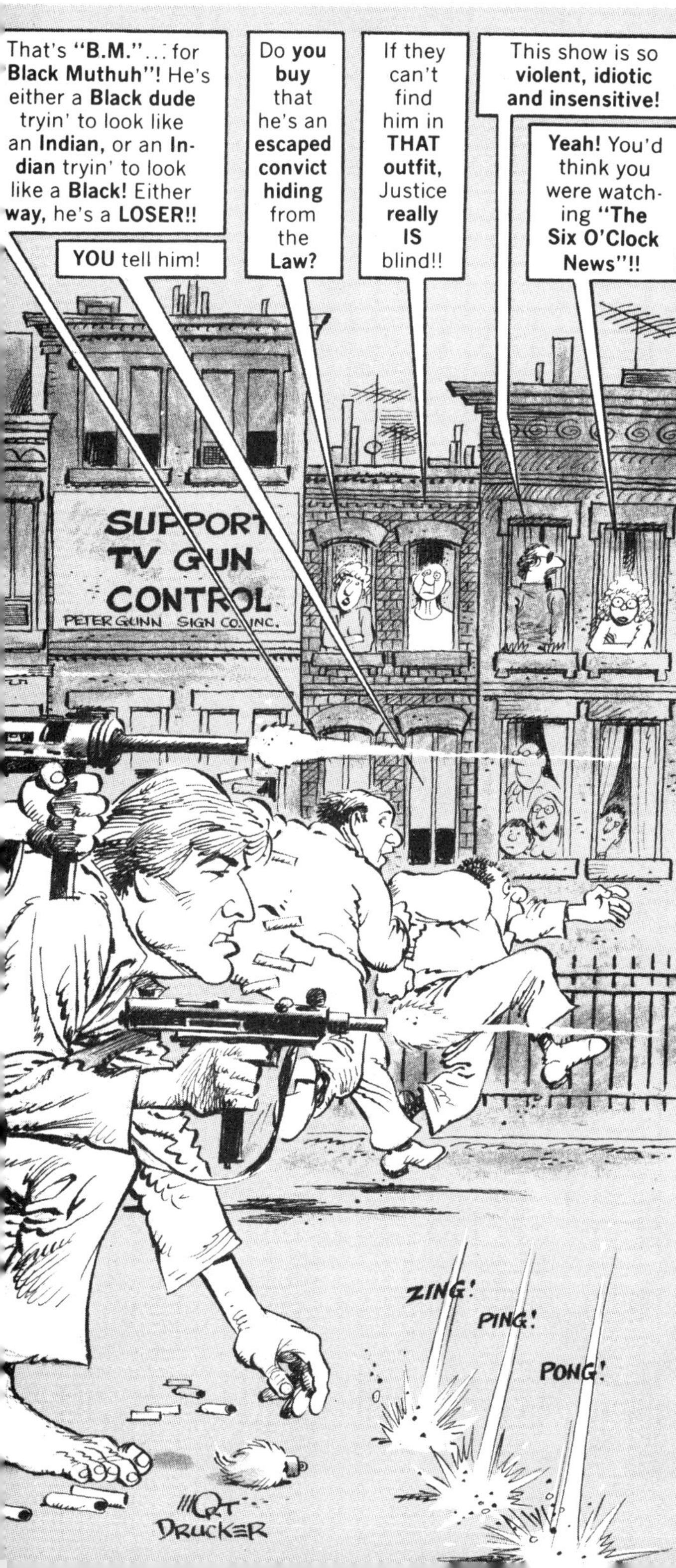

That's "B.M."... for Black Muthuh"! He's either a Black dude tryin' to look like an Indian, or an Indian tryin' to look like a Black! Either way, he's a LOSER!!
YOU tell him!
Do you buy that he's an escaped convict hiding from the Law?
If they can't find him in THAT outfit, Justice really IS blind!!
This show is so violent, idiotic and insensitive!
Yeah! You'd think you were watching "The Six O'Clock News"!!
SUPPORT TV GUN CONTROL
PETER GUNN SIGN CO. INC.
ZING!
PING!
PONG!
MORT DRUCKER

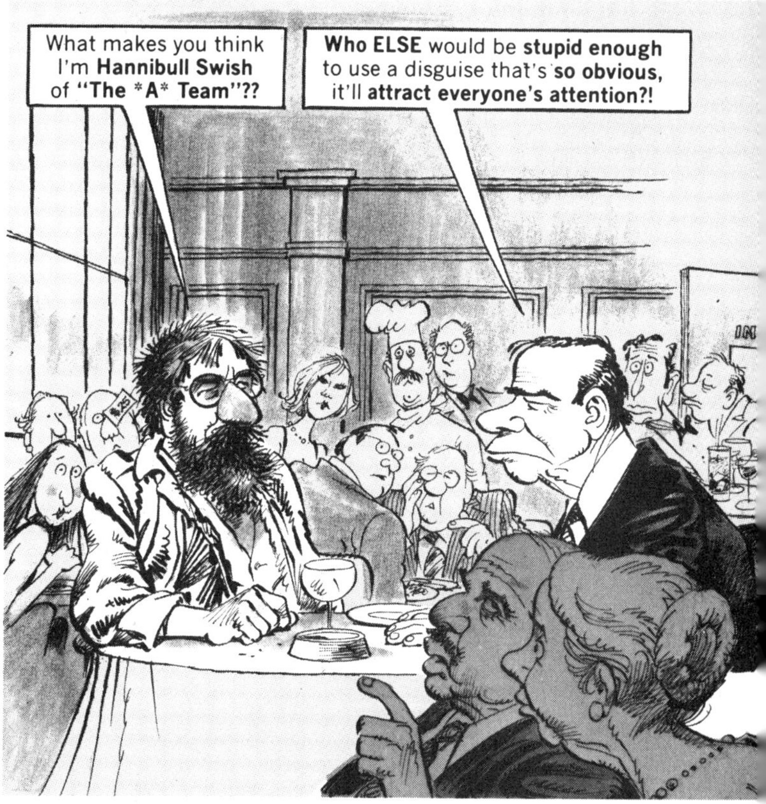

What makes you think I'm Hannibull Swish of "The *A* Team"??
Who ELSE would be stupid enough to use a disguise that's so obvious, it'll attract everyone's attention?!

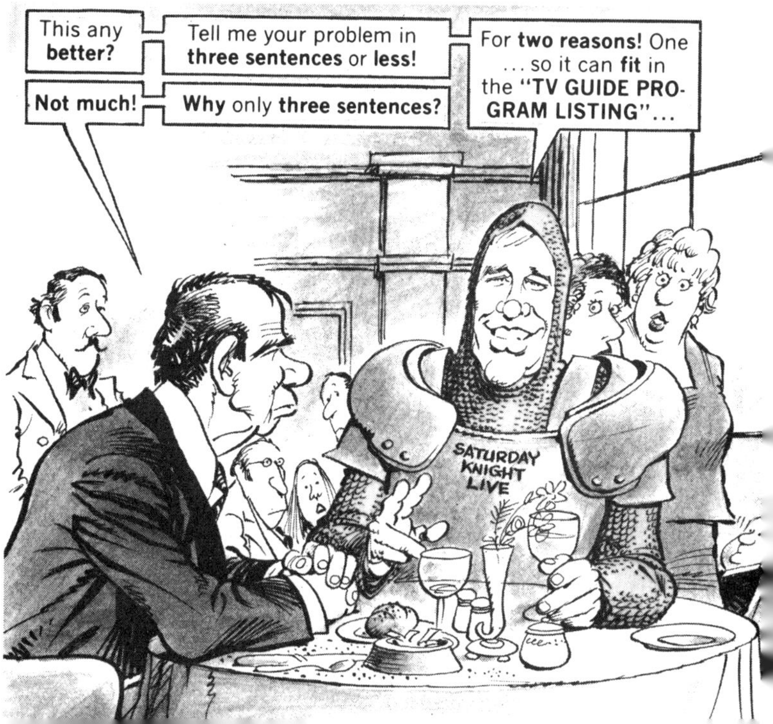

This any better?
Tell me your problem in three sentences or less!
For two reasons! One ... so it can fit in the "TV GUIDE PROGRAM LISTING"...
Not much!
Why only three sentences?
SATURDAY KNIGHT LIVE

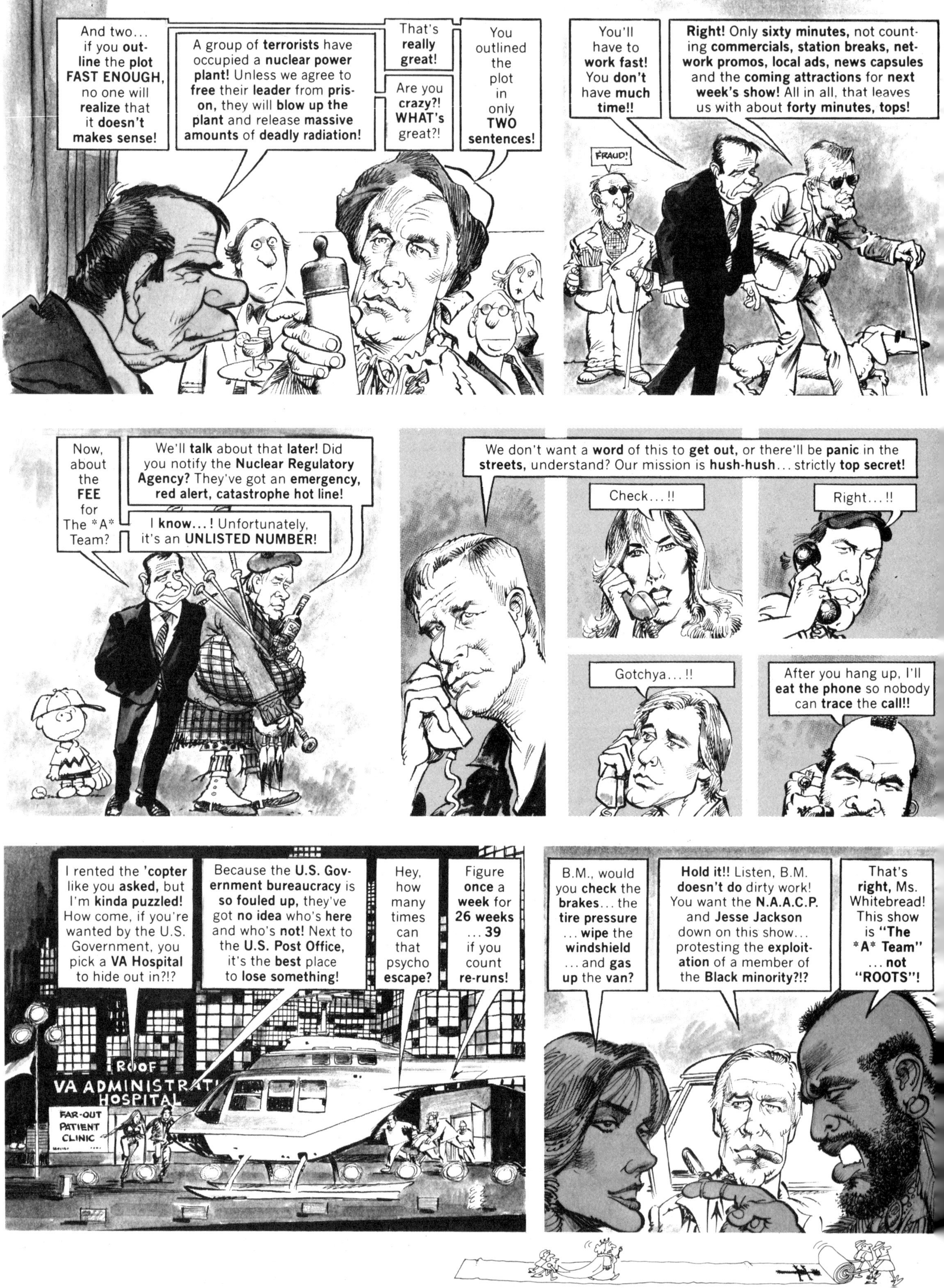
And two... if you outline the plot FAST ENOUGH, no one will realize that it doesn't makes sense!
A group of terrorists have occupied a nuclear power plant! Unless we agree to free their leader from prison, they will blow up the plant and release massive amounts of deadly radiation!
That's really great!
Are you crazy?! WHAT's great?!
You outlined the plot in only TWO sentences!
FRAUD!
You'll have to work fast! You don't have much time!!
Right! Only sixty minutes, not counting commercials, station breaks, network promos, local ads, news capsules and the coming attractions for next week's show! All in all, that leaves us with about forty minutes, tops!
Now, about the FEE for The *A* Team?
We'll talk about that later! Did you notify the Nuclear Regulatory Agency? They've got an emergency, red alert, catastrophe hot line!
I know...! Unfortunately, it's an UNLISTED NUMBER!
We don't want a word of this to get out, or there'll be panic in the streets, understand? Our mission is hush-hush... strictly top secret!
Check...!!
Right...!!
Gotchya...!!
After you hang up, I'll eat the phone so nobody can trace the call!!
I rented the 'copter like you asked, but I'm kinda puzzled! How come, if you're wanted by the U.S. Government, you pick a VA Hospital to hide out in?!?
Because the U.S. Government bureaucracy is so fouled up, they've got no idea who's here and who's not! Next to the U.S. Post Office, it's the best place to lose something!
Hey, how many times can that psycho escape?
Figure once a week for 26 weeks ...39 if you count re-runs!
ROOF
VA ADMINISTRAT
HOSPITAL
FAR-OUT PATIENT CLINIC
B.M., would you check the brakes... the tire pressure ...wipe the windshield ...and gas up the van?
Hold it!! Listen, B.M. doesn't do dirty work! You want the N.A.A.C.P. and Jesse Jackson down on this show... protesting the exploitation of a member of the Black minority?!?
That's right, Ms. Whitebread! This show is "The *A* Team" ...not "ROOTS"!

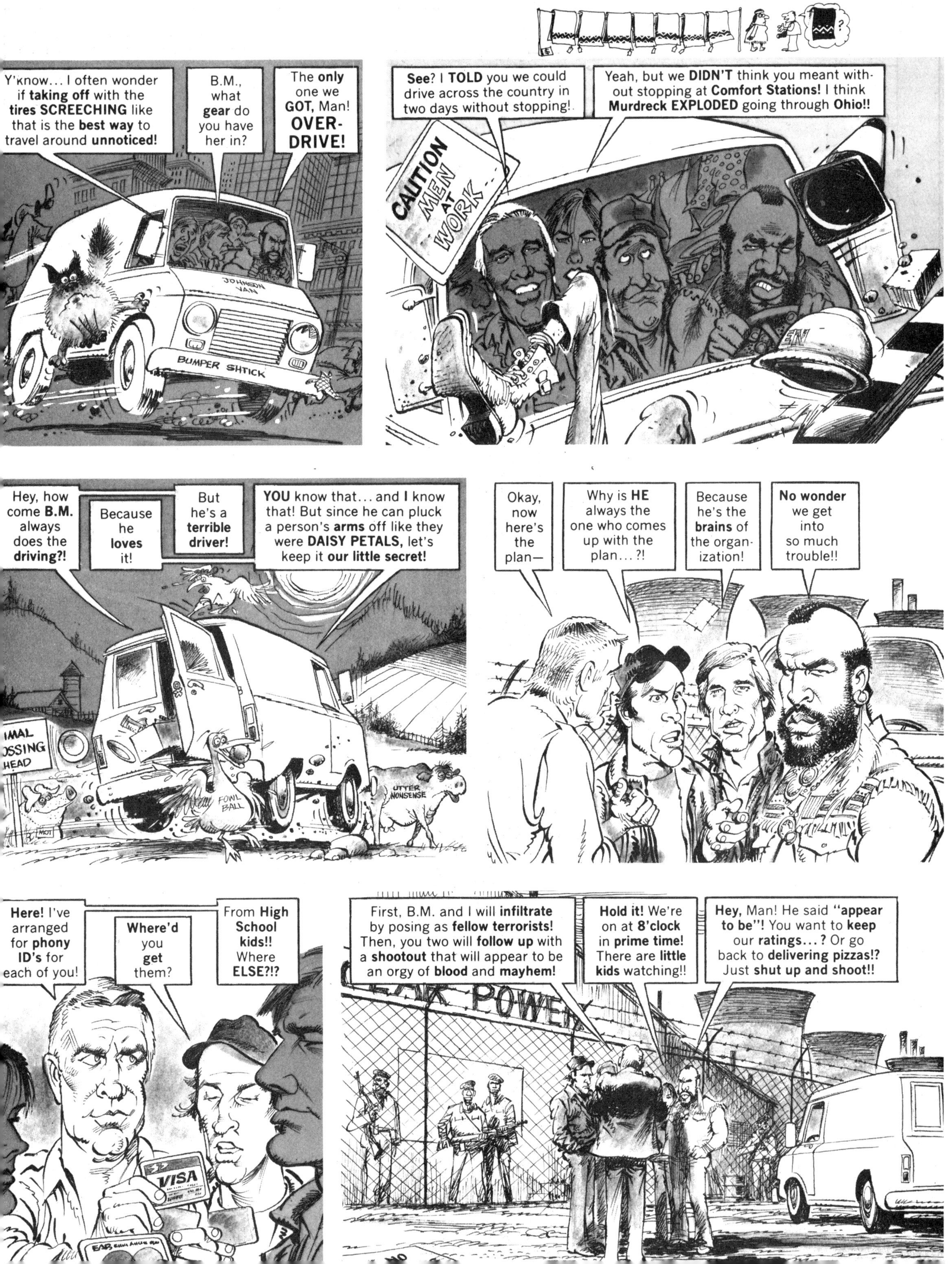

Y'know... I often wonder if taking off with the tires SCREECHING like that is the best way to travel around unnoticed!
B.M., what gear do you have her in?
The only one we GOT, Man! OVER-DRIVE!
JOHNSON VAN
BUMPER SHTICK
See? I TOLD you we could drive across the country in two days without stopping!
Yeah, but we DIDN'T think you meant without stopping at Comfort Stations! I think Murdreck EXPLODED going through Ohio!!
CAUTION MEN AT WORK
Hey, how come B.M. always does the driving?!
Because he loves it!
But he's a terrible driver!
YOU know that... and I know that! But since he can pluck a person's arms off like they were DAISY PETALS, let's keep it our little secret!
FOWL BALL
UTTER NONSENSE
Okay, now here's the plan—
Why is HE always the one who comes up with the plan... ?!
Because he's the brains of the organ-ization!
No wonder we get into so much trouble!!
Here! I've arranged for phony ID's for each of you!
Where'd you get them?
From High School kids!! Where ELSE?!?
VISA
First, B.M. and I will infiltrate by posing as fellow terrorists! Then, you two will follow up with a shootout that will appear to be an orgy of blood and mayhem!
Hold it! We're on at 8'clock in prime time! There are little kids watching!!
Hey, Man! He said "appear to be"! You want to keep our ratings... ? Or go back to delivering pizzas!? Just shut up and shoot!!

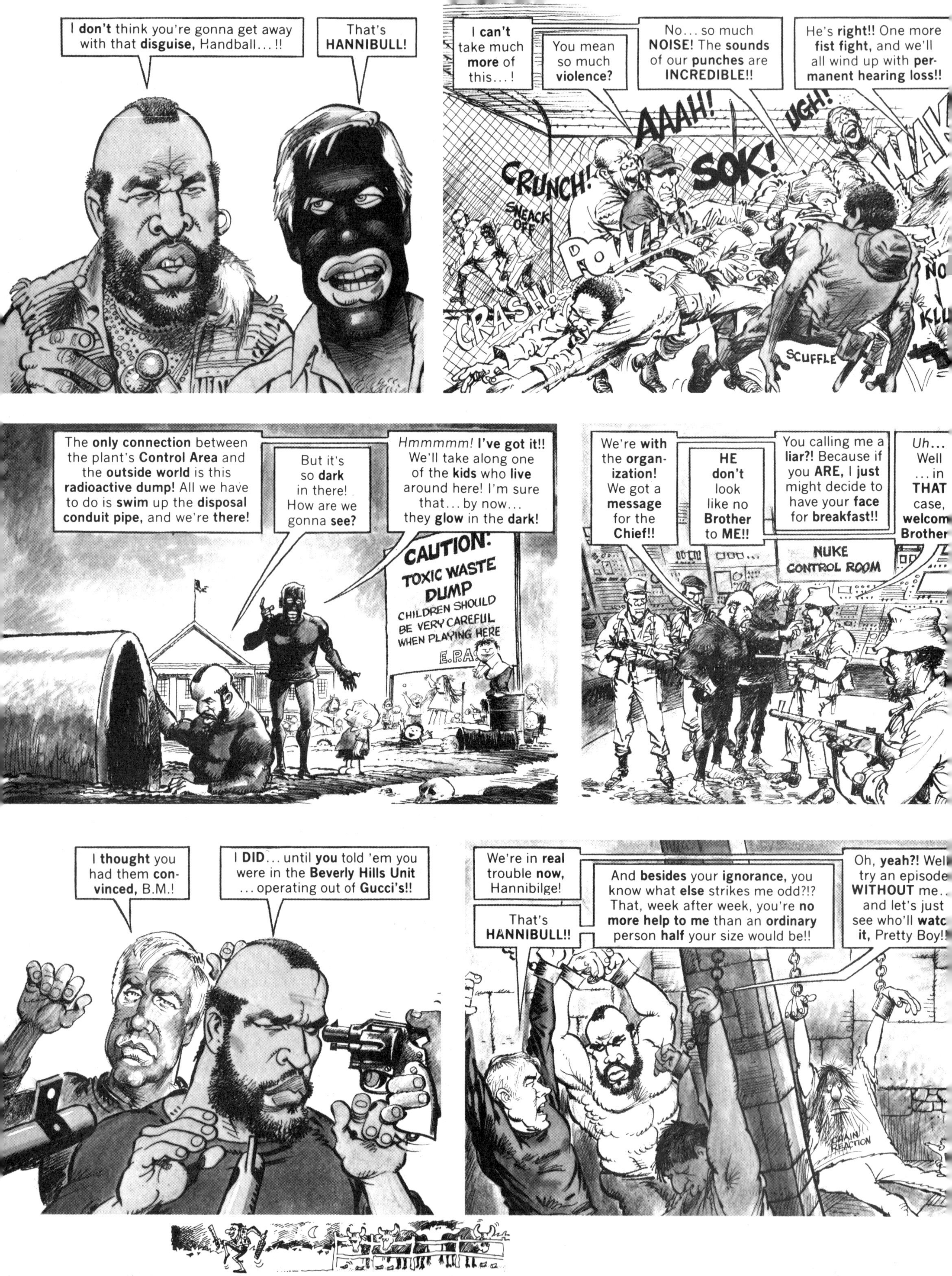

I **don't** think you're gonna get away with that **disguise,** Handball...!!
That's **HANNIBULL!**
I **can't** take much **more** of this...!
You mean so much **violence?**
No... so much **NOISE!** The **sounds** of our **punches** are **INCREDIBLE!!**
He's **right!!** One more **fist fight,** and we'll all wind up with **permanent hearing loss!!**
AAAH!
UGH!
SOK!
CRUNCH!
SNEACK OFF
POW!!
CRASH!
SCUFFLE
The **only connection** between the plant's **Control Area** and the **outside world** is this **radioactive dump!** All we have to do is **swim** up the **disposal conduit pipe,** and we're **there!**
But it's so **dark** in there! How are we gonna **see?**
Hmmmmm! **I've got it!!** We'll take along one of the **kids** who **live** around here! I'm sure that... by now... they **glow** in the **dark!**
CAUTION: TOXIC WASTE DUMP
CHILDREN SHOULD BE VERY CAREFUL WHEN PLAYING HERE
E.P.A.
We're **with** the **organization!** We got a **message** for the **Chief!!**
HE don't look like no **Brother** to **ME!!**
You calling me a **liar?!** Because if you **ARE,** I **just** might decide to have your **face** for **breakfast!!**
NUKE CONTROL ROOM
I **thought** you had them **convinced,** B.M.!
I **DID**... until **you** told 'em you were in the **Beverly Hills Unit** ... operating out of **Gucci's!!**
We're in **real** trouble **now,** Hannibilge!
That's **HANNIBULL!!**
And **besides** your **ignorance,** you know what **else** strikes me odd?!? That, week after week, you're **no more help to me** than an **ordinary** person **half** your size would be!!
CHAIN REACTION

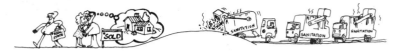

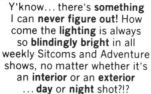

SOLD
SANITATION
SANITATION
SANITATION
Y'know... there's **something** I can **never figure out!** How come the **lighting** is always so **blindingly bright** in all weekly Sitcoms and Adventure shows, no matter whether it's an **interior** or an **exterior** ... **day** or **night** shot?!?
Ahh, **who cares!?!** Listen, I've got a **plan** that I'm **sure** will **work!**
Okay... but **only** if it's **zany, idiotic** and **completely impossible** in **real life!!** Is it... ?!?
Does a **cabbie pick his NOSE** waiting for the **light** to change?!
Gee, that's a **pretty dangerous mission!!** How come you made **HER** do it... ?!?
Since we **can't** use **B.M.** for dirty jobs, the **woman** is the **only** member of an **exploited group** we've **got!**
SWISH!
NUCLEAR AND TUNA FISSION
Okay, gang! Here comes our usual **violent, climatic shootout**... along with our **weekly big surprise!**
What surprise??
That with all these **explosions, crashes** and **gunfire,** no one ever **gets killed** on this show!!
CHOMP!
RATTAT
TAT TAT TAT!
BRAT TAT!
VIP
VIP
BLAM!
Thanks for not only doing a **great job,** but **also** for demonstrating that people with **below-average intelligence** can **also** serve their country! Now, as for the **money** we owe you for this mission...
Forget it... !!
FORGET IT... ?!?
There you go AGAIN!! How we gonna pay for renting that **'copter,** the **transportation** we used, the **ammunition** we burned, the **living expenses** we incurred, the **private property** we destroyed... ?!
We'll **ALWAYS** be **fugitives on the lam!!**
From the **Govern-ment!!**
No... from all the **Collection Agencies** that are after us to **pay** the **enormous BILLS** we keep run-ning up on these idiotic missions!
BILLS
BILLS

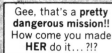

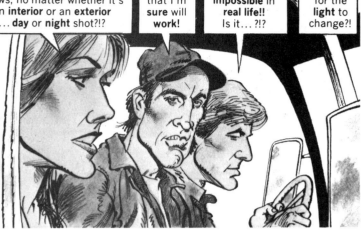

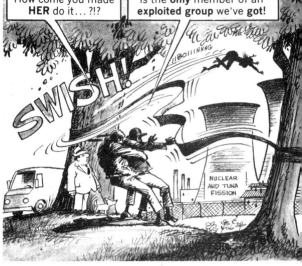

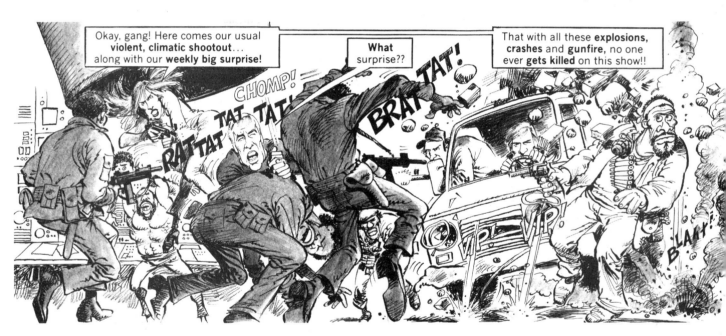

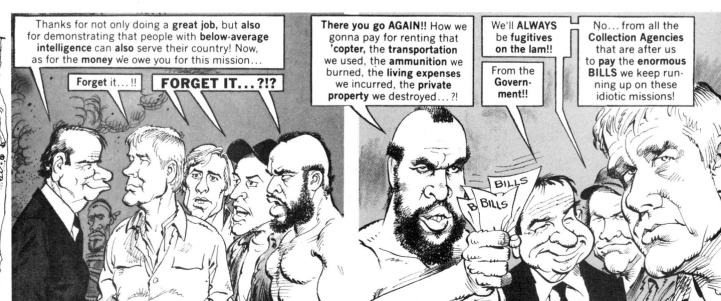

And now a new MAD feature! A look back at a TV show that just refuses to die!

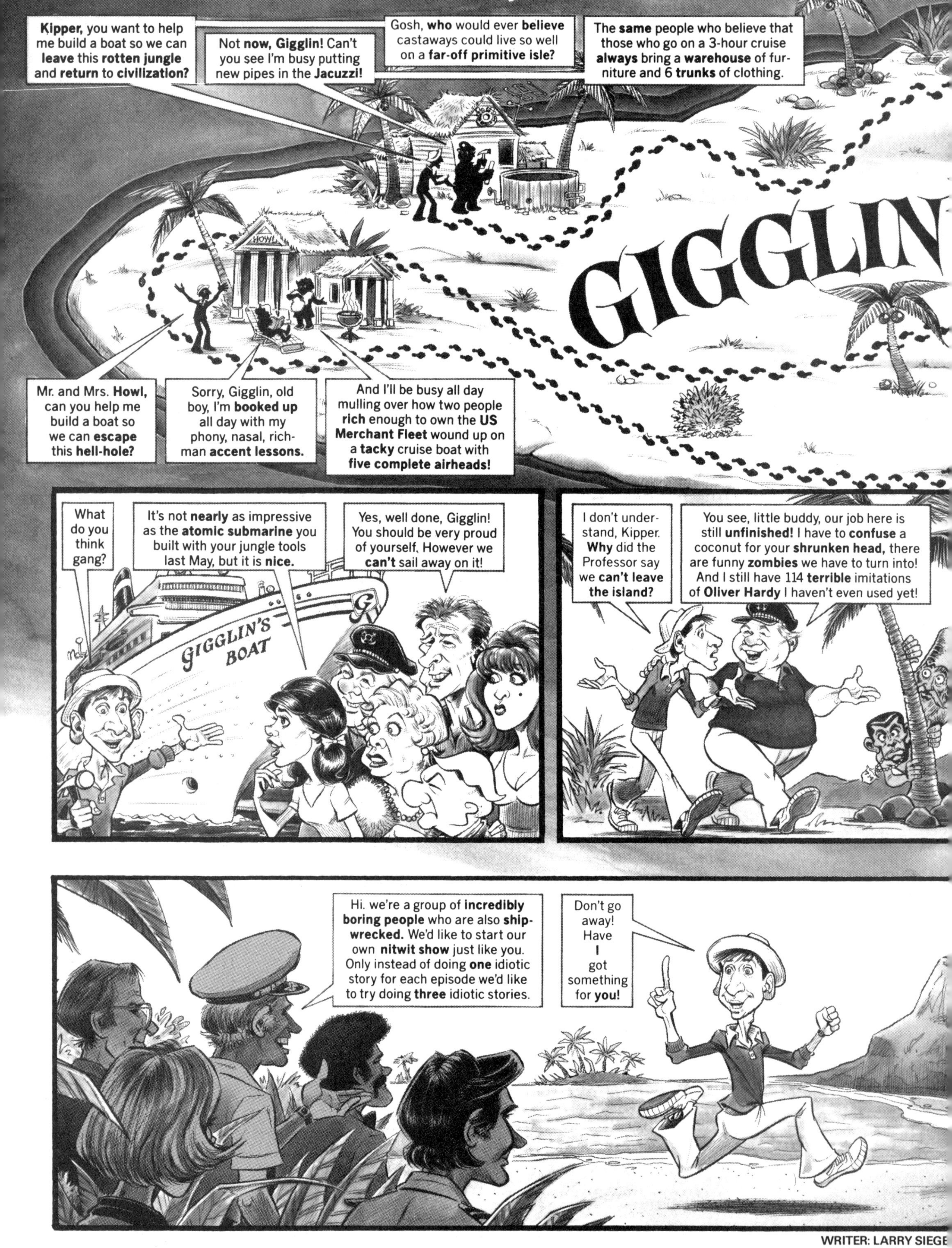

Kipper, you want to help me build a boat so we can leave this rotten jungle and return to civilization?
Not now, Gigglin! Can't you see I'm busy putting new pipes in the Jacuzzi!
Gosh, who would ever believe castaways could live so well on a far-off primitive isle?
The same people who believe that those who go on a 3-hour cruise always bring a warehouse of furniture and 6 trunks of clothing.
GIGGLIN
HOWL
Mr. and Mrs. Howl, can you help me build a boat so we can escape this hell-hole?
Sorry, Gigglin, old boy, I'm booked up all day with my phony, nasal, rich-man accent lessons.
And I'll be busy all day mulling over how two people rich enough to own the US Merchant Fleet wound up on a tacky cruise boat with five complete airheads!
What do you think gang?
It's not nearly as impressive as the atomic submarine you built with your jungle tools last May, but it is nice.
Yes, well done, Gigglin! You should be very proud of yourself. However we can't sail away on it!
GIGGLIN'S BOAT
I don't understand, Kipper. Why did the Professor say we can't leave the island?
You see, little buddy, our job here is still unfinished! I have to confuse a coconut for your shrunken head, there are funny zombies we have to turn into! And I still have 114 terrible imitations of Oliver Hardy I haven't even used yet!
Hi. we're a group of incredibly boring people who are also shipwrecked. We'd like to start our own nitwit show just like you. Only instead of doing one idiotic story for each episode we'd like to try doing three idiotic stories.
Don't go away! Have I got something for you!

WRITER: LARRY SIEGE

A BAD CASE OF THE RE-RUNS DEPT.

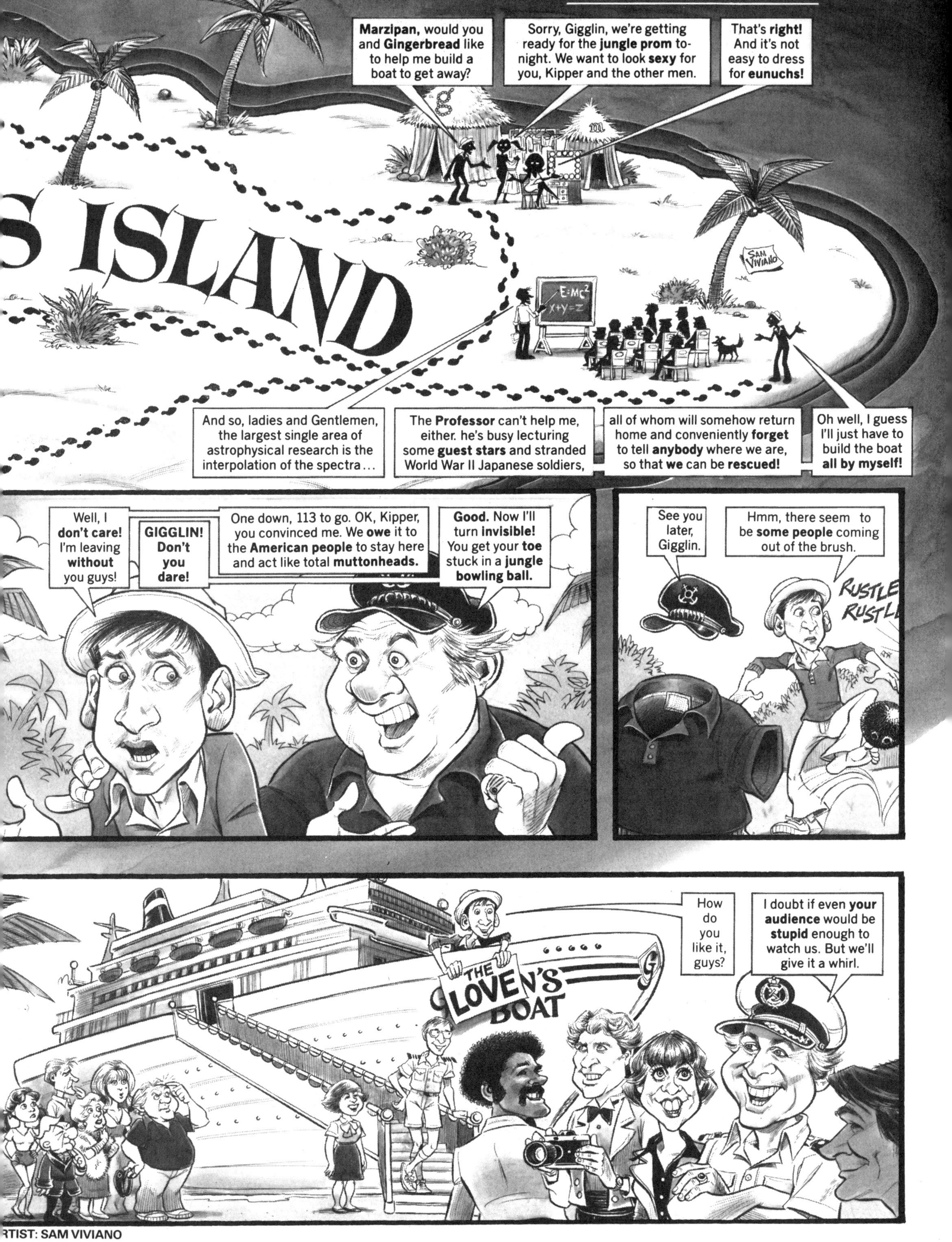

Marzipan, would you and Gingerbread like to help me build a boat to get away?
Sorry, Gigglin, we're getting ready for the jungle prom tonight. We want to look sexy for you, Kipper and the other men.
That's right! And it's not easy to dress for eunuchs!
S ISLAND
E=MC²
X+Y=Z
SAM VIVIANO
And so, ladies and Gentlemen, the largest single area of astrophysical research is the interpolation of the spectra...
The Professor can't help me, either. he's busy lecturing some guest stars and stranded World War II Japanese soldiers,
all of whom will somehow return home and conveniently forget to tell anybody where we are, so that we can be rescued!
Oh well, I guess I'll just have to build the boat all by myself!
Well, I don't care! I'm leaving without you guys!
GIGGLIN! Don't you dare!
One down, 113 to go. OK, Kipper, you convinced me. We owe it to the American people to stay here and act like total muttonheads.
Good. Now I'll turn invisible! You get your toe stuck in a jungle bowling ball.
See you later, Gigglin.
Hmm, there seem to be some people coming out of the brush.
RUSTLE
RUSTLE
THE LOVEN'S BOAT
How do you like it, guys?
I doubt if even your audience would be stupid enough to watch us. But we'll give it a whirl.

ARTIST: SAM VIVIANO

A BAD CASE OF THE RE-RUNS DEPT.

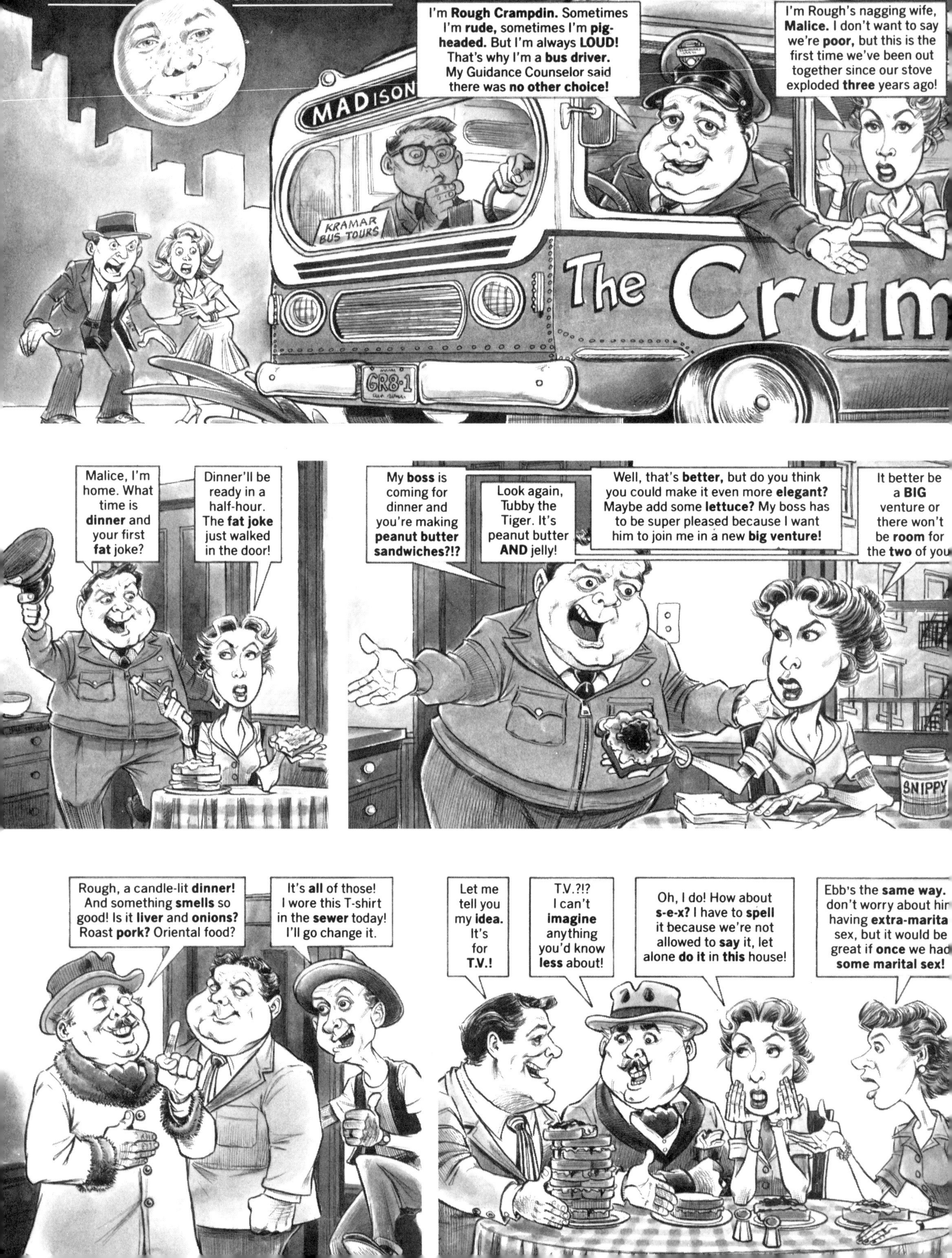

I'm Rough Crampdin. Sometimes I'm rude, sometimes I'm pig-headed. But I'm always LOUD! That's why I'm a bus driver. My Guidance Counselor said there was no other choice!
I'm Rough's nagging wife, Malice. I don't want to say we're poor, but this is the first time we've been out together since our stove exploded three years ago!
MADison
KRAMAR BUS TOURS
GR8-1
The Crum
Malice, I'm home. What time is dinner and your first fat joke?
Dinner'll be ready in a half-hour. The fat joke just walked in the door!
My boss is coming for dinner and you're making peanut butter sandwiches?!?
Look again, Tubby the Tiger. It's peanut butter AND jelly!
Well, that's better, but do you think you could make it even more elegant? Maybe add some lettuce? My boss has to be super pleased because I want him to join me in a new big venture!
It better be a BIG venture or there won't be room for the two of you
SNIPPY
Rough, a candle-lit dinner! And something smells so good! Is it liver and onions? Roast pork? Oriental food?
It's all of those! I wore this T-shirt in the sewer today! I'll go change it.
Let me tell you my idea. It's for T.V.!
T.V.?!? I can't imagine anything you'd know less about!
Oh, I do! How about s-e-x? I have to spell it because we're not allowed to say it, let alone do it in this house!
Ebb's the same way. don't worry about hi having extra-marita sex, but it would be great if once we ha some marital sex!

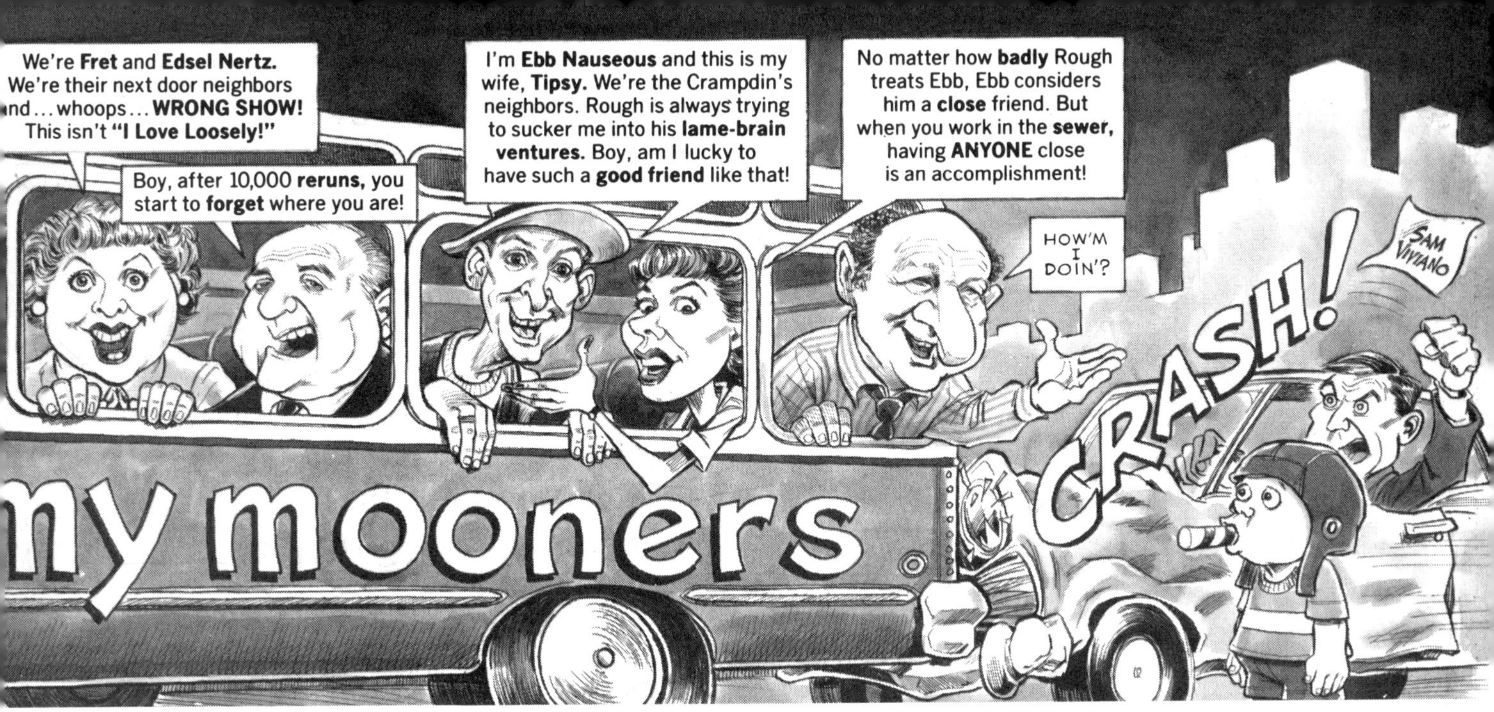
We're Fret and Edsel Nertz. We're their next door neighbors nd... whoops... WRONG SHOW! This isn't "I Love Loosely!"
Boy, after 10,000 reruns, you start to forget where you are!
I'm Ebb Nauseous and this is my wife, Tipsy. We're the Crampdin's neighbors. Rough is always trying to sucker me into his lame-brain ventures. Boy, am I lucky to have such a good friend like that!
No matter how badly Rough treats Ebb, Ebb considers him a close friend. But when you work in the sewer, having ANYONE close is an accomplishment!
HOW'M I DOIN'?
SAM VIVIANO
CRASH!
my mooners

WRITER: LARRY SIEGEL ARTIST: SAM VIVIANO

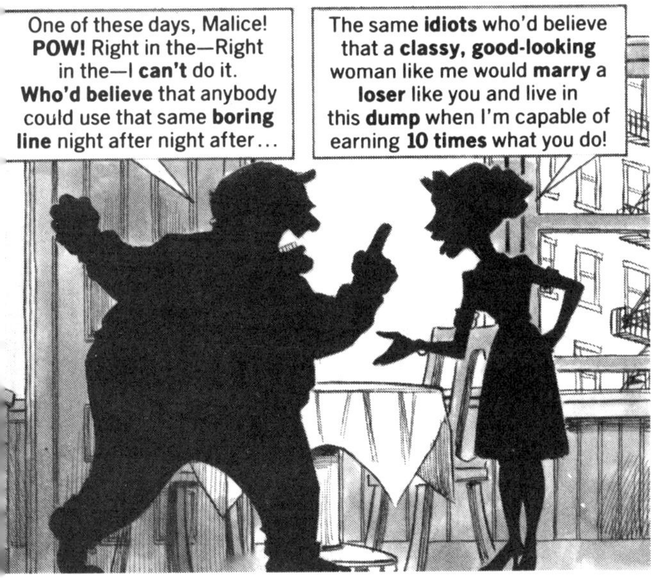
One of these days, Malice! POW! Right in the—Right in the—I can't do it. Who'd believe that anybody could use that same boring line night after night after...
The same idiots who'd believe that a classy, good-looking woman like me would marry a loser like you and live in this dump when I'm capable of earning 10 times what you do!

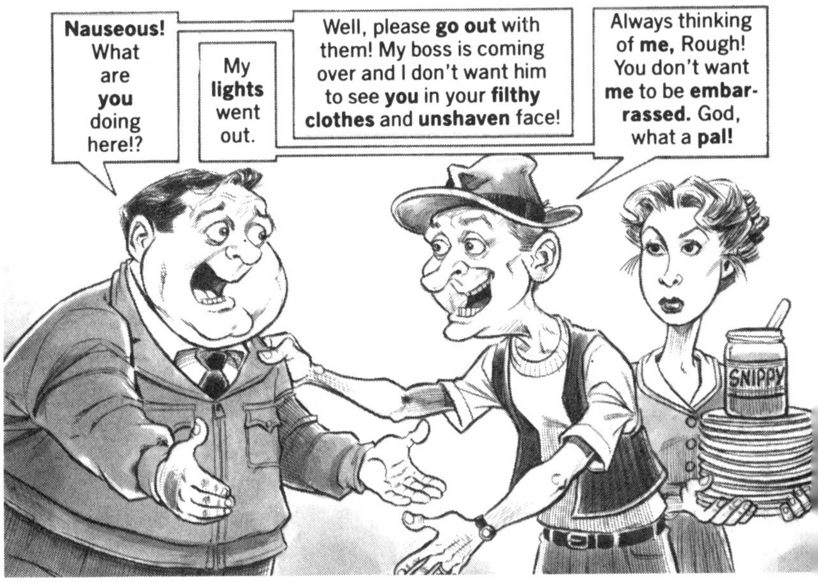
Nauseous! What are you doing here!?
My lights went out.
Well, please go out with them! My boss is coming over and I don't want him to see you in your filthy clothes and unshaven face!
Always thinking of me, Rough! You don't want me to be embarrassed. God, what a pal!
SNIPPY

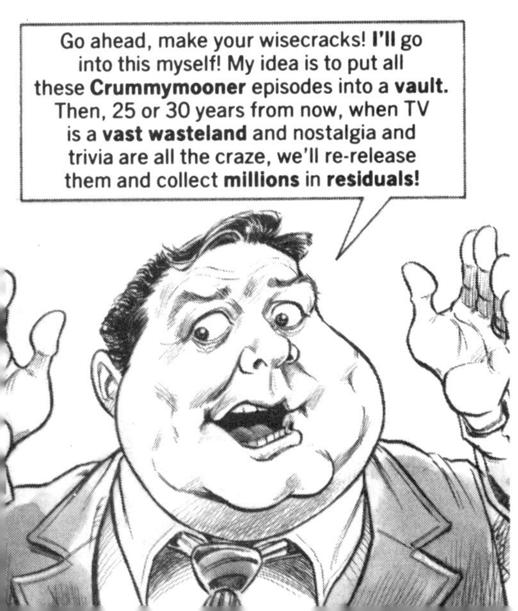
Go ahead, make your wisecracks! I'll go into this myself! My idea is to put all these Crummymooner episodes into a vault. Then, 25 or 30 years from now, when TV is a vast wasteland and nostalgia and trivia are all the craze, we'll re-release them and collect millions in residuals!

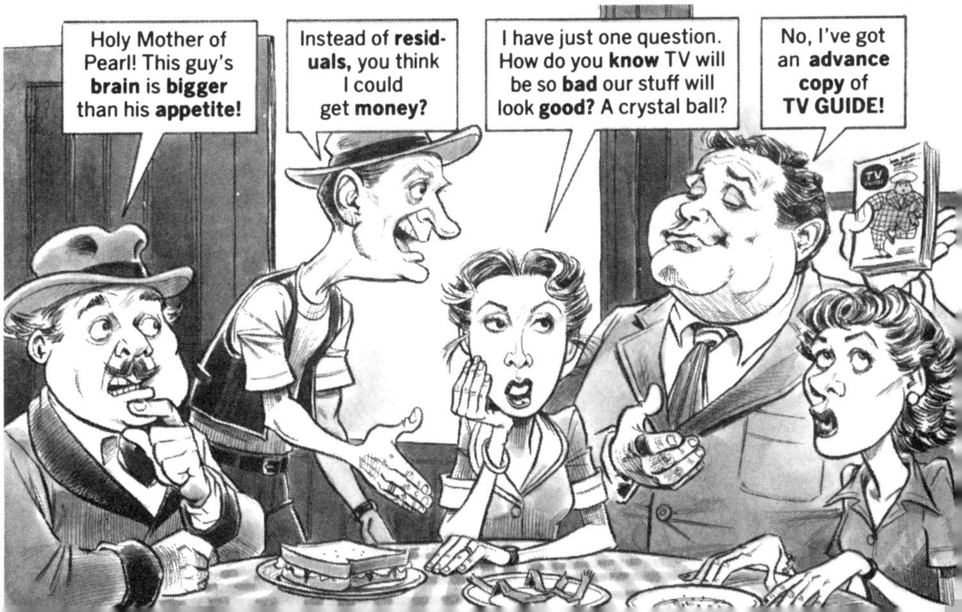
Holy Mother of Pearl! This guy's brain is bigger than his appetite!
Instead of residuals, you think I could get money?
I have just one question. How do you know TV will be so bad our stuff will look good? A crystal ball?
No, I've got an advance copy of TV GUIDE!
TV

FOPS AND ROBBERS DEPT.

Nowadays it costs a lot of money to be an undercover cop, especially in Florida! High rents? Pay-offs to squealers? Chicken feed! No, the big bucks have to be spent for the trendiest and most over-priced designer fashions and hair styles or you lose your job! In other words, you gotta pay the...

MIAMI PRICE

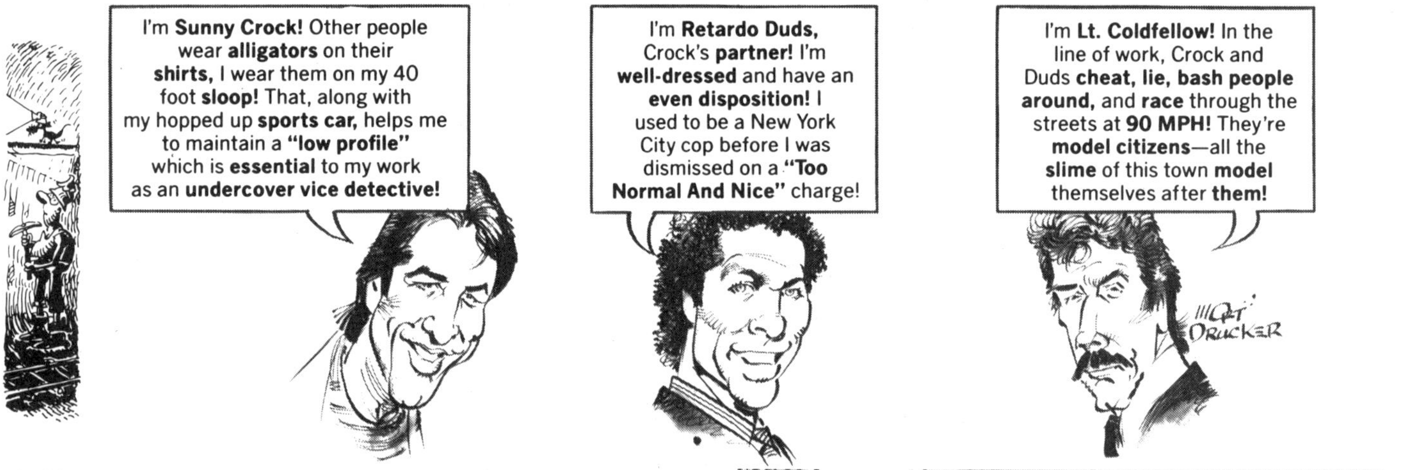
I'm **Sunny Crock!** Other people wear **alligators** on their **shirts,** I wear them on my 40 foot **sloop!** That, along with my hopped up **sports car,** helps me to maintain a **"low profile"** which is **essential** to my work as an **undercover vice detective!**
I'm **Retardo Duds,** Crock's **partner!** I'm **well-dressed** and have an **even disposition!** I used to be a New York City cop before I was dismissed on a **"Too Normal And Nice"** charge!
I'm **Lt. Coldfellow!** In the line of work, Crock and Duds **cheat, lie, bash people around,** and **race** through the streets at **90 MPH!** They're **model citizens**—all the **slime** of this town **model** themselves after **them!**
MORT DRUCKER

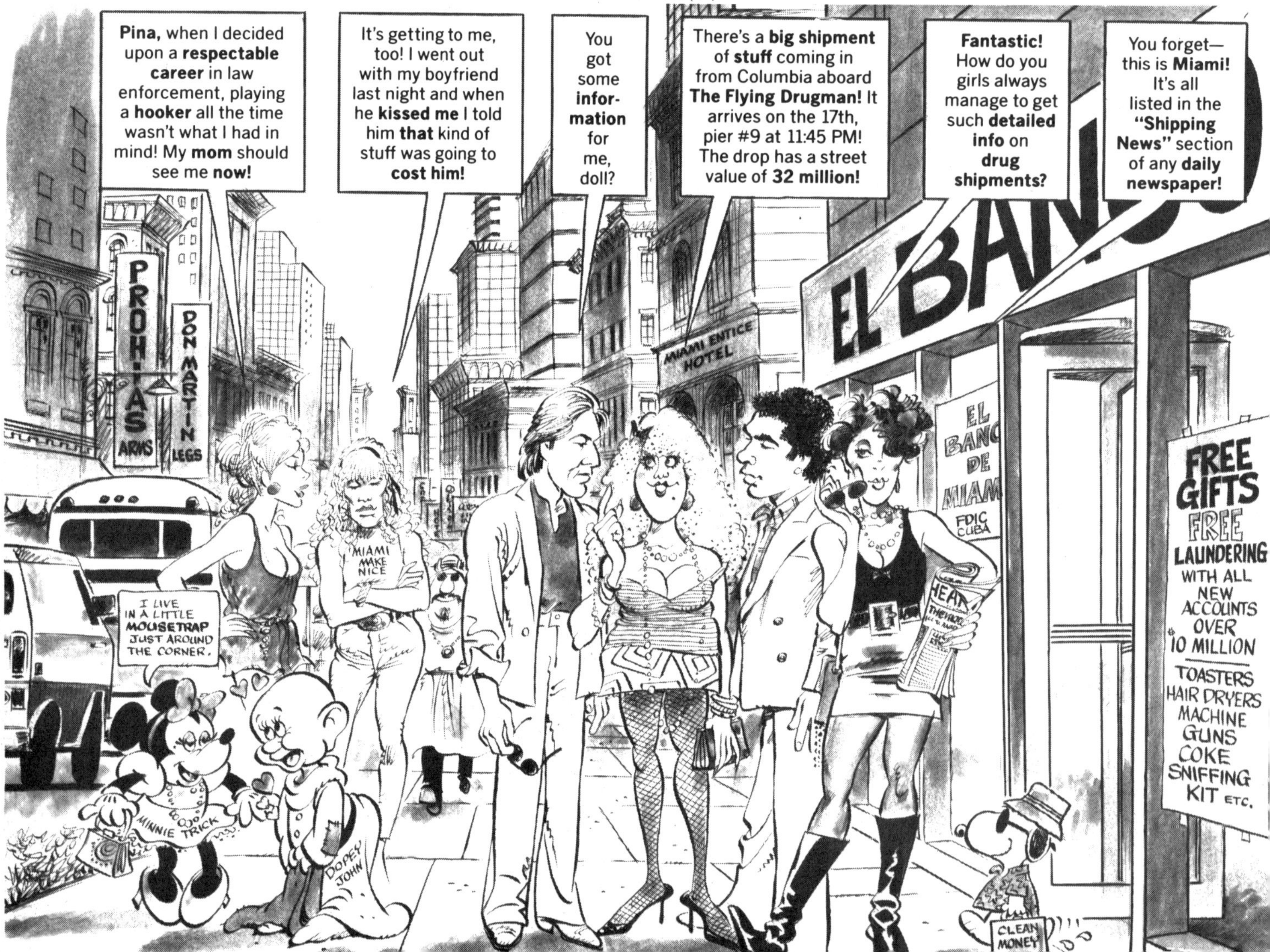
Pina, when I decided upon a **respectable career** in law enforcement, playing a **hooker** all the time wasn't what I had in mind! My **mom** should see me **now!**
It's getting to me, too! I went out with my boyfriend last night and when he **kissed me** I told him **that** kind of stuff was going to **cost him!**
You got some **information** for me, doll?
There's a **big shipment** of **stuff** coming in from Columbia aboard **The Flying Drugman!** It arrives on the 17th, pier #9 at 11:45 PM! The drop has a street value of **32 million!**
Fantastic! How do you girls always manage to get such **detailed info** on **drug shipments?**
You forget—this is **Miami!** It's all listed in the **"Shipping News"** section of any **daily newspaper!**
PROHI-TAS ARMS
DON MARTIN LEGS
MIAMI ENTICE HOTEL
EL BAN
EL BANC DE MIAM
FDIC CUBA
MIAMI MAKE NICE
I LIVE IN A LITTLE MOUSETRAP JUST AROUND THE CORNER.
MINNIE TRICK
DOPEY JOHN
FREE GIFTS FREE LAUNDERING WITH ALL NEW ACCOUNTS OVER $10 MILLION
TOASTERS HAIR DRYERS MACHINE GUNS COKE SNIFFING KIT ETC.
CLEAN MONEY

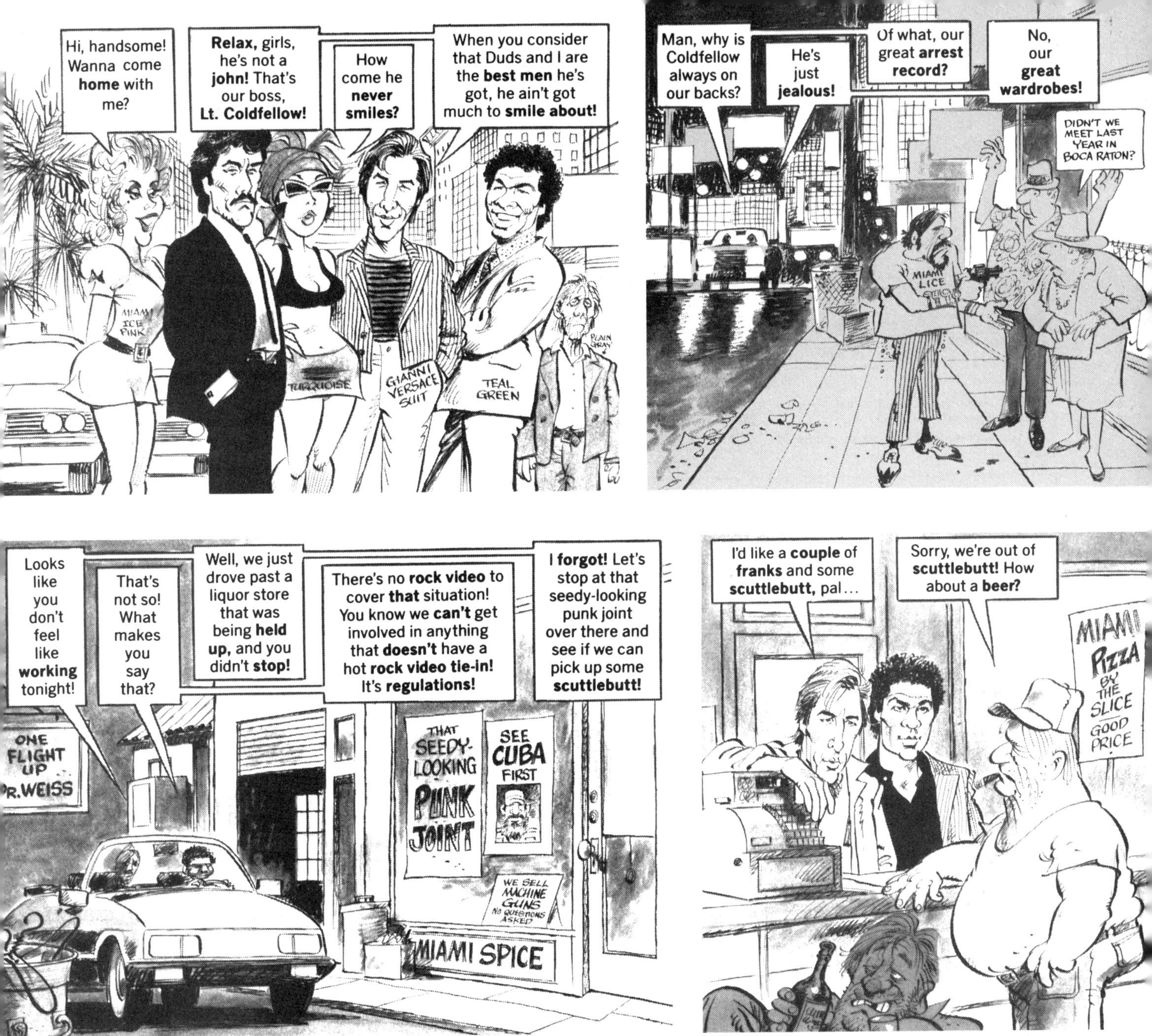
Hi, handsome! Wanna come **home** with me?
Relax, girls, he's not a **john!** That's our boss, **Lt. Coldfellow!**
How come he **never smiles?**
When you consider that Duds and I are the **best men** he's got, he ain't got much to **smile about!**
MIAMI ICE PINK
TURQUOISE
GIANNI VERSACE SUIT
TEAL GREEN
PLAIN GRAY
Man, why is Coldfellow always on our backs?
He's just **jealous!**
Of what, our great **arrest record?**
No, our **great wardrobes!**
DIDN'T WE MEET LAST YEAR IN BOCA RATON?
MIAMI LICE
Looks like you don't feel like **working** tonight!
That's not so! What makes you say that?
Well, we just drove past a liquor store that was being **held up,** and you didn't **stop!**
There's no **rock video** to cover **that** situation! You know we **can't** get involved in anything that **doesn't** have a hot **rock video tie-in!** It's **regulations!**
I **forgot!** Let's stop at that seedy-looking punk joint over there and see if we can pick up some **scuttlebutt!**
ONE FLIGHT UP DR. WEISS
THAT SEEDY-LOOKING PUNK JOINT
SEE CUBA FIRST
WE SELL MACHINE GUNS NO QUESTIONS ASKED
MIAMI SPICE
I'd like a **couple** of **franks** and some **scuttlebutt,** pal...
Sorry, we're out of **scuttlebutt!** How about a **beer?**
MIAMI PIZZA BY THE SLICE GOOD PRICE

ARTIST: MORT DRUCKER WRITER: LOU SILVERSTONE

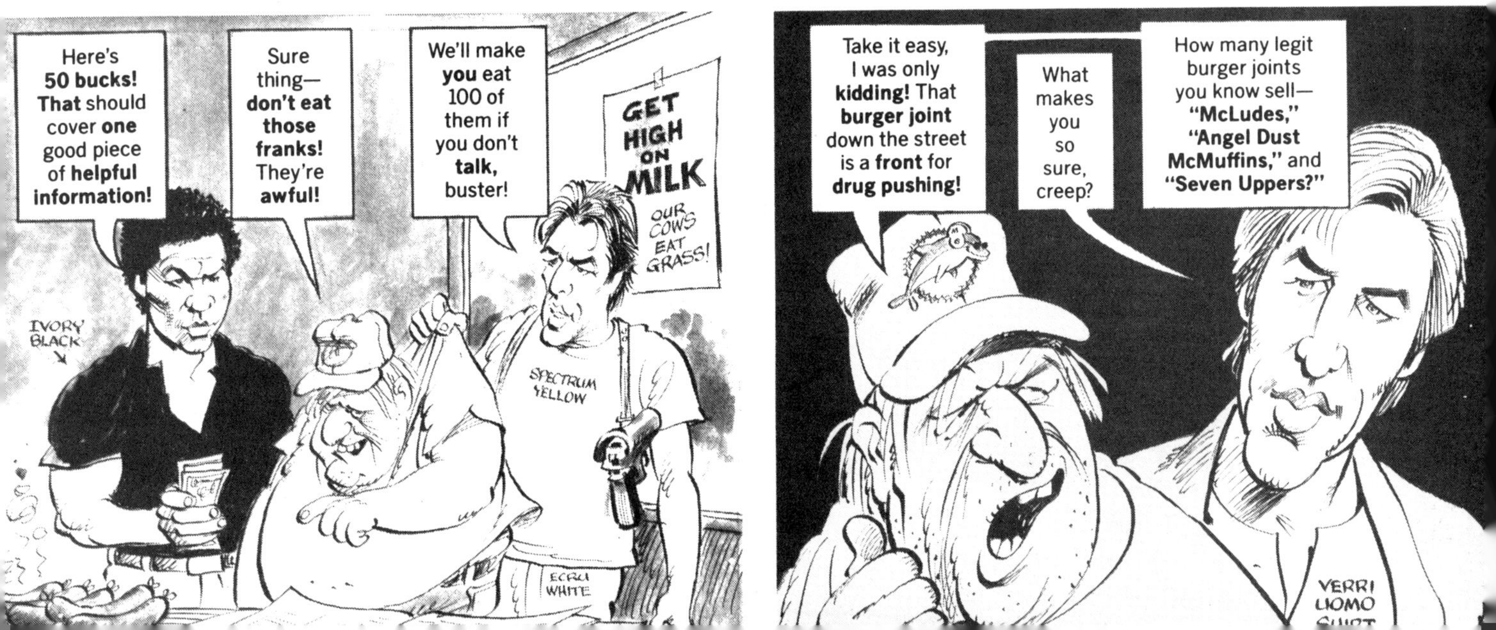
Here's **50 bucks! That** should cover **one** good piece of **helpful information!**
Sure thing— **don't eat those franks!** They're **awful!**
We'll make **you** eat 100 of them if you don't **talk,** buster!
GET HIGH ON MILK
OUR COWS EAT GRASS!
IVORY BLACK
SPECTRUM YELLOW
ECRU WHITE
Take it easy, I was only **kidding!** That **burger joint** down the street is a **front** for **drug pushing!**
What makes you so sure, creep?
How many legit burger joints you know sell— **"McLudes," "Angel Dust McMuffins,"** and **"Seven Uppers?"**
VERRI UOMO SUIT

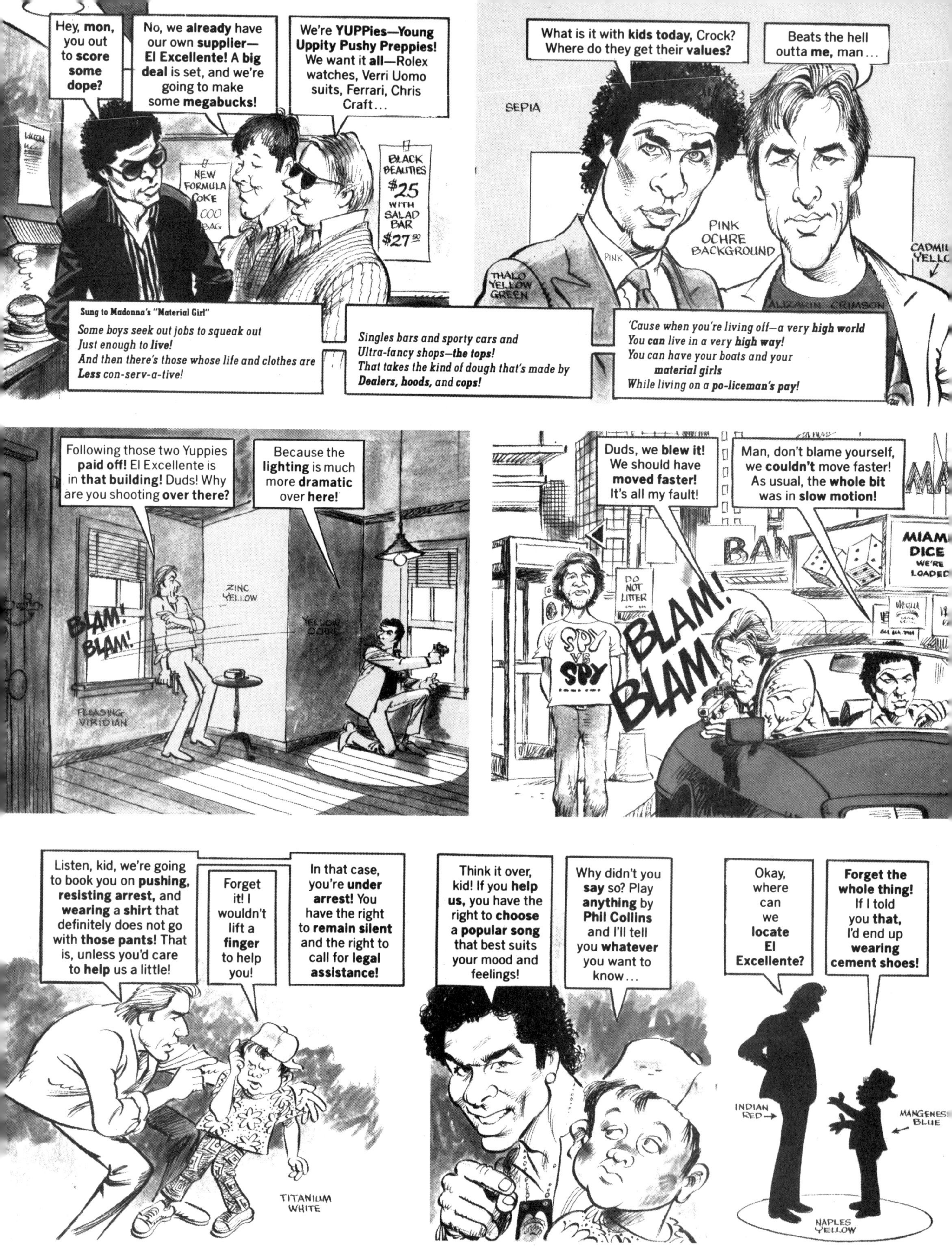
Hey, mon, you out to score some dope?
No, we already have our own supplier—El Excellente! A big deal is set, and we're going to make some megabucks!
We're YUPPies—Young Uppity Pushy Preppies! We want it all—Rolex watches, Verri Uomo suits, Ferrari, Chris Craft...
NEW FORMULA COKE
BLACK BEAUTIES $25 WITH SALAD BAR $27.50
What is it with kids today, Crock? Where do they get their values?
Beats the hell outta me, man...
SEPIA
PINK OCHRE BACKGROUND
PINK
THALO YELLOW GREEN
ALIZARIN CRIMSON
Sung to Madonna's "Material Girl"
Some boys seek out jobs to squeak out
Just enough to live!
And then there's those whose life and clothes are
Less con-serv-a-tive!
Singles bars and sporty cars and
Ultra-fancy shops—the tops!
That takes the kind of dough that's made by
Dealers, hoods, and cops!
'Cause when you're living off—a very high world
You can live in a very high way!
You can have your boats and your
material girls
While living on a po-liceman's pay!
Following those two Yuppies paid off! El Excellente is in that building! Duds! Why are you shooting over there?
Because the lighting is much more dramatic over here!
ZINC YELLOW
YELLOW OCRE
BLAM! BLAM!
PLEASING VIRIDIAN
Duds, we blew it! We should have moved faster! It's all my fault!
Man, don't blame yourself, we couldn't move faster! As usual, the whole bit was in slow motion!
DICE WE'RE LOADED
DO NOT LITTER
SPY VS SPY
BLAM! BLAM!
Listen, kid, we're going to book you on pushing, resisting arrest, and wearing a shirt that definitely does not go with those pants! That is, unless you'd care to help us a little!
Forget it! I wouldn't lift a finger to help you!
In that case, you're under arrest! You have the right to remain silent and the right to call for legal assistance!
TITANIUM WHITE
Think it over, kid! If you help us, you have the right to choose a popular song that best suits your mood and feelings!
Why didn't you say so? Play anything by Phil Collins and I'll tell you whatever you want to know...
Okay, where can we locate El Excellente?
Forget the whole thing! If I told you that, I'd end up wearing cement shoes!
INDIAN RED
MANGENESE BLUE
NAPLES YELLOW

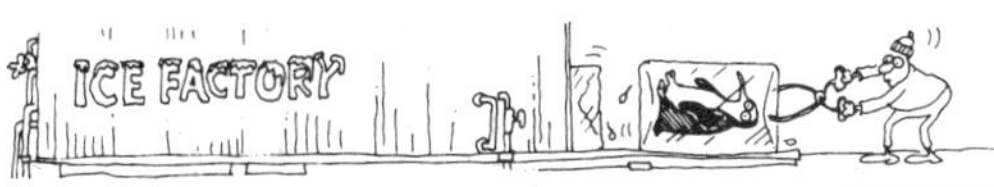
ICE FACTORY

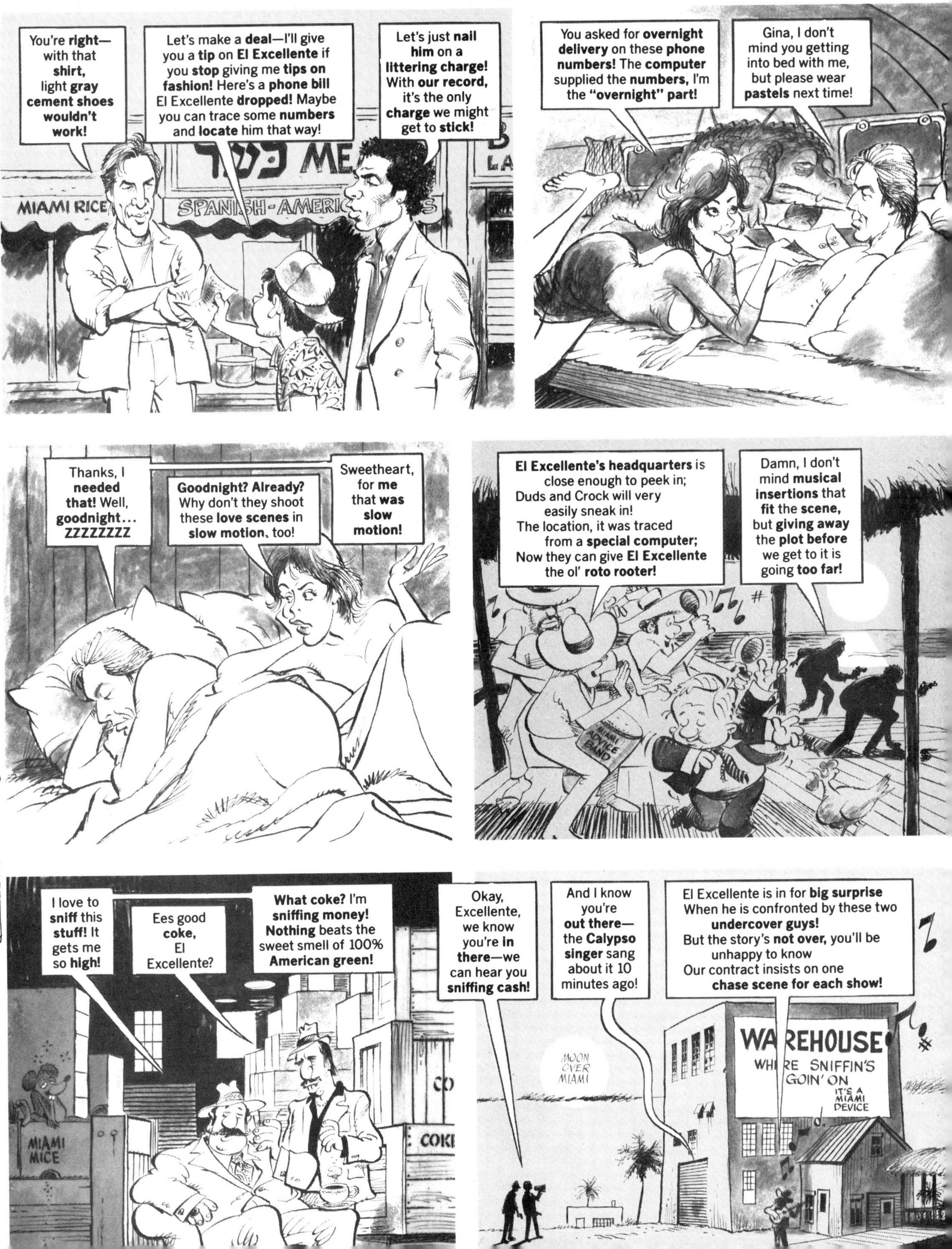
You're right—with that shirt, light gray cement shoes wouldn't work!
Let's make a deal—I'll give you a tip on El Excellente if you stop giving me tips on fashion! Here's a phone bill El Excellente dropped! Maybe you can trace some numbers and locate him that way!
Let's just nail him on a littering charge! With our record, it's the only charge we might get to stick!
MIAMI RICE
SPANISH-AMERIC
You asked for overnight delivery on these phone numbers! The computer supplied the numbers, I'm the "overnight" part!
Gina, I don't mind you getting into bed with me, but please wear pastels next time!
Thanks, I needed that! Well, goodnight... ZZZZZZZZ
Goodnight? Already? Why don't they shoot these love scenes in slow motion, too!
Sweetheart, for me that was slow motion!
El Excellente's headquarters is close enough to peek in; Duds and Crock will very easily sneak in! The location, it was traced from a special computer; Now they can give El Excellente the ol' roto rooter!
Damn, I don't mind musical insertions that fit the scene, but giving away the plot before we get to it is going too far!
MIAMI ADVICE BAND
I love to sniff this stuff! It gets me so high!
Ees good coke, El Excellente?
What coke? I'm sniffing money! Nothing beats the sweet smell of 100% American green!
MIAMI MICE
COKE
Okay, Excellente, we know you're in there—we can hear you sniffing cash!
And I know you're out there—the Calypso singer sang about it 10 minutes ago!
El Excellente is in for big surprise When he is confronted by these two undercover guys! But the story's not over, you'll be unhappy to know Our contract insists on one chase scene for each show!
MOON OVER MIAMI
WAREHOUSE WHERE SNIFFIN'S GOIN' ON
IT'S A MIAMI DEVICE

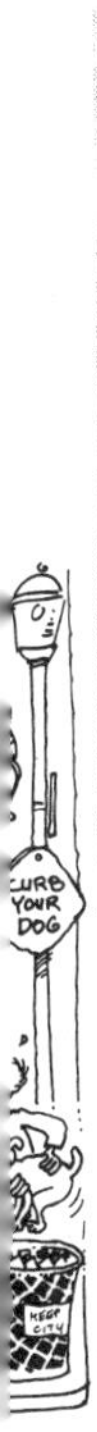
CURB YOUR DOG

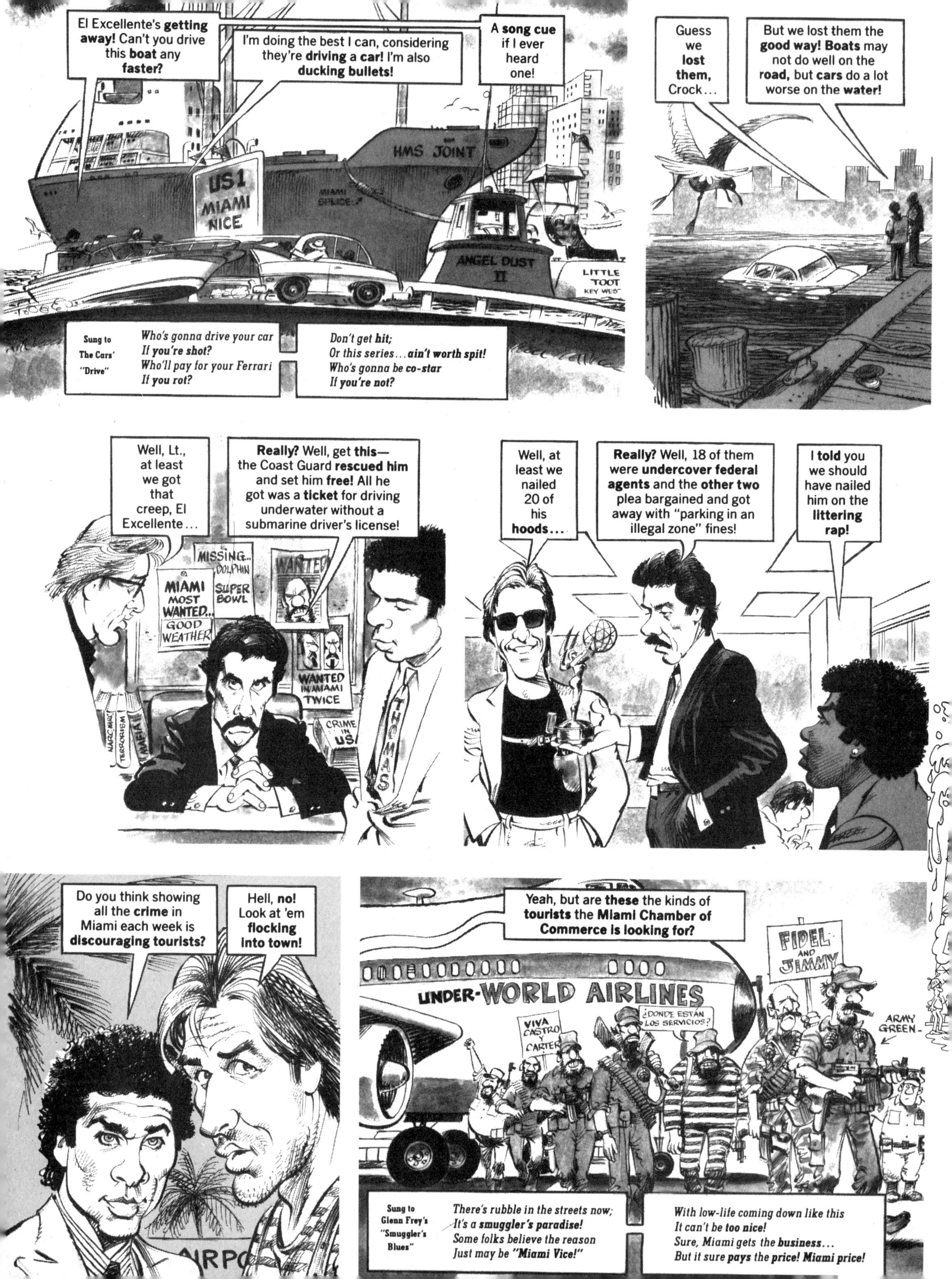

El Excellente's **getting away!** Can't you drive this **boat** any **faster?**
I'm doing the best I can, considering they're **driving a car!** I'm also **ducking bullets!**
A **song cue** if I ever heard one!
HMS JOINT
US1 MIAMI NICE
ANGEL DUST II
LITTLE TOOT
Sung to The Cars' "Drive"
Who's gonna drive your car
If you're ***shot?***
Who'll pay for your Ferrari
If you ***rot?***
Don't get ***hit;***
Or this series... ***ain't worth spit!***
Who's gonna be ***co-star***
If you're ***not?***
Guess we **lost them,** Crock...
But we lost them the **good way! Boats** may not do well on the **road,** but **cars** do a lot worse on the **water!**
Well, Lt., at least we got that creep, El Excellente...
Really? Well, get **this**— the Coast Guard **rescued him** and set him **free!** All he got was a **ticket** for driving underwater without a submarine driver's license!
MISSING... DOLPHIN
SUPER BOWL
MIAMI MOST WANTED... GOOD WEATHER
WANTED
WANTED IN MIAMI TWICE
CRIME IN US
TERRORISM
MAFIA
THOMAS
Well, at least we nailed 20 of his **hoods...**
Really? Well, 18 of them were **undercover federal agents** and the **other two** plea bargained and got away with "parking in an illegal zone" fines!
I **told** you we should have nailed him on the **littering rap!**
Do you think showing all the **crime** in Miami each week is **discouraging tourists?**
Hell, **no!** Look at 'em **flocking into town!**
AIRPO
Yeah, but are **these** the kinds of **tourists** the **Miami Chamber of Commerce is looking for?**
UNDER-WORLD AIRLINES
VIVA CASTRO Y CARTER
¿DONDE ESTAN LOS SERVICIOS?
FIDEL AND JIMMY
ARMY GREEN-
Sung to Glenn Frey's "Smuggler's Blues"
There's rubble in the streets now;
It's a ***smuggler's paradise!***
Some folks believe the reason
Just may be ***"Miami Vice!"***
With low-life coming down like this
It can't be ***too nice!***
Sure, Miami gets the ***business...***
But it sure ***pays*** *the* ***price! Miami price!***

INN-SIPID TV DEPARTMENT

A few years ago, Bob Newhart played the part of a bumbling husband with a sensible wife and some dopey friends. But you can't stand still in the TV Sitcom business! So Bob made a dramatic career change. Now, he's a bumbling husband with a sensible wife and some *new* dopey friends. In a mind-blowing change of format, one of the mildest, most ineffective psychologists in Chicago has now become one of the mildest, most ineffective innkeepers in Vermont! Yes, it's a new series! But it's a...

Not-So-New-Hart

ARTIST: ANGELO TORRES WRITER: ARNIE KOGEN

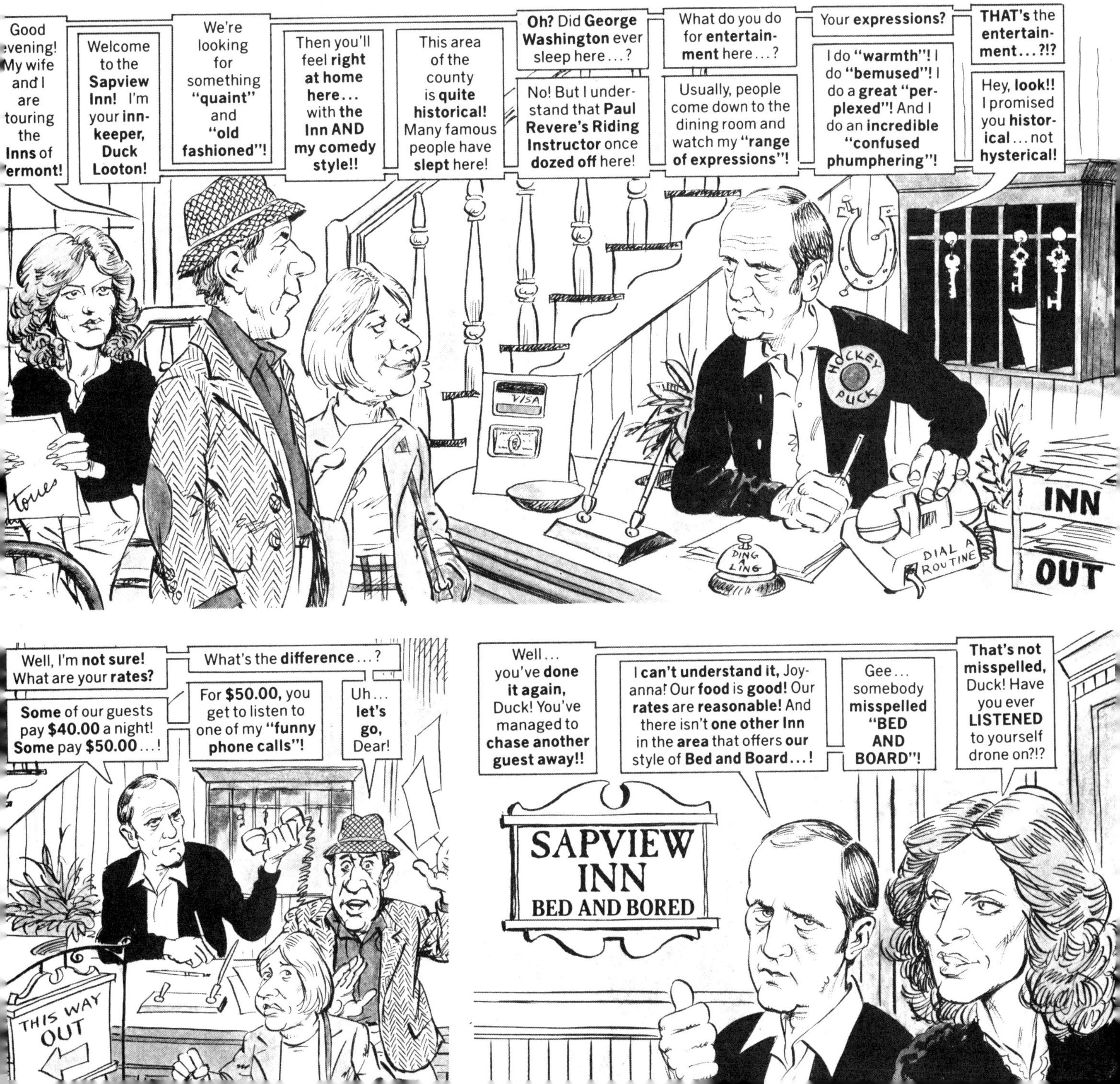
Good vening! My wife and I are touring the Inns of ermont!
Welcome to the Sapview Inn! I'm your innkeeper, Duck Looton!
We're looking for something "quaint" and "old fashioned"!
Then you'll feel right at home here... with the Inn AND my comedy style!!
This area of the county is quite historical! Many famous people have slept here!
Oh? Did George Washington ever sleep here...?
No! But I understand that Paul Revere's Riding Instructor once dozed off here!
What do you do for entertainment here...?
Usually, people come down to the dining room and watch my "range of expressions"!
Your expressions?
I do "warmth"! I do "bemused"! I do a great "perplexed"! And I do an incredible "confused phumphering"!
THAT's the entertainment...?!?
Hey, look!! I promised you historical... not hysterical!
VISA
HOCKEY PUCK
DING A LING
DIAL A ROUTINE
INN
OUT
Well, I'm not sure! What are your rates?
Some of our guests pay $40.00 a night! Some pay $50.00...!
What's the difference...?
For $50.00, you get to listen to one of my "funny phone calls"!
Uh... let's go, Dear!
THIS WAY OUT
Well... you've done it again, Duck! You've managed to chase another guest away!!
I can't understand it, Joyanna! Our food is good! Our rates are reasonable! And there isn't one other Inn in the area that offers our style of Bed and Board...!
SAPVIEW INN BED AND BORED
Gee... somebody misspelled "BED AND BOARD"!
That's not misspelled, Duck! Have you ever LISTENED to yourself drone on?!?

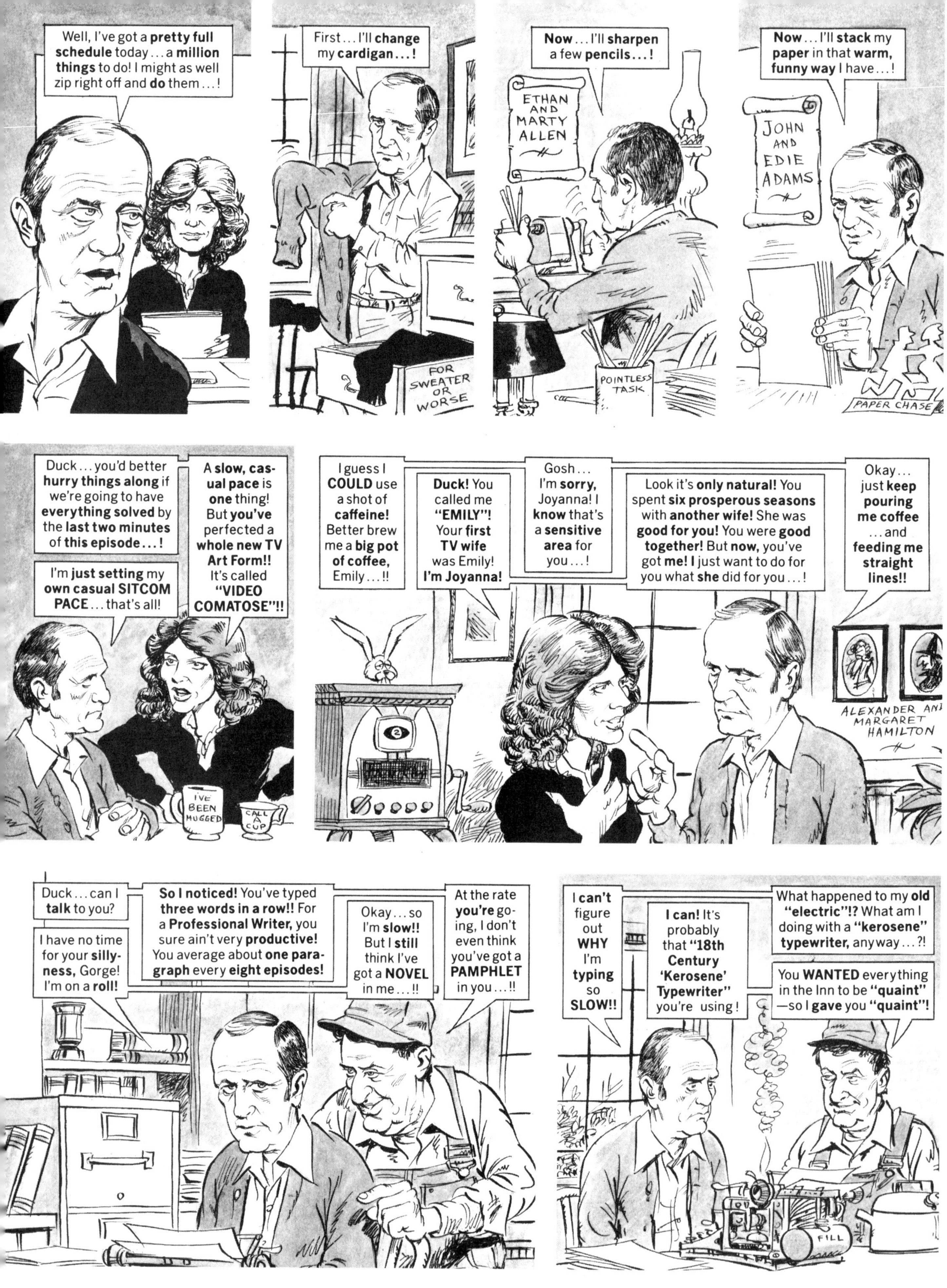
Well, I've got a **pretty full schedule** today . . . a **million things** to do! I might as well zip right off and **do** them . . . !
First . . . I'll **change** my **cardigan . . . !**
FOR SWEATER OR WORSE
Now . . . I'll **sharpen** a few **pencils . . . !**
ETHAN AND MARTY ALLEN
POINTLESS TASK
Now . . . I'll **stack** my **paper** in that **warm, funny way** I have . . . !
JOHN AND EDIE ADAMS
PAPER CHASE
Duck . . . you'd better **hurry things along** if we're going to have **everything solved** by the **last two minutes** of **this episode . . . !**
I'm **just setting** my **own casual SITCOM PACE** . . . that's all!
A **slow, casual pace** is **one** thing! But **you've** perfected a **whole new TV Art Form!!** It's called **"VIDEO COMATOSE"!!**
I'VE BEEN MUGGED
CALL A CUP
I guess I **COULD** use a shot of **caffeine!** Better brew me a **big pot of coffee,** Emily . . . !!
Duck! You called me **"EMILY"!** Your **first TV wife** was Emily! **I'm Joyanna!**
Gosh . . . I'm **sorry,** Joyanna! I **know** that's a **sensitive area** for you . . . !
Look it's **only natural!** You spent **six prosperous seasons** with **another wife!** She was **good for you!** You were **good together!** But **now,** you've got **me!** I just want to do for you what **she** did for you . . . !
Okay . . . just **keep pouring me coffee** . . . and **feeding me straight lines!!**
ALEXANDER AND MARGARET HAMILTON
Duck . . . can I **talk** to you?
I have no time for your **silly-ness,** Gorge! I'm on a **roll!**
So I noticed! You've typed **three words in a row!!** For a **Professional Writer,** you sure ain't very **productive!** You average about **one para-graph** every **eight episodes!**
Okay . . . so I'm **slow!!** But I **still** think I've got a **NOVEL** in me . . . !!
At the rate **you're** go-ing, I don't even think you've got a **PAMPHLET** in you . . . !!
I **can't** figure out **WHY** I'm **typing** so **SLOW!!**
I can! It's probably that **"18th Century 'Kerosene' Typewriter"** you're using!
What happened to my **old "electric"!?** What am I doing with a **"kerosene" typewriter,** anyway . . . ?!
You **WANTED** everything in the Inn to be **"quaint"** —so I **gave** you **"quaint"!**
FILL

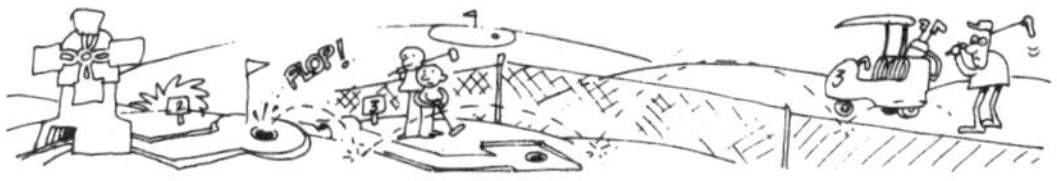
FLOP!

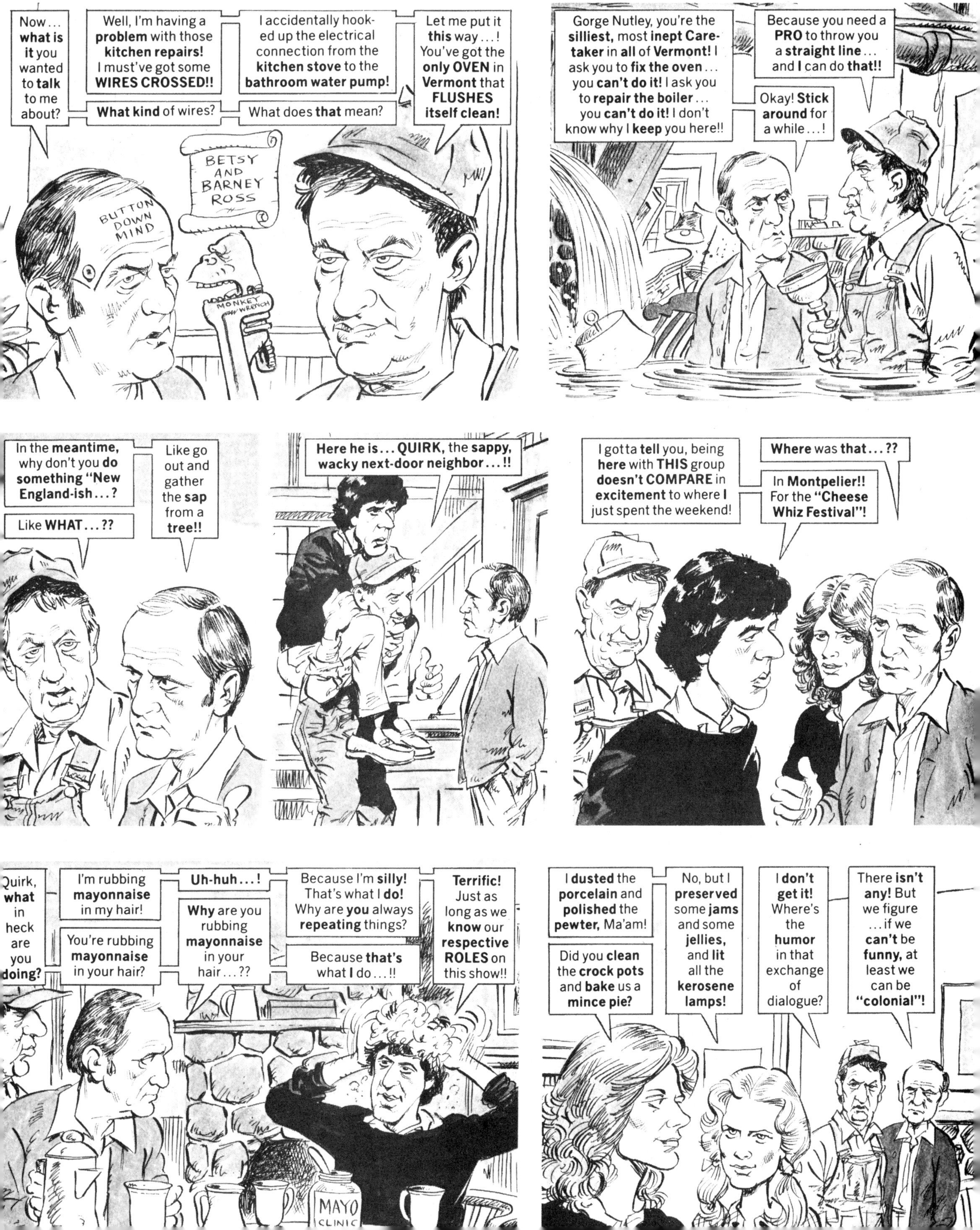
Now... what is it you wanted to talk to me about?
Well, I'm having a problem with those kitchen repairs! I must've got some WIRES CROSSED!!
What kind of wires?
I accidentally hooked up the electrical connection from the kitchen stove to the bathroom water pump!
What does that mean?
Let me put it this way...! You've got the only OVEN in Vermont that FLUSHES itself clean!
BUTTON DOWN MIND
BETSY AND BARNEY ROSS
MONKEY WRENCH
Gorge Nutley, you're the silliest, most inept Caretaker in all of Vermont! I ask you to fix the oven... you can't do it! I ask you to repair the boiler... you can't do it! I don't know why I keep you here!!
Okay! Stick around for a while...!
Because you need a PRO to throw you a straight line... and I can do that!!
In the meantime, why don't you do something "New England-ish...?
Like WHAT...??
Like go out and gather the sap from a tree!!
Here he is... QUIRK, the sappy, wacky next-door neighbor...!!
I gotta tell you, being here with THIS group doesn't COMPARE in excitement to where I just spent the weekend!
Where was that...??
In Montpelier!! For the "Cheese Whiz Festival"!
Quirk, what in heck are you doing?
I'm rubbing mayonnaise in my hair!
You're rubbing mayonnaise in your hair?
Uh-huh...!
Why are you rubbing mayonnaise in your hair...??
Because I'm silly! That's what I do! Why are you always repeating things?
Because that's what I do...!!
Terrific! Just as long as we know our respective ROLES on this show!!
MAYO CLINIC
I dusted the porcelain and polished the pewter, Ma'am!
Did you clean the crock pots and bake us a mince pie?
No, but I preserved some jams and some jellies, and lit all the kerosene lamps!
I don't get it! Where's the humor in that exchange of dialogue?
There isn't any! But we figure ...if we can't be funny, at least we can be "colonial"!

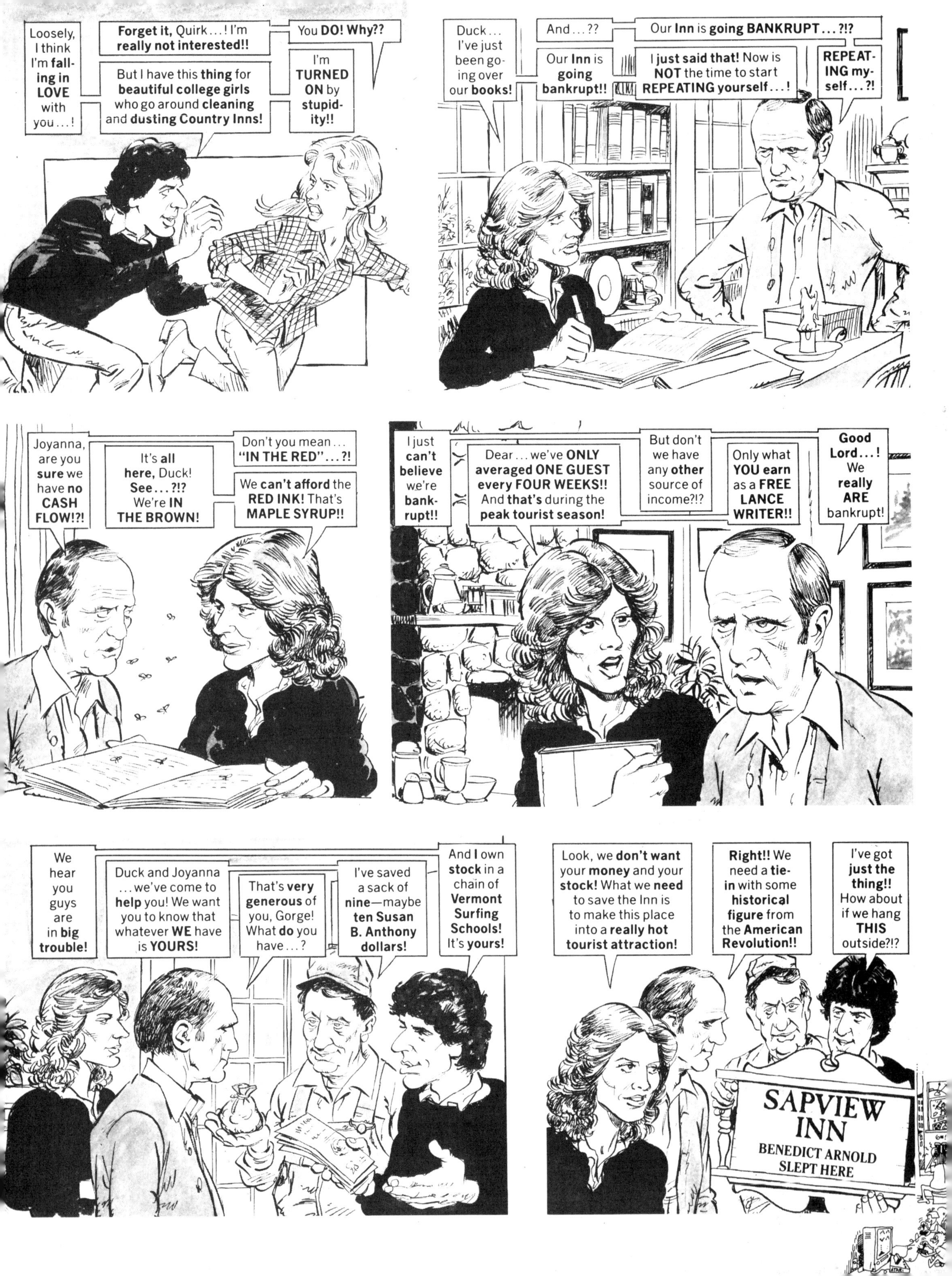
Loosely, I think I'm falling in LOVE with you...!
Forget it, Quirk...! I'm really not interested!!
You DO! Why??
But I have this thing for beautiful college girls who go around cleaning and dusting Country Inns!
I'm TURNED ON by stupidity!!
Duck... I've just been going over our books!
And...??
Our Inn is going BANKRUPT...?!?
Our Inn is going bankrupt!!
I just said that! Now is NOT the time to start REPEATING yourself...!
REPEATING myself...?!
Joyanna, are you sure we have no CASH FLOW!?!
It's all here, Duck! See...?!? We're IN THE BROWN!
Don't you mean... "IN THE RED"...?!
We can't afford the RED INK! That's MAPLE SYRUP!!
I just can't believe we're bankrupt!!
Dear... we've ONLY averaged ONE GUEST every FOUR WEEKS!! And that's during the peak tourist season!
But don't we have any other source of income?!?
Only what YOU earn as a FREE LANCE WRITER!!
Good Lord...! We really ARE bankrupt!
We hear you guys are in big trouble!
Duck and Joyanna ...we've come to help you! We want you to know that whatever WE have is YOURS!
That's very generous of you, Gorge! What do you have...?
I've saved a sack of nine—maybe ten Susan B. Anthony dollars!
And I own stock in a chain of Vermont Surfing Schools! It's yours!
Look, we don't want your money and your stock! What we need to save the Inn is to make this place into a really hot tourist attraction!
Right!! We need a tie-in with some historical figure from the American Revolution!!
I've got just the thing!! How about if we hang THIS outside?!?
SAPVIEW INN
BENEDICT ARNOLD SLEPT HERE

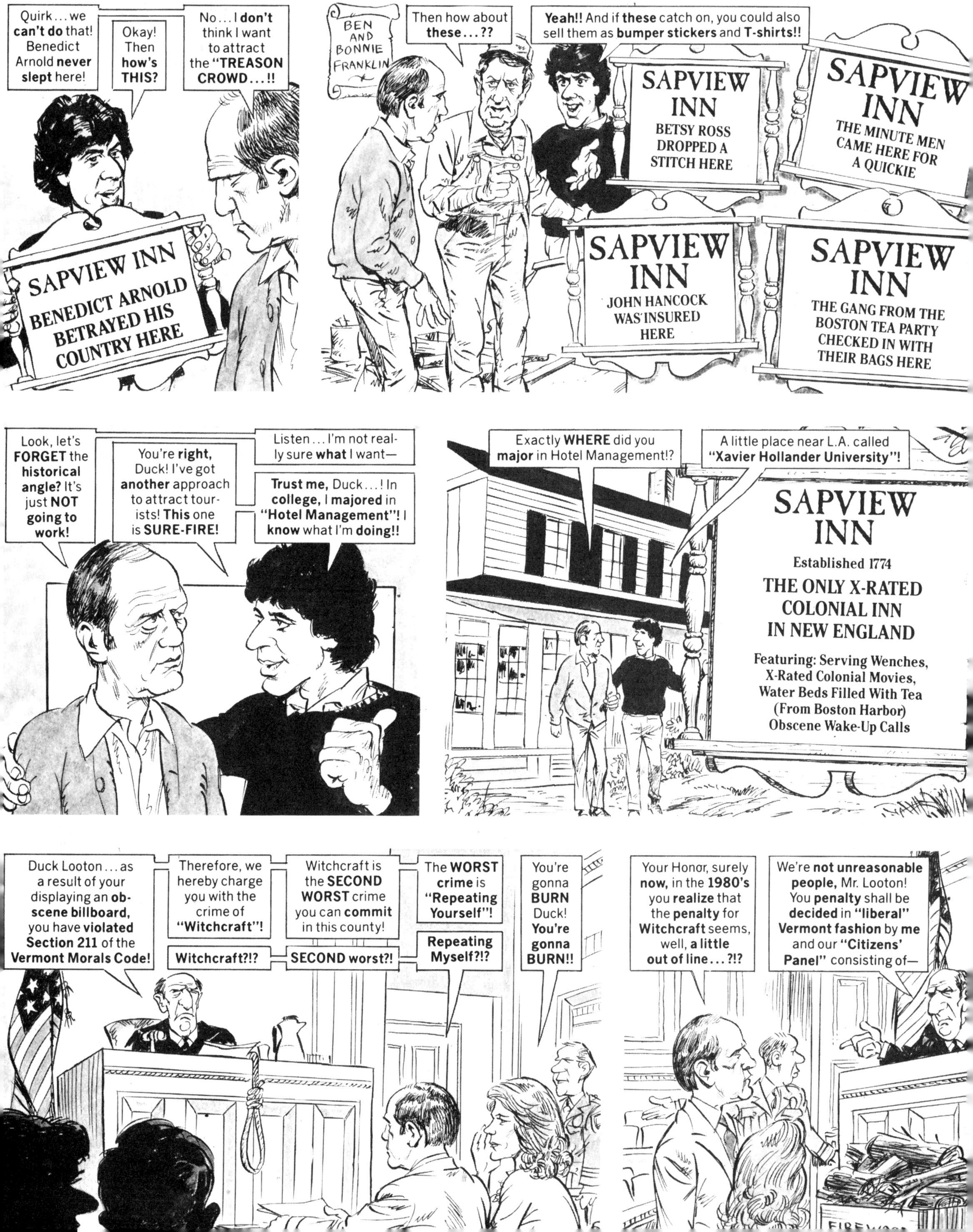

Quirk... we can't do that! Benedict Arnold never slept here!
Okay! Then how's THIS?
SAPVIEW INN
BENEDICT ARNOLD BETRAYED HIS COUNTRY HERE
No... I don't think I want to attract the "TREASON CROWD...!!
BEN AND BONNIE FRANKLIN
Then how about these...??
Yeah!! And if these catch on, you could also sell them as bumper stickers and T-shirts!!
SAPVIEW INN
BETSY ROSS DROPPED A STITCH HERE
SAPVIEW INN
THE MINUTE MEN CAME HERE FOR A QUICKIE
SAPVIEW INN
JOHN HANCOCK WAS INSURED HERE
SAPVIEW INN
THE GANG FROM THE BOSTON TEA PARTY CHECKED IN WITH THEIR BAGS HERE
Look, let's FORGET the historical angle? It's just NOT going to work!
You're right, Duck! I've got another approach to attract tourists! This one is SURE-FIRE!
Listen... I'm not really sure what I want—
Trust me, Duck...! In college, I majored in "Hotel Management"! I know what I'm doing!!
Exactly WHERE did you major in Hotel Management!?
A little place near L.A. called "Xavier Hollander University"!
SAPVIEW INN
Established 1774
THE ONLY X-RATED COLONIAL INN IN NEW ENGLAND
Featuring: Serving Wenches, X-Rated Colonial Movies, Water Beds Filled With Tea (From Boston Harbor) Obscene Wake-Up Calls
Duck Looton... as a result of your displaying an obscene billboard, you have violated Section 211 of the Vermont Morals Code!
Therefore, we hereby charge you with the crime of "Witchcraft"!
Witchcraft?!?
Witchcraft is the SECOND WORST crime you can commit in this county!
SECOND worst?!
The WORST crime is "Repeating Yourself"!
Repeating Myself?!?
You're gonna BURN Duck! You're gonna BURN!!
Your Honor, surely now, in the 1980's you realize that the penalty for Witchcraft seems, well, a little out of line...?!?
We're not unreasonable people, Mr. Looton! You penalty shall be decided in "liberal" Vermont fashion by me and our "Citizens' Panel" consisting of—

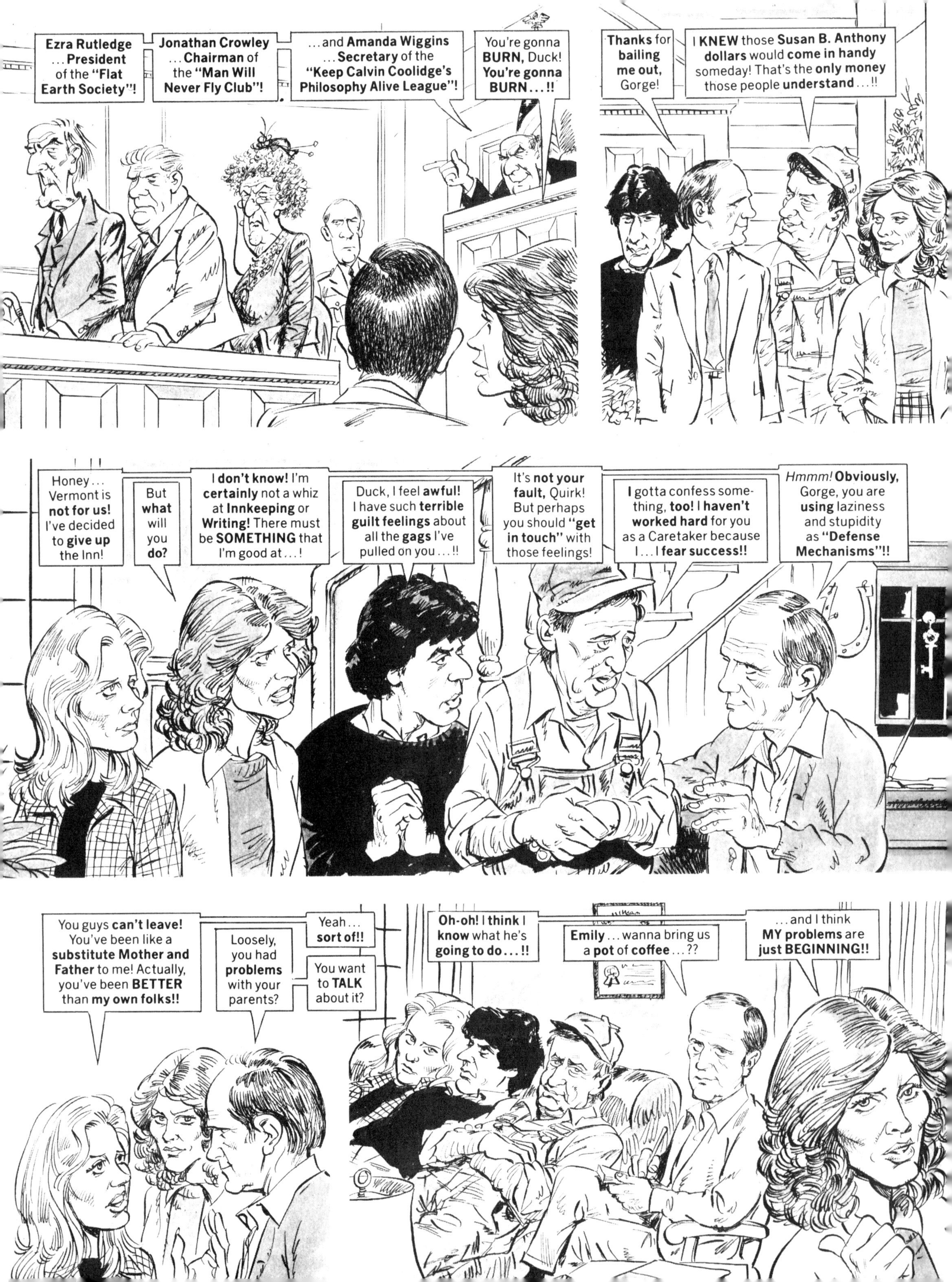
Ezra Rutledge ...President of the "Flat Earth Society"!
Jonathan Crowley ...Chairman of the "Man Will Never Fly Club"!
...and Amanda Wiggins ...Secretary of the "Keep Calvin Coolidge's Philosophy Alive League"!
You're gonna BURN, Duck! You're gonna BURN...!!
Thanks for bailing me out, Gorge!
I KNEW those Susan B. Anthony dollars would come in handy someday! That's the only money those people understand...!!
Honey... Vermont is not for us! I've decided to give up the Inn!
But what will you do?
I don't know! I'm certainly not a whiz at Innkeeping or Writing! There must be SOMETHING that I'm good at...!
Duck, I feel awful! I have such terrible guilt feelings about all the gags I've pulled on you...!!
It's not your fault, Quirk! But perhaps you should "get in touch" with those feelings!
I gotta confess something, too! I haven't worked hard for you as a Caretaker because I... I fear success!!
Hmmm! Obviously, Gorge, you are using laziness and stupidity as "Defense Mechanisms"!!
You guys can't leave! You've been like a substitute Mother and Father to me! Actually, you've been BETTER than my own folks!!
Loosely, you had problems with your parents?
Yeah... sort of!!
You want to TALK about it?
Oh-oh! I think I know what he's going to do...!!
Emily... wanna bring us a pot of coffee...??
...and I think MY problems are just BEGINNING!!

SLEUTH DECAY DEPT.

MURDER SHE HOPES

WRITER: DICK DE BARTOLO ARTIST: ANGELO TORRES

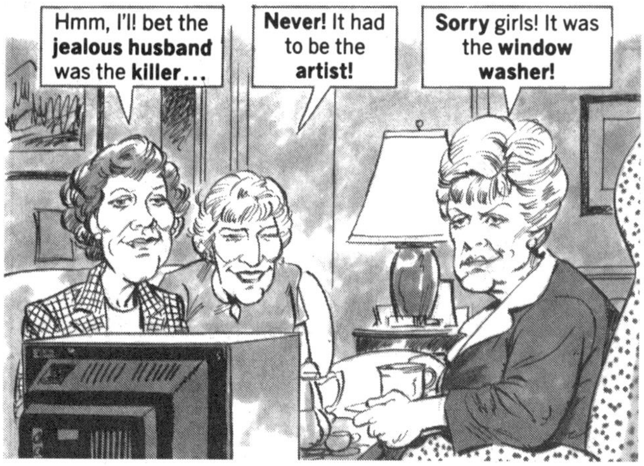
Hmm, I'll bet the jealous husband was the killer...
Never! It had to be the artist!
Sorry girls! It was the window washer!

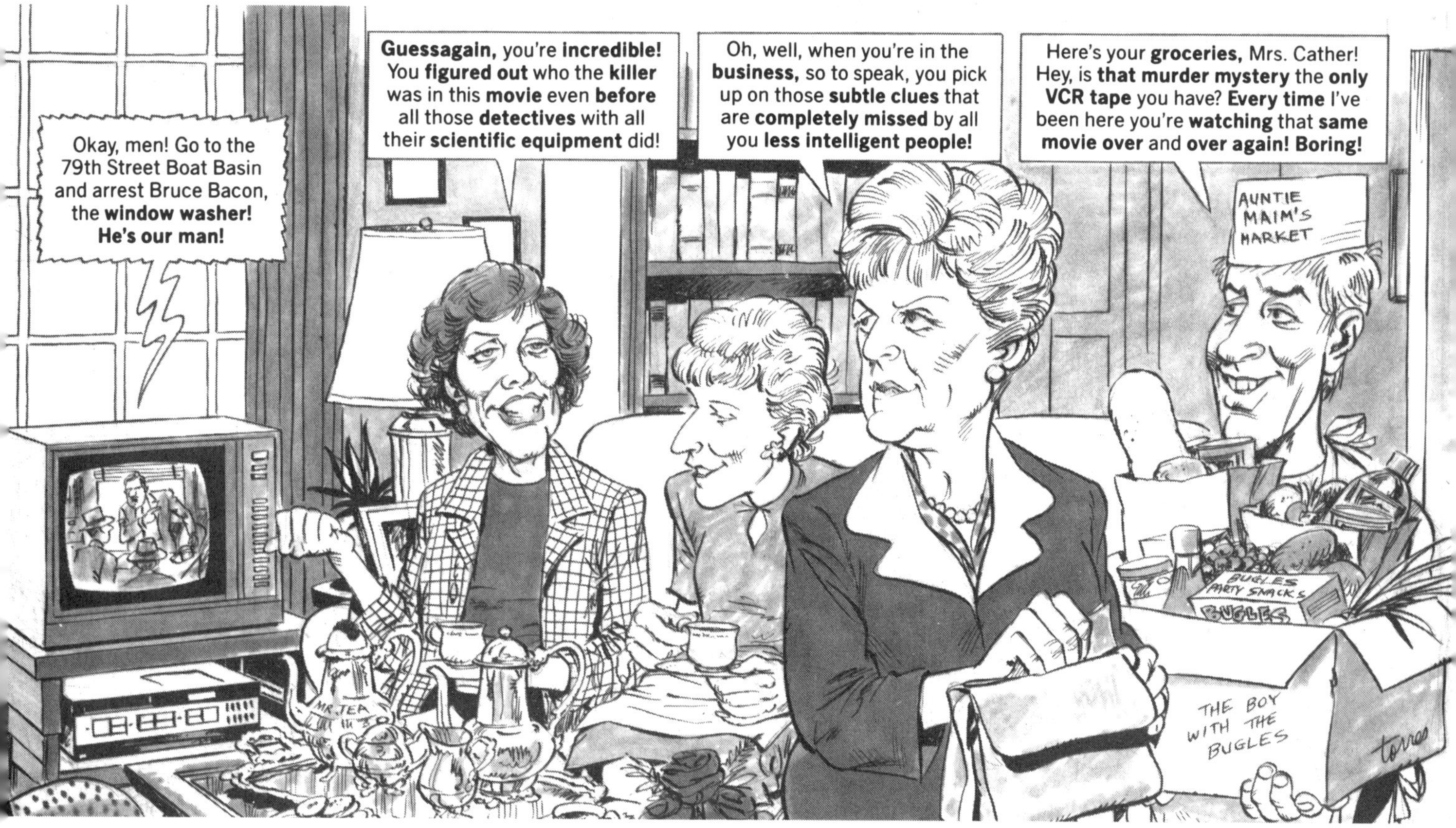
Okay, men! Go to the 79th Street Boat Basin and arrest Bruce Bacon, the window washer! He's our man!
Guessagain, you're incredible! You figured out who the killer was in this movie even before all those detectives with all their scientific equipment did!
Oh, well, when you're in the business, so to speak, you pick up on those subtle clues that are completely missed by all you less intelligent people!
Here's your groceries, Mrs. Cather! Hey, is that murder mystery the only VCR tape you have? Every time I've been here you're watching that same movie over and over again! Boring!
AUNTIE MAIM'S MARKET
MR. TEA
BUGLES PARTY SNACKS
BUGLES
THE BOY WITH THE BUGLES
torres

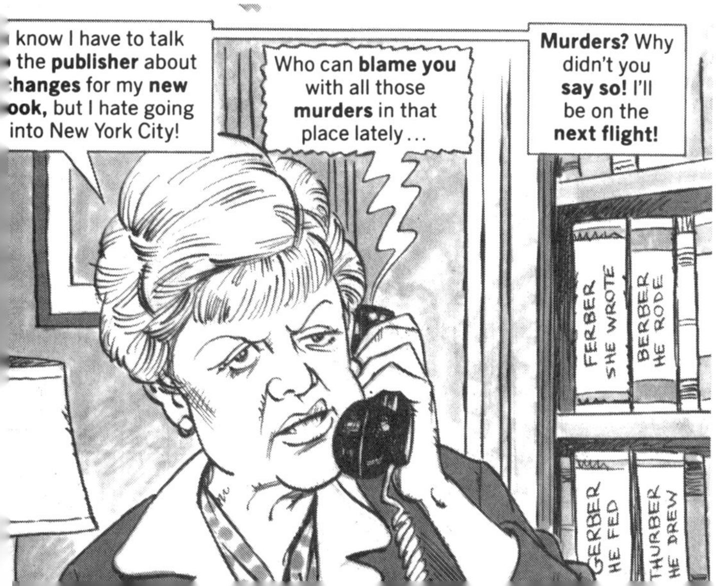
know I have to talk the publisher about hanges for my new ook, but I hate going into New York City!
Who can blame you with all those murders in that place lately...
Murders? Why didn't you say so! I'll be on the next flight!
FERBER SHE WROTE
BERBER HE RODE
GERBER HE FED
THURBER HE DREW

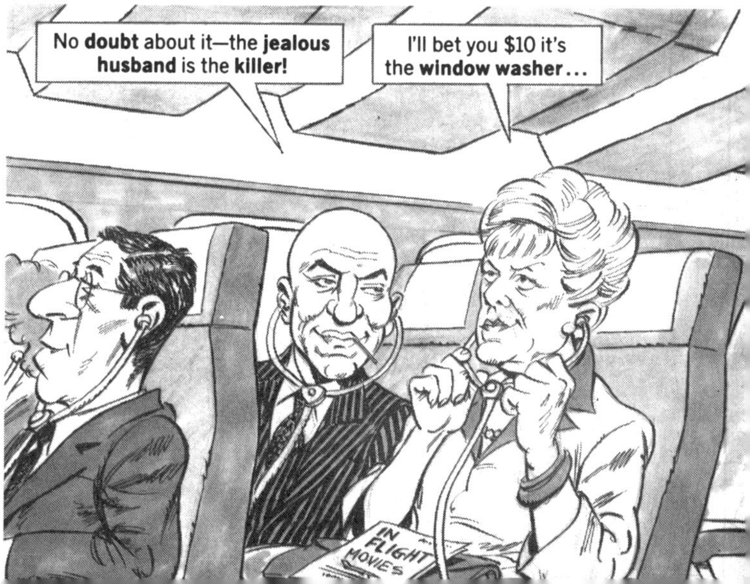
No doubt about it—the jealous husband is the killer!
I'll bet you $10 it's the window washer...
IN FLIGHT MOVIES

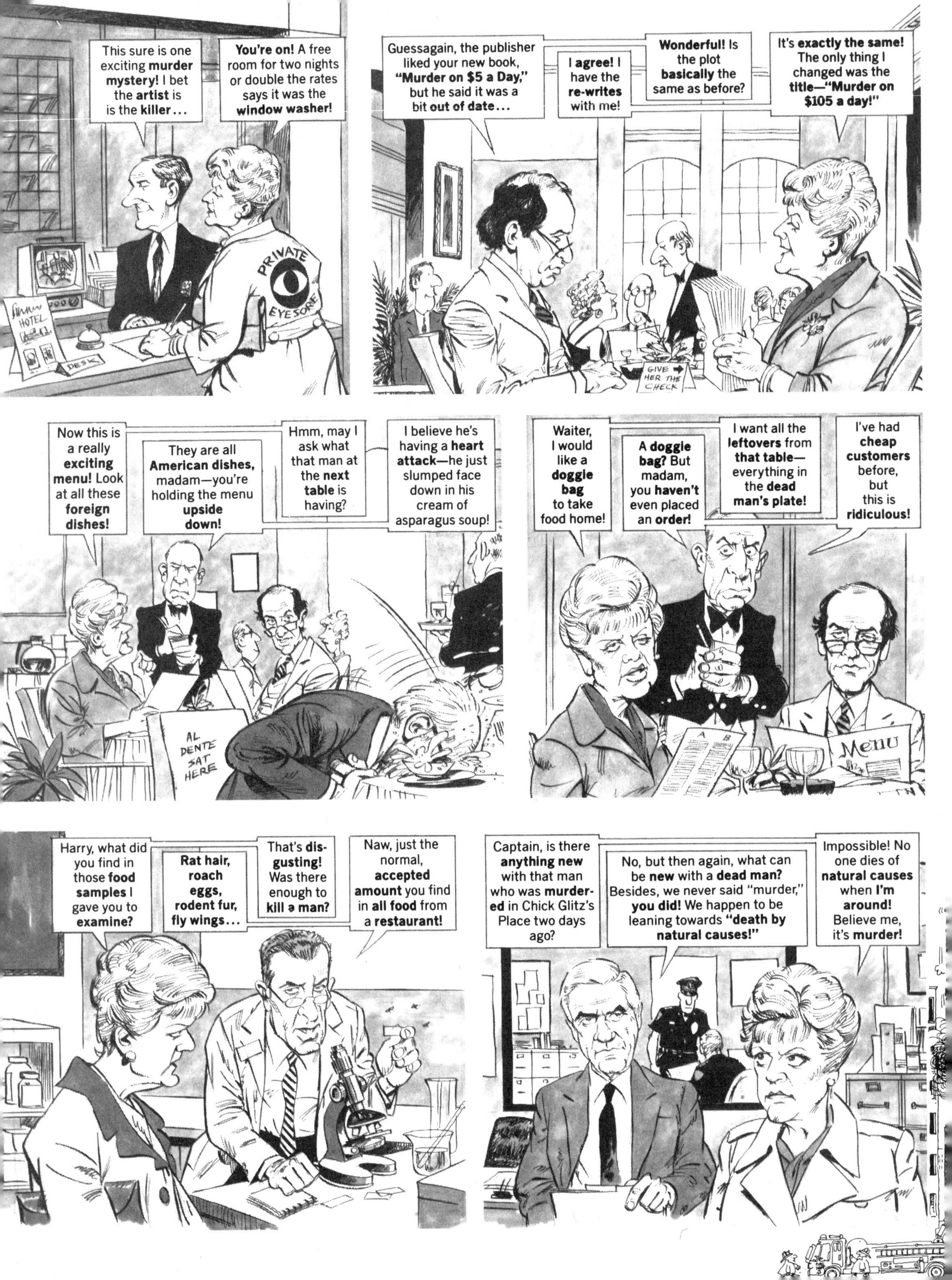
This sure is one exciting **murder mystery!** I bet the **artist** is is the **killer...**
You're on! A free room for two nights or double the rates says it was the **window washer!**
HOTEL
DESK
PRIVATE EYESORE
Guessagain, the publisher liked your new book, **"Murder on $5 a Day,"** but he said it was a bit **out of date...**
I **agree!** I have the **re-writes** with me!
Wonderful! Is the plot **basically** the same as before?
It's **exactly the same!** The only thing I changed was the **title—"Murder on $105 a day!"**
GIVE HER THE CHECK
Now this is a really **exciting menu!** Look at all these **foreign dishes!**
They are all **American dishes,** madam—you're holding the menu **upside down!**
Hmm, may I ask what that man at the **next table** is having?
I believe he's having a **heart attack**—he just slumped face down in his cream of asparagus soup!
AL DENTE SAT HERE
Waiter, I would like a **doggie bag** to take food home!
A doggie bag? But madam, you **haven't** even placed an **order!**
I want all the **leftovers** from **that table**—everything in the **dead man's plate!**
I've had **cheap customers** before, but this is **ridiculous!**
Menu
Harry, what did you find in those **food samples** I gave you to **examine?**
Rat hair, roach eggs, rodent fur, fly wings...
That's **dis-gusting!** Was there enough to **kill a man?**
Naw, just the normal, **accepted amount** you find in **all food** from a **restaurant!**
Captain, is there **anything new** with that man who was **murder-ed** in Chick Glitz's Place two days ago?
No, but then again, what can be **new** with a **dead man?** Besides, we never said "murder," **you did!** We happen to be leaning towards **"death by natural causes!"**
Impossible! No one dies of **natural causes** when **I'm around!** Believe me, it's **murder!**

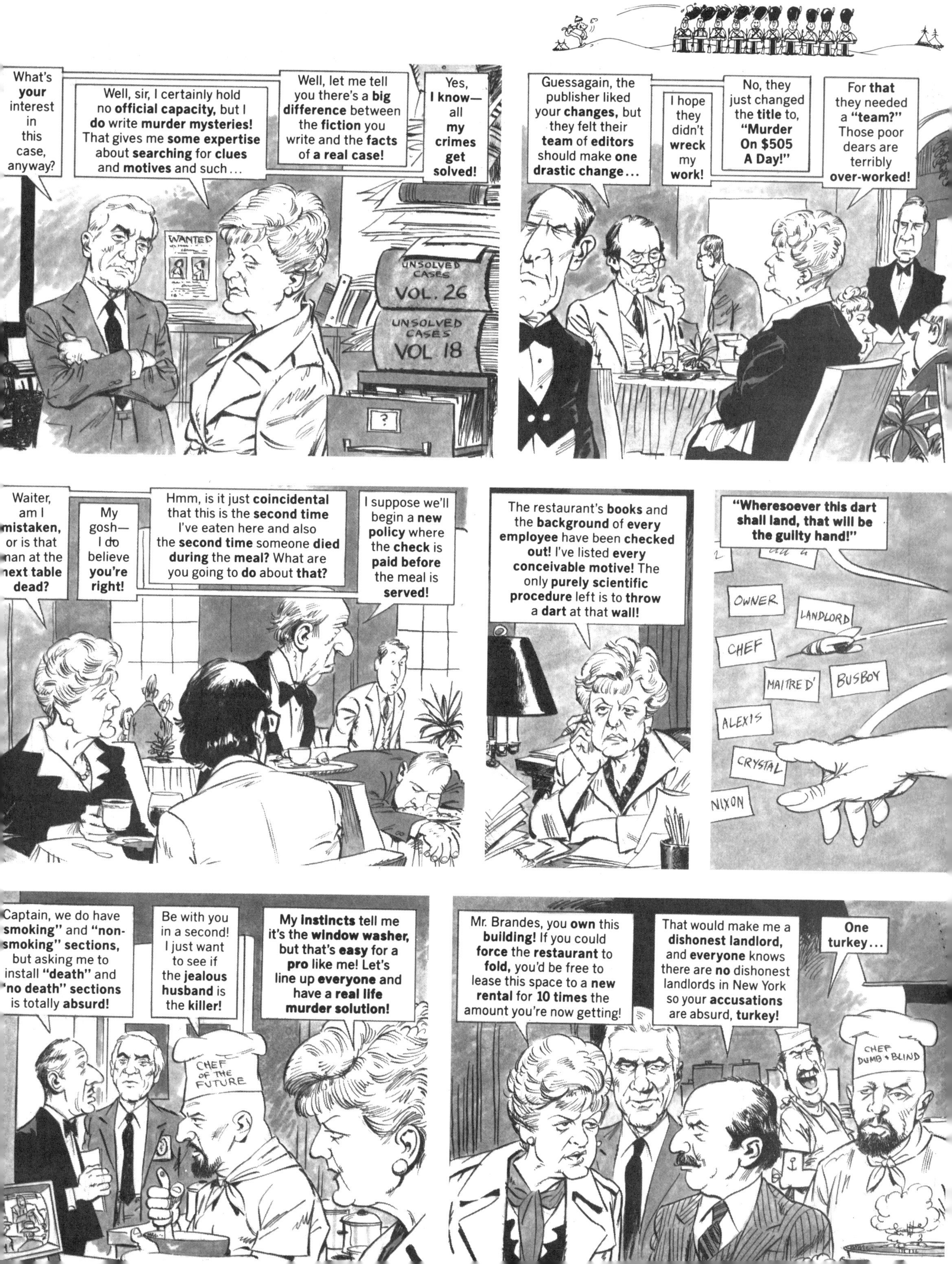

What's your interest in this case, anyway?
Well, sir, I certainly hold no official capacity, but I do write murder mysteries! That gives me some expertise about searching for clues and motives and such...
Well, let me tell you there's a big difference between the fiction you write and the facts of a real case!
Yes, I know—all my crimes get solved!
WANTED
UNSOLVED CASES VOL. 26
UNSOLVED CASES VOL 18
?
Guessagain, the publisher liked your changes, but they felt their team of editors should make one drastic change...
I hope they didn't wreck my work!
No, they just changed the title to, "Murder On $505 A Day!"
For that they needed a "team?" Those poor dears are terribly over-worked!
Waiter, am I mistaken, or is that nan at the next table dead?
My gosh—I do believe you're right!
Hmm, is it just coincidental that this is the second time I've eaten here and also the second time someone died during the meal? What are you going to do about that?
I suppose we'll begin a new policy where the check is paid before the meal is served!
The restaurant's books and the background of every employee have been checked out! I've listed every conceivable motive! The only purely scientific procedure left is to throw a dart at that wall!
"Wheresoever this dart shall land, that will be the guilty hand!"
OWNER
LANDLORD
CHEF
MAITRE D'
BUSBOY
ALEXIS
CRYSTAL
NIXON
Captain, we do have smoking" and "non-smoking" sections, but asking me to install "death" and no death" sections is totally absurd!
Be with you in a second! I just want to see if the jealous husband is the killer!
CHEF OF THE FUTURE
My instincts tell me it's the window washer, but that's easy for a pro like me! Let's line up everyone and have a real life murder solution!
Mr. Brandes, you own this building! If you could force the restaurant to fold, you'd be free to lease this space to a new rental for 10 times the amount you're now getting!
That would make me a dishonest landlord, and everyone knows there are no dishonest landlords in New York so your accusations are absurd, turkey!
One turkey...
CHEF DUMB & BLIND

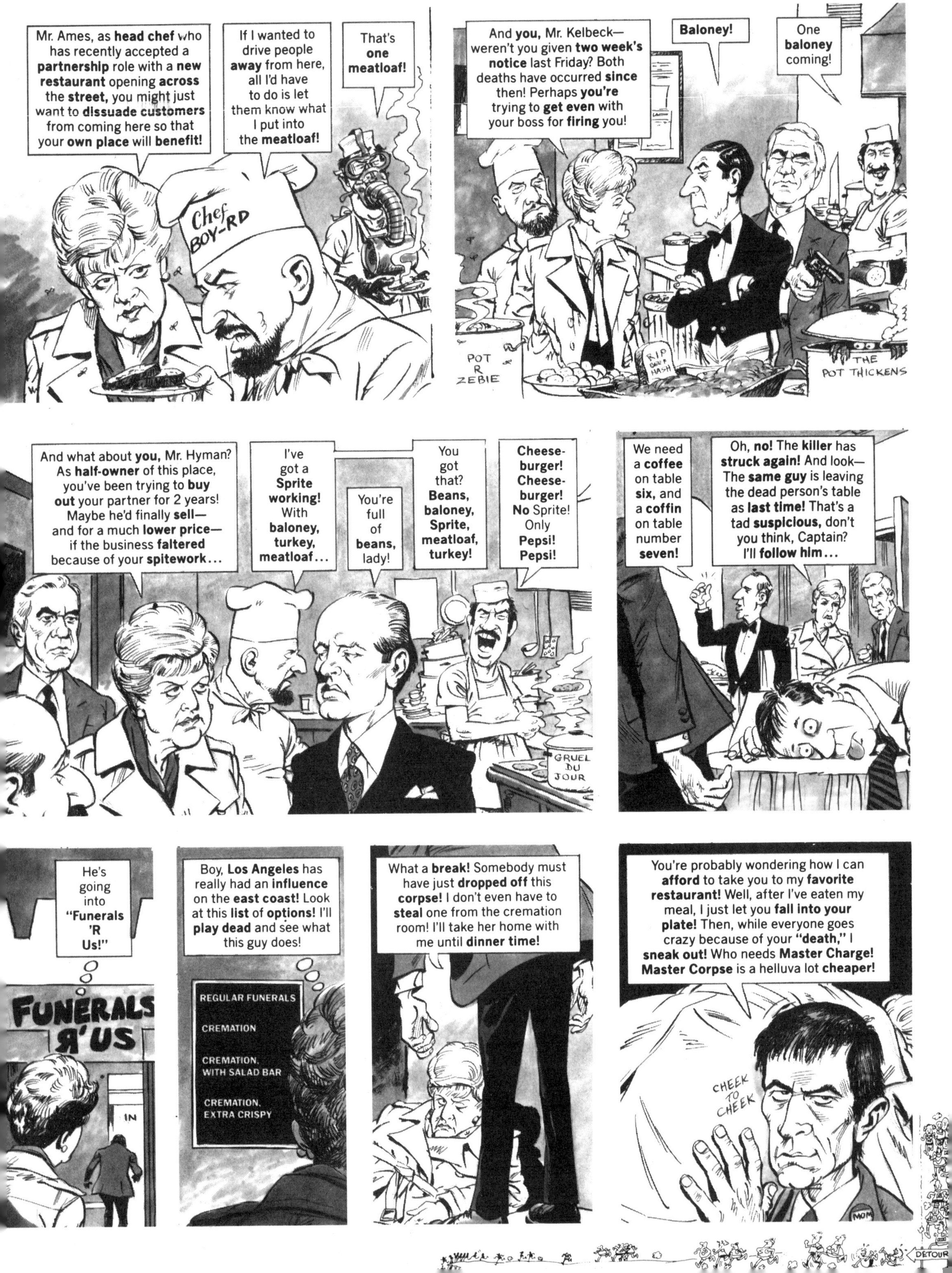

Mr. Ames, as head chef who has recently accepted a partnership role with a new restaurant opening across the street, you might just want to dissuade customers from coming here so that your own place will benefit!
If I wanted to drive people away from here, all I'd have to do is let them know what I put into the meatloaf!
That's one meatloaf!
Chef BOY-RD
And you, Mr. Kelbeck—weren't you given two week's notice last Friday? Both deaths have occurred since then! Perhaps you're trying to get even with your boss for firing you!
Baloney!
One baloney coming!
POT R ZEBIE
RIP
THE POT THICKENS
And what about you, Mr. Hyman? As half-owner of this place, you've been trying to buy out your partner for 2 years! Maybe he'd finally sell—and for a much lower price—if the business faltered because of your spitework...
I've got a Sprite working! With baloney, turkey, meatloaf...
You're full of beans, lady!
You got that? Beans, baloney, Sprite, meatloaf, turkey!
Cheese-burger! Cheese-burger! No Sprite! Only Pepsi! Pepsi!
GRUEL DU JOUR
We need a coffee on table six, and a coffin on table number seven!
Oh, no! The killer has struck again! And look—The same guy is leaving the dead person's table as last time! That's a tad suspicious, don't you think, Captain? I'll follow him...
He's going into "Funerals 'R Us!"
FUNERALS Я'US
IN
Boy, Los Angeles has really had an influence on the east coast! Look at this list of options! I'll play dead and see what this guy does!
REGULAR FUNERALS
CREMATION
CREMATION, WITH SALAD BAR
CREMATION, EXTRA CRISPY
What a break! Somebody must have just dropped off this corpse! I don't even have to steal one from the cremation room! I'll take her home with me until dinner time!
You're probably wondering how I can afford to take you to my favorite restaurant! Well, after I've eaten my meal, I just let you fall into your plate! Then, while everyone goes crazy because of your "death," I sneak out! Who needs Master Charge! Master Corpse is a helluva lot cheaper!
CHEEK TO CHEEK
MOM
DETOUR

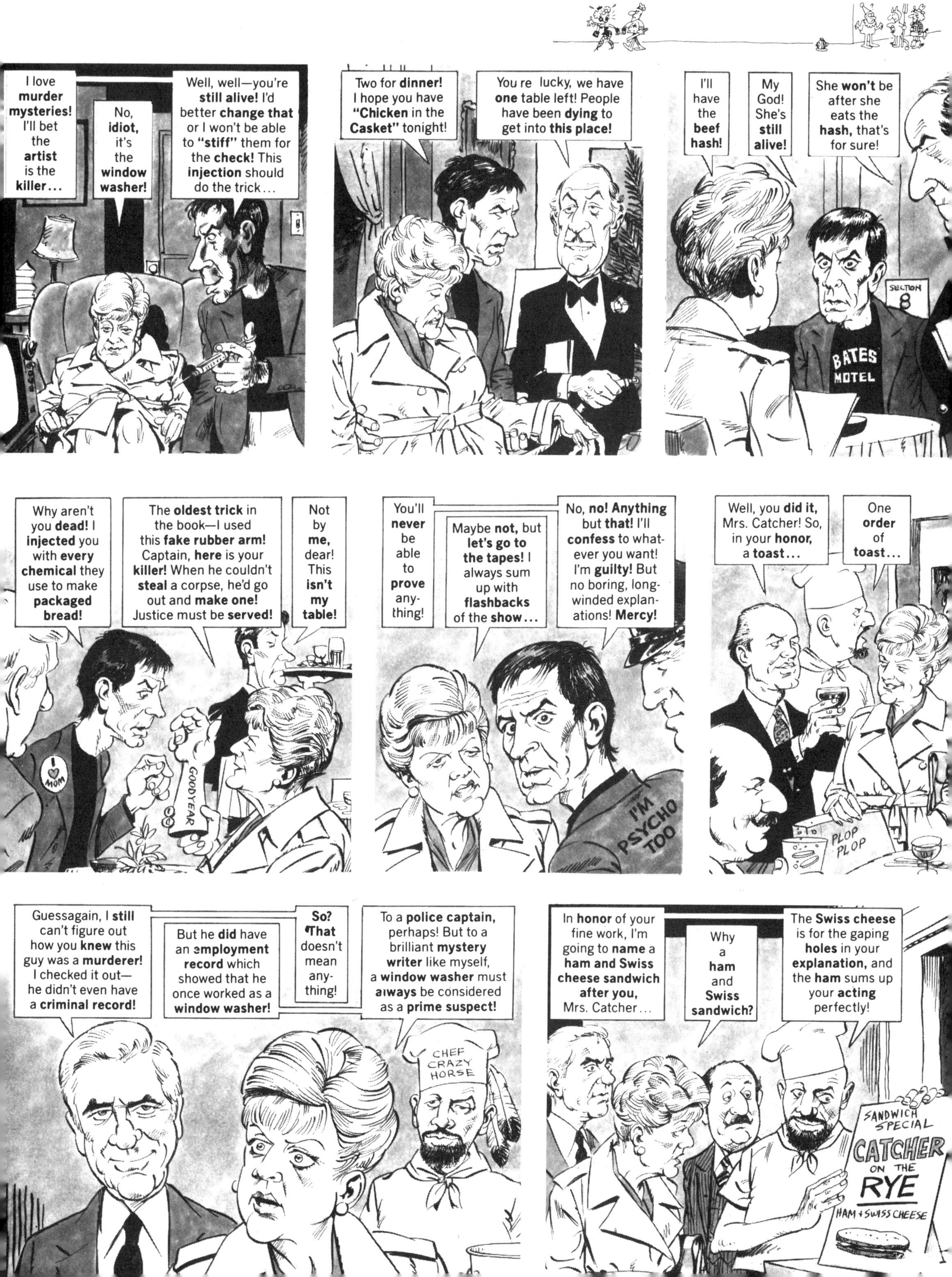
I love murder mysteries! I'll bet the artist is the killer...
No, idiot, it's the window washer!
Well, well—you're still alive! I'd better change that or I won't be able to "stiff" them for the check! This injection should do the trick...
Two for dinner! I hope you have "Chicken in the Casket" tonight!
You're lucky, we have one table left! People have been dying to get into this place!
I'll have the beef hash!
My God! She's still alive!
She won't be after she eats the hash, that's for sure!
SECTION 8
BATES MOTEL
Why aren't you dead! I injected you with every chemical they use to make packaged bread!
The oldest trick in the book—I used this fake rubber arm! Captain, here is your killer! When he couldn't steal a corpse, he'd go out and make one! Justice must be served!
Not by me, dear! This isn't my table!
I ♥ MOM
GOODYEAR
You'll never be able to prove anything!
Maybe not, but let's go to the tapes! I always sum up with flashbacks of the show...
No, no! Anything but that! I'll confess to whatever you want! I'm guilty! But no boring, long-winded explanations! Mercy!
I'M PSYCHO TOO
Well, you did it, Mrs. Catcher! So, in your honor, a toast...
One order of toast...
PLOP PLOP
Guessagain, I still can't figure out how you knew this guy was a murderer! I checked it out—he didn't even have a criminal record!
But he did have an employment record which showed that he once worked as a window washer!
So? That doesn't mean anything!
To a police captain, perhaps! But to a brilliant mystery writer like myself, a window washer must always be considered as a prime suspect!
CHEF CRAZY HORSE
In honor of your fine work, I'm going to name a ham and Swiss cheese sandwich after you, Mrs. Catcher...
Why a ham and Swiss sandwich?
The Swiss cheese is for the gaping holes in your explanation, and the ham sums up your acting perfectly!
SANDWICH SPECIAL
CATCHER ON THE RYE
HAM + SWISS CHEESE

MIRACLE DIP DEPT.

There's a syrupy, sickeningly sweet television show on the air that exploits the sick, elderly and needy. It's about a goody-two shoes angel who reforms non-believers and restores their faith by spouting a few well-worn clichés in each episode. It's true he may be showing them the road to salvation, but he's leading the rest of us down a...

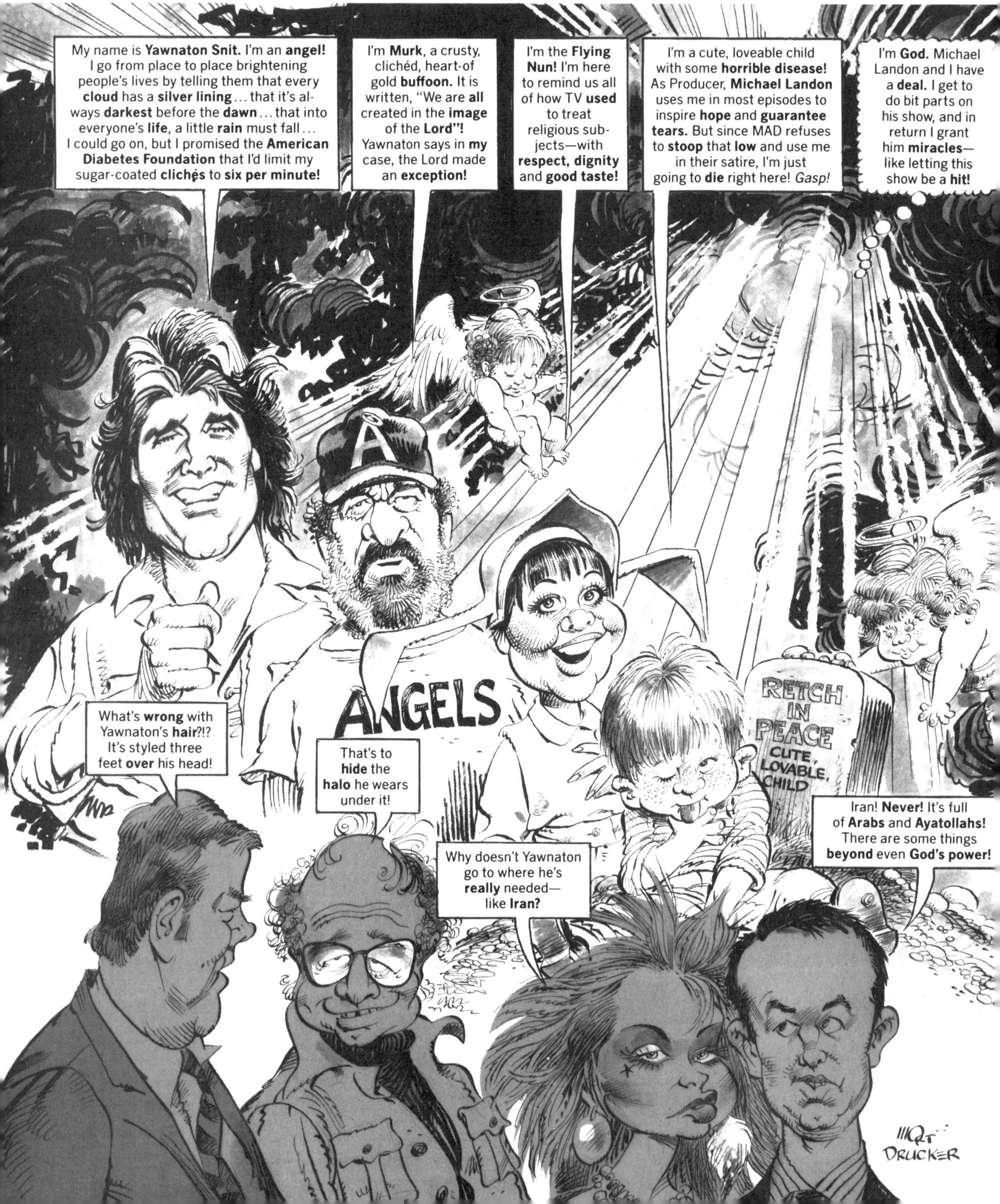

My name is Yawnaton Snit. I'm an angel! I go from place to place brightening people's lives by telling them that every cloud has a silver lining... that it's always darkest before the dawn... that into everyone's life, a little rain must fall... I could go on, but I promised the American Diabetes Foundation that I'd limit my sugar-coated clichés to six per minute!
I'm Murk, a crusty, clichéd, heart-of gold buffoon. It is written, "We are all created in the image of the Lord"! Yawnaton says in my case, the Lord made an exception!
I'm the Flying Nun! I'm here to remind us all of how TV used to treat religious subjects—with respect, dignity and good taste!
I'm a cute, loveable child with some horrible disease! As Producer, Michael Landon uses me in most episodes to inspire hope and guarantee tears. But since MAD refuses to stoop that low and use me in their satire, I'm just going to die right here! Gasp!
I'm God. Michael Landon and I have a deal. I get to do bit parts on his show, and in return I grant him miracles—like letting this show be a hit!
ANGELS
RETCH IN PEACE CUTE, LOVABLE, CHILD
What's wrong with Yawnaton's hair?!? It's styled three feet over his head!
That's to hide the halo he wears under it!
Why doesn't Yawnaton go to where he's really needed—like Iran?
Iran! Never! It's full of Arabs and Ayatollahs! There are some things beyond even God's power!
MORT DRUCKER

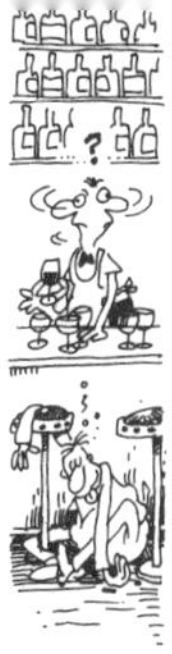

HIGHWAY TO HEAVING

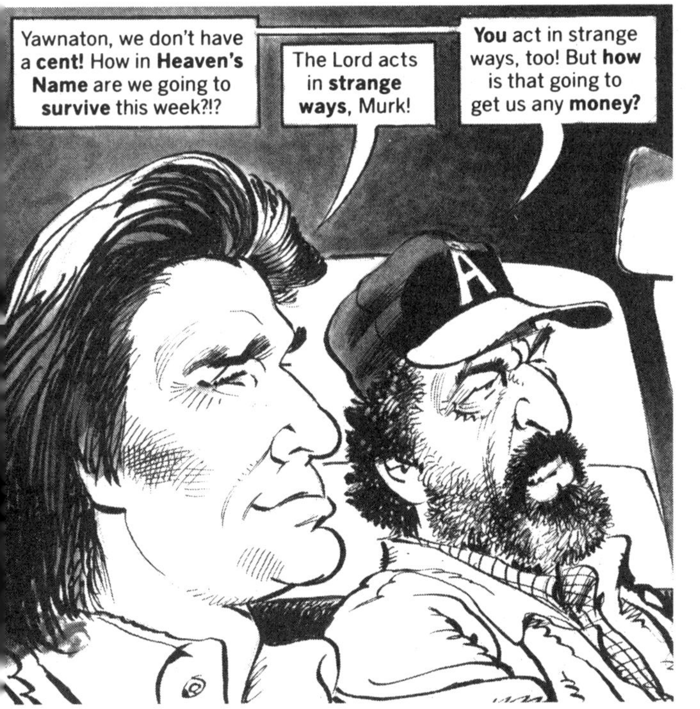

Yawnaton, we don't have a **cent!** How in **Heaven's Name** are we going to **survive** this week?!?
The Lord acts in **strange ways**, Murk!
You act in strange ways, too! But **how** is that going to get us any **money?**

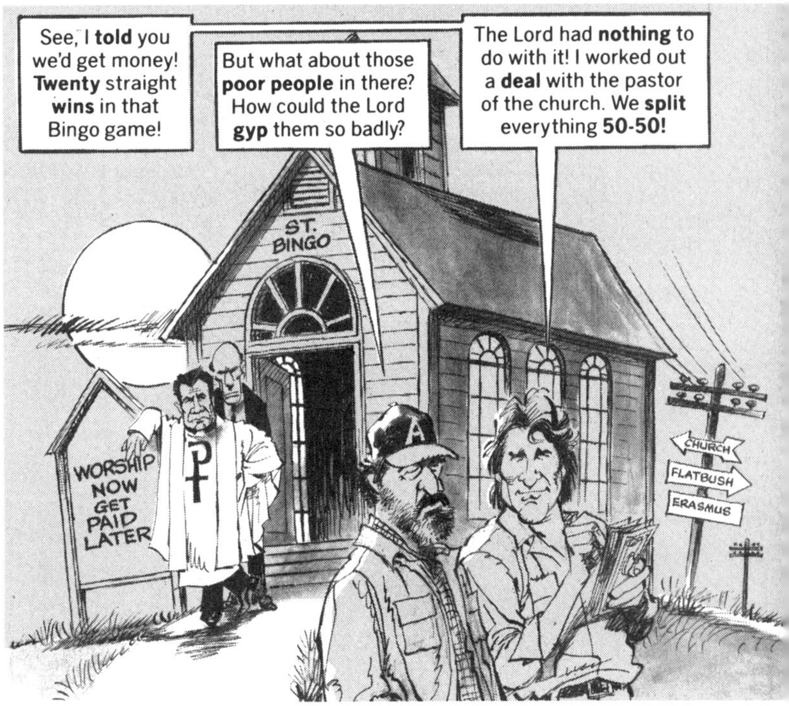

See, I **told** you we'd get money! **Twenty** straight **wins** in that Bingo game!
But what about those **poor people** in there? How could the Lord **gyp** them so badly?
The Lord had **nothing** to do with it! I worked out a **deal** with the pastor of the church. We **split** everything **50-50!**
ST. BINGO
WORSHIP NOW GET PAID LATER
CHURCH
FLATBUSH
ERASMUS

ARTIST: MORT DRUCKER WRITER: DICK DE BARTOLO

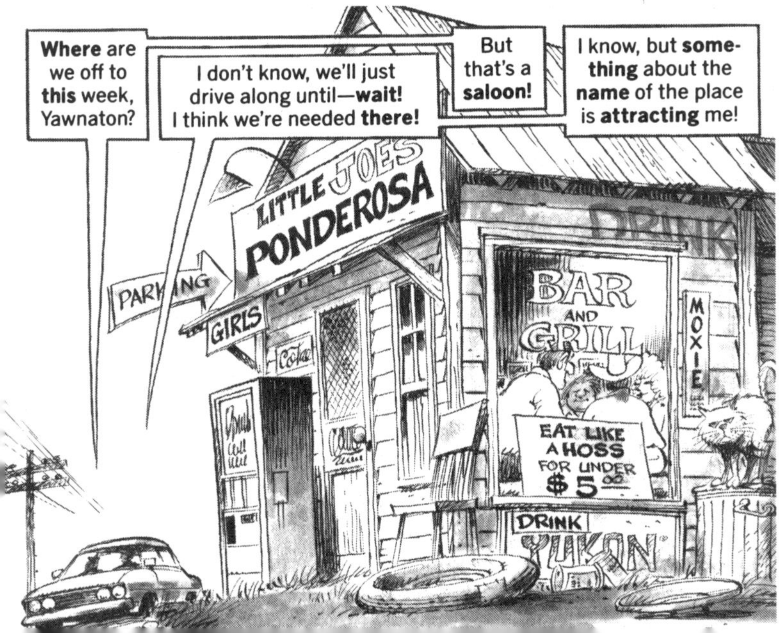

Where are we off to **this** week, Yawnaton?
I don't know, we'll just drive along until—**wait!** I think we're needed **there!**
But that's a **saloon!**
I know, but **something** about the **name** of the place is **attracting** me!
LITTLE JOES PONDEROSA
PARKING
GIRLS
BAR AND GRILL
MOXIE
EAT LIKE A HOSS FOR UNDER $5.00
DRINK
YUKON

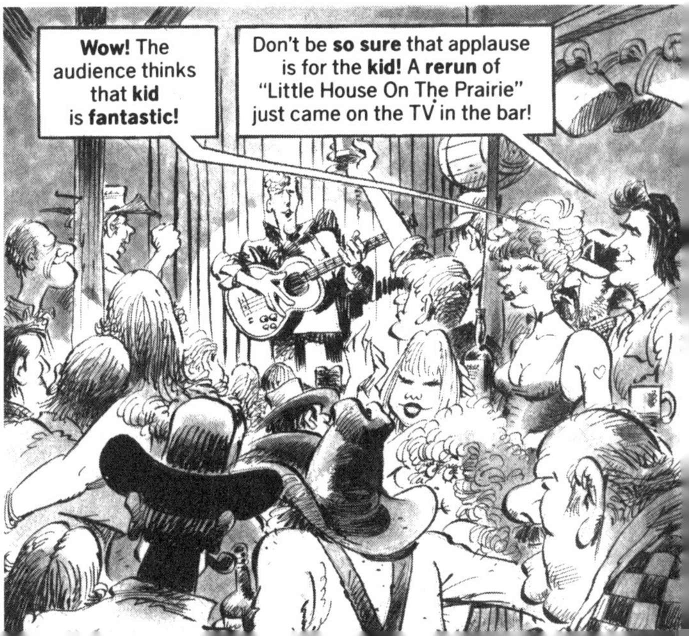

Wow! The audience thinks that **kid** is **fantastic!**
Don't be **so sure** that applause is for the **kid!** A **rerun** of "Little House On The Prairie" just came on the TV in the bar!

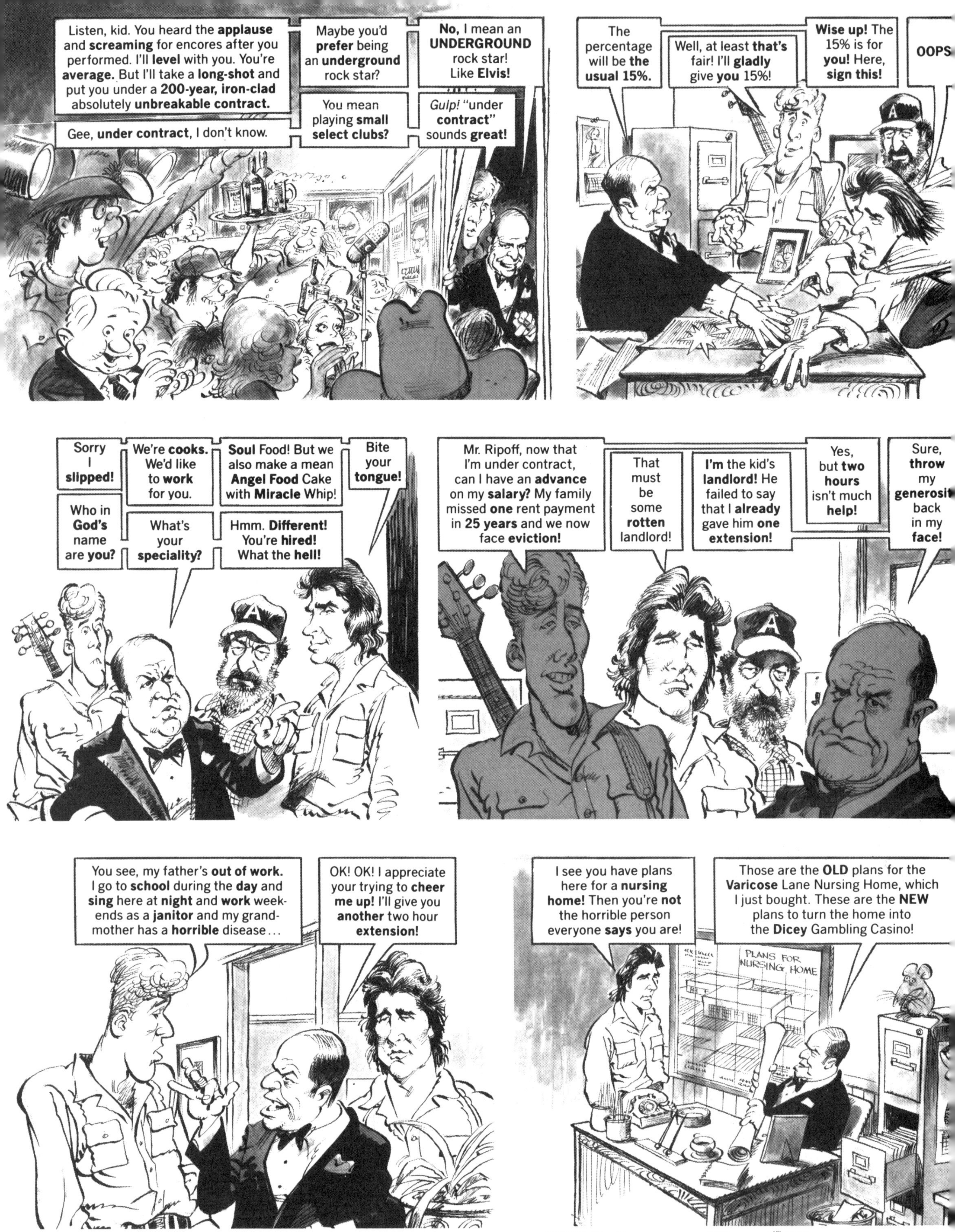
Listen, kid. You heard the applause and screaming for encores after you performed. I'll level with you. You're average. But I'll take a long-shot and put you under a 200-year, iron-clad absolutely unbreakable contract.
Gee, under contract, I don't know.
Maybe you'd prefer being an underground rock star?
You mean playing small select clubs?
No, I mean an UNDERGROUND rock star! Like Elvis!
Gulp! "under contract" sounds great!
The percentage will be the usual 15%.
Well, at least that's fair! I'll gladly give you 15%!
Wise up! The 15% is for you! Here, sign this!
OOPS
Sorry I slipped!
Who in God's name are you?
We're cooks. We'd like to work for you.
What's your speciality?
Soul Food! But we also make a mean Angel Food Cake with Miracle Whip!
Hmm. Different! You're hired! What the hell!
Bite your tongue!
Mr. Ripoff, now that I'm under contract, can I have an advance on my salary? My family missed one rent payment in 25 years and we now face eviction!
That must be some rotten landlord!
I'm the kid's landlord! He failed to say that I already gave him one extension!
Yes, but two hours isn't much help!
Sure, throw my generosit back in my face!
You see, my father's out of work. I go to school during the day and sing here at night and work week-ends as a janitor and my grand-mother has a horrible disease...
OK! OK! I appreciate your trying to cheer me up! I'll give you another two hour extension!
I see you have plans here for a nursing home! Then you're not the horrible person everyone says you are!
Those are the OLD plans for the Varicose Lane Nursing Home, which I just bought. These are the NEW plans to turn the home into the Dicey Gambling Casino!
PLANS FOR NURSING HOME
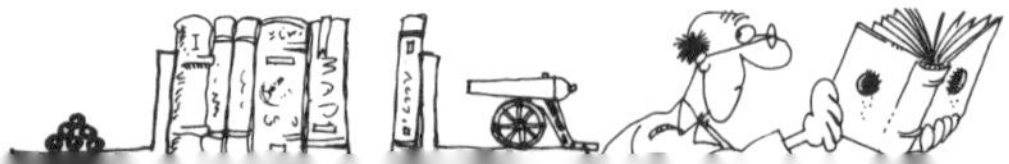

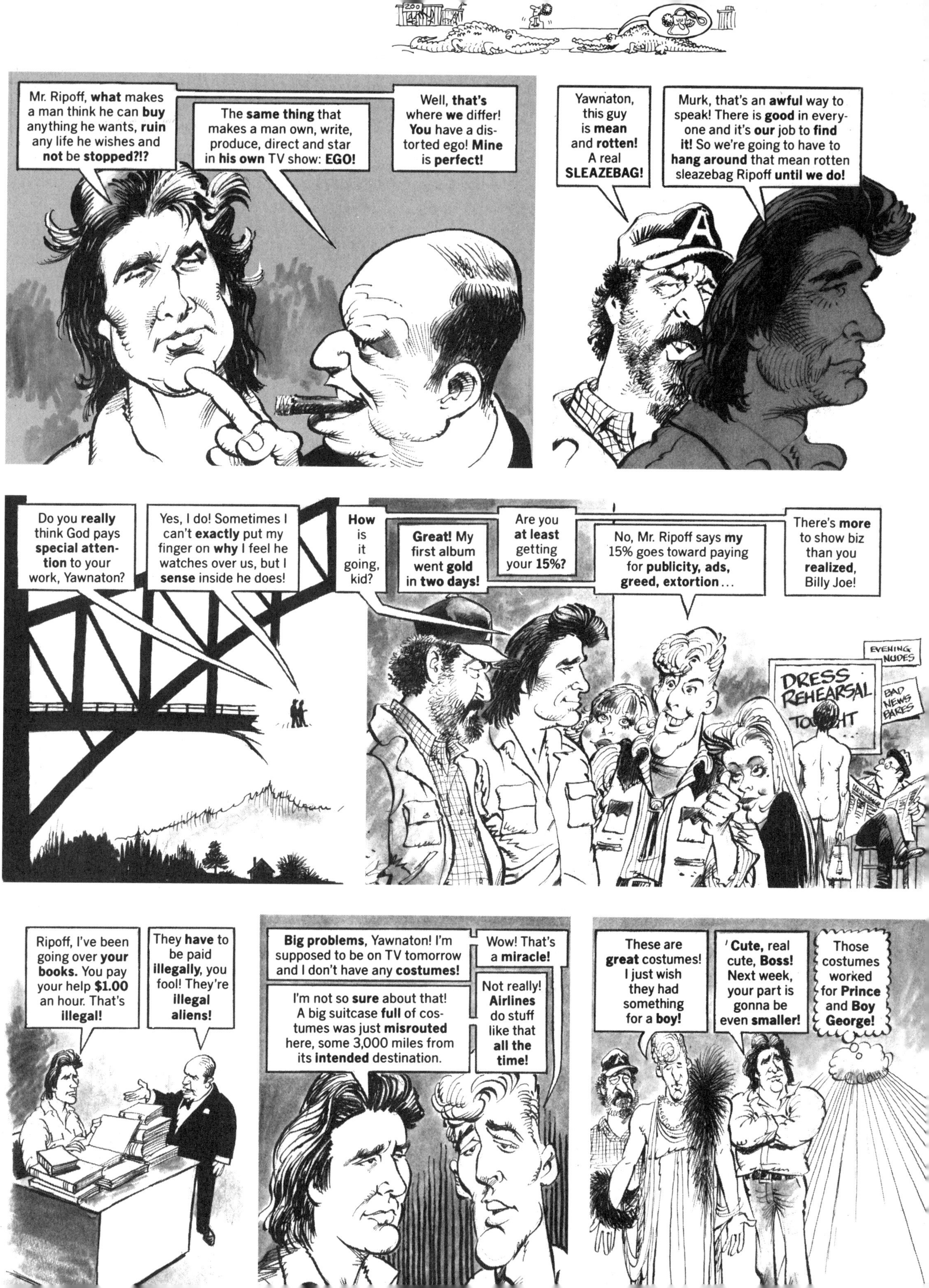

ZOO
Mr. Ripoff, **what** makes a man think he can **buy** anything he wants, **ruin** any life he wishes and **not** be **stopped?!?**
The **same thing** that makes a man own, write, produce, direct and star in **his own** TV show: **EGO!**
Well, **that's** where **we** differ! **You** have a distorted ego! **Mine** is **perfect!**
Yawnaton, this guy is **mean** and **rotten!** A real **SLEAZEBAG!**
Murk, that's an **awful** way to speak! There is **good** in everyone and it's **our** job to **find it!** So we're going to have to **hang around** that mean rotten sleazebag Ripoff **until we do!**
Do you **really** think God pays **special attention** to your work, Yawnaton?
Yes, I do! Sometimes I can't **exactly** put my finger on **why** I feel he watches over us, but I **sense** inside he does!
How is it going, kid?
Great! My first album went **gold** in **two days!**
Are you **at least** getting your **15%?**
No, Mr. Ripoff says **my** 15% goes toward paying for **publicity, ads, greed, extortion**...
There's **more** to show biz than you **realized**, Billy Joe!
EVENING NUDES
DRESS REHEARSAL
BAD NEWS BARES
Ripoff, I've been going over **your books.** You pay your help **$1.00** an hour. That's **illegal!**
They **have** to be paid **illegally**, you fool! They're **illegal aliens!**
Big problems, Yawnaton! I'm supposed to be on TV tomorrow and I don't have any **costumes!**
Wow! That's a **miracle!**
I'm not so **sure** about that! A big suitcase **full** of costumes was just **misrouted** here, some 3,000 miles from its **intended** destination.
Not really! **Airlines** do stuff like that **all the time!**
These are **great** costumes! I just wish they had something for a **boy!**
'**Cute,** real cute, **Boss!** Next week, your part is gonna be even **smaller!**
Those costumes worked for **Prince** and **Boy George!**

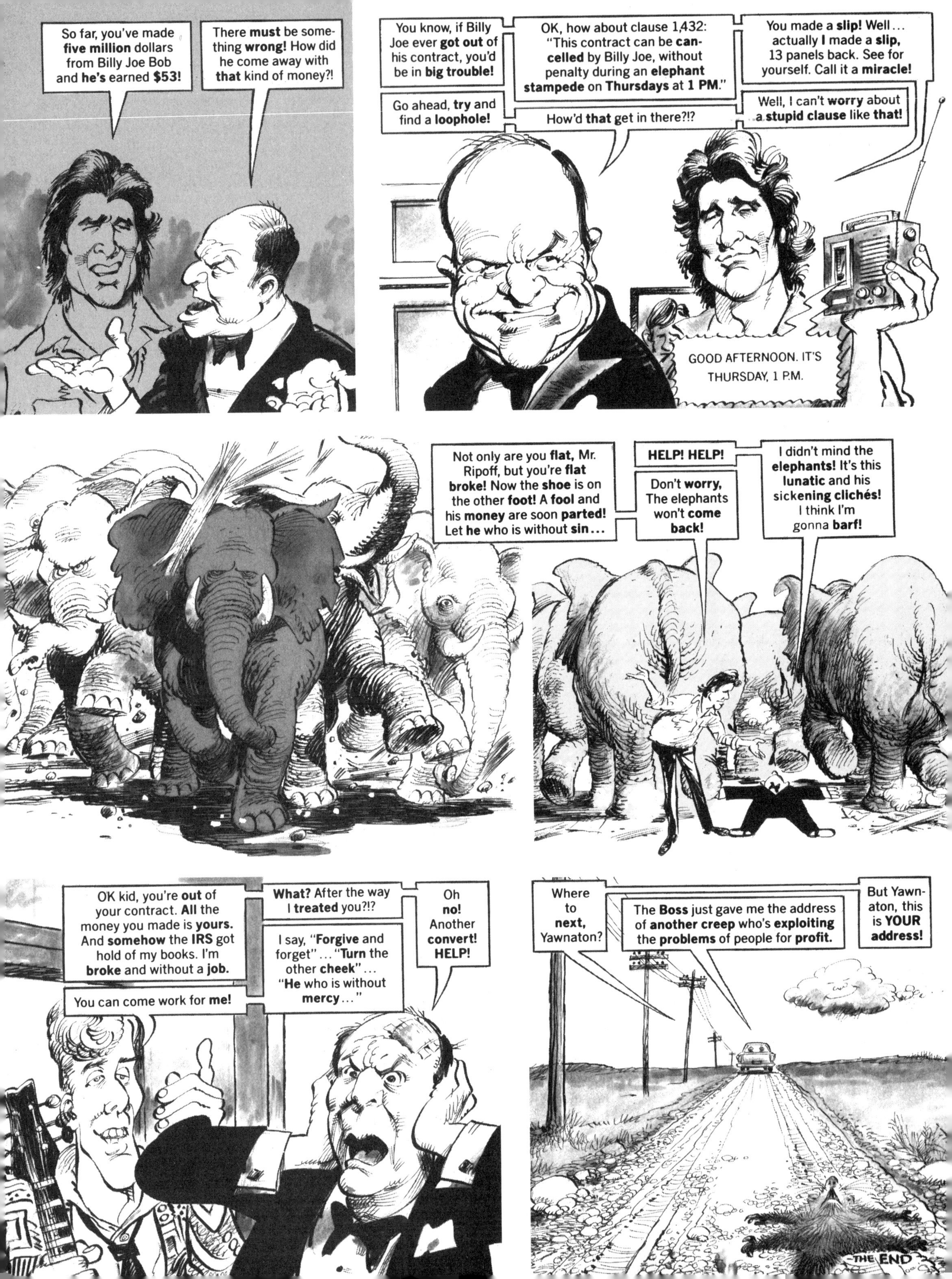
So far, you've made **five million** dollars from Billy Joe Bob and **he's** earned **$53!**
There **must** be some-thing **wrong!** How did he come away with **that** kind of money?!
You know, if Billy Joe ever **got out** of his contract, you'd be in **big trouble!**
Go ahead, **try** and find a **loophole!**
OK, how about clause 1,432: "This contract can be **can-celled** by Billy Joe, without penalty during an **elephant stampede** on **Thursdays** at **1 PM**."
How'd **that** get in there?!?
You made a **slip!** Well… actually **I** made a **slip,** 13 panels back. See for yourself. Call it a **miracle!**
Well, I can't **worry** about a **stupid clause** like **that!**
GOOD AFTERNOON. IT'S THURSDAY, 1 P.M.
Not only are you **flat,** Mr. Ripoff, but you're **flat broke!** Now the **shoe** is on the other **foot!** A **fool** and his **money** are soon **parted!** Let **he** who is without **sin**…
HELP! HELP!
Don't **worry,** The elephants won't **come back!**
I didn't mind the **elephants!** It's this **lunatic** and his sickening **clichés!** I think I'm gonna **barf!**
OK kid, you're **out** of your contract. **All** the money you made is **yours.** And **somehow** the **IRS** got hold of my books. I'm **broke** and without a **job.**
You can come work for **me!**
What? After the way I **treated** you?!?
I say, "**Forgive** and forget"… "**Turn** the other **cheek**"… "**He** who is without **mercy**…"
Oh **no!** Another **convert! HELP!**
Where to **next,** Yawnaton?
The **Boss** just gave me the address of **another creep** who's **exploiting** the **problems** of people for **profit.**
But Yawn-aton, this is **YOUR address!**
THE END

MAY THE FORCE BE WITH TWO DEPT.

When it comes to police shows on TV, the networks have been very successful in feeding us viewers a steady diet of cop "teams," a pair of dedicated crimefighters with colorful personalities and even more colorful names: Cagney & Lacey, Simon & Simon, Hardcastle & McCormick, Scarecrow & Mrs. King, Starsky & Hutch, Macgruder & Loud, Tenspeed & Brownshoe, and so on. We figure it won't be long before network execs *really* reach the bottom of the barrel and get so gimmicky in their lame attempts to attract viewers that they introduce these...

UPCOMING TV COP "TEAMS"

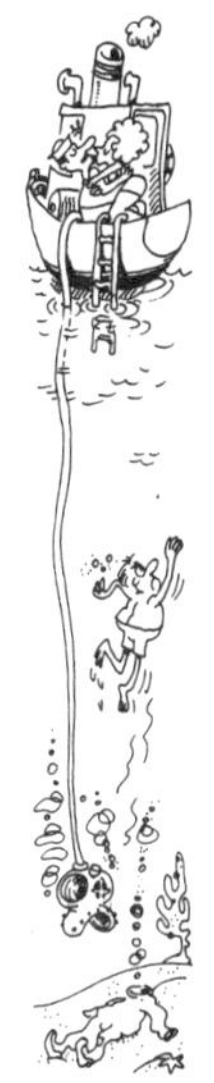

ARTIST: JACK DAVIS WRITER: CHARLIE KADAU

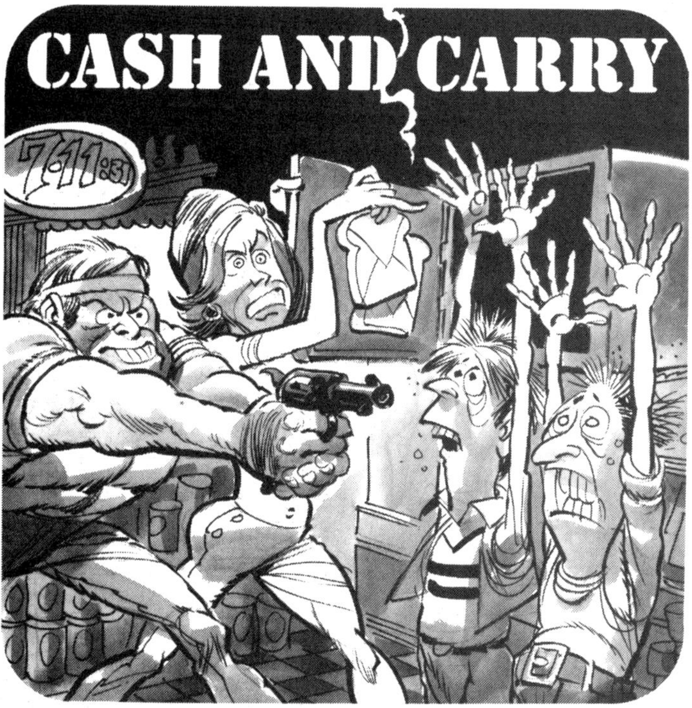
CASH AND CARRY
7-11

Cash is Sgt. Augie "Cash" Pooster. Carry is Det. Gloria "Carry" Bunting. Together, they keep the aisles of Detroit's 7-11 stores safe for middle-of-the-night shoppers. In the first episode, the team is pushed to its breaking point as Cash and Carry come face to face with a gang of thugs who heat their sandwiches in the store's microwave *before* paying for them.

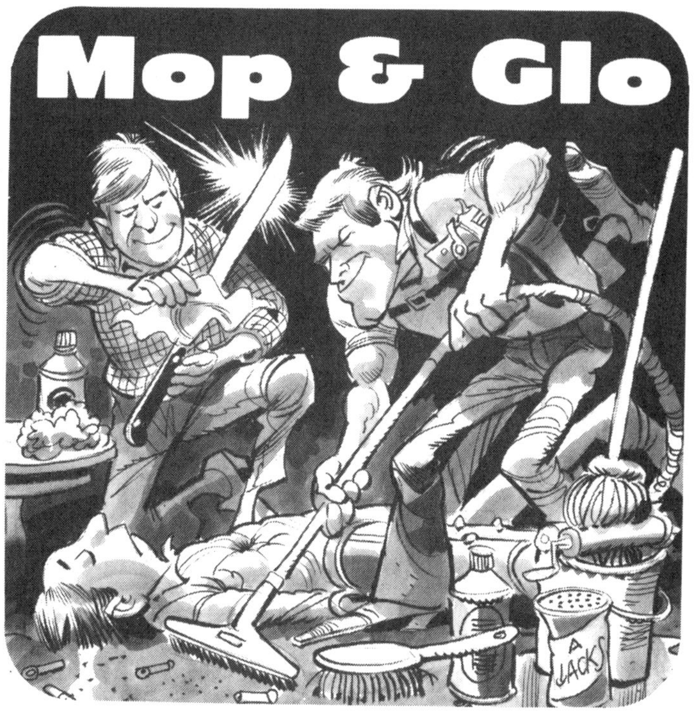
Mop & Glo
JACKS

Victor Mop and Walter Glo are the two top forensics experts at the FBI. The catch? They're also compulsive neat-freaks. At murder scenes, after dusting for fingerprints, they can't keep themselves from polishing, mopping and vacuuming. Since the producers are so confident that Mop & Glo will be a hit, they've already begun work on a spinoff series called Spic And Span.

BITCH & MOAN

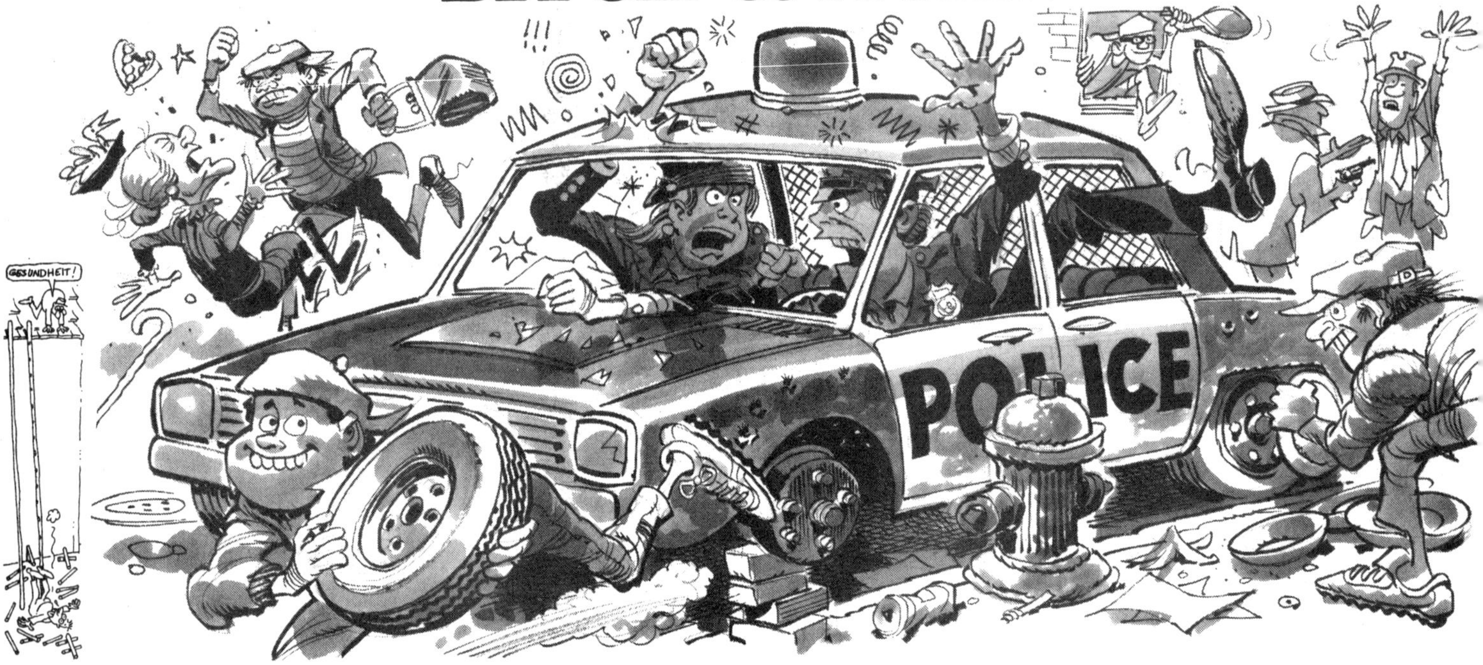
GESUNDHEIT!
POLICE

In this series' pilot episode, rookie cops Douglas Bitch and Cindy Moan are assigned to the same squad car, leaving them more than enough time for their favorite activity: complaining! Whether it be about their itchy uniforms, their hard-nosed sergeant, the lousy shift, the crummy pension plan, each other's bad habits, or anything else that comes to mind, Bitch and Moan do nothing but grumble for 60 solid minutes.

BACON & EGGS

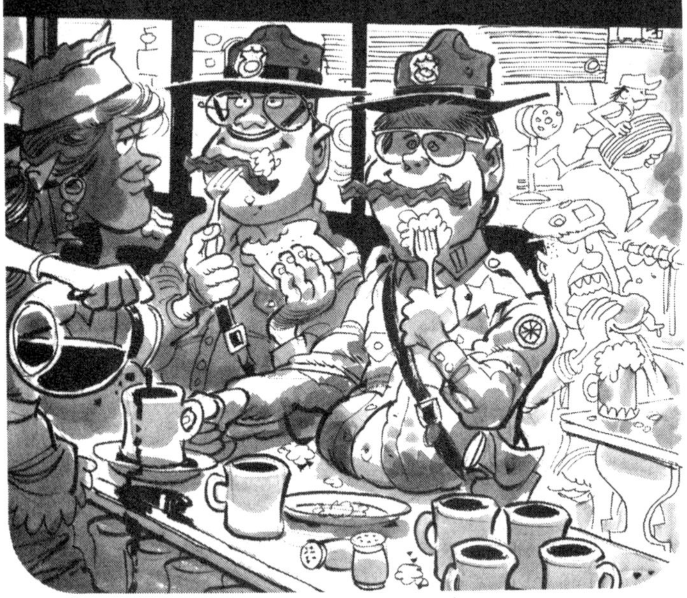

As soon as Harlan County Deputies Jack Bacon and Andy Eggs go on duty, they head straight for Edna's Diner, where they spend the next eight hours belly-up to the counter enjoying breakfast, chatter with truckers and Edna's bottomless coffee pot. In the unlikely case smugglers, hijackers or serial killers stop by, they've got to deal with Jack and Andy!

SURF & TURF

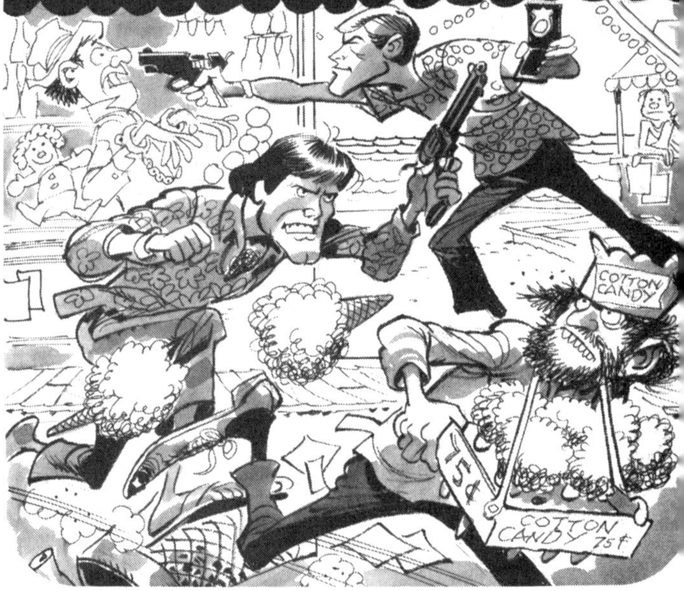
COTTON CANDY
75¢
COTTON CANDY 75¢

Asbury Park's Danny Surf and Danny Turf are Private Investigators who share the same first name and only accept cases which can be solved without leaving the beach or boardwalk area. Because of this, most episodes revolve around car keys lost in the sand, rigged amusement pier arcade games and illegal taffy operations.

BLACK & DECKER

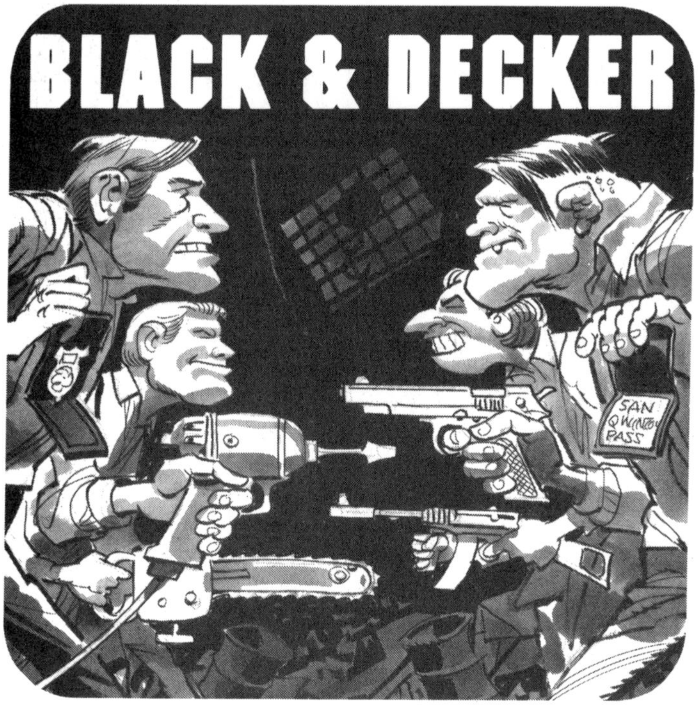

Dazed & Confused

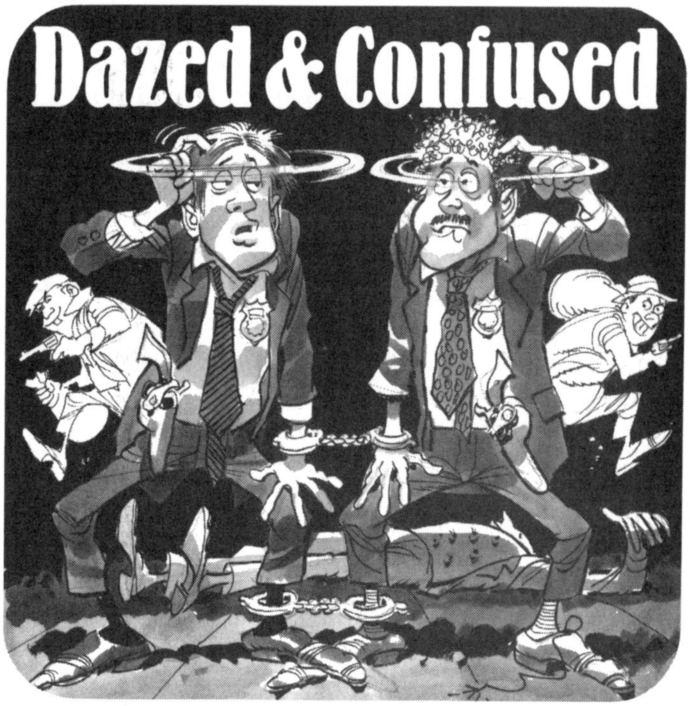

Plainclothes detectives Leo Black and Harry Decker work undercover for the Chicago Police Department. Unable to carry handguns, billy clubs or handcuffs, they use power tools to protect themselves and bring outlaws to justice. This season, Black and Decker foil a hijacking with a power drill, uncover corruption in City Hall with a sabre saw and round up a prostitution ring using an orbital sander. A must-see for crime buffs and carpenters alike.

When a case that really isn't important comes up, it's assigned to detectives Chet "Dazed" Harris and Cliff "Confused" Anderson. The pair can always be counted on to not only misunderstand their instructions, but to completely forget who they're looking for. They become handcuffed to each other at least twice each episode and frequently misplace their squad car. Despite this, they solve a case each week—but not necessarily the one they're trying to.

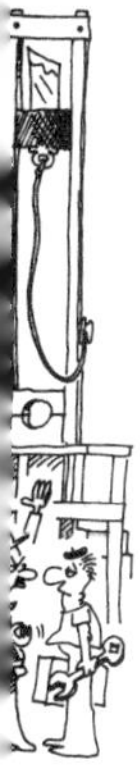

Dead & Buried

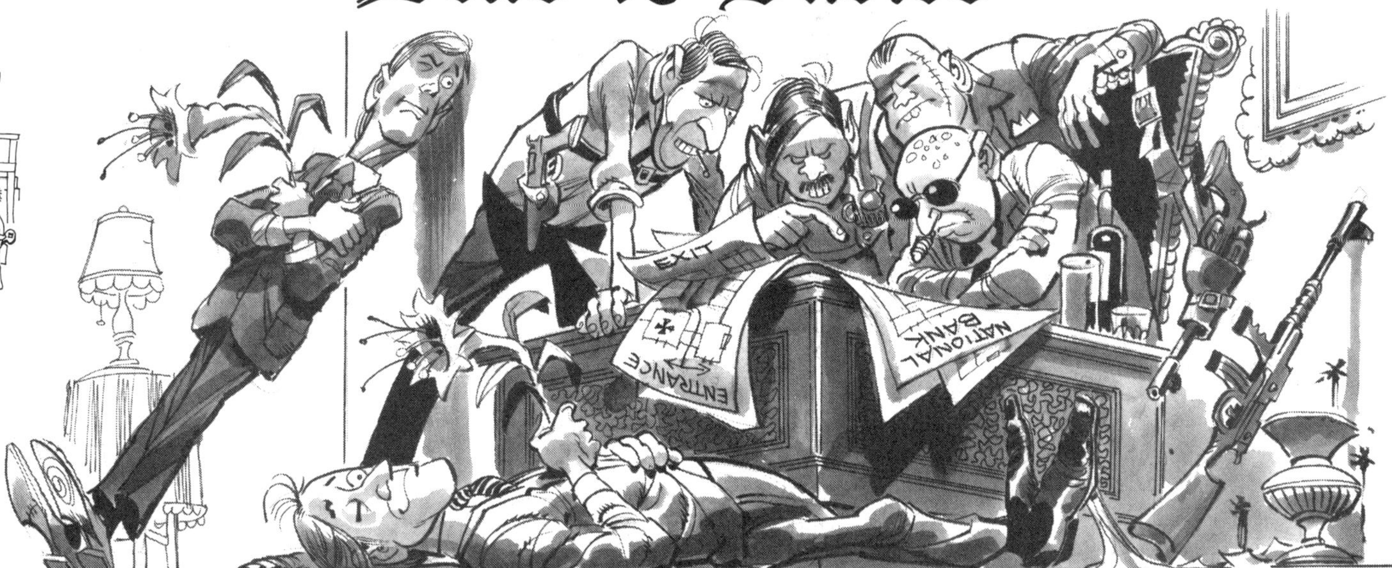
EXIT
ENTRANCE
NATIONAL BANK

Dick Dead and Barry Buried are not your average run-of-the-mill private eyes. Using East Indian breath control techniques, they can remain completely stiff and motionless for hours at a time. This, coupled with their ability to give off the smell of decaying flesh, makes them the perfect pair for infiltrating hideouts of organized crime kingpins, who have no misgivings about revealing their secret plans in the presence of what they think are corpses.

SCORN ON THE COS DEPT.

Once a year, MAD's evil staff rounds up a new collection of revered celebrities and ho lowed institutions, and then takes pot shots at them in our annual Nasty File. Normall we have to search the earth for victims so beloved that no one but us would dare to i

The COSBY SH

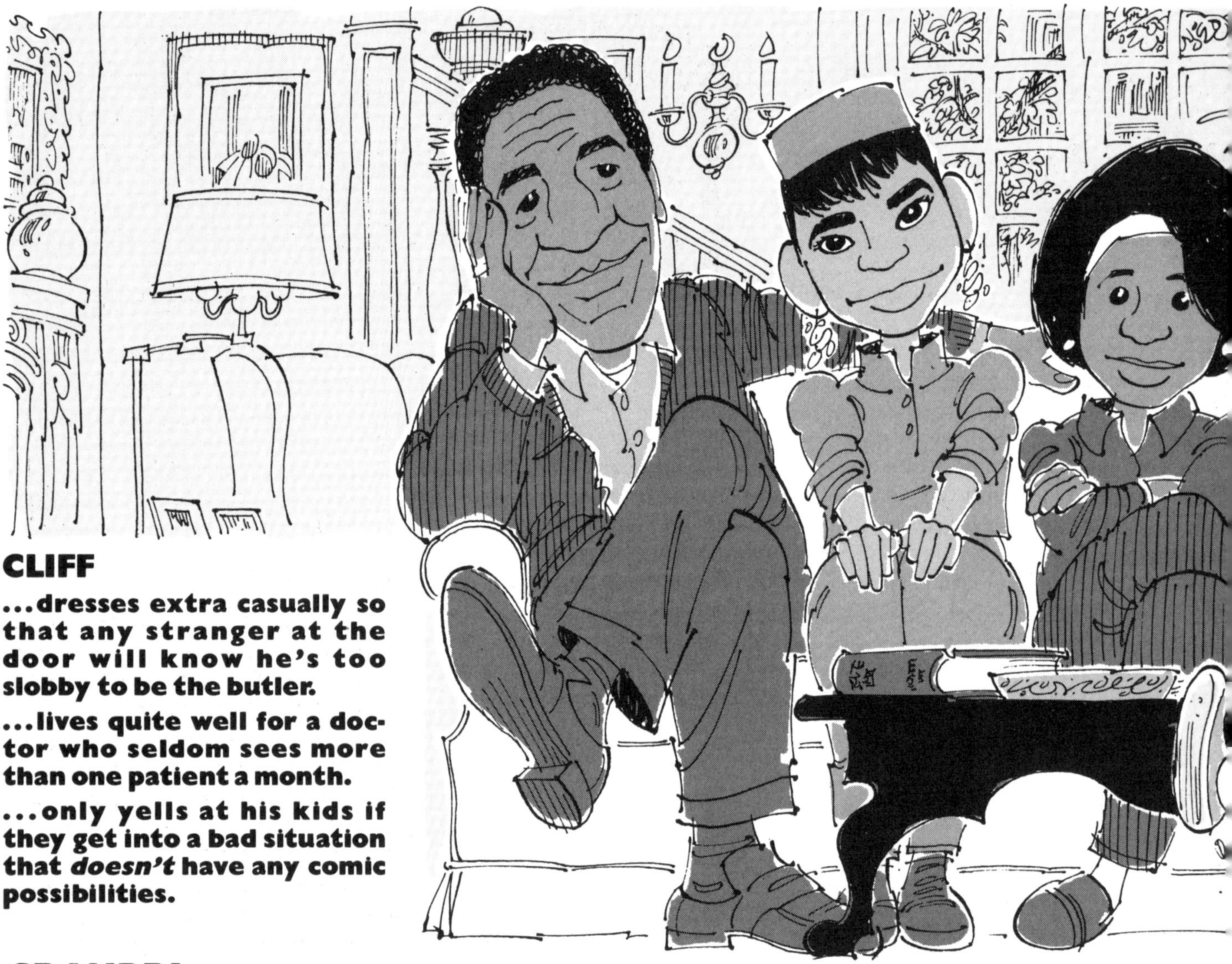

CLIFF

...dresses extra casually so that any stranger at the door will know he's too slobby to be the butler.

...lives quite well for a doctor who seldom sees more than one patient a month.

...only yells at his kids if they get into a bad situation that *doesn't* have any comic possibilities.

GRANDPA HUXTABLE

...avoids portraying a racial stereotype by depicting a dull, whiny, forgetful old Senior Citizen stereotype.

...displayed his one and only outburst of humor over 45 years ago when he decided to name his son Heathcliff.

...is the sort of man who makes his grandchildren thankful that he lives across town.

DENISE

...has a good head on her shoulders, but it belongs to her boyfriend.

...seems less like a member of the family and more like someone who's just there haunting the house.

...manages to make a "fashion statement" on every show. And that statement is: "PLEASE HELP ME!!"

VANESSA

...looks perpetually wo ried—as would any girl wh knows that she's doomed t be next in line for Denise hand-me-downs.

...sometimes suffers fro an identity crisis becaus people tend to confuse h with the wallpaper.

...scores points for equalit by being as vapid as ar white kid on a sit-com!

ult them. But this year, we got lucky. The Nation's sweethearts are all together, right nder our noses—on television! And they've got about as much chance for mercy as a long-ailed cat in a roomful of rockers when we begin firing away with a special edition of MAD's

OW Nasty File

ARTIST: PAUL COKER WRITER: TOM KOCH

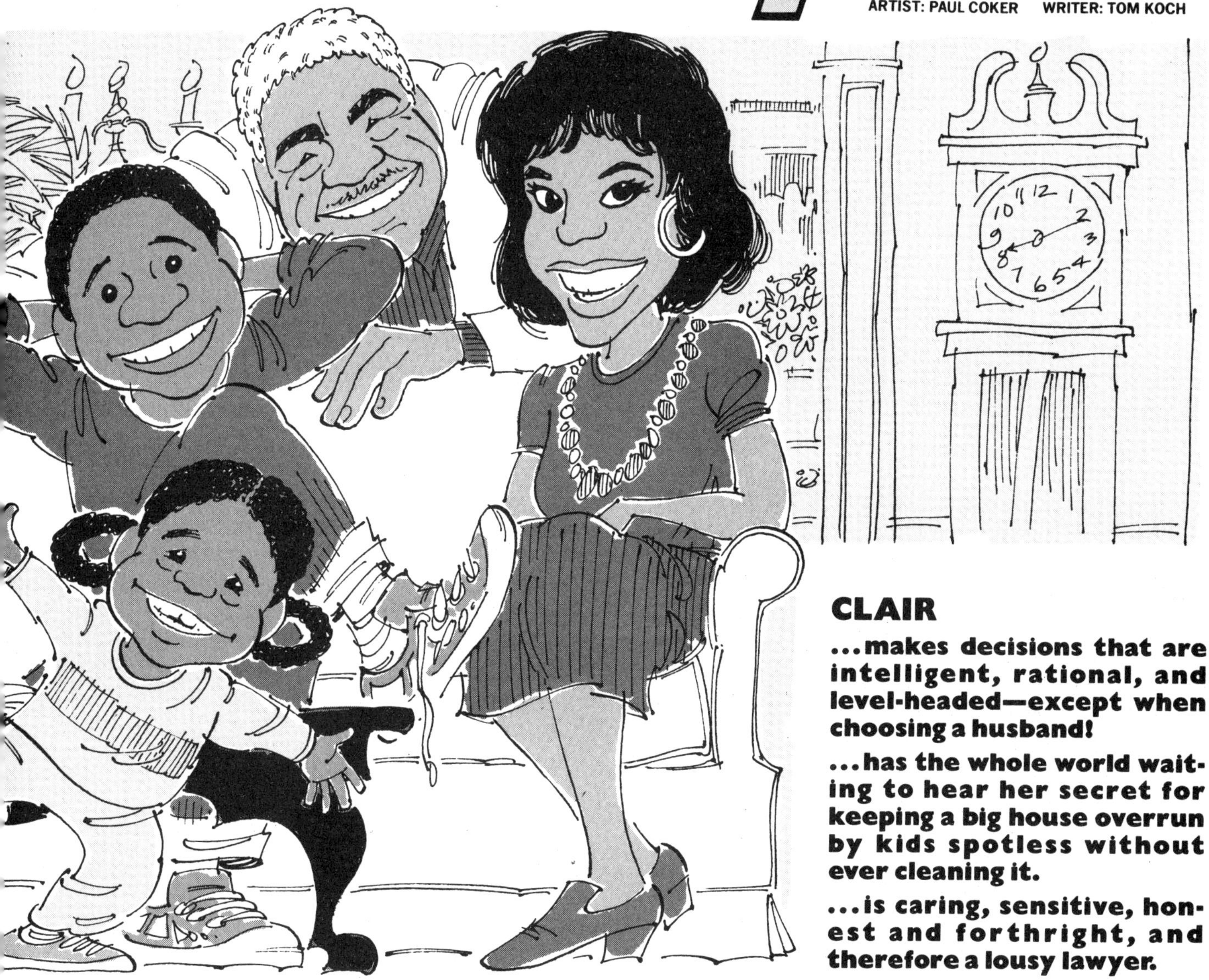

10 12 1
2
9 3
8 4
7 6 5

CLAIR

...makes decisions that are intelligent, rational, and level-headed—except when choosing a husband!

...has the whole world waiting to hear her secret for keeping a big house overrun by kids spotless without ever cleaning it.

...is caring, sensitive, honest and forthright, and therefore a lousy lawyer.

UDY

.would be worth about $50 the open market, figur-g ham at $1.29 a lb.

.keeps her hair braided so ghtly that the tiniest vi-ation could make her eyes p out completely.

.should plan to elope with nmanuel Lewis when she ows up since they ob-ously deserve each other.

THEO

...is clumsy, stubborn and slow—in other words, just like his father.

...consistently ranks near the top of his class, but only alphabetically.

...helps the world appreciate teenagers for what they really are—deceitful, lazy and oversexed.

THE HUXTABLE HOME

...houses a small fortune in fragile furniture and a gang of fumbling children.

...is the type of well-kept New York brownstone that J.R. Ewing would live in—if he could afford it.

...is the only house in Manhattan that has both (a) a basketball hoop on the garage, and (b) a garage.

A BAD CASE OF THE RE-RUNS DEPT.

The problem: Not enough good, current TV hits for MAD to parody!

The Solution: Go back and make fun of old TV shows that are still being played to death!

Another problem: Not enough copy to fill this boring introduction.

The solution: This extra line which doesn't say anything.

NOW there's enough copy, so here's our version of…

"I Love Luny"

I'm glad you guys stopped by! **Sicky** is at the club **auditioning** male **singers** for his new nightclub act.

What are **you** waiting for? Put on a **fake moustache** and **dress up** like a man and we'll go down to the audition and **fool** Sicky!

Nah, Sicky won't **fall** for that **old routine!**

I don't see why not! He's **fallen** for it **2,000 times before!**

Luny, **I can't** understand why you're not going to **louse-up** Sicky's audition with one of your **hilarious male impersonations!**

I'm staying **home** and making one of my **hilarious meals** instead—**chili!**

Chili's not hilarious!

It is when you make it with **Mexican jump beans!** If you want to try som get a ladder a **scrape** a littl off the ceilin

ARTIST: ANGELO TOR

How did the **audition** go, Sicky?

Okay, but there was **one singer** that was **so bad,** I thought it was Luny in **disguise!**

How did you **know** it really **wasn't** me?

I was able to get him **off** the stage in 15 seconds. If it was **you,** youse would've stayed on stage **15 minutes milking** the bit!

So **what** did you finally do with the **lousy singer?**

When I found out he was from **Cuba,** I told him I'd give him **air fare** back if he'd give up singing **forever.**

Well… did he **go** for it?

Not only did he **agre** but he **promised** no o in his **family** would sing, so I gave him money for **15 fares** home. I'm no **dumm**

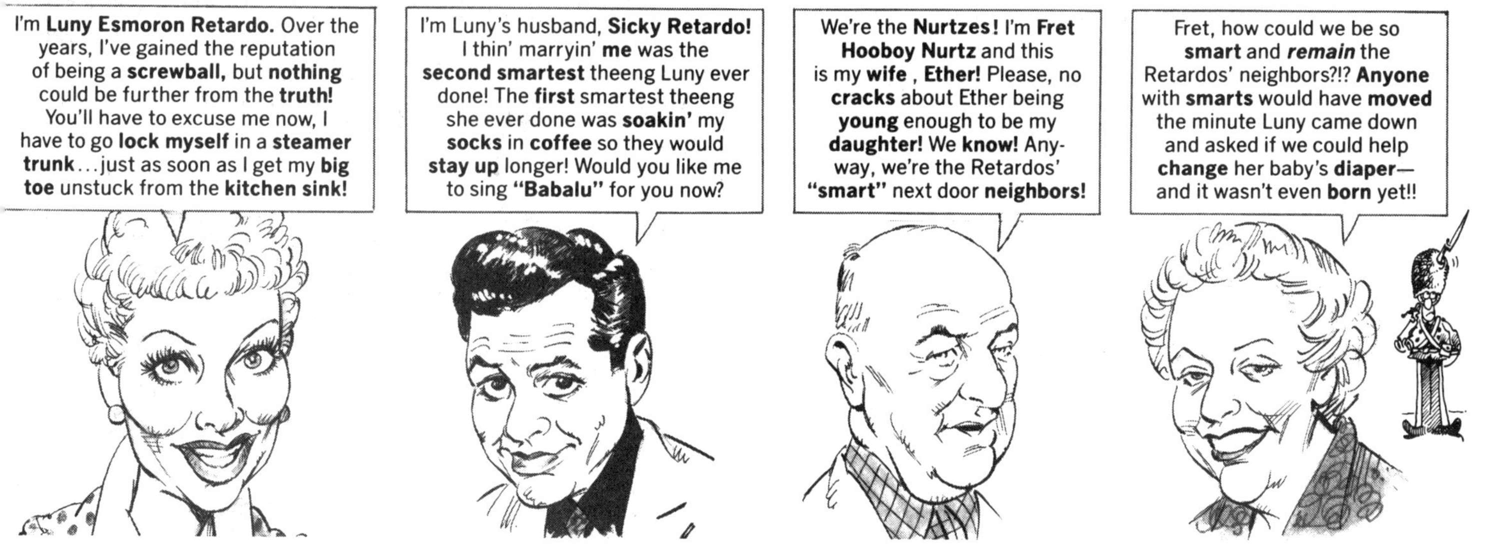
I'm Luny Esmoron Retardo. Over the years, I've gained the reputation of being a screwball, but nothing could be further from the truth! You'll have to excuse me now, I have to go lock myself in a steamer trunk...just as soon as I get my big toe unstuck from the kitchen sink!
I'm Luny's husband, Sicky Retardo! I thin' marryin' me was the second smartest theeng Luny ever done! The first smartest theeng she ever done was soakin' my socks in coffee so they would stay up longer! Would you like me to sing "Babalu" for you now?
We're the Nurtzes! I'm Fret Hooboy Nurtz and this is my wife , Ether! Please, no cracks about Ether being young enough to be my daughter! We know! Anyway, we're the Retardos' "smart" next door neighbors!
Fret, how could we be so smart and remain the Retardos' neighbors?!? Anyone with smarts would have moved the minute Luny came down and asked if we could help change her baby's diaper—and it wasn't even born yet!!

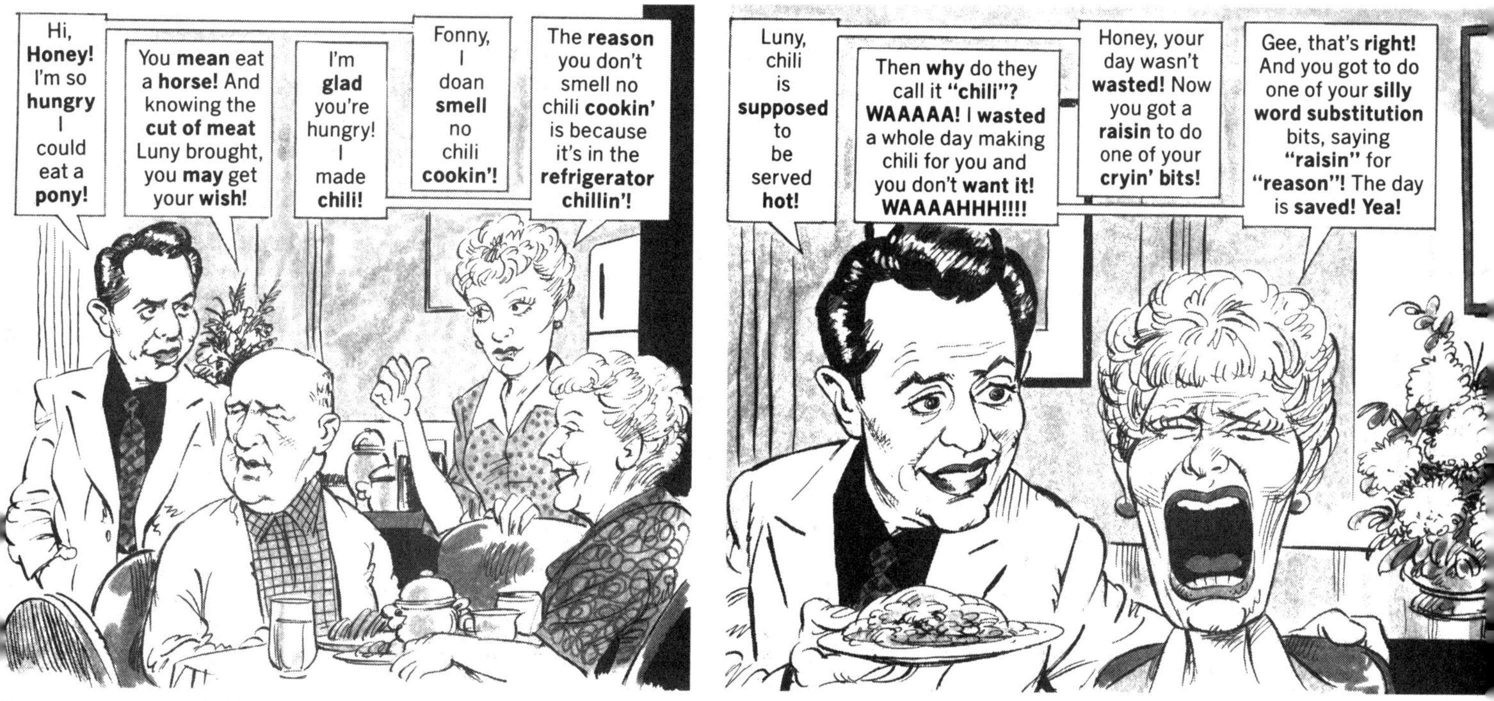
Hi, Honey! I'm so hungry I could eat a pony!
You mean eat a horse! And knowing the cut of meat Luny brought, you may get your wish!
I'm glad you're hungry! I made chili!
Fonny, I doan smell no chili cookin'!
The reason you don't smell no chili cookin' is because it's in the refrigerator chillin'!
Luny, chili is supposed to be served hot!
Then why do they call it "chili"? WAAAAA! I wasted a whole day making chili for you and you don't want it! WAAAAHHH!!!!
Honey, your day wasn't wasted! Now you got a raisin to do one of your cryin' bits!
Gee, that's right! And you got to do one of your silly word substitution bits, saying "raisin" for "reason"! The day is saved! Yea!

RITER: LOU SILVERSTONE

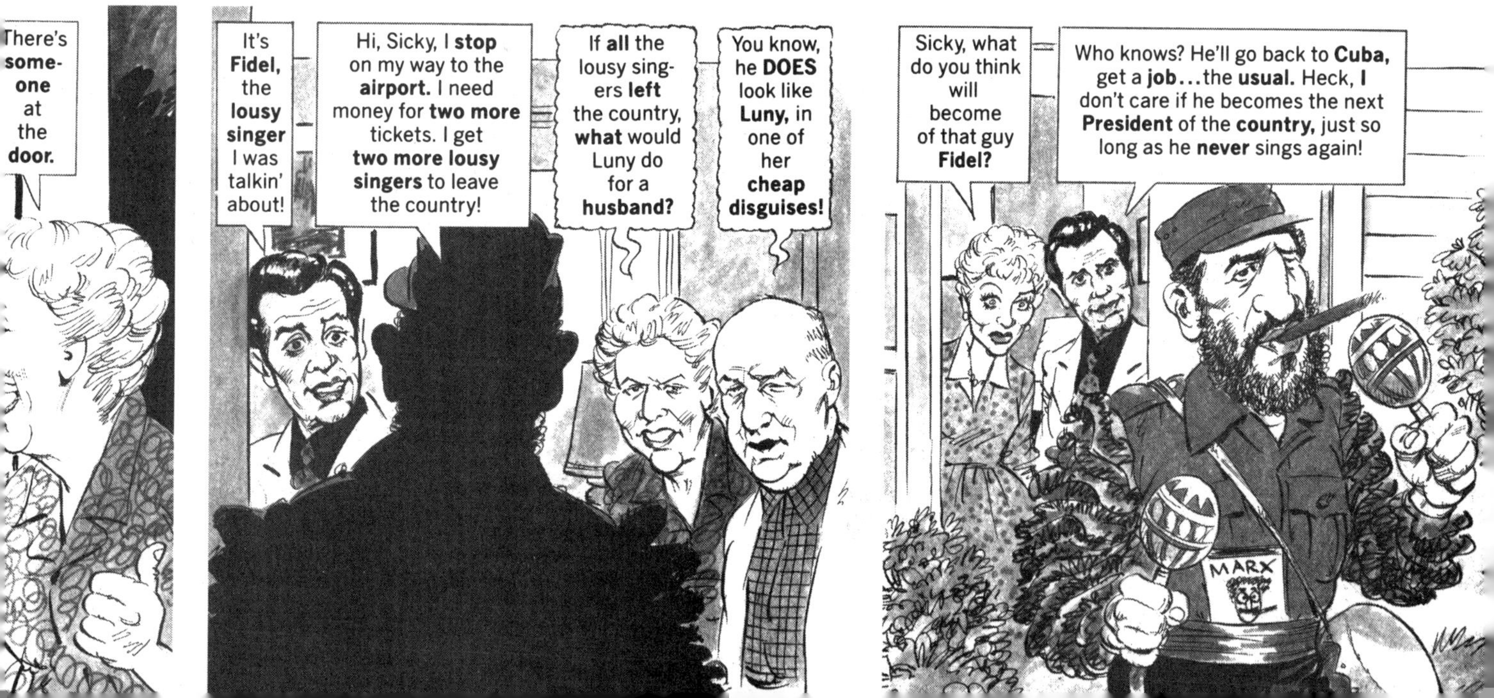
There's someone at the door.
It's Fidel, the lousy singer I was talkin' about!
Hi, Sicky, I stop on my way to the airport. I need money for two more tickets. I get two more lousy singers to leave the country!
If all the lousy singers left the country, what would Luny do for a husband?
You know, he DOES look like Luny, in one of her cheap disguises!
Sicky, what do you think will become of that guy Fidel?
Who knows? He'll go back to Cuba, get a job...the usual. Heck, I don't care if he becomes the next President of the country, just so long as he never sings again!
MARX

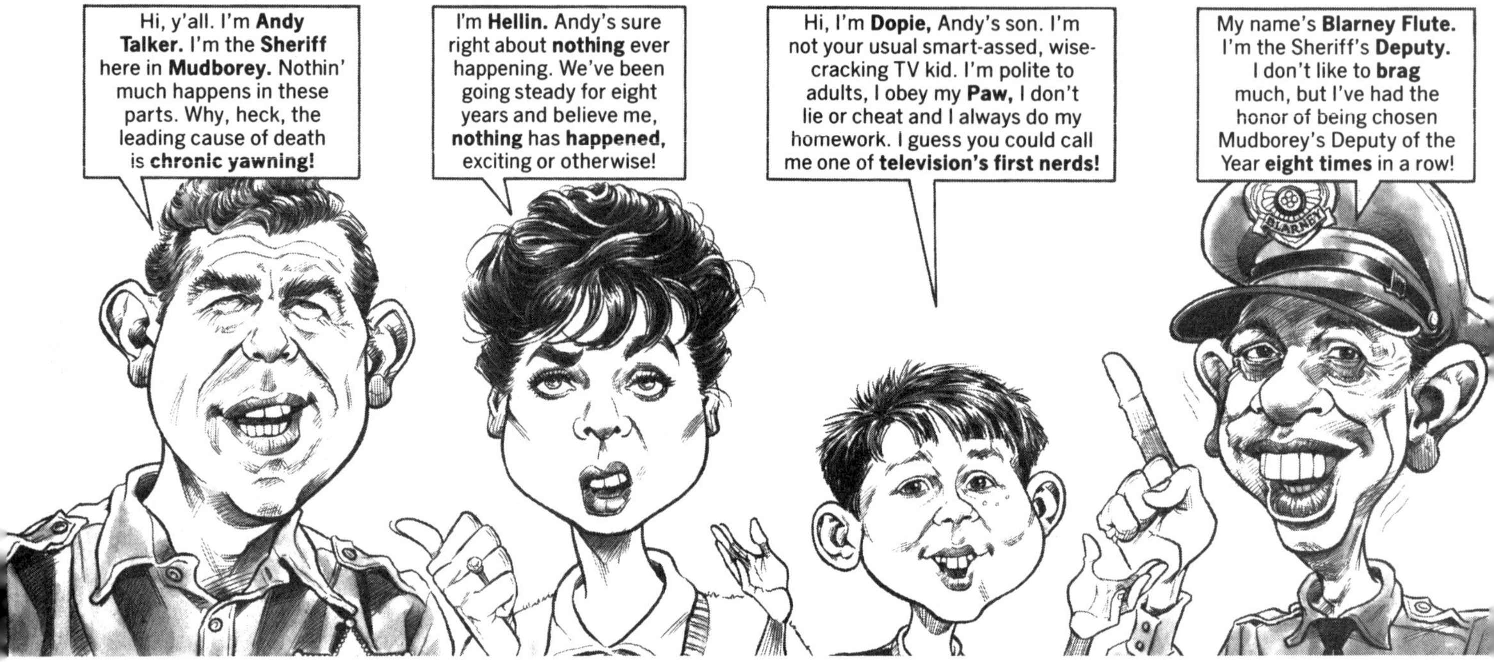

Hi, y'all. I'm **Andy Talker.** I'm the **Sheriff** here in **Mudborey.** Nothin' much happens in these parts. Why, heck, the leading cause of death is **chronic yawning!**
I'm **Hellin.** Andy's sure right about **nothing** ever happening. We've been going steady for eight years and believe me, **nothing** has **happened,** exciting or otherwise!
Hi, I'm **Dopie,** Andy's son. I'm not your usual smart-assed, wise-cracking TV kid. I'm polite to adults, I obey my **Paw,** I don't lie or cheat and I always do my homework. I guess you could call me one of **television's first nerds!**
My name's **Blarney Flute.** I'm the Sheriff's **Deputy.** I don't like to **brag** much, but I've had the honor of being chosen Mudborey's Deputy of the Year **eight times** in a row!
BLARNEY

ARTIST: SAM VIVIANO WRITER: LOU SILVERSTONE

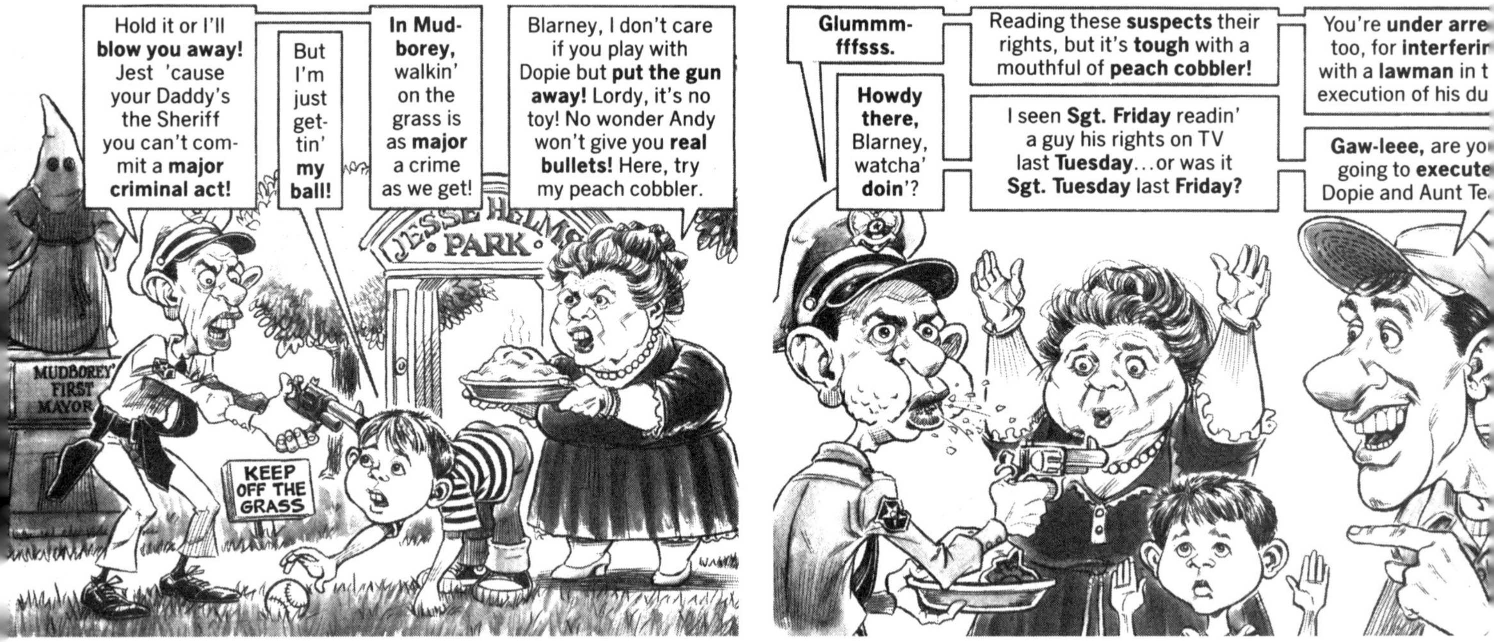

Hold it or I'll **blow you away!** Jest 'cause your Daddy's the Sheriff you can't commit a **major criminal act!**
But I'm just gettin' **my ball!**
In Mudborey, walkin' on the grass is as **major** a crime as we get!
Blarney, I don't care if you play with Dopie but **put the gun away!** Lordy, it's no toy! No wonder Andy won't give you **real bullets!** Here, try my peach cobbler.
JESSE HELMS PARK
MUDBOREY'S FIRST MAYOR
KEEP OFF THE GRASS
Glummm-fffsss.
Reading these **suspects** their rights, but it's **tough** with a mouthful of **peach cobbler!**
Howdy there, Blarney, watcha' **doin'**?
I seen **Sgt. Friday** readin' a guy his rights on TV last **Tuesday**...or was it **Sgt. Tuesday** last **Friday?**
You're **under arre** too, for **interferin** with a **lawman** in t execution of his du
Gaw-leee, are yo going to **execute** Dopie and Aunt Te

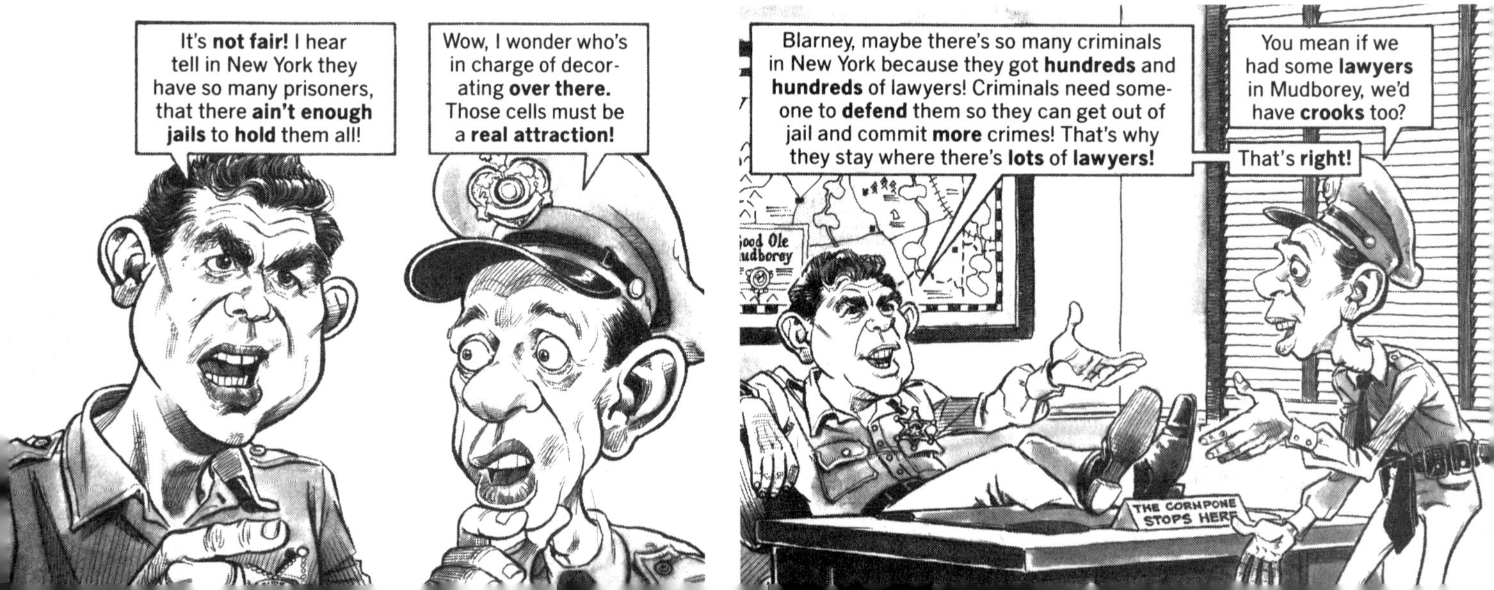

It's **not fair!** I hear tell in New York they have so many prisoners, that there **ain't enough jails** to **hold** them all!
Wow, I wonder who's in charge of decorating **over there.** Those cells must be a **real attraction!**
Blarney, maybe there's so many criminals in New York because they got **hundreds** and **hundreds** of lawyers! Criminals need someone to **defend** them so they can get out of jail and commit **more** crimes! That's why they stay where there's **lots of lawyers!**
You mean if we had some **lawyers** in Mudborey, we'd have **crooks** too?
That's **right!**
THE CORNPONE STOPS HERE

A BAD CASE OF THE RE-RUNS DEPT.

THE ANDY GRINNING SHOW

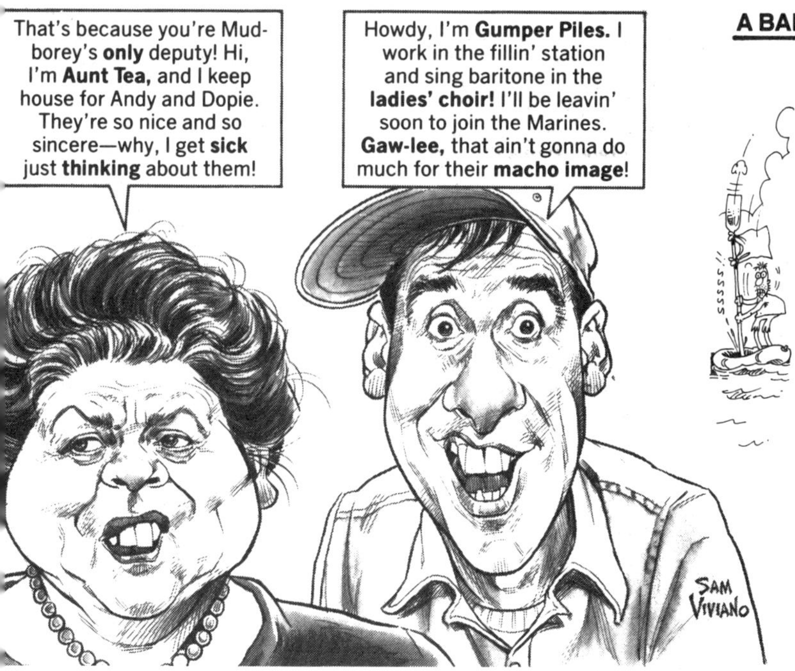

That's because you're Mudborey's **only** deputy! Hi, I'm **Aunt Tea,** and I keep house for Andy and Dopie. They're so nice and so sincere—why, I get **sick** just **thinking** about them!
Howdy, I'm **Gumper Piles.** I work in the fillin' station and sing baritone in the **ladies' choir!** I'll be leavin' soon to join the Marines. **Gaw-lee,** that ain't gonna do much for their **macho image**!
SAM VIVIANO

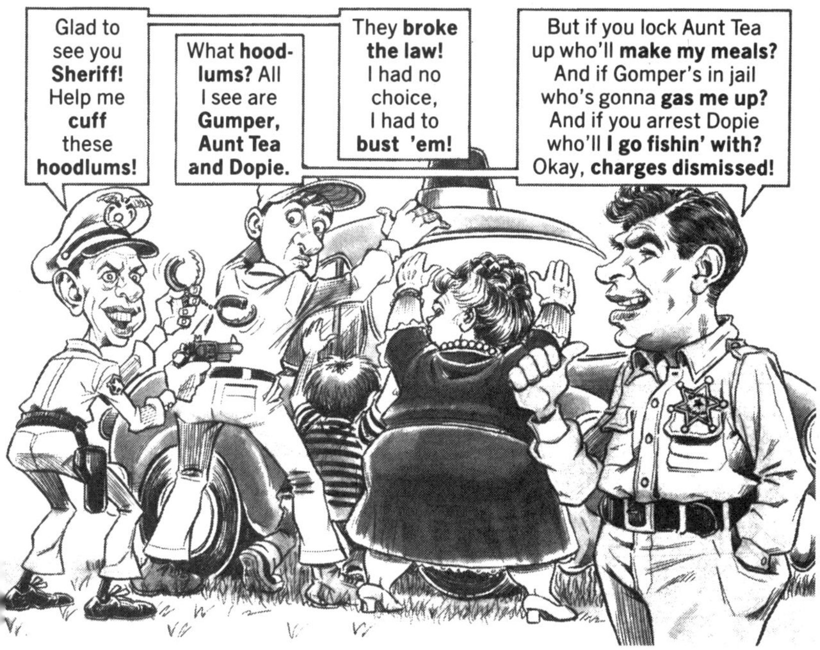

Glad to see you **Sheriff!** Help me **cuff** these **hoodlums!**
What **hoodlums?** All I see are **Gumper, Aunt Tea and Dopie.**
They **broke the law!** I had no choice, I had to **bust 'em!**
But if you lock Aunt Tea up who'll **make my meals?** And if Gomper's in jail who's gonna **gas me up?** And if you arrest Dopie who'll **I go fishin' with?** Okay, **charges dismissed!**

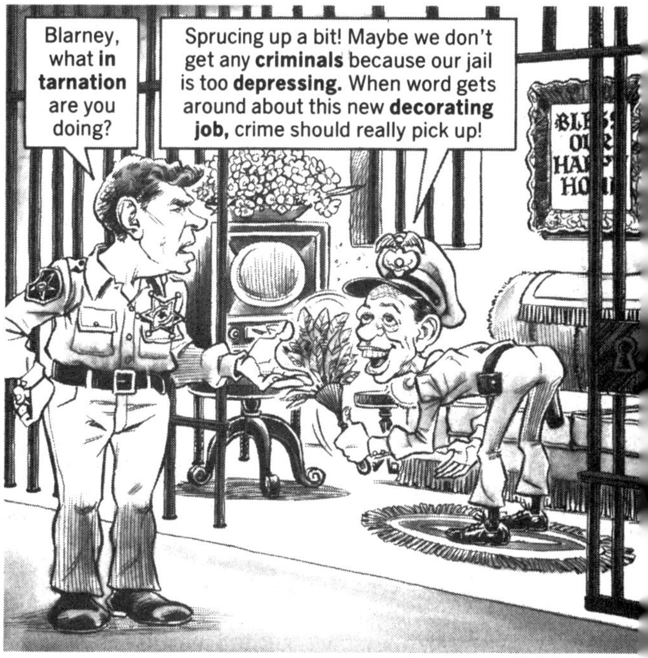

Blarney, what **in tarnation** are you doing?
Sprucing up a bit! Maybe we don't get any **criminals** because our jail is too **depressing.** When word gets around about this new **decorating job,** crime should really pick up!

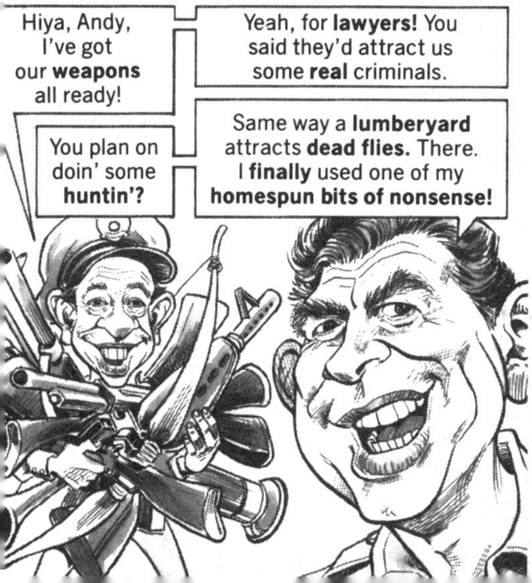

Hiya, Andy, I've got our **weapons** all ready!
Yeah, for **lawyers!** You said they'd attract us some **real** criminals.
You plan on doin' some **huntin'?**
Same way a **lumberyard** attracts **dead flies.** There. I **finally** used one of my **homespun bits of nonsense!**

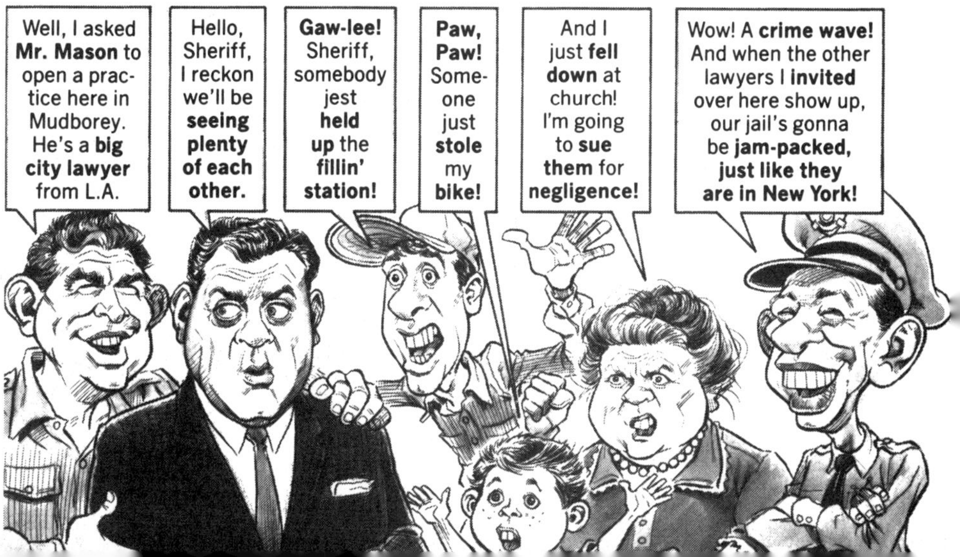

Well, I asked **Mr. Mason** to open a practice here in Mudborey. He's a **big city lawyer** from L.A.
Hello, Sheriff, I reckon we'll be **seeing plenty of each other.**
Gaw-lee! Sheriff, somebody jest **held up** the **fillin' station!**
Paw, Paw! Someone just **stole** my **bike!**
And I just **fell down** at church! I'm going to **sue them** for **negligence!**
Wow! A **crime wave!** And when the other lawyers I **invited** over here show up, our jail's gonna be **jam-packed, just like they are in New York!**

WIMP-LASH DEPT.

A MAD PEEK BEH

PEE-WEE'S

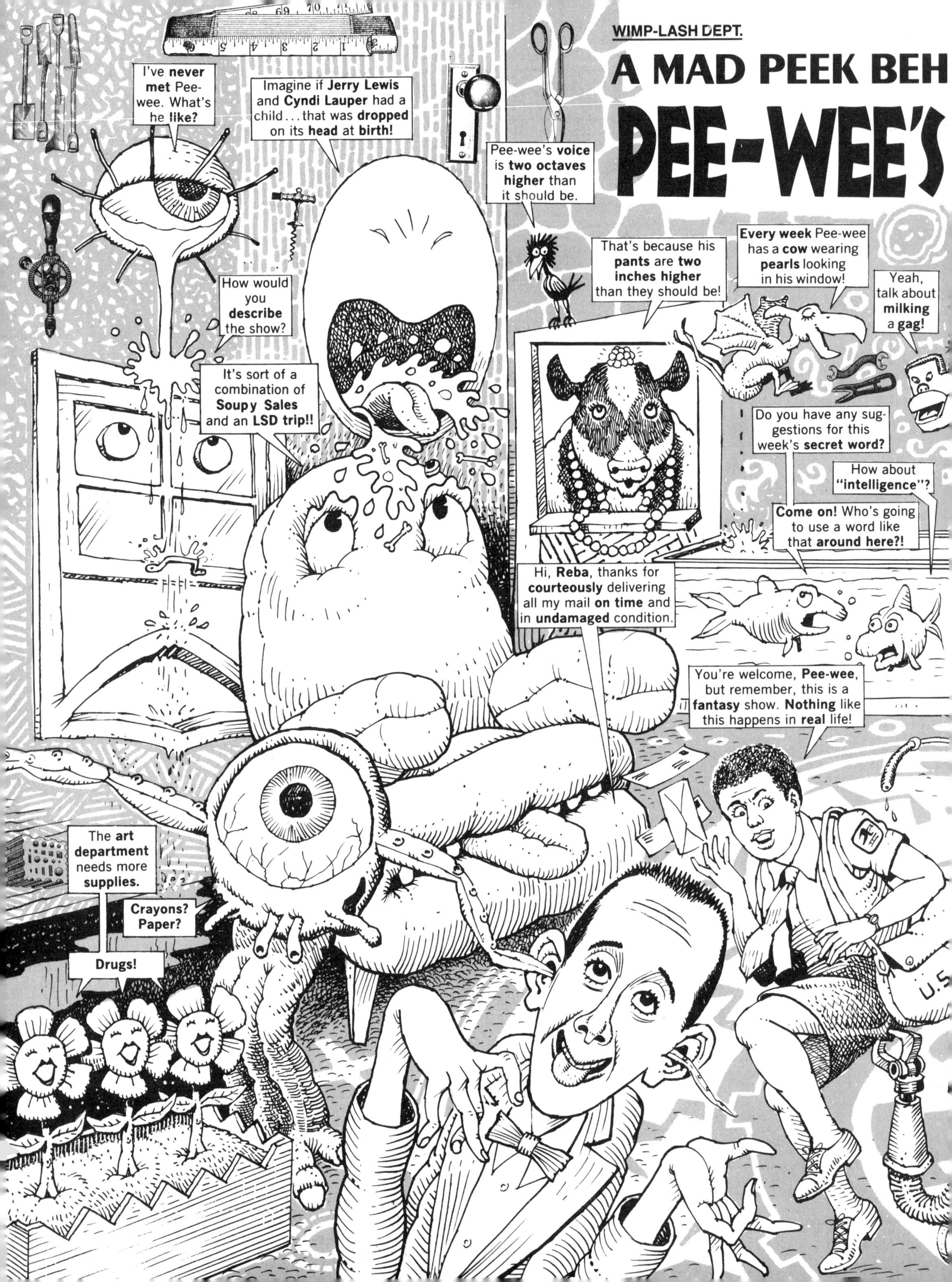

I've **never met** Pee-wee. What's he **like?**
Imagine if **Jerry Lewis** and **Cyndi Lauper** had a child . . . that was **dropped** on its **head** at **birth!**
Pee-wee's **voice** is **two octaves higher** than it should be.
That's because his **pants** are **two inches higher** than they should be!
Every week Pee-wee has a **cow** wearing **pearls** looking in his window!
Yeah, talk about **milking** a **gag!**
How would you **describe** the show?
It's sort of a combination of **Soupy Sales** and an **LSD trip!!**
Do you have any suggestions for this week's **secret word?**
How about **"intelligence"?**
Come on! Who's going to use a word like that **around here?!**
Hi, **Reba**, thanks for **courteously** delivering all my mail **on time** and in **undamaged** condition.
You're welcome, **Pee-wee**, but remember, this is a **fantasy** show. **Nothing** like this happens in **real** life!
The **art department** needs more **supplies.**
Crayons? Paper?
Drugs!

THE SCENES AT

LAYHOUSE

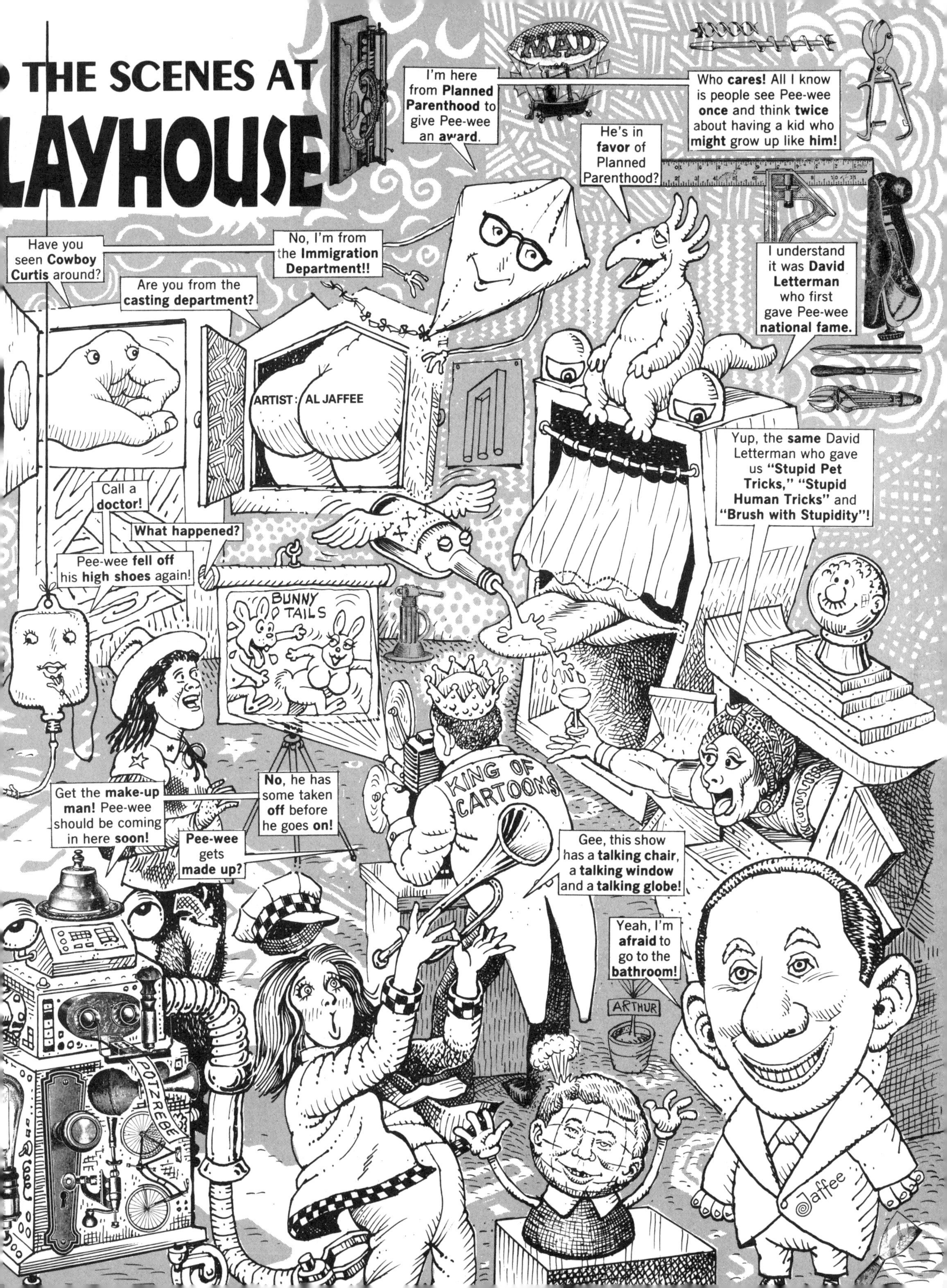

I'm here from **Planned Parenthood** to give Pee-wee an **award**.
Who **cares!** All I know is people see Pee-wee **once** and think **twice** about having a kid who **might** grow up like **him!**
He's in **favor** of Planned Parenthood?
Have you seen **Cowboy Curtis** around?
No, I'm from the **Immigration Department!!**
Are you from the **casting department?**
ARTIST : AL JAFFEE
I understand it was **David Letterman** who first gave Pee-wee **national fame.**
Yup, the **same** David Letterman who gave us **"Stupid Pet Tricks," "Stupid Human Tricks"** and **"Brush with Stupidity"!**
Call a **doctor!**
What happened?
Pee-wee **fell off** his **high shoes** again!
BUNNY TAILS
KING OF CARTOONS
Get the **make-up man!** Pee-wee should be coming in here **soon!**
No, he has some taken **off** before he goes **on!**
Pee-wee gets **made up?**
Gee, this show has a **talking chair**, a **talking window** and a **talking globe!**
Yeah, I'm **afraid** to go to the **bathroom!**
ARTHUR
POTZREBIE
Jaffee

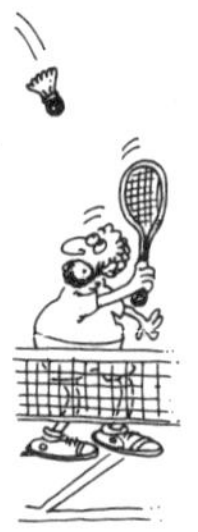

EYEWITNESS RUSE DEPT.

Hey, schmucks! Why do you assume, as you watch your local TV Newscast, that th anchormen and reporters are all top journalists bringing you the very latest in pro fessionally gathered information? We'll tell you why! Because the station managemen

TRICKS OF THE TRAI

ARTIST: GEORGE WOODBRID

DISPLAYS OF TIME IN FOREIGN CITIES

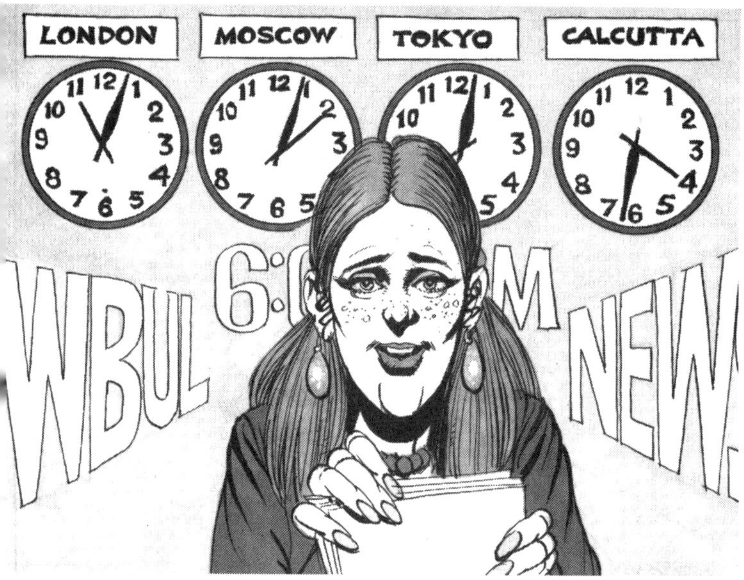
LONDON
MOSCOW
TOKYO
CALCUTTA
WBUL

This is an obvious trick employed by many local TV News Departments to hoodwink their viewers. If you doubt it, just ask yourself, "Why does this station in Ames, Iowa, which has no reporter in Calcutta, India, and has never carried a story about Calcutta, India, need to keep its staff aware of the exact time now in Calcutta, India?"

REMOTES FROM REPORTERS IN THE FIELD

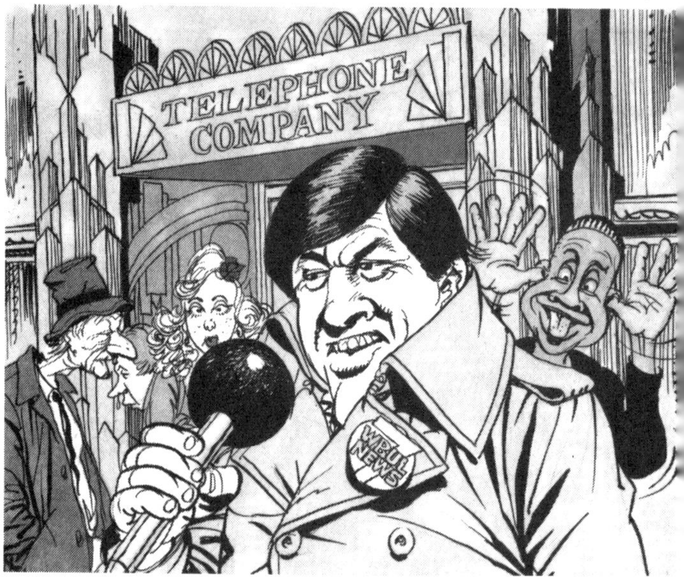
TELEPHONE COMPANY
WBUL NEWS

Why does the TV Newsman who's telling you about an increase in phone rates need to be seen standing in front of the Telephone Building? Obviously, he doesn't want you to suspect that he's read the story in the morning paper, just like you. So beware of this form of "on-the-spot reporting" that comes from a spot that isn't exactly "on the spot" where the spot news occurred.

ANALYSIS OF EVENTS BY LOCAL EXPERTS

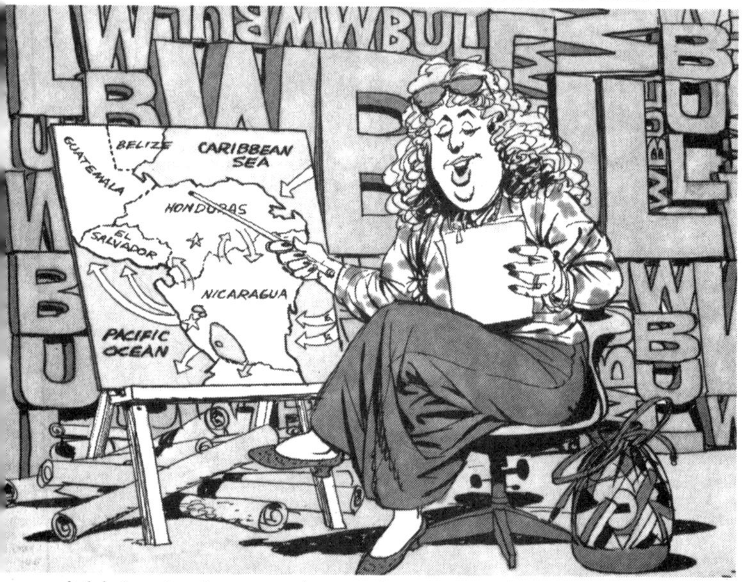
BELIZE
CARIBBEAN SEA
GUATEMALA
HONDURAS
EL SALVADOR
NICARAGUA
PACIFIC OCEAN

A high school economics teacher may understand the National Debt almost enough to analyze it on TV, but be skeptical of lesser experts, like the local garage mechanic who's called in to explain what went wrong with today's space launch, or the real estate salesman who makes economic predictions, or the station manager's wife who was last week's expert on El Salvador and this week's authority on food preservatives.

INTERVIEWS OF "THE MAN IN THE STREET"

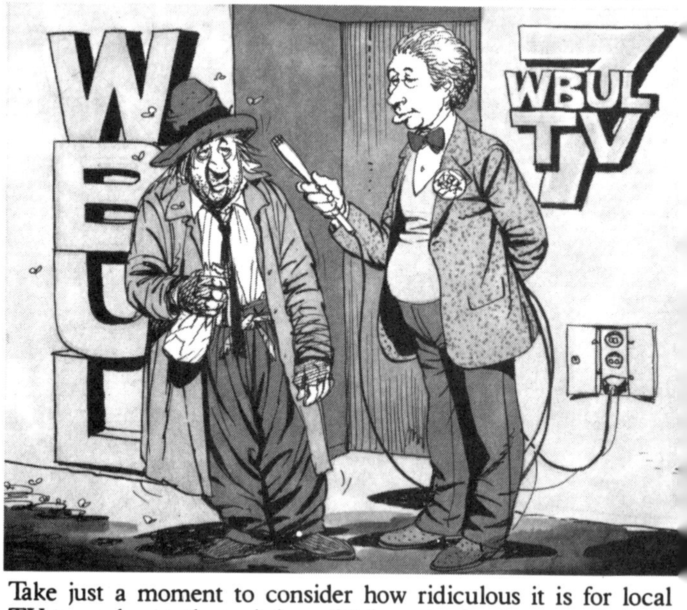
WBUL TV

Take just a moment to consider how ridiculous it is for local TV to seek out the opinion of "the man in the street" about some late news development. People chosen at random obviously don't know any more about an event than you do, so why waste time airing their views? Because it's an easy story that can be done right in front of the studio while the station's only mobile unit is out of action getting a lube job! That's why!

uses a whole bagful of gimmicks, props, double-talk and outright tricks to create the illusion that its news people know what they're doing! As part of MAD's ongoing campaign to protect the public from its own gullibility, let's take a hard look at:

E IN LOCAL TV NEWS

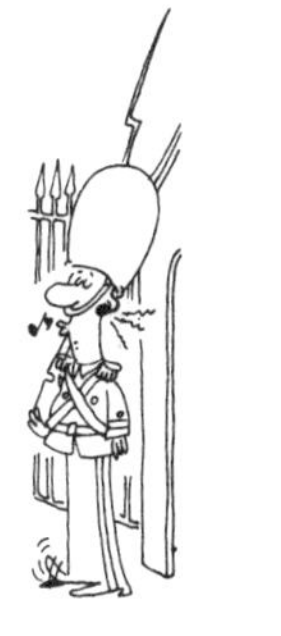

WRITER: TOM KOCH

EXTENDED COVERAGE OF LURID STORIES

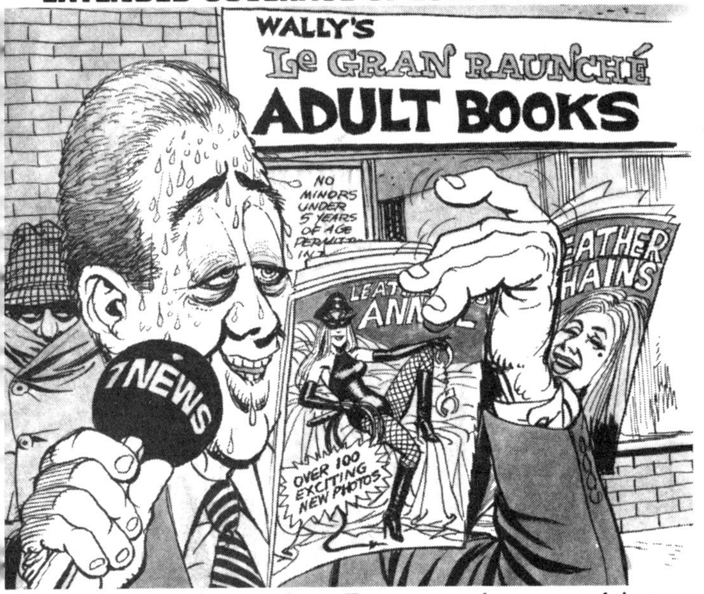
WALLY'S
Le GRAN' RAUNCHÉ
ADULT BOOKS
NO MINORS UNDER 5 YEARS OF AGE
7NEWS
OVER 100 EXCITING NEW PHOTOS

If the day's total news from Europe can be reported in two sentences, ask yourself why it takes a four-part "investigative series" to cover the town's only porno store. Such lengthy "studies" are even more suspect when they come at the same time that the other local station is doing an in-depth report on "Shower Facilities at the Women's Prison."

NEEDLESS USE OF NEWS HELICOPTERS

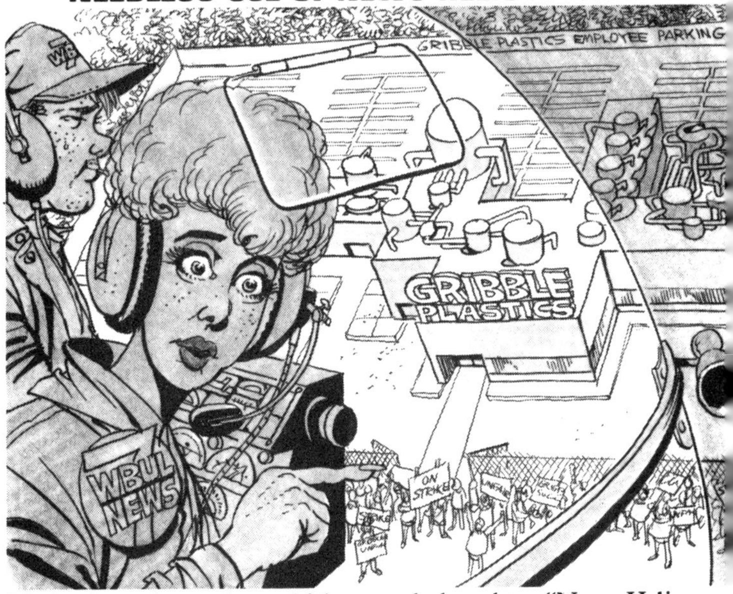
GRIBBLE PLASTICS EMPLOYEE PARKING
GRIBBLE PLASTICS
WBUL NEWS
ON STRIKE

Notice how the station, which recently bought a "News Helicopter" amid much ballyhoo, now uses the chopper to make stories that don't really require helicopter coverage appear more sensational. Example: Overhead shot of a factory parking lot to illustrate how striking employees who didn't report to work today also didn't drive their cars to work.

FLAUNTED USE OF MYSTERIOUS EARPIECES

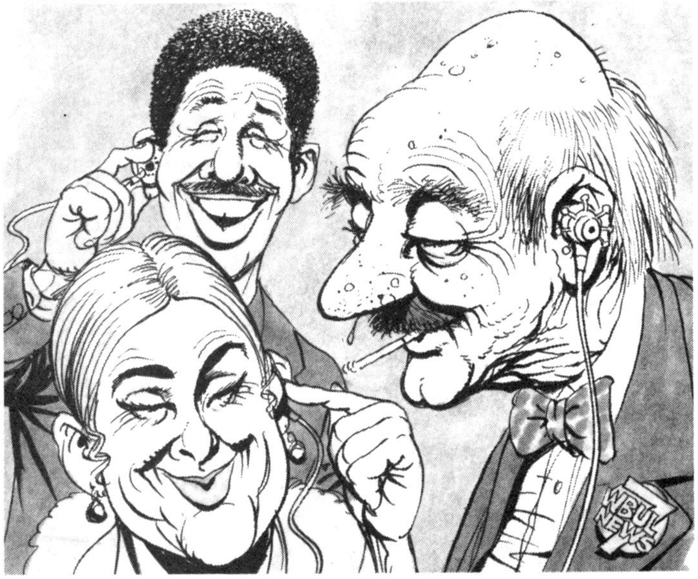
WBUL NEWS

Anchormen at even tiny TV stations are now copying network news stars by wearing poorly concealed earphones attached to long cords. This is to make you think that they're very important people who use the gadgets to remain in constant communication with directors and other flunkies! In truth, anchormen who wear earpieces are just bored with their show and are listening to something better on transistor radios.

DRAMATIC USE OF NEWSROOM ATMOSPHERE

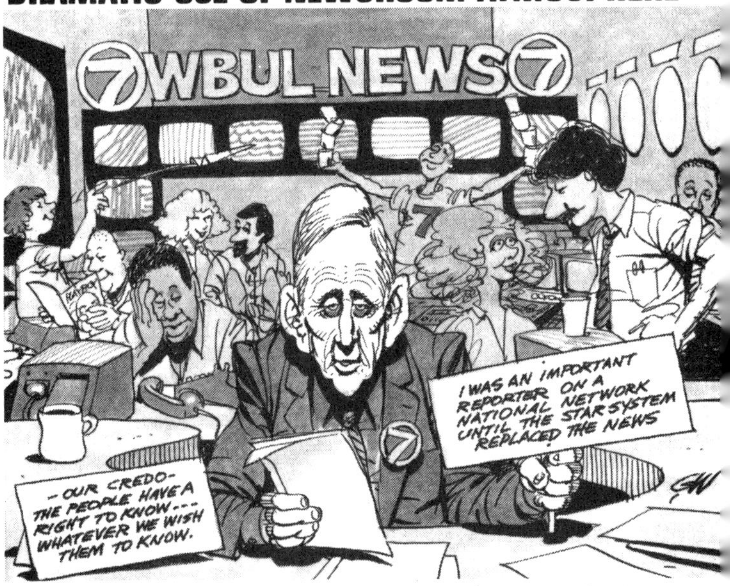
7 WBUL NEWS 7
I WAS AN IMPORTANT REPORTER ON A NATIONAL NETWORK UNTIL THE STAR SYSTEM REPLACED THE NEWS
—OUR CREDO— THE PEOPLE HAVE A RIGHT TO KNOW... WHATEVER WE WISH THEM TO KNOW.

Televising direct from the newsroom is a common bit of hokum employed by local stations to make you believe you're getting the latest hot-off-the-wire news. To puncture this myth, just watch the newswriters visible in the background, and note that they aren't writing news. Instead, they're talking, or eating, or tossing darts, or doing any of the other things that newswriters do on the job when they think no one's watching them.

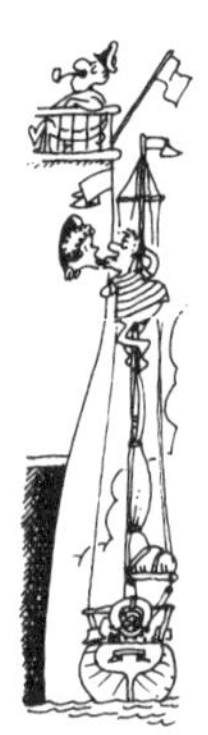

HIPPOCRATIC OAFS DEPT.

Here we go with MAD's version of the medical TV series about a fictional hospi tal where the doctors and nurses are more concerned with their own problems thar those of their patients. Hmmm, that sounds just like a *real* hospital! It's a fictional hospital where the administrators are more interested in making a prof

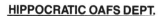

ST. HEAL

ARTIST: MORT DRUCKE

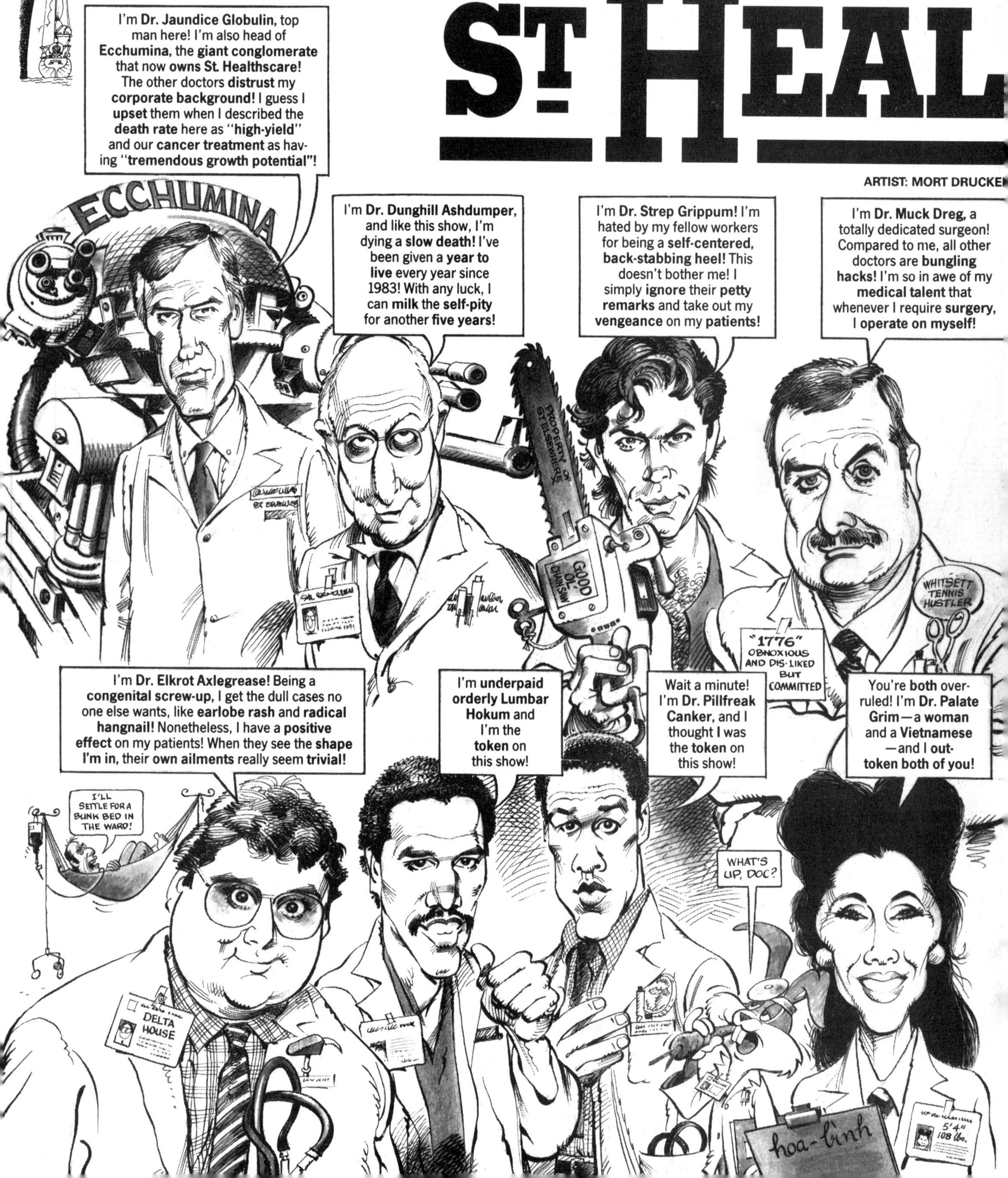
I'm Dr. Jaundice Globulin, top man here! I'm also head of Ecchumina, the giant conglomerate that now owns St. Healthscare! The other doctors distrust my corporate background! I guess I upset them when I described the death rate here as "high-yield" and our cancer treatment as having "tremendous growth potential"!
ECCHUMINA
I'm Dr. Dunghill Ashdumper, and like this show, I'm dying a slow death! I've been given a year to live every year since 1983! With any luck, I can milk the self-pity for another five years!
I'm Dr. Strep Grippum! I'm hated by my fellow workers for being a self-centered, back-stabbing heel! This doesn't bother me! I simply ignore their petty remarks and take out my vengeance on my patients!
PROPERTY OF ST. ELSEWHERE
GOOD OL' CHAINSAW
I'm Dr. Muck Dreg, a totally dedicated surgeon! Compared to me, all other doctors are bungling hacks! I'm so in awe of my medical talent that whenever I require surgery, I operate on myself!
WHITSETT TENNIS HUSTLER
"1776" OBNOXIOUS AND DIS-LIKED BUT COMMITTED
I'm Dr. Elkrot Axlegrease! Being a congenital screw-up, I get the dull cases no one else wants, like earlobe rash and radical hangnail! Nonetheless, I have a positive effect on my patients! When they see the shape I'm in, their own ailments really seem trivial!
I'LL SETTLE FOR A BUNK BED IN THE WARD!
DELTA HOUSE
I'm underpaid orderly Lumbar Hokum and I'm the token on this show!
Wait a minute! I'm Dr. Pillfreak Canker, and I thought I was the token on this show!
WHAT'S UP, DOC?
You're both over-ruled! I'm Dr. Palate Grim—a woman and a Vietnamese—and I out-token both of you!
hoa-binh
5'4" 108 lbs.

t than healing the sick. Hey, *that's* like a real hospital too! It's a fictional hospital where patients receive inferior treatment from a bunch of wisecracking, unqualified medical trainees. Uh-oh, *that's* painfully real! Since this "fictional" TV show is so much like real life, you now know why we call it...

HSCARE

RITER: FRANK JACOBS

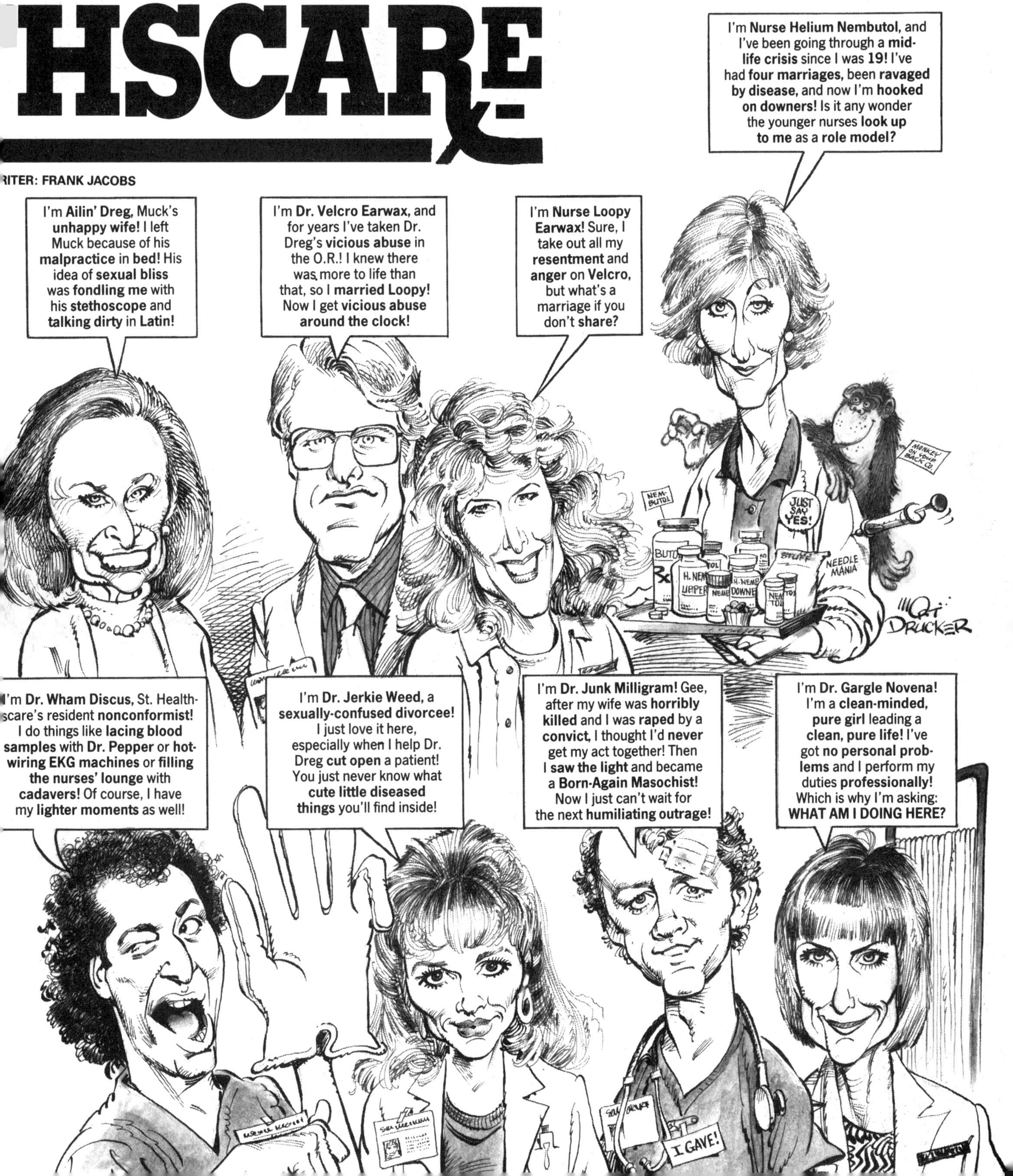

I'm Ailin' Dreg, Muck's unhappy wife! I left Muck because of his malpractice in bed! His idea of sexual bliss was fondling me with his stethoscope and talking dirty in Latin!
I'm Dr. Velcro Earwax, and for years I've taken Dr. Dreg's vicious abuse in the O.R.! I knew there was more to life than that, so I married Loopy! Now I get vicious abuse around the clock!
I'm Nurse Loopy Earwax! Sure, I take out all my resentment and anger on Velcro, but what's a marriage if you don't share?
I'm Nurse Helium Nembutol, and I've been going through a mid-life crisis since I was 19! I've had four marriages, been ravaged by disease, and now I'm hooked on downers! Is it any wonder the younger nurses look up to me as a role model?
JUST SAY YES!
NEEDLE MANIA
DRUCKER
I'm Dr. Wham Discus, St. Health-scare's resident nonconformist! I do things like lacing blood samples with Dr. Pepper or hot-wiring EKG machines or filling the nurses' lounge with cadavers! Of course, I have my lighter moments as well!
I'm Dr. Jerkie Weed, a sexually-confused divorcee! I just love it here, especially when I help Dr. Dreg cut open a patient! You just never know what cute little diseased things you'll find inside!
I'm Dr. Junk Milligram! Gee, after my wife was horribly killed and I was raped by a convict, I thought I'd never get my act together! Then I saw the light and became a Born-Again Masochist! Now I just can't wait for the next humiliating outrage!
I'm Dr. Gargle Novena! I'm a clean-minded, pure girl leading a clean, pure life! I've got no personal problems and I perform my duties professionally! Which is why I'm asking: WHAT AM I DOING HERE?
I GAVE!

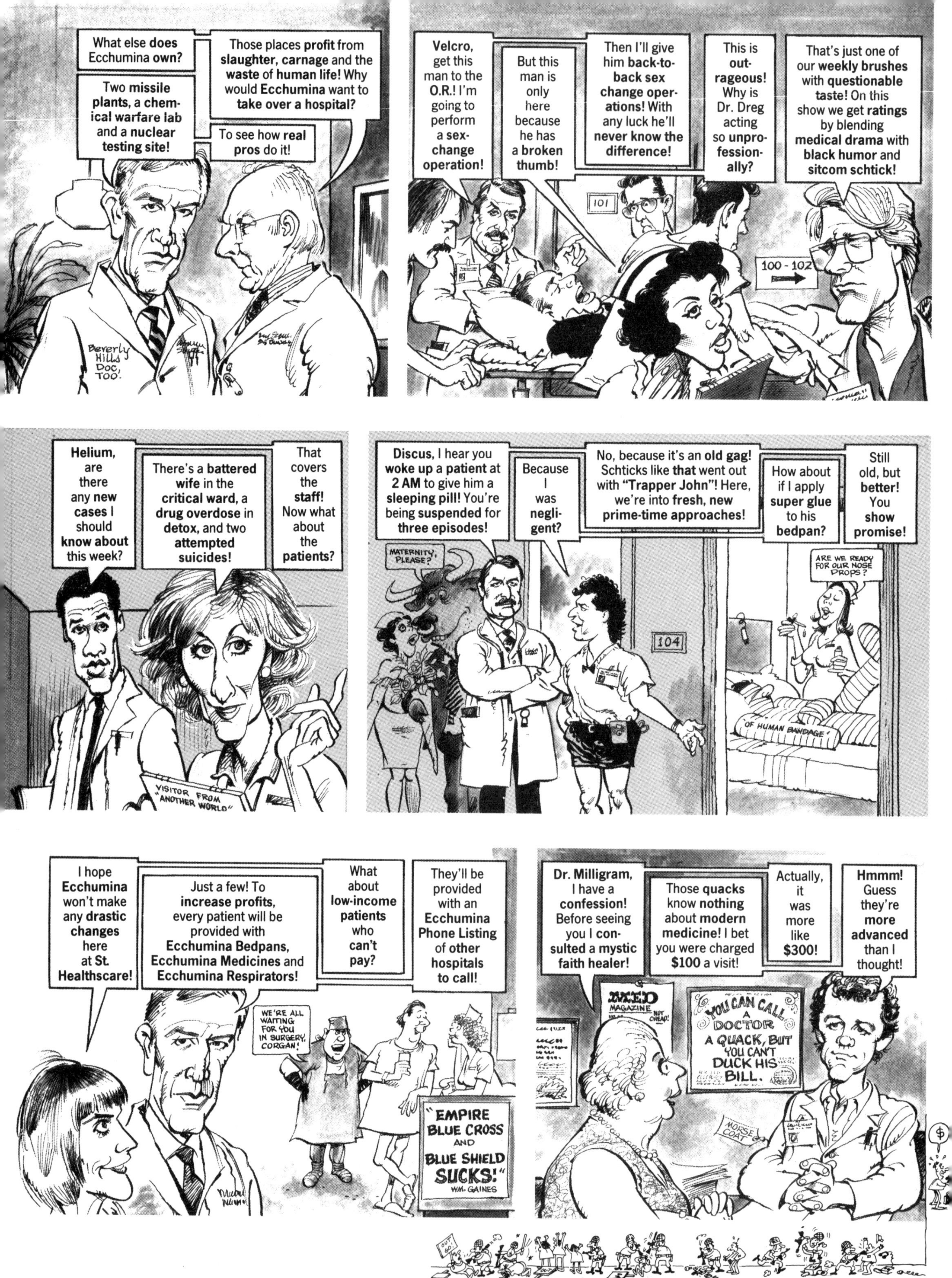

What else does Ecchumina own?
Two missile plants, a chemical warfare lab and a nuclear testing site!
Those places profit from slaughter, carnage and the waste of human life! Why would Ecchumina want to take over a hospital?
To see how real pros do it!
Beverly Hills Doc, Too.
Velcro, get this man to the O.R.! I'm going to perform a sex-change operation!
But this man is only here because he has a broken thumb!
Then I'll give him back-to-back sex change operations! With any luck he'll never know the difference!
This is outrageous! Why is Dr. Dreg acting so unprofessionally?
That's just one of our weekly brushes with questionable taste! On this show we get ratings by blending medical drama with black humor and sitcom schtick!
101
100 - 102
Helium, are there any new cases I should know about this week?
There's a battered wife in the critical ward, a drug overdose in detox, and two attempted suicides!
That covers the staff! Now what about the patients?
VISITOR FROM "ANOTHER WORLD"
Discus, I hear you woke up a patient at 2 AM to give him a sleeping pill! You're being suspended for three episodes!
Because I was negligent?
No, because it's an old gag! Schticks like that went out with "Trapper John"! Here, we're into fresh, new prime-time approaches!
How about if I apply super glue to his bedpan?
Still old, but better! You show promise!
MATERNITY, PLEASE?
104
ARE WE READY FOR OUR NOSE DROPS?
"OF HUMAN BANDAGE"
I hope Ecchumina won't make any drastic changes here at St. Healthscare!
Just a few! To increase profits, every patient will be provided with Ecchumina Bedpans, Ecchumina Medicines and Ecchumina Respirators!
What about low-income patients who can't pay?
They'll be provided with an Ecchumina Phone Listing of other hospitals to call!
WE'RE ALL WAITING FOR YOU IN SURGERY, CORGAN!
"EMPIRE BLUE CROSS AND BLUE SHIELD SUCKS!"
W.M. GAINES
Dr. Milligram, I have a confession! Before seeing you I consulted a mystic faith healer!
Those quacks know nothing about modern medicine! I bet you were charged $100 a visit!
Actually, it was more like $300!
Hmmm! Guess they're more advanced than I thought!
MAD MAGAZINE NOT CHEAP!
YOU CAN CALL A DOCTOR A QUACK, BUT YOU CAN'T DUCK HIS BILL.

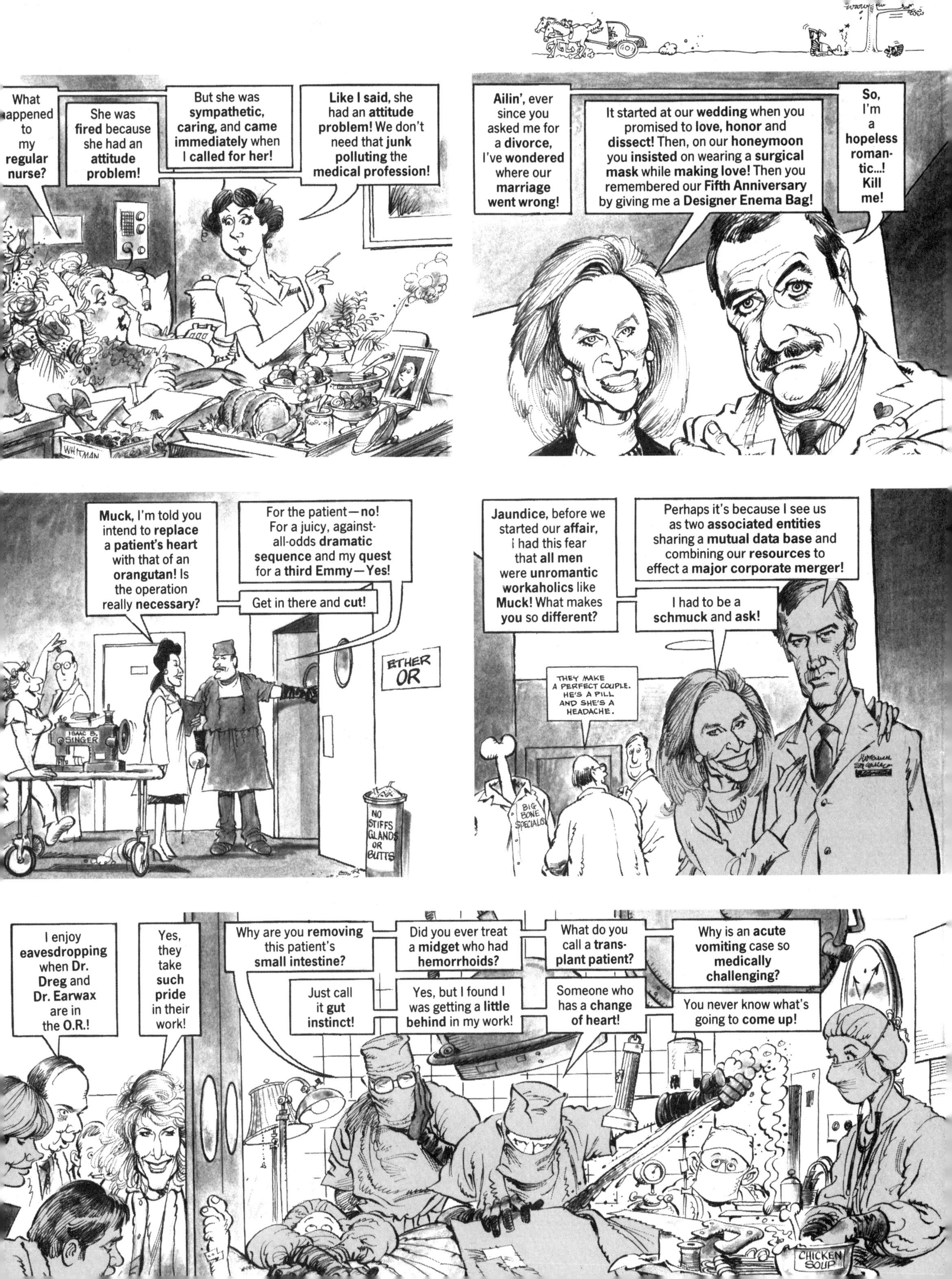

What appened to my regular nurse?
She was fired because she had an attitude problem!
But she was sympathetic, caring, and came immediately when I called for her!
Like I said, she had an attitude problem! We don't need that junk polluting the medical profession!
WHITMAN
Ailin', ever since you asked me for a divorce, I've wondered where our marriage went wrong!
It started at our wedding when you promised to love, honor and dissect! Then, on our honeymoon you insisted on wearing a surgical mask while making love! Then you remembered our Fifth Anniversary by giving me a Designer Enema Bag!
So, I'm a hopeless romantic...! Kill me!
Muck, I'm told you intend to replace a patient's heart with that of an orangutan! Is the operation really necessary?
For the patient—no! For a juicy, against-all-odds dramatic sequence and my quest for a third Emmy—Yes!
Get in there and cut!
ISAAC B. SINGER
ETHER OR
NO STIFFS GLANDS OR BUTTS
Jaundice, before we started our affair, I had this fear that all men were unromantic workaholics like Muck! What makes you so different?
Perhaps it's because I see us as two associated entities sharing a mutual data base and combining our resources to effect a major corporate merger!
I had to be a schmuck and ask!
THEY MAKE A PERFECT COUPLE. HE'S A PILL AND SHE'S A HEADACHE.
BIG BONE SPECIALIST
I enjoy eavesdropping when Dr. Dreg and Dr. Earwax are in the O.R.!
Yes, they take such pride in their work!
Why are you removing this patient's small intestine?
Just call it gut instinct!
Did you ever treat a midget who had hemorrhoids?
Yes, but I found I was getting a little behind in my work!
What do you call a transplant patient?
Someone who has a change of heart!
Why is an acute vomiting case so medically challenging?
You never know what's going to come up!
CHICKEN SOUP

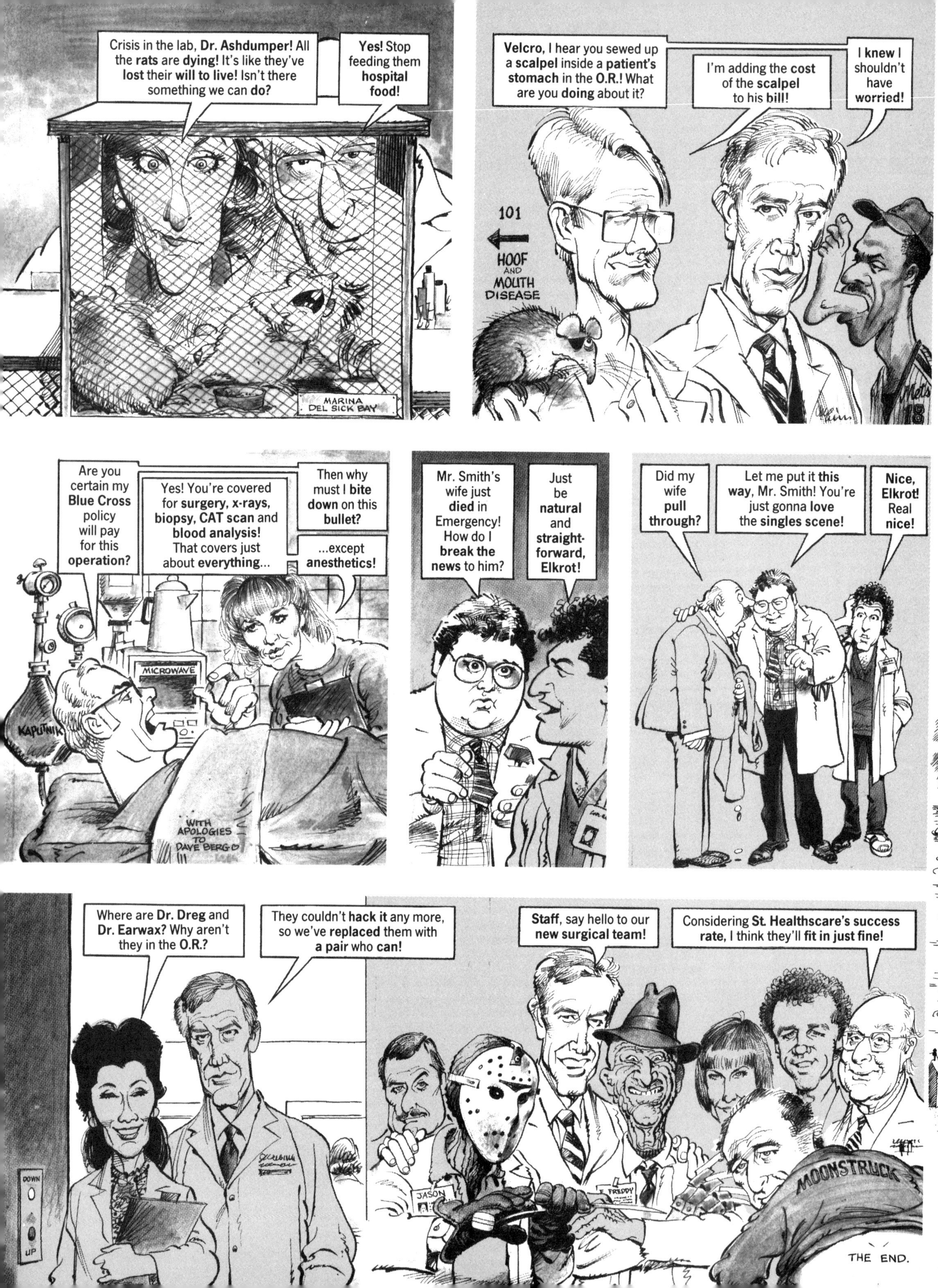
Crisis in the lab, Dr. Ashdumper! All the rats are dying! It's like they've lost their will to live! Isn't there something we can do?
Yes! Stop feeding them hospital food!
MARINA DEL SICK BAY
Velcro, I hear you sewed up a scalpel inside a patient's stomach in the O.R.! What are you doing about it?
I'm adding the cost of the scalpel to his bill!
I knew I shouldn't have worried!
101
HOOF AND MOUTH DISEASE
Mets 18
Are you certain my Blue Cross policy will pay for this operation?
Yes! You're covered for surgery, x-rays, biopsy, CAT scan and blood analysis! That covers just about everything...
Then why must I bite down on this bullet?
...except anesthetics!
MICROWAVE
KAPUTNIK
WITH APOLOGIES TO DAVE BERG
Mr. Smith's wife just died in Emergency! How do I break the news to him?
Just be natural and straight-forward, Elkrot!
Did my wife pull through?
Let me put it this way, Mr. Smith! You're just gonna love the singles scene!
Nice, Elkrot! Real nice!
Where are Dr. Dreg and Dr. Earwax? Why aren't they in the O.R.?
They couldn't hack it any more, so we've replaced them with a pair who can!
DOWN
UP
Staff, say hello to our new surgical team!
Considering St. Healthscare's success rate, I think they'll fit in just fine!
JASON
FREDDY
MOONSTRUCK
THE END.

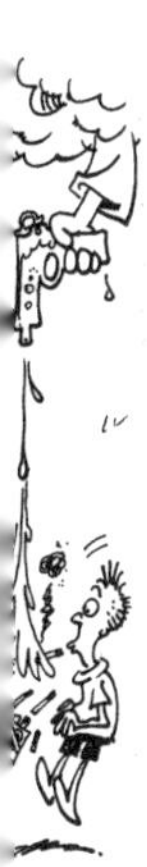

A CRASS ACT DEPT.

What do you get when you take a sexist, under-employed husband, a conniving wife, a promiscuous teenage daughter, and a horny son? You get one of TV's most popular sitcoms! Apparently a lot of viewers identify with couples who are miserable, low-class and . . .

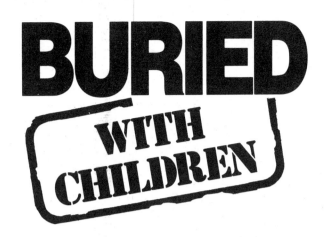

BURIED WITH CHILDREN

ARTIST: SAM VIVIANO WRITER: DENNIS SNEE

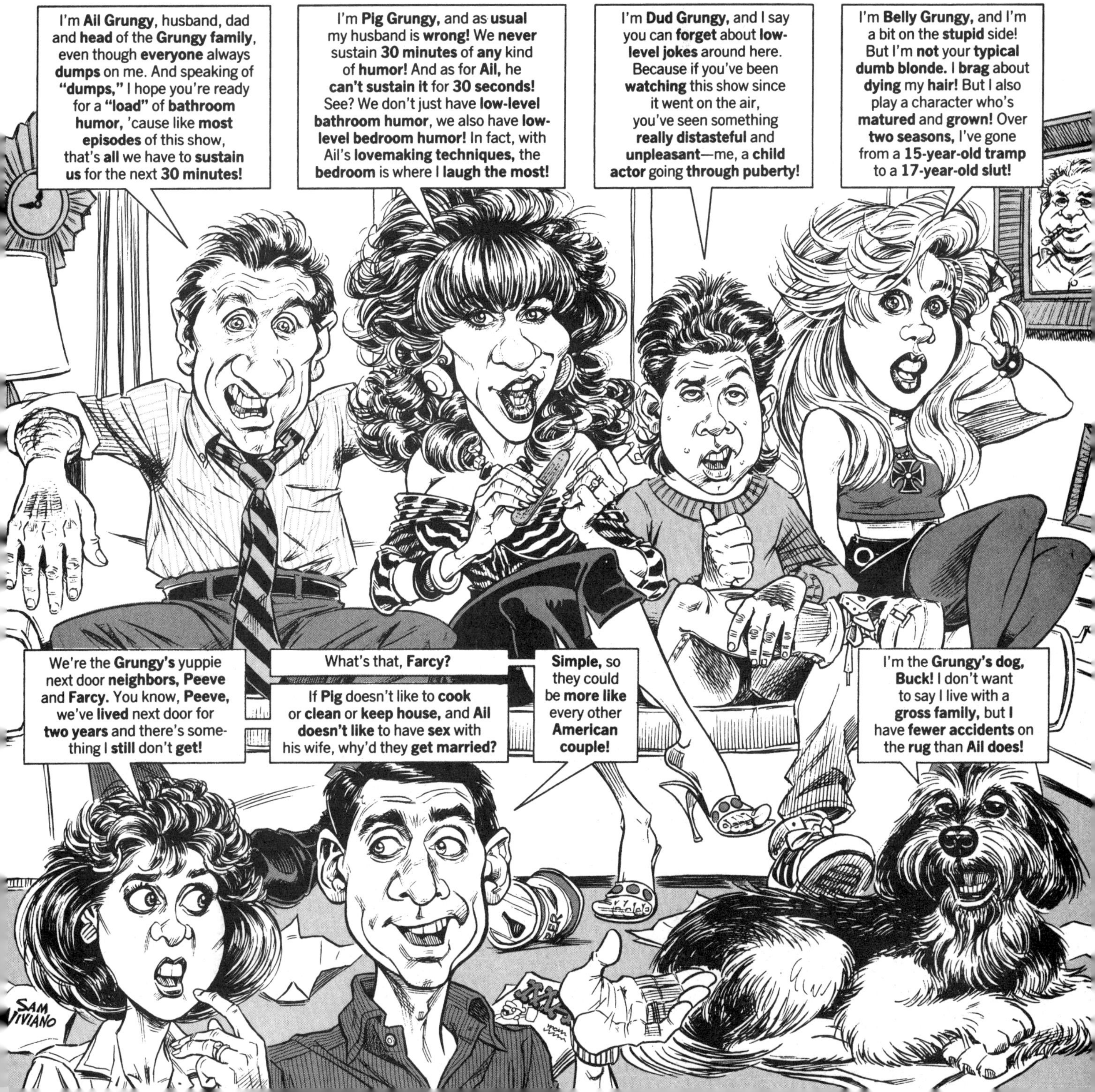

I'm Ail Grungy, husband, dad and head of the Grungy family, even though everyone always dumps on me. And speaking of "dumps," I hope you're ready for a "load" of bathroom humor, 'cause like most episodes of this show, that's all we have to sustain us for the next 30 minutes!
I'm Pig Grungy, and as usual my husband is wrong! We never sustain 30 minutes of any kind of humor! And as for Ail, he can't sustain it for 30 seconds! See? We don't just have low-level bathroom humor, we also have low-level bedroom humor! In fact, with Ail's lovemaking techniques, the bedroom is where I laugh the most!
I'm Dud Grungy, and I say you can forget about low-level jokes around here. Because if you've been watching this show since it went on the air, you've seen something really distasteful and unpleasant—me, a child actor going through puberty!
I'm Belly Grungy, and I'm a bit on the stupid side! But I'm not your typical dumb blonde. I brag about dying my hair! But I also play a character who's matured and grown! Over two seasons, I've gone from a 15-year-old tramp to a 17-year-old slut!
We're the Grungy's yuppie next door neighbors, Peeve and Farcy. You know, Peeve, we've lived next door for two years and there's something I still don't get!
What's that, Farcy?
If Pig doesn't like to cook or clean or keep house, and Ail doesn't like to have sex with his wife, why'd they get married?
Simple, so they could be more like every other American couple!
I'm the Grungy's dog, Buck! I don't want to say I live with a gross family, but I have fewer accidents on the rug than Ail does!
SAM VIVIANO

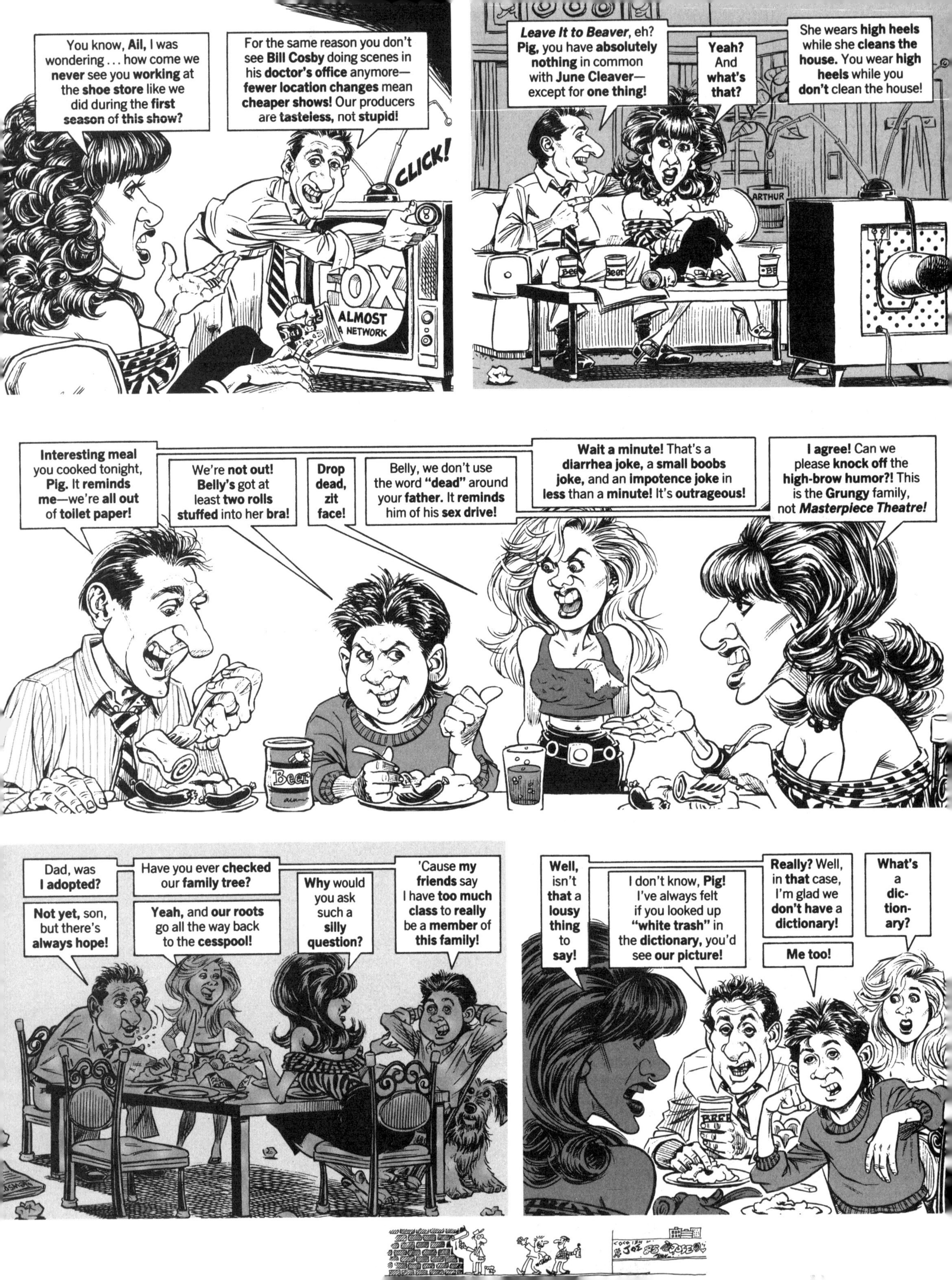

You know, Ail, I was wondering . . . how come we never see you working at the shoe store like we did during the first season of this show?
For the same reason you don't see Bill Cosby doing scenes in his doctor's office anymore—fewer location changes mean cheaper shows! Our producers are tasteless, not stupid!
CLICK!
FOX
ALMOST A NETWORK
Leave It to Beaver, eh? Pig, you have absolutely nothing in common with June Cleaver—except for one thing!
Yeah? And what's that?
She wears high heels while she cleans the house. You wear high heels while you don't clean the house!
ARTHUR
Beer
Interesting meal you cooked tonight, Pig. It reminds me—we're all out of toilet paper!
We're not out! Belly's got at least two rolls stuffed into her bra!
Drop dead, zit face!
Belly, we don't use the word "dead" around your father. It reminds him of his sex drive!
Wait a minute! That's a diarrhea joke, a small boobs joke, and an impotence joke in less than a minute! It's outrageous!
I agree! Can we please knock off the high-brow humor?! This is the Grungy family, not Masterpiece Theatre!
Beer
Dad, was I adopted?
Not yet, son, but there's always hope!
Have you ever checked our family tree?
Yeah, and our roots go all the way back to the cesspool!
Why would you ask such a silly question?
'Cause my friends say I have too much class to really be a member of this family!
Well, isn't that a lousy thing to say!
I don't know, Pig! I've always felt if you looked up "white trash" in the dictionary, you'd see our picture!
Really? Well, in that case, I'm glad we don't have a dictionary!
Me too!
What's a dic-tion-ary?
BEER

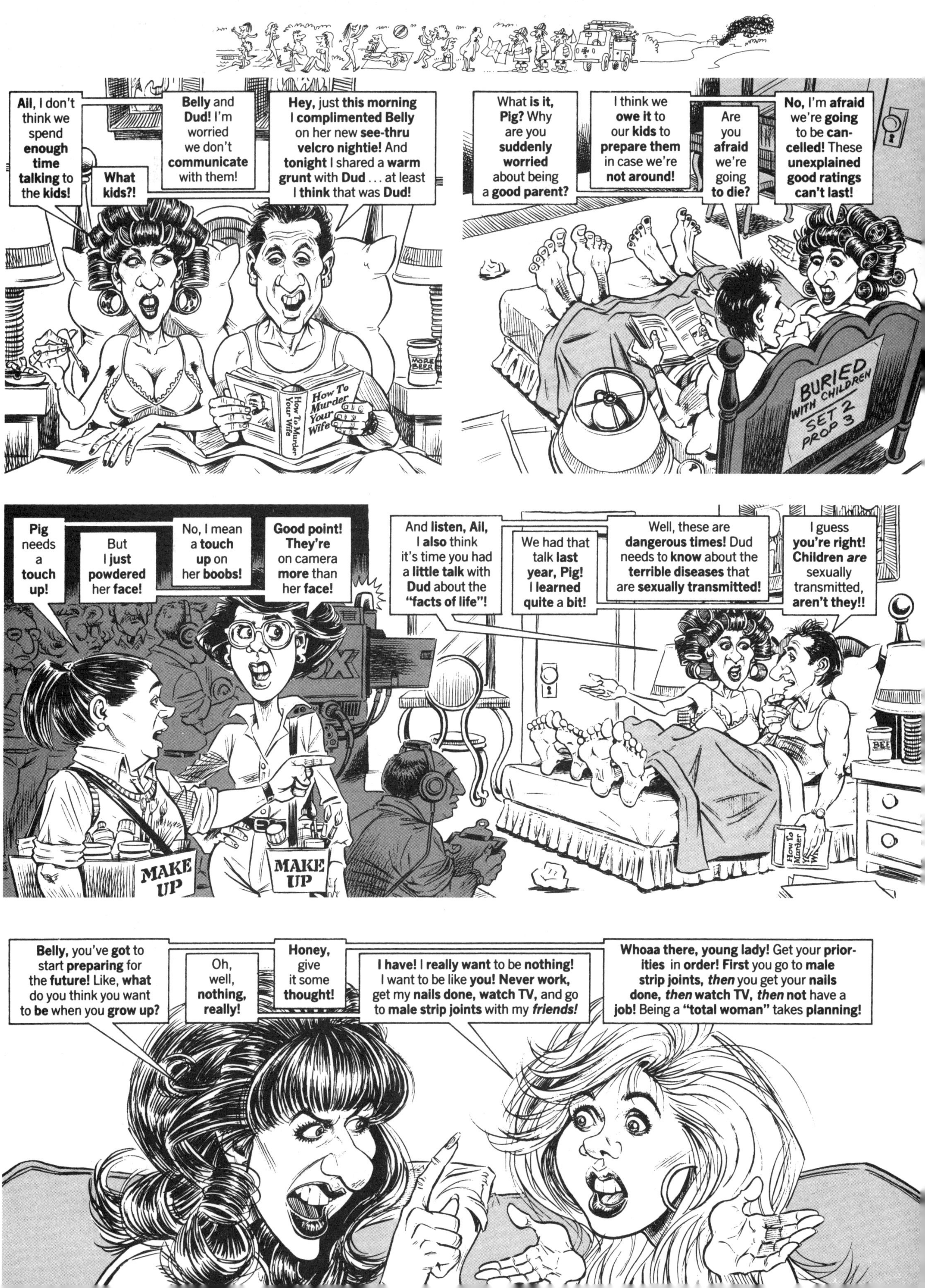

Ail, I don't think we spend enough time talking to the kids!
Belly and Dud! I'm worried we don't communicate with them!
What kids?!
Hey, just this morning I complimented Belly on her new see-thru velcro nightie! And tonight I shared a warm grunt with Dud . . . at least I think that was Dud!
MORE BEER
How To Murder Your Wife
How To Murder Your Wife
What is it, Pig? Why are you suddenly worried about being a good parent?
I think we owe it to our kids to prepare them in case we're not around!
Are you afraid we're going to die?
No, I'm afraid we're going to be cancelled! These unexplained good ratings can't last!
BURIED WITH CHILDREN
SET 2 PROP 3
Pig needs a touch up!
But I just powdered her face!
No, I mean a touch up on her boobs!
Good point! They're on camera more than her face!
MAKE UP
MAKE UP
And listen, Ail, I also think it's time you had a little talk with Dud about the "facts of life"!
We had that talk last year, Pig! I learned quite a bit!
Well, these are dangerous times! Dud needs to know about the terrible diseases that are sexually transmitted!
I guess you're right! Children are sexually transmitted, aren't they!!
Belly, you've got to start preparing for the future! Like, what do you think you want to be when you grow up?
Oh, well, nothing, really!
Honey, give it some thought!
I have! I really want to be nothing! I want to be like you! Never work, get my nails done, watch TV, and go to male strip joints with my friends!
Whoaa there, young lady! Get your priorities in order! First you go to male strip joints, then you get your nails done, then watch TV, then not have a job! Being a "total woman" takes planning!

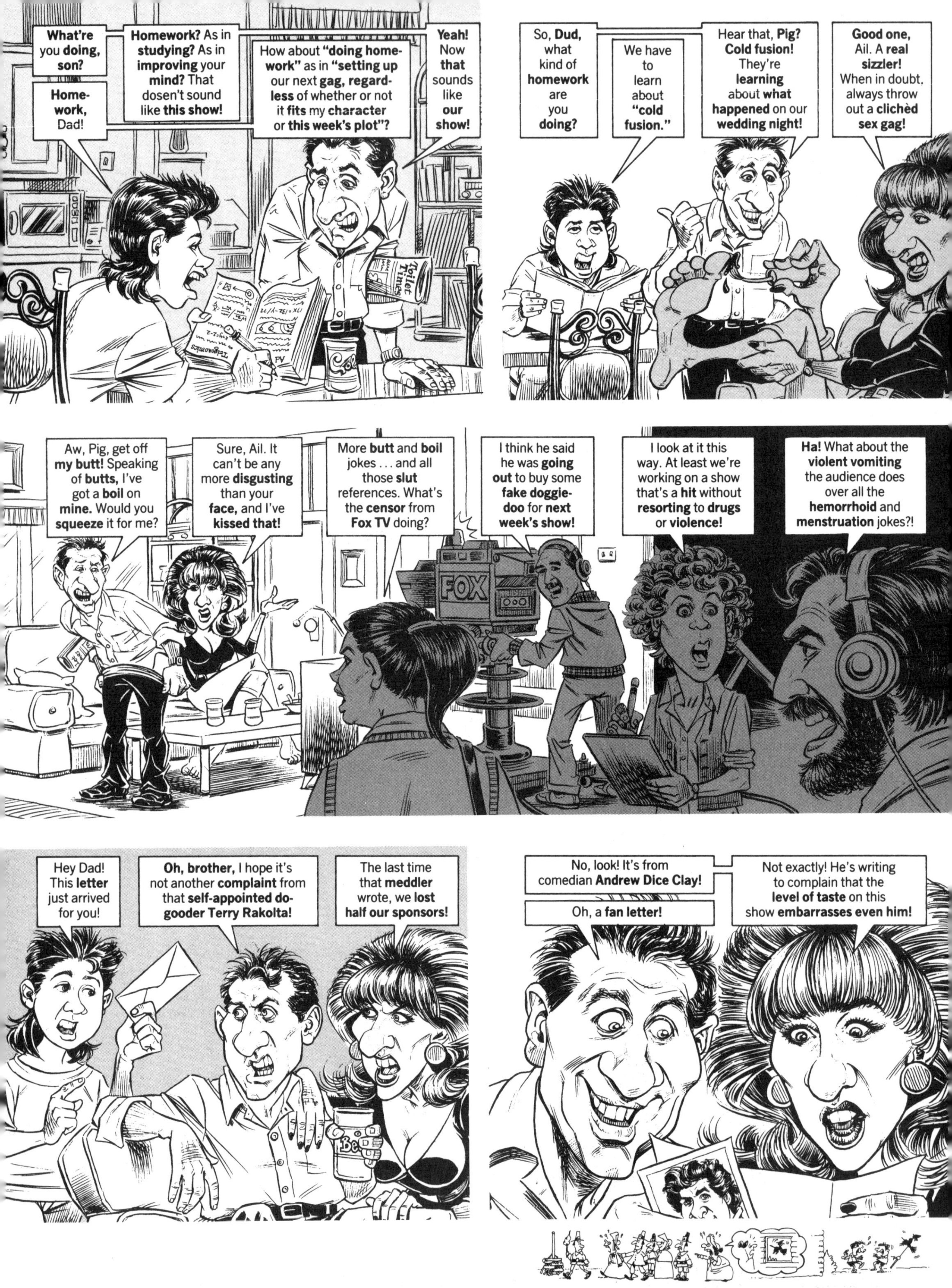
What're you doing, son?
Home-work, Dad!
Homework? As in studying? As in improving your mind? That dosen't sound like this show!
How about "doing home-work" as in "setting up our next gag, regard-less of whether or not it fits my character or this week's plot"?
Yeah! Now that sounds like our show!
Toilet Times
So, Dud, what kind of homework are you doing?
We have to learn about "cold fusion."
Hear that, Pig? Cold fusion! They're learning about what happened on our wedding night!
Good one, Ail. A real sizzler! When in doubt, always throw out a clichèd sex gag!
Aw, Pig, get off my butt! Speaking of butts, I've got a boil on mine. Would you squeeze it for me?
Sure, Ail. It can't be any more disgusting than your face, and I've kissed that!
More butt and boil jokes . . . and all those slut references. What's the censor from Fox TV doing?
I think he said he was going out to buy some fake doggie-doo for next week's show!
FOX
I look at it this way. At least we're working on a show that's a hit without resorting to drugs or violence!
Ha! What about the violent vomiting the audience does over all the hemorrhoid and menstruation jokes?!
Hey Dad! This letter just arrived for you!
Oh, brother, I hope it's not another complaint from that self-appointed do-gooder Terry Rakolta!
The last time that meddler wrote, we lost half our sponsors!
No, look! It's from comedian Andrew Dice Clay!
Oh, a fan letter!
Not exactly! He's writing to complain that the level of taste on this show embarrasses even him!

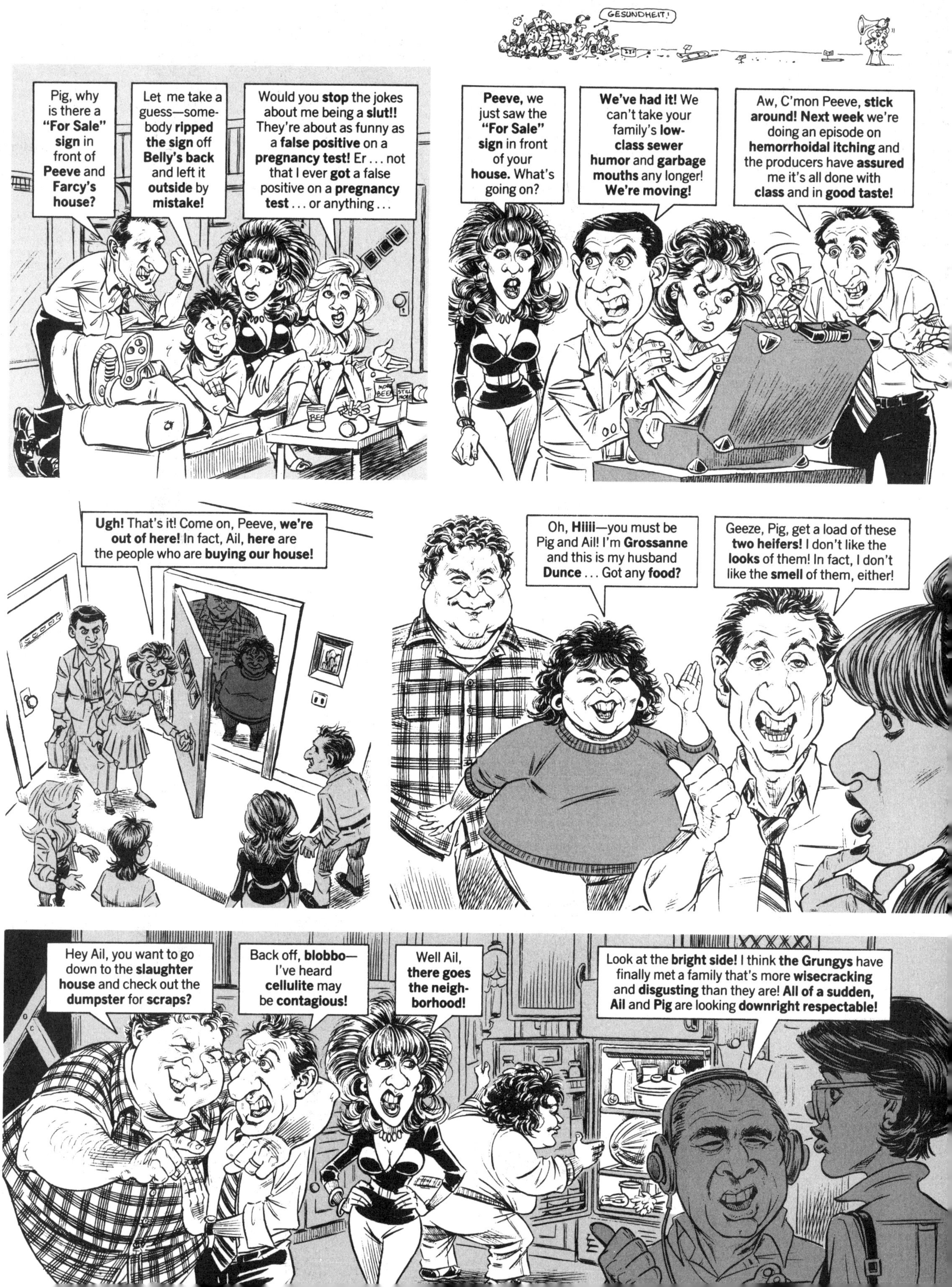
GESUNDHEIT!
Pig, why is there a "For Sale" sign in front of Peeve and Farcy's house?
Let me take a guess—somebody ripped the sign off Belly's back and left it outside by mistake!
Would you stop the jokes about me being a slut!! They're about as funny as a false positive on a pregnancy test! Er . . . not that I ever got a false positive on a pregnancy test . . . or anything . . .
Peeve, we just saw the "For Sale" sign in front of your house. What's going on?
We've had it! We can't take your family's low-class sewer humor and garbage mouths any longer! We're moving!
Aw, C'mon Peeve, stick around! Next week we're doing an episode on hemorrhoidal itching and the producers have assured me it's all done with class and in good taste!
Ugh! That's it! Come on, Peeve, we're out of here! In fact, Ail, here are the people who are buying our house!
Oh, Hiiii—you must be Pig and Ail! I'm Grossanne and this is my husband Dunce . . . Got any food?
Geeze, Pig, get a load of these two heifers! I don't like the looks of them! In fact, I don't like the smell of them, either!
Hey Ail, you want to go down to the slaughter house and check out the dumpster for scraps?
Back off, blobbo—I've heard cellulite may be contagious!
Well Ail, there goes the neighborhood!
Look at the bright side! I think the Grungys have finally met a family that's more wisecracking and disgusting than they are! All of a sudden, Ail and Pig are looking downright respectable!

SLAM DANSON DEPT.

I'm **Fresser Brain, Psychiatrist!** They say that after **seven years** a marriage often has problems! It's called the **Seven Year Itch!** I'm here to see what happens to a **TV sitcom** after seven years! Is there an **"itch"** here, too? Well, if there is, you can be sure MAD will **scratch it** with a **second round of...**

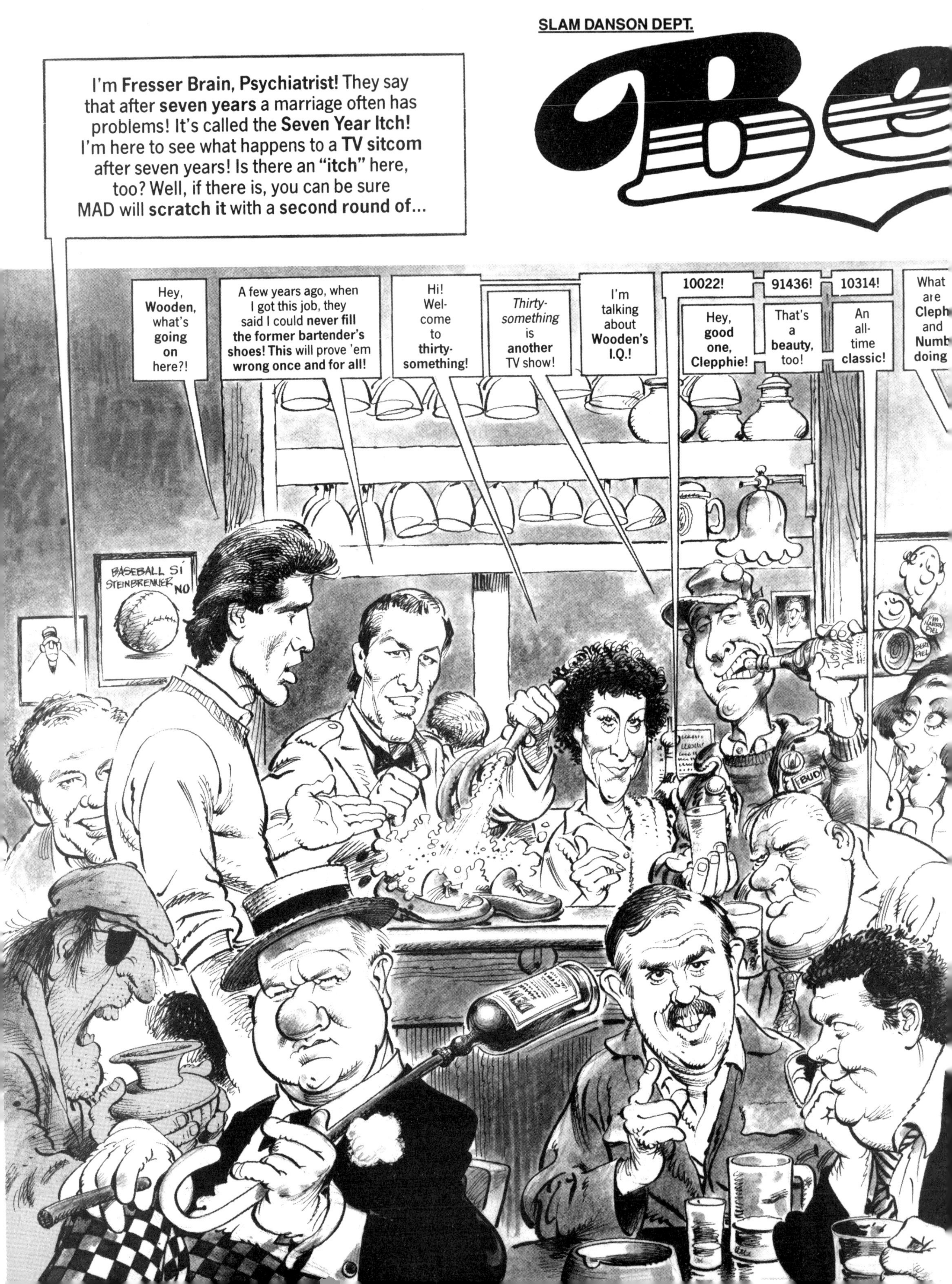

Hey, Wooden, what's going on here?!
A few years ago, when I got this job, they said I could never fill the former bartender's shoes! This will prove 'em wrong once and for all!
Hi! Wel-come to thirty-something!
Thirty-something is another TV show!
I'm talking about Wooden's I.Q.!
10022!
Hey, good one, Clepphie!
91436!
That's a beauty, too!
10314!
An all-time classic!
What are Cleph and Numb doing
BASEBALL SÍ STEINBRENNER NO
BUD

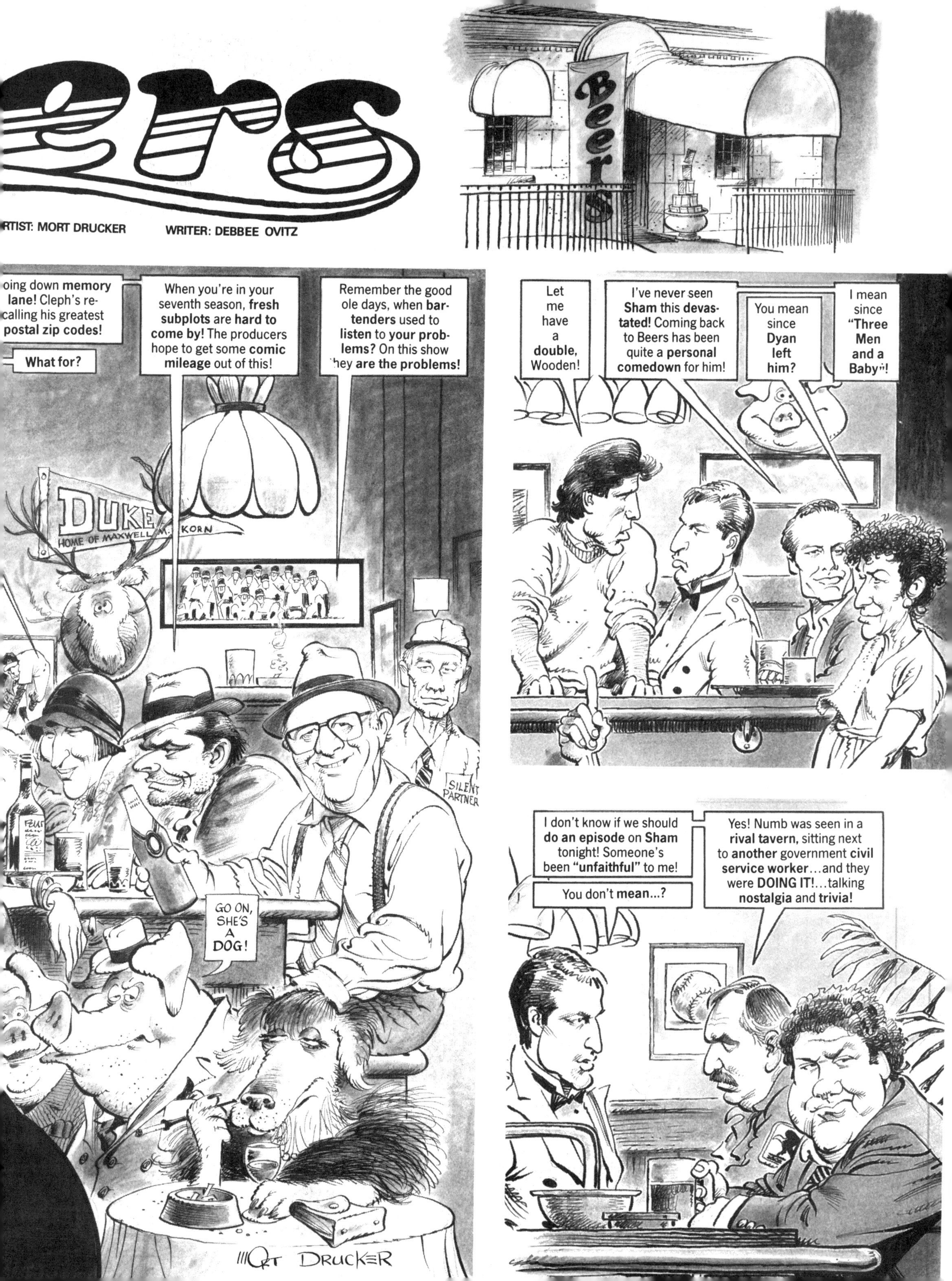
ers
RTIST: MORT DRUCKER
WRITER: DEBBEE OVITZ
Beers
oing down memory lane! Cleph's re-calling his greatest postal zip codes!
What for?
When you're in your seventh season, fresh subplots are hard to come by! The producers hope to get some comic mileage out of this!
Remember the good ole days, when bar-tenders used to listen to your prob-lems? On this show 'hey are the problems!
DUKE
HOME OF MAXWELL M. KORN
SILENT PARTNER
GO ON, SHE'S A DOG!
MORT DRUCKER
Let me have a double, Wooden!
I've never seen Sham this devas-tated! Coming back to Beers has been quite a personal comedown for him!
You mean since Dyan left him?
I mean since "Three Men and a Baby"!
I don't know if we should do an episode on Sham tonight! Someone's been "unfaithful" to me!
You don't mean...?
Yes! Numb was seen in a rival tavern, sitting next to another government civil service worker...and they were DOING IT!...talking nostalgia and trivia!

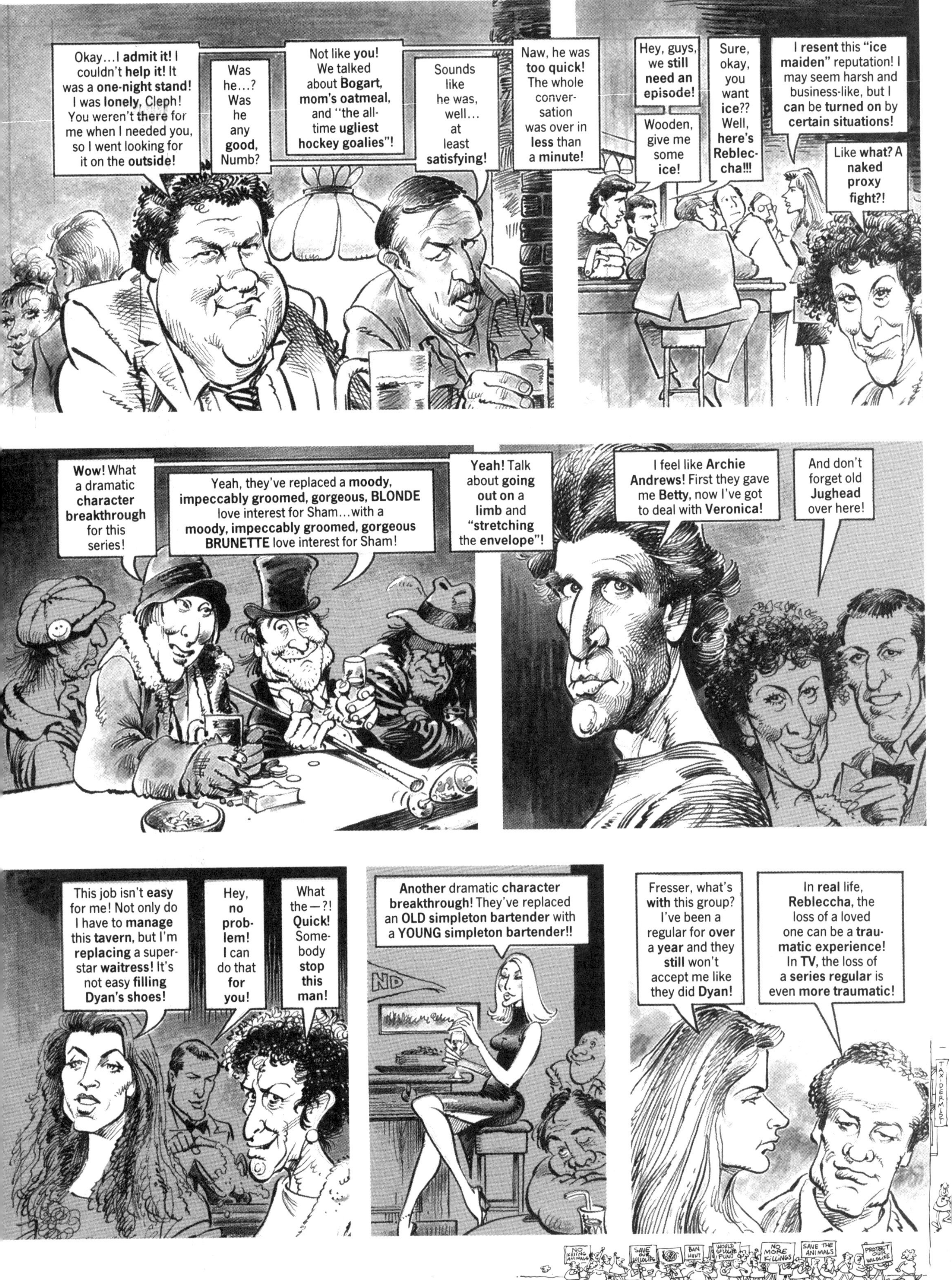

Okay...I admit it! I couldn't help it! It was a one-night stand! I was lonely, Cleph! You weren't there for me when I needed you, so I went looking for it on the outside!
Was he...? Was he any good, Numb?
Not like you! We talked about Bogart, mom's oatmeal, and "the all-time ugliest hockey goalies"!
Sounds like he was, well... at least satisfying!
Naw, he was too quick! The whole conversation was over in less than a minute!
Hey, guys, we still need an episode!
Wooden, give me some ice!
Sure, okay, you want ice?? Well, here's Reblec-cha!!!
I resent this "ice maiden" reputation! I may seem harsh and business-like, but I can be turned on by certain situations!
Like what? A naked proxy fight?!
Wow! What a dramatic character breakthrough for this series!
Yeah, they've replaced a moody, impeccably groomed, gorgeous, BLONDE love interest for Sham...with a moody, impeccably groomed, gorgeous BRUNETTE love interest for Sham!
Yeah! Talk about going out on a limb and "stretching the envelope"!
I feel like Archie Andrews! First they gave me Betty, now I've got to deal with Veronica!
And don't forget old Jughead over here!
This job isn't easy for me! Not only do I have to manage this tavern, but I'm replacing a super-star waitress! It's not easy filling Dyan's shoes!
Hey, no prob-lem! I can do that for you!
What the—?! Quick! Some-body stop this man!
Another dramatic character breakthrough! They've replaced an OLD simpleton bartender with a YOUNG simpleton bartender!!
Fresser, what's with this group? I've been a regular for over a year and they still won't accept me like they did Dyan!
In real life, Rebleccha, the loss of a loved one can be a trau-matic experience! In TV, the loss of a series regular is even more traumatic!
TAXIDERMIST
NO KILLING ANIMALS
SAVE OUR WILDLIFE
BAN HUNT
WORLD WILDLIFE FUND
NO MORE KILLINGS
SAVE THE ANIMALS
PROTECT OUR WILDLIFE

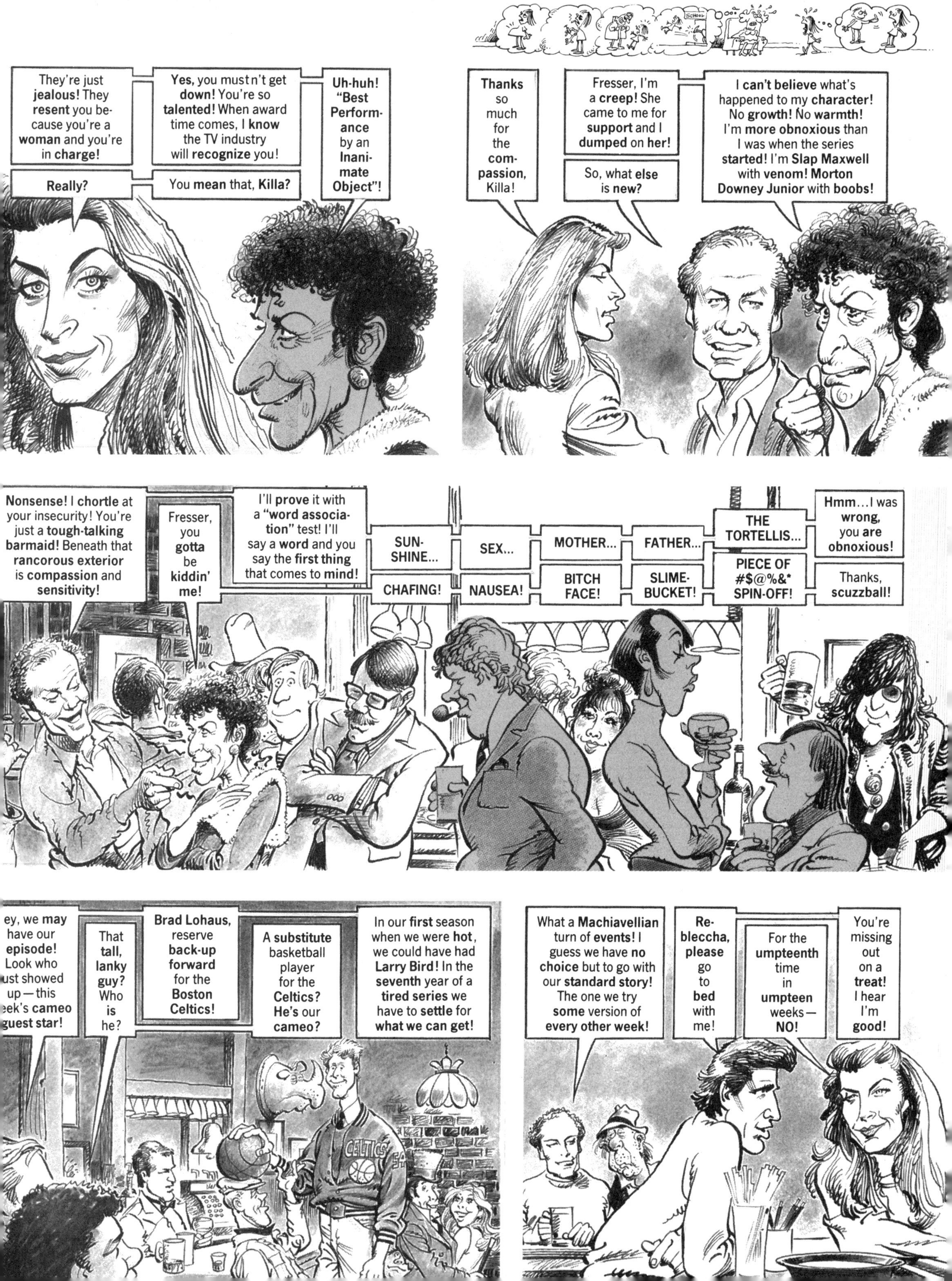

SCHOOL
They're just jealous! They resent you because you're a woman and you're in charge!
Really?
Yes, you must n't get down! You're so talented! When award time comes, I know the TV industry will recognize you!
You mean that, Killa?
Uh-huh! "Best Performance by an Inanimate Object"!
Thanks so much for the compassion, Killa!
Fresser, I'm a creep! She came to me for support and I dumped on her!
So, what else is new?
I can't believe what's happened to my character! No growth! No warmth! I'm more obnoxious than I was when the series started! I'm Slap Maxwell with venom! Morton Downey Junior with boobs!
Nonsense! I chortle at your insecurity! You're just a tough-talking barmaid! Beneath that rancorous exterior is compassion and sensitivity!
Fresser, you gotta be kiddin' me!
I'll prove it with a "word association" test! I'll say a word and you say the first thing that comes to mind!
SUNSHINE...
CHAFING!
SEX...
NAUSEA!
MOTHER...
BITCH FACE!
FATHER...
SLIME-BUCKET!
THE TORTELLIS...
PIECE OF #$@%&* SPIN-OFF!
Hmm...I was wrong, you are obnoxious!
Thanks, scuzzball!
ey, we may have our episode! Look who ust showed up—this eek's cameo guest star!
That tall, lanky guy? Who is he?
Brad Lohaus, reserve back-up forward for the Boston Celtics!
A substitute basketball player for the Celtics? He's our cameo?
In our first season when we were hot, we could have had Larry Bird! In the seventh year of a tired series we have to settle for what we can get!
CELTICS
What a Machiavellian turn of events! I guess we have no choice but to go with our standard story! The one we try some version of every other week!
Rebleccha, please go to bed with me!
For the umpteenth time in umpteen weeks—NO!
You're missing out on a treat! I hear I'm good!

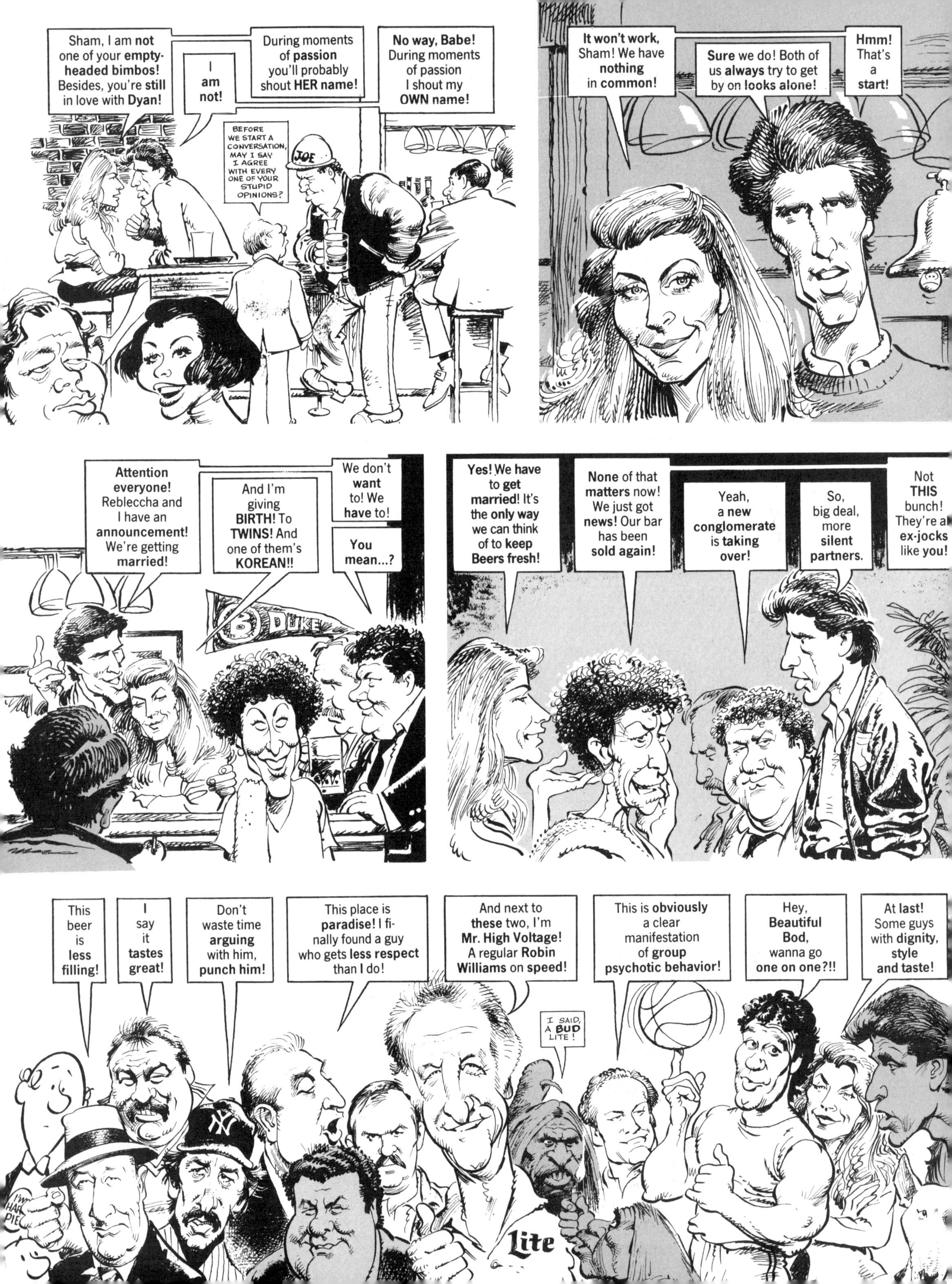
Sham, I am not one of your empty-headed bimbos! Besides, you're still in love with Dyan!
I am not!
During moments of passion you'll probably shout HER name!
No way, Babe! During moments of passion I shout my OWN name!
BEFORE WE START A CONVERSATION, MAY I SAY I AGREE WITH EVERY ONE OF YOUR STUPID OPINIONS?
JOE
It won't work, Sham! We have nothing in common!
Sure we do! Both of us always try to get by on looks alone!
Hmm! That's a start!
Attention everyone! Rebleccha and I have an announcement! We're getting married!
And I'm giving BIRTH! To TWINS! And one of them's KOREAN!!
We don't want to! We have to!
You mean...?
DUKE
Yes! We have to get married! It's the only way we can think of to keep Beers fresh!
None of that matters now! We just got news! Our bar has been sold again!
Yeah, a new conglomerate is taking over!
So, big deal, more silent partners.
Not THIS bunch! They're a ex-jocks like you!
This beer is less filling!
I say it tastes great!
Don't waste time arguing with him, punch him!
This place is paradise! I finally found a guy who gets less respect than I do!
And next to these two, I'm Mr. High Voltage! A regular Robin Williams on speed!
I SAID, A BUD LITE!
This is obviously a clear manifestation of group psychotic behavior!
Hey, Beautiful Bod, wanna go one on one?!!
At last! Some guys with dignity, style and taste!
Lite

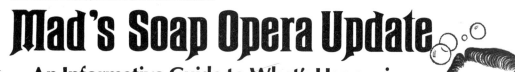

Mad's Soap Opera Update

An Informative Guide to What's Happening on Your Favorite Daytime Dramas

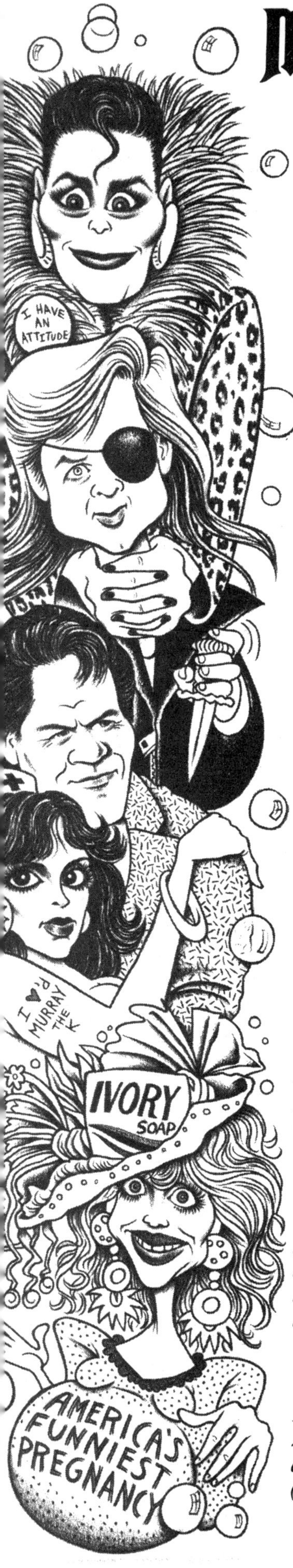
I HAVE AN ATTITUDE
I ♥ P.J. MURRAY THE K
IVORY SOAP
AMERICA'S FUNNIEST PREGNANCY

MAUL MY CHILDREN

Victor told Frank he was secretly married to every woman in Detroit. Shane and Johnny's plan against Cal backfired when Jennifer discovered them auditioning yodelers. Dane's nightmares about robot hens continued.

THE YOUNG AND THE RUSTLESS

When no one was watching, Beth let the air out of Tim's steady date. Kitty's plans to mass market Frederico's edible lawn furniture hit an unexpected snag when Uncle Chip decided to invest his money in Cassandra's new line of novelty neck braces. Kathleen told Margo he wondered why he had a girl's name.

DAYS OF OUR LIES

In an attempt to learn more about Henderson's past, Becky hypnotized his parrot's therapist. Phyllis charged Reed with refusing to reveal the identity of the man Rusty thought was responsible for Betty's Aunt going to Wally's bungalow with the Vancouver Canucks. Kent demanded that everyone stop putting butter in his hat.

ANOTHER WHIRL

Randy mistook Butch's aunt for an old sofa and sent her out to be reupholstered. At confession, Cliff revealed that he was the man responsible for those Infiniti car commercials. Julie invited a horse on a ski weekend.

LUSTING

Mike was miraculously spared when his earmuffs exploded at the Yeast Festival. Bill was named Oral Surgeon of the Year, even though he works at a Stuckey's. On the day before elections, Congressman Toomey was seen strapping hams to local school children.

MISGUIDING LIGHT

Despondent over Frank's passion for recaulking, Blake attempted suicide using a garlic press. Kayla informed Kyle that the only way he could win Morgan's love was by convincing her that he was Casey Kasem's skin consultant. Jan told Jimmy Lee that he would only be allowed to use one name, like everyone else in town.

AS THE WORLD RETURNS

A newcomer named Jimmy Lee said he would stay in town if they allowed him to use both of his names. In an unsuccessful attempt to appear older and gain entrance into the town's hot new nightclub, Timmy had varicose veins tattooed on his legs. In a flashback sequence, Kirk sold towels to Patrick Henry.

GENERALLY HOSPITABLE

Hilda was alarmed when Doctor Knuckles arrived for her appendectomy in a Zamboni machine. Nurse Rene assured Wilton that the fluid dripping from his elbow was peach juice, and then offered him a glass. Everyone in town was killed. (Last show of series.)

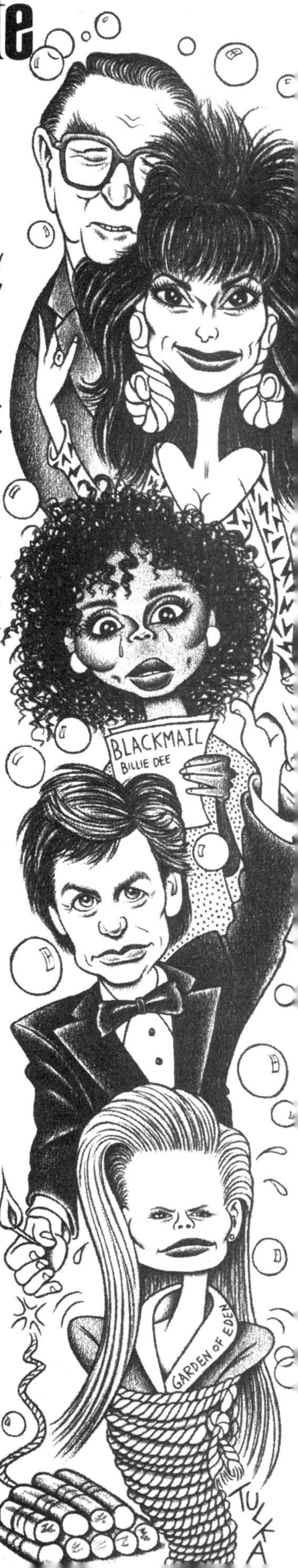
BLACKMAIL
BILLIE DEE
GARDEN OF EDEN
TULKA

ARTIST: RICK TULKA WRITERS: CHARLIE KADAU AND JOE RAIOLA

ANGST FOR NOTHING DEPT.

There's a hot ensemble-cast show that just won a slew of Emmys! It's the kind of show that most viewers seem to either love or hate, or love to hate! It's dark, it's moody, it's depressing, it's...

thirtysuffe

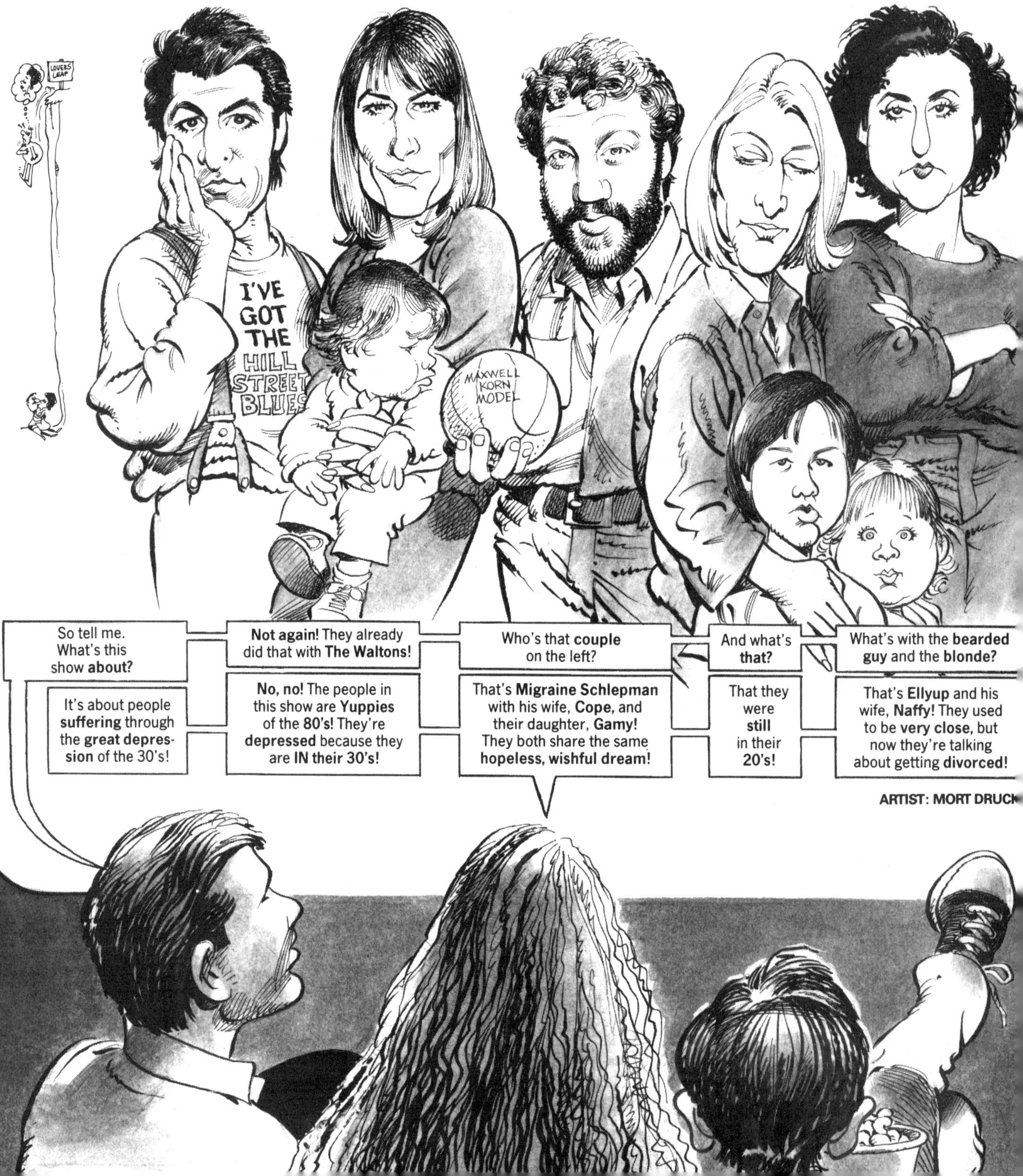

LOVERS LEAP
I'VE GOT THE HILL STREET BLUES
MAXWELL KORN MODEL
So tell me. What's this show **about?**
It's about people **suffering** through the **great depression** of the 30's!
Not again! They already did that with **The Waltons!**
No, no! The people in this show are **Yuppies** of the **80's!** They're **depressed** because they are **IN their 30's!**
Who's that **couple** on the left?
That's **Migraine Schlepman** with his wife, **Cope,** and their daughter, **Gamy!** They both share the same **hopeless, wishful dream!**
And what's **that?**
That they were **still** in their **20's!**
What's with the **bearded guy** and the **blonde?**
That's **Ellyup** and his wife, **Naffy!** They used to be **very close,** but now they're talking about getting **divorced!**

ARTIST: MORT DRUCK

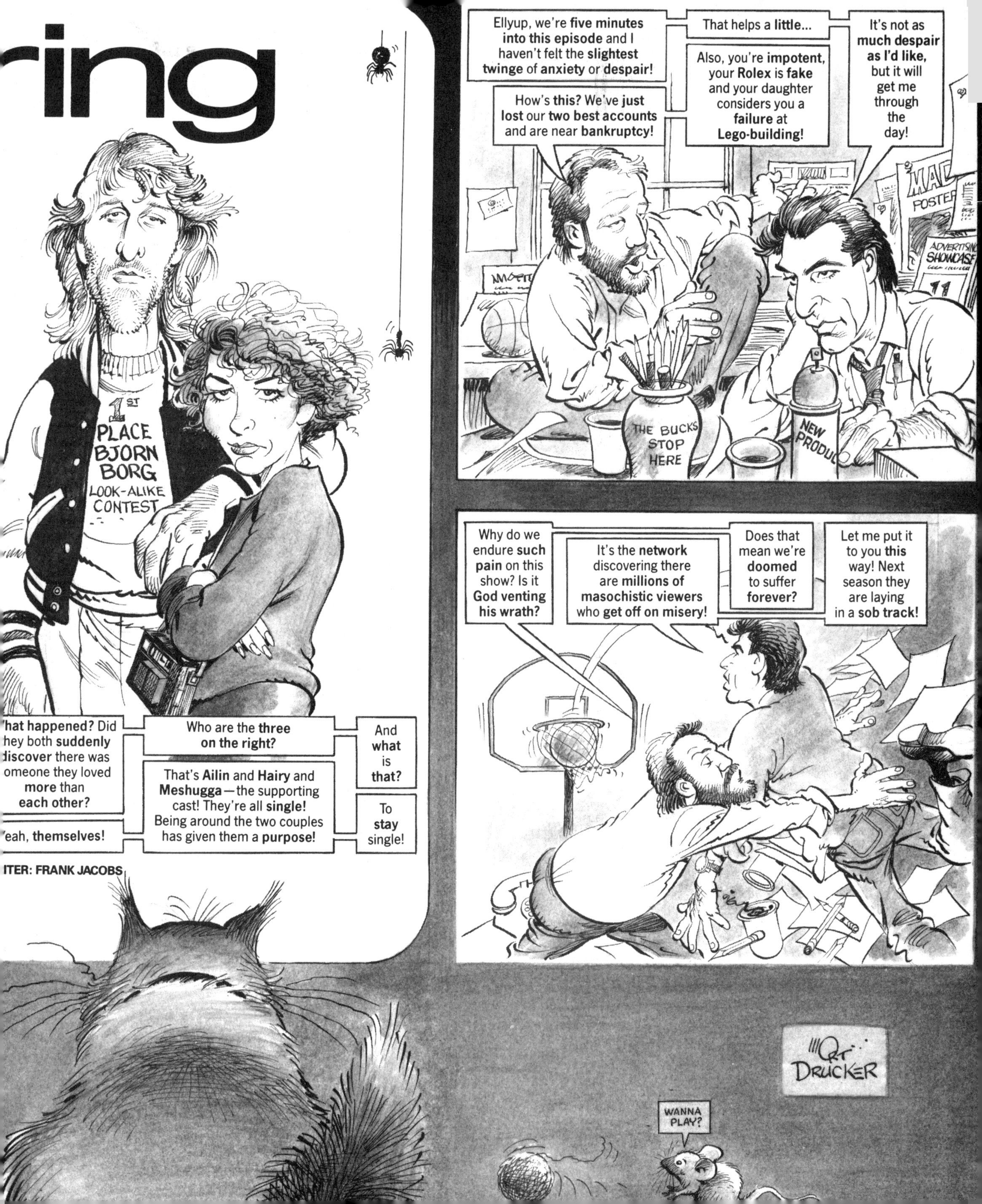
ring
1ST PLACE BJORN BORG LOOK-ALIKE CONTEST
'hat happened? Did hey both suddenly discover there was omeone they loved more than each other?
'eah, themselves!
Who are the three on the right?
That's Ailin and Hairy and Meshugga—the supporting cast! They're all single! Being around the two couples has given them a purpose!
And what is that?
To stay single!
ITER: FRANK JACOBS
Ellyup, we're five minutes into this episode and I haven't felt the slightest twinge of anxiety or despair!
How's this? We've just lost our two best accounts and are near bankruptcy!
That helps a little...
Also, you're impotent, your Rolex is fake and your daughter considers you a failure at Lego-building!
It's not as much despair as I'd like, but it will get me through the day!
THE BUCKS STOP HERE
NEW PRODU
POSTER
ADVERTISING SHOWCASE
Why do we endure such pain on this show? Is it God venting his wrath?
It's the network discovering there are millions of masochistic viewers who get off on misery!
Does that mean we're doomed to suffer forever?
Let me put it to you this way! Next season they are laying in a sob track!
DRUCKER
WANNA PLAY?

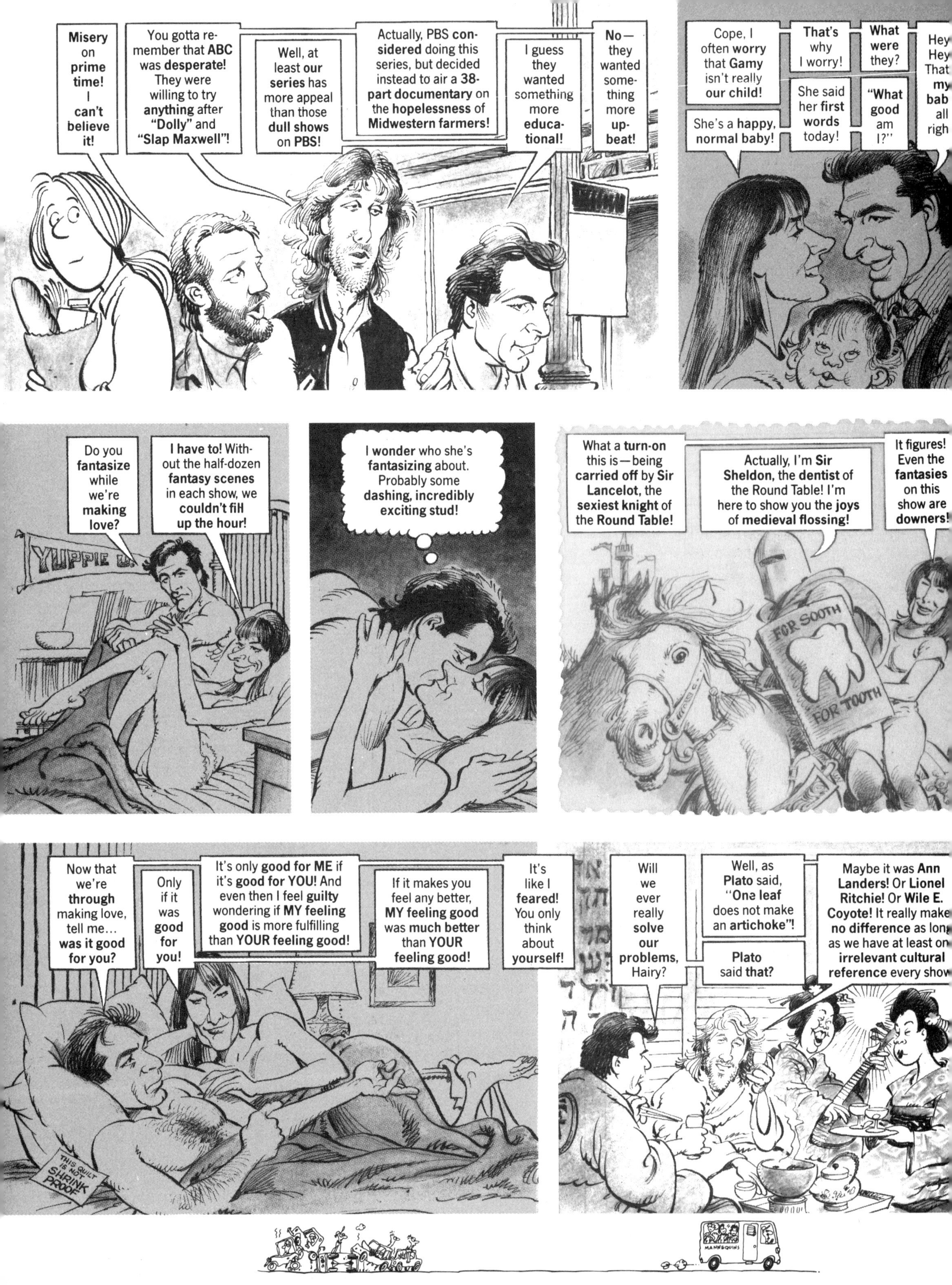

Misery on prime time! I can't believe it!
You gotta re-member that ABC was desperate! They were willing to try anything after "Dolly" and "Slap Maxwell"!
Well, at least our series has more appeal than those dull shows on PBS!
Actually, PBS con-sidered doing this series, but decided instead to air a 38-part documentary on the hopelessness of Midwestern farmers!
I guess they wanted something more educa-tional!
No—they wanted some-thing more up-beat!
Cope, I often worry that Gamy isn't really our child!
She's a happy, normal baby!
That's why I worry!
She said her first words today!
What were they?
"What good am I?"
Hey Hey That my bab all righ
Do you fantasize while we're making love?
I have to! With-out the half-dozen fantasy scenes in each show, we couldn't fill up the hour!
YUPPIE U.
I wonder who she's fantasizing about. Probably some dashing, incredibly exciting stud!
What a turn-on this is—being carried off by Sir Lancelot, the sexiest knight of the Round Table!
Actually, I'm Sir Sheldon, the dentist of the Round Table! I'm here to show you the joys of medieval flossing!
It figures! Even the fantasies on this show are downers!
FOR SOOTH
FOR TOOTH
Now that we're through making love, tell me… was it good for you?
Only if it was good for you!
It's only good for ME if it's good for YOU! And even then I feel guilty wondering if MY feeling good is more fulfilling than YOUR feeling good!
If it makes you feel any better, MY feeling good was much better than YOUR feeling good!
It's like I feared! You only think about yourself!
THIS QUILT IS NOT SHRINK PROOF
Will we ever really solve our problems, Hairy?
Well, as Plato said, "One leaf does not make an artichoke"!
Plato said that?
Maybe it was Ann Landers! Or Lionel Ritchie! Or Wile E. Coyote! It really make no difference as lon as we have at least on irrelevant cultural reference every shov
MANNEQUINS

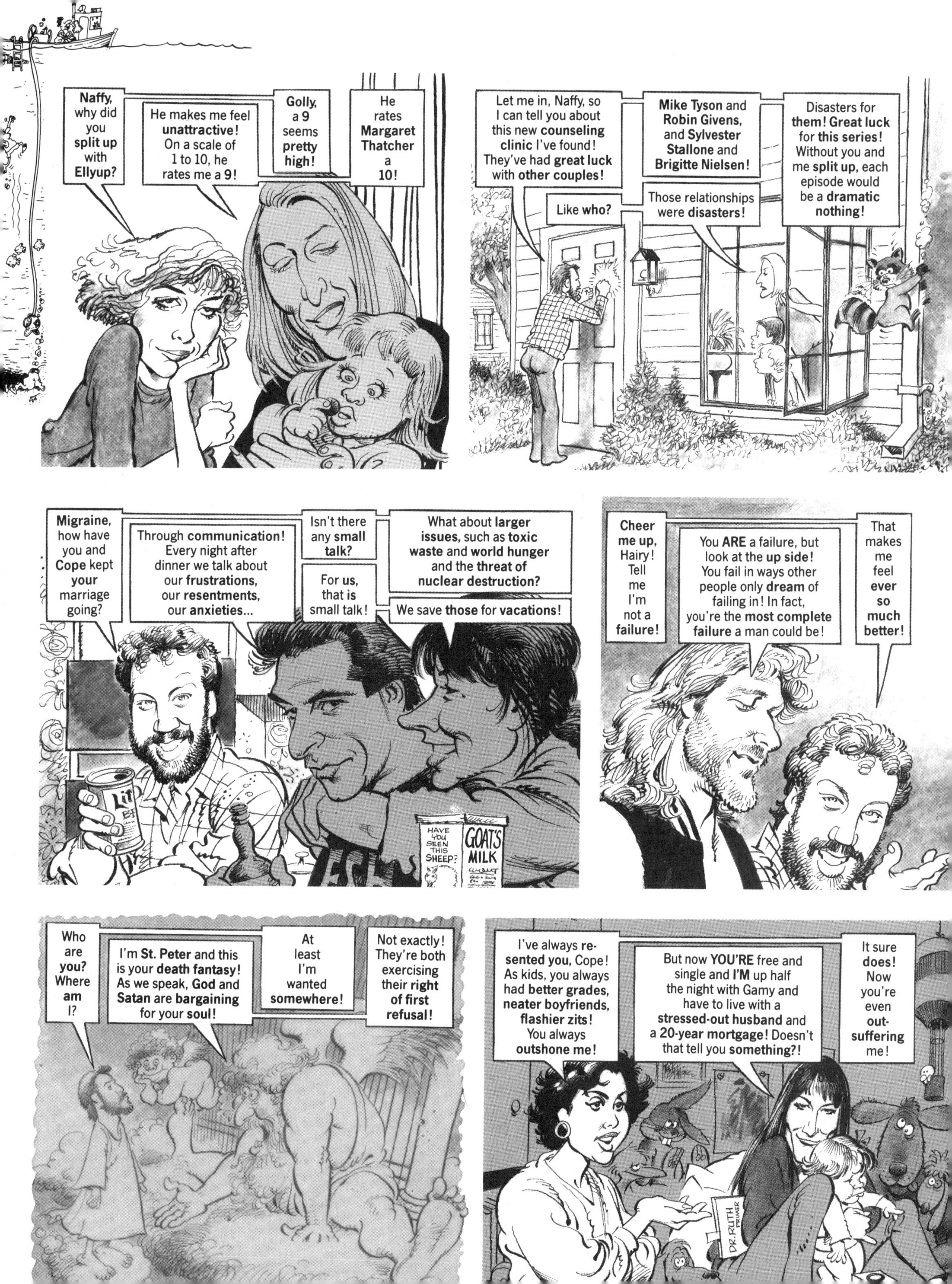
Naffy, why did you split up with Ellyup?
He makes me feel unattractive! On a scale of 1 to 10, he rates me a 9!
Golly, a 9 seems pretty high!
He rates Margaret Thatcher a 10!
Let me in, Naffy, so I can tell you about this new counseling clinic I've found! They've had great luck with other couples!
Like who?
Mike Tyson and Robin Givens, and Sylvester Stallone and Brigitte Nielsen!
Those relationships were disasters!
Disasters for them! Great luck for this series! Without you and me split up, each episode would be a dramatic nothing!
Migraine, how have you and Cope kept your marriage going?
Through communication! Every night after dinner we talk about our frustrations, our resentments, our anxieties...
Isn't there any small talk?
What about larger issues, such as toxic waste and world hunger and the threat of nuclear destruction?
For us, that is small talk!
We save those for vacations!
HAVE YOU SEEN THIS SHEEP?
GOAT'S MILK
Cheer me up, Hairy! Tell me I'm not a failure!
You ARE a failure, but look at the up side! You fail in ways other people only dream of failing in! In fact, you're the most complete failure a man could be!
That makes me feel ever so much better!
Who are you? Where am I?
I'm St. Peter and this is your death fantasy! As we speak, God and Satan are bargaining for your soul!
At least I'm wanted somewhere!
Not exactly! They're both exercising their right of first refusal!
I've always resented you, Cope! As kids, you always had better grades, neater boyfriends, flashier zits! You always outshone me!
But now YOU'RE free and single and I'M up half the night with Gamy and have to live with a stressed-out husband and a 20-year mortgage! Doesn't that tell you something?!
It sure does! Now you're even out-suffering me!
DR. RUTH PRIMER

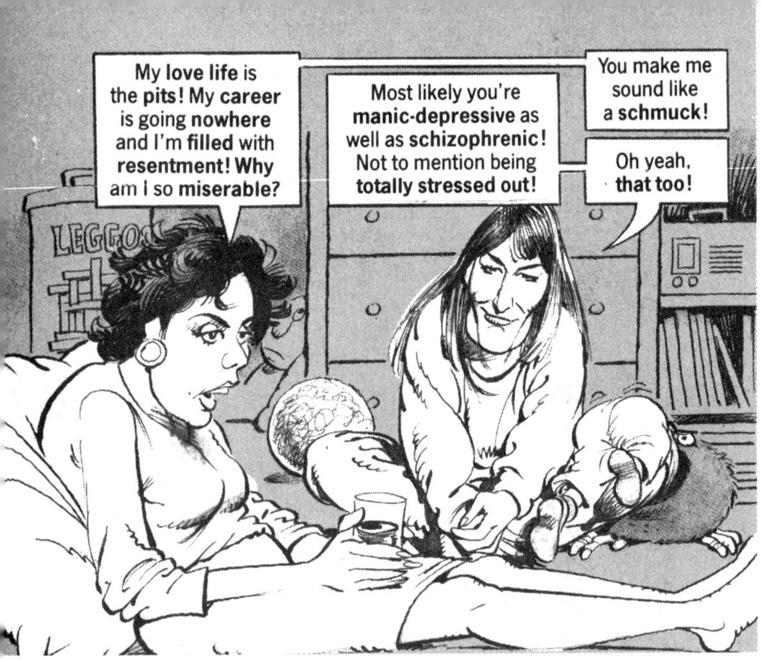
My love life is the pits! My career is going nowhere and I'm filled with resentment! Why am I so miserable?
Most likely you're manic-depressive as well as schizophrenic! Not to mention being totally stressed out!
You make me sound like a schmuck!
Oh yeah, that too!
LEGGOS

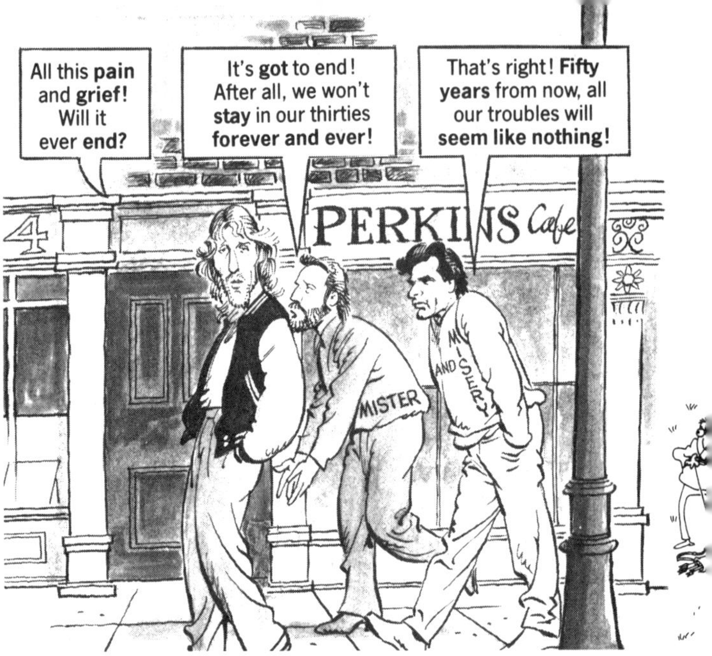
All this pain and grief! Will it ever end?
It's got to end! After all, we won't stay in our thirties forever and ever!
That's right! Fifty years from now, all our troubles will seem like nothing!
4
PERKINS Cafe
MISTER
AND MISERY

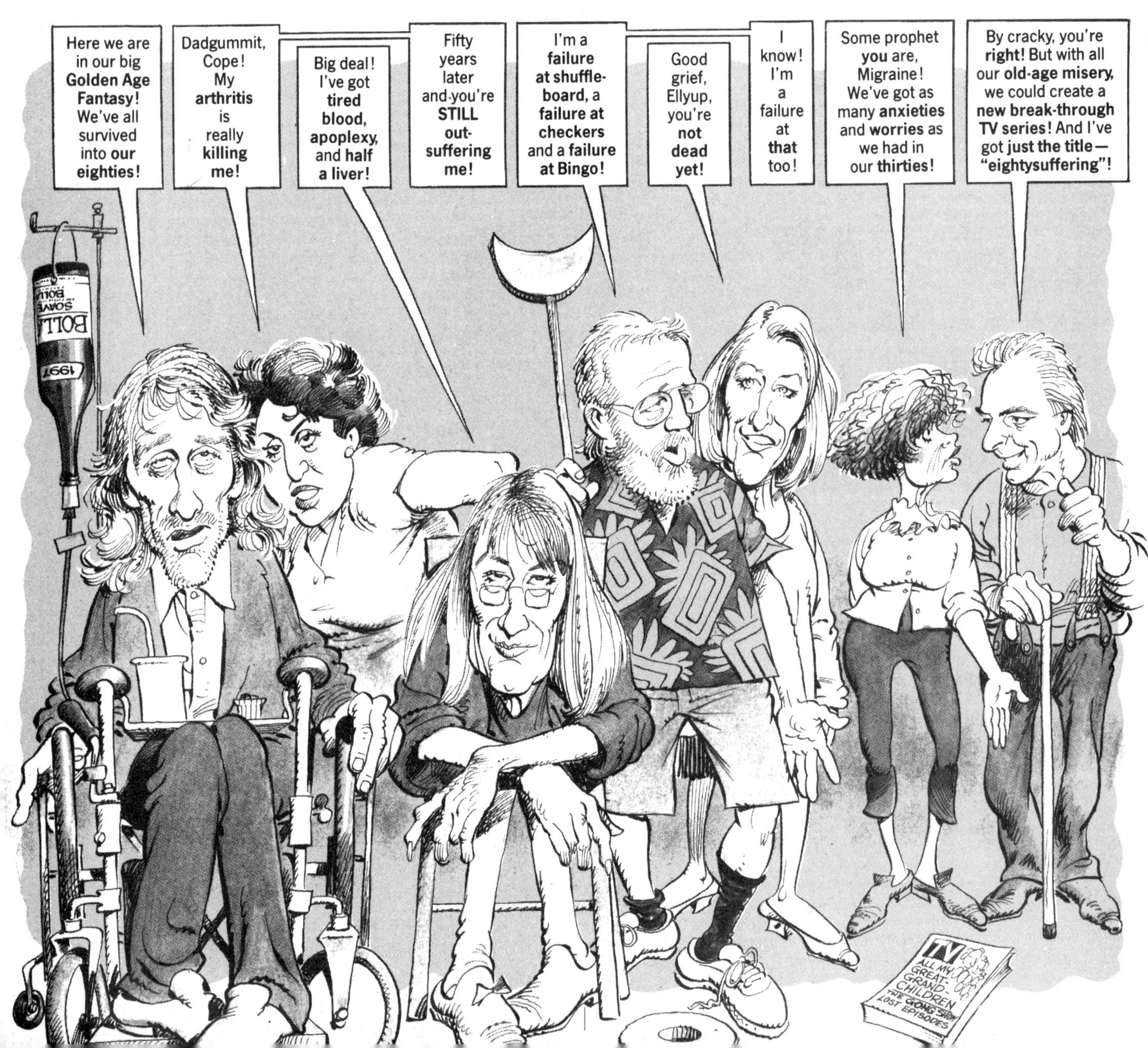
Here we are in our big Golden Age Fantasy! We've all survived into our eighties!
Dadgummit, Cope! My arthritis is really killing me!
Big deal! I've got tired blood, apoplexy, and half a liver!
Fifty years later and you're STILL out-suffering me!
I'm a failure at shuffle-board, a failure at checkers and a failure at Bingo!
Good grief, Ellyup, you're not dead yet!
I know! I'm a failure at that too!
Some prophet you are, Migraine! We've got as many anxieties and worries as we had in our thirties!
By cracky, you're right! But with all our old-age misery, we could create a new break-through TV series! And I've got just the title — "eightysuffering"!
TV
ALL MY GREAT-GRANDCHILDREN
THE GONG SHOW LOST EPISODES

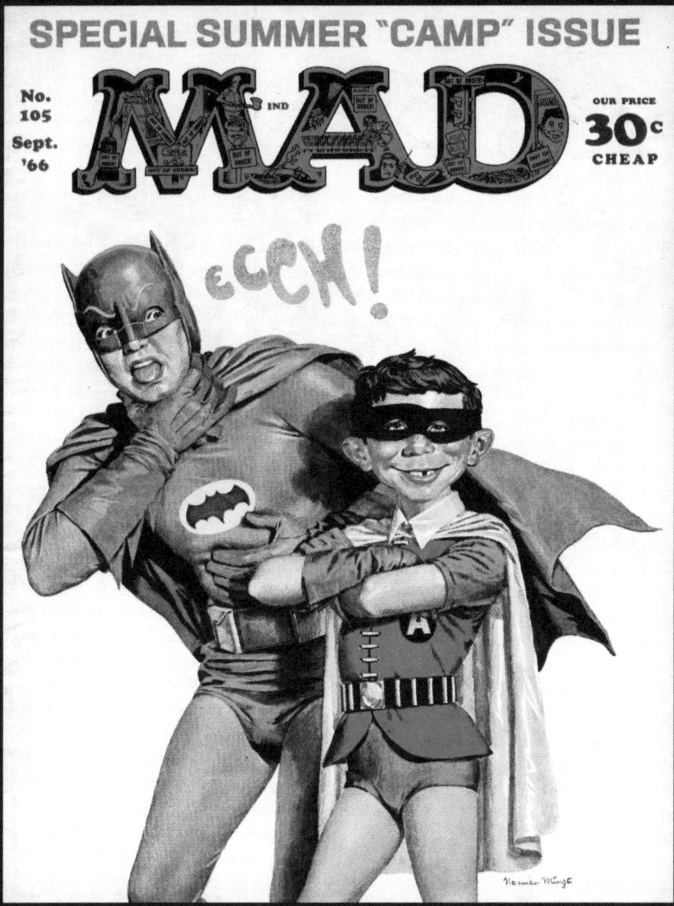
SPECIAL SUMMER "CAMP" ISSUE
No. 105 Sept. '66
MAD
IND
OUR PRICE 30¢ CHEAP
ECCH!

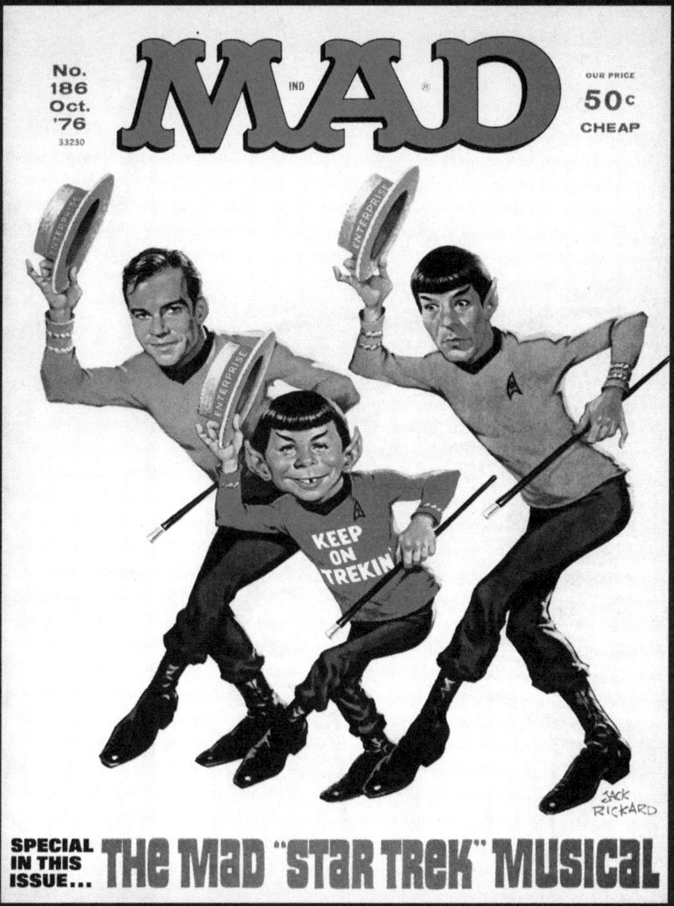
No. 186 Oct. '76
33230
MAD
IND
OUR PRICE 50¢ CHEAP
ENTERPRISE
KEEP ON TREKIN'
JACK RICKARD
SPECIAL IN THIS ISSUE... THE MAD "STAR TREK" MUSICAL

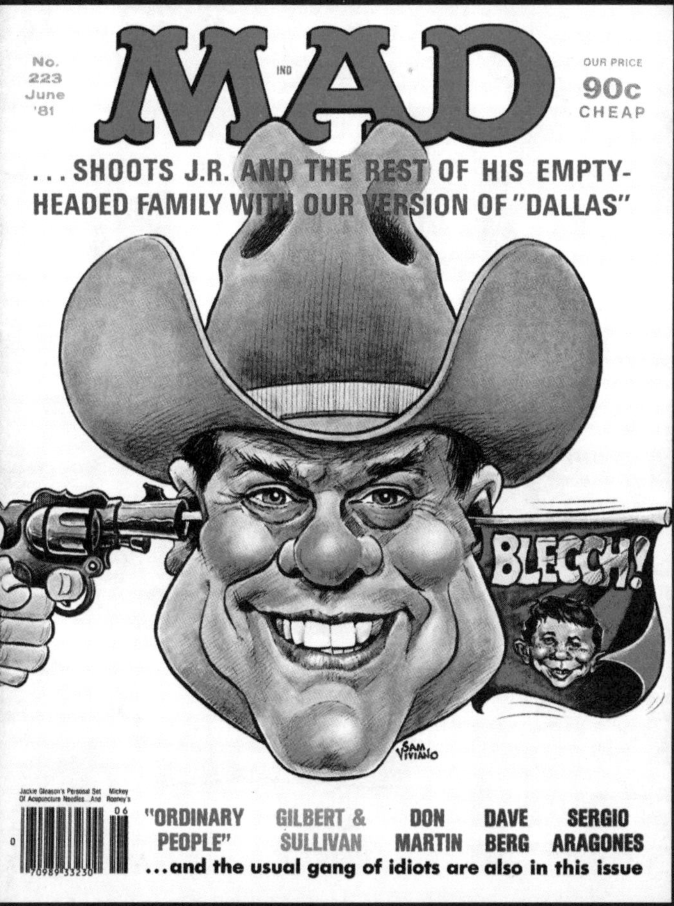
No. 223 June '81
MAD
IND
OUR PRICE 90¢ CHEAP
...SHOOTS J.R. AND THE REST OF HIS EMPTY-HEADED FAMILY WITH OUR VERSION OF "DALLAS"
BLECCH!
SAM VIVIANO
Jackie Gleason's Personal Set Of Acupuncture Needles... And Mickey Rooney's
"ORDINARY PEOPLE"
GILBERT & SULLIVAN
DON MARTIN
DAVE BERG
SERGIO ARAGONES
...and the usual gang of idiots are also in this issue

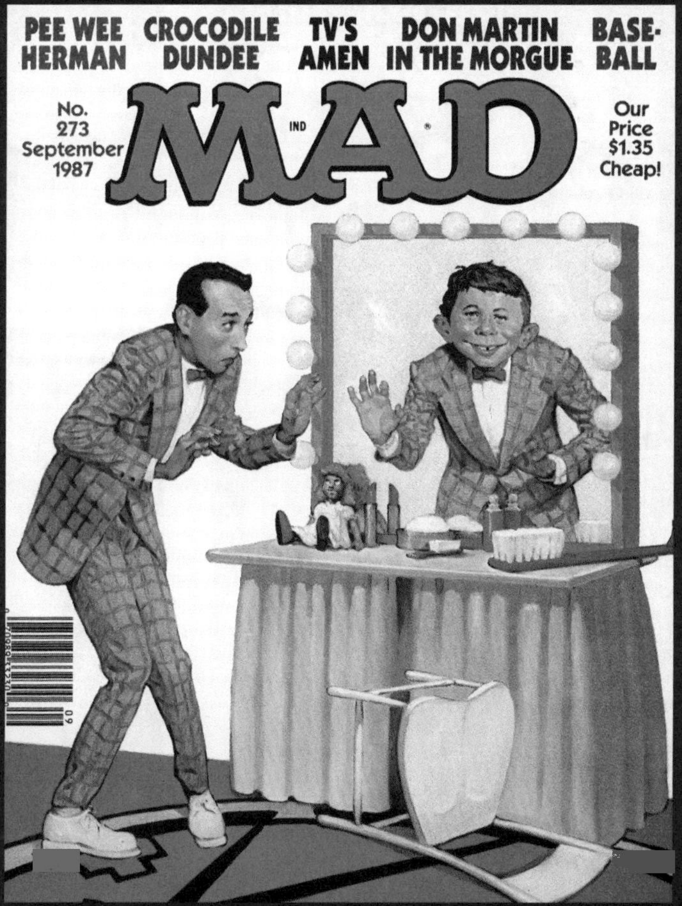
PEE WEE HERMAN
CROCODILE DUNDEE
TV'S AMEN
DON MARTIN IN THE MORGUE
BASE-BALL
No. 273 September 1987
MAD
IND
Our Price $1.35 Cheap!

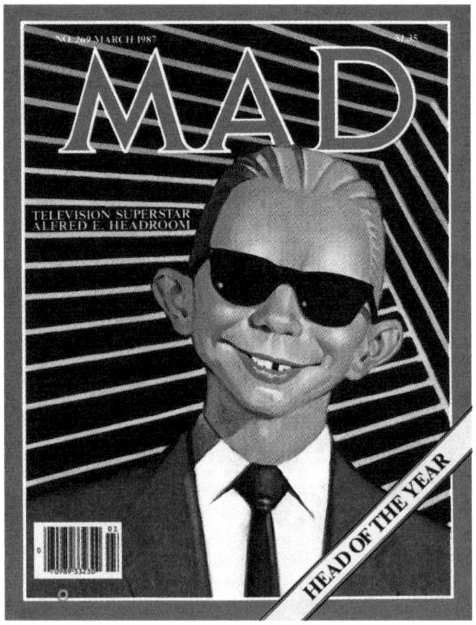
NO.269 MARCH 1987
$1.35
MAD
TELEVISION SUPERSTAR
ALFRED E. HEADROOM
HEAD OF THE YEAR

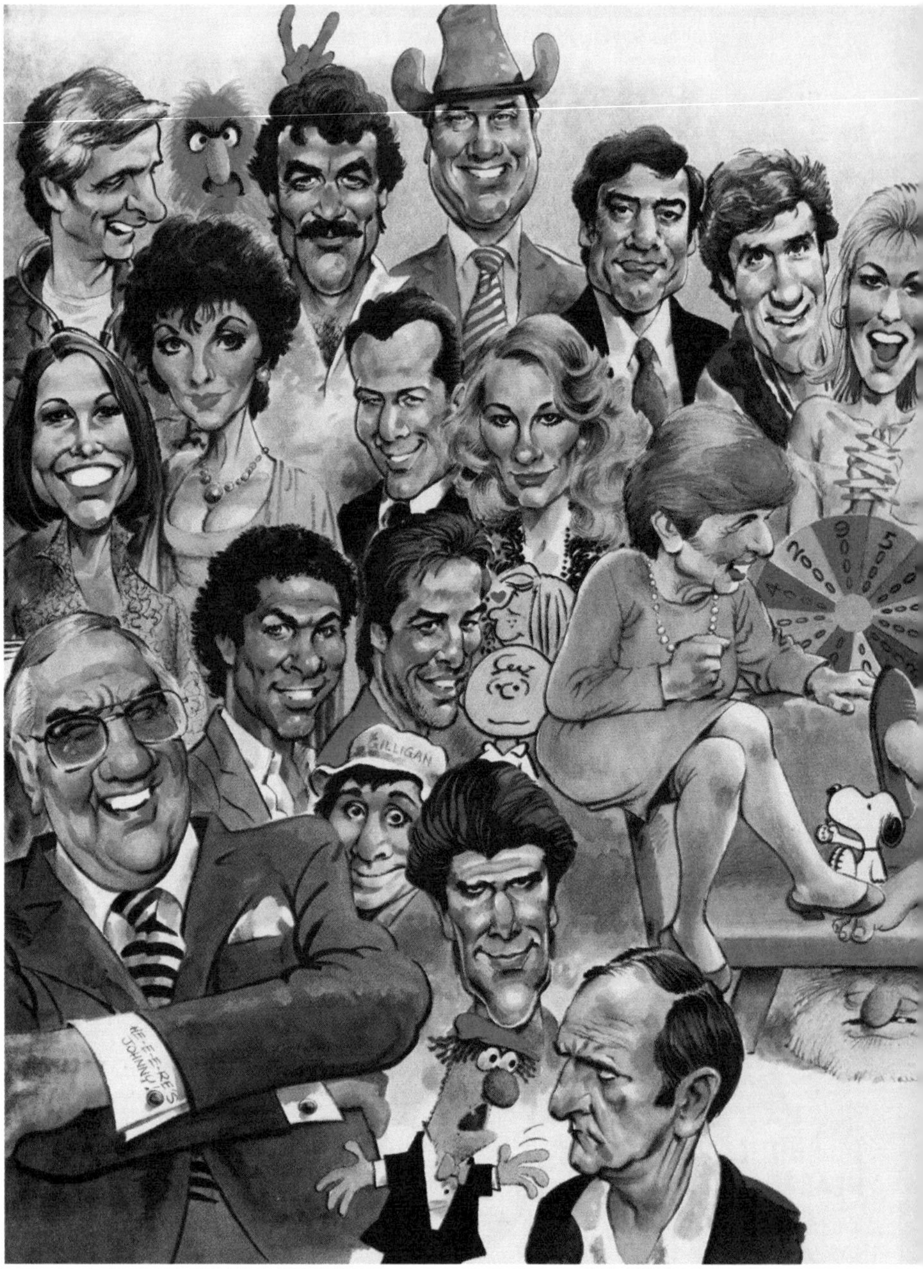
GILLIGAN

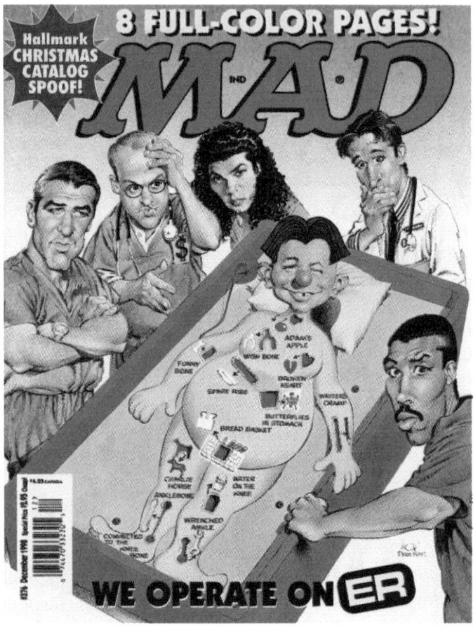
8 FULL-COLOR PAGES!
Hallmark CHRISTMAS CATALOG SPOOF!
MAD
WE OPERATE ON ER

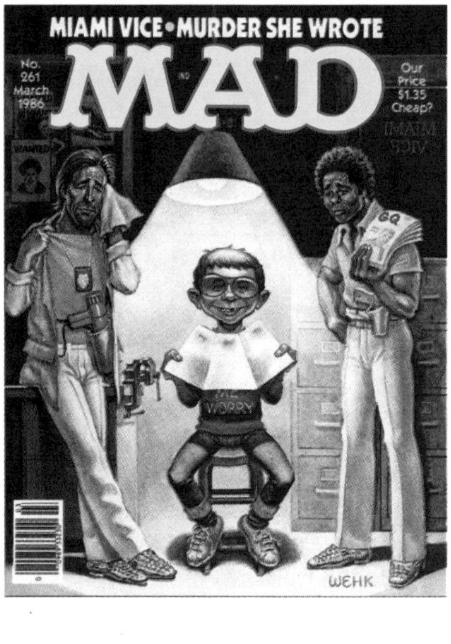
MIAMI VICE • MURDER SHE WROTE
No. 261 March 1986
MAD
Our Price $1.35 Cheap?
WEHK

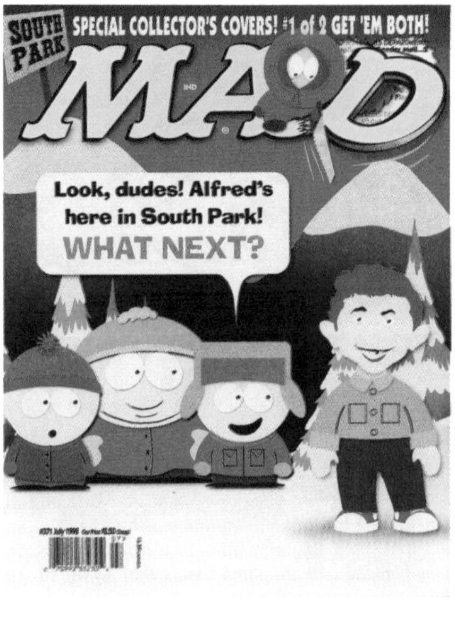
SOUTH PARK
SPECIAL COLLECTOR'S COVERS! #1 of 2 GET 'EM BOTH!
MAD
Look, dudes! Alfred's here in South Park!
WHAT NEXT?

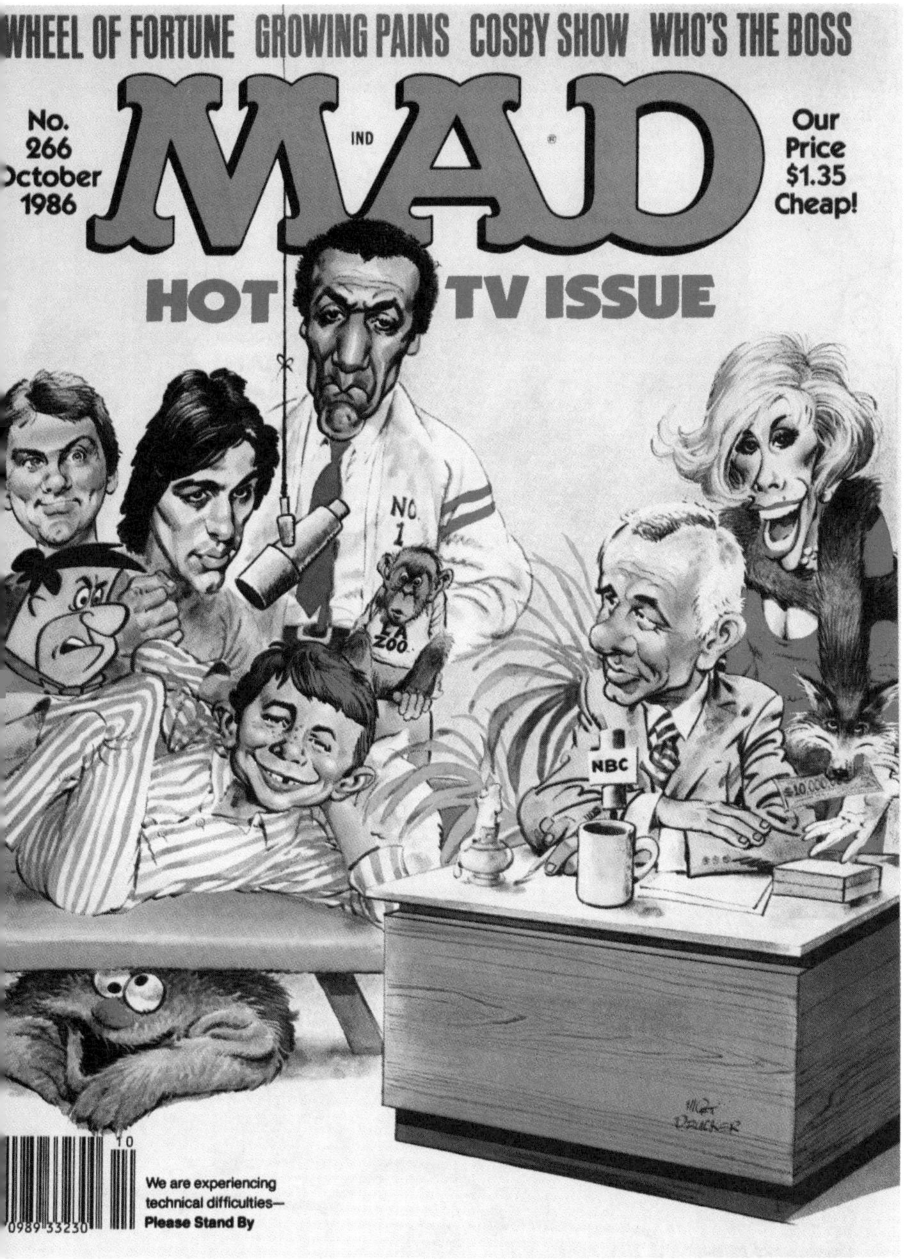
WHEEL OF FORTUNE GROWING PAINS COSBY SHOW WHO'S THE BOSS
MAD
No. 266 October 1986
Our Price $1.35 Cheap!
HOT TV ISSUE
NO. 1
LA ZOO
NBC
We are experiencing technical difficulties—
Please Stand By
DRUCKER

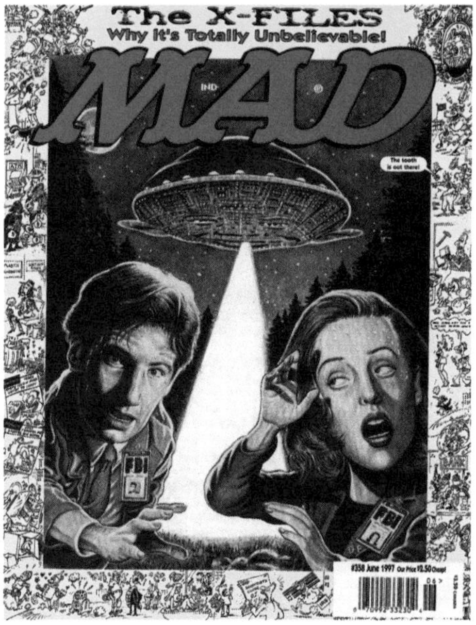
The X-FILES
Why It's Totally Unbelievable!
MAD
The truth is not there!
FBI

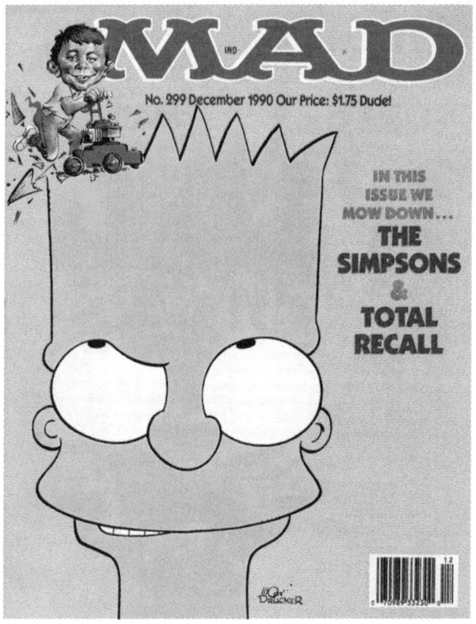
MAD
No. 299 December 1990 Our Price: $1.75 Dude!
IN THIS ISSUE WE MOW DOWN...
THE SIMPSONS
&
TOTAL RECALL
DRUCKER

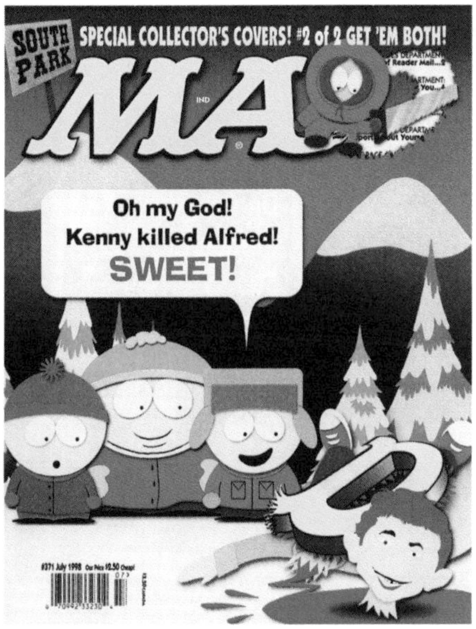
SOUTH PARK
SPECIAL COLLECTOR'S COVERS! #2 of 2 GET 'EM BOTH!
MAD
Oh my God!
Kenny killed Alfred!
SWEET!

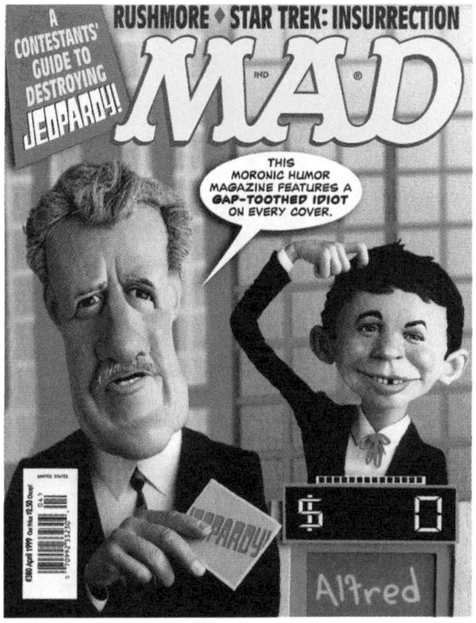
RUSHMORE ♦ STAR TREK: INSURRECTION
A CONTESTANTS' GUIDE TO DESTROYING JEOPARDY!
MAD
THIS MORONIC HUMOR MAGAZINE FEATURES A GAP-TOOTHED IDIOT ON EVERY COVER.
$ 0
Alfred

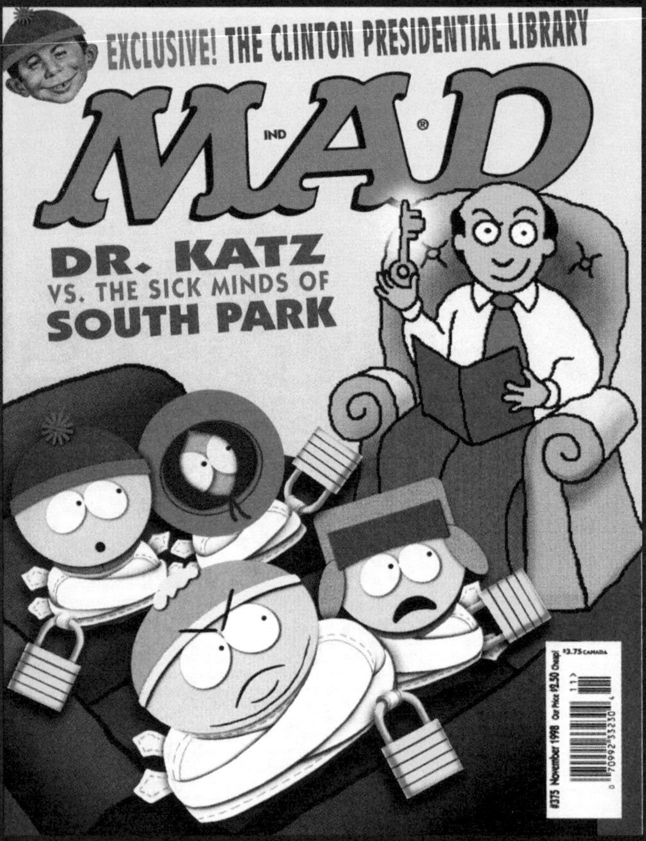
EXCLUSIVE! THE CLINTON PRESIDENTIAL LIBRARY
MAD
DR. KATZ
VS. THE SICK MINDS OF
SOUTH PARK
#375 November 1998 Our Price $2.50 Cheap!
$3.75 CANADA

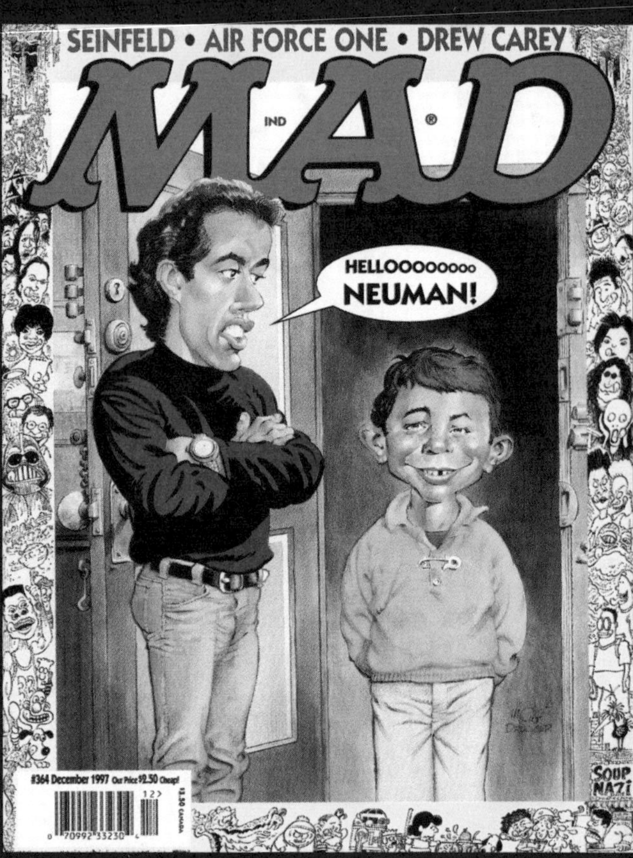
SEINFELD • AIR FORCE ONE • DREW CAREY
MAD
HELLOOOOOOOO
NEUMAN!
SOUP NAZI
#364 December 1997 Our Price $2.50 Cheap!

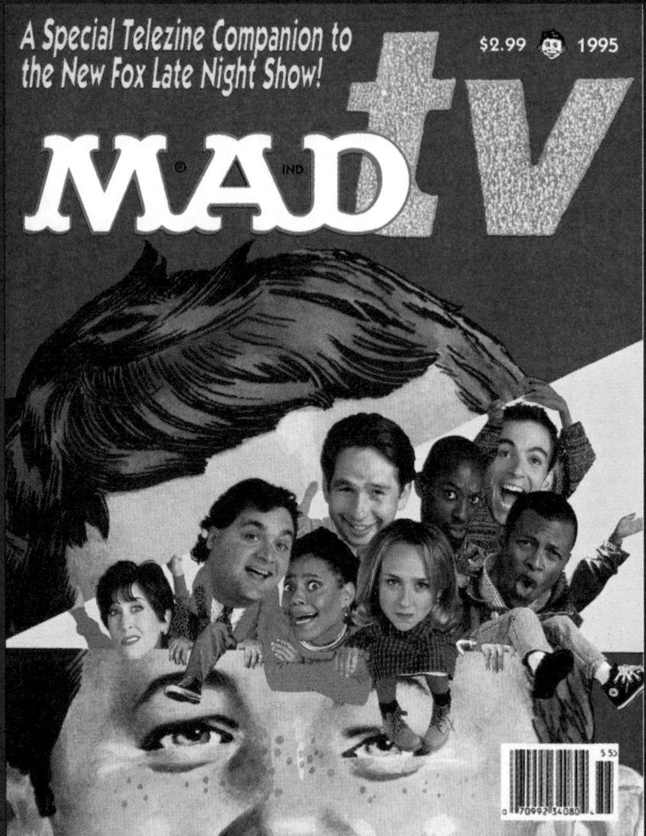
A Special Telezine Companion to
the New Fox Late Night Show!
$2.99 1995
MAD tv

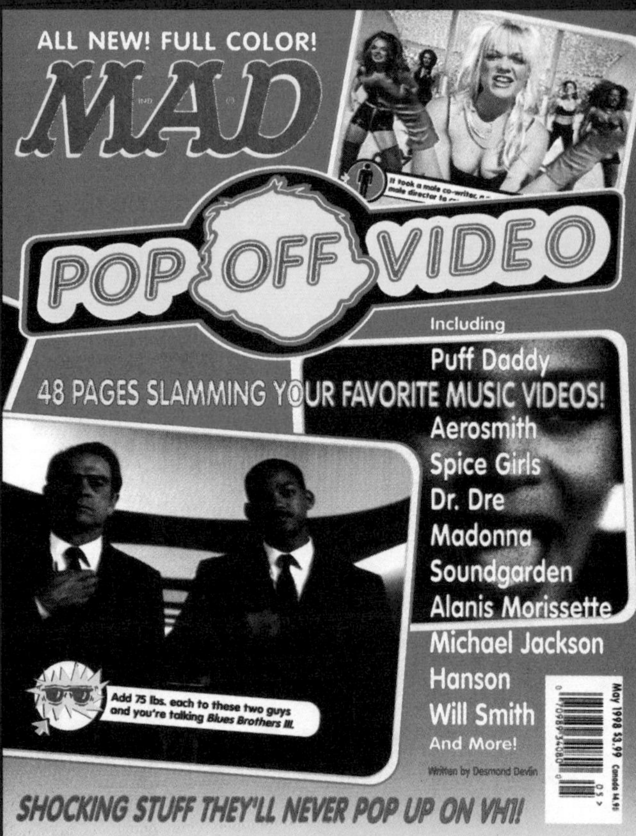
ALL NEW! FULL COLOR!
MAD
POP OFF VIDEO
Including
Puff Daddy
48 PAGES SLAMMING YOUR FAVORITE MUSIC VIDEOS!
Aerosmith
Spice Girls
Dr. Dre
Madonna
Soundgarden
Alanis Morissette
Michael Jackson
Hanson
Will Smith
And More!
Written by Desmond Devlin
Add 75 lbs. each to these two guys
and you're talking Blues Brothers III.
May 1998 $3.99 Canada $4.95
SHOCKING STUFF THEY'LL NEVER POP UP ON VH1!

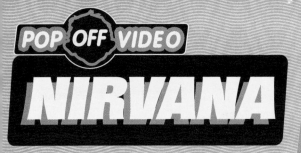

POP OFF VIDEO

NIRVANA

COME AS YOU ARE

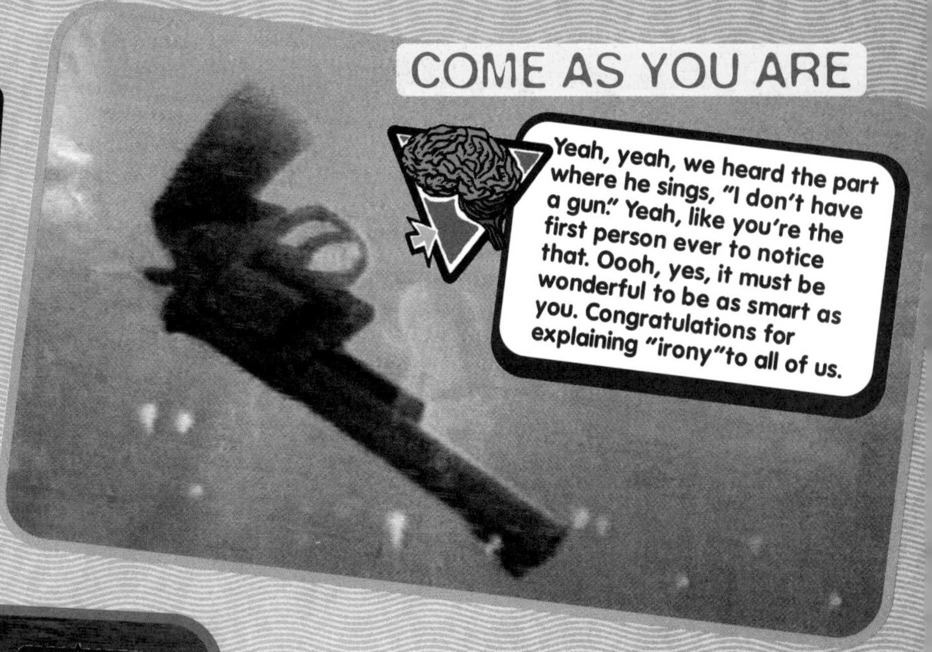

Yeah, yeah, we heard the part where he sings, "I don't have a gun." Yeah, like you're the first person ever to notice that. Oooh, yes, it must be wonderful to be as smart as you. Congratulations for explaining "irony" to all of us.

ALL APOLOGIES

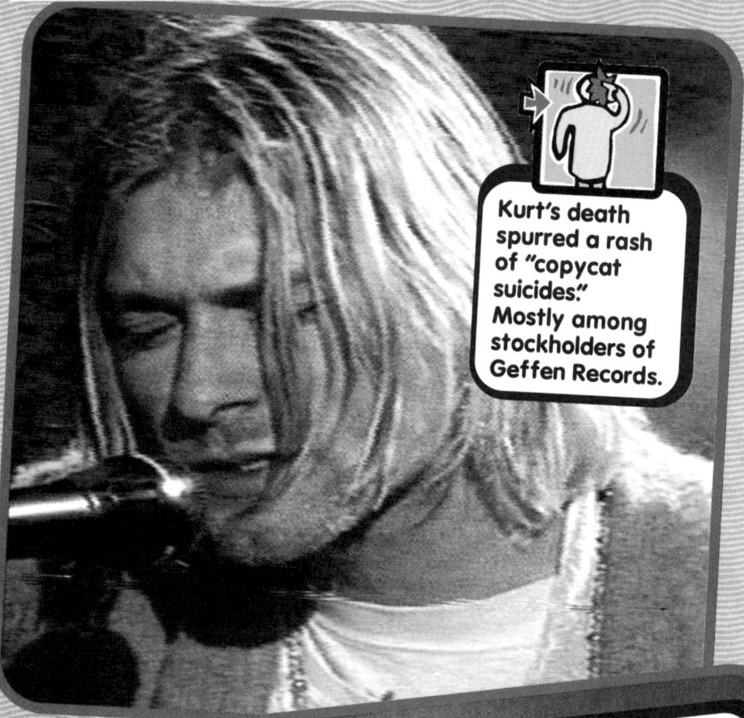

Kurt's death spurred a rash of "copycat suicides." Mostly among stockholders of Geffen Records.

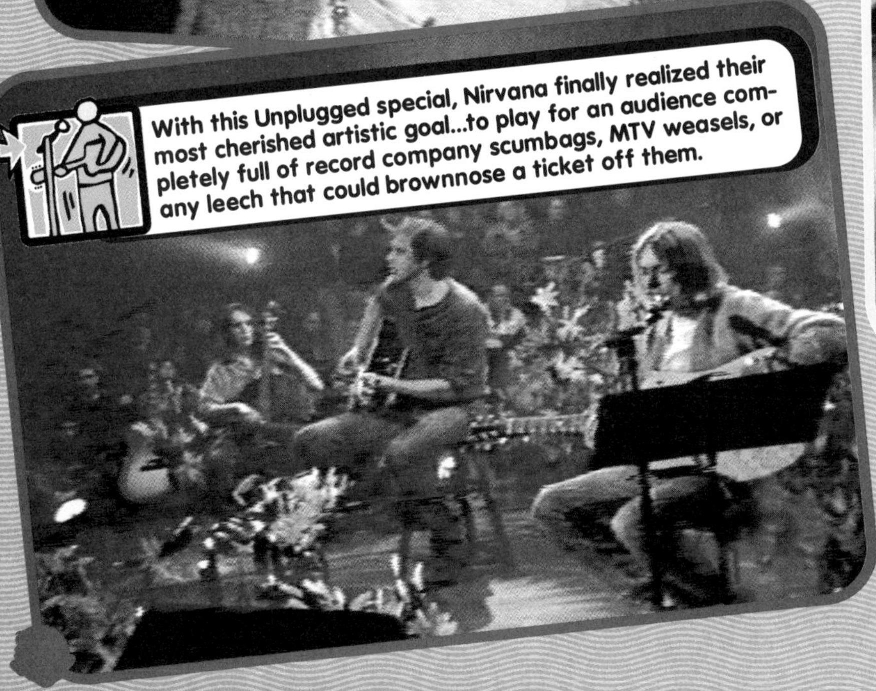

With this Unplugged special, Nirvana finally realized their most cherished artistic goal...to play for an audience completely full of record company scumbags, MTV weasels, or any leech that could brownnose a ticket off them.

IN BLOOM

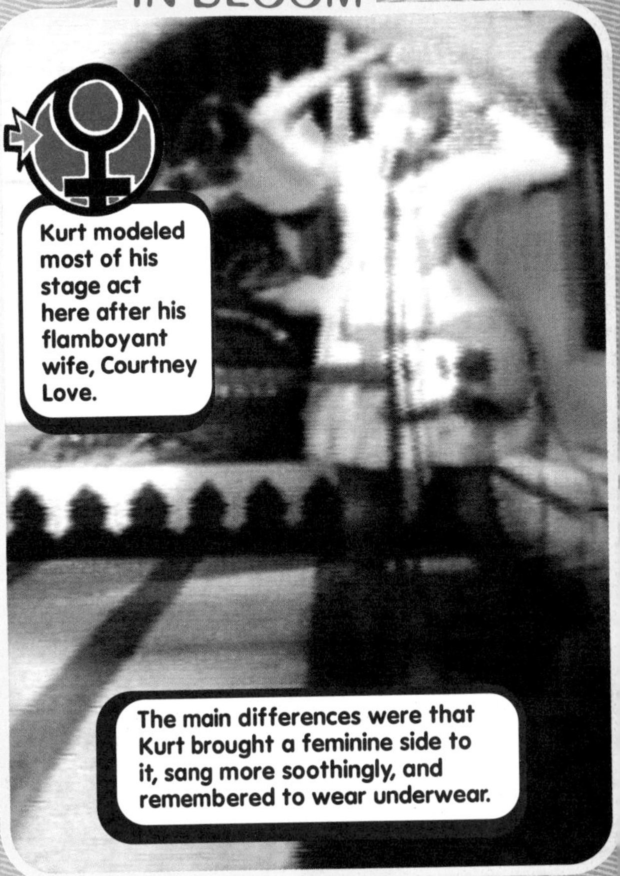

Kurt modeled most of his stage act here after his flamboyant wife, Courtney Love.

The main differences were that Kurt brought a feminine side to it, sang more soothingly, and remembered to wear underwear.

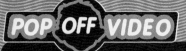

POP OFF VIDEO

ALANIS MORISSETTE

IRONIC

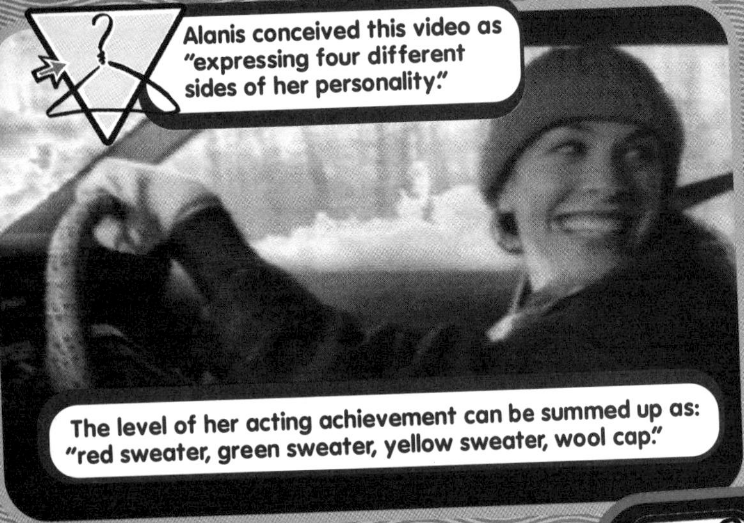

Alanis conceived this video as "expressing four different sides of her personality."

The level of her acting achievement can be summed up as: "red sweater, green sweater, yellow sweater, wool cap."

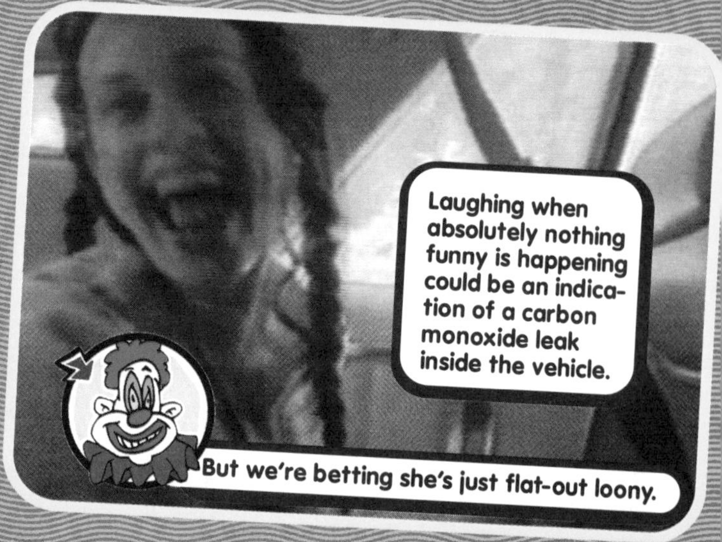

Laughing when absolutely nothing funny is happening could be an indication of a carbon monoxide leak inside the vehicle.

But we're betting she's just flat-out loony.

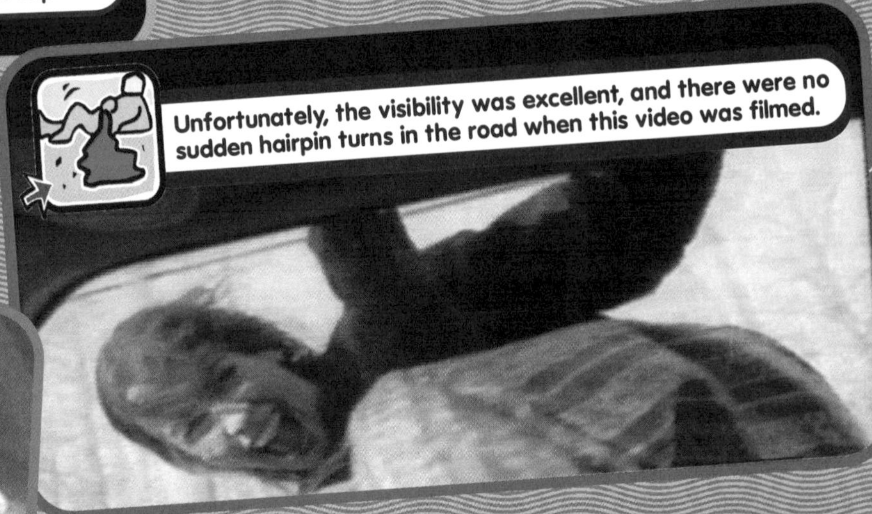

Unfortunately, the visibility was excellent, and there were no sudden hairpin turns in the road when this video was filmed.

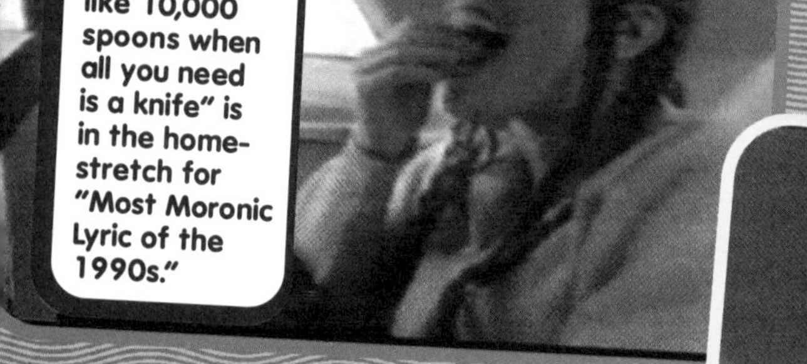

With very little time left in the decade to lose its lead, "It's like 10,000 spoons when all you need is a knife" is in the home-stretch for "Most Moronic Lyric of the 1990s."

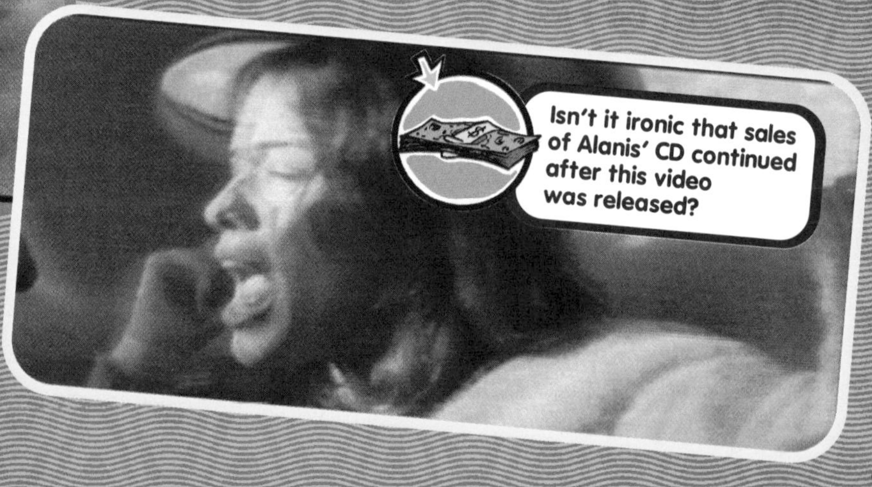

Isn't it ironic that sales of Alanis' CD continued after this video was released?

POP OFF VIDEO

SPICE GIRLS

SAY YOU'LL BE THERE

It took a male co-writer, a male producer and a male director to create this tribute to "Girl Power."

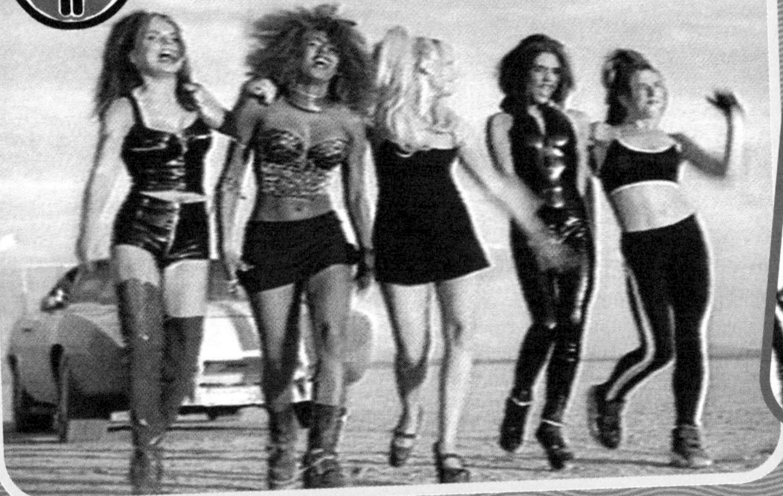

The Spice Girls' 1997 musical performance on *Saturday Night Live* got the most laughs of any segment since Belushi left.

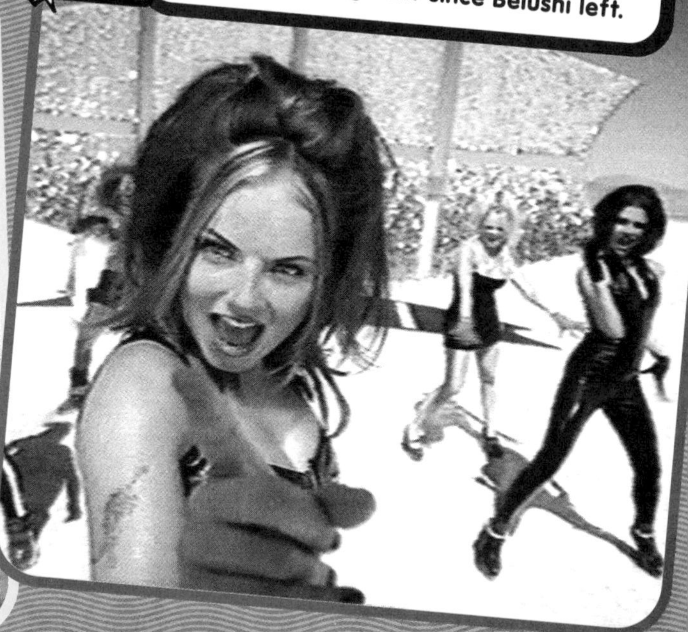

When the Girls sing "Tell me, will this déjà vu never end," they are tapping into an entire school of French philosophical thought, embodied by Marcel Proust's *Remembrance of Things Past*, another work which seeks to use the inner self as a basis for comparing art and the literal world.

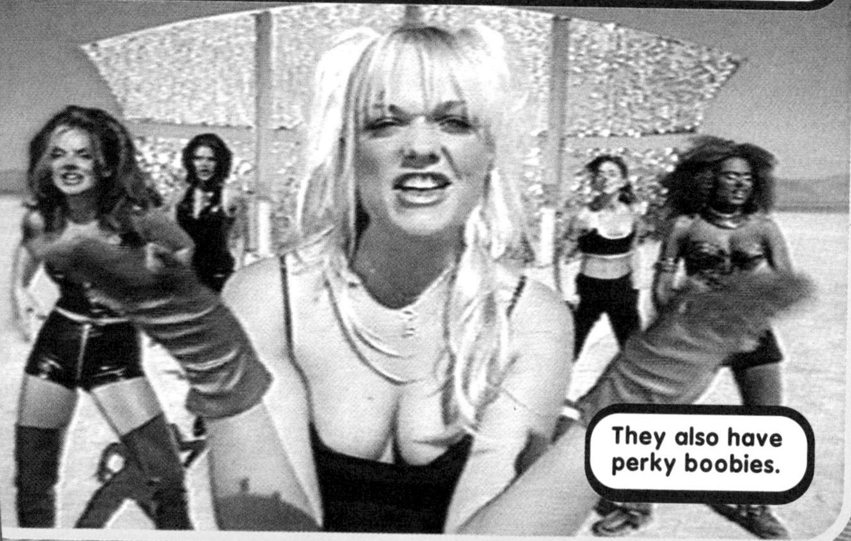

They also have perky boobies.

The most advanced futuristic technology yet seen in video-making was used here — not the rayguns or the vehicles, but the machine to get all five women's voices in the same key.

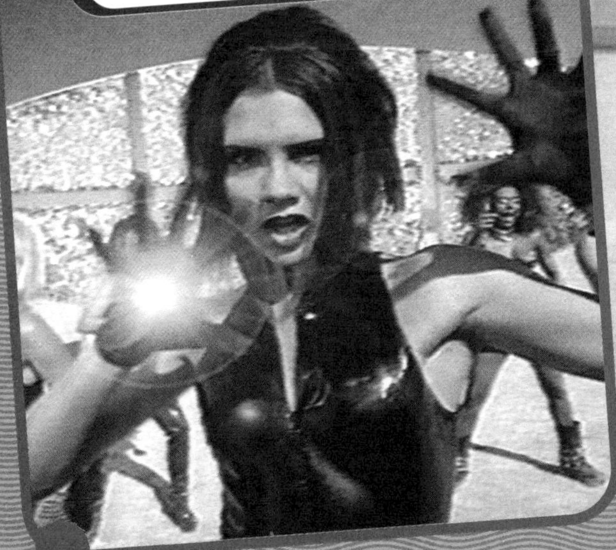

A 📺 SCENE WE'D LIKE TO SEE

Good morning, Mr. Phelps! The man you are looking at has become a **serious threat** to the **Impossible Mission Force.**

He has squandered **millions of dollars of government funds** on such useless and extravagant contrivances as laser-beam fountain pens, radar wrist watches, closed-circuit mini-TV cameras embedded in belt buckles, and invisible sneakers . . .

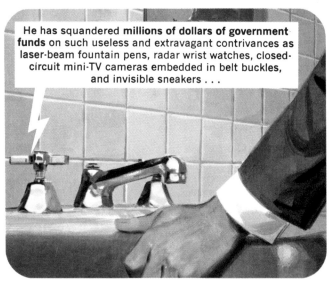

In addition, he has created an unusual **high-risk factor** by ordering his co-workers to perform **needlessly complex** and **dangerous tasks** in order to carry out assignments that could have been accomplished relatively safely and simply.

In other words, Mr. Phelps . . . **YOU'RE FIRED!!**

Good luck in your next TV series, Jim . . .

This sink will self-destruct in five seconds . . .

ARTIST: JOHN CULLEN MURPHY WRITER: CHEVY CHASE

WHO ON TV IS SURPASSING RUSH LIMBAUGH OR INTELLECTUAL SOCIAL COMMENTARY?

HERE WE GO WITH ANOTHER RIDICULOUS

MAD FOLD-IN

Rush Limbaugh is a TV hit due to his thought-provoking right wing extremist views. But now, Americans are turning to a new source for views that surpass Limbaugh for wit, originality and intelligence. To find out what exactly this competition is, fold page in as shown.

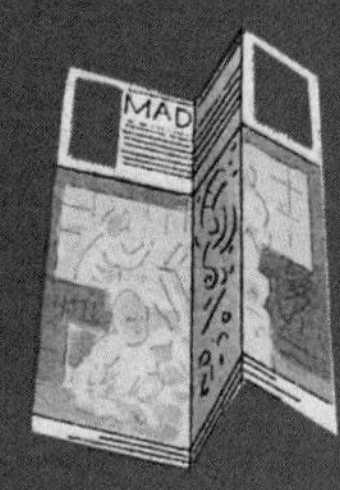

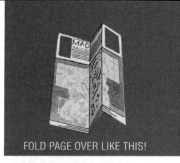

FOLD PAGE OVER LIKE THIS!

A▶ FOLD THIS SECTION OVER LEFT ◀B FOLD BACK SO "A" MEETS "B"

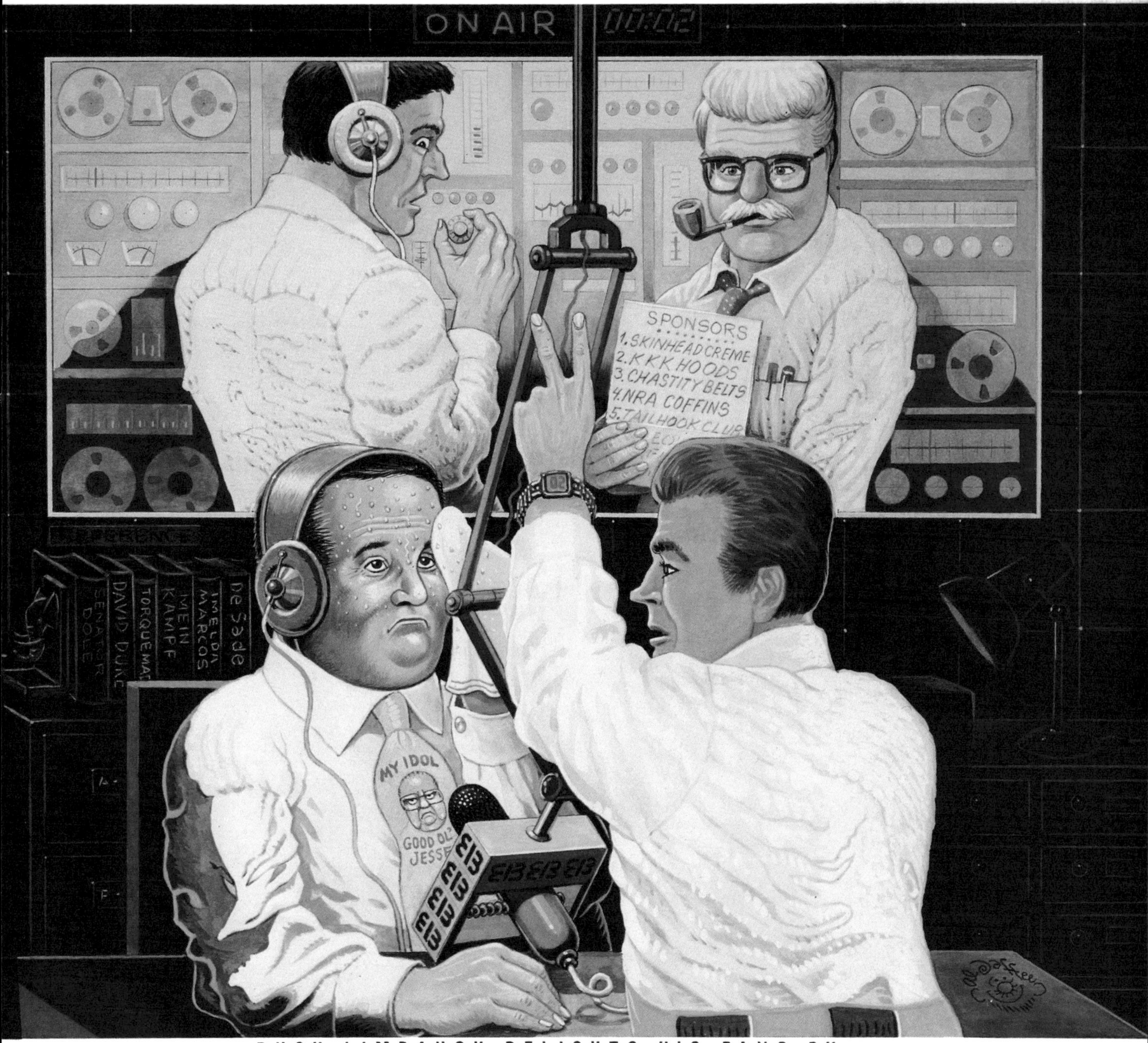

ON AIR
SPONSORS
1. SKINHEAD CREME
2. KKK HOODS
3. CHASTITY BELTS
4. NRA COFFINS
5. TAILHOOK CLUB
DAVID DUKE
SENATOR DOLE
TORQUEMADA
MEIN KAMPF
IMELDA MARCOS
De Sade
MY IDOL
GOOD OL' JESSE

RUSH LIMBAUGH DELIGHTS HIS FANS BY BEATING UP ON HIS ENEMIES. HIS ENORMOUS IN-VISIBLE LOYAL AUDIENCE LOVES VENEMOUS HATE AND BIGOTRY. THEY GET OFF ON ATTACKS THAT'RE UTT-ERLY MERCILESS TO LIBERALS, FEMINISTS, HOMOSEXUALS, AND OTHERS THEY FEAR AND DREAD.

A▶ ◀B

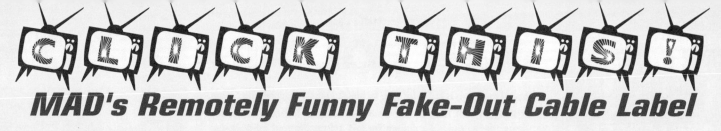

CLICK THIS!

MAD's Remotely Funny Fake-Out Cable Label

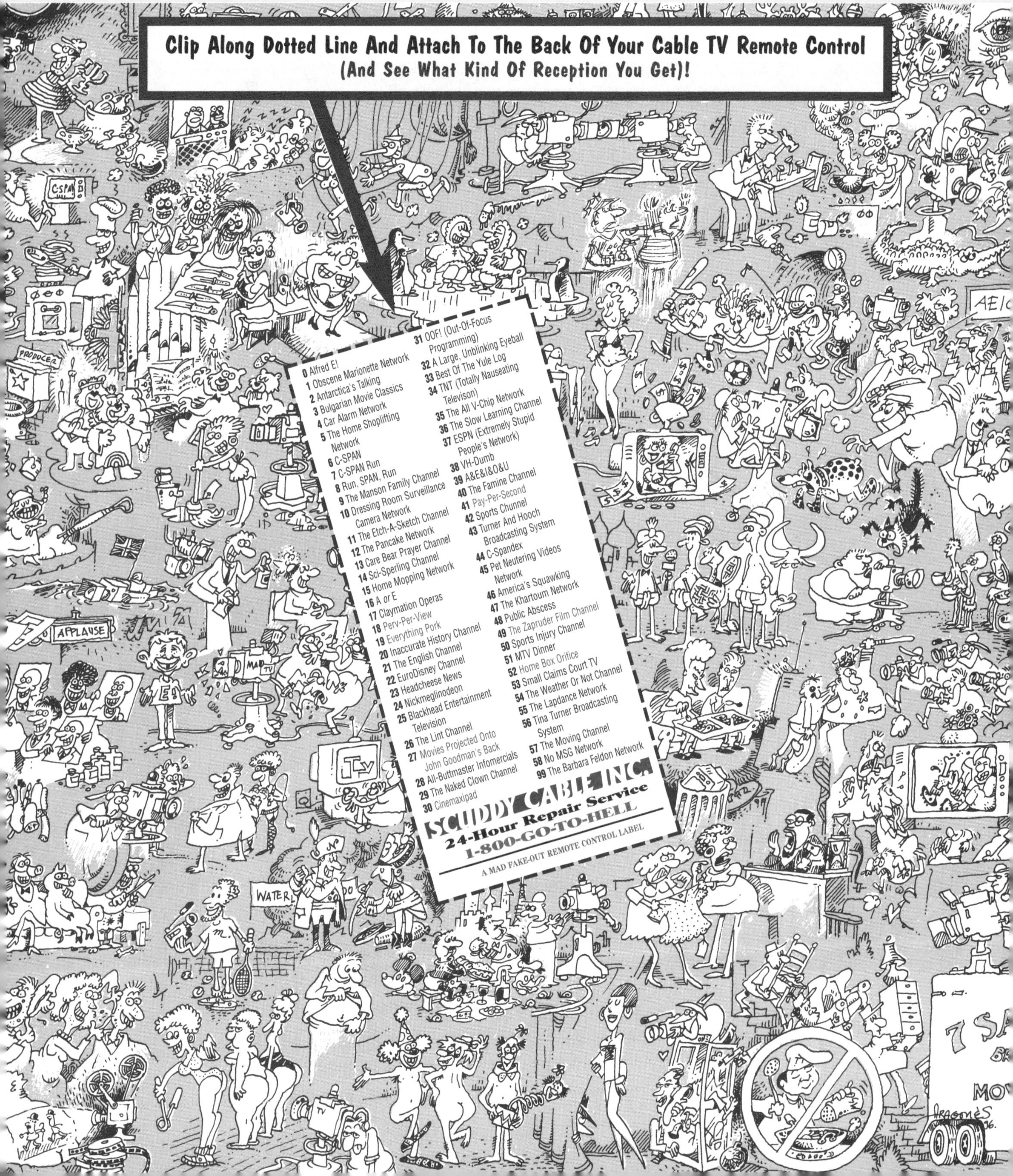

Clip Along Dotted Line And Attach To The Back Of Your Cable TV Remote Control
(And See What Kind Of Reception You Get)!
0 Alfred E!
1 Obscene Marionette Network
2 Antarctica's Talking
3 Bulgarian Movie Classics
4 Car Alarm Network
5 The Home Shoplifting Network
6 C-SPAN
7 C-SPAN Run
8 Run, SPAN, Run
9 The Manson Family Channel
10 Dressing Room Surveillance Camera Network
11 The Etch-A-Sketch Channel
12 The Pancake Network
13 Care Bear Prayer Channel
14 Sci-Sperling Channel
15 Home Mopping Network
16 A or E
17 Claymation Operas
18 Perv-Per-View
19 Everything Pork
20 Inaccurate History Channel
21 The English Channel
22 EuroDisney News
23 Headcheese News
24 Nickmeglinodeon
25 Blackhead Entertainment Television
26 The Lint Channel
27 Movies Projected Onto John Goodman's Back
28 All-Buttmaster Infomercials
29 The Naked Clown Channel
30 Cinemaxipad
31 OOF! (Out-Of-Focus Programming)
32 A Large, Unblinking Eyeball
33 Best Of The Yule Log
34 TNT (Totally Nauseating Television)
35 The All V-Chip Network
36 The Slow Learning Channel
37 ESPN (Extremely Stupid People's Network)
38 VH-Dumb
39 A&E&I&O&U
40 The Famine Channel
41 Pay-Per-Second
42 Sports Chunnel
43 Turner And Hooch Broadcasting System
44 C-Spandex
45 Pet Neutering Videos Network
46 America's Squawking
47 The Khartoum Network
48 Public Abscess
49 The Zapruder Film Channel
50 Sports Injury Channel
51 MTV Dinner
52 Home Box Orifice
53 Small Claims Court TV
54 The Weather Or Not Channel
55 The Lapdance Network
56 Tina Turner Broadcasting System
57 The Moving Channel
58 No MSG Network
99 The Barbara Feldon Network
SCUDDY CABLE INC.
24-Hour Repair Service
1-800-GO-TO-HELL
A MAD FAKE-OUT REMOTE CONTROL LABEL
PRODUCER
APPLAUSE
WATER

VHAT AREA OF THE COUNTRY LEADS THE NATION IN EATH SENTENCES?

HERE WE GO WITH ANOTHER RIDICULOUS

MAD FOLD-IN

More and more states have brought back the death penalty. You can't open a paper today without reading about them strapping another prisoner into Old Sparky, turning up the juice and frying him until smoke comes out his ears and ankles. To find out where death sentences are meted out with unbridled enthusiasm, fold page in as shown.

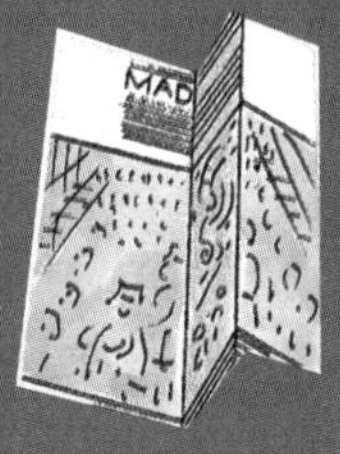

FOLD PAGE OVER LIKE THIS!

A ▶ FOLD THIS SECTION OVER LEFT ◀ B FOLD BACK SO "A" MEETS "B"

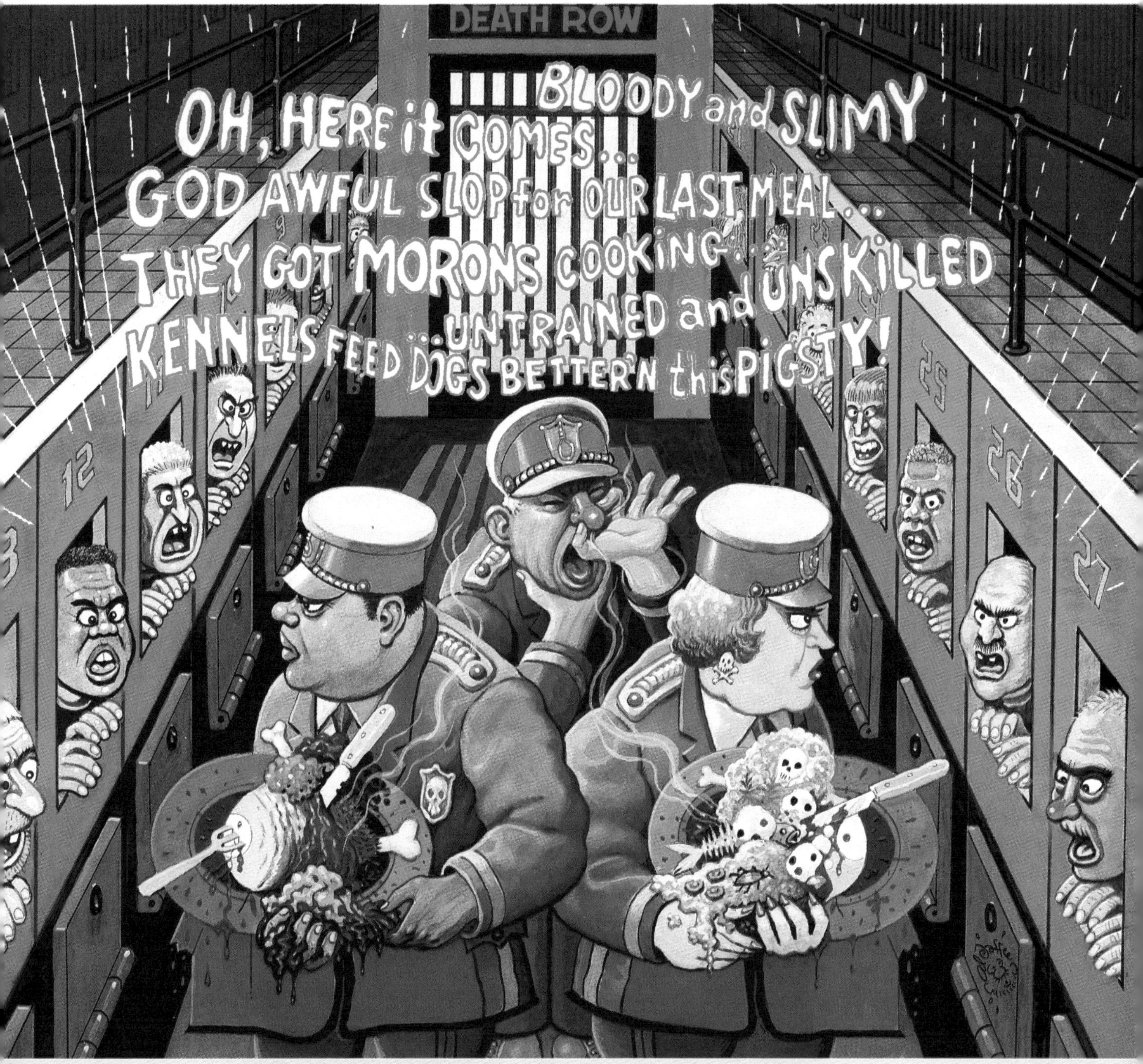

DEATH ROW
OH, HERE it COMES... BLOODY and SLIMY
GOD AWFUL SLOP for OUR LAST MEAL...
THEY GOT MORONS COOKING... UNTRAINED and UNSKILLED
KENNELS FEED DOGS BETTER'N this PIGSTY!

MANY OF US KNOW ABOUT ONE UNFORTUNATE SOUL WHO'LL BE FACING A SENTENCE OF DEATH PARTICULARLY GRUESOME, SADISTIC AND SICK

A ▶ ◀ B

ARTIST AND WRITER: AL JAFFEE

SNAPPY ANSWERS TO STUPID QUESTIONS ON THE SET OF MAD TV

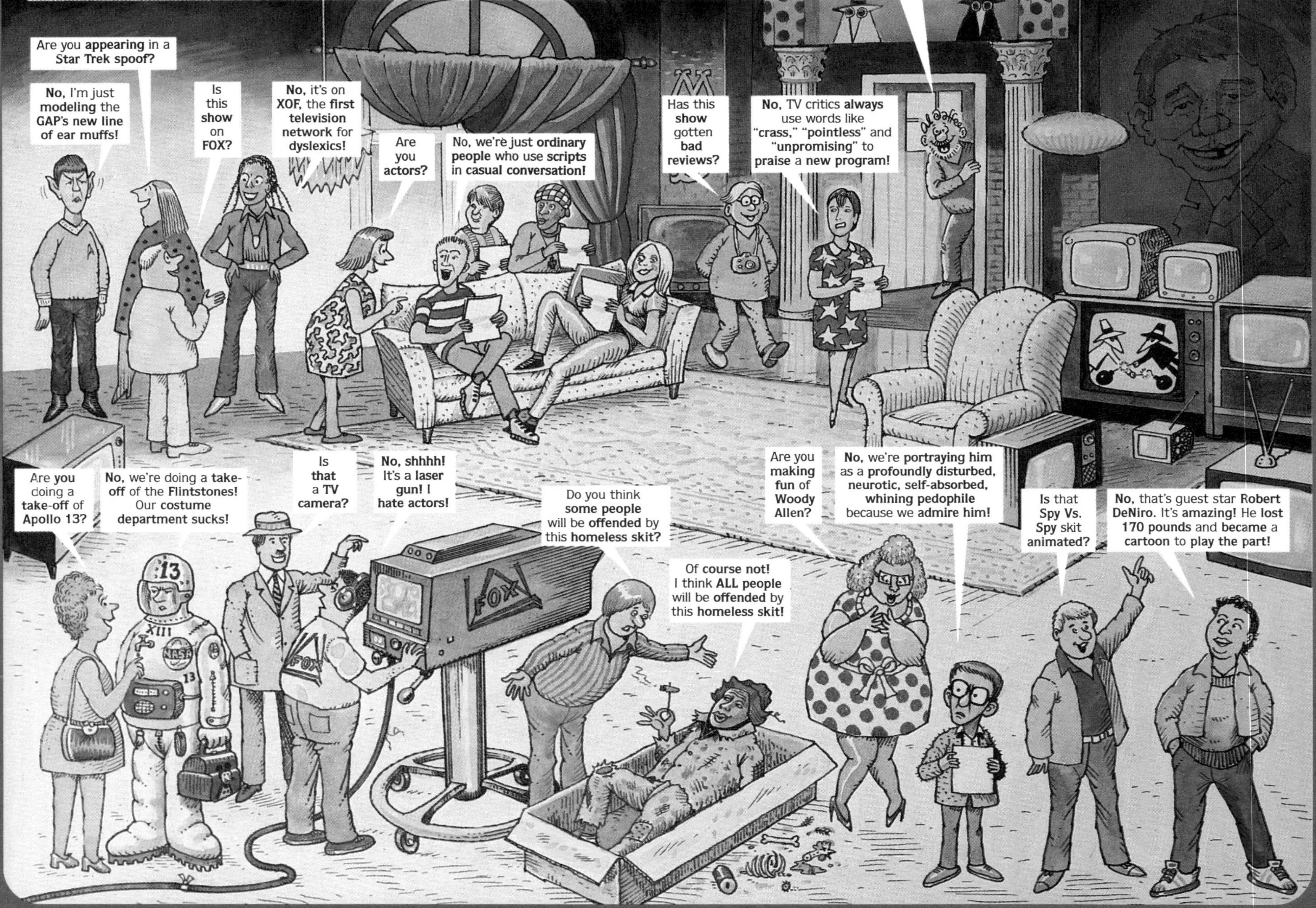

Are you appearing in a Star Trek spoof?
No, I'm just modeling the GAP's new line of ear muffs!
Is this show on FOX?
No, it's on XOF, the first television network for dyslexics!
Are you actors?
No, we're just ordinary people who use scripts in casual conversation!
Has this show gotten bad reviews?
No, TV critics always use words like "crass," "pointless" and "unpromising" to praise a new program!
Are you doing a take-off of Apollo 13?
No, we're doing a take-off of the Flintstones! Our costume department sucks!
Is that a TV camera?
No, shhhh! It's a laser gun! I hate actors!
Do you think some people will be offended by this homeless skit?
Of course not! I think ALL people will be offended by this homeless skit!
Are you making fun of Woody Allen?
No, we're portraying him as a profoundly disturbed, neurotic, self-absorbed, whining pedophile because we admire him!
Is that Spy Vs. Spy skit animated?
No, that's guest star Robert DeNiro. It's amazing! He lost 170 pounds and became a cartoon to play the part!

ARTIST & WRITER: AL JAFFEE

PLEASE PHRASE YOUR ANSWER AS A FORM OF AGGRESSION DEPT.

Answer:
He's the most pompous game show host on television.

Question:
Who is Alex Trebek?

For a guy who's about a step and a half up from "small-town weatherman" on the TV food chain, *Jeopardy!* host Alex Trebek is awfully snooty. Each night ol' Al looms smugly behind his podium in his complimentary Perry Ellis wardrobe, ready to look down his mustache at the first player who accidentally mispronounces "Machu Pichu"! Well, it's time to fight back and put Canada's fourteenth most-important celebrity in his place with MAD's guide to...

11 WAYS JEOPARDY! CONTESTANTS CAN REALLY PISS OFF ALEX TREBEK

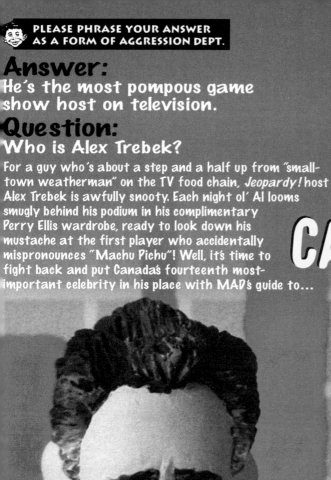

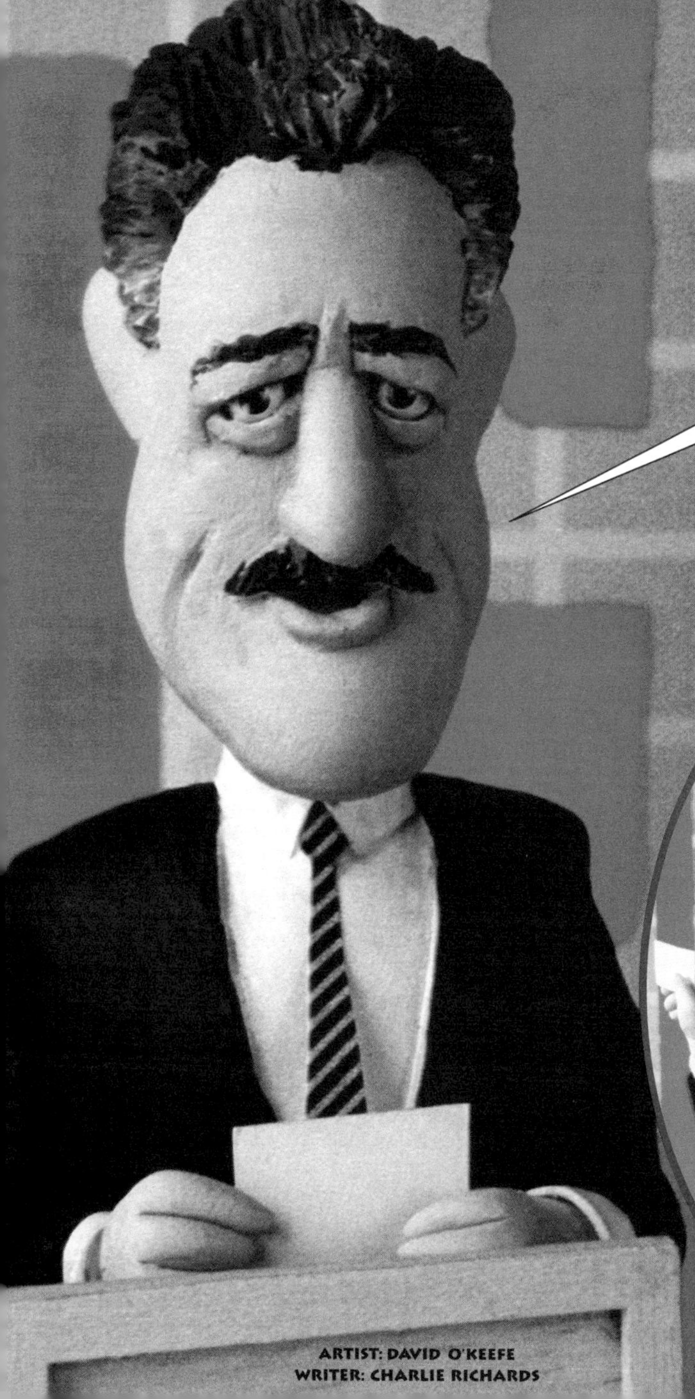
I'm Alex Trebek. Let's play *Jeopardy!*

1. Ask for categories that aren't there.

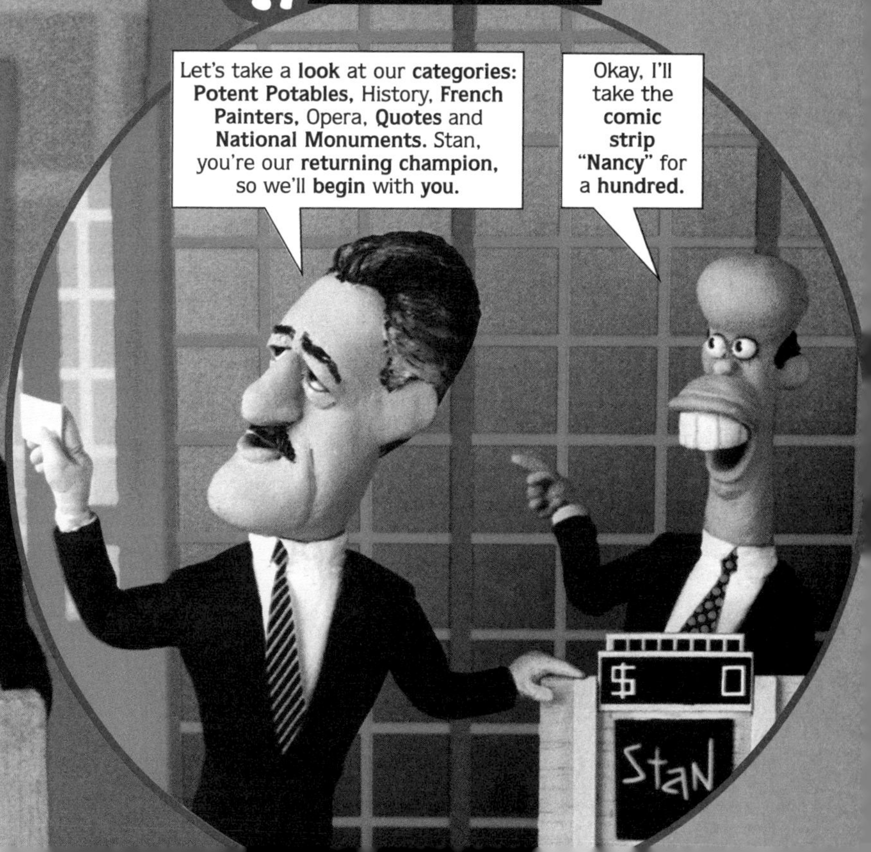
Let's take a look at our categories: Potent Potables, History, French Painters, Opera, Quotes and National Monuments. Stan, you're our returning champion, so we'll begin with you.
Okay, I'll take the comic strip "Nancy" for a hundred.
$ 0
Stan

ARTIST: DAVID O'KEEFE
WRITER: CHARLIE RICHARDS

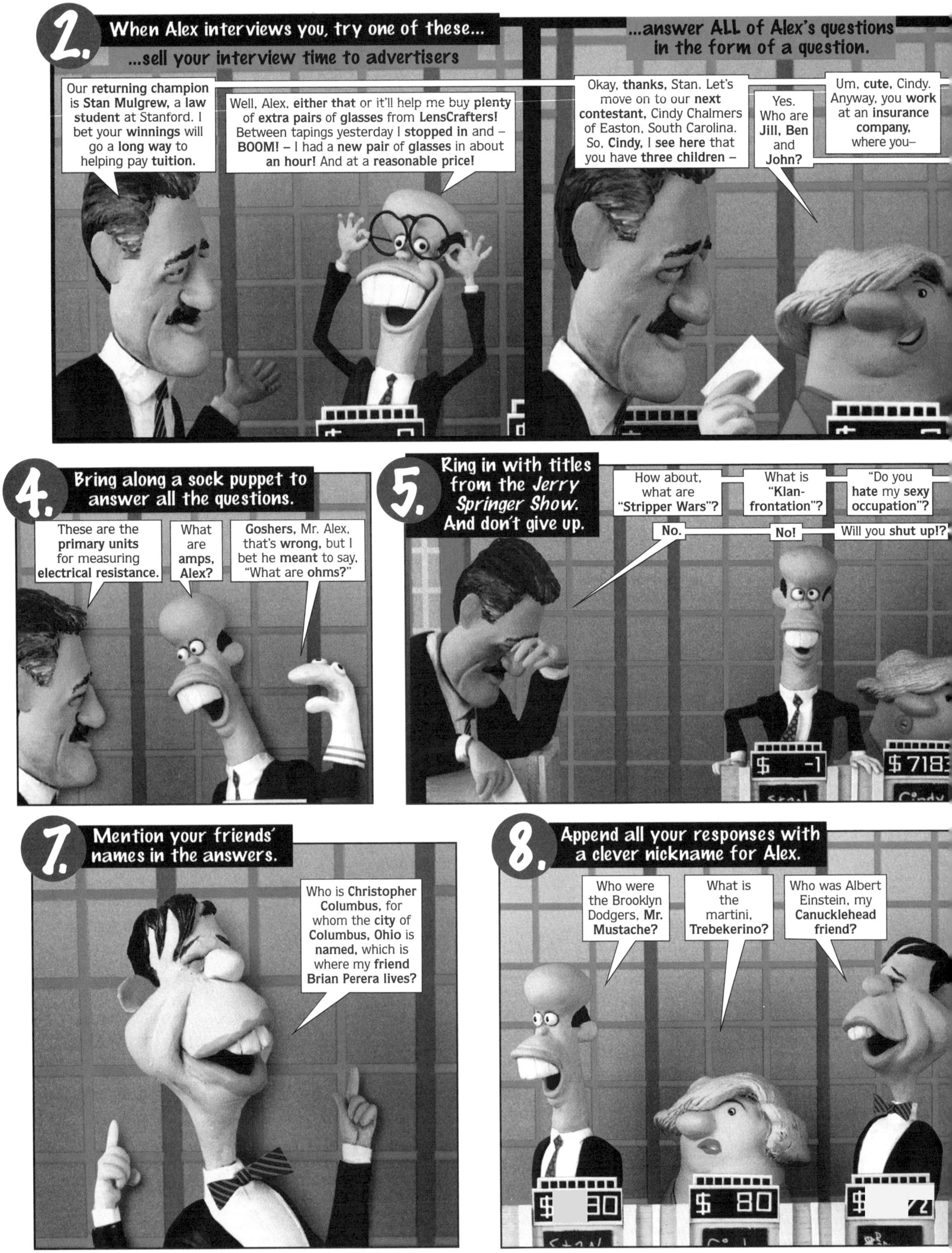

2.
When Alex interviews you, try one of these...
...sell your interview time to advertisers
Our returning champion is Stan Mulgrew, a law student at Stanford. I bet your winnings will go a long way to helping pay tuition.
Well, Alex, either that or it'll help me buy plenty of extra pairs of glasses from LensCrafters! Between tapings yesterday I stopped in and – BOOM! – I had a new pair of glasses in about an hour! And at a reasonable price!
...answer ALL of Alex's questions in the form of a question.
Okay, thanks, Stan. Let's move on to our next contestant, Cindy Chalmers of Easton, South Carolina. So, Cindy, I see here that you have three children –
Yes. Who are Jill, Ben and John?
Um, cute, Cindy. Anyway, you work at an insurance company, where you–
4.
Bring along a sock puppet to answer all the questions.
These are the primary units for measuring electrical resistance.
What are amps, Alex?
Goshers, Mr. Alex, that's wrong, but I bet he meant to say, "What are ohms?"
5.
Ring in with titles from the Jerry Springer Show. And don't give up.
How about, what are "Stripper Wars"?
No.
What is "Klan-frontation"?
No!
"Do you hate my sexy occupation"?
Will you shut up!?
$ -1
$ 718
7.
Mention your friends' names in the answers.
Who is Christopher Columbus, for whom the city of Columbus, Ohio is named, which is where my friend Brian Perera lives?
8.
Append all your responses with a clever nickname for Alex.
Who were the Brooklyn Dodgers, Mr. Mustache?
What is the martini, Trebekerino?
Who was Albert Einstein, my Canucklehead friend?
$ 80

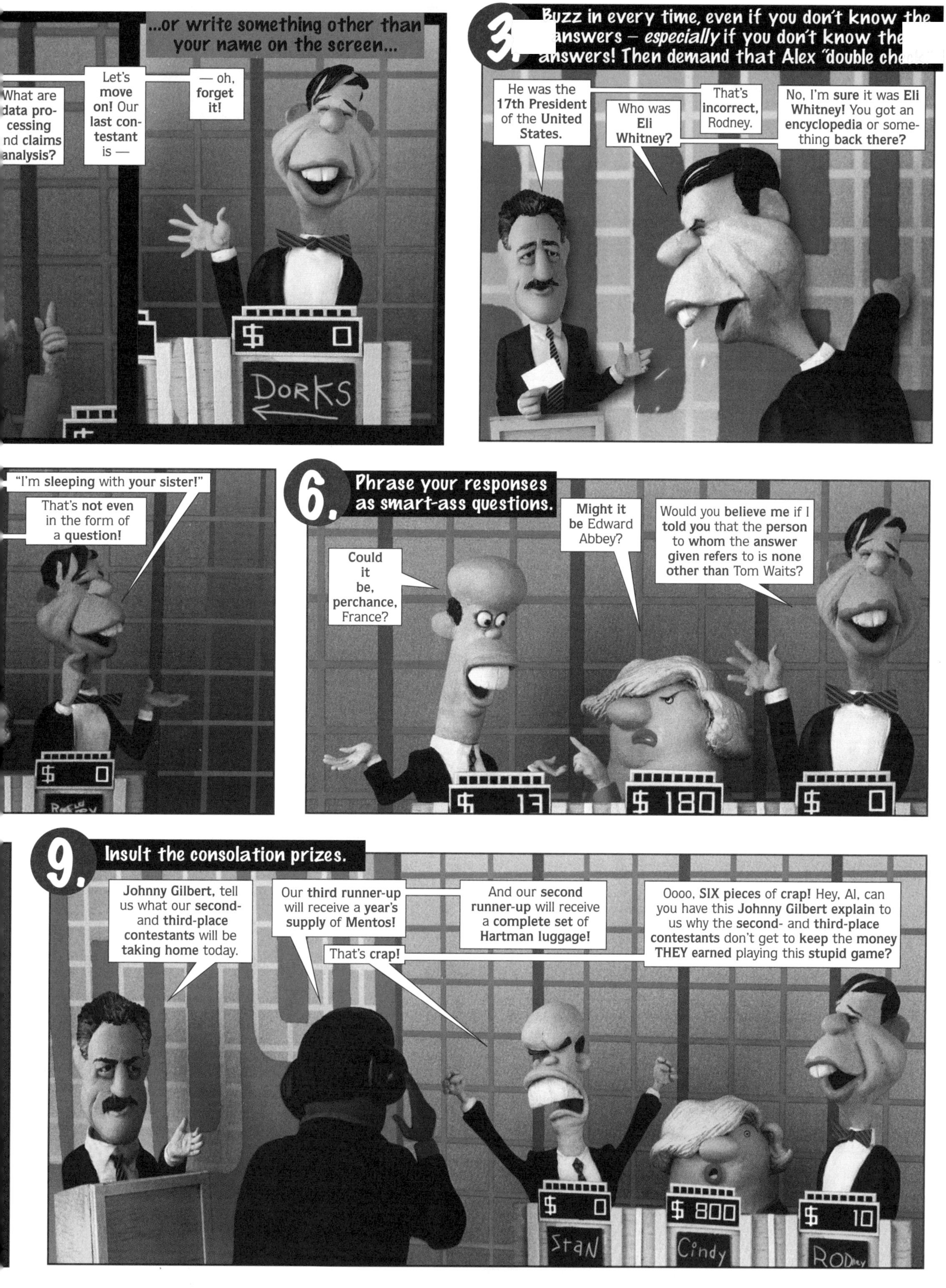

...or write something other than your name on the screen...
What are data processing and claims analysis?
Let's move on! Our last contestant is —
— oh, forget it!
$ 0
DORKS
3. Buzz in every time, even if you don't know the answers – *especially* if you don't know the answers! Then demand that Alex "double ch
He was the 17th President of the United States.
That's incorrect, Rodney.
Who was Eli Whitney?
No, I'm sure it was Eli Whitney! You got an encyclopedia or something back there?
"I'm sleeping with your sister!"
That's not even in the form of a question!
$ 0
6. Phrase your responses as smart-ass questions.
Could it be, perchance, France?
Might it be Edward Abbey?
Would you believe me if I told you that the person to whom the answer given refers to is none other than Tom Waits?
$ 13
$ 180
$ 0
9. Insult the consolation prizes.
Johnny Gilbert, tell us what our second- and third-place contestants will be taking home today.
Our third runner-up will receive a year's supply of Mentos!
And our second runner-up will receive a complete set of Hartman luggage!
That's crap!
Oooo, SIX pieces of crap! Hey, Al, can you have this Johnny Gilbert explain to us why the second- and third-place contestants don't get to keep the money THEY earned playing this stupid game?
$ 0
$ 800
$ 10
Stan
Cindy
RODney

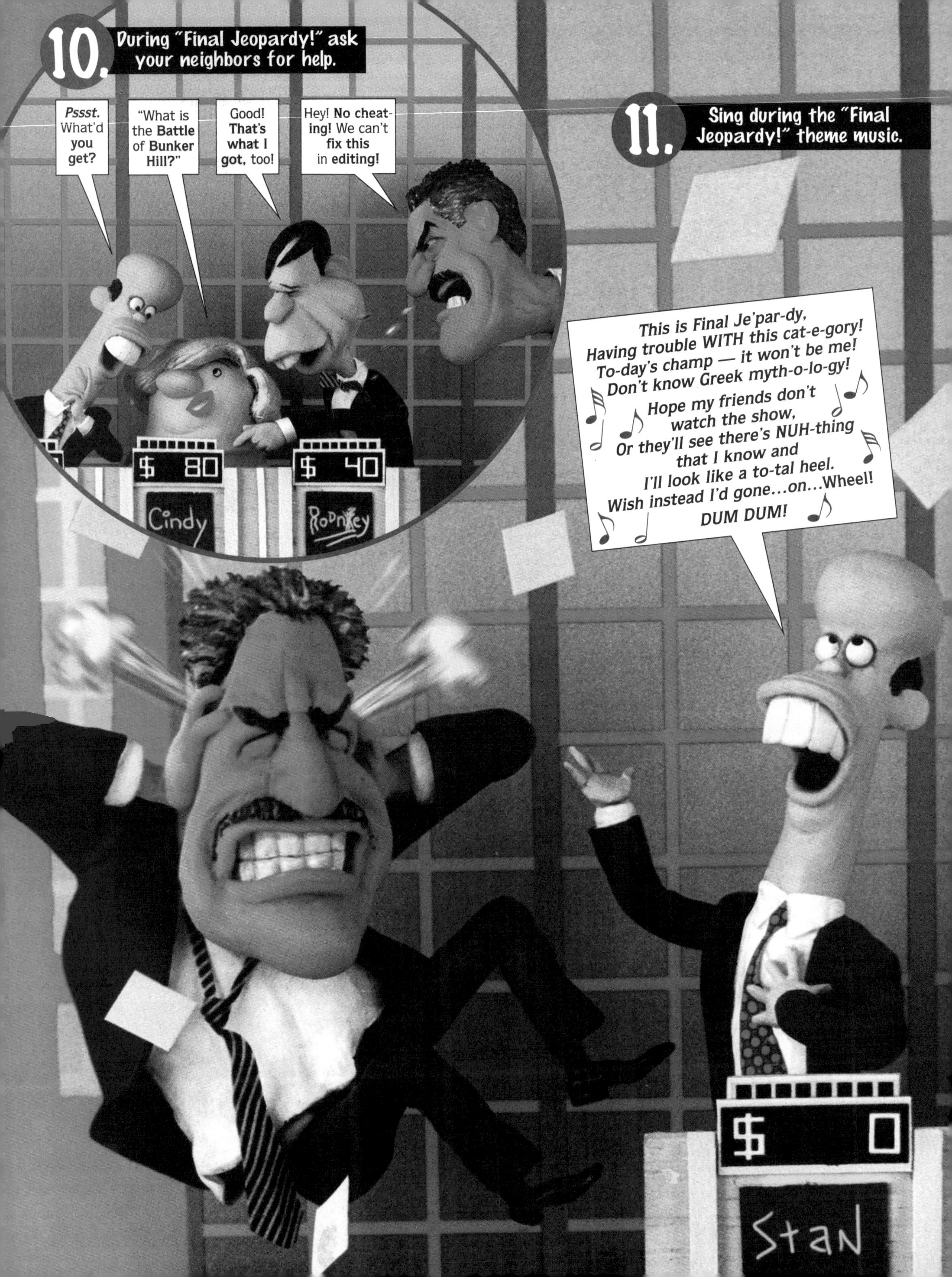

10. During "Final Jeopardy!" ask your neighbors for help.
Pssst. What'd you get?
"What is the Battle of Bunker Hill?"
Good! That's what I got, too!
Hey! No cheating! We can't fix this in editing!
$ 80
Cindy
$ 40
Rodney
11. Sing during the "Final Jeopardy!" theme music.
This is Final Je'par-dy, Having trouble WITH this cat-e-gory! To-day's champ — it won't be me! Don't know Greek myth-o-lo-gy! Hope my friends don't watch the show, Or they'll see there's NUH-thing that I know and I'll look like a to-tal heel. Wish instead I'd gone...on...Wheel! DUM DUM!
$ 0
Stan

FLOP, FLOP, QUIZ, QUIZ DEPT.

One way filthy rich TV game show producers become even more filthy rich is by spinning their shows off into home-version board games. We think this is outrageous! WE want to be the ones who get filthy rich! So we're offering our new version of a popular game show spinoff. Here's

MAD'S HOME VERSION OF JEOPARDY!

WRITER: J. PRETE

TELEVISION	POTPOURRI	THE MOVIES	CURRENT EVENTS	FOREIGN PHRASES	MUSIC
100 TV'S "ODD COUPLE"	100 SHE IS OFTEN REFERRED TO AS "OLD GLORY"	100 GROUP NAME FOR YOUNG H'WOOD ACTORS IN FILMS "ST. ELMO'S FIRE" & "THE BREAKFAST CLUB"	100 SCENE WHERE THE NICARAGUAN CONTRAS' MOST BITTER BATTLE TO DATE HAS BEEN FOUGHT	100 IN MEXICO: "¿OLVÍDATE DE LAS MILLAS POR GALÓN, CUANTAS PERSONAS CABEN EN EL BAÚL?"	100 OLD MCDONALD HAD ONE
200 BIG BIRD IS ONE OF THE MOST FAMOUS OF THESE	200 SCIENTISTS SAY IT ACTUALLY TAKES 23 HRS., 56 MIN. & 4.1 SEC. TO BE COMPLETED	200 HE WON BEST ACTOR IN 1985	200 IN NEW YORK CITY, (718) & (212)	200 IN ITALY: "CHI L'HA APPRESO SULLA 'STUTUA DI DAVID'?"	200 HE MADE PURPLE RAIN
300 IT FOLLOWS "THE TONIGHT SHOW" ACROSS MOST OF THE U.S.	300 IT BEGAN "LONG AGO, IN A GALAXY FAR, FAR AWAY..."	300 THE FULL NAMES OF THE THREE STOOGES	300 FOR MANY AMERICANS, HE AND NANCY ARE THE PERFECT COUPLE	300 IN AUSTRIA: "NA GAUT—SO HABN WIR AN NAZI ALS BUNDESPRÄSIDENT GWÄHLT—DER MANN BRAUCHTE EBEN AN POSTEN!"	300 SCIENTISTS SAY IT CONTAINS EVERY COLOR IN THE SPECTRUM
400 THEY BECAME FAMOUS AS "TWO WILD & CRAZY GUYS"	400 ACCORDING TO THE OLD ADAGE, THIS "KEEPS THE DOCTOR AWAY"	400 MOVIE INDUSTRY EXPERTS SAY IT WILL PROBABLY TOP $10 IN 2 YEARS	400 THE TERM FOR AN ATTACHMENT TO A BILL GOING THROUGH CONGRESS	400 IN FRANCE: "AU CUL LES AMERLOS! DONNE AUX TERRORISTS CE QU'IL VEULT!"	400 FEMALE SINGING GROUP OF WHICH VANNA WHITE IS FORMER MEMBER
500 GERALDO RIVERA FOUND NOTHING WHEN HE OPENED THIS	500 HE DEFEATED JIMMY CARTER IN 1980	500 FOR STAR TREK'S CAPTAIN KIRK, IT REPRESENTS "THE FINAL FRONTIER"	500 AS A TEAM, THE NY METS HIT 127 OF THESE IN 1986	500 IN LEBANESE: هل أنا منجره! أم أنه كان انفجار سياره آخر!	500 CHAKA KHAN AND WANG CHUNG, FOR EXAMPLE

(ANSWERS ON REVERSE)

MAD'S HOME VERSION OF JEOPARDY! ANSWERS

And remember, your answer* MUST *be in the form of a question!

TELEVISION	POTPOURRI	THE MOVIES	CURRENT EVENTS	FOREIGN PHRASES	MUSIC
100 WHO ARE DIANE SAWYER & MORLEY SAFER?	100 WHO IS JOAN COLLINS?	100 WHO ARE THE HAS-BEENS?	100 WHAT IS THE UNITED STATES SENATE FINANCE COMMITTEE ROOM?	100 WHAT IS, "FORGET ABOUT THE GAS MILEAGE, HOW MANY PEOPLE CAN FIT IN THE TRUNK?"	100 WHAT IS A GOITER?
200 WHAT ARE JOAN RIVERS LOOKALIKES?	200 WHAT IS THE SUPER BOWL'S PRE-GAME & WRAP-UP SHOW?	200 WHO IS KLAUS VON BULOW?	200 WHAT IS THE NO. OF FELONS ARRESTED EVERY HOUR, & THE NO. OF THOSE WHO WILL EVER SEE THE INSIDE OF A JAIL?	200 WHAT IS, "WHO HUNG THAT ON THE 'STATUE OF DAVID'?"	200 WHO IS THE CHIEF ENGINEER AT CHERNOBYL?
300 WHAT IS 10 MINUTES OF FOOLING AROUND WITH YOUR WIFE?	300 WHAT IS THE LIFE STORY OF RONALD REAGAN?	300 WHAT ARE "DAN RATHER," "PETER JENNINGS" & "TOM BROKAW"?	300 WHO IS SLUGGO?	300 WHAT IS, "OK, SO WE ELECTED A NAZI PRESIDENT OF OUR COUNTRY. THE MAN NEEDED A JOB!"	300 WHAT IS CYNDI LAUPER'S HAIR?
400 WHO ARE OLIVER NORTH & JOHN POINDEXTER?	400 WHAT IS NO MEDICAL INSURANCE COVERAGE?	400 WHAT IS THE PRICE OF A MEDIUM-SIZE POPCORN, NO BUTTER?	400 WHAT IS A BRIBE?	400 WHAT IS, "SCREW THE AMERICANS! GIVE THE TERRORISTS WHATEVER THEY WANT!"	400 WHO ARE THE POINTER SISTERS?
500 WHAT IS HIS FAN MAIL FILE?	500 WHO IS JIMMY CARTER?	500 WHAT IS LT. UHURA'S BEDROOM?	500 WHAT ARE OPPOSING PLAYERS, ABUSIVE FANS AND OFF-DUTY HOUSTON POLICEMEN?	500 WHAT IS, "AM I CRAZY, OR WAS THAT ANOTHER CAR BOMB?"	500 WHAT ARE TWO SOUNDS MADE BY OPRAH WINFREY WHEN PUTTING ON HER PANTYHOSE?

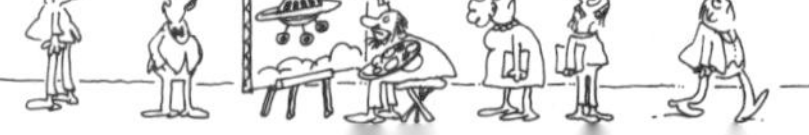

What's the world's most-watched TV show? *Roseanne*? *Seinfeld*? *Studs*? Guess again! It's not as subtle as *Studs*! It's a syndicated show about LA lifeguards that has 140 million viewers worldwide! Why are people fascinated with this show? We'll give you a hint! They're not tuning in to see schools of flounder! They're watching it because it's...

BABEWATCH

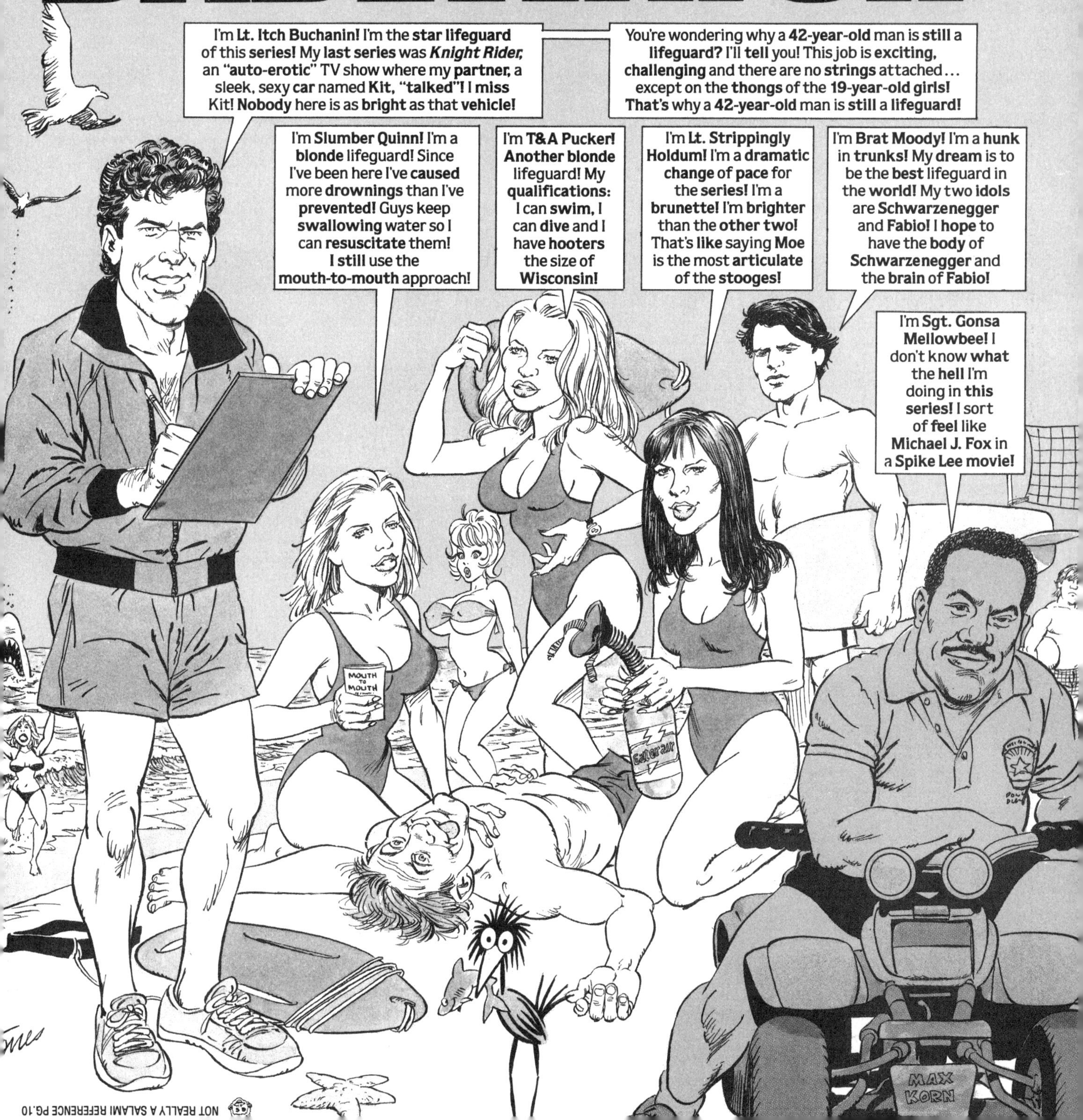
I'm Lt. Itch Buchanin! I'm the star lifeguard of this series! My last series was *Knight Rider*, an "auto-erotic" TV show where my partner, a sleek, sexy car named Kit, "talked"! I miss Kit! Nobody here is as bright as that vehicle!
You're wondering why a 42-year-old man is still a lifeguard? I'll tell you! This job is exciting, challenging and there are no strings attached... except on the thongs of the 19-year-old girls! That's why a 42-year-old man is still a lifeguard!
I'm Slumber Quinn! I'm a blonde lifeguard! Since I've been here I've caused more drownings than I've prevented! Guys keep swallowing water so I can resuscitate them! I still use the mouth-to-mouth approach!
I'm T&A Pucker! Another blonde lifeguard! My qualifications: I can swim, I can dive and I have hooters the size of Wisconsin!
I'm Lt. Strippingly Holdum! I'm a dramatic change of pace for the series! I'm a brunette! I'm brighter than the other two! That's like saying Moe is the most articulate of the stooges!
I'm Brat Moody! I'm a hunk in trunks! My dream is to be the best lifeguard in the world! My two idols are Schwarzenegger and Fabio! I hope to have the body of Schwarzenegger and the brain of Fabio!
I'm Sgt. Gonsa Mellowbee! I don't know what the hell I'm doing in this series! I sort of feel like Michael J. Fox in a Spike Lee movie!
MOUTH TO MOUTH
Gaterair
MAX KORN
NOT REALLY A SALAMI REFERENCE PG.10

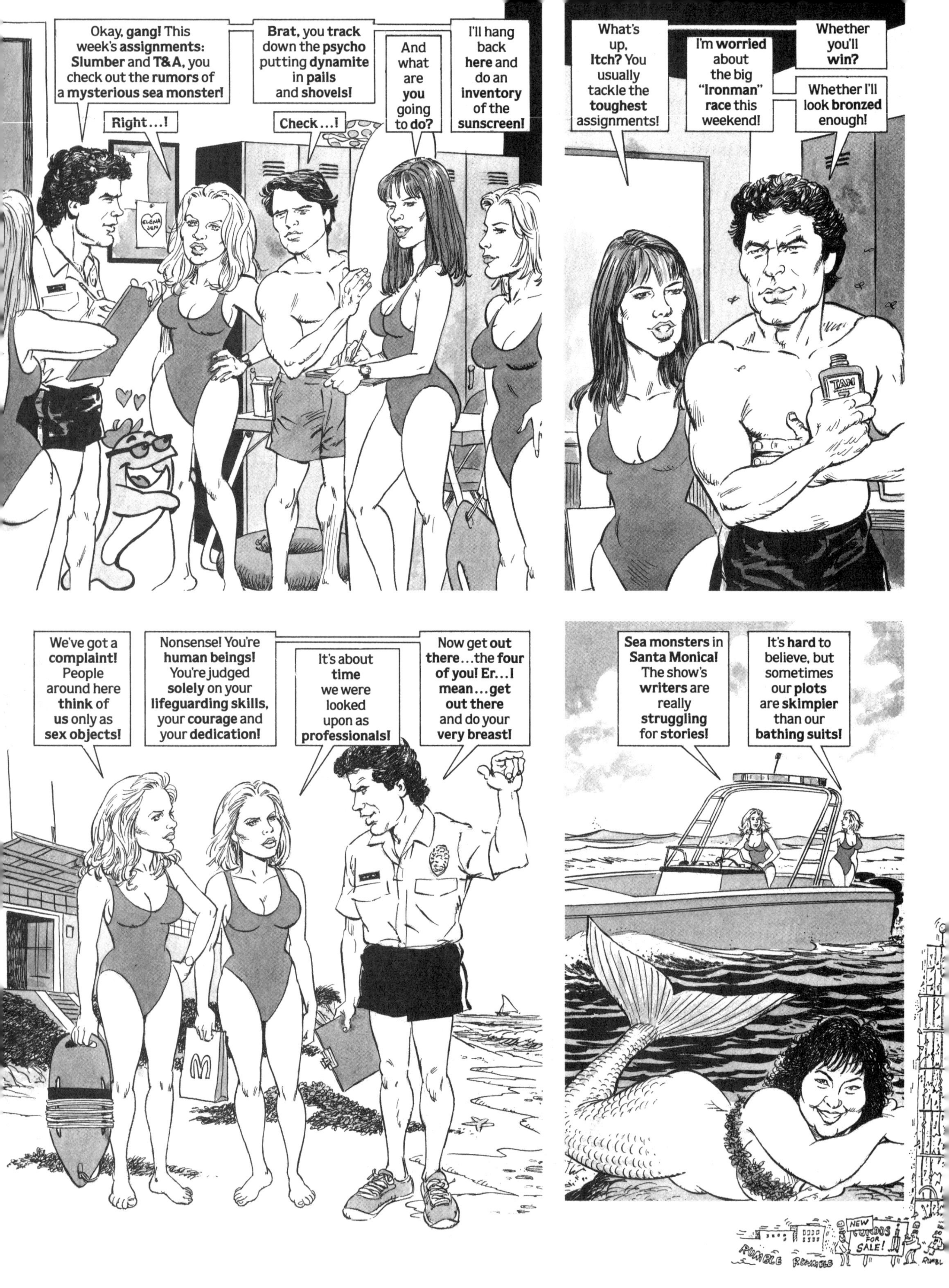

Okay, gang! This week's assignments: Slumber and T&A, you check out the rumors of a mysterious sea monster!
Right...!
Brat, you track down the psycho putting dynamite in pails and shovels!
Check...!
And what are you going to do?
I'll hang back here and do an inventory of the sunscreen!
ELENA JEN
What's up, Itch? You usually tackle the toughest assignments!
I'm worried about the big "Ironman" race this weekend!
Whether you'll win?
Whether I'll look bronzed enough!
TAN
We've got a complaint! People around here think of us only as sex objects!
Nonsense! You're human beings! You're judged solely on your lifeguarding skills, your courage and your dedication!
It's about time we were looked upon as professionals!
Now get out there...the four of you! Er...I mean...get out there and do your very breast!
Sea monsters in Santa Monica! The show's writers are really struggling for stories!
It's hard to believe, but sometimes our plots are skimpier than our bathing suits!
NEW CONDOS FOR SALE!
RUMBLE
RUMBLE
RUMBL

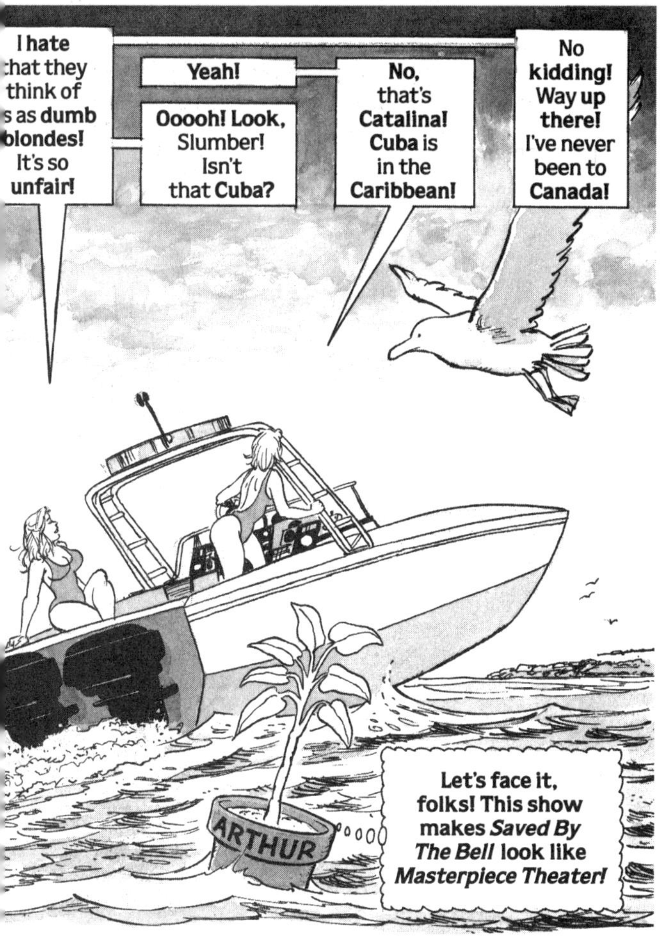
I hate
:hat they
think of
s as dumb
blondes!
It's so
unfair!
Yeah!
Ooooh! Look, Slumber! Isn't that Cuba?
No, that's Catalina! Cuba is in the Caribbean!
No kidding! Way up there! I've never been to Canada!
Let's face it, folks! This show makes *Saved By The Bell* look like *Masterpiece Theater!*
ARTHUR

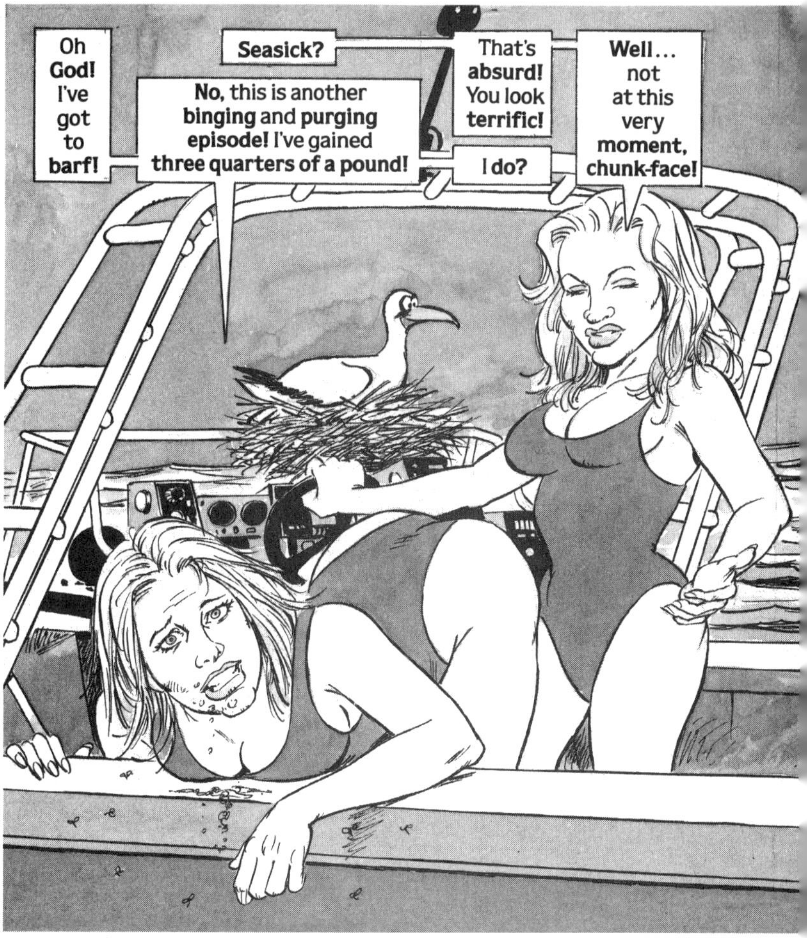
Oh God! I've got to barf!
Seasick?
No, this is another binging and purging episode! I've gained three quarters of a pound!
That's absurd! You look terrific!
I do?
Well... not at this very moment, chunk-face!

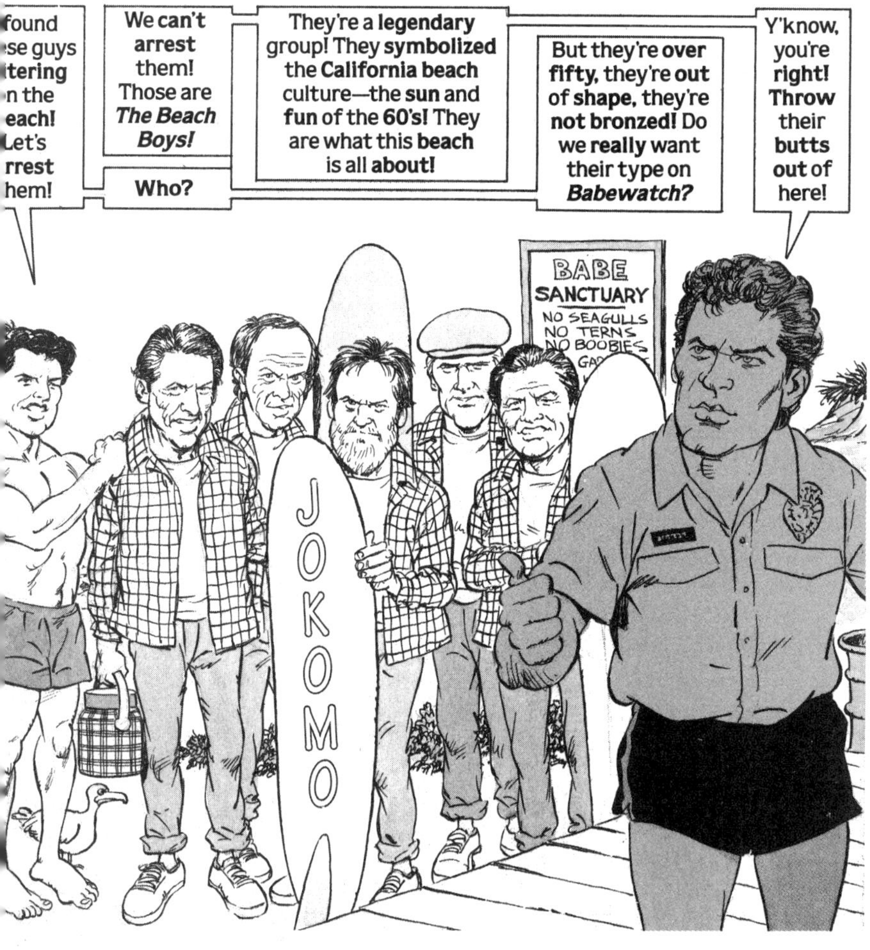
found
se guys
tering
n the
each!
et's
rrest
hem!
We can't arrest them! Those are *The Beach Boys!*
Who?
They're a legendary group! They symbolized the California beach culture—the sun and fun of the 60's! They are what this beach is all about!
But they're over fifty, they're out of shape, they're not bronzed! Do we really want their type on *Babewatch?*
Y'know, you're right! Throw their butts out of here!
BABE SANCTUARY
NO SEAGULLS
NO TERNS
NO BOOBIES
JOKOMO

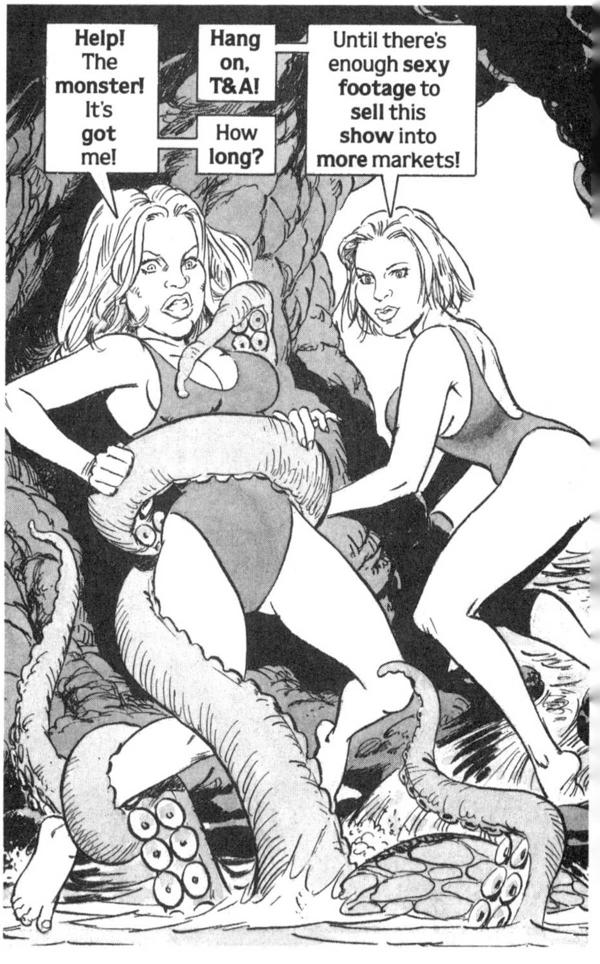
Help! The monster! It's got me!
Hang on, T&A!
How long?
Until there's enough sexy footage to sell this show into more markets!

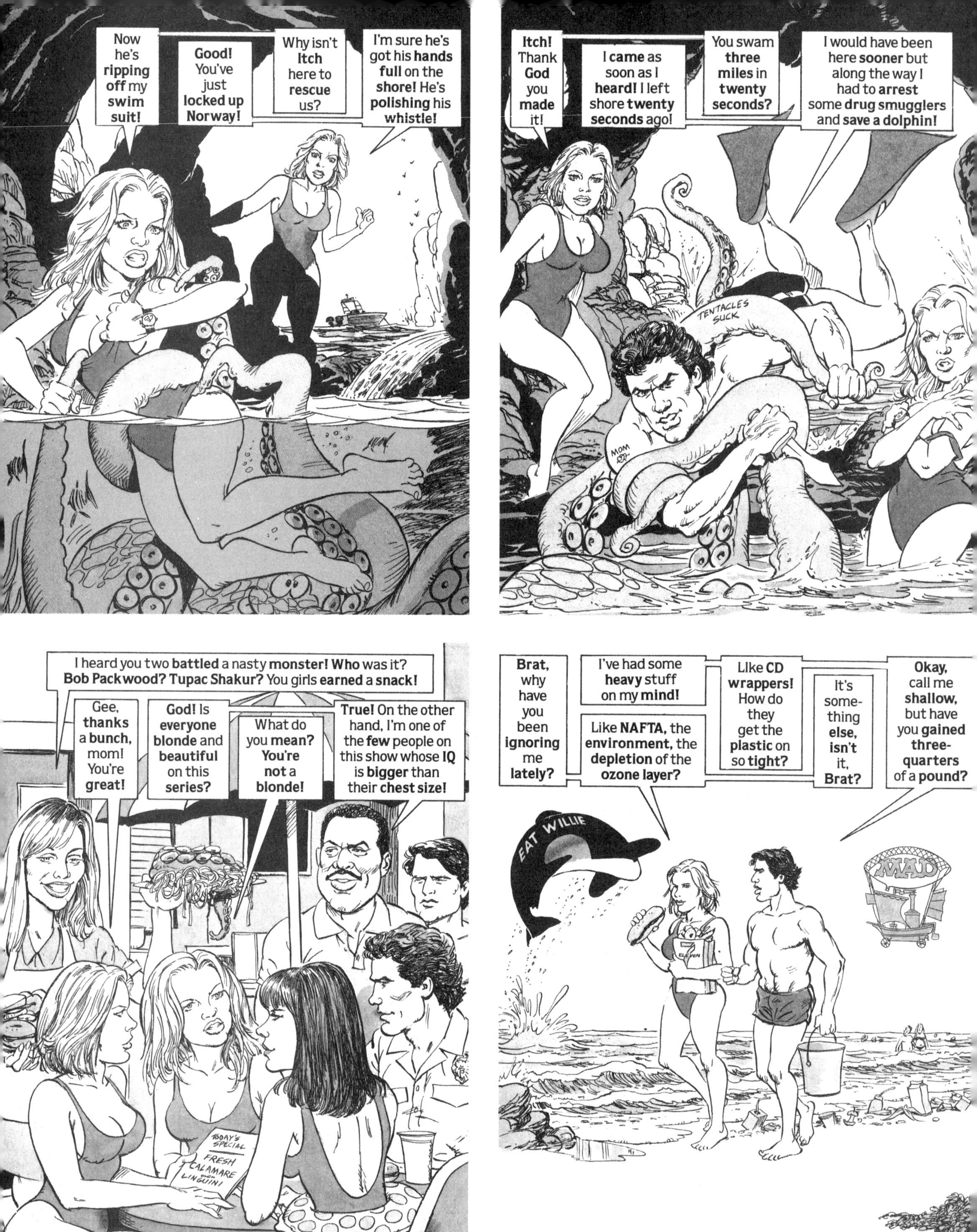
Now he's ripping off my swim suit!
Good! You've just locked up Norway!
Why isn't Itch here to rescue us?
I'm sure he's got his hands full on the shore! He's polishing his whistle!
Itch! Thank God you made it!
I came as soon as I heard! I left shore twenty seconds ago!
You swam three miles in twenty seconds?
I would have been here sooner but along the way I had to arrest some drug smugglers and save a dolphin!
TENTACLES SUCK
MOM
I heard you two battled a nasty monster! Who was it? Bob Packwood? Tupac Shakur? You girls earned a snack!
Gee, thanks a bunch, mom! You're great!
God! Is everyone blonde and beautiful on this series?
What do you mean? You're not a blonde!
True! On the other hand, I'm one of the few people on this show whose IQ is bigger than their chest size!
TODAY'S SPECIAL
FRESH CALAMARE
LINGUINI
Brat, why have you been ignoring me lately?
I've had some heavy stuff on my mind!
Like NAFTA, the environment, the depletion of the ozone layer?
Like CD wrappers! How do they get the plastic on so tight?
It's something else, isn't it, Brat?
Okay, call me shallow, but have you gained three-quarters of a pound?
EAT WILLIE
MAD

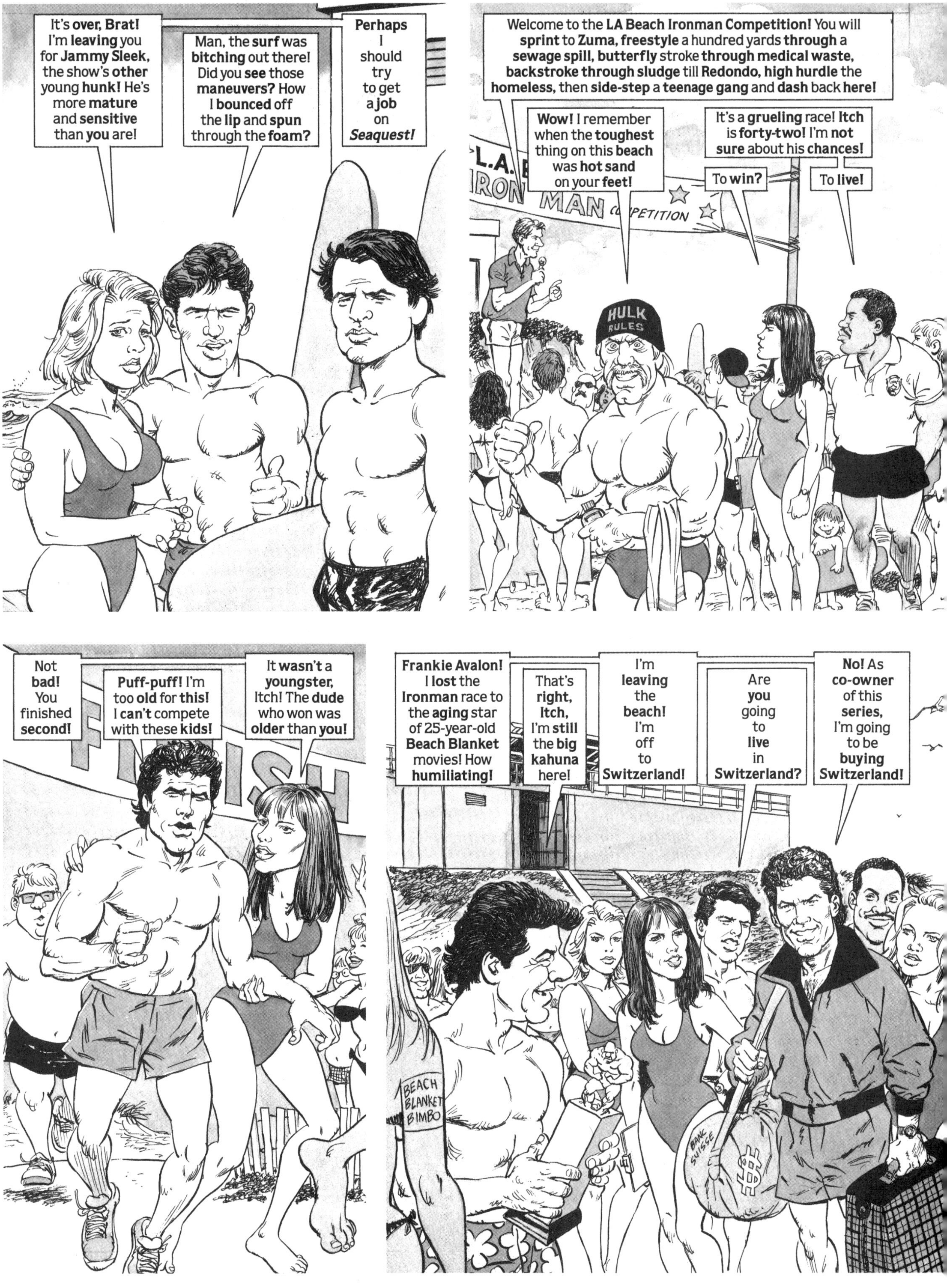
It's over, Brat! I'm leaving you for Jammy Sleek, the show's other young hunk! He's more mature and sensitive than you are!
Man, the surf was bitching out there! Did you see those maneuvers? How I bounced off the lip and spun through the foam?
Perhaps I should try to get a job on Seaquest!
Welcome to the LA Beach Ironman Competition! You will sprint to Zuma, freestyle a hundred yards through a sewage spill, butterfly stroke through medical waste, backstroke through sludge till Redondo, high hurdle the homeless, then side-step a teenage gang and dash back here!
Wow! I remember when the toughest thing on this beach was hot sand on your feet!
It's a grueling race! Itch is forty-two! I'm not sure about his chances!
To win?
To live!
IRON MAN COMPETITION
HULK RULES
Not bad! You finished second!
Puff-puff! I'm too old for this! I can't compete with these kids!
It wasn't a youngster, Itch! The dude who won was older than you!
Frankie Avalon! I lost the Ironman race to the aging star of 25-year-old Beach Blanket movies! How humiliating!
That's right, Itch, I'm still the big kahuna here!
I'm leaving the beach! I'm off to Switzerland!
Are you going to live in Switzerland?
No! As co-owner of this series, I'm going to be buying Switzerland!
BEACH BLANKET BIMBO
BANC SUISSE

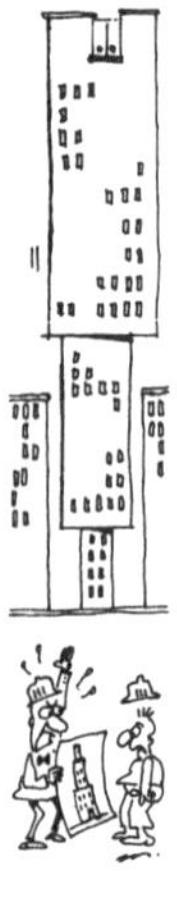

OUR FEATURES PRESENTATION DEPT.

People in the public eye are constantly concerned with their image. They hire expensiv
Beauty Consultants and Wardrobe Experts to advise them how to present themselves in th

USING THE SI
TO UPDATE STA

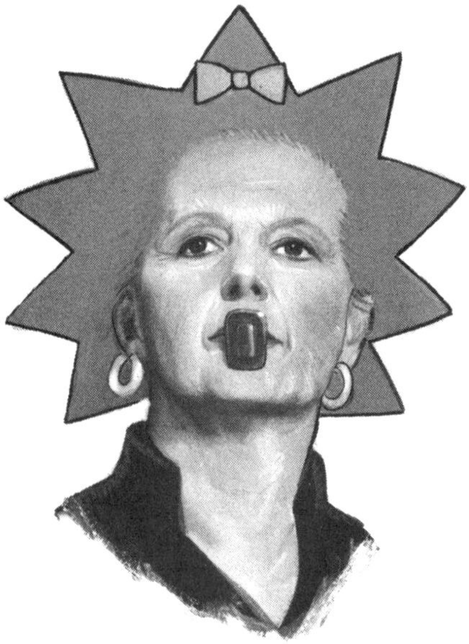

MARGARET THATCHER

Margaret—Maggie, it's a natural! The pacifier might even stop the fiesty Prime Minister from talking about new taxes that cause her fellow Britons to riot!

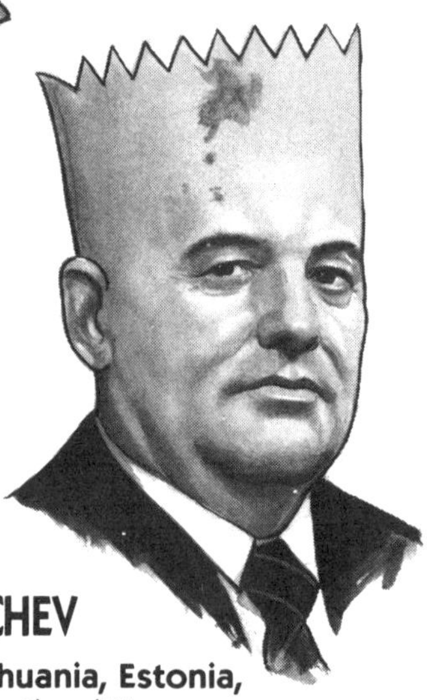

MIKHAIL GORBACHEV

Mikhail's troubles in Latvia, Lithuania, Estonia, Azerbaijan, Byelorussia or Mongolia will be over when he shows his countrymen that he's really a fun guy with his new Bart Simpson look. You'll notice it goes perfectly with his zany birthmark.

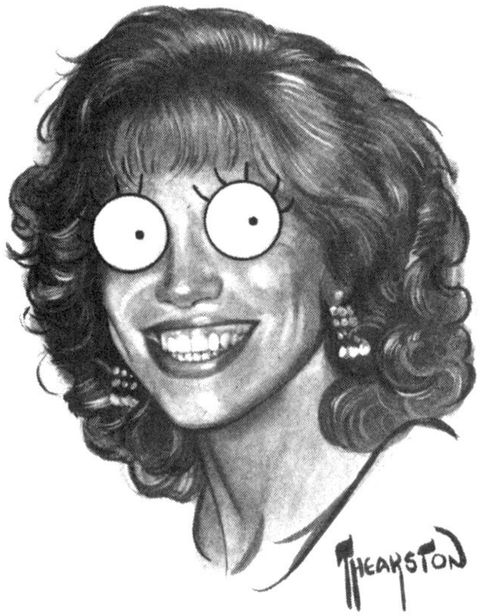
THEAKSTON

CARLY SIMON

When forty-ish Carly tries singing sexy songs, she looks like your maiden aunt gone berserk! To make her image more youthful, she can hide her crows feet by using the Simpsons eye implants!

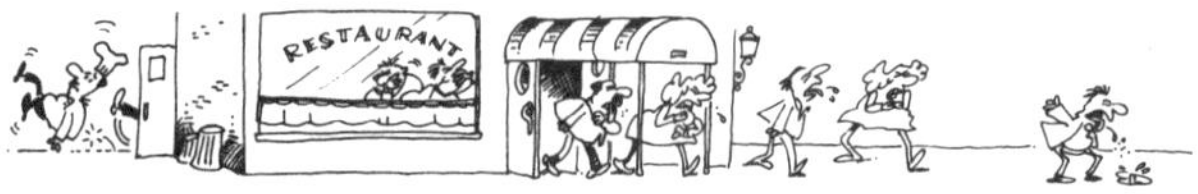
RESTAURANT

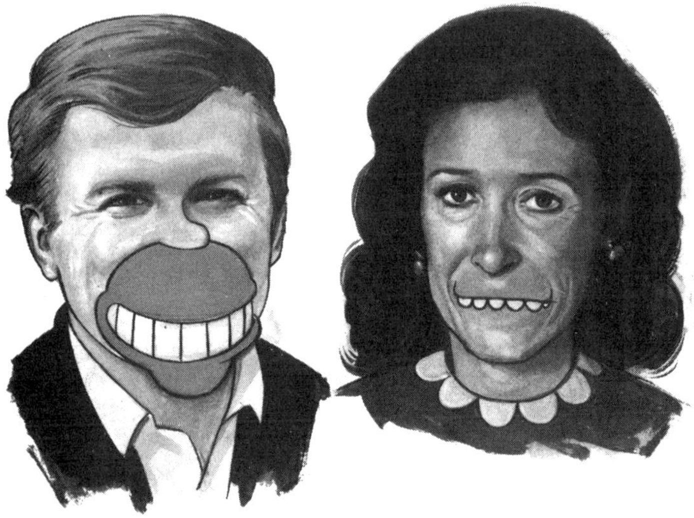

DAN & MARILYN QUAYLE

Nineteen-ninety-six isn't so far off that the Quayles shouldn't be thinking about taking over the White House. The Simpson mouth formation will give Dan and Marilyn the simple look that perfectly compliments their political philosophy.

ARTIST: GREG THEAKSTON WRITER: STAN HART

ost appealing fashion. Well, celebrities of the world unite! Stop wasting your money! AD has a plan to enhance your public image! With a little plastic surgery you can be...

PSON LOOK
E APPEARANCES

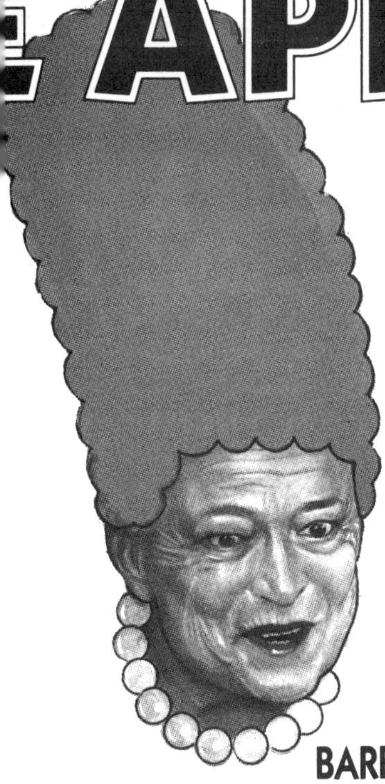

BARBARA BUSH

Vhy should the First Lady just stand in the shadow f her husband when she could upstage him as effec-ively as Nancy Reagan did Ronnie? With the Marge impson beehive, Barbara is sure to be noticed at he next State Dinner or Presidential photo-op.

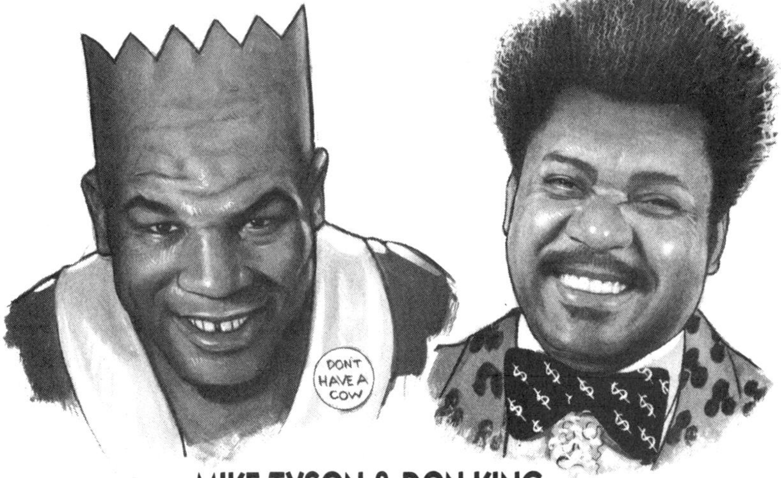
DON'T HAVE A COW

MIKE TYSON & DON KING

To make people forget his knockout loss to Buster Douglas, ex-champ Mike Tyson has to look like a winner. Promoter Don King is fine just as he is!

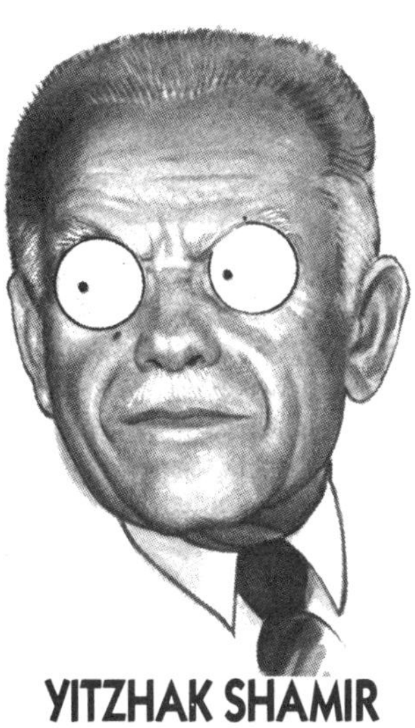

YITZHAK SHAMIR

ne Middle East can sure use a laugh for change and Israeli Prime Minister, itzhak Shamir, is just the fellow to rovide it! Even the Arabs will get a arge out of his loveable Simpson eyes!

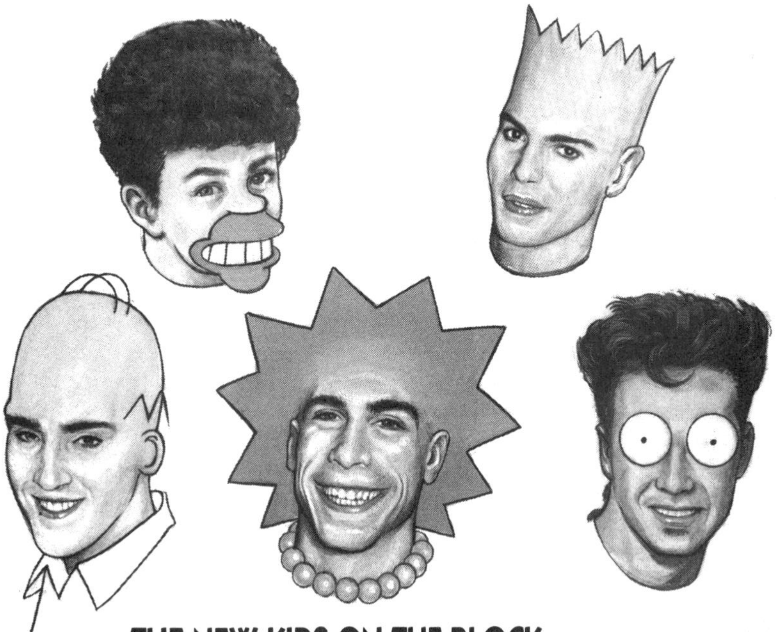

THE NEW KIDS ON THE BLOCK

Fame can be fleeting and The New Kids on the Block could get to be The Old Kids on the Block very quickly. To hold on to their already dwindling popularity, we suggest NKOTB get a complete "Simpsonization."

THE HYPE OF ABSURDITY DEPT.

IF IT WERE
ENTER
T O H

ARTIST: RICK TUL

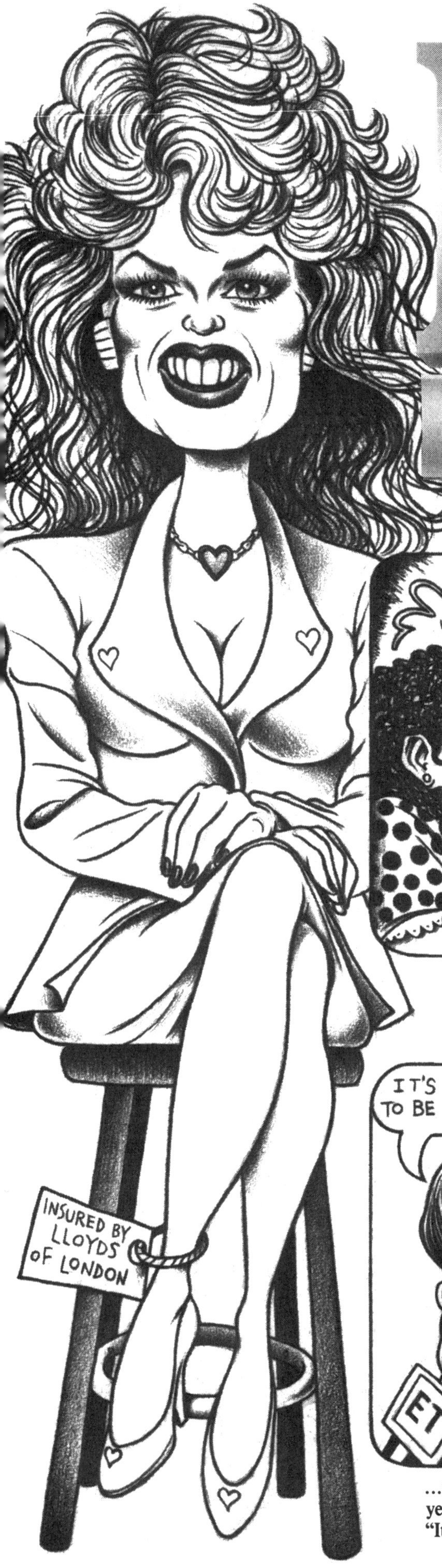

INSURED BY LLOYDS OF LONDON

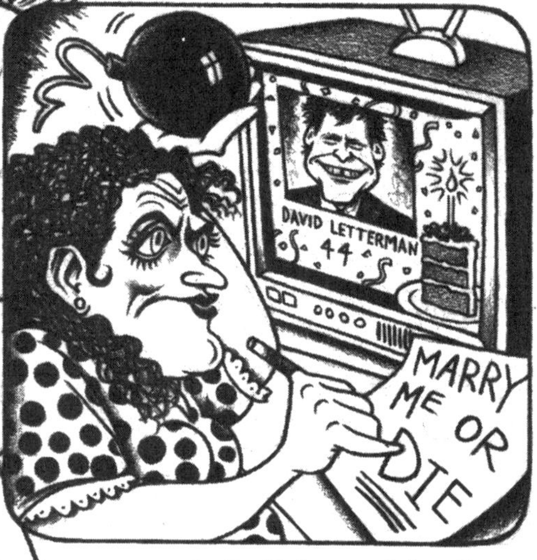

DAVID LETTERMAN 44
MARRY ME OR DIE

...psychotic "obsessed fans" wouldn't know when to send those "special" Birthday death-threats!

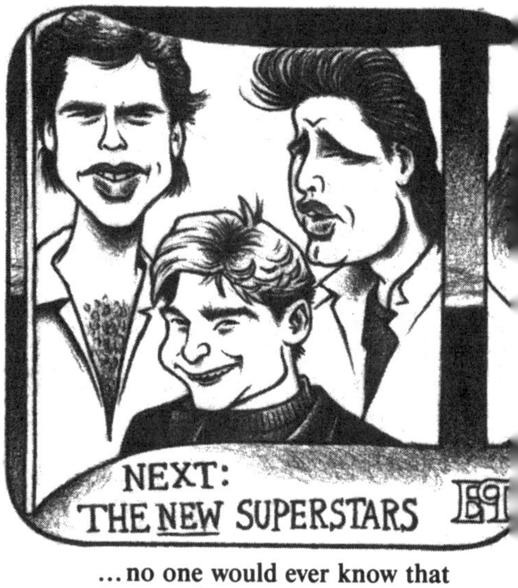

NEXT: THE NEW SUPERSTARS

...no one would ever know that Lorenzo Lamas, Corey Feldman or Peter DeLuise are "famous"!

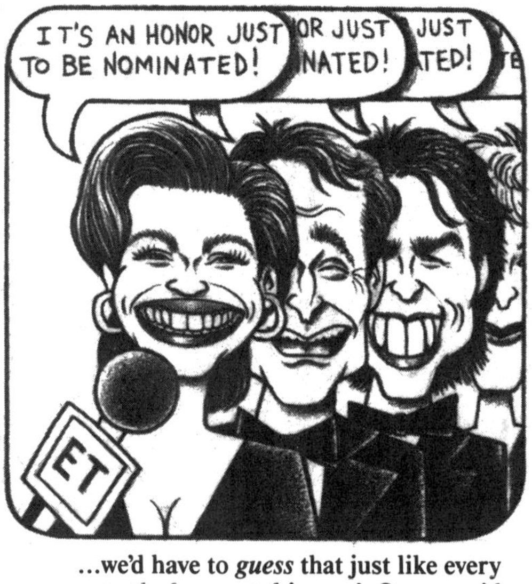

IT'S AN HONOR JUST TO BE NOMINATED!
OR JUST NATED!
JUST TED!
ET

...we'd have to *guess* that just like every year, the losers at this year's Oscars said "It was an honor just to be nominated!"

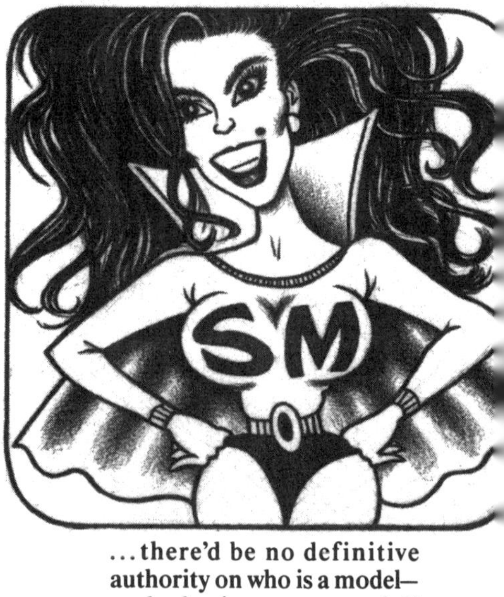

SM

...there'd be no definitive authority on who is a model—and who is a *super*model!

T FOR
NMENT
G H T

RITER: MIKE SNIDER

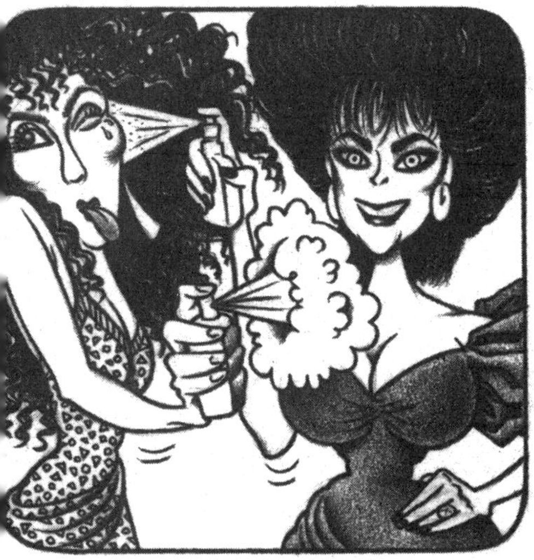

... actresses launching their own brand of perfume would have to *buy* commercial time!

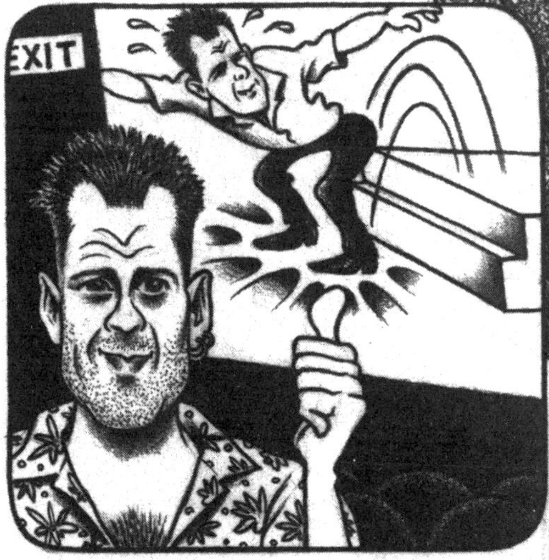
EXIT

..."macho" actors would have no place to brag about the one undangerous little stunt in a movie they did themselves!

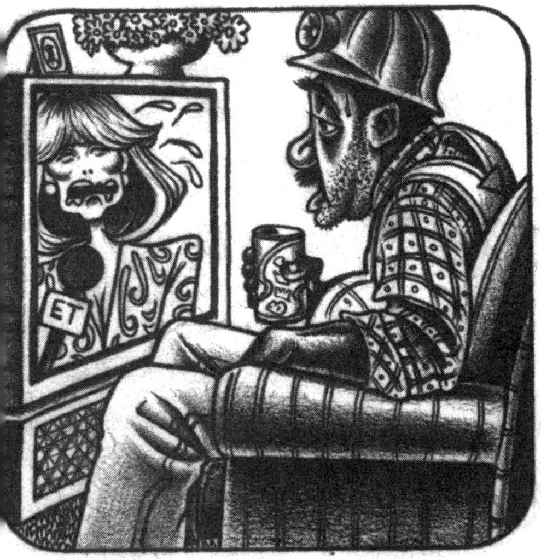
ET

... coal miners, factory workers and the like would never get to hear about what a grueling job acting is!

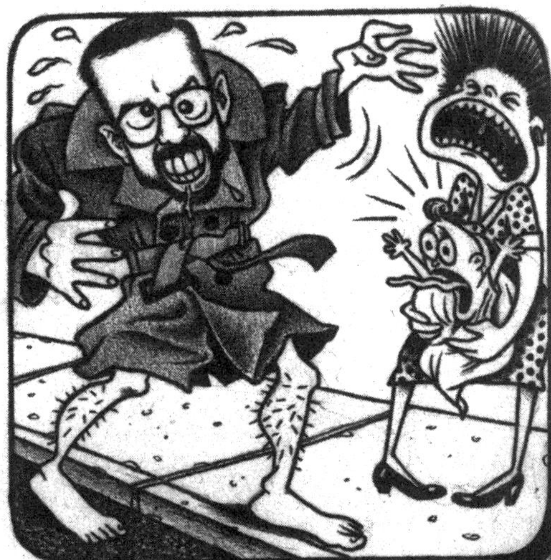

... Leonard Maltin would be roaming around free, and probably worth keeping an eye on!

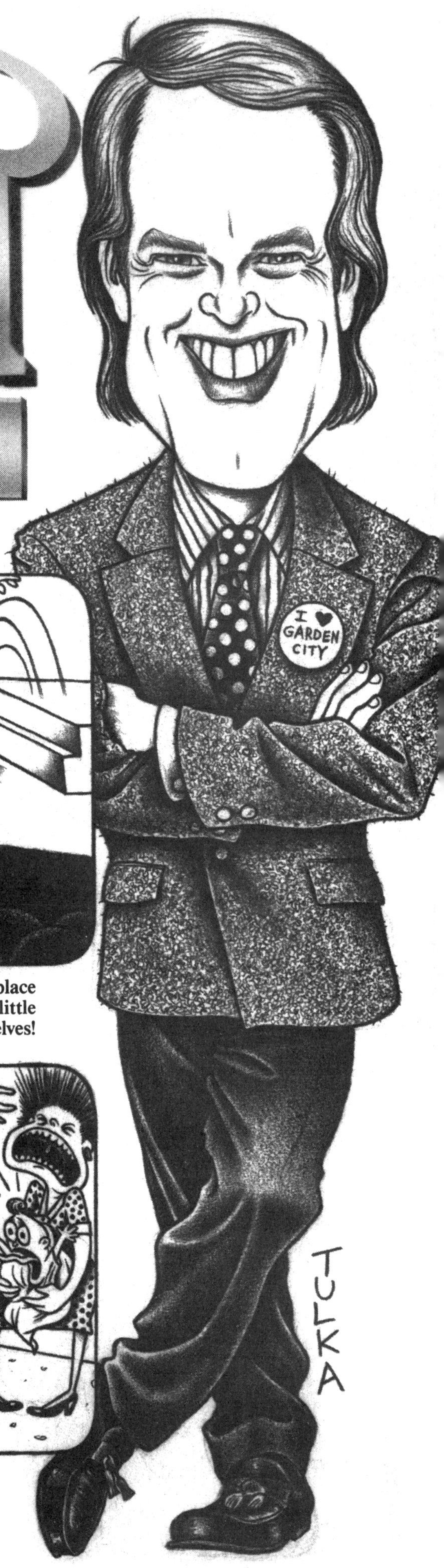
I ♥ GARDEN CITY
TULKA

YOUR GUEST IS AS GOOD AS MINE DEPT.

THE MAD GUIDE TO DOING WELL NOT DOING WELL ON TV TALK SHOWS

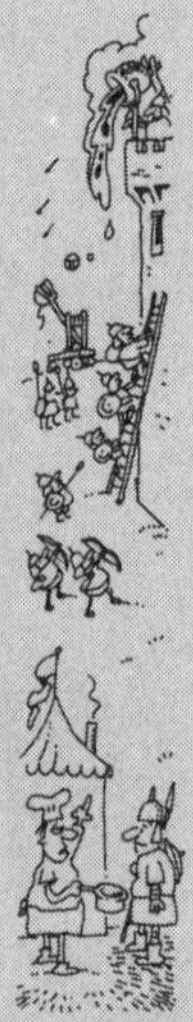

ARTIST: MORT DRUCKER WRITER: GREG ECKLER

People who dot their i's with smiley faces or hearts… **Suck!**

DAVID LETTERMAN

TO DO WELL:

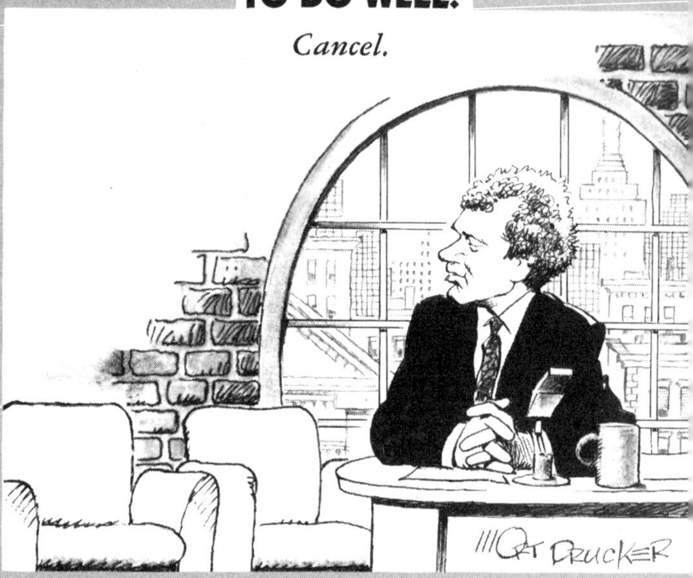

Cancel.

TO NOT DO WELL:

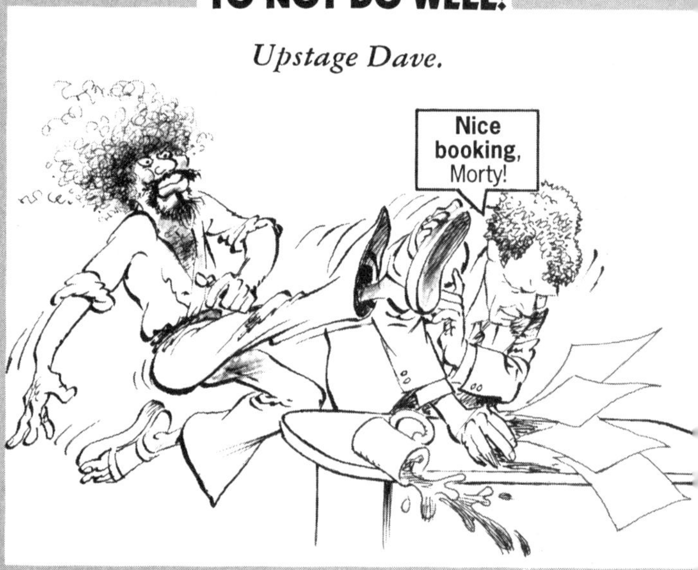
Nice booking, Morty!

Upstage Dave.

TO NOT DO WELL:

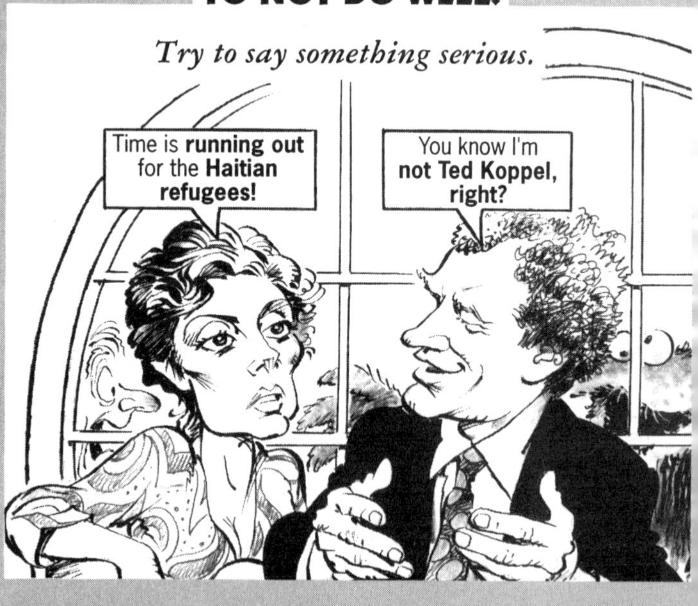
Time is **running out** for the **Haitian refugees!**
You know I'm **not Ted Koppel, right?**

Try to say something serious.

ARSENIO HALL

TO DO WELL:

Mention the basketball game you were at last week, using only the first name of the star players.

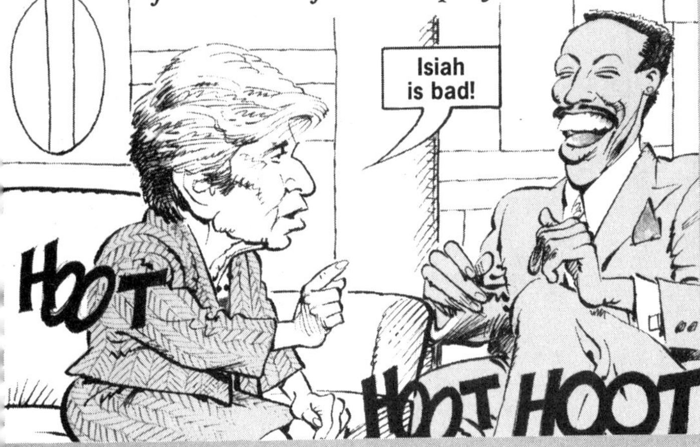

Isiah is bad!
HOOT
HOOT HOOT

TO DO WELL:

Praise the acting talent of the rapper who had a small role in your film.

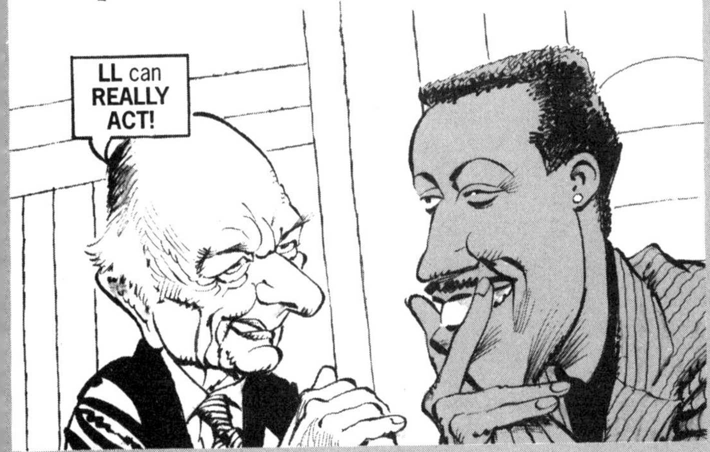

LL can REALLY ACT!

TO NOT DO WELL:

Talk at length about pro hockey.

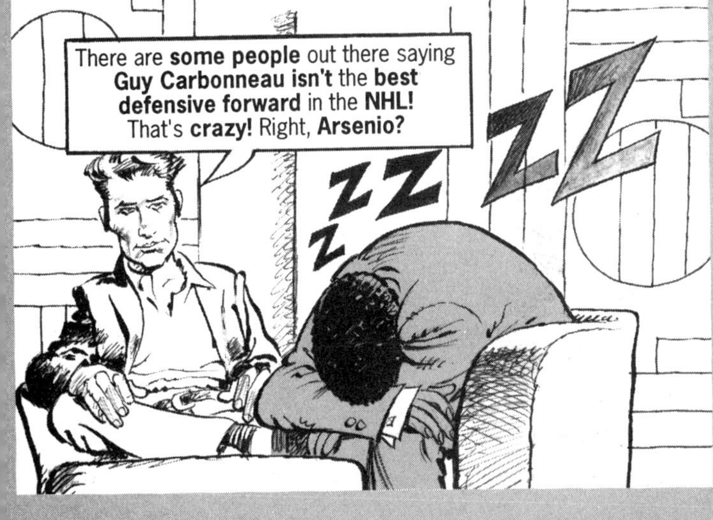

There are some people out there saying Guy Carbonneau isn't the best defensive forward in the NHL! That's crazy! Right, Arsenio?
ZZZ

JAY LENO

TO DO WELL:

Let Jay jump on your punchlines.

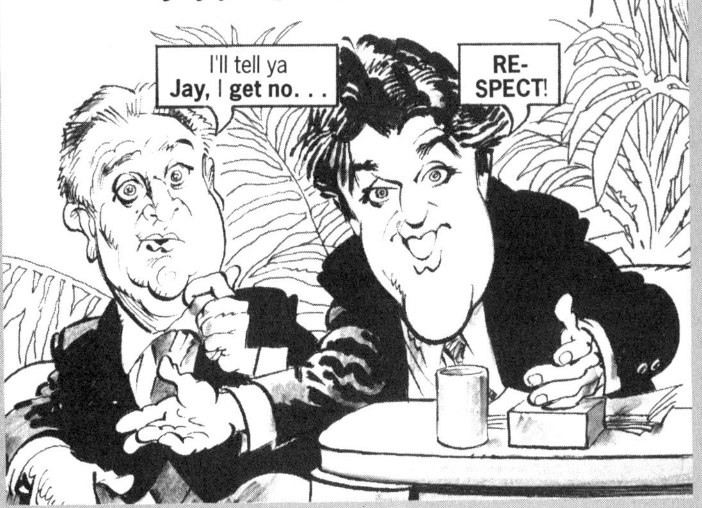

I'll tell ya Jay, I get no. . .
RE-SPECT!

TO NOT DO WELL:

Quote motorcycle accident and death statistics.

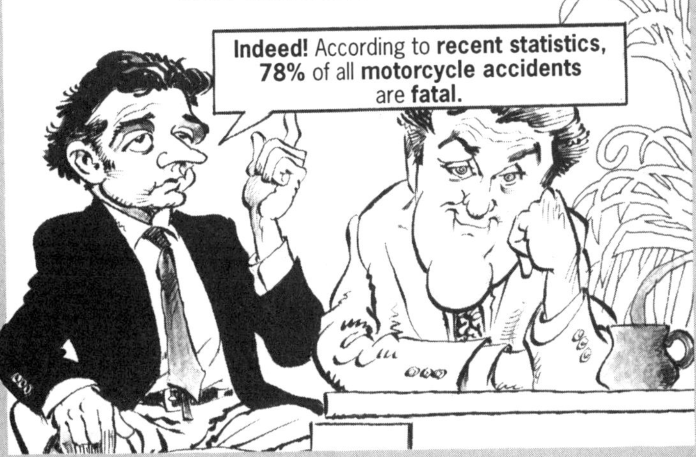

Indeed! According to recent statistics, 78% of all motorcycle accidents are fatal.

TO NOT DO WELL:

Ask inappropriate questions.

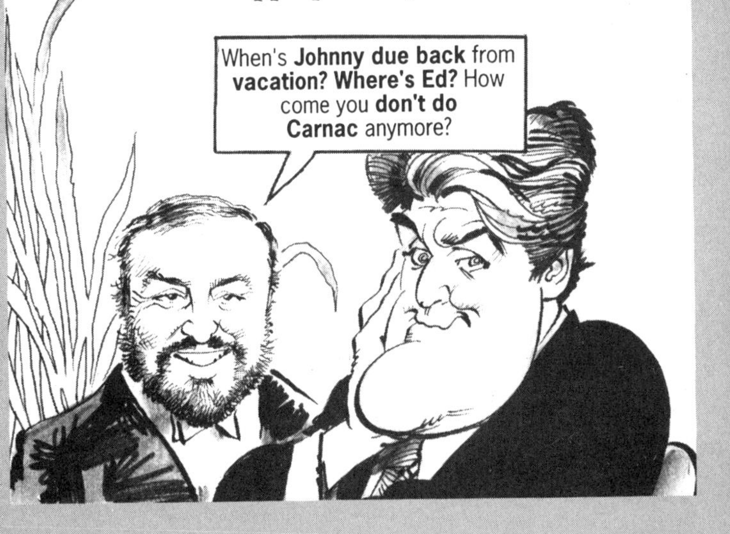

When's Johnny due back from vacation? Where's Ed? How come you don't do Carnac anymore?

OPRAH WINFREY

TO DO WELL:

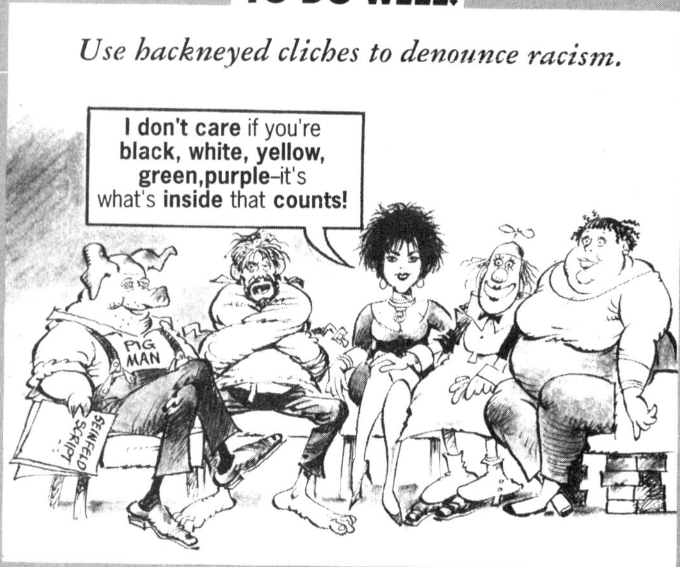
Use hackneyed cliches to denounce racism.
I don't care if you're **black, white, yellow, green,purple**–it's what's **inside** that **counts!**
PIG MAN
SEINFELD SCRIPT!

TO DO WELL:

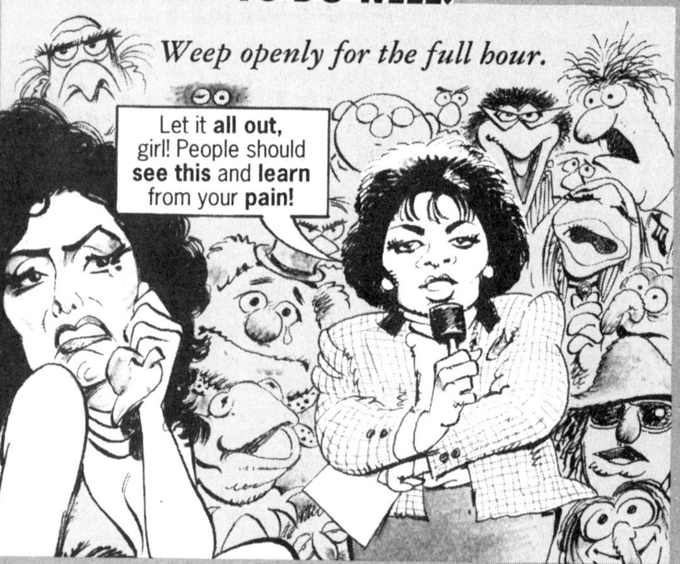
Weep openly for the full hour.
Let it **all out,** girl! People should **see this** and **learn** from your **pain!**

TO NOT DO WELL:

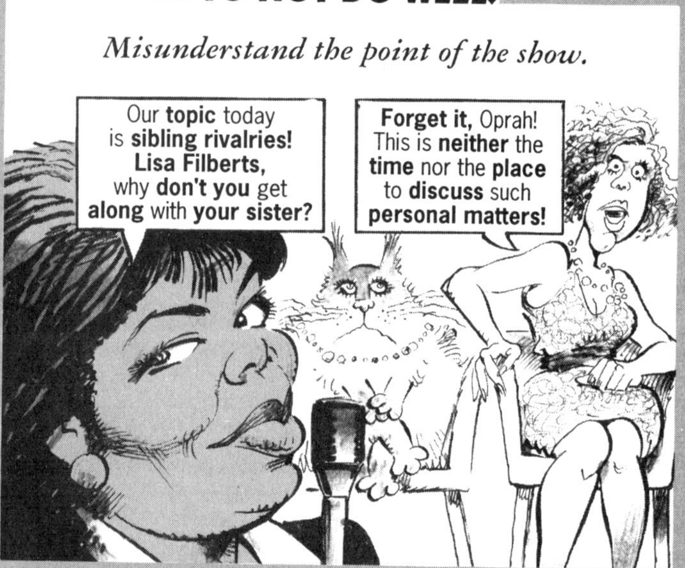
Misunderstand the point of the show.
Our **topic** today is **sibling rivalries! Lisa Filberts,** why **don't you** get **along** with **your sister?**
Forget it, Oprah! This is **neither** the **time** nor the **place** to **discuss** such **personal matters!**

PHIL DONAHUE

TO DO WELL:

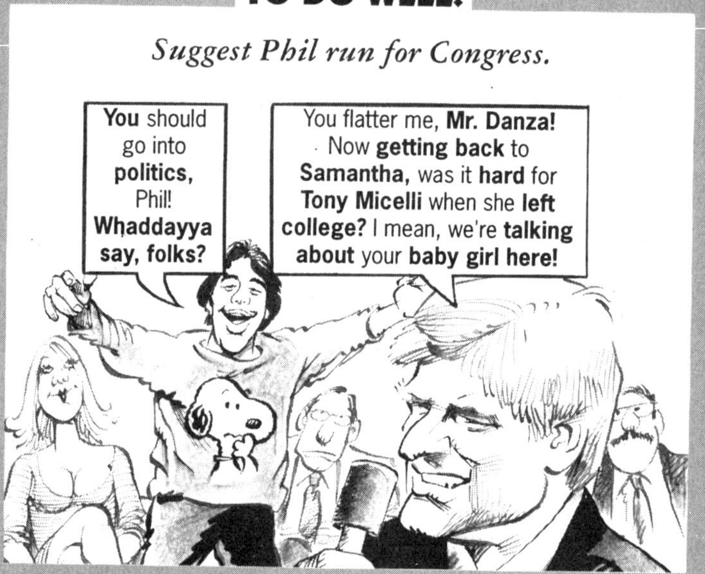
Suggest Phil run for Congress.
You should go into **politics,** Phil! **Whaddayya say, folks?**
You flatter me, **Mr. Danza!** Now **getting back** to **Samantha,** was it **hard** for **Tony Micelli** when she **left college?** I mean, we're **talking about** your **baby girl here!**

TO DO WELL:

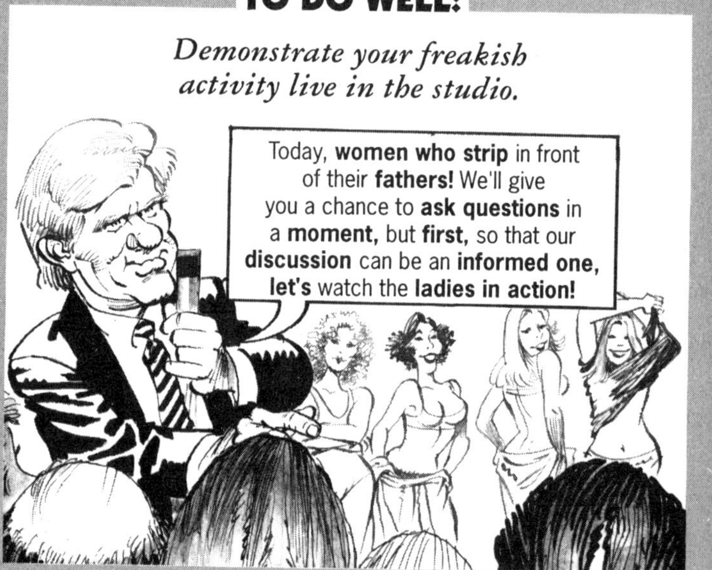
Demonstrate your freakish activity live in the studio.
Today, **women who strip** in front of their **fathers!** We'll give you a chance to **ask questions** in a **moment,** but **first,** so that our **discussion** can be an **informed one, let's** watch the **ladies in action!**

TO NOT DO WELL:

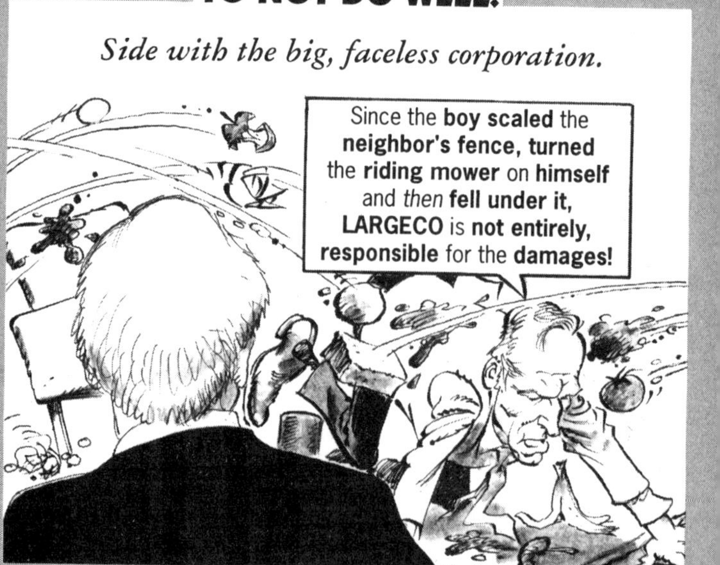
Side with the big, faceless corporation.
Since the **boy scaled** the **neighbor's fence, turned** the **riding mower on himself** and *then* **fell under it, LARGECO** is **not entirely, responsible** for the **damages!**

SHRINK RAPPED DEPT.

Remember Cheers? Remember your least favorite character? The self centered and annoyingly egotistical psychologist whose foppish character should have been killed off when Shelley Long left! But nope, despite all those beers with Norm and Cliff, he didn't DWI off the New England thruway! He's still on, in his own show no less! And the bad news is, he's even...

FLAKIER

ARTIST: PAUL COKER WRITER: DICK DEBARTOLO

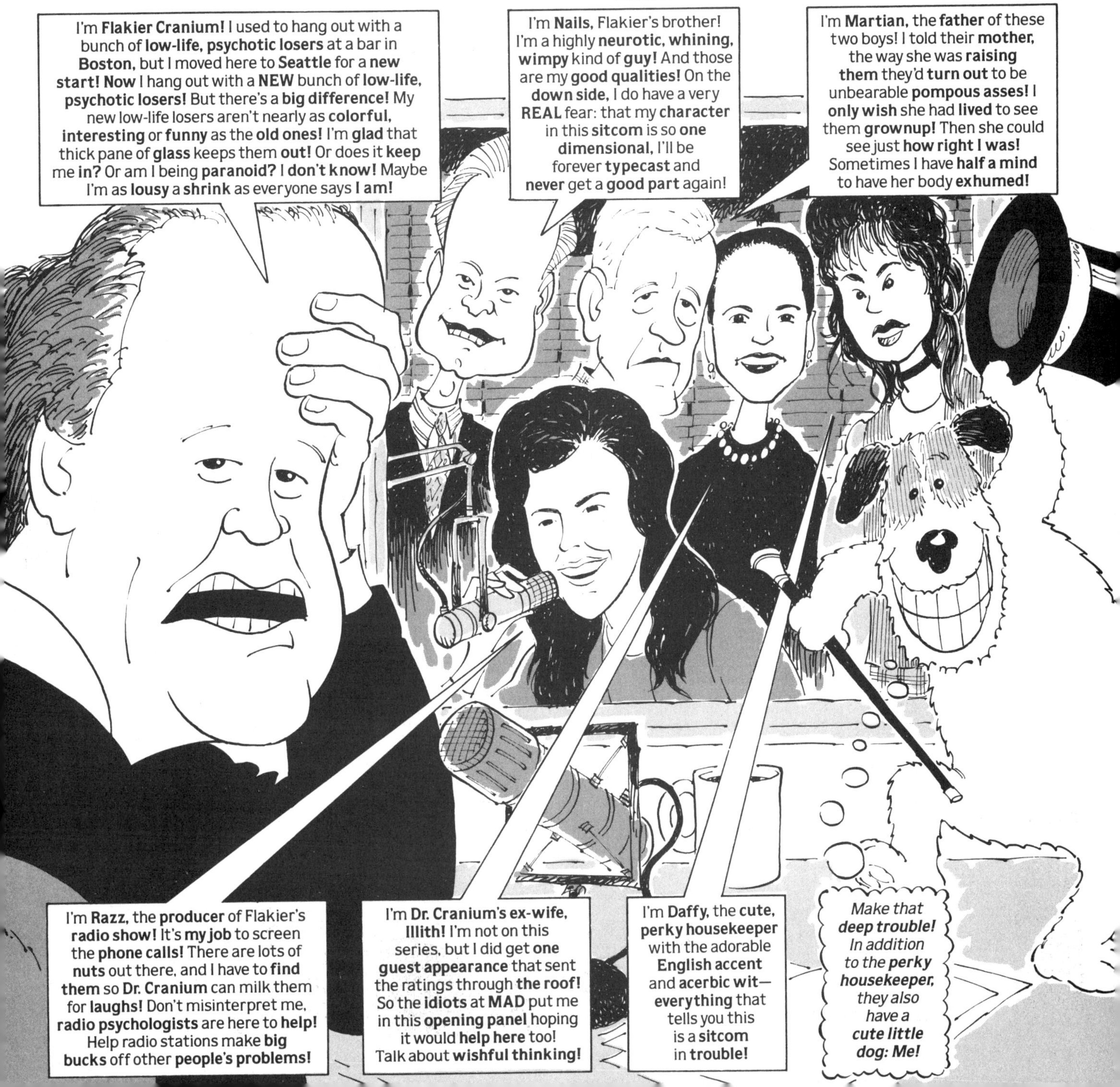
I'm **Flakier Cranium!** I used to hang out with a bunch of **low-life, psychotic losers** at a bar in **Boston,** but I moved here to **Seattle** for a **new start! Now** I hang out with a **NEW** bunch of **low-life, psychotic losers!** But there's a **big difference!** My new low-life losers aren't nearly as **colorful, interesting** or **funny** as the **old ones!** I'm **glad** that thick pane of **glass** keeps them **out!** Or does it **keep** me **in?** Or am I being **paranoid?** I **don't know!** Maybe I'm as **lousy** a **shrink** as everyone says **I am!**
I'm **Nails,** Flakier's brother! I'm a highly **neurotic, whining, wimpy** kind of **guy!** And those are my **good qualities!** On the **down side,** I do have a very **REAL** fear: that my **character** in this **sitcom** is so **one dimensional,** I'll be forever **typecast** and **never** get a **good part** again!
I'm **Martian,** the **father** of these two boys! I told their **mother,** the way she was **raising them** they'd **turn out** to be unbearable **pompous asses!** I **only wish** she had **lived** to see them **grownup!** Then she could see just **how right I was!** Sometimes I have **half a mind** to have her body **exhumed!**
I'm **Razz,** the **producer** of Flakier's **radio show!** It's **my job** to screen the **phone calls!** There are lots of **nuts** out there, and I have to **find them** so **Dr. Cranium** can milk them for **laughs!** Don't misinterpret me, **radio psychologists** are here to **help!** Help radio stations make **big bucks** off other **people's problems!**
I'm **Dr. Cranium's ex-wife, Illith!** I'm not on this series, but I did get **one guest appearance** that sent the ratings through **the roof!** So the **idiots** at **MAD** put me in this **opening panel** hoping it would **help here** too! Talk about **wishful thinking!**
I'm **Daffy,** the **cute, perky housekeeper** with the adorable **English accent** and **acerbic wit— everything** that tells you this is a **sitcom** in **trouble!**
Make that ***deep trouble!*** *In addition to the* ***perky housekeeper,*** *they also have a* ***cute little dog: Me!***

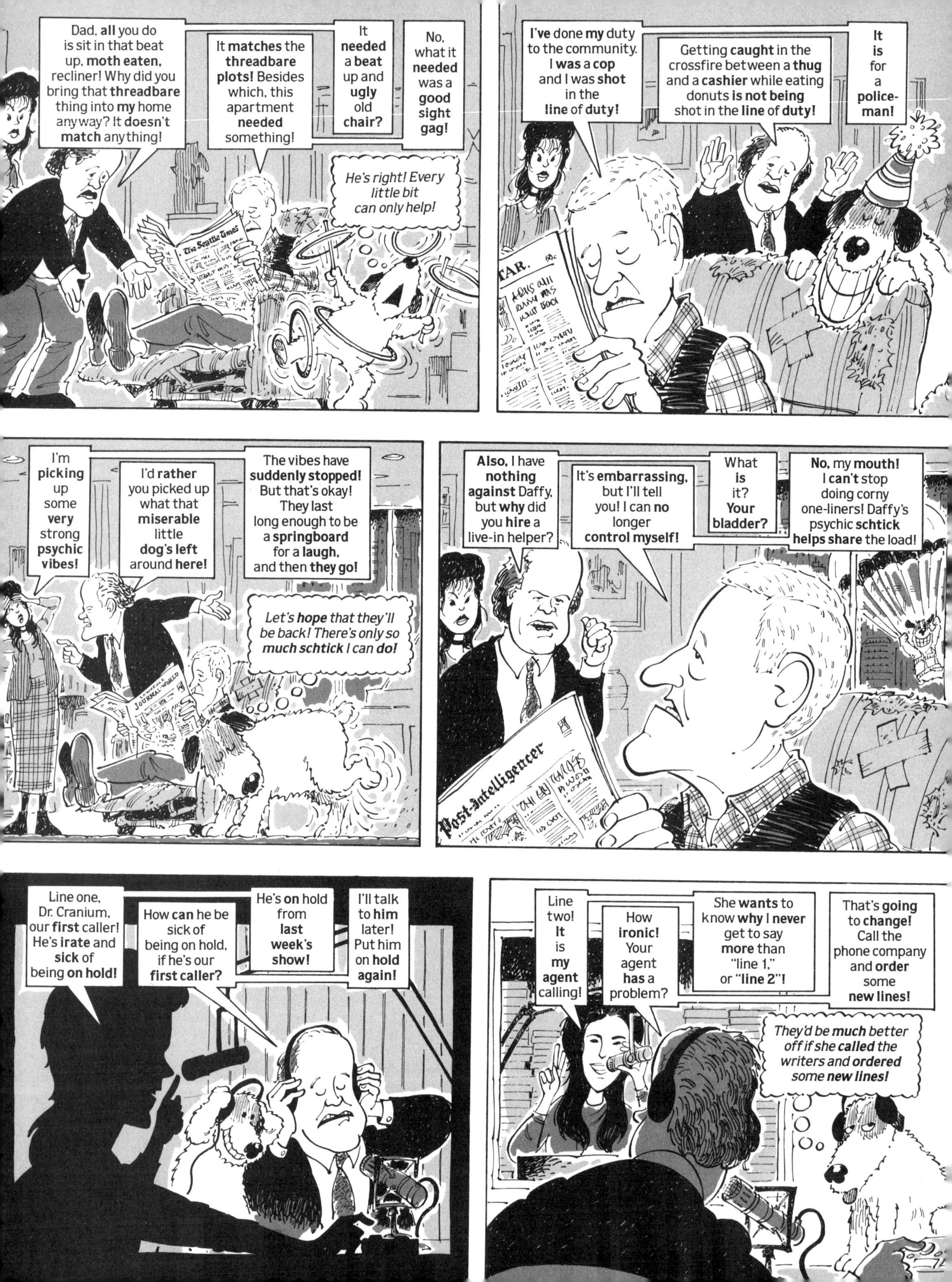

Dad, all you do is sit in that beat up, moth eaten, recliner! Why did you bring that threadbare thing into my home anyway? It doesn't match anything!
It matches the threadbare plots! Besides which, this apartment needed something!
It needed a beat up and ugly old chair?
No, what it needed was a good sight gag!
He's right! Every little bit can only help!
The Seattle Times
I've done my duty to the community. I was a cop and I was shot in the line of duty!
Getting caught in the crossfire between a thug and a cashier while eating donuts is not being shot in the line of duty!
It is for a policeman!
I'm picking up some very strong psychic vibes!
I'd rather you picked up what that miserable little dog's left around here!
The vibes have suddenly stopped! But that's okay! They last long enough to be a springboard for a laugh, and then they go!
Let's hope that they'll be back! There's only so much schtick I can do!
Also, I have nothing against Daffy, but why did you hire a live-in helper?
It's embarrassing, but I'll tell you! I can no longer control myself!
What is it? Your bladder?
No, my mouth! I can't stop doing corny one-liners! Daffy's psychic schtick helps share the load!
Post-Intelligencer
Line one, Dr. Cranium, our first caller! He's irate and sick of being on hold!
How can he be sick of being on hold, if he's our first caller?
He's on hold from last week's show!
I'll talk to him later! Put him on hold again!
Line two! It is my agent calling!
How ironic! Your agent has a problem?
She wants to know why I never get to say more than "line 1," or "line 2"!
That's going to change! Call the phone company and order some new lines!
They'd be much better off if she called the writers and ordered some new lines!

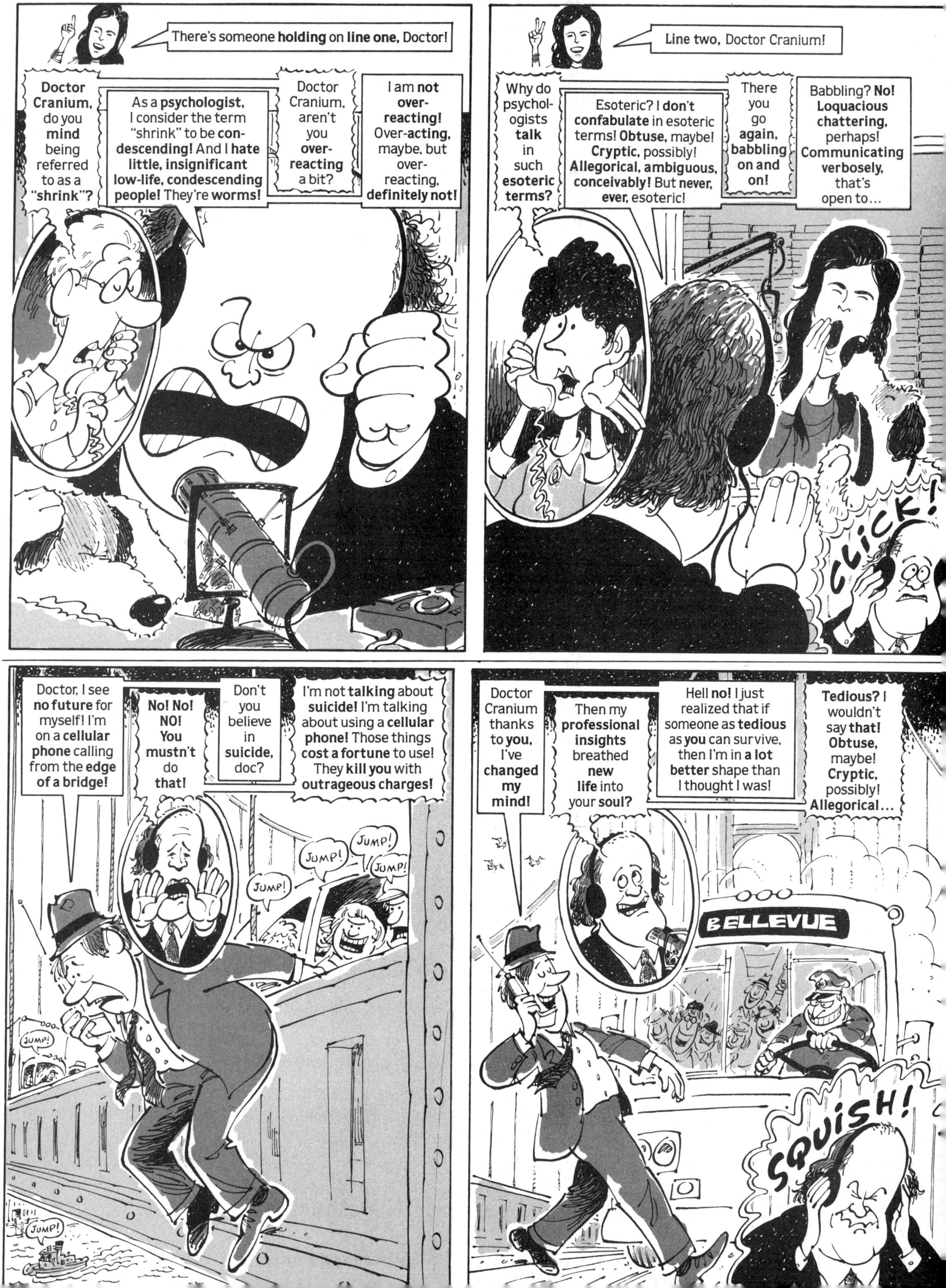

There's someone holding on line one, Doctor!
Doctor Cranium, do you mind being referred to as a "shrink"?
As a psychologist, I consider the term "shrink" to be condescending! And I hate little, insignificant low-life, condescending people! They're worms!
Doctor Cranium, aren't you over-reacting a bit?
I am not over-reacting! Over-acting, maybe, but over-reacting, definitely not!
Line two, Doctor Cranium!
Why do psychologists talk in such esoteric terms?
Esoteric? I don't confabulate in esoteric terms! Obtuse, maybe! Cryptic, possibly! Allegorical, ambiguous, conceivably! But never, ever, esoteric!
There you go again, babbling on and on!
Babbling? No! Loquacious chattering, perhaps! Communicating verbosely, that's open to…
CLICK!
Doctor, I see no future for myself! I'm on a cellular phone calling from the edge of a bridge!
No! No! NO! You mustn't do that!
Don't you believe in suicide, doc?
I'm not talking about suicide! I'm talking about using a cellular phone! Those things cost a fortune to use! They kill you with outrageous charges!
JUMP!
JUMP!
JUMP!
JUMP!
JUMP!
JUMP!
Doctor Cranium thanks to you, I've changed my mind!
Then my professional insights breathed new life into your soul?
Hell no! I just realized that if someone as tedious as you can survive, then I'm in a lot better shape than I thought I was!
Tedious? I wouldn't say that! Obtuse, maybe! Cryptic, possibly! Allegorical…
BELLEVUE
SQUISH!

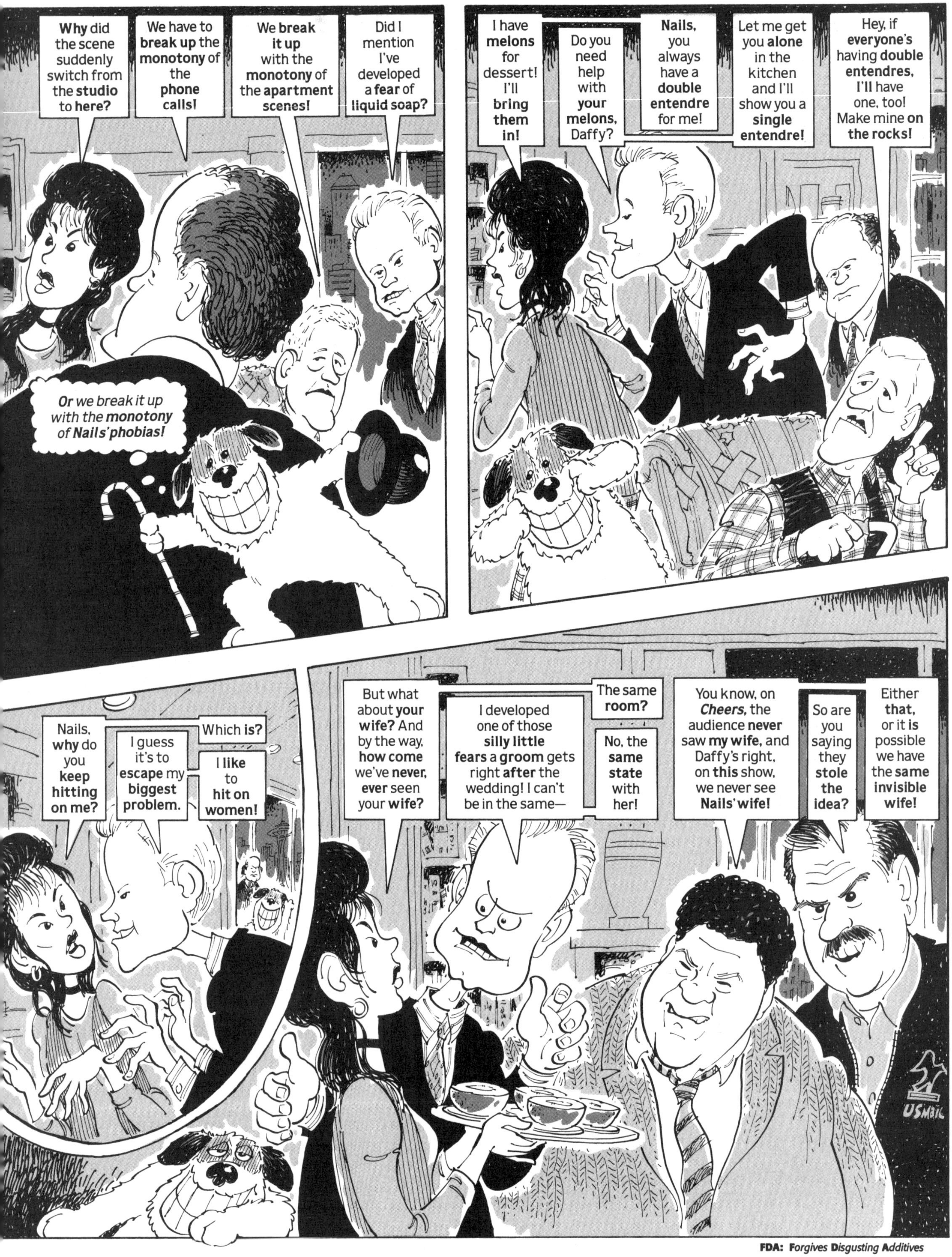
Why did the scene suddenly switch from the studio to here?
We have to break up the monotony of the phone calls!
We break it up with the monotony of the apartment scenes!
Did I mention I've developed a fear of liquid soap?
Or we break it up with the monotony of Nails' phobias!
I have melons for dessert! I'll bring them in!
Do you need help with your melons, Daffy?
Nails, you always have a double entendre for me!
Let me get you alone in the kitchen and I'll show you a single entendre!
Hey, if everyone's having double entendres, I'll have one, too! Make mine on the rocks!
Nails, why do you keep hitting on me?
I guess it's to escape my biggest problem.
Which is?
I like to hit on women!
But what about your wife? And by the way, how come we've never, ever seen your wife?
I developed one of those silly little fears a groom gets right after the wedding! I can't be in the same—
The same room?
No, the same state with her!
You know, on Cheers, the audience never saw my wife, and Daffy's right, on this show, we never see Nails' wife!
So are you saying they stole the idea?
Either that, or it is possible we have the same invisible wife!

FDA: *Forgives Disgusting Additives*

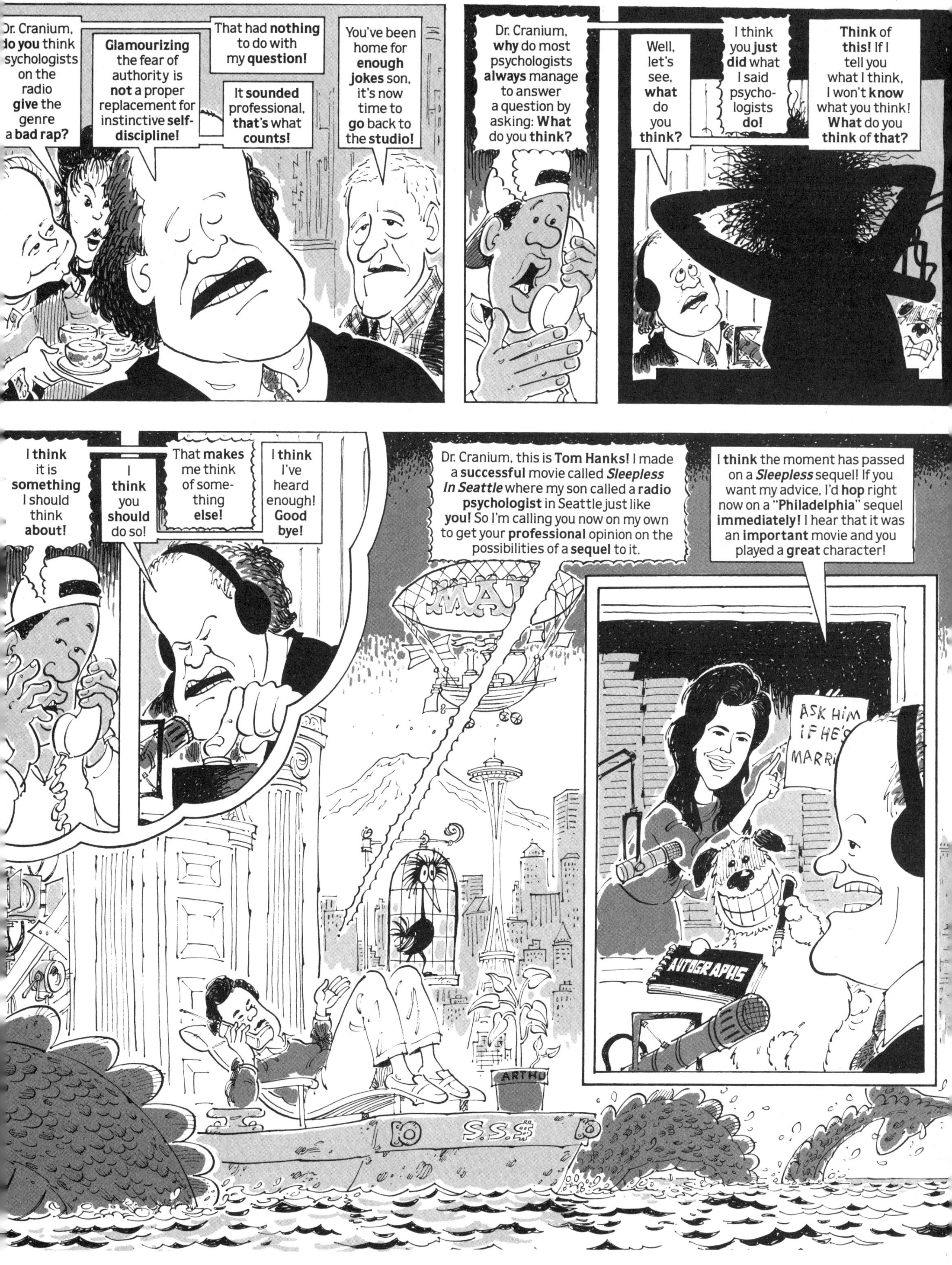
Dr. Cranium, do you think sychologists on the radio give the genre a bad rap?
Glamourizing the fear of authority is not a proper replacement for instinctive self-discipline!
That had nothing to do with my question!
It sounded professional, that's what counts!
You've been home for enough jokes son, it's now time to go back to the studio!
Dr. Cranium, why do most psychologists always manage to answer a question by asking: What do you think?
Well, let's see, what do you think?
I think you just did what I said psycho-logists do!
Think of this! If I tell you what I think, I won't know what you think! What do you think of that?
I think it is something I should think about!
I think you should do so!
That makes me think of some-thing else!
I think I've heard enough! Good bye!
Dr. Cranium, this is Tom Hanks! I made a successful movie called Sleepless In Seattle where my son called a radio psychologist in Seattle just like you! So I'm calling you now on my own to get your professional opinion on the possibilities of a sequel to it.
I think the moment has passed on a Sleepless sequel! If you want my advice, I'd hop right now on a "Philadelphia" sequel immediately! I hear that it was an important movie and you played a great character!
ASK HIM IF HE'S MARRI
AUTOGRAPHS
S.S.$
ARTHU

Doctor Cranium, I'm so **lonely!** I spend weeks and months just **sitting** at **home alone!** Do you have any **advice?**
The **question** here is, **why** are you **lonely?** I **suggest** you **spend** some time at **home alone** and **think about it!**
Geez! I know your **advice** is **free**, but it's still a **rip-off!**
Do you think me **talking** to people while I'm **sitting** on the **toilet** bowl is **gross?**
Gross doesn't begin to describe such **anal oriented behavior!** It's **vulgar, odorous** and **tasteless!** And I **know** who you **are—Howard!**
Did I **mention** I made **three million dollars** doing **exactly that** on my **New Year's Eve Special!**
Three million dollars? Thanks for the **call**, Mr. Stern! He **seems** like a **decent** guy, doesn't he? Hmmm, **three million dollars**... Razz, have them **install a line** in the **men's room!**
If you'd like to talk to a **lesbian, sado-masochist,** or if you want to talk to **me direct**, dial **1-900-52-FLAKIER!** Remember **all calls** are **$4.95 a minute!** And tonight's theme: **Professional Ethics, Or Big Bucks**—has been **postponed indefinitely!**
Dr. Cranium, do you feel **your work** stands on its **own**, or do you **owe others** for **your success?**
With **rare exception**, a person's body of work is **greatly influenced** by **others!** So, to be **honest**, my **success** is only about **99%** my **own** doing, **give** or **take 1%!**
Glad to **hear it**, because I'm a **Programing Exec** at **NBC**, and we're **moving** another **show** into the **slot following** the **mega-hit, Seinfeld!** Your **new lead-in** will be **DATELINE NBC!**
NO! You **can't do that!** Being moved from my **familiar surroundings** would **cut deep** into my **psyche!** And **deeper** into my **bank account!** You **mustn't forget** what **Freud** said: "I have a **huge mortgage** on my **house**, and **society won't get well** until I **pay it off!** So **PLEASE—leave my show where it is!**"

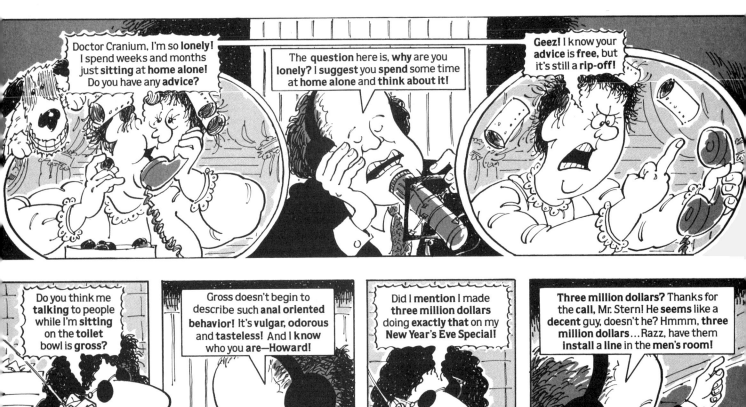

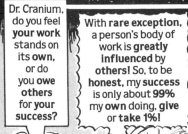

COMPULSIVE RAMBLER DEPT.

We're sick and tired of people blasting Rosie O'Donnell for not being a hard-hitting talk show host! Okay, so some of her questions are soft enough to make Kathie Lee Gifford look like an investigative journalist! And maybe Rosie does kiss so much celebrity ass, she should use Preparation H for lip balm! But we know in our heart of hearts that the former Betty Flintstone can ask the tough questions of today's newsmakers, as you'll see when...

ROSIE O'DONNELL
GRILLS SOME NON-SHOWBIZ GUESTS

NELSON MANDELA

Nelson, you spent a **quarter** of a **century** being **beaten** and starved in **South African prisons.** Did you have a **radio** and **escape tunnel** like they had on *Hogan's Heroes*?

To me, there is **no uglier word** than "apartheid." See, the audience **agrees with me.** So let's make it a **BETTER** word! *Apartheid, apartheid, bo-bartheid, banana fana fo fartheid, me mi mo martheid...*

In 1993, you **split** the **Nobel Peace Prize** with **F.W. deKlerk,** and I said, "**Oh no!** It's **happened again!** That's just like when **Barbra Streisand** had to split the **Best Actress Oscar** with **Katherine Hepburn!**" I mean, I am sorry. **No offense** to Kate, and I hope she **comes on the show,** but there is only **ONE** Streisand, and we are so **darn lucky** to **have her!** Hmmm, I guess I made a **little speech** defending **what I believe. Just like YOU,** Nellie!

JOHN GOTTI

You had your **boss shot down** and **took over** the **family.** That reminds me of a **little trivia** — remember the **name** of Lucy's boss on *The Lucy Show*? Give up? Wait, I **heard it** from the **audience!** Mr. Mooney, **that's right!** You see, they **always know!**

It came out in **court** that **innocent people** got **murdered** by **accident,** based on **your orders.** That is **SUCH** a coincidence, because only **yesterday,** I **totally forgot** to say who the **guests** were before I went to **commercial!** So you see, **everybody,** even stars, sometimes **make mistakes!**

You just **snapped your fingers,** had other **human beings killed,** and a lot of people **never** got to **say** goodbye to the **people they love.** It's **just like that** episode of *M*A*S*H* — you know, remember the **first one** with B.J., where **Hawkeye just misses** saying goodbye to Trapper John by like **FIVE** minutes? Is that like the **best show?** I have **every one** on **tape!**

ARTIST: DREW FRIEDMAN   WRITER: DESMOND DEVLIN

ROSIE O'DONNELL

GRILLS SOME NON-SHOWBIZ GUESTS

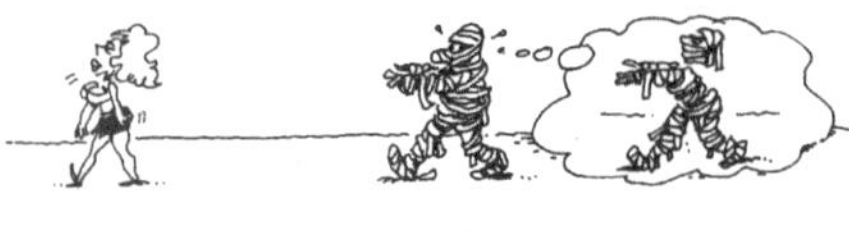

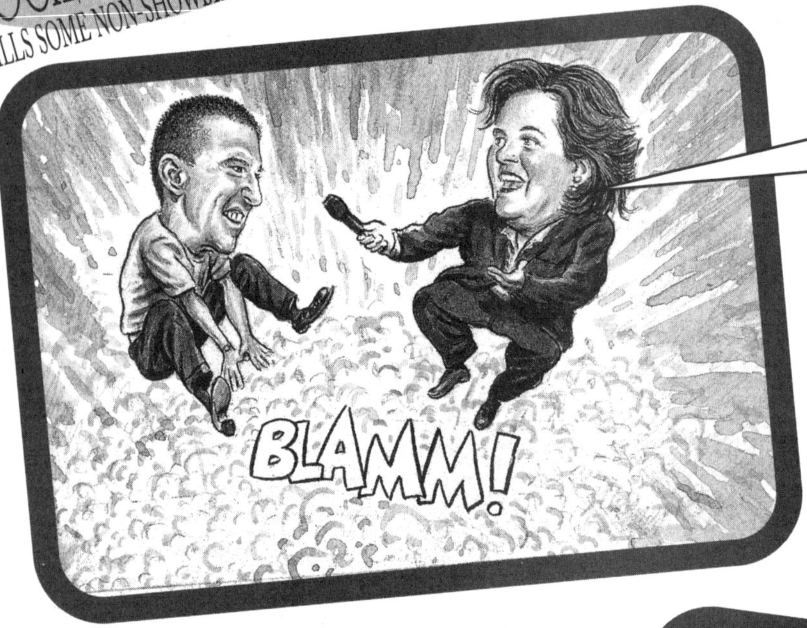
BLAMM!

TIMOTHY McVEIGH

You're accused of snuffing out the lives of babies with glycerin and fertilizer. And speaking of fertilizer — pardon my French — how can Madonna WIN a Golden Globe, and not even get an Oscar NOMINATION? Where is the criminal trial THERE, hmm?

They say you lit the fuse just five minutes before the explosion, and ran. I get winded just walking through the curtains, y'know? Have you ever thought about doing an exercise video?

You were so close to the devastation that the blood and smoke got into your clothes. Did you try cold water and lemon juice?

CHARLES MANSON

You claimed to hear secret messages in Beatles songs, so what did you think about that Beatles reunion? Wasn't that new song great?

Hey, remember that old Almond Joy commercial — *sometimes you feel like a nut, sometimes you don't*! C'mon, Charlie, sing!

You ordered the slaughter of innocent people, including a woman who was eight months pregnant, and bathed the walls of their homes in hot blood! So I gotta ask — what makes Charlie Manson cry?

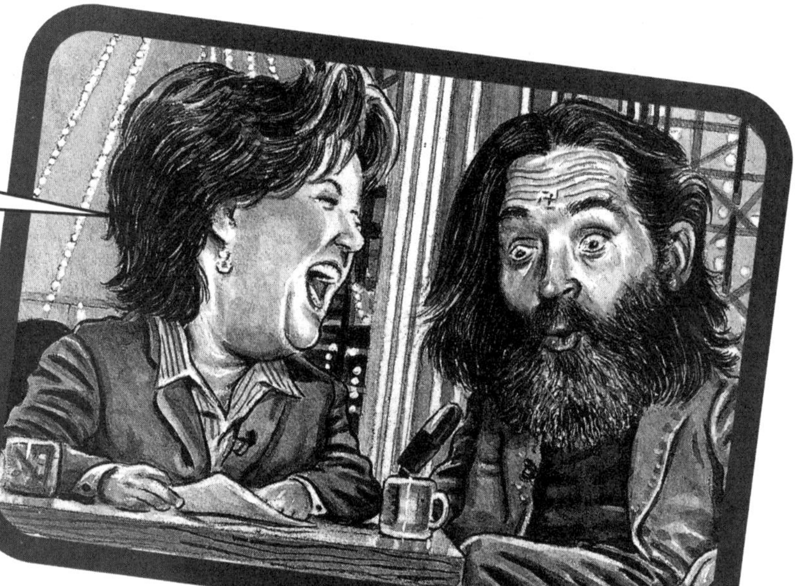

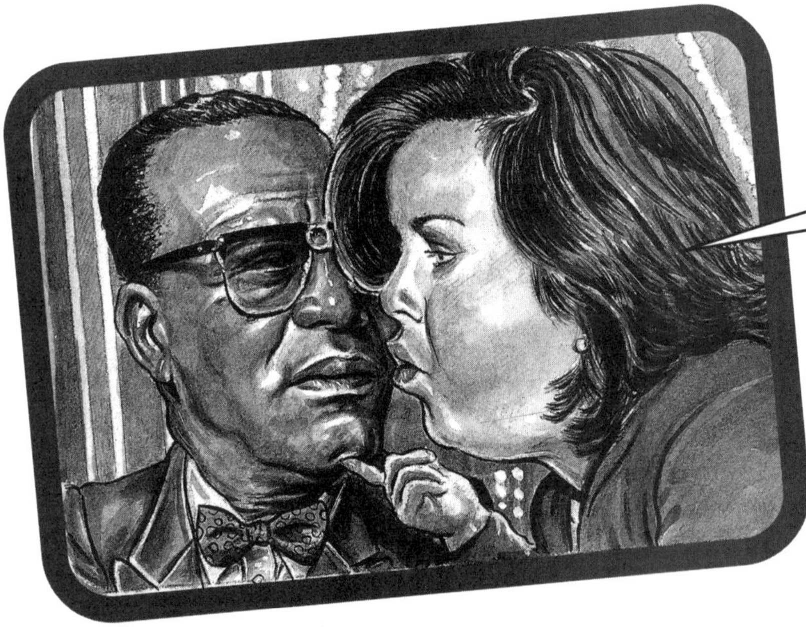

LOUIS FARRAKHAN

Love, love, LOVE the bow tie, Louie! Did you get the idea from Yogi Bear?

I just want to say that I would have been SO against that whole slavery thing!

You've been quoted as hating whites, hating black traitors, hating the Jews. You know what I hate? Cell phones in the movie theater! Totally annoying, am I right? People, take it out to the candy counter, and let me watch my Tommy, okay? Thank you, next!

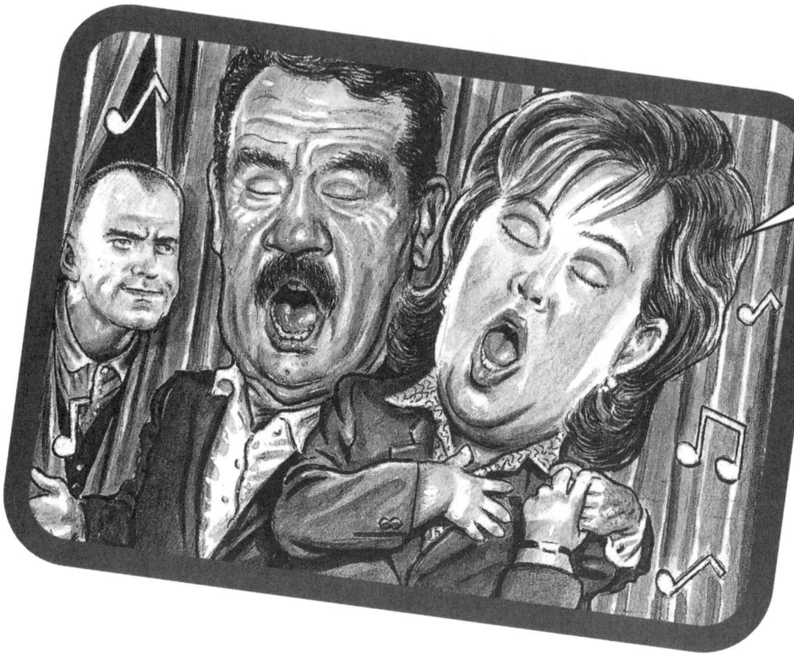

SADAAM HUSSEIN

Sing with me, Saddy! *Let me tell you 'bout* ***Ahab the Arab****, the sheik of the* ***burning sand!*** Okay, **I'LL sing,** and **YOU** do the **camel noises!**

You tricked your **own son-in-laws** into **returning** to **Iraq,** just so you could **have them killed** by **assassins!** That whole **violence thing** is **so big** these days. **Big, big, BIG!** It's just **ca-razy!** Have you ever met **Quentin Tarantino?**

Your army **opened** up **Kuwait's oil pipes** and **drained them** into the **Persian Gulf,** intentionally causing **incredible ecological damage.** So I guess you're more of a **"country person"** than a **"beach person,"** huh?

MOTHER TERESA

You've **dedicated** your **existence** on this planet to **helping** the **starving. For me,** starving is when I have to eat **regular Oreos** instead of the **Double-Stuff!** HA! **Joke, people!**

This is going to be **so awesome** — after this **special facial makeover,** you are going to **look 85 again!**

Now, Terry, **somebody told me** you like to **wash people's feet.** See, the **audience** knows **what's coming.** I hope you **don't mind,** but my **producer** picked **three people** from the **audience,** I **got your soap** right here — **LET'S BRING 'EM OUT!**

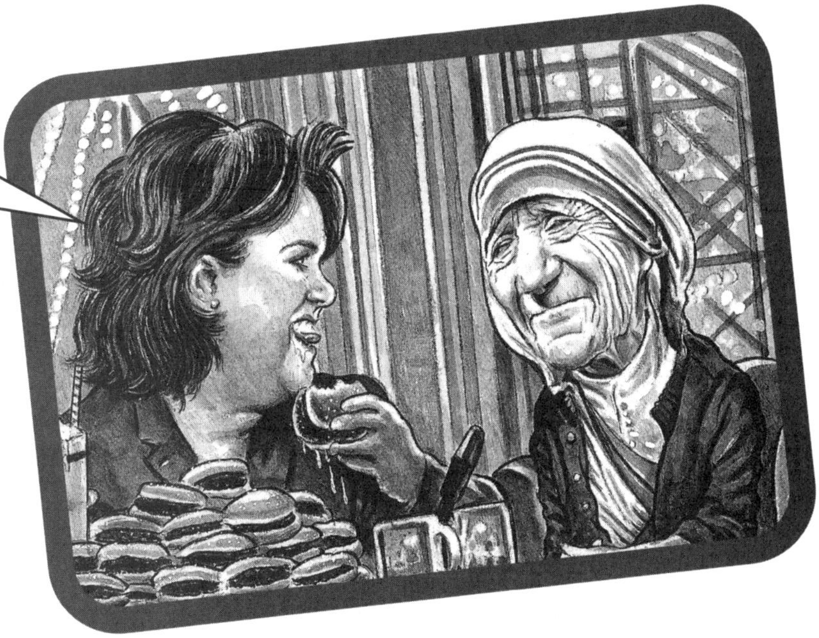

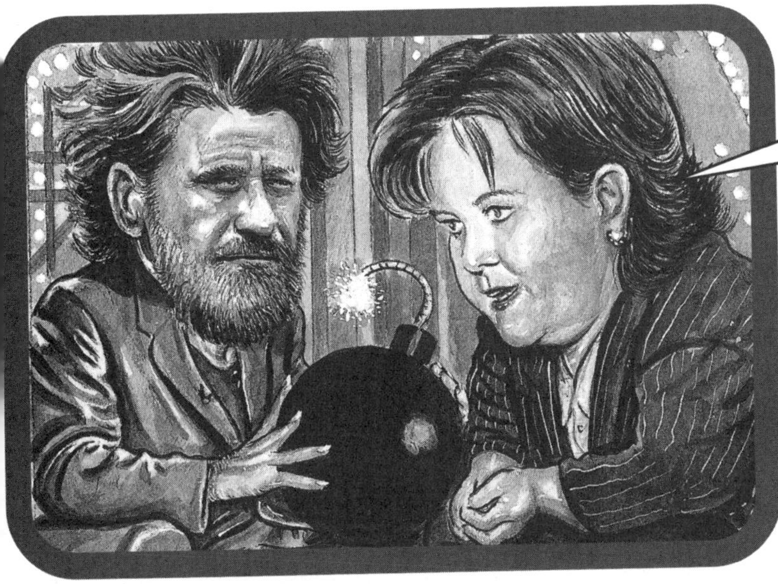

THE UNABOMBER

You've been **fighting** a **battle** against the **forces** of **technology** you say have **doomed our society** — hey, how about the **clock** on my **VCR? 12:00, 12:00, 12:00**...don't you **HATE** that?

Now you're looking at **spendin'** the **rest** of **your life** in a **10-by-12 cell,** all because **your brother turned you in!** I guess you've got one of those **Wally/Beaver relationships,** huh?

You're an **expert** on **bombs** — what did you **think** of ***Showgirls?***

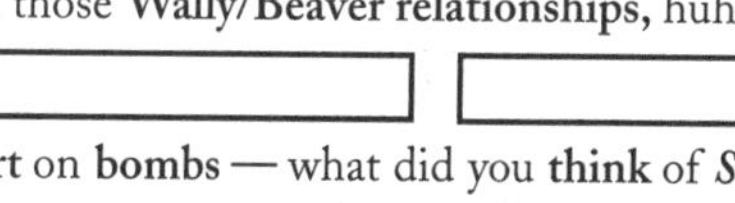

NEWTWORK TELEVISION DEPT.

Let's face it: in today's ultra-conservative political climate, Muppets have become an endangered species. If Newt "The Pompous, Egocentric, Revolting Blowhard" Gingrich has his way, Congress will soon cut the financial lifeline to PBS, putting Big Bird, Kermit and friends out of work. The sad truth is that in order to protect their jobs, the Muppets may have to alter their insidious left-wing agenda of teaching children to read and spell, and make certain "compromises." Here's what their show may look like...

When SESAME STREET Caves In to the *Radical Right*

ARTIST: SAM VIVIANO

WRITER: FRANK JACOBS

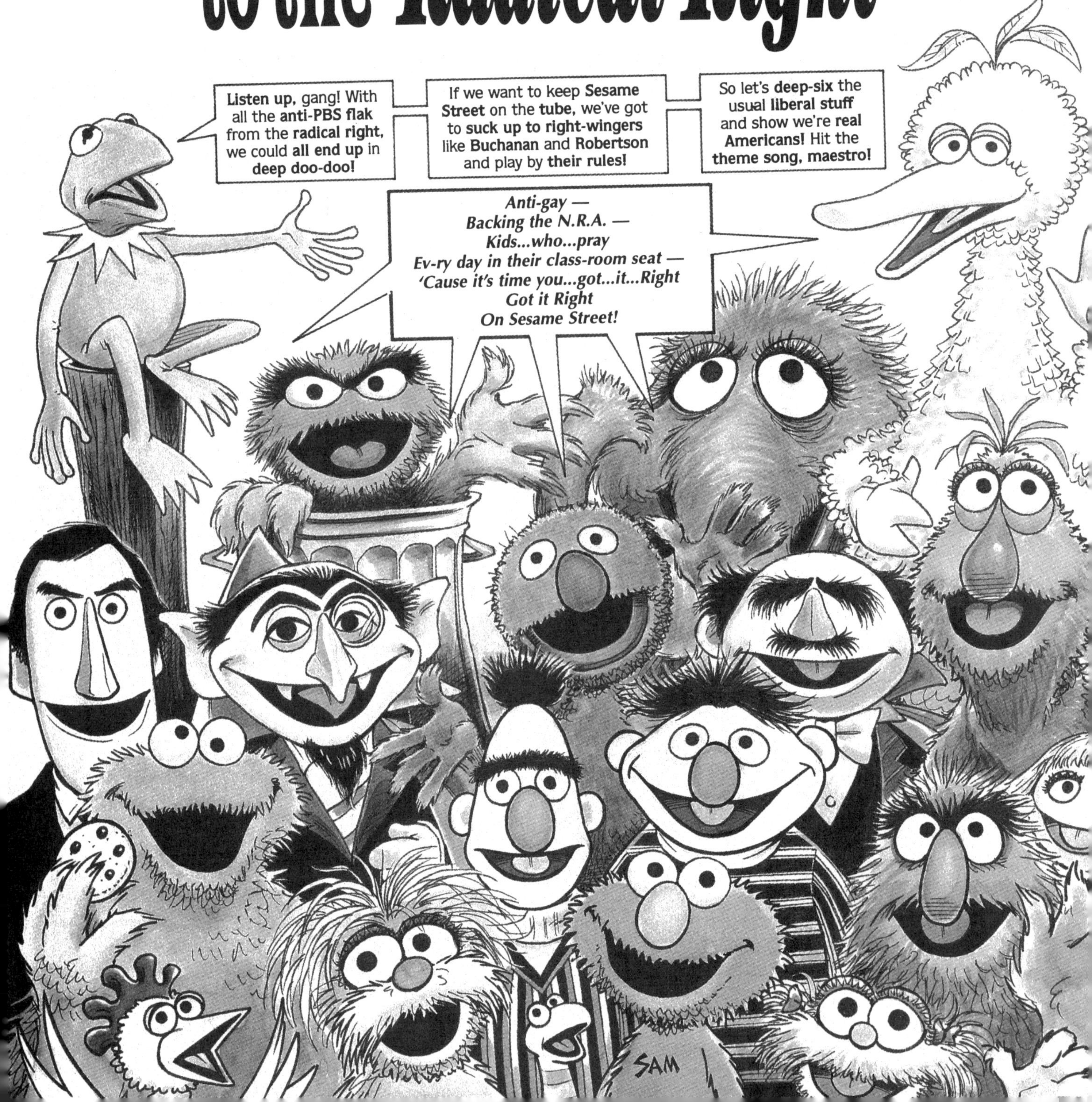

Listen up, gang! With all the anti-PBS flak from the radical right, we could all end up in deep doo-doo!
If we want to keep Sesame Street on the tube, we've got to suck up to right-wingers like Buchanan and Robertson and play by their rules!
So let's deep-six the usual liberal stuff and show we're real Americans! Hit the theme song, maestro!
Anti-gay — Backing the N.R.A. — Kids...who...pray Ev-ry day in their class-room seat — 'Cause it's time you...got...it...Right Got it Right On Sesame Street!
SAM

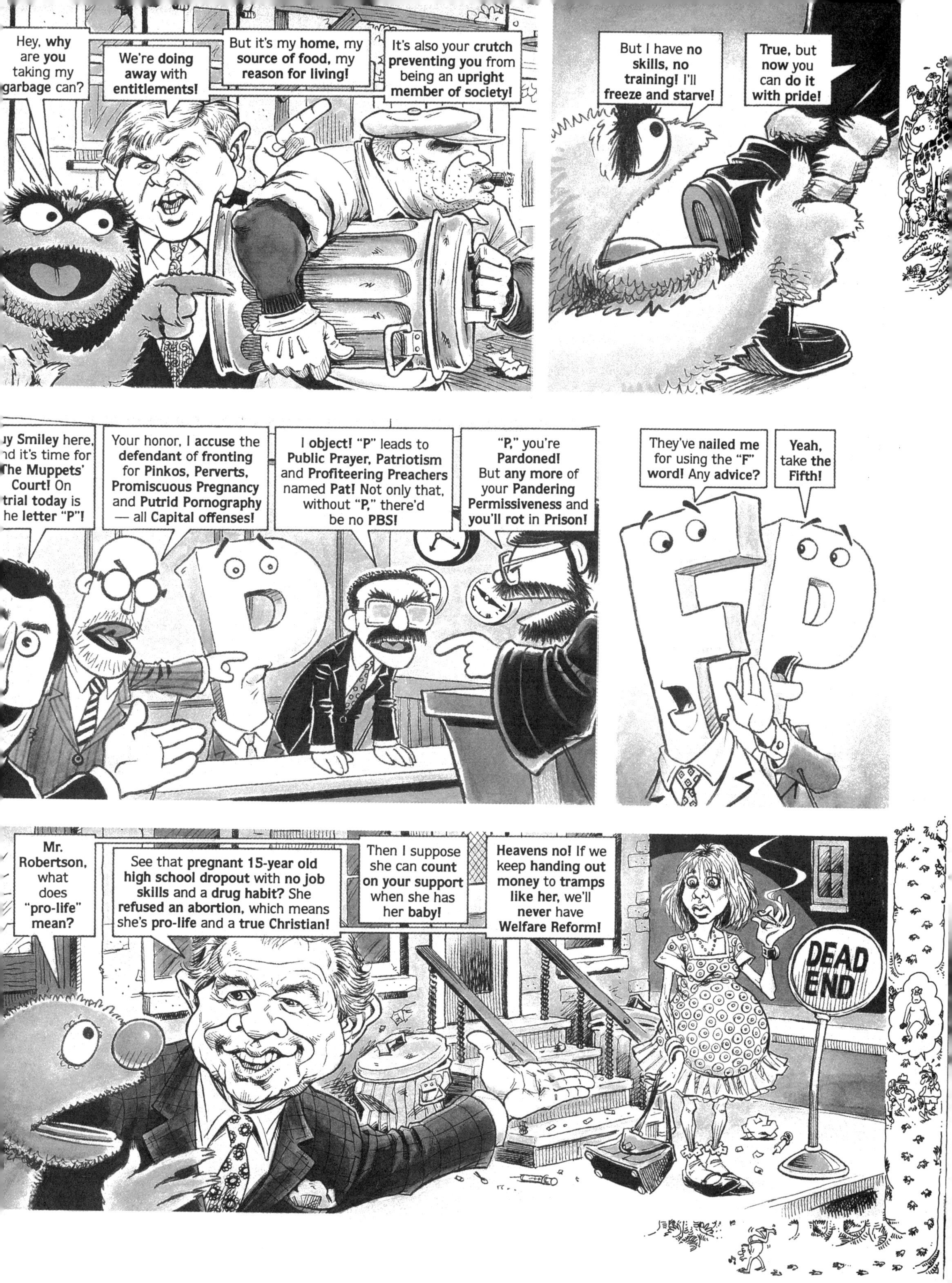

Hey, why are you taking my garbage can?
We're doing away with entitlements!
But it's my home, my source of food, my reason for living!
It's also your crutch preventing you from being an upright member of society!
But I have no skills, no training! I'll freeze and starve!
True, but now you can do it with pride!
y Smiley here, nd it's time for The Muppets' Court! On trial today is he letter "P"!
Your honor, I accuse the defendant of fronting for Pinkos, Perverts, Promiscuous Pregnancy and Putrid Pornography — all Capital offenses!
I object! "P" leads to Public Prayer, Patriotism and Profiteering Preachers named Pat! Not only that, without "P," there'd be no PBS!
"P," you're Pardoned! But any more of your Pandering Permissiveness and you'll rot in Prison!
They've nailed me for using the "F" word! Any advice?
Yeah, take the Fifth!
Mr. Robertson, what does "pro-life" mean?
See that pregnant 15-year old high school dropout with no job skills and a drug habit? She refused an abortion, which means she's pro-life and a true Christian!
Then I suppose she can count on your support when she has her baby!
Heavens no! If we keep handing out money to tramps like her, we'll never have Welfare Reform!
DEAD END

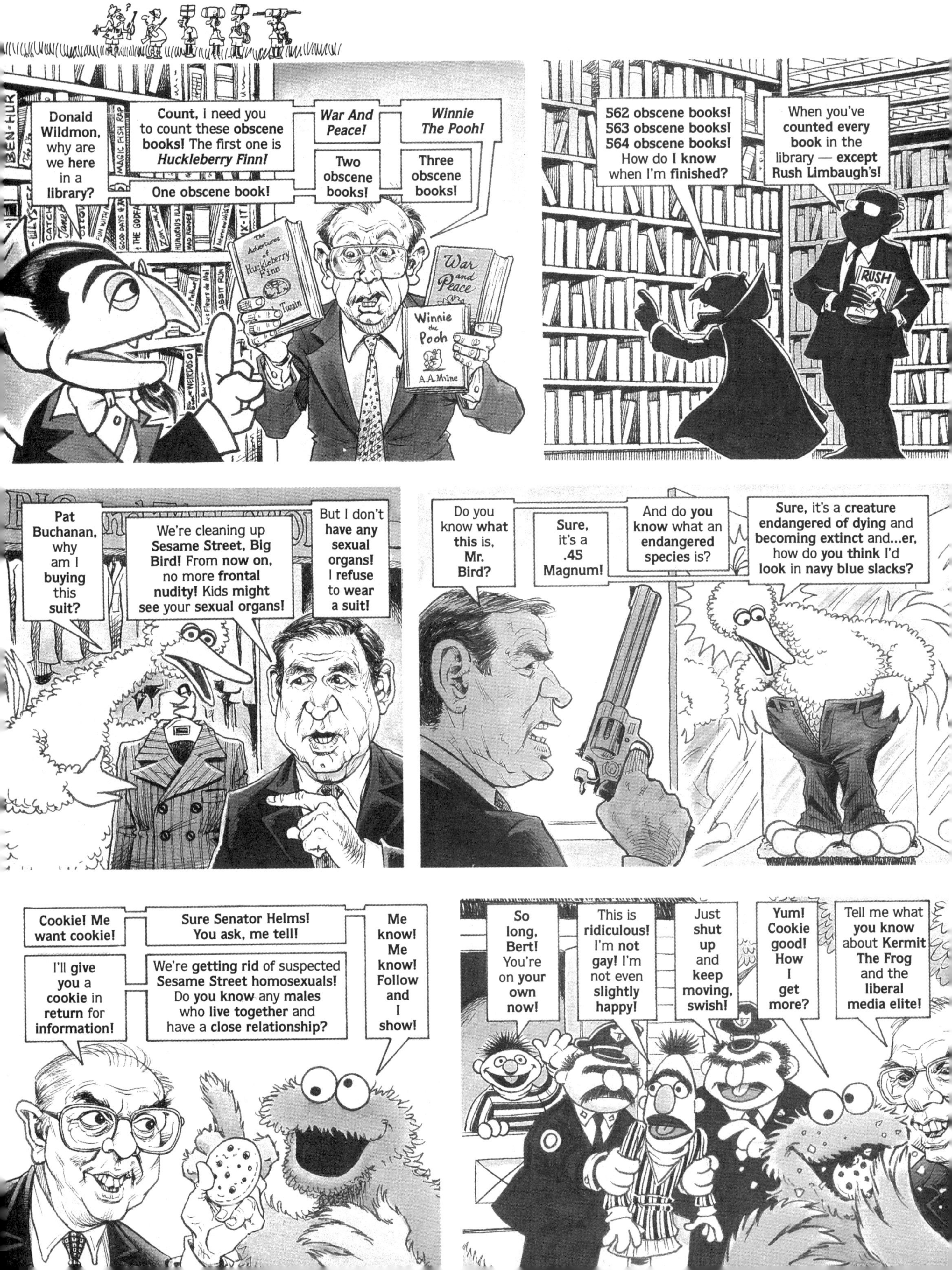

Donald Wildmon, why are we here in a library?
Count, I need you to count these obscene books! The first one is Huckleberry Finn!
One obscene book!
War And Peace!
Two obscene books!
Winnie The Pooh!
Three obscene books!
The Adventures of Huckleberry Finn
Twain
War and Peace
Winnie the Pooh
A.A. Milne
BEN-HUR
WEIRDOS
562 obscene books! 563 obscene books! 564 obscene books! How do I know when I'm finished?
When you've counted every book in the library — except Rush Limbaugh's!
RUSH
Pat Buchanan, why am I buying this suit?
We're cleaning up Sesame Street, Big Bird! From now on, no more frontal nudity! Kids might see your sexual organs!
But I don't have any sexual organs! I refuse to wear a suit!
Do you know what this is, Mr. Bird?
Sure, it's a .45 Magnum!
And do you know what an endangered species is?
Sure, it's a creature endangered of dying and becoming extinct and...er, how do you think I'd look in navy blue slacks?
Cookie! Me want cookie!
Sure Senator Helms! You ask, me tell!
I'll give you a cookie in return for information!
We're getting rid of suspected Sesame Street homosexuals! Do you know any males who live together and have a close relationship?
Me know! Me know! Follow and I show!
So long, Bert! You're on your own now!
This is ridiculous! I'm not gay! I'm not even slightly happy!
Just shut up and keep moving, swish!
Yum! Cookie good! How I get more?
Tell me what you know about Kermit The Frog and the liberal media elite!

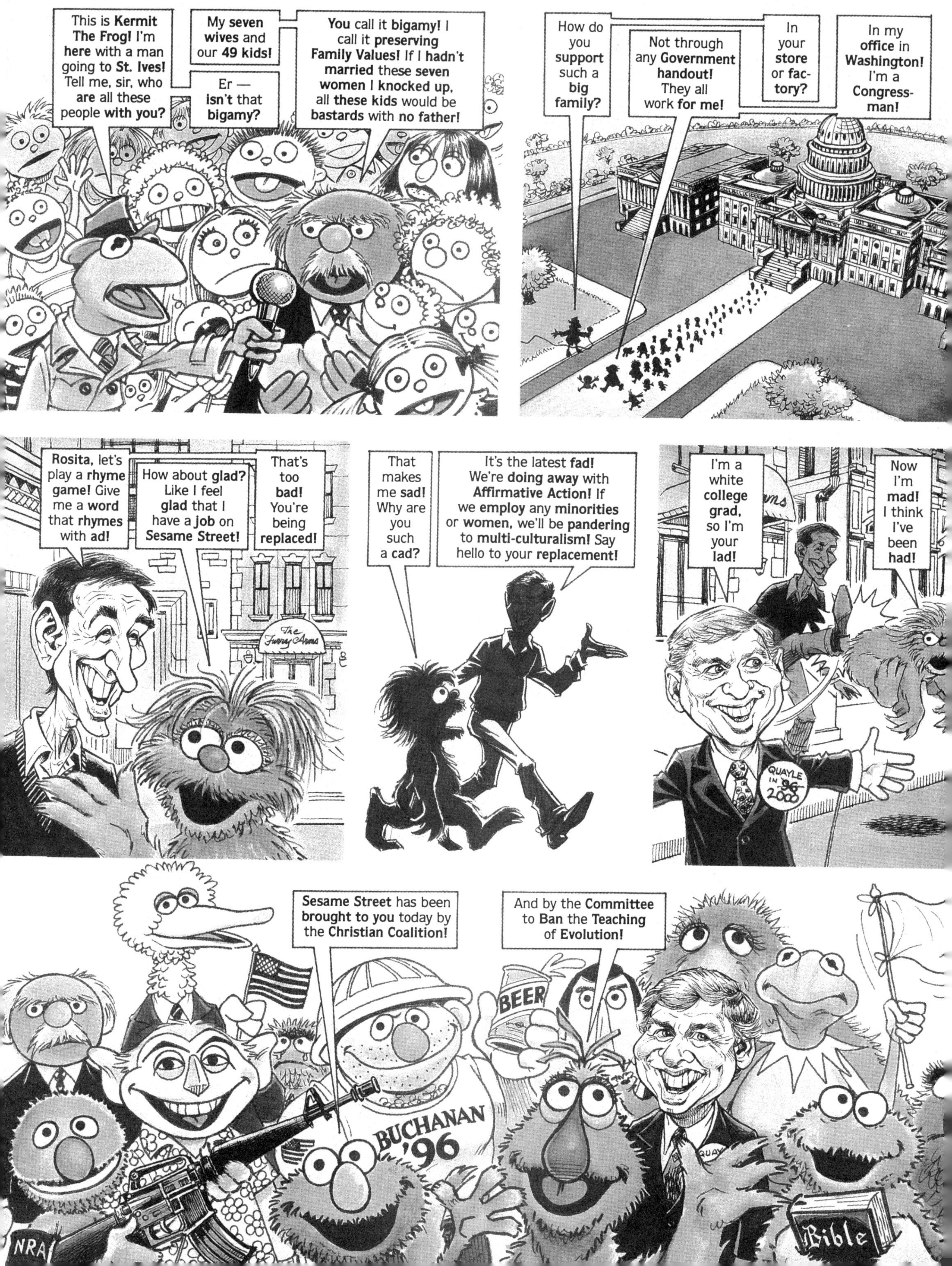

This is Kermit The Frog! I'm here with a man going to St. Ives! Tell me, sir, who are all these people with you?
My seven wives and our 49 kids!
Er — isn't that bigamy?
You call it bigamy! I call it preserving Family Values! If I hadn't married these seven women I knocked up, all these kids would be bastards with no father!
How do you support such a big family?
Not through any Government handout! They all work for me!
In your store or factory?
In my office in Washington! I'm a Congressman!
Rosita, let's play a rhyme game! Give me a word that rhymes with ad!
How about glad? Like I feel glad that I have a job on Sesame Street!
That's too bad! You're being replaced!
The Furry Arms
That makes me sad! Why are you such a cad?
It's the latest fad! We're doing away with Affirmative Action! If we employ any minorities or women, we'll be pandering to multi-culturalism! Say hello to your replacement!
I'm a white college grad, so I'm your lad!
Now I'm mad! I think I've been had!
QUAYLE IN 96 2000
Sesame Street has been brought to you today by the Christian Coalition!
And by the Committee to Ban the Teaching of Evolution!
BEER
BUCHANAN '96
NRA
Bible

AND THEY CALL IT YUPPIE LOVE DEPT.

What's this show about?
It's about every-day stuff...rela-tionships, in-laws, getting stuck in bathrooms, finding a lost sock...
Sounds remarkably like another popular situation comedy — *Seinfeld!*
There's a differ-ence! *Seinfeld* does shows about "nothing"!
And this show...?
This show does nothing about "nothing"!

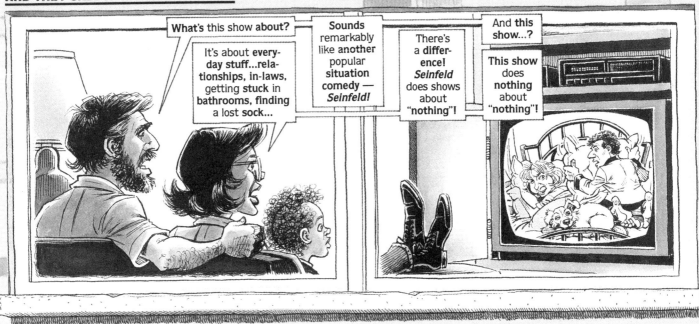

...and that's the problem! On the surface, this popular sitcom has all the ingredients of a great show: a cool New York apartment as its setting, a cute, lovable couple as its main characters, and their uncontrollable sex drive as a plot device! In fact, the only thing this sitcom is missing is JOKES! It's like the producers are looking viewers in the eye and saying...

Too Bad About You

Pill, what are you doing?
Fluff-ing!
You're fluff-ing?
Yeah! Fluffing!
Well, it's keep-ing me up!
I must fluff! I'm a fluff addict!
There are fluff support groups!
I'm trying to find the "cool spot" on my pillow!
I under-stand! Don't fluff!
It's a need! It's a want! It's a thing! It's a want-thing!
Stop it! Stop fluff-ing!
I must have a cool spot! I gotta fluff!
If you love me, don't fluff!
I lov you. but I'm fluf ing

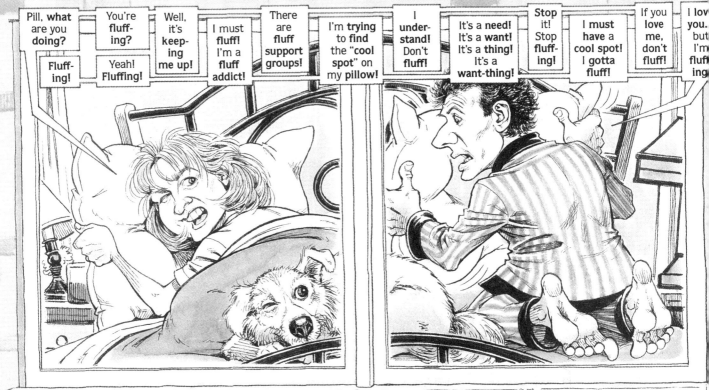

ARTIST: SAM VIVIANO WRITER: JOSH GORDON

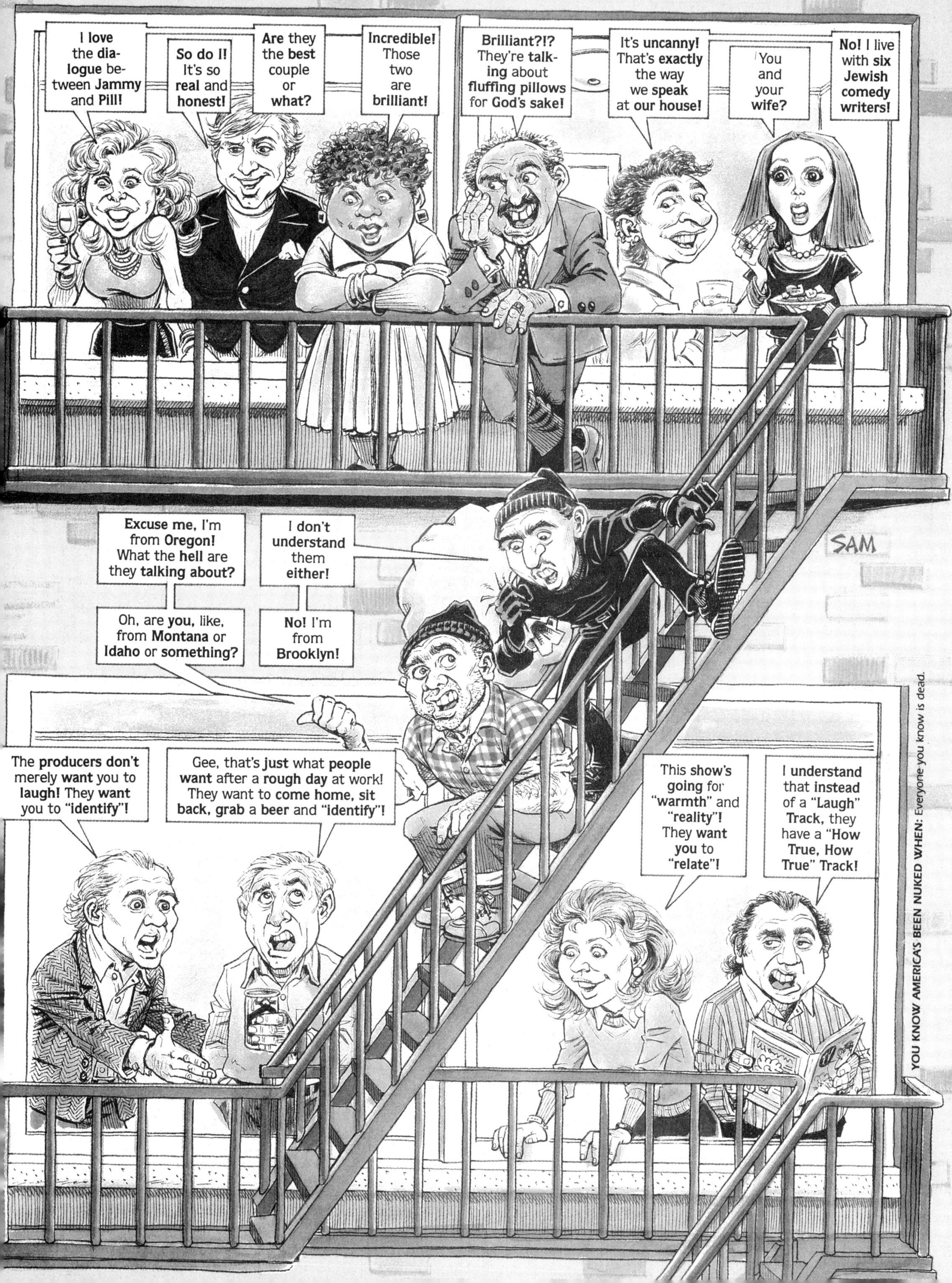

I love the dialogue between Jammy and Pill!
So do I! It's so real and honest!
Are they the best couple or what?
Incredible! Those two are brilliant!
Brilliant?!? They're talking about fluffing pillows for God's sake!
It's uncanny! That's exactly the way we speak at our house!
You and your wife?
No! I live with six Jewish comedy writers!
Excuse me, I'm from Oregon! What the hell are they talking about?
Oh, are you, like, from Montana or Idaho or something?
I don't understand them either!
No! I'm from Brooklyn!
SAM
The producers don't merely want you to laugh! They want you to "identify"!
Gee, that's just what people want after a rough day at work! They want to come home, sit back, grab a beer and "identify"!
This show's going for "warmth" and "reality"! They want you to "relate"!
I understand that instead of a "Laugh" Track, they have a "How True, How True" Track!

YOU KNOW AMERICA'S BEEN NUKED WHEN: Everyone you know is dead.

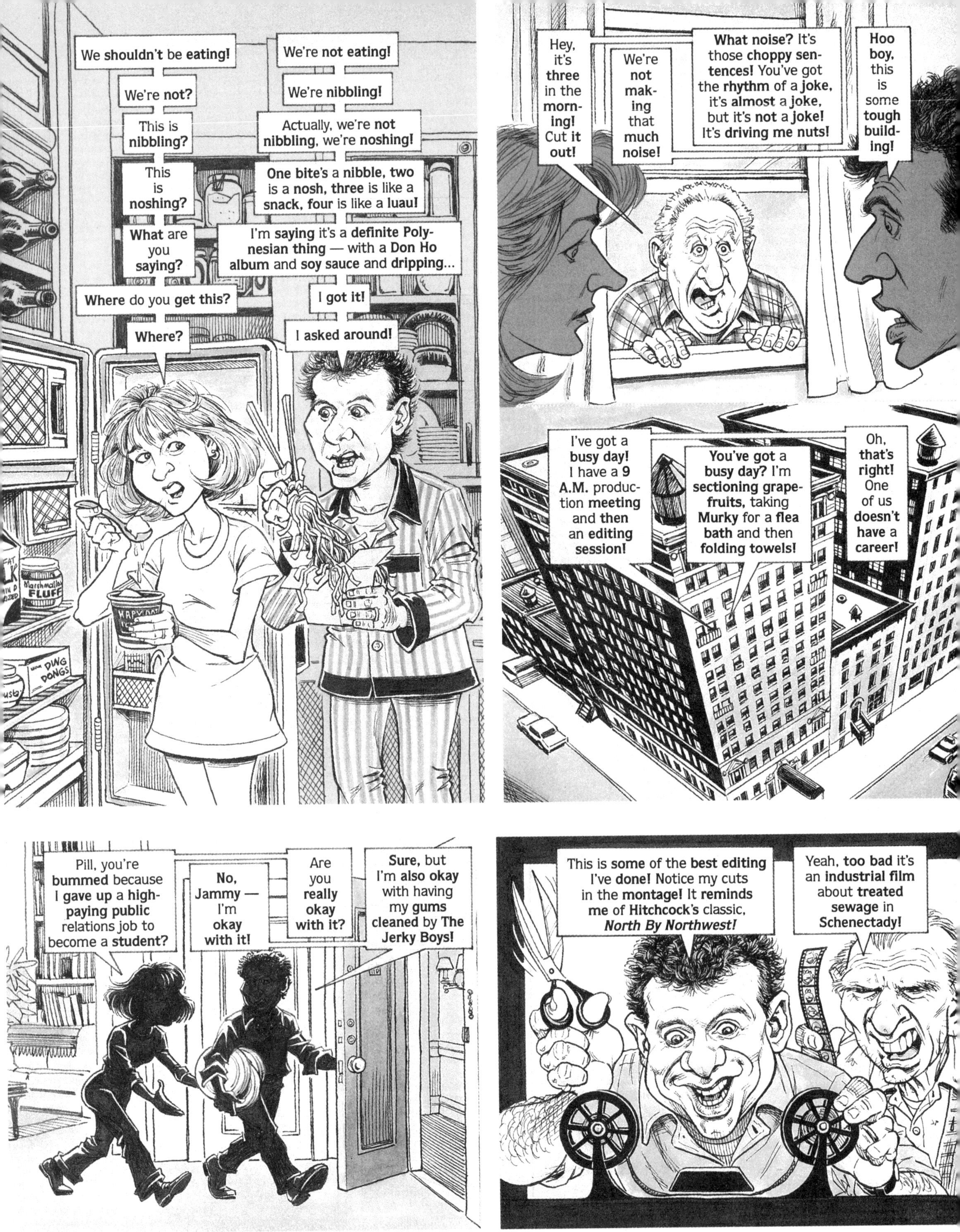
We shouldn't be eating!
We're not eating!
We're not?
We're nibbling!
This is nibbling?
Actually, we're not nibbling, we're noshing!
This is noshing?
One bite's a nibble, two is a nosh, three is like a snack, four is like a luau!
What are you saying?
I'm saying it's a definite Polynesian thing — with a Don Ho album and soy sauce and dripping...
Where do you get this?
I got it!
Where?
I asked around!
Marshmallow FLUFF
DING DONGS
Hey, it's three in the morning! Cut it out!
We're not making that much noise!
What noise? It's those choppy sentences! You've got the rhythm of a joke, it's almost a joke, but it's not a joke! It's driving me nuts!
Hoo boy, this is some tough building!
I've got a busy day! I have a 9 A.M. production meeting and then an editing session!
You've got a busy day? I'm sectioning grapefruits, taking Murky for a flea bath and then folding towels!
Oh, that's right! One of us doesn't have a career!
Pill, you're bummed because I gave up a high-paying public relations job to become a student?
No, Jammy — I'm okay with it!
Are you really okay with it?
Sure, but I'm also okay with having my gums cleaned by The Jerky Boys!
This is some of the best editing I've done! Notice my cuts in the montage! It reminds me of Hitchcock's classic, *North By Northwest!*
Yeah, too bad it's an industrial film about treated sewage in Schenectady!

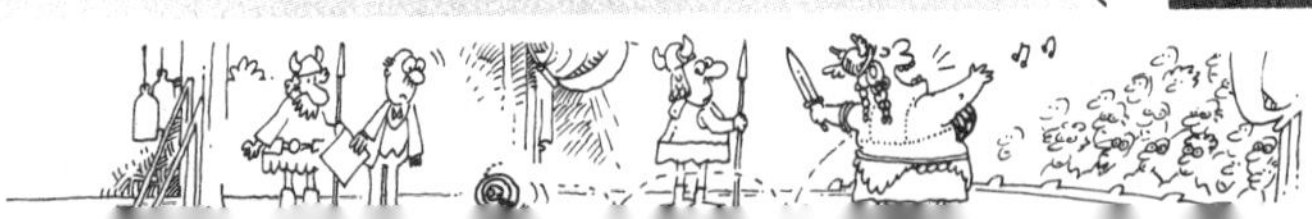

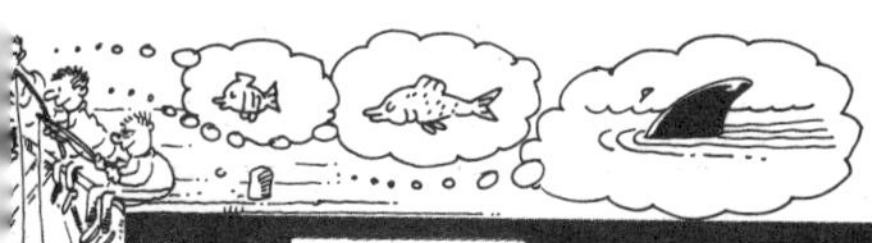

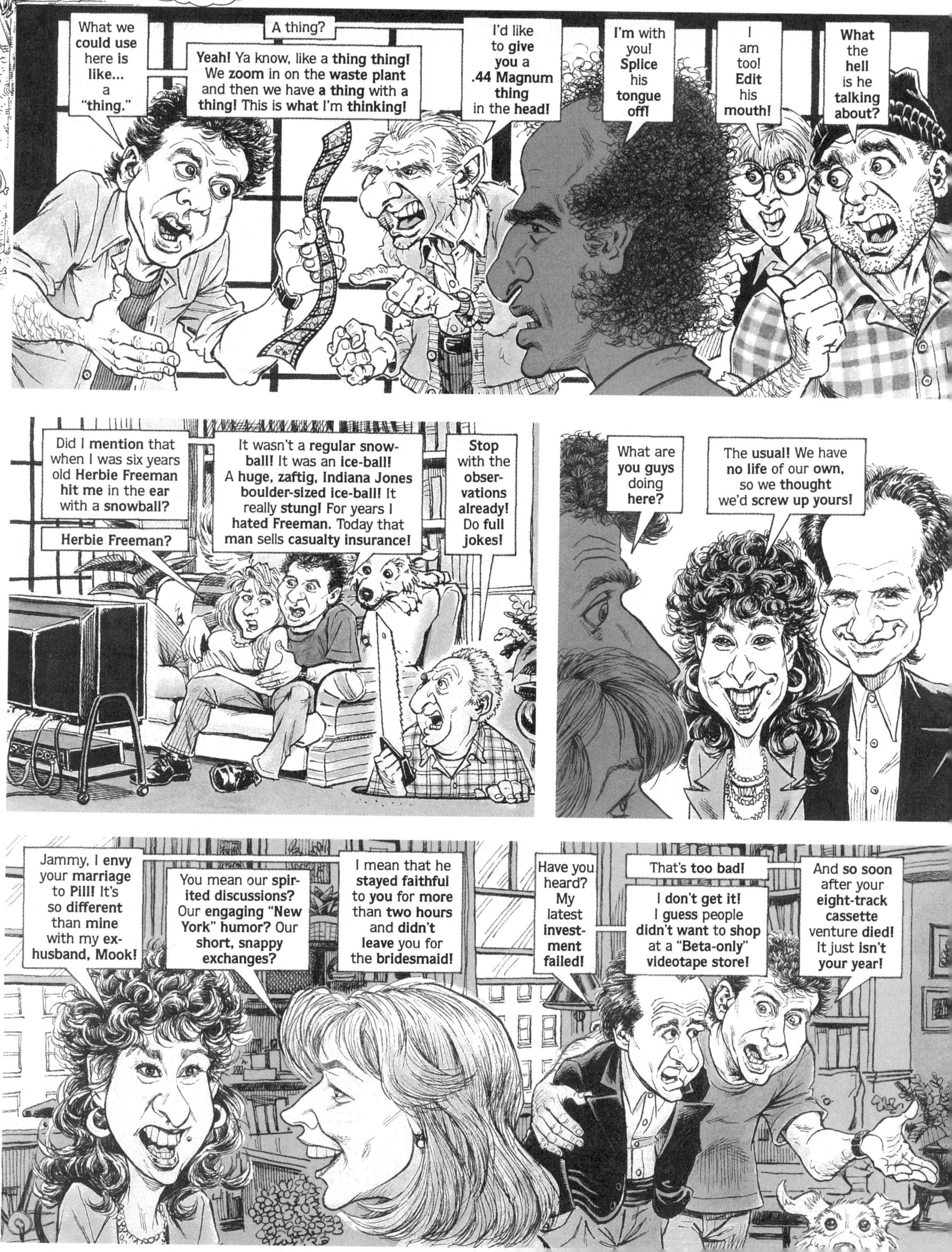

What we could use here is like... a "thing."
A thing?
Yeah! Ya know, like a thing thing! We zoom in on the waste plant and then we have a thing with a thing! This is what I'm thinking!
I'd like to give you a .44 Magnum thing in the head!
I'm with you! Splice his tongue off!
I am too! Edit his mouth!
What the hell is he talking about?
Did I mention that when I was six years old Herbie Freeman hit me in the ear with a snowball?
Herbie Freeman?
It wasn't a regular snow-ball! It was an ice-ball! A huge, zaftig, Indiana Jones boulder-sized ice-ball! It really stung! For years I hated Freeman. Today that man sells casualty insurance!
Stop with the obser-vations already! Do full jokes!
What are you guys doing here?
The usual! We have no life of our own, so we thought we'd screw up yours!
Jammy, I envy your marriage to Pill! It's so different than mine with my ex-husband, Mook!
You mean our spir-ited discussions? Our engaging "New York" humor? Our short, snappy exchanges?
I mean that he stayed faithful to you for more than two hours and didn't leave you for the bridesmaid!
Have you heard? My latest invest-ment failed!
That's too bad!
I don't get it! I guess people didn't want to shop at a "Beta-only" videotape store!
And so soon after your eight-track cassette venture died! It just isn't your year!

YOU KNOW AMERICA'S BEEN NUKED WHEN: You ask Elle Macpherson to have sex with you and she says "Yes."

YOU KNOW AMERICA'S BEEN NUKED WHEN: People are running through the streets rioting and looting even though no racially-charged trial verdict has been handed down.

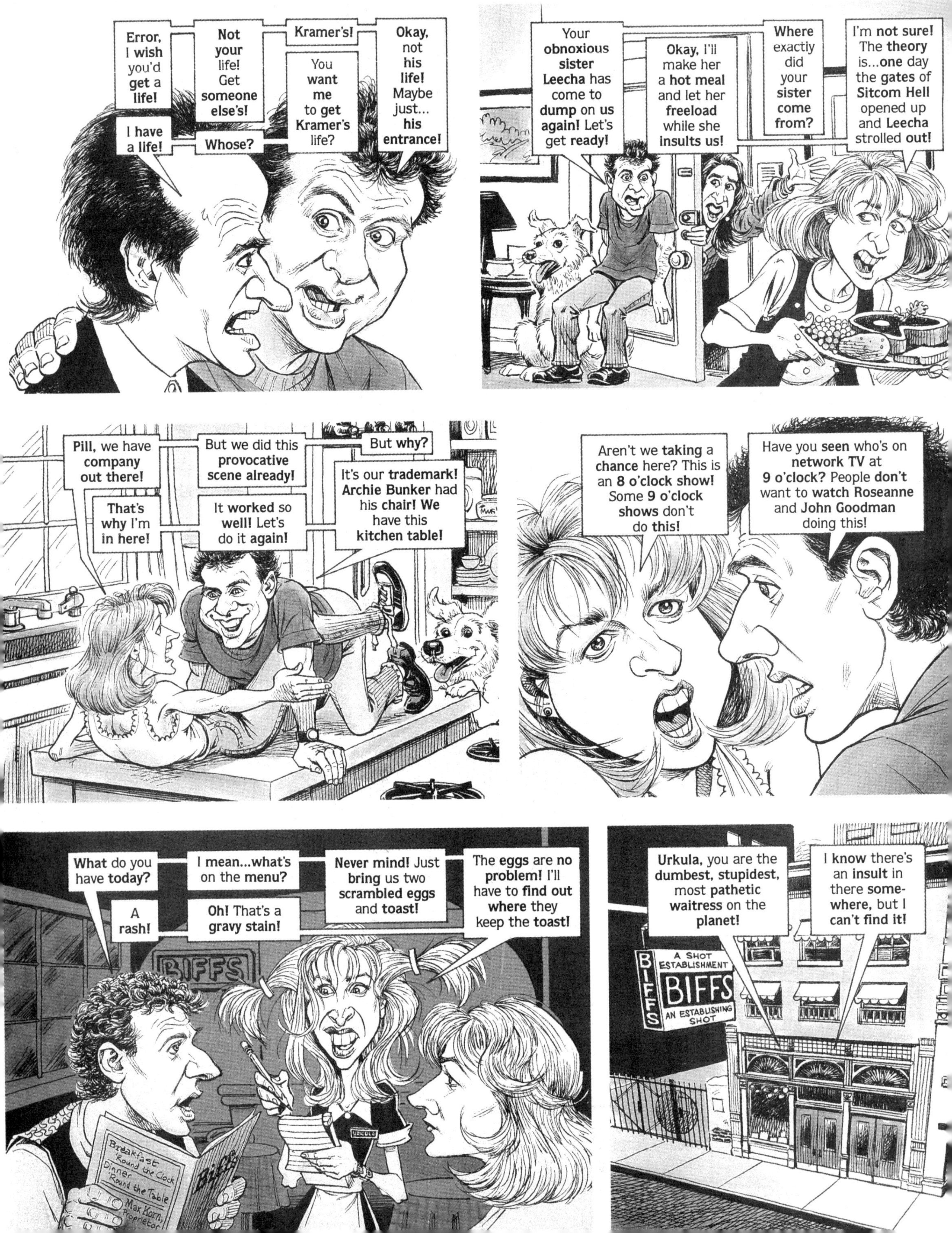

Error, I wish you'd get a life!
I have a life!
Not your life! Get someone else's!
Whose?
Kramer's!
You want me to get Kramer's life?
Okay, not his life! Maybe just... his entrance!
Your obnoxious sister Leecha has come to dump on us again! Let's get ready!
Okay, I'll make her a hot meal and let her freeload while she insults us!
Where exactly did your sister come from?
I'm not sure! The theory is...one day the gates of Sitcom Hell opened up and Leecha strolled out!
Pill, we have company out there!
That's why I'm in here!
But we did this provocative scene already!
It worked so well! Let's do it again!
But why?
It's our trademark! Archie Bunker had his chair! We have this kitchen table!
Aren't we taking a chance here? This is an 8 o'clock show! Some 9 o'clock shows don't do this!
Have you seen who's on network TV at 9 o'clock? People don't want to watch Roseanne and John Goodman doing this!
What do you have today?
A rash!
I mean...what's on the menu?
Oh! That's a gravy stain!
Never mind! Just bring us two scrambled eggs and toast!
The eggs are no problem! I'll have to find out where they keep the toast!
BIFFS
Breakfast 'Round the Clock
Dinner 'Round the Table
Max Korn, Proprietor
Biffs
URKULA
Urkula, you are the dumbest, stupidest, most pathetic waitress on the planet!
I know there's an insult in there some-where, but I can't find it!
BIFFS
A SHOT ESTABLISHMENT
BIFFS
AN ESTABLISHING SHOT

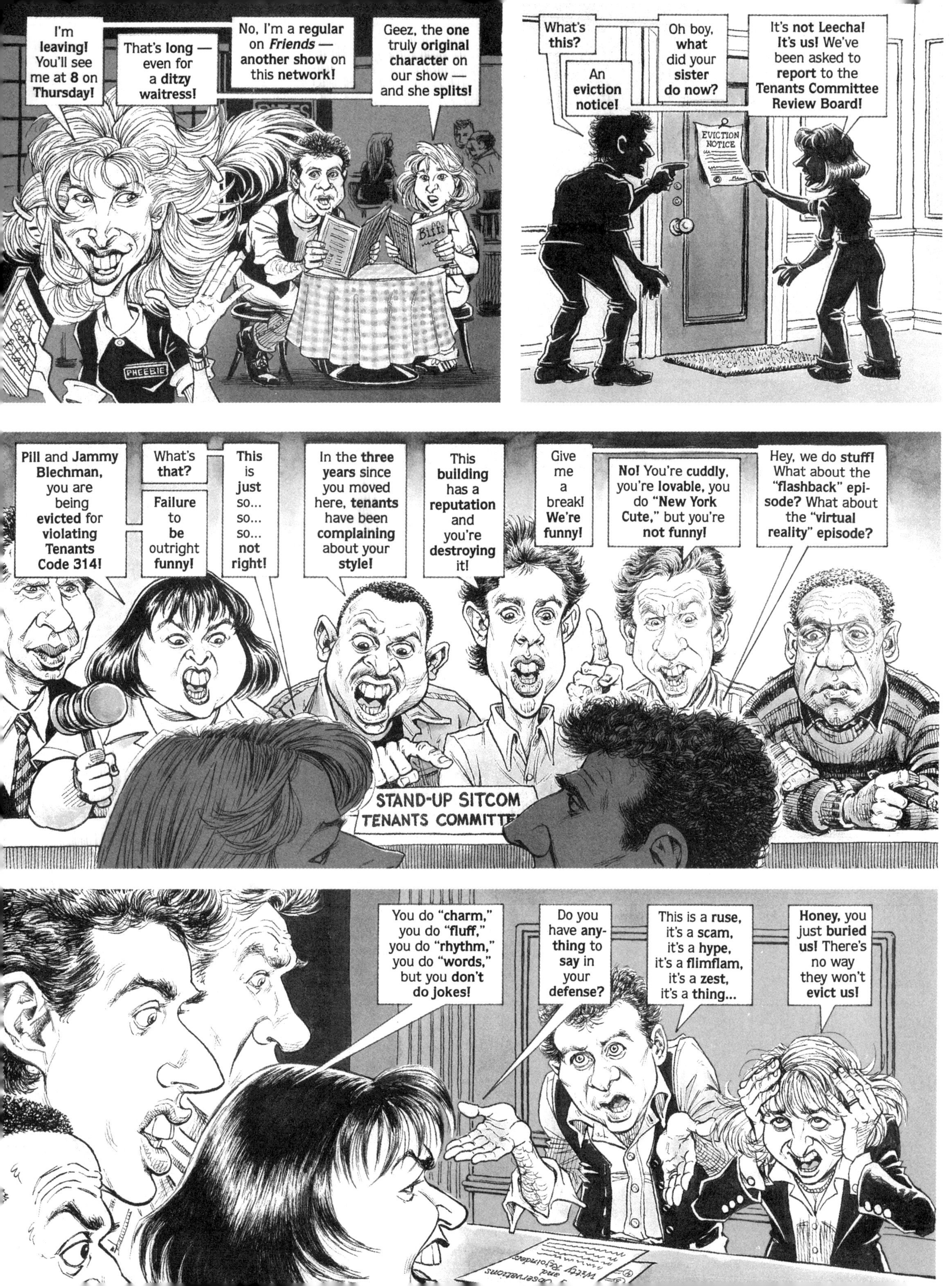
I'm leaving! You'll see me at 8 on Thursday!
That's long — even for a ditzy waitress!
No, I'm a regular on Friends — another show on this network!
Geez, the one truly original character on our show — and she splits!
PHEEBIE
Biffs
What's this?
An eviction notice!
Oh boy, what did your sister do now?
It's not Leecha! It's us! We've been asked to report to the Tenants Committee Review Board!
EVICTION NOTICE
Pill and Jammy Blechman, you are being evicted for violating Tenants Code 314!
What's that?
Failure to be outright funny!
This is just so... so... so... not right!
In the three years since you moved here, tenants have been complaining about your style!
This building has a reputation and you're destroying it!
Give me a break! We're funny!
No! You're cuddly, you're lovable, you do "New York Cute," but you're not funny!
Hey, we do stuff! What about the "flashback" episode? What about the "virtual reality" episode?
STAND-UP SITCOM TENANTS COMMITTE
You do "charm," you do "fluff," you do "rhythm," you do "words," but you don't do jokes!
Do you have anything to say in your defense?
This is a ruse, it's a scam, it's a hype, it's a flimflam, it's a zest, it's a thing...
Honey, you just buried us! There's no way they won't evict us!

EVERYBODY WANTS TO FOOL THE WORLD DEPT.

Okay MAD fans, Get out your dictionary and your guide to obscure references, 'cause it's time...

DENNIS MILLER RANTS ABOUT DENNIS MILLER

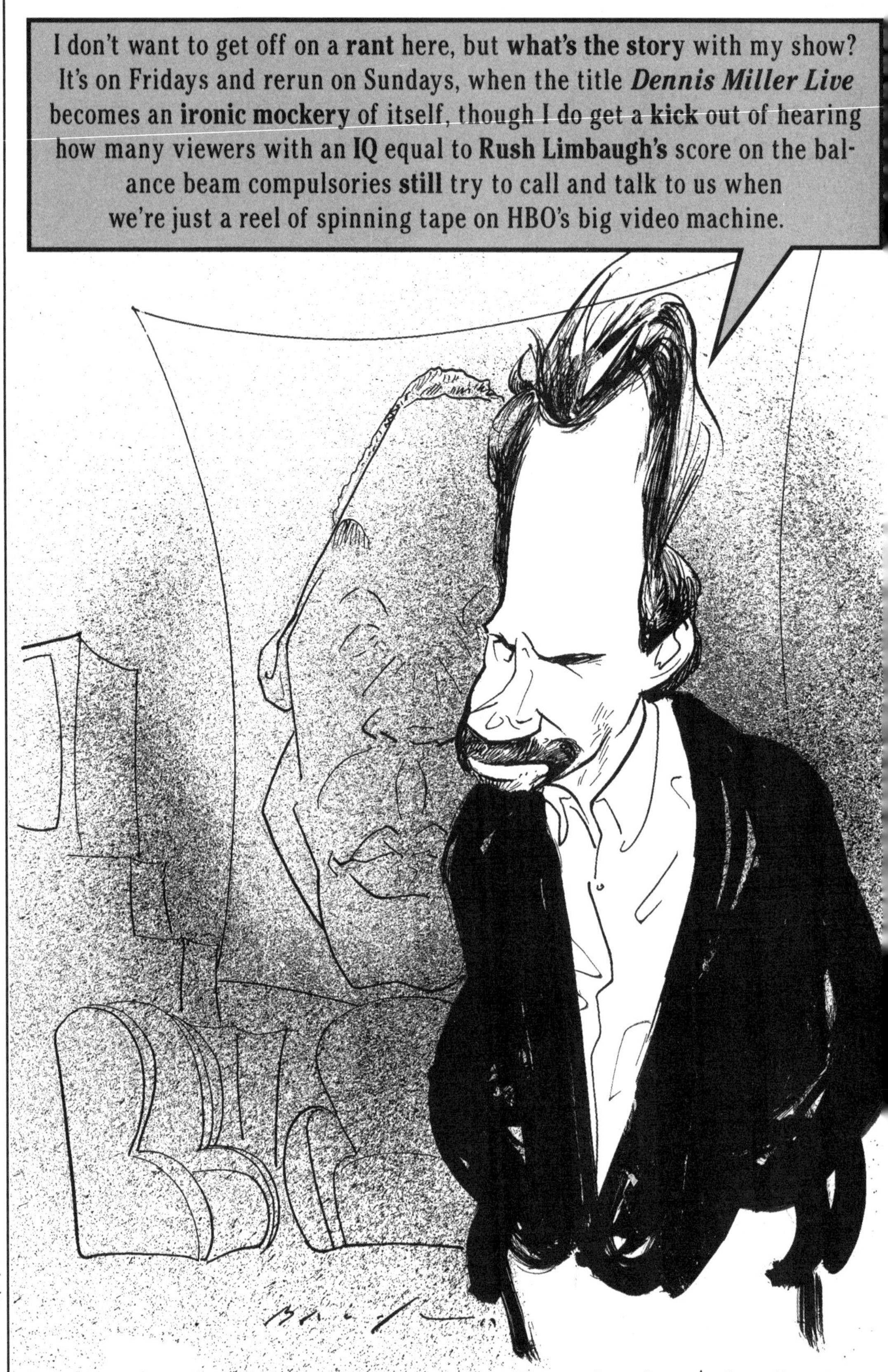
I don't want to get off on a **rant** here, but **what's the story** with my show? It's on Fridays and rerun on Sundays, when the title *Dennis Miller Live* becomes an **ironic mockery** of itself, though I do get a **kick** out of hearing how many viewers with an **IQ** equal to **Rush Limbaugh's** score on the balance beam compulsories **still** try to call and talk to us when we're just a reel of spinning tape on HBO's big video machine.

You know the drill: I come out, under-dressed and frequently unshaven to the audience's immediate Pavlovian reaction to the **applause sign** – without which, let's face it, our talk shows would be little more than a young **Martin Short** in his attic with a tape recorder. Yeah, the applause sign. If it wasn't here, our performer **egos** would be bruised more than a peach manhandled by **O.J.** in one of his flashback moods. That's something else I do: no matter how **tenuous** the connection, I always mention **The Juice** at least once a show so I can say, "You're a bad, bad man, O.J. A bad, bad, bad, bad man." Why? Because, it kills, which is, in itself, a semi-quasi joke if you really **ratchet up the magnification** on that petri dish I call my sense of humor.

ARTIST: STEVE BRODNER WRITER: BUTCH D'AMBROSIO

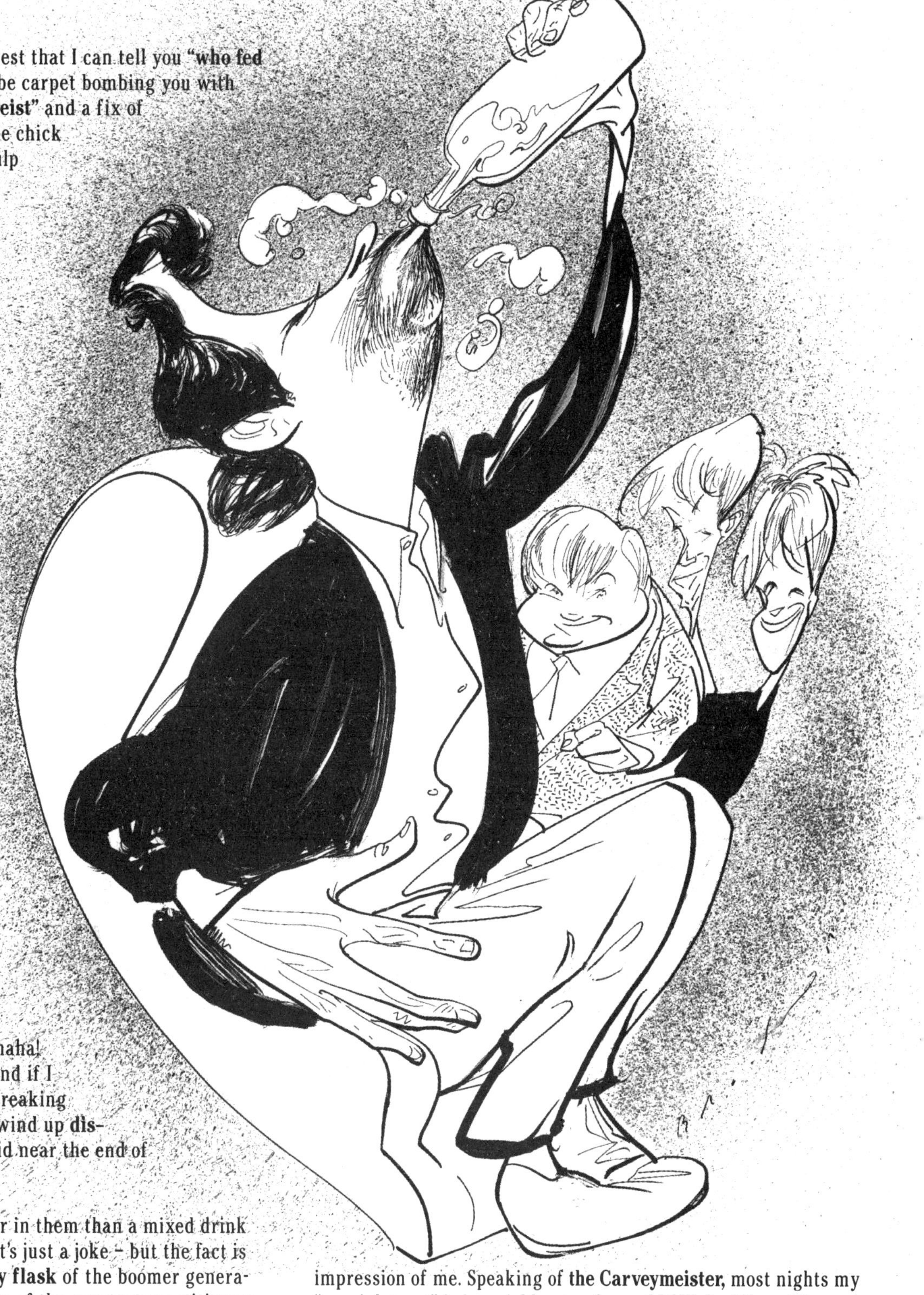

Next, I'm arrogant enough to suggest that I can tell you **"who fed it and who ate it."** In reality, I'll be carpet bombing you with payloads of big SAT words like **"zeitgeist"** and a fix of minutiae as **fabulously obscure** as the chick who sings the song on the radio in Pulp Fiction before **Bruce Willis** meets **The Gimp.** Truth be told, by the end of the show you still don't know who fed it and who ate it. I'm just espousing my pragmatic, utilitarian ideas and you're buying them like coke fiends buy tissues. You're running with the **bull#$%*** because between all the big words like "pragmatism" and "utilitarianism," I say stuff like **bull#$%***. I swear so much because, frankly, I want viewers, and I'm hoping some people might haphazardly channel-surf onto my program and think it's an all-white episode of Def Comedy Jam. Besides, it's in my contract, Babe.

And what's the deal with my **bottled water?** Seems like I'm sipping it, slugging it, or otherwise chugging it for a full 3 minutes out of every 28-minute show! Am I so busy I can't stop by the water cooler before I go on? Now, I don't want to get off on a diatribe here – you kids thought I was going to say **"rant,"** didn't you? Yeah, I know, a routine is called a "routine" for a reason. Ah hahaha! But the fact is I'm already **in** a rant, and if I started another one, I'd probably be breaking some **obscure metaphysical law** and wind up **dissolving** into myself like **Ron Silver** did near the end of *Timecop*.

Sure, all our bodies have more water in them than a mixed drink at the **Viper Room** – Deppy, baby, it's just a joke – but the fact is bottled water has become the **whiskey flask** of the boomer generation. And, I myself admit that I am one of the greatest practitioners of this self-induced, self-important anti-tap water **paranoia,** this belief that without a plastic bottle of that sparkling mineral mountain stream ménage à trois of Hydrogen and Oxygen known as **l'acqua,** you're nothing in everybody else's eyes. As **Freud** said, "Sometimes a cigar is just a cigar, but eight ounces of Evian is my way of showing you I'm well off enough to plunk down a buck twenty-five for each cool, clear, refreshing swig of put-out-the-fire water I swallow." **Besides,** each sip I take is one less joke we have to write!

After I finish the **"rant"** portion of the show I stand there, self-conciously shaking my head only slightly less than Dana Carvey's impression of me. Speaking of **the Carveymeister,** most nights my "special guest" is invariably one of my **old SNL buddies.** Like **Chris Farley.** I thank him for coming on and using my show to plug his new "road picture" with the Spadester. Or **David Spade.** I thank him for coming on and using my show to plug the remake of his previous "road picture" with the Farleycane. Farley, man! He's one funny, fat bastard, and I always loved watching him sweat over at 30 Rock. I love those guys. **I really do.** Actually, I have to say that because I'm beholden to **Lorne Michaels** to have someone from every one of his little SNL spinoff projects on to **shill away**, because they say I copped his **"Weekend Update"** and turned it into my **"Big Screen."** Which is absolutely not true. There I sat behind a desk. Here I stand in front of a big TV!

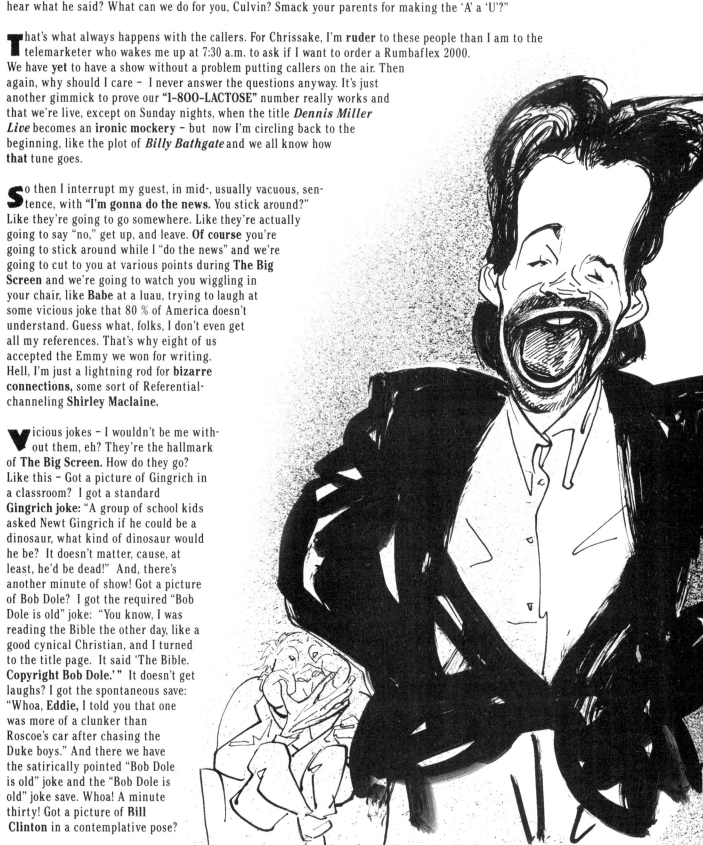

Then, I ask you, why do we **always** do the next part of the show exactly the same way when it never works? You know: after a couple of minutes of trying to talk to my guest about the week's "topic," which is only slightly more difficult than **Sisyphus** trying to get that stone up the hill, what do we do? Go to callers. Here's what it sounds like – "Okay, we got a caller. Line 2. Culvin Mushnick, watching in Fresno. How you doing out there in Fresno tonight, Culv? They still got that great little rib joint, Slimbo's, there? Great #$&*ing carrion for the carnivores." "I'm fine, Dennis. I just wanted to say I love your show and –" **"What's your $#%@ing question, Culvin?"** "I think you're the funniest, most intelligent person on TV and –" "Hey, so do I, now, what's your question?" "(Crackle crackle) thinks if (fuzz crackle) euthanasia (crackle click)–" "Culv, you out there? What happened? Did you hear what he said? What can we do for you, Culvin? Smack your parents for making the 'A' a 'U'?"

That's what always happens with the callers. For Chrissake, I'm **ruder** to these people than I am to the telemarketer who wakes me up at 7:30 a.m. to ask if I want to order a Rumbaflex 2000. We have **yet** to have a show without a problem putting callers on the air. Then again, why should I care – I never answer the questions anyway. It's just another gimmick to prove our **"1-800-LACTOSE"** number really works and that we're live, except on Sunday nights, when the title *Dennis Miller Live* becomes an **ironic mockery** – but now I'm circling back to the beginning, like the plot of *Billy Bathgate* and we all know how **that** tune goes.

So then I interrupt my guest, in mid-, usually vacuous, sentence, with **"I'm gonna do the news.** You stick around?" Like they're going to go somewhere. Like they're actually going to say "no," get up, and leave. **Of course** you're going to stick around while I "do the news" and we're going to cut to you at various points during **The Big Screen** and we're going to watch you wiggling in your chair, like **Babe** at a luau, trying to laugh at some vicious joke that 80 % of America doesn't understand. Guess what, folks, I don't even get all my references. That's why eight of us accepted the Emmy we won for writing. Hell, I'm just a lightning rod for **bizarre connections,** some sort of Referential-channeling **Shirley Maclaine.**

Vicious jokes – I wouldn't be me without them, eh? They're the hallmark of **The Big Screen.** How do they go? Like this – Got a picture of Gingrich in a classroom? I got a standard **Gingrich joke:** "A group of school kids asked Newt Gingrich if he could be a dinosaur, what kind of dinosaur would he be? It doesn't matter, cause, at least, he'd be dead!" And, there's another minute of show! Got a picture of Bob Dole? I got the required "Bob Dole is old" joke: "You know, I was reading the Bible the other day, like a good cynical Christian, and I turned to the title page. It said 'The Bible. **Copyright Bob Dole.'** " It doesn't get laughs? I got the spontaneous save: "Whoa, **Eddie,** I told you that one was more of a clunker than Roscoe's car after chasing the Duke boys." And there we have the satirically pointed "Bob Dole is old" joke and the "Bob Dole is old" joke save. Whoa! A minute thirty! Got a picture of **Bill Clinton** in a contemplative pose?

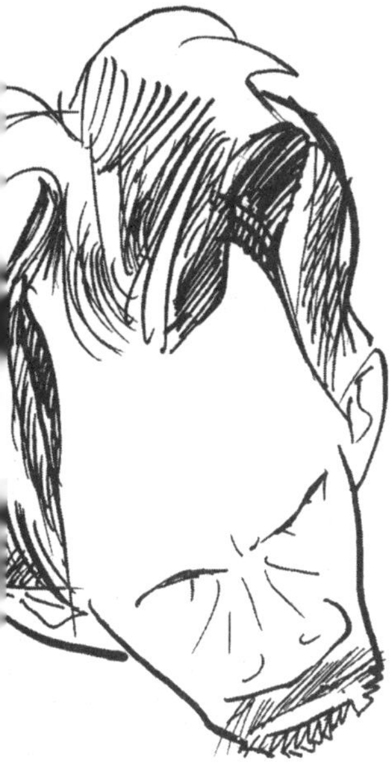

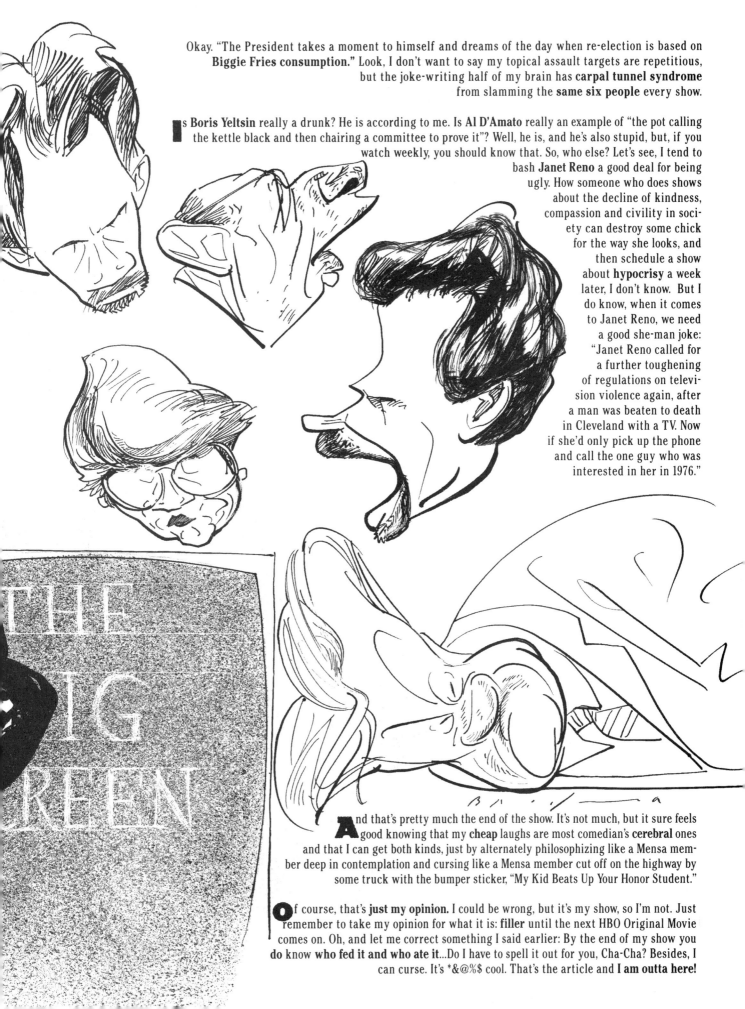

Okay. "The President takes a moment to himself and dreams of the day when re-election is based on **Biggie Fries consumption."** Look, I don't want to say my topical assault targets are repetitious, but the joke-writing half of my brain has **carpal tunnel syndrome** from slamming the **same six people** every show.

Is **Boris Yeltsin** really a drunk? He is according to me. Is **Al D'Amato** really an example of "the pot calling the kettle black and then chairing a committee to prove it"? Well, he is, and he's also stupid, but, if you watch weekly, you should know that. So, who else? Let's see, I tend to bash **Janet Reno** a good deal for being ugly. How someone who does shows about the decline of kindness, compassion and civility in society can destroy some chick for the way she looks, and then schedule a show about **hypocrisy** a week later, I don't know. But I do know, when it comes to Janet Reno, we need a good she-man joke: "Janet Reno called for a further toughening of regulations on television violence again, after a man was beaten to death in Cleveland with a TV. Now if she'd only pick up the phone and call the one guy who was interested in her in 1976."

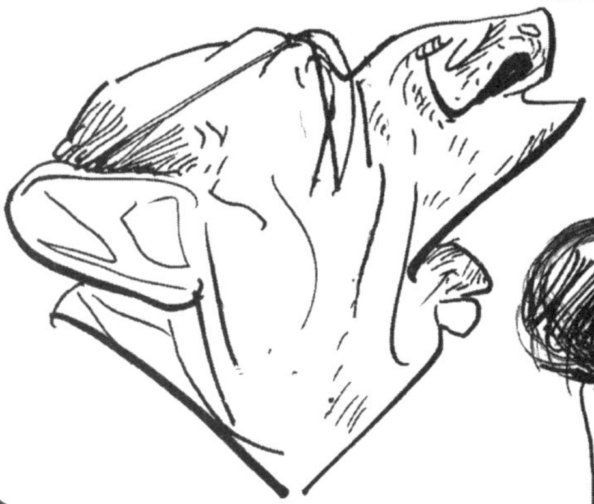

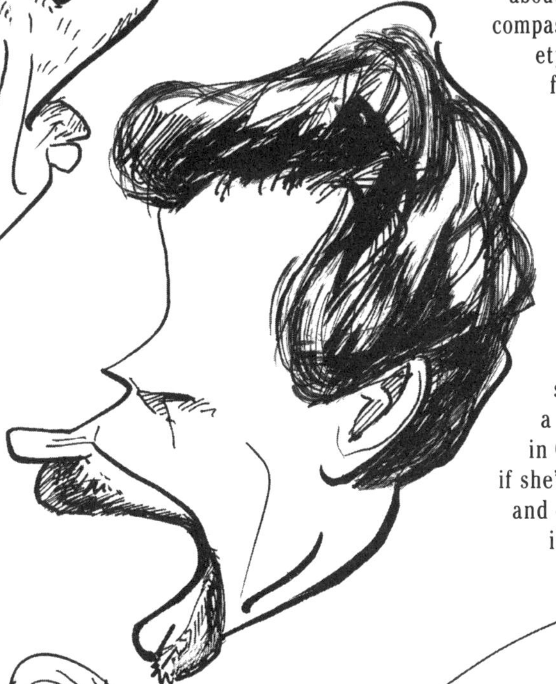

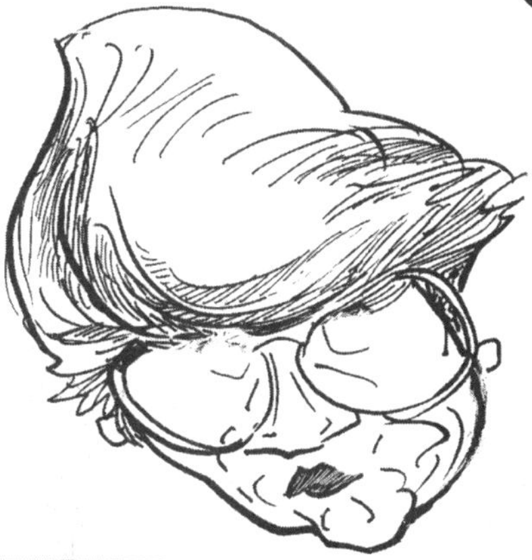

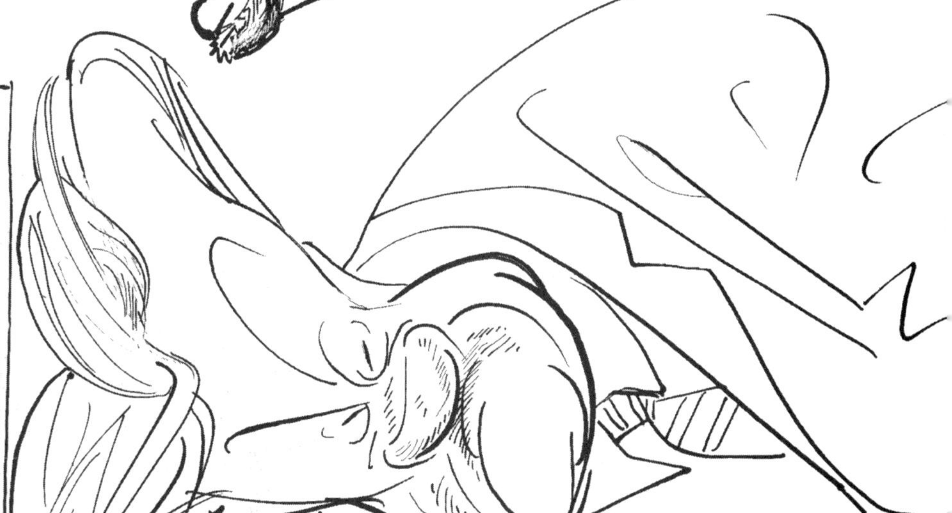

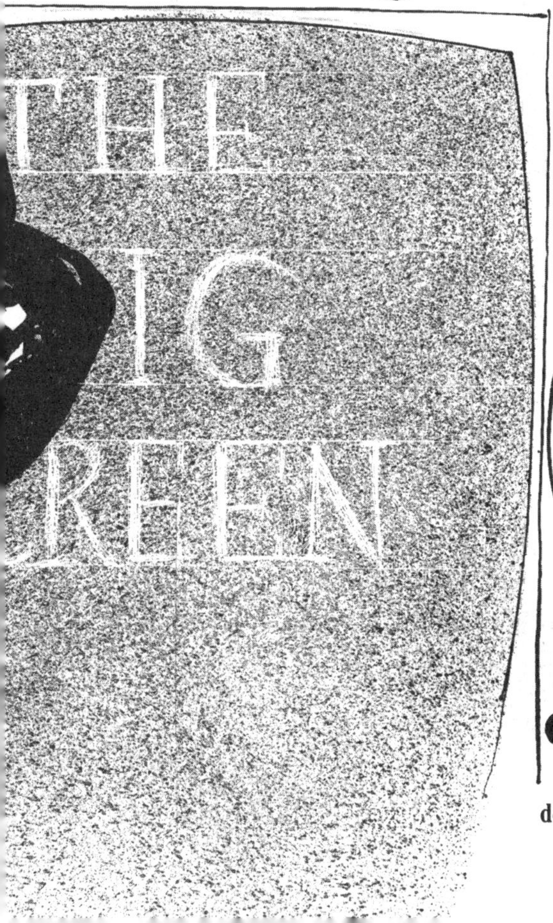
THE
IG
REEN

And that's pretty much the end of the show. It's not much, but it sure feels good knowing that my **cheap** laughs are most comedian's **cerebral** ones and that I can get both kinds, just by alternately philosophizing like a Mensa member deep in contemplation and cursing like a Mensa member cut off on the highway by some truck with the bumper sticker, "My Kid Beats Up Your Honor Student."

Of course, that's **just my opinion.** I could be wrong, but it's my show, so I'm not. Just remember to take my opinion for what it is: **filler** until the next HBO Original Movie comes on. Oh, and let me correct something I said earlier: By the end of my show you **do know who fed it and who ate it**...Do I have to spell it out for you, Cha-Cha? Besides, I can curse. It's *&@%$ cool. That's the article and **I am outta here!**

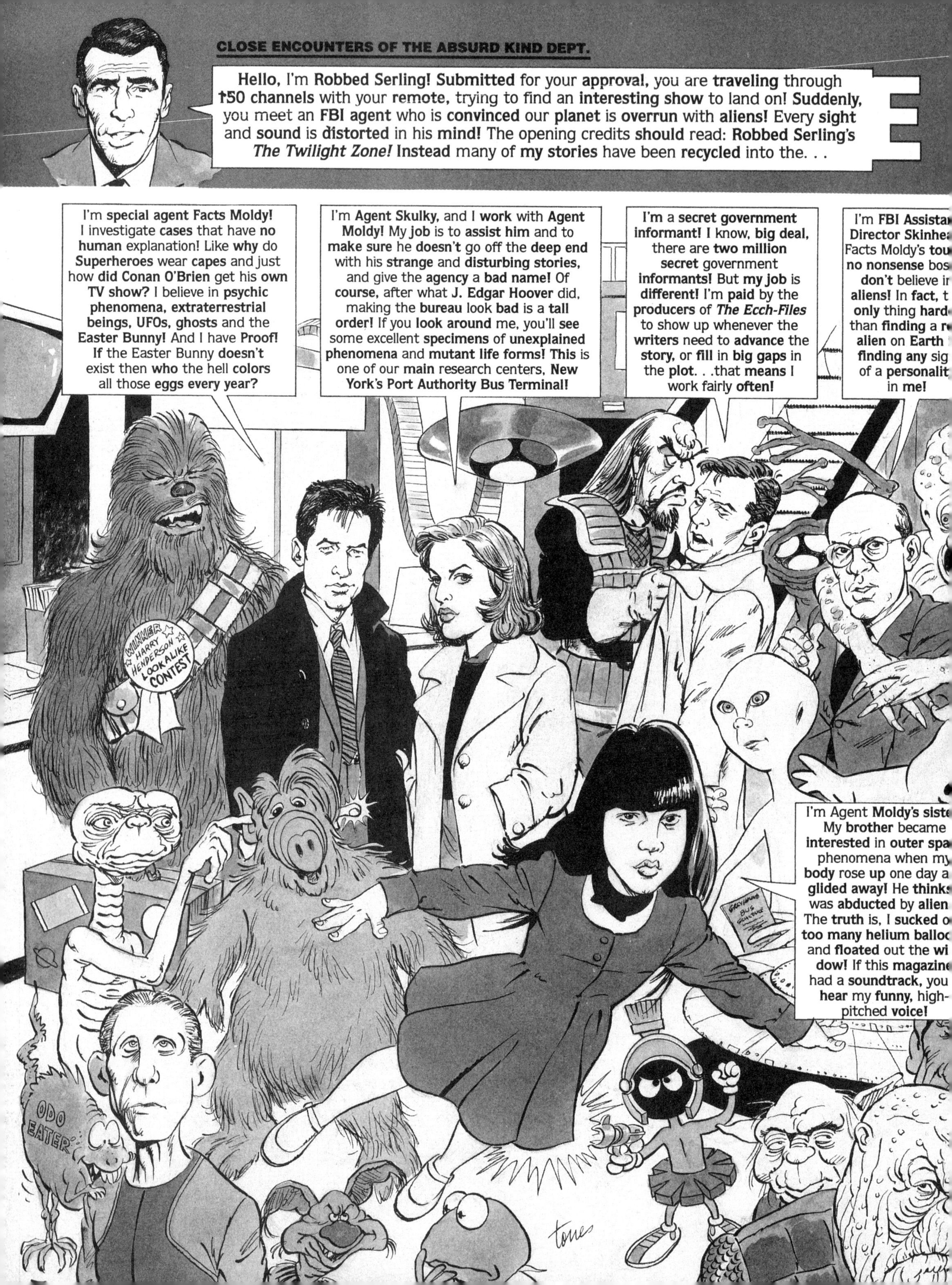

CLOSE ENCOUNTERS OF THE ABSURD KIND DEPT.
Hello, I'm Robbed Serling! Submitted for your approval, you are traveling through 150 channels with your remote, trying to find an interesting show to land on! Suddenly, you meet an FBI agent who is convinced our planet is overrun with aliens! Every sight and sound is distorted in his mind! The opening credits should read: Robbed Serling's *The Twilight Zone!* Instead many of my stories have been recycled into the. . .
I'm special agent Facts Moldy! I investigate cases that have no human explanation! Like why do Superheroes wear capes and just how did Conan O'Brien get his own TV show? I believe in psychic phenomena, extraterrestrial beings, UFOs, ghosts and the Easter Bunny! And I have Proof! If the Easter Bunny doesn't exist then who the hell colors all those eggs every year?
I'm Agent Skulky, and I work with Agent Moldy! My job is to assist him and to make sure he doesn't go off the deep end with his strange and disturbing stories, and give the agency a bad name! Of course, after what J. Edgar Hoover did, making the bureau look bad is a tall order! If you look around me, you'll see some excellent specimens of unexplained phenomena and mutant life forms! This is one of our main research centers, New York's Port Authority Bus Terminal!
I'm a secret government informant! I know, big deal, there are two million secret government informants! But my job is different! I'm paid by the producers of *The Ecch-Files* to show up whenever the writers need to advance the story, or fill in big gaps in the plot. . .that means I work fairly often!
I'm FBI Assista Director Skinhe Facts Moldy's tou no nonsense bos don't believe ir aliens! In fact, t only thing hard than finding a r alien on Earth finding any sig of a personalit in me!
WINNER HARRY HENDERSON LOOK ALIKE CONTEST
I'm Agent Moldy's siste My brother became interested in outer spa phenomena when my body rose up one day a glided away! He think was abducted by alien The truth is, I sucked o too many helium ballo and floated out the wi dow! If this magazine had a soundtrack, you hear my funny, high-pitched voice!
ODO EATER
torres

CH-FILES

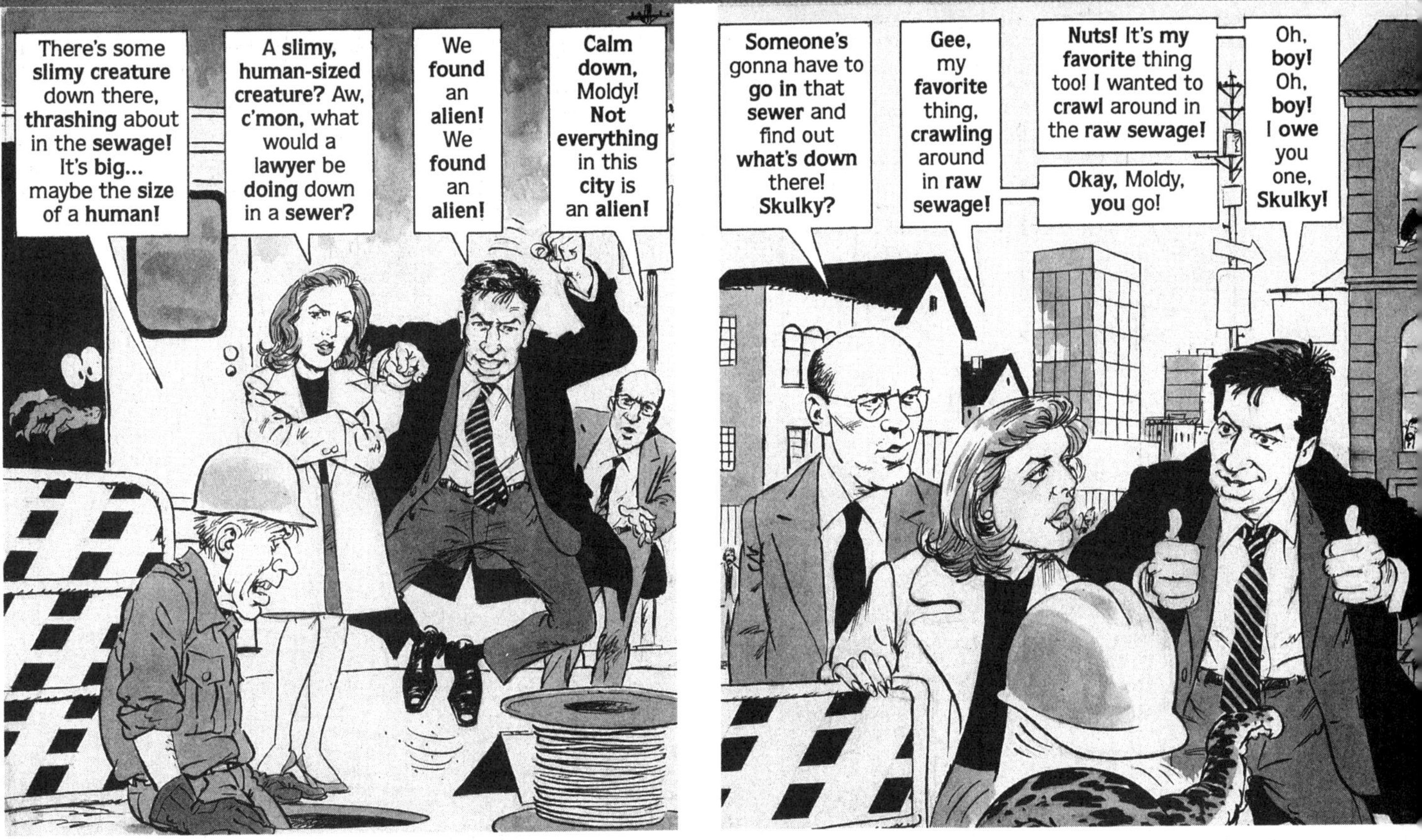

There's some slimy creature down there, thrashing about in the sewage! It's big... maybe the size of a human!
A slimy, human-sized creature? Aw, c'mon, what would a lawyer be doing down in a sewer?
We found an alien! We found an alien!
Calm down, Moldy! Not everything in this city is an alien!
Someone's gonna have to go in that sewer and find out what's down there! Skulky?
Gee, my favorite thing, crawling around in raw sewage!
Nuts! It's my favorite thing too! I wanted to crawl around in the raw sewage!
Okay, Moldy, you go!
Oh, boy! Oh, boy! I owe you one, Skulky!

ARTIST: ANGELO TORRES WRITER: DICK DEBARTOLO

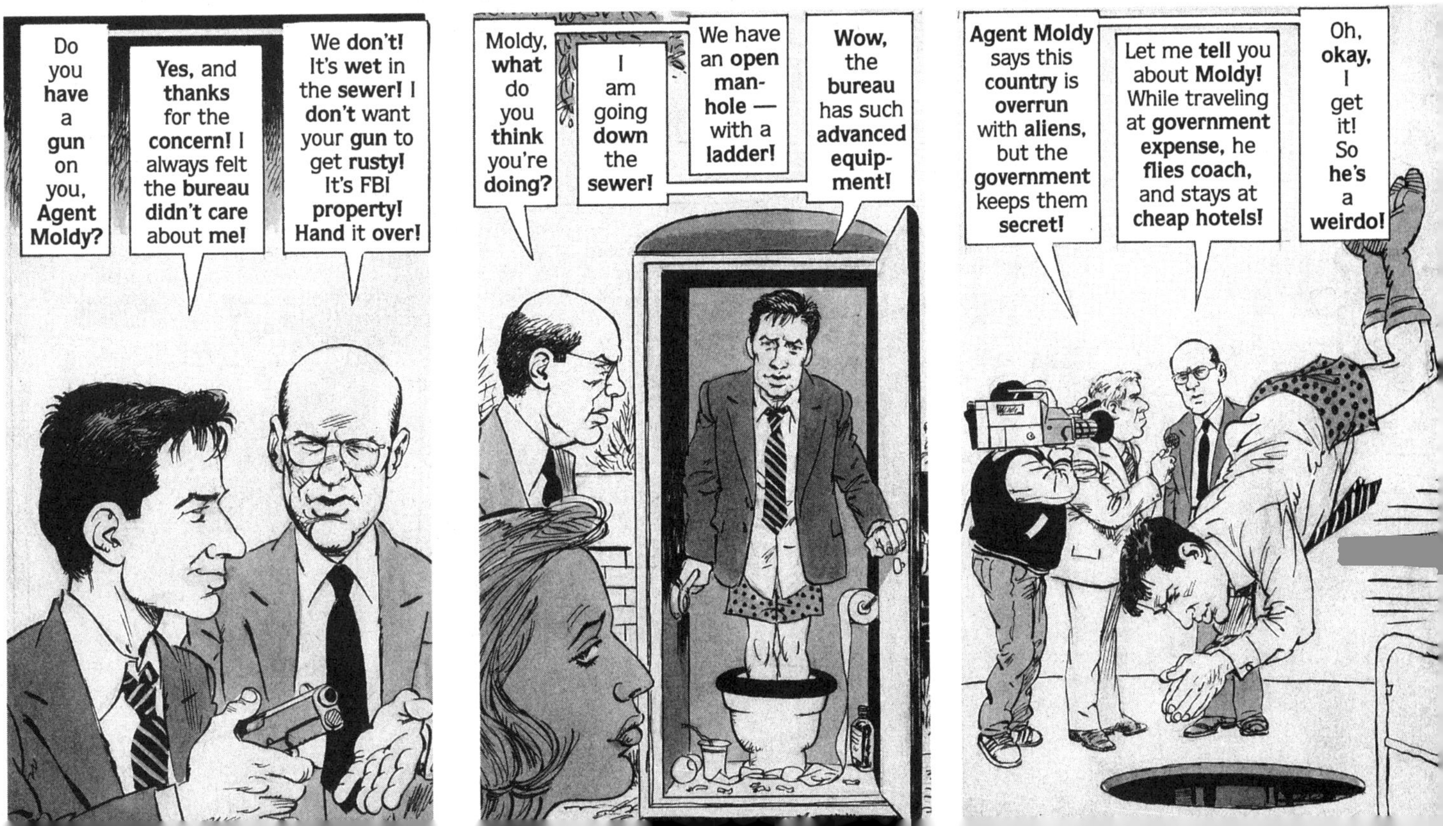

Do you have a gun on you, Agent Moldy?
Yes, and thanks for the concern! I always felt the bureau didn't care about me!
We don't! It's wet in the sewer! I don't want your gun to get rusty! It's FBI property! Hand it over!
Moldy, what do you think you're doing?
I am going down the sewer!
We have an open man-hole — with a ladder!
Wow, the bureau has such advanced equip-ment!
Agent Moldy says this country is overrun with aliens, but the government keeps them secret!
Let me tell you about Moldy! While traveling at government expense, he flies coach, and stays at cheap hotels!
Oh, okay, I get it! So he's a weirdo!

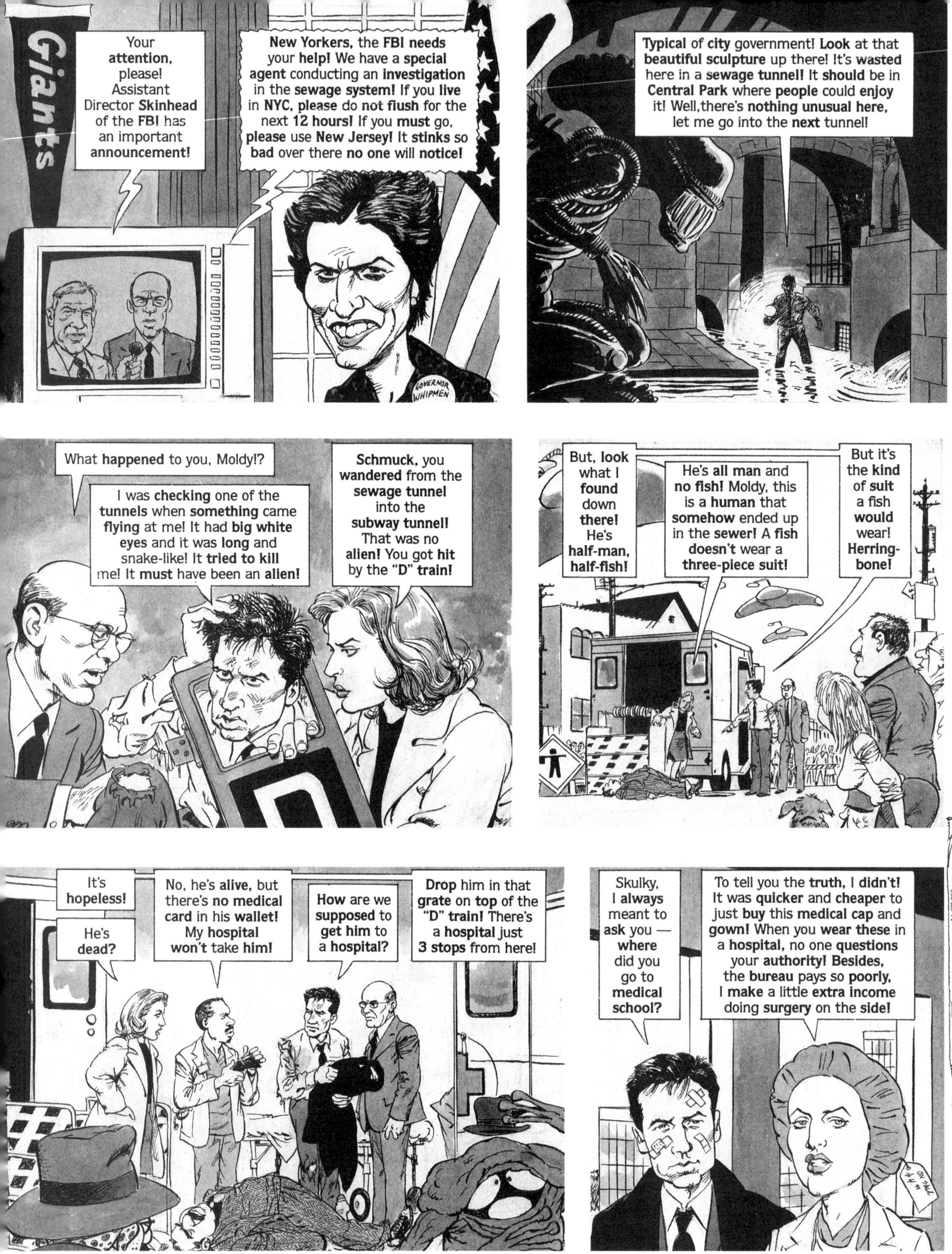
Giants
Your attention, please! Assistant Director Skinhead of the FBI has an important announcement!
New Yorkers, the FBI needs your help! We have a special agent conducting an investigation in the sewage system! If you live in NYC, please do not flush for the next 12 hours! If you must go, please use New Jersey! It stinks so bad over there no one will notice!
GOVERNOR WHIPMEN
Typical of city government! Look at that beautiful sculpture up there! It's wasted here in a sewage tunnel! It should be in Central Park where people could enjoy it! Well,there's nothing unusual here, let me go into the next tunnel!
What happened to you, Moldy!?
I was checking one of the tunnels when something came flying at me! It had big white eyes and it was long and snake-like! It tried to kill me! It must have been an alien!
Schmuck, you wandered from the sewage tunnel into the subway tunnel! That was no alien! You got hit by the "D" train!
But, look what I found down there! He's half-man, half-fish!
He's all man and no fish! Moldy, this is a human that somehow ended up in the sewer! A fish doesn't wear a three-piece suit!
But it's the kind of suit a fish would wear! Herring-bone!
It's hopeless!
He's dead?
No, he's alive, but there's no medical card in his wallet! My hospital won't take him!
How are we supposed to get him to a hospital?
Drop him in that grate on top of the "D" train! There's a hospital just 3 stops from here!
Skulky, I always meant to ask you — where did you go to medical school?
To tell you the truth, I didn't! It was quicker and cheaper to just buy this medical cap and gown! When you wear these in a hospital, no one questions your authority! Besides, the bureau pays so poorly, I make a little extra income doing surgery on the side!
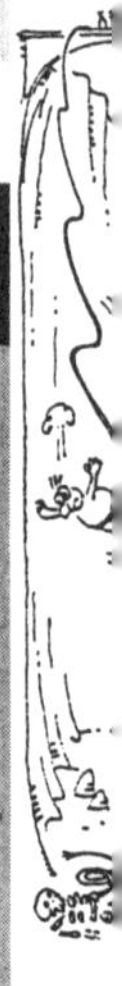
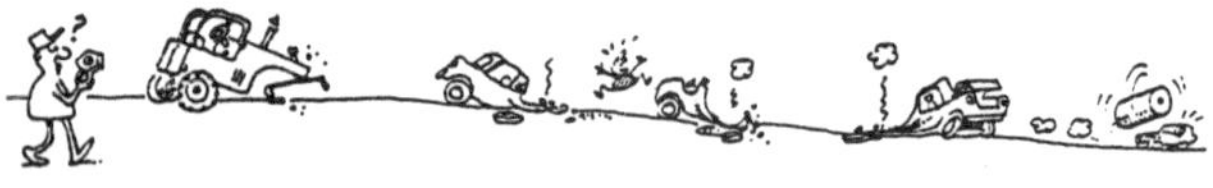

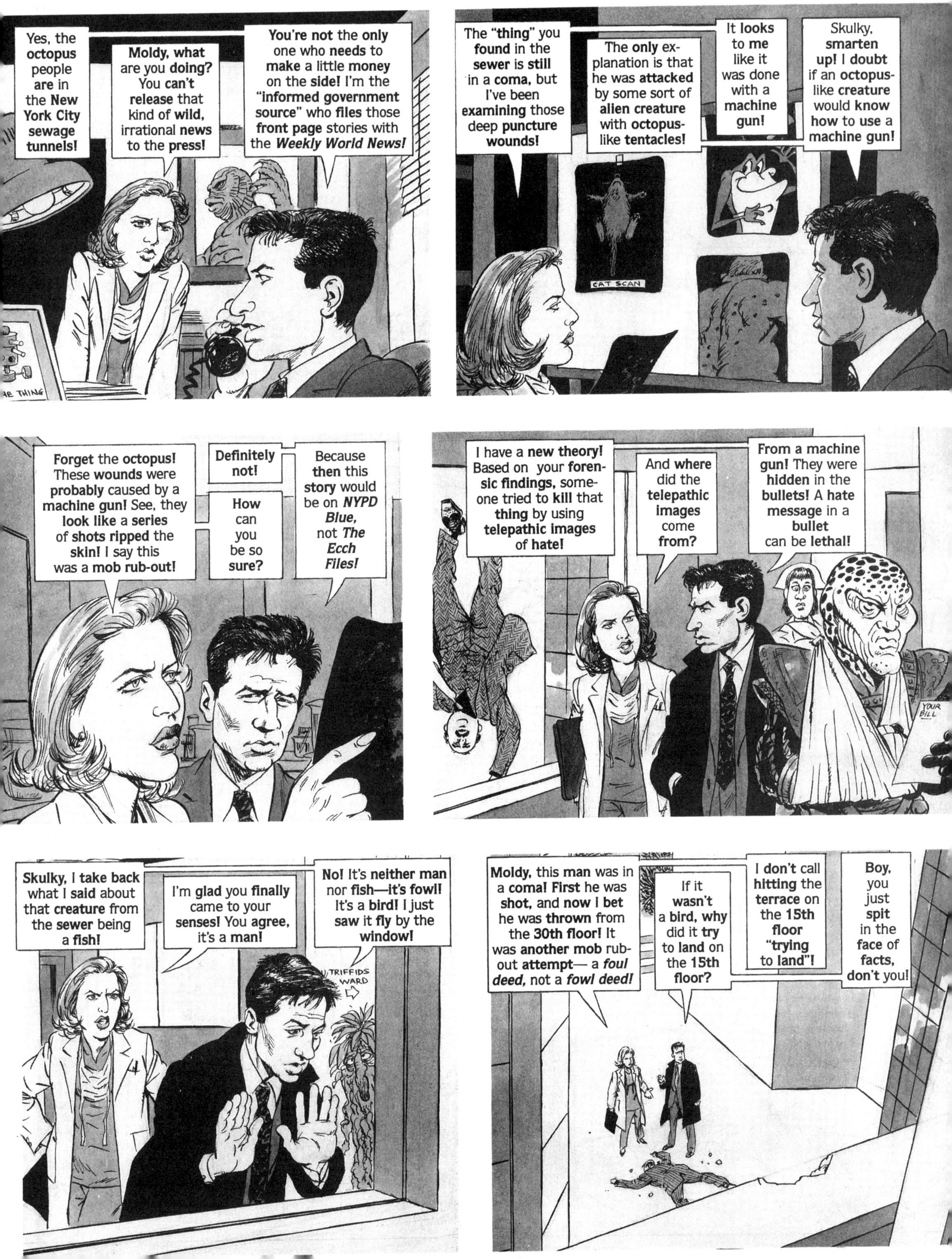

Yes, the octopus people are in the New York City sewage tunnels!
Moldy, what are you doing? You can't release that kind of wild, irrational news to the press!
You're not the only one who needs to make a little money on the side! I'm the "informed government source" who files those front page stories with the *Weekly World News!*
The "thing" you found in the sewer is still in a coma, but I've been examining those deep puncture wounds!
The only explanation is that he was attacked by some sort of alien creature with octopus-like tentacles!
CAT SCAN
It looks to me like it was done with a machine gun!
Skulky, smarten up! I doubt if an octopus-like creature would know how to use a machine gun!
Forget the octopus! These wounds were probably caused by a machine gun! See, they look like a series of shots ripped the skin! I say this was a mob rub-out!
Definitely not!
How can you be so sure?
Because then this story would be on *NYPD Blue,* not *The Ecch Files!*
I have a new theory! Based on your forensic findings, someone tried to kill that thing by using telepathic images of hate!
And where did the telepathic images come from?
From a machine gun! They were hidden in the bullets! A hate message in a bullet can be lethal!
YOUR BILL
Skulky, I take back what I said about that creature from the sewer being a fish!
I'm glad you finally came to your senses! You agree, it's a man!
No! It's neither man nor fish—it's fowl! It's a bird! I just saw it fly by the window!
TRIFFIDS WARD
Moldy, this man was in a coma! First he was shot, and now I bet he was thrown from the 30th floor! It was another mob rub-out attempt— a *foul deed,* not a *fowl deed!*
If it wasn't a bird, why did it try to land on the 15th floor?
I don't call hitting the terrace on the 15th floor "trying to land"!
Boy, you just spit in the face of facts, don't you!

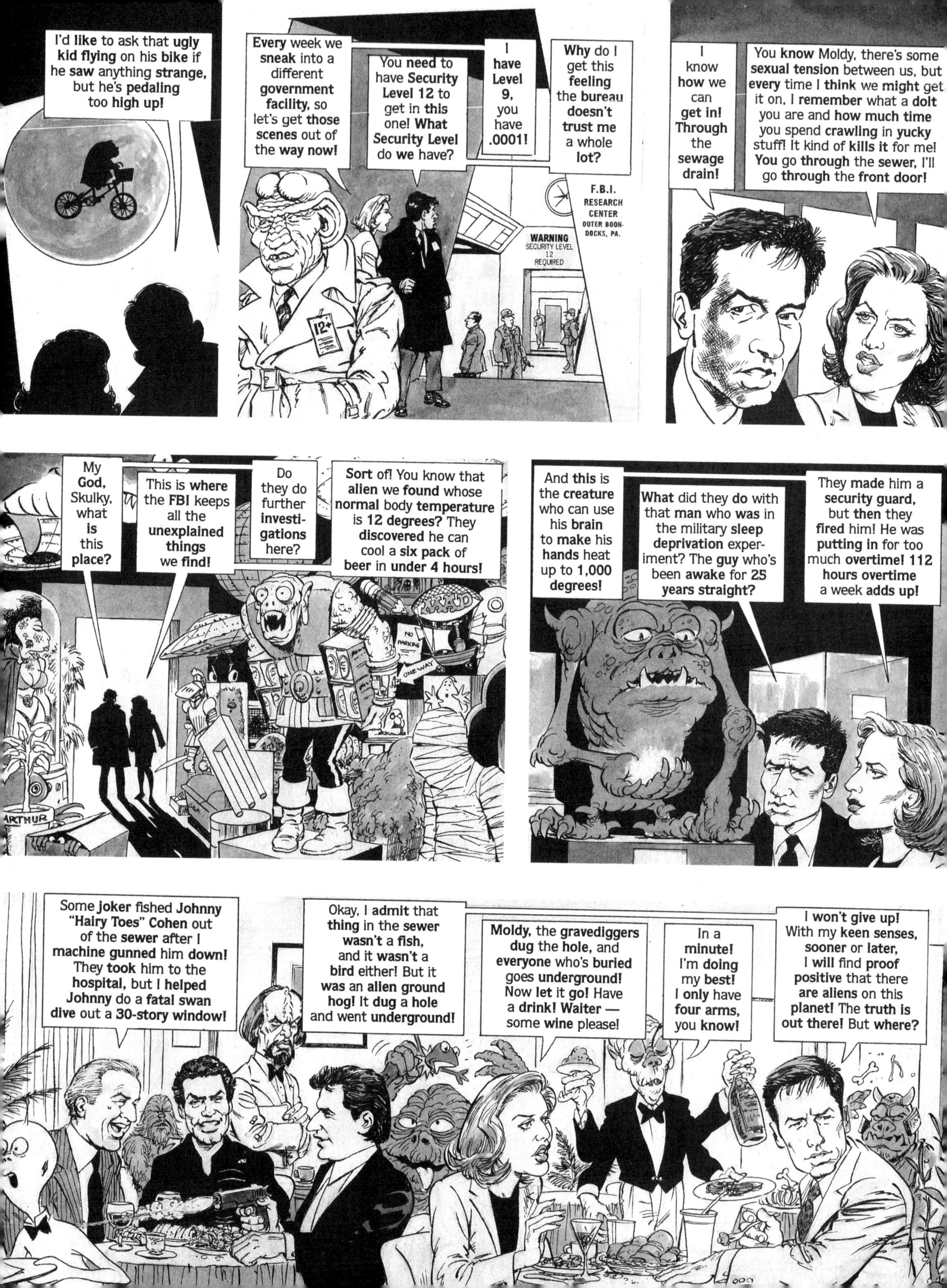
I'd like to ask that ugly kid flying on his bike if he saw anything strange, but he's pedaling too high up!
Every week we sneak into a different government facility, so let's get those scenes out of the way now!
You need to have Security Level 12 to get in this one! What Security Level do we have?
I have Level 9, you have .0001!
Why do I get this feeling the bureau doesn't trust me a whole lot?
F.B.I. RESEARCH CENTER OUTER BOONDOCKS, PA.
WARNING SECURITY LEVEL 12 REQUIRED
12+
I know how we can get in! Through the sewage drain!
You know Moldy, there's some sexual tension between us, but every time I think we might get it on, I remember what a dolt you are and how much time you spend crawling in yucky stuff! It kind of kills it for me! You go through the sewer, I'll go through the front door!
My God, Skulky, what is this place?
This is where the FBI keeps all the unexplained things we find!
Do they do further investigations here?
Sort of! You know that alien we found whose normal body temperature is 12 degrees? They discovered he can cool a six pack of beer in under 4 hours!
NO PARKING
ONE WAY
ARTHUR
And this is the creature who can use his brain to make his hands heat up to 1,000 degrees!
What did they do with that man who was in the military sleep deprivation experiment? The guy who's been awake for 25 years straight?
They made him a security guard, but then they fired him! He was putting in for too much overtime! 112 hours overtime a week adds up!
Some joker fished Johnny "Hairy Toes" Cohen out of the sewer after I machine gunned him down! They took him to the hospital, but I helped Johnny do a fatal swan dive out a 30-story window!
Okay, I admit that thing in the sewer wasn't a fish, and it wasn't a bird either! But it was an alien ground hog! It dug a hole and went underground!
Moldy, the gravediggers dug the hole, and everyone who's buried goes underground! Now let it go! Have a drink! Waiter — some wine please!
In a minute! I'm doing my best! I only have four arms, you know!
I won't give up! With my keen senses, sooner or later, I will find proof positive that there are aliens on this planet! The truth is out there! But where?

GAYWATCH DEPT.

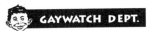

Now that Ellen DeGeneres' sitcom character, Ellen Morgan, has boldly proclaimed her gayness, we figure it won't be long before other programs use the same controversial gimmick to cash in on the ratings bonanza! Yup, it's sure to make for interesting viewing...

WHEN OTHER TV SHOWS FINALLY COME OUT OF THE CLOSET

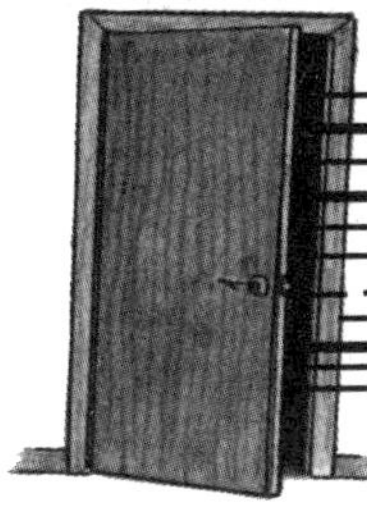

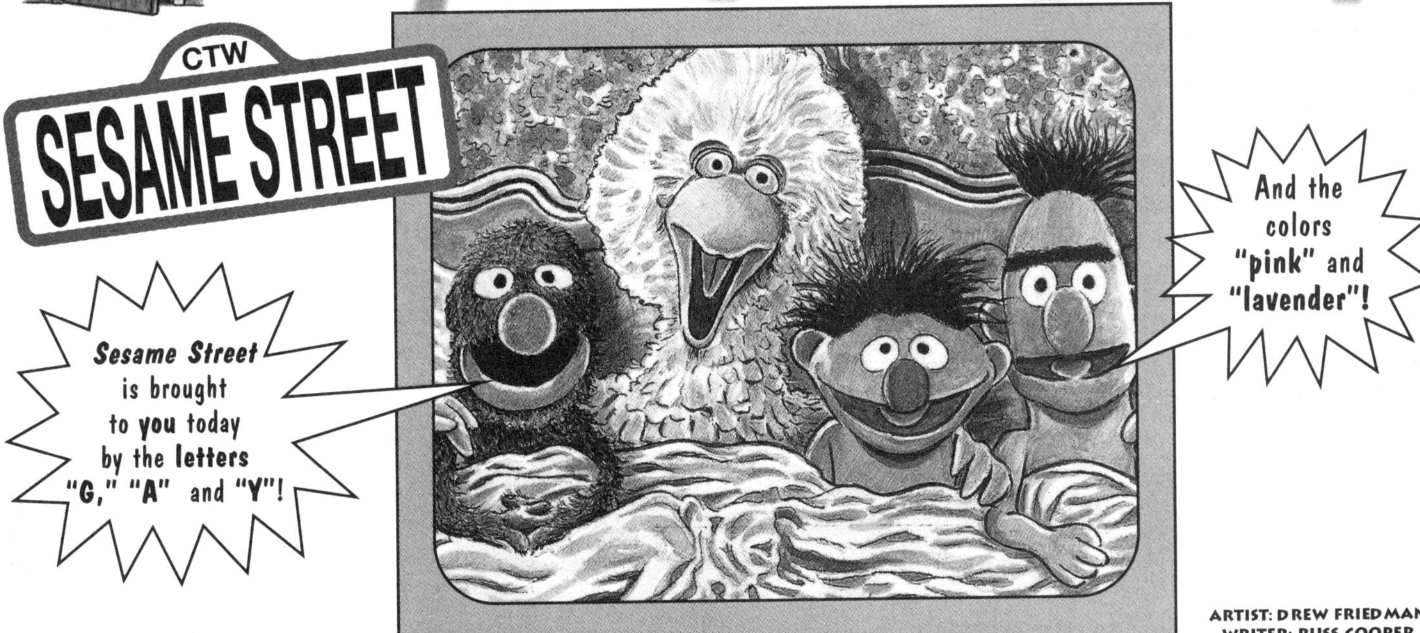
CTW
SESAME STREET
Sesame Street is brought to you today by the letters "G," "A" and "Y"!
And the colors "pink" and "lavender"!

ARTIST: DREW FRIEDMAN
WRITER: RUSS COOPER

LATE SHOW with David Letterman

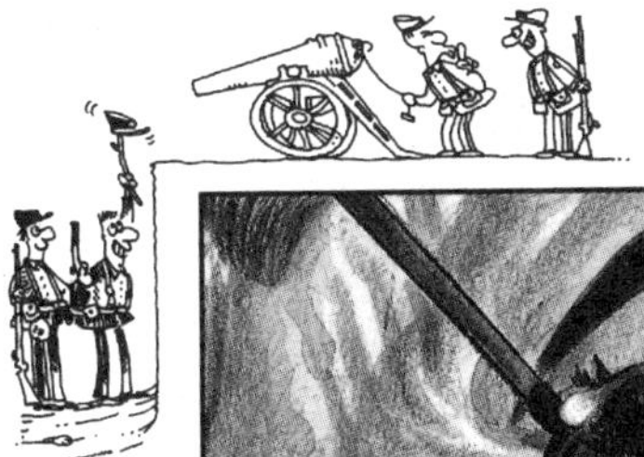

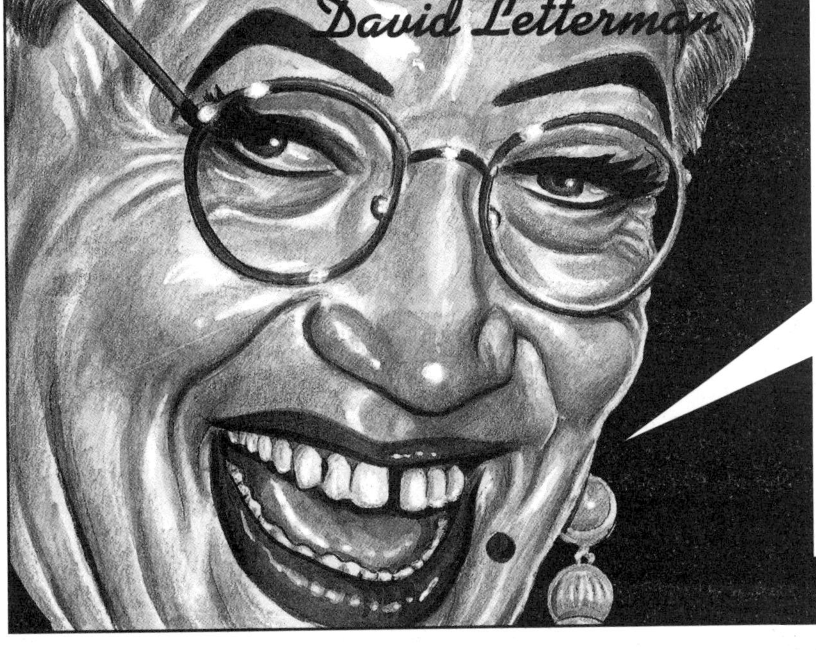

Here are the **Top 10 Changes** in *Late Show* now that I've **come out** of the **closet**:

10. **Home Office Moving to San Francisco**
9. **New Segment: Brush With RuPaul**
8. **The CBS Orchestra Now Playing All-Bette Midler Repertoire**
7. **A Lot More Mujibur and Sirajul, If You Know What We Mean!**
6. **New Nightly Feature: Can A Guy In A Bear Suit Get Into A Turkish Bath?**
5. **Two Words: Butt-Cam**
4. **Stupid Gay Tricks**
3. **From Now On, We'll Be Playing "May We See Your Homo-Erotic Photos, Please?"**
2. **Good-bye, Paul Schaffer – Hello, Elton John!**

And the **number one change** in *Late Show* now that I've **come out** of the **closet**:

1. **Mom Won't Take My Calls Anymore!**

WHEN OTHER TV SHOWS FINALLY COME OUT OF THE CLOSET

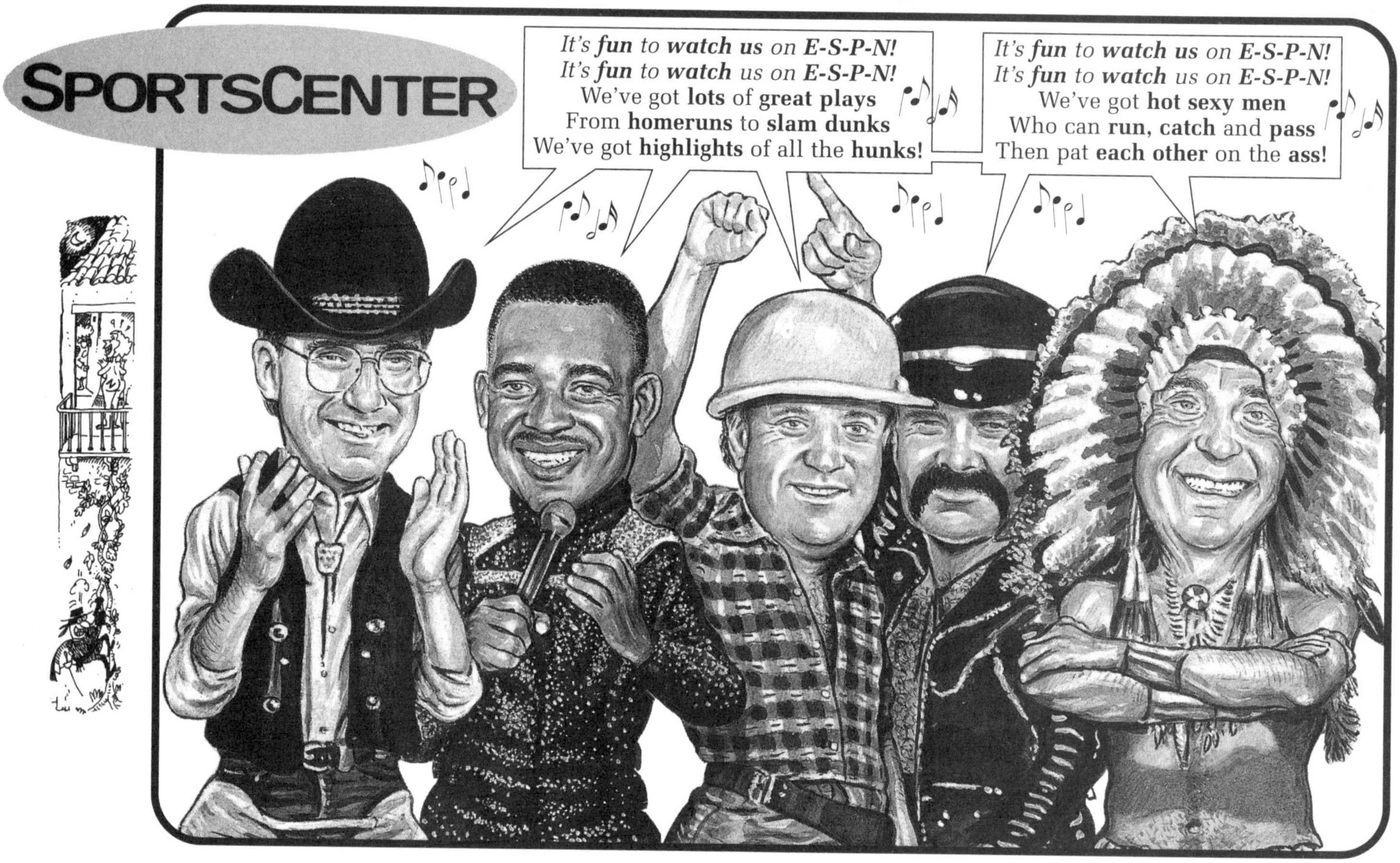
SPORTSCENTER
It's fun to watch us on E-S-P-N!
It's fun to watch us on E-S-P-N!
We've got lots of great plays
From homeruns to slam dunks
We've got highlights of all the hunks!
It's fun to watch us on E-S-P-N!
It's fun to watch us on E-S-P-N!
We've got hot sexy men
Who can run, catch and pass
Then pat each other on the ass!

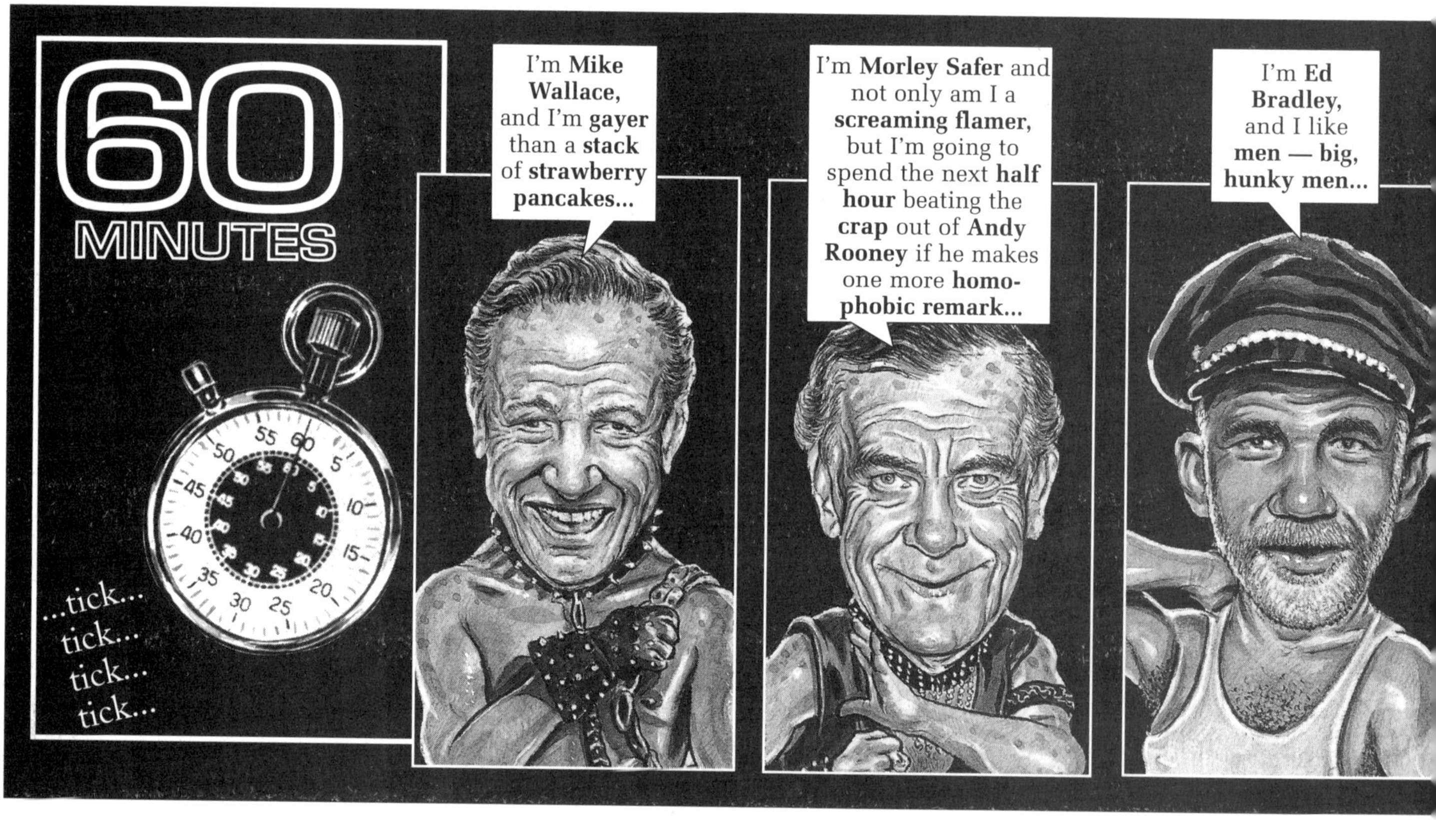
60 MINUTES
...tick...
tick...
tick...
tick...
I'm Mike Wallace, and I'm gayer than a stack of strawberry pancakes...
I'm Morley Safer and not only am I a screaming flamer, but I'm going to spend the next half hour beating the crap out of Andy Rooney if he makes one more homophobic remark...
I'm Ed Bradley, and I like men — big, hunky men...

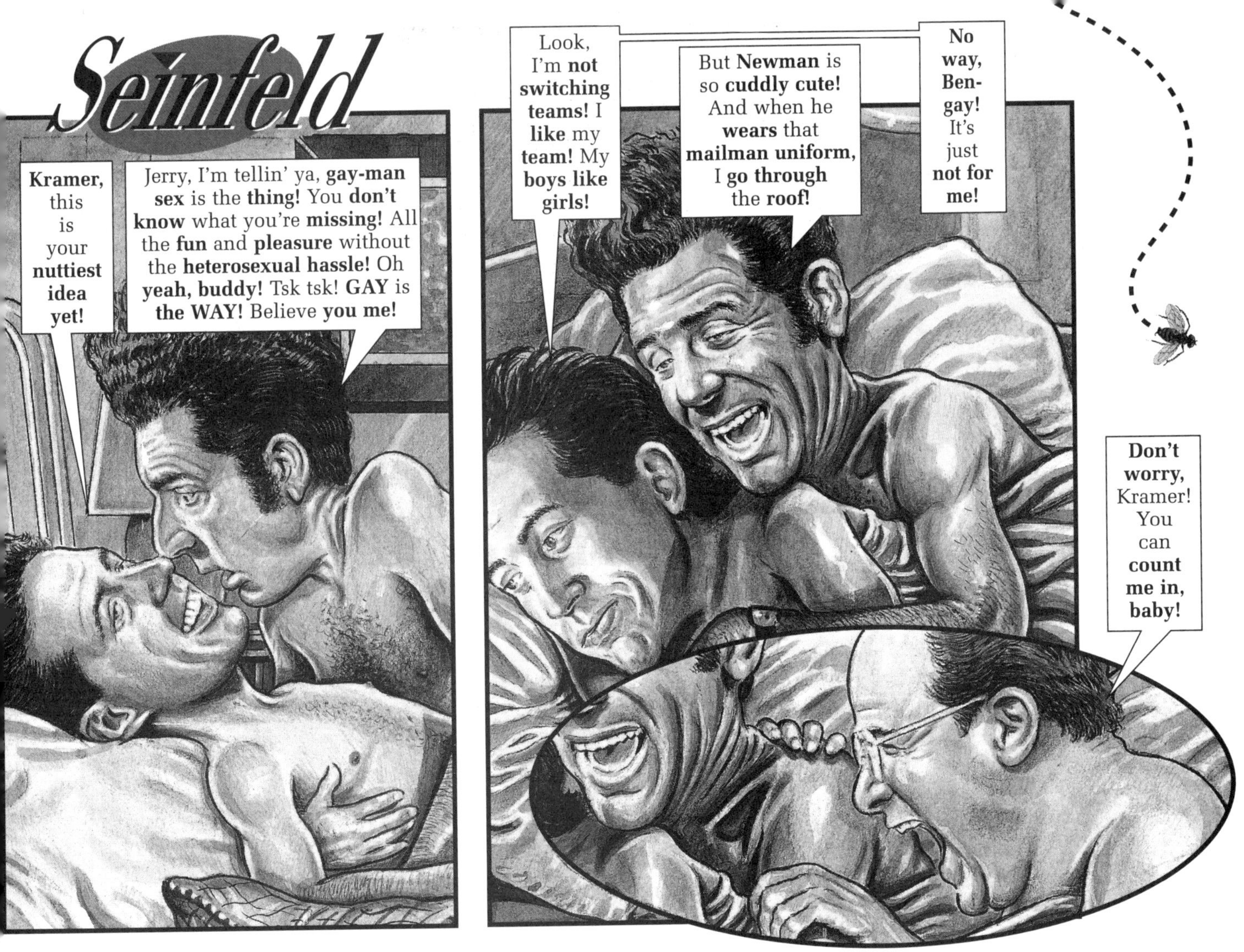
Seinfeld
Kramer, this is your nuttiest idea yet!
Jerry, I'm tellin' ya, gay-man sex is the thing! You don't know what you're missing! All the fun and pleasure without the heterosexual hassle! Oh yeah, buddy! Tsk tsk! GAY is the WAY! Believe you me!
Look, I'm not switching teams! I like my team! My boys like girls!
But Newman is so cuddly cute! And when he wears that mailman uniform, I go through the roof!
No way, Ben-gay! It's just not for me!
Don't worry, Kramer! You can count me in, baby!

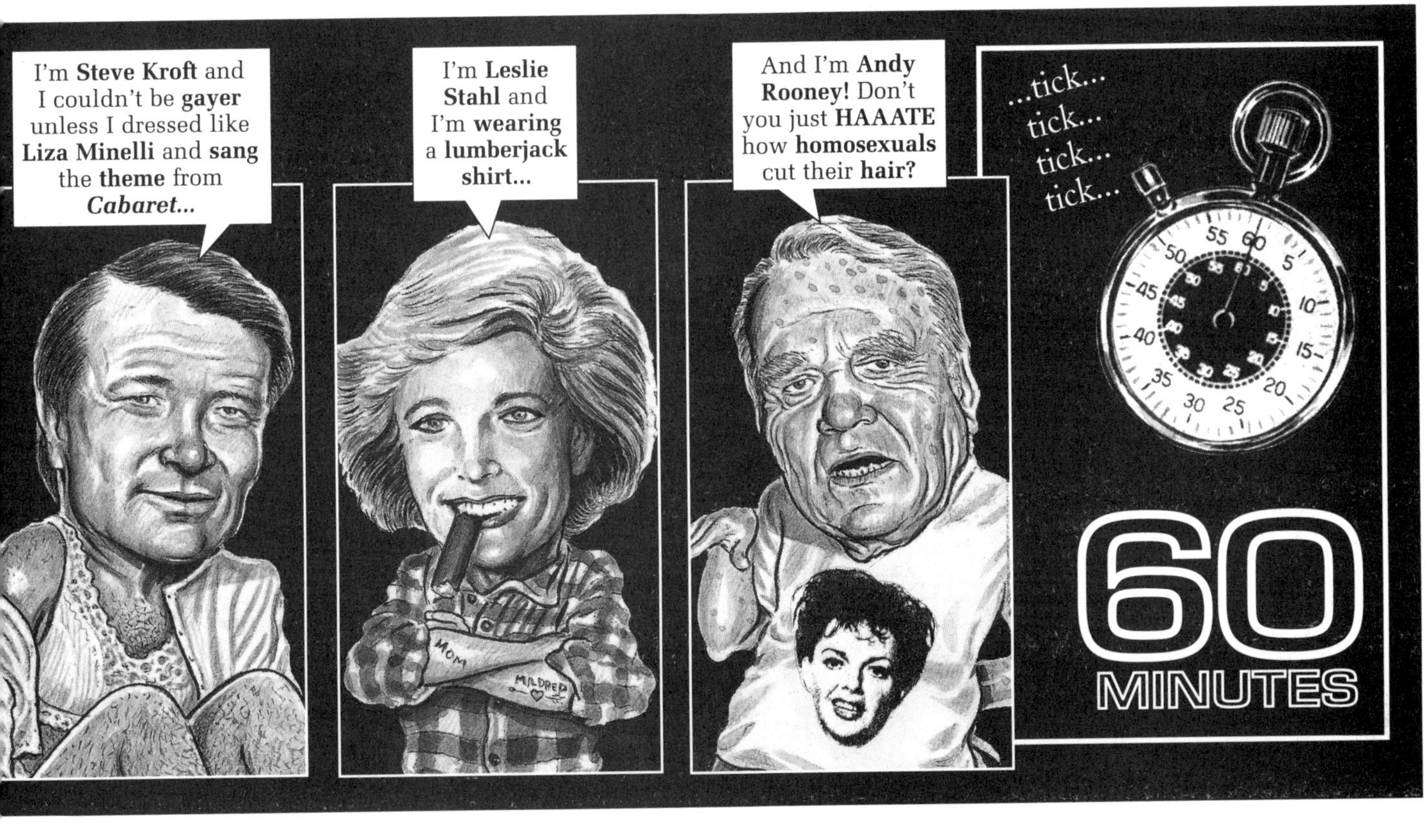
I'm Steve Kroft and I couldn't be gayer unless I dressed like Liza Minelli and sang the theme from *Cabaret...*
I'm Leslie Stahl and I'm wearing a lumberjack shirt...
MOM
MILDRED
And I'm Andy Rooney! Don't you just HAAATE how homosexuals cut their hair?
...tick... tick... tick... tick...
60 MINUTES

DRAWN OUT TRAUMAS DEPT.

In the '60s, TV gave us cute caring doctors like Ben Casey and Dr. Kildare. In the '70s, Marcus Welby M.D., kind and fatherly. And in the '80s, it was the wacky but lovable gang at St. Elsewhere. But this is the '90s. Health care reform is dead. And nowhere is it deader than on NBC's new hospital drama. In this medical zoo, patients check in sick and they leave the place...

Sick

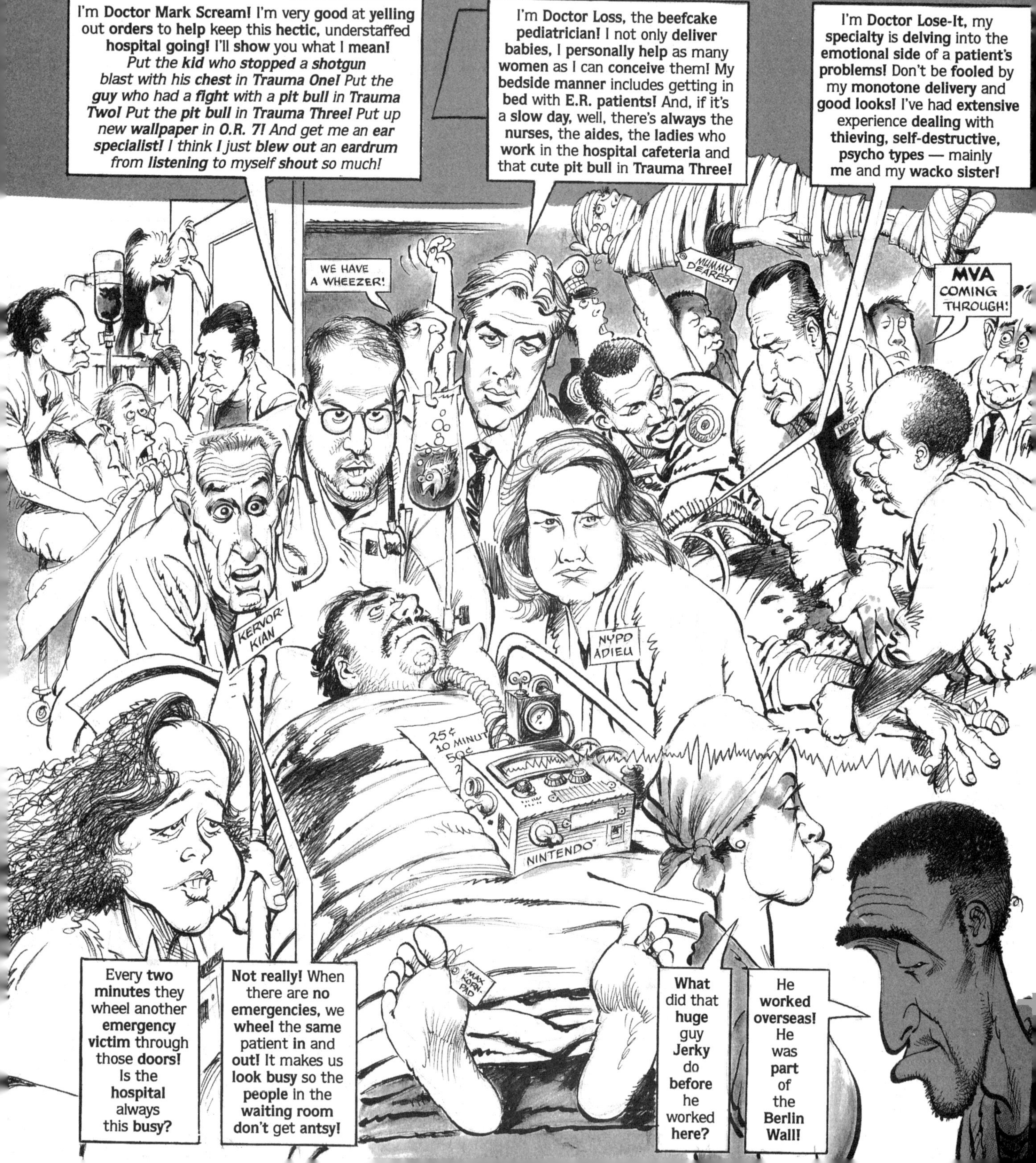

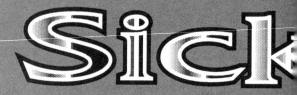

I'm Doctor Mark Scream! I'm very good at yelling out orders to help keep this hectic, understaffed hospital going! I'll show you what I mean! Put the kid who stopped a shotgun blast with his chest in Trauma One! Put the guy who had a fight with a pit bull in Trauma Two! Put the pit bull in Trauma Three! Put up new wallpaper in O.R. 7! And get me an ear specialist! I think I just blew out an eardrum from listening to myself shout so much!
I'm Doctor Loss, the beefcake pediatrician! I not only deliver babies, I personally help as many women as I can conceive them! My bedside manner includes getting in bed with E.R. patients! And, if it's a slow day, well, there's always the nurses, the aides, the ladies who work in the hospital cafeteria and that cute pit bull in Trauma Three!
I'm Doctor Lose-It, my specialty is delving into the emotional side of a patient's problems! Don't be fooled by my monotone delivery and good looks! I've had extensive experience dealing with thieving, self-destructive, psycho types — mainly me and my wacko sister!
WE HAVE A WHEEZER!
MUMMY DEAREST
MVA COMING THROUGH!
KERVOR-KIAN
NYPD ADIEU
NINTENDO
Every two minutes they wheel another emergency victim through those doors! Is the hospital always this busy?
Not really! When there are no emergencies, we wheel the same patient in and out! It makes us look busy so the people in the waiting room don't get antsy!
What did that huge guy Jerky do before he worked here?
He worked overseas! He was part of the Berlin Wall!

ER

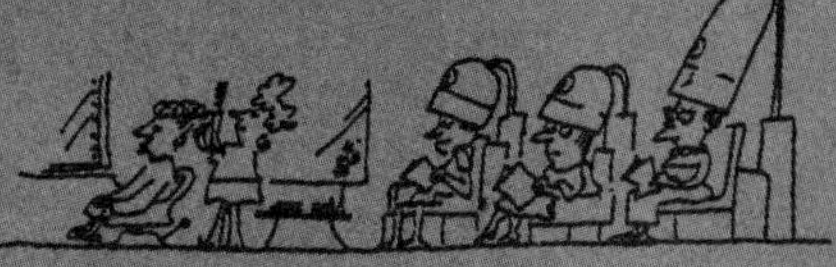

ARTIST: MORT DRUCKER WRITER: DICK DEBARTOLO

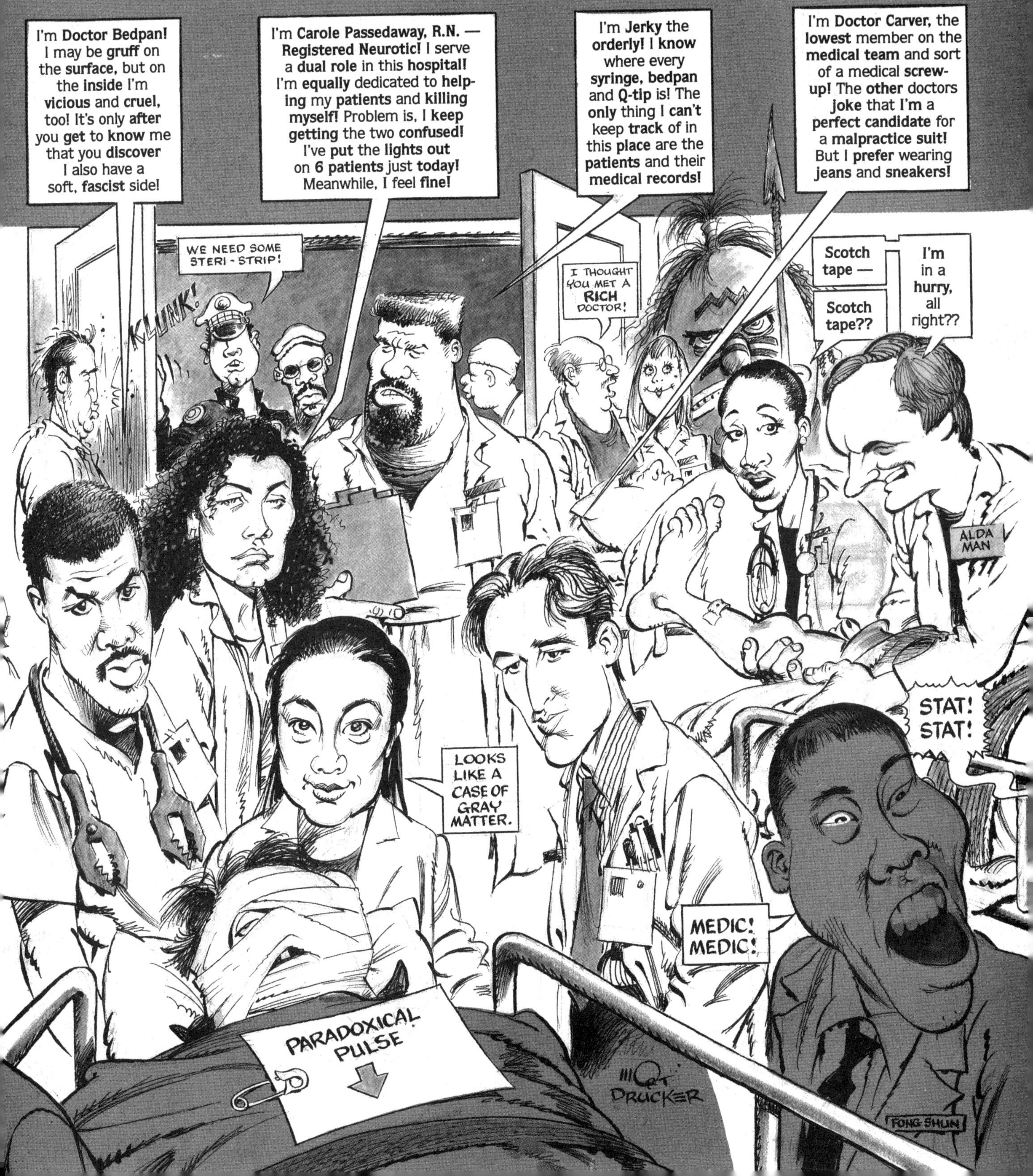

I'm Doctor Bedpan! I may be gruff on the surface, but on the inside I'm vicious and cruel, too! It's only after you get to know me that you discover I also have a soft, fascist side!
I'm Carole Passedaway, R.N. — Registered Neurotic! I serve a dual role in this hospital! I'm equally dedicated to help-ing my patients and killing myself! Problem is, I keep getting the two confused! I've put the lights out on 6 patients just today! Meanwhile, I feel fine!
I'm Jerky the orderly! I know where every syringe, bedpan and Q-tip is! The only thing I can't keep track of in this place are the patients and their medical records!
I'm Doctor Carver, the lowest member on the medical team and sort of a medical screw-up! The other doctors joke that I'm a perfect candidate for a malpractice suit! But I prefer wearing jeans and sneakers!
WE NEED SOME STERI-STRIP!
KLUNK!
I THOUGHT YOU MET A RICH DOCTOR!
Scotch tape —
Scotch tape??
I'm in a hurry, all right??
ALDA MAN
STAT! STAT!
LOOKS LIKE A CASE OF GRAY MATTER.
MEDIC! MEDIC!
PARADOXICAL PULSE
MORT DRUCKER
FONG SHUN

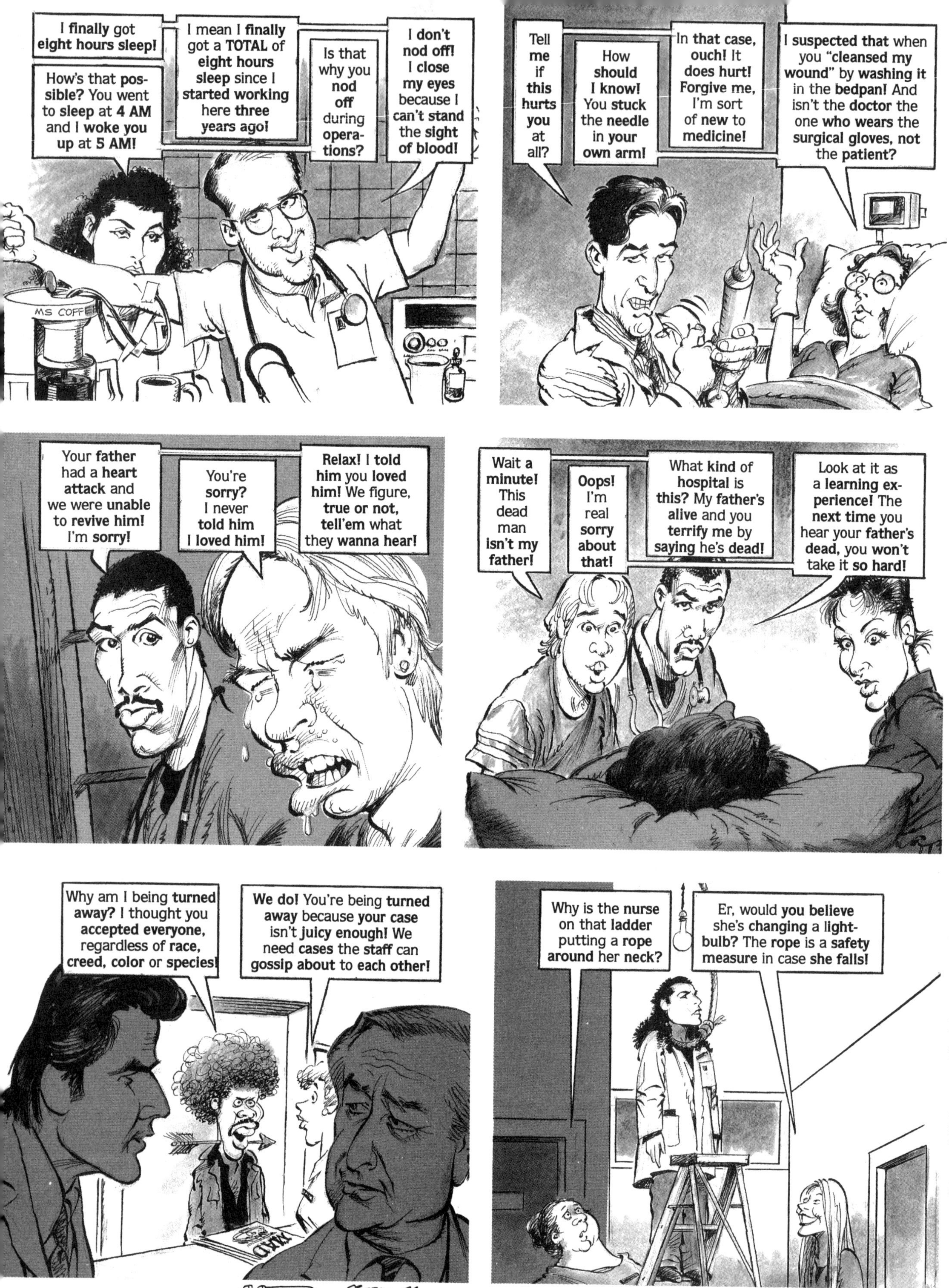
I finally got eight hours sleep!
How's that possible? You went to sleep at 4 AM and I woke you up at 5 AM!
I mean I finally got a TOTAL of eight hours sleep since I started working here three years ago!
Is that why you nod off during operations?
I don't nod off! I close my eyes because I can't stand the sight of blood!
MS COFF
Tell me if this hurts you at all?
How should I know! You stuck the needle in your own arm!
In that case, ouch! It does hurt! Forgive me, I'm sort of new to medicine!
I suspected that when you "cleansed my wound" by washing it in the bedpan! And isn't the doctor the one who wears the surgical gloves, not the patient?
Your father had a heart attack and we were unable to revive him! I'm sorry!
You're sorry? I never told him I loved him!
Relax! I told him you loved him! We figure, true or not, tell'em what they wanna hear!
Wait a minute! This dead man isn't my father!
Oops! I'm real sorry about that!
What kind of hospital is this? My father's alive and you terrify me by saying he's dead!
Look at it as a learning experience! The next time you hear your father's dead, you won't take it so hard!
Why am I being turned away? I thought you accepted everyone, regardless of race, creed, color or species!
We do! You're being turned away because your case isn't juicy enough! We need cases the staff can gossip about to each other!
Why is the nurse on that ladder putting a rope around her neck?
Er, would you believe she's changing a lightbulb? The rope is a safety measure in case she falls!

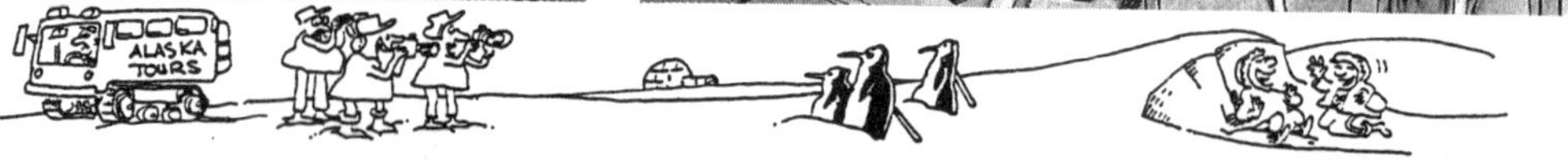
ALASKA TOURS

Between O.J.'s lawyers and the L.A. prosecutors, the public's perception of lawyers as a vipers' nest of money-sucking, evidence-hiding, egomaniacal sewer slugs is only confirmed...***So What's the Problem?***

Psychologically damaging conditions, overcrowding, and insufficient amenities force our nation's prisoners to live in a squalor unfit for a workhorse...*So What's the Problem?*

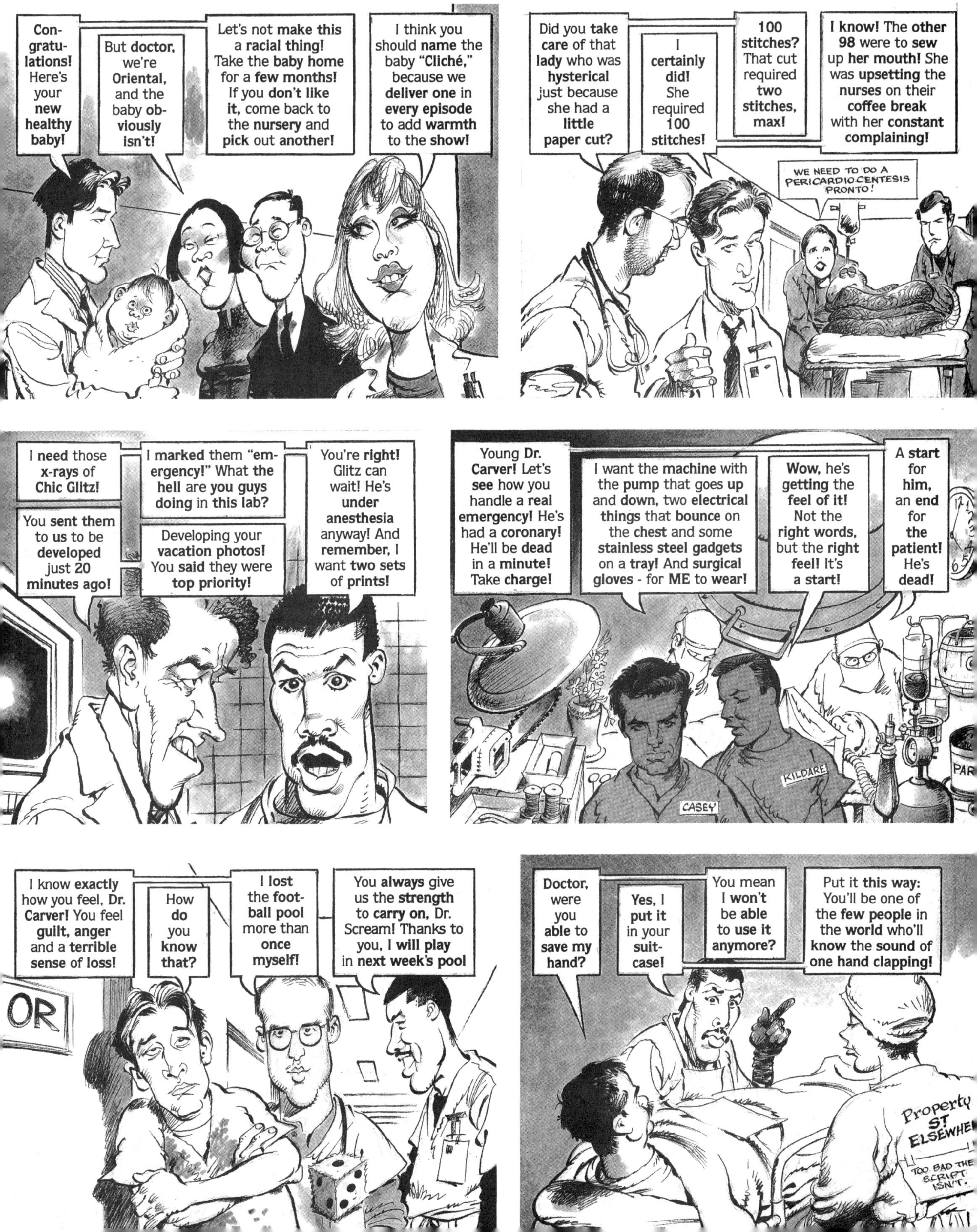

Congratulations! Here's your new healthy baby!
But doctor, we're Oriental, and the baby obviously isn't!
Let's not make this a racial thing! Take the baby home for a few months! If you don't like it, come back to the nursery and pick out another!
I think you should name the baby "Cliché," because we deliver one in every episode to add warmth to the show!
Did you take care of that lady who was hysterical just because she had a little paper cut?
I certainly did! She required 100 stitches!
100 stitches? That cut required two stitches, max!
I know! The other 98 were to sew up her mouth! She was upsetting the nurses on their coffee break with her constant complaining!
WE NEED TO DO A PERICARDIO CENTESIS PRONTO!
I need those x-rays of Chic Glitz!
I marked them "emergency!" What the hell are you guys doing in this lab?
You sent them to us to be developed just 20 minutes ago!
Developing your vacation photos! You said they were top priority!
You're right! Glitz can wait! He's under anesthesia anyway! And remember, I want two sets of prints!
Young Dr. Carver! Let's see how you handle a real emergency! He's had a coronary! He'll be dead in a minute! Take charge!
I want the machine with the pump that goes up and down, two electrical things that bounce on the chest and some stainless steel gadgets on a tray! And surgical gloves - for ME to wear!
Wow, he's getting the feel of it! Not the right words, but the right feel! It's a start!
A start for him, an end for the patient! He's dead!
CASEY
KILDARE
I know exactly how you feel, Dr. Carver! You feel guilt, anger and a terrible sense of loss!
How do you know that?
I lost the football pool more than once myself!
You always give us the strength to carry on, Dr. Scream! Thanks to you, I will play in next week's pool
OR
Doctor, were you able to save my hand?
Yes, I put it in your suitcase!
You mean I won't be able to use it anymore?
Put it this way: You'll be one of the few people in the world who'll know the sound of one hand clapping!
Property ST ELSEWHE
TOO BAD THE SCRIPT ISN'T.

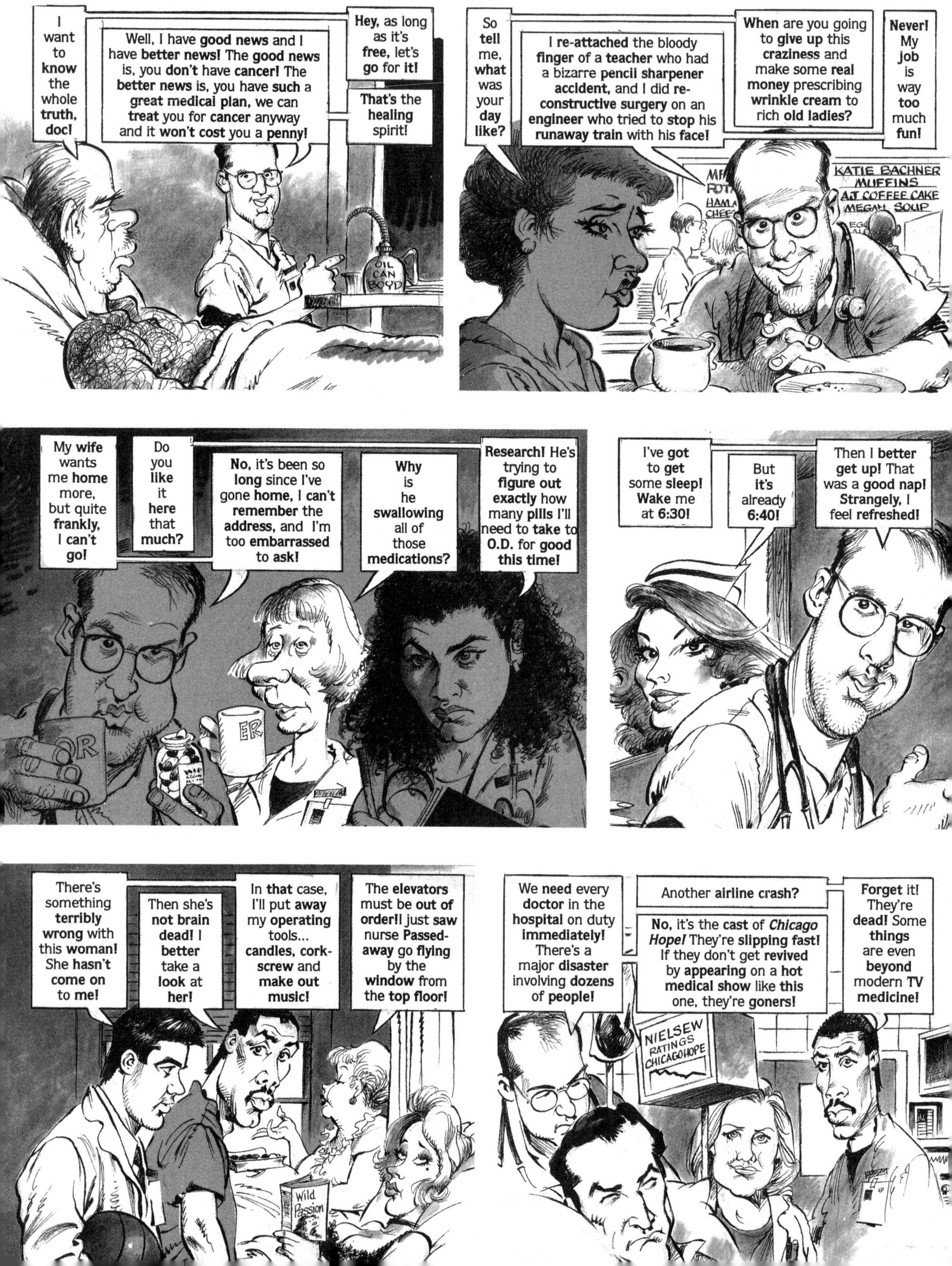
I want to know the whole truth, doc!
Well, I have good news and I have better news! The good news is, you don't have cancer! The better news is, you have such a great medical plan, we can treat you for cancer anyway and it won't cost you a penny!
Hey, as long as it's free, let's go for it!
That's the healing spirit!
OIL CAN BOYD
So tell me, what was your day like?
I re-attached the bloody finger of a teacher who had a bizarre pencil sharpener accident, and I did re-constructive surgery on an engineer who tried to stop his runaway train with his face!
When are you going to give up this craziness and make some real money prescribing wrinkle cream to rich old ladies?
Never! My job is way too much fun!
KATIE BACHNER MUFFINS
AJ COFFEE CAKE
MEGAN SOUP
My wife wants me home more, but quite frankly, I can't go!
Do you like it here that much?
No, it's been so long since I've gone home, I can't remember the address, and I'm too embarrassed to ask!
Why is he swallowing all of those medications?
Research! He's trying to figure out exactly how many pills I'll need to take to O.D. for good this time!
OR
ER
I've got to get some sleep! Wake me at 6:30!
But it's already 6:40!
Then I better get up! That was a good nap! Strangely, I feel refreshed!
There's something terribly wrong with this woman! She hasn't come on to me!
Then she's not brain dead! I better take a look at her!
In that case, I'll put away my operating tools... candles, cork-screw and make out music!
The elevators must be out of order! I just saw nurse Passed-away go flying by the window from the top floor!
Wild Passion
We need every doctor in the hospital on duty immediately! There's a major disaster involving dozens of people!
Another airline crash?
No, it's the cast of *Chicago Hope!* They're slipping fast! If they don't get revived by appearing on a hot medical show like this one, they're goners!
Forget it! They're dead! Some things are even beyond modern TV medicine!
NIELSEW RATINGS CHICAGOHOPE

GRIEVING LAS VEGAS DEPT.

MAD'S CELEBRITY CAUSE-OF-DEATH BETTING ODDS

Our team of crack oddsmakers gives you the latest Vegas line on how one of today's biggest stars is going to sign off for the last time!

THIS MONTH'S FUTURE AUTOPSY RECIPIENT:

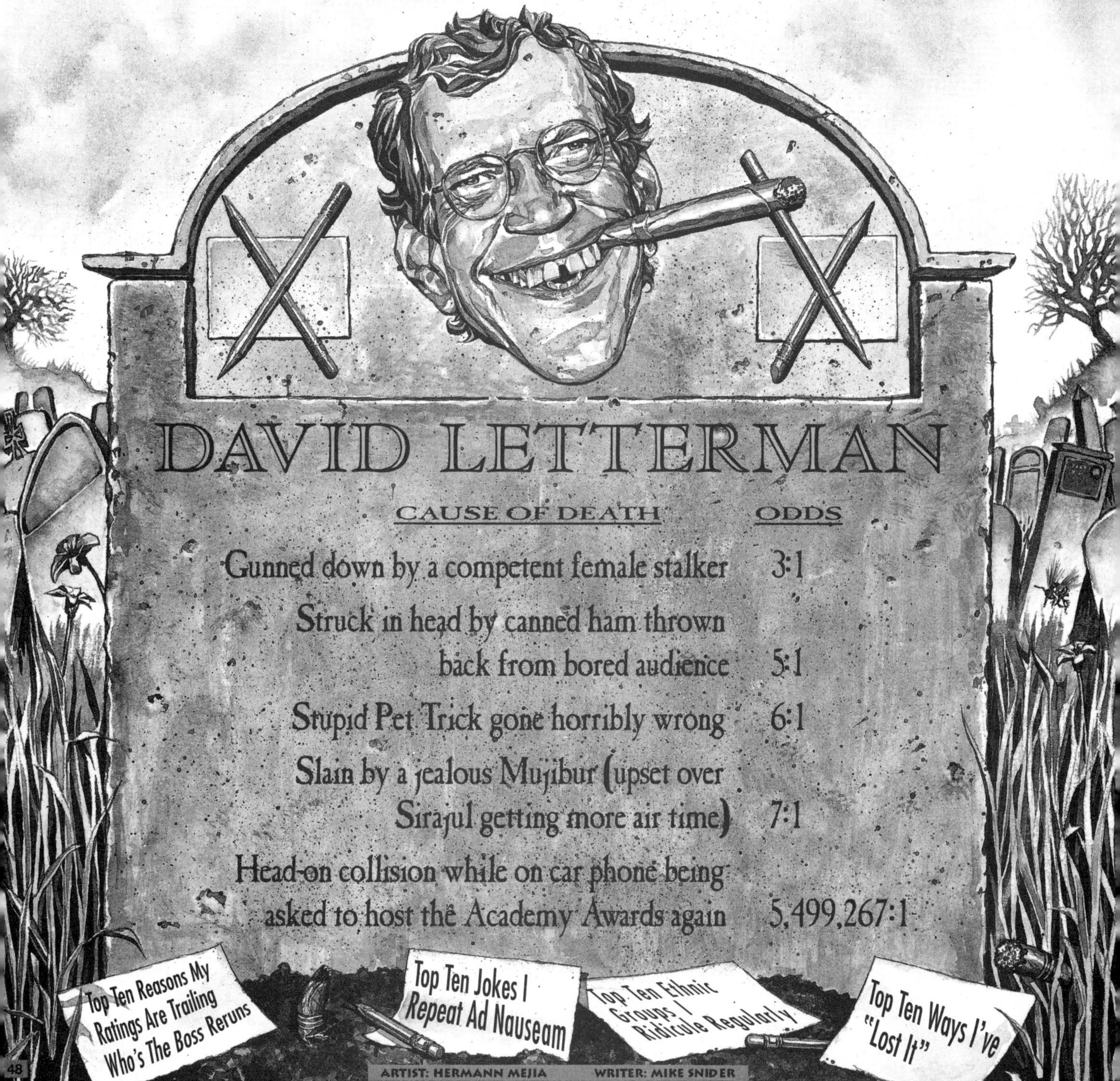
DAVID LETTERMAN
CAUSE OF DEATH
ODDS
Gunned down by a competent female stalker 3:1
Struck in head by canned ham thrown back from bored audience 5:1
Stupid Pet Trick gone horribly wrong 6:1
Slain by a jealous Mujibur (upset over Sirajul getting more air time) 7:1
Head-on collision while on car phone being asked to host the Academy Awards again 5,499,267:1
Top Ten Reasons My Ratings Are Trailing Who's The Boss Reruns
Top Ten Jokes I Repeat Ad Nauseam
Top Ten Ethnic Groups I Ridicule Regularly
Top Ten Ways I've "Lost It"

ARTIST: HERMANN MEJIA WRITER: MIKE SNIDER

GENERATION ECCH DEPT.

And now a show about six twentysomethings! They're single, they're attractive, they're witty, they're bonding, and they've got something great going for them: it's called Thursday night on NBC! The amazing thing is they claim it's all platonic and there's no hanky-panky going on between them. (Yeah, right! And the Pope was born in Guatemala!) Whatever they claim, we know them for what they really are—sex...

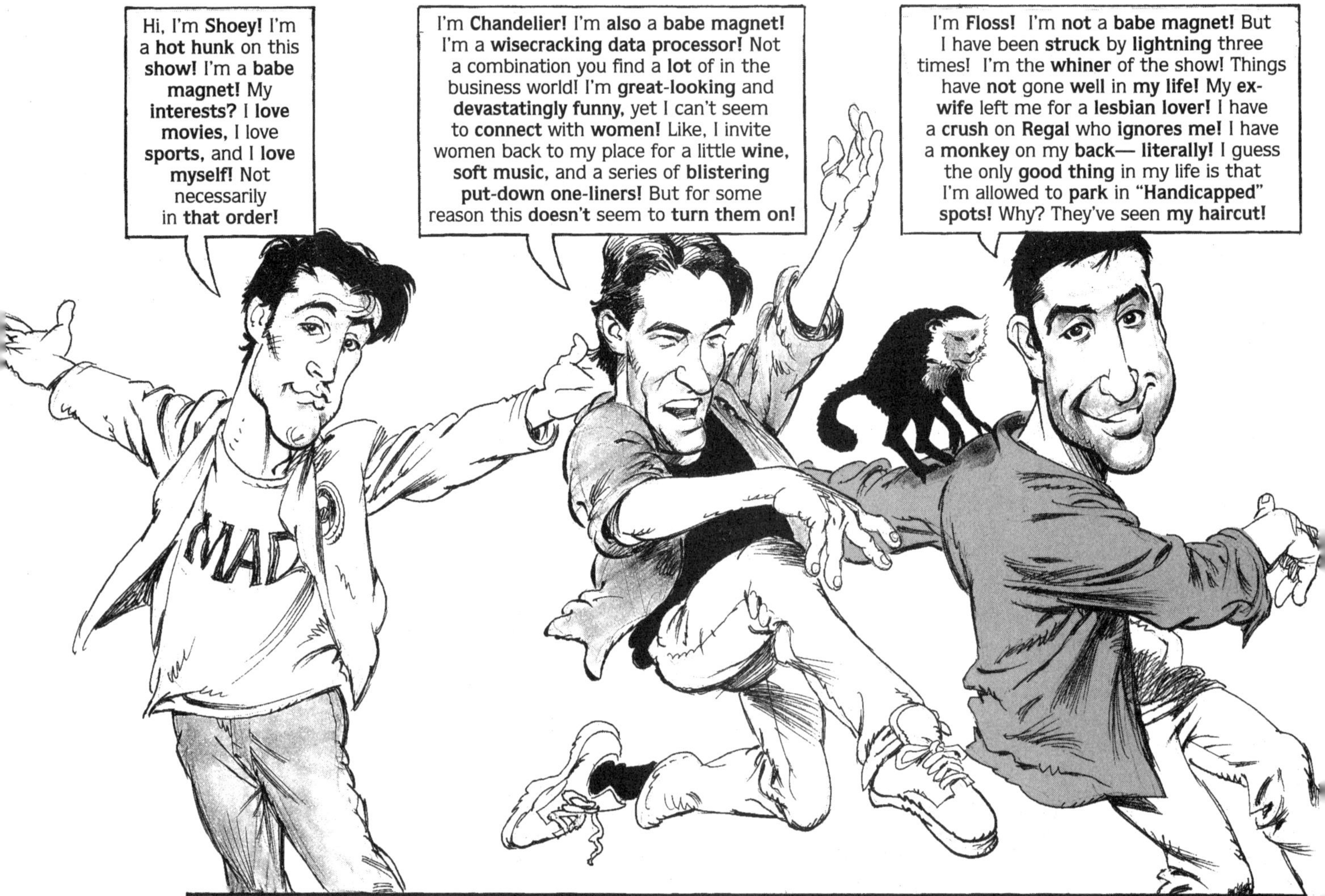
Hi, I'm Shoey! I'm a hot hunk on this show! I'm a babe magnet! My interests? I love movies, I love sports, and I love myself! Not necessarily in that order!
I'm Chandelier! I'm also a babe magnet! I'm a wisecracking data processor! Not a combination you find a lot of in the business world! I'm great-looking and devastatingly funny, yet I can't seem to connect with women! Like, I invite women back to my place for a little wine, soft music, and a series of blistering put-down one-liners! But for some reason this doesn't seem to turn them on!
I'm Floss! I'm not a babe magnet! But I have been struck by lightning three times! I'm the whiner of the show! Things have not gone well in my life! My ex-wife left me for a lesbian lover! I have a crush on Regal who ignores me! I have a monkey on my back— literally! I guess the only good thing in my life is that I'm allowed to park in "Handicapped" spots! Why? They've seen my haircut!
MAD

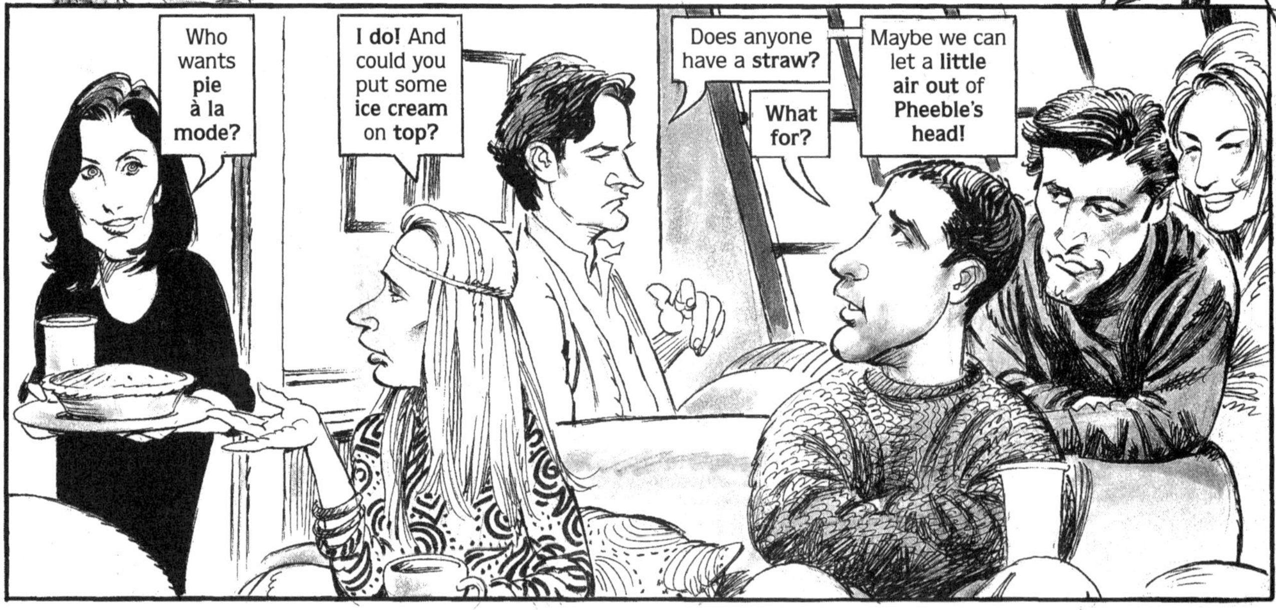
Who wants pie à la mode?
I do! And could you put some ice cream on top?
Does anyone have a straw?
What for?
Maybe we can let a little air out of Pheeble's head!

ARTIST: MORT DRUCKER WRITER: JOSH GORDON

f·i·e·n·d·s

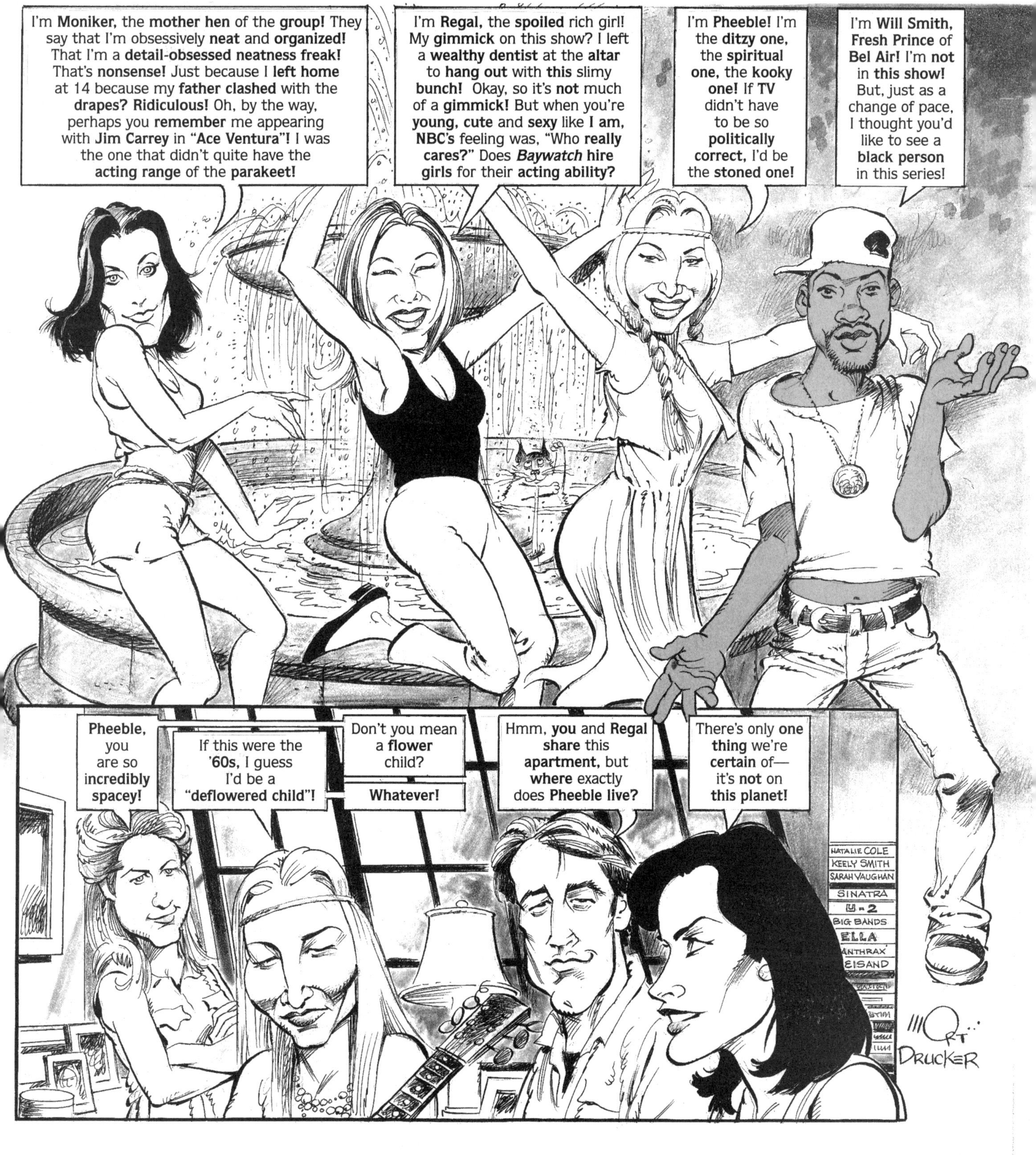

I'm Moniker, the mother hen of the group! They say that I'm obsessively neat and organized! That I'm a detail-obsessed neatness freak! That's nonsense! Just because I left home at 14 because my father clashed with the drapes? Ridiculous! Oh, by the way, perhaps you remember me appearing with Jim Carrey in "Ace Ventura"! I was the one that didn't quite have the acting range of the parakeet!
I'm Regal, the spoiled rich girl! My gimmick on this show? I left a wealthy dentist at the altar to hang out with this slimy bunch! Okay, so it's not much of a gimmick! But when you're young, cute and sexy like I am, NBC's feeling was, "Who really cares?" Does Baywatch hire girls for their acting ability?
I'm Pheeble! I'm the ditzy one, the spiritual one, the kooky one! If TV didn't have to be so politically correct, I'd be the stoned one!
I'm Will Smith, Fresh Prince of Bel Air! I'm not in this show! But, just as a change of pace, I thought you'd like to see a black person in this series!
Pheeble, you are so incredibly spacey!
If this were the '60s, I guess I'd be a "deflowered child"!
Don't you mean a flower child?
Whatever!
Hmm, you and Regal share this apartment, but where exactly does Pheeble live?
There's only one thing we're certain of—it's not on this planet!
NATALIE COLE
KEELY SMITH
SARAH VAUGHAN
SINATRA
U-2
BIG BANDS
ELLA
ANTHRAX
MORT DRUCKER

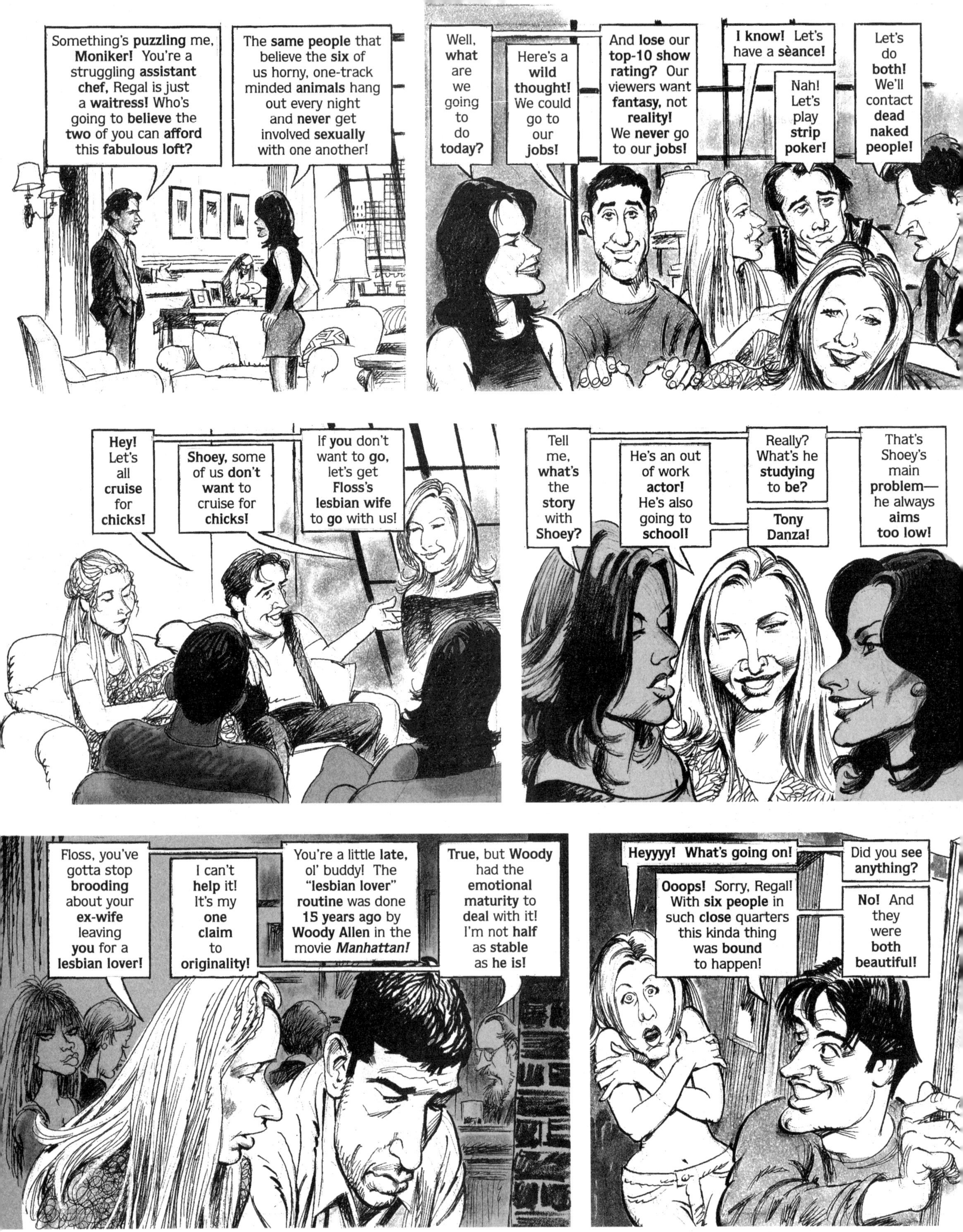
Something's puzzling me, Moniker! You're a struggling assistant chef, Regal is just a waitress! Who's going to believe the two of you can afford this fabulous loft?
The same people that believe the six of us horny, one-track minded animals hang out every night and never get involved sexually with one another!
Well, what are we going to do today?
Here's a wild thought! We could go to our jobs!
And lose our top-10 show rating? Our viewers want fantasy, not reality! We never go to our jobs!
I know! Let's have a sèance!
Nah! Let's play strip poker!
Let's do both! We'll contact dead naked people!
Hey! Let's all cruise for chicks!
Shoey, some of us don't want to cruise for chicks!
If you don't want to go, let's get Floss's lesbian wife to go with us!
Tell me, what's the story with Shoey?
He's an out of work actor! He's also going to school!
Really? What's he studying to be?
Tony Danza!
That's Shoey's main problem— he always aims too low!
Floss, you've gotta stop brooding about your ex-wife leaving you for a lesbian lover!
I can't help it! It's my one claim to originality!
You're a little late, ol' buddy! The "lesbian lover" routine was done 15 years ago by Woody Allen in the movie *Manhattan!*
True, but Woody had the emotional maturity to deal with it! I'm not half as stable as he is!
Heyyyy! What's going on!
Ooops! Sorry, Regal! With six people in such close quarters this kinda thing was bound to happen!
Did you see anything?
No! And they were both beautiful!

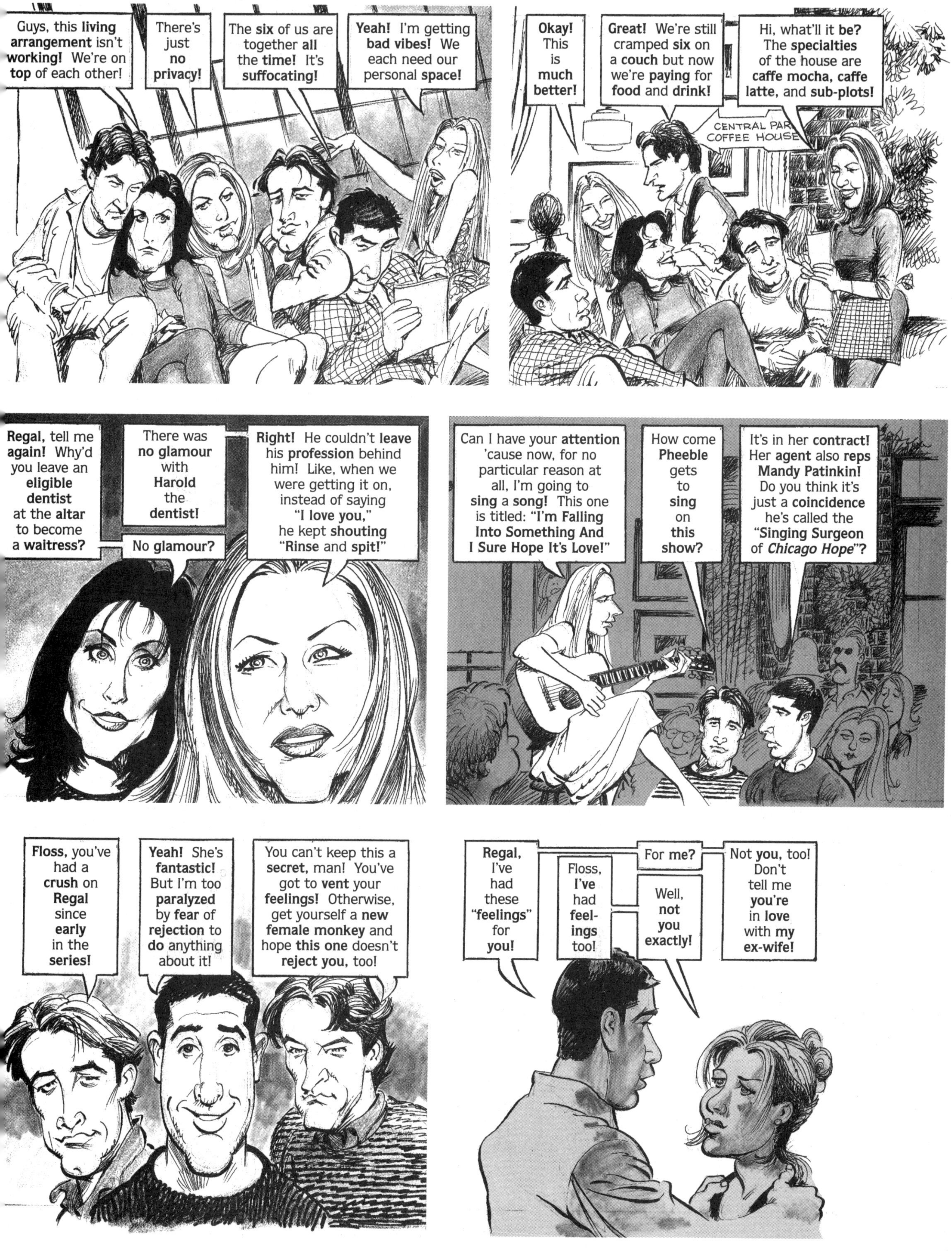
Guys, this living arrangement isn't working! We're on top of each other!
There's just no privacy!
The six of us are together all the time! It's suffocating!
Yeah! I'm getting bad vibes! We each need our personal space!
Okay! This is much better!
Great! We're still cramped six on a couch but now we're paying for food and drink!
Hi, what'll it be? The specialties of the house are caffe mocha, caffe latte, and sub-plots!
CENTRAL PAR
COFFEE HOUSE
Regal, tell me again! Why'd you leave an eligible dentist at the altar to become a waitress?
There was no glamour with Harold the dentist!
No glamour?
Right! He couldn't leave his profession behind him! Like, when we were getting it on, instead of saying "I love you," he kept shouting "Rinse and spit!"
Can I have your attention 'cause now, for no particular reason at all, I'm going to sing a song! This one is titled: "I'm Falling Into Something And I Sure Hope It's Love!"
How come Pheeble gets to sing on this show?
It's in her contract! Her agent also reps Mandy Patinkin! Do you think it's just a coincidence he's called the "Singing Surgeon of Chicago Hope"?
Floss, you've had a crush on Regal since early in the series!
Yeah! She's fantastic! But I'm too paralyzed by fear of rejection to do anything about it!
You can't keep this a secret, man! You've got to vent your feelings! Otherwise, get yourself a new female monkey and hope this one doesn't reject you, too!
Regal, I've had these "feelings" for you!
Floss, I've had feel-ings too!
For me?
Well, not you exactly!
Not you, too! Don't tell me you're in love with my ex-wife!

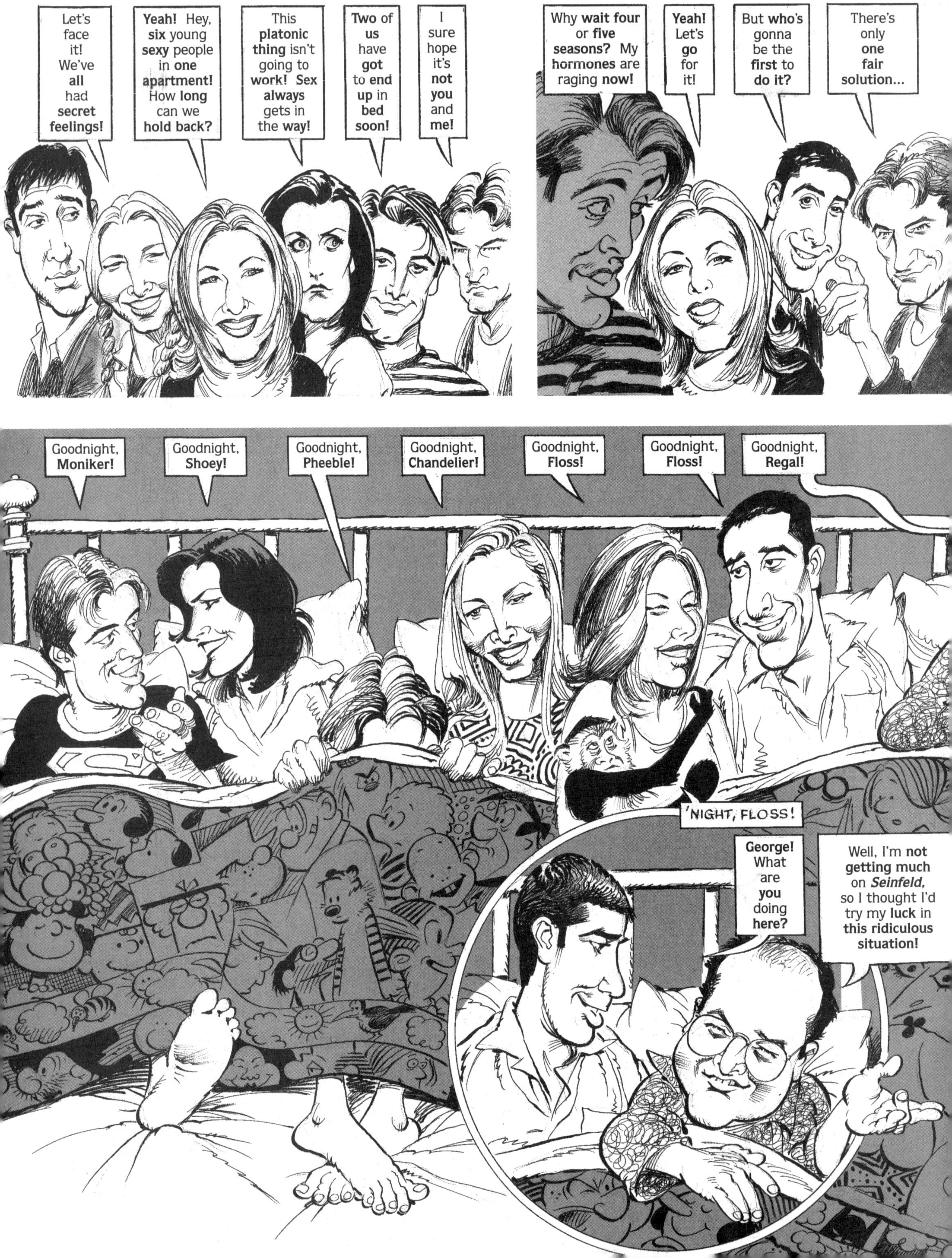
Let's face it! We've all had secret feelings!
Yeah! Hey, six young sexy people in one apartment! How long can we hold back?
This platonic thing isn't going to work! Sex always gets in the way!
Two of us have got to end up in bed soon!
I sure hope it's not you and me!
Why wait four or five seasons? My hormones are raging now!
Yeah! Let's go for it!
But who's gonna be the first to do it?
There's only one fair solution...
Goodnight, Moniker!
Goodnight, Shoey!
Goodnight, Pheeble!
Goodnight, Chandelier!
Goodnight, Floss!
Goodnight, Floss!
Goodnight, Regal!
'NIGHT, FLOSS!
George! What are you doing here?
Well, I'm not getting much on *Seinfeld,* so I thought I'd try my luck in this ridiculous situation!

THE IRRATIONAL INQUIRER DEPT.

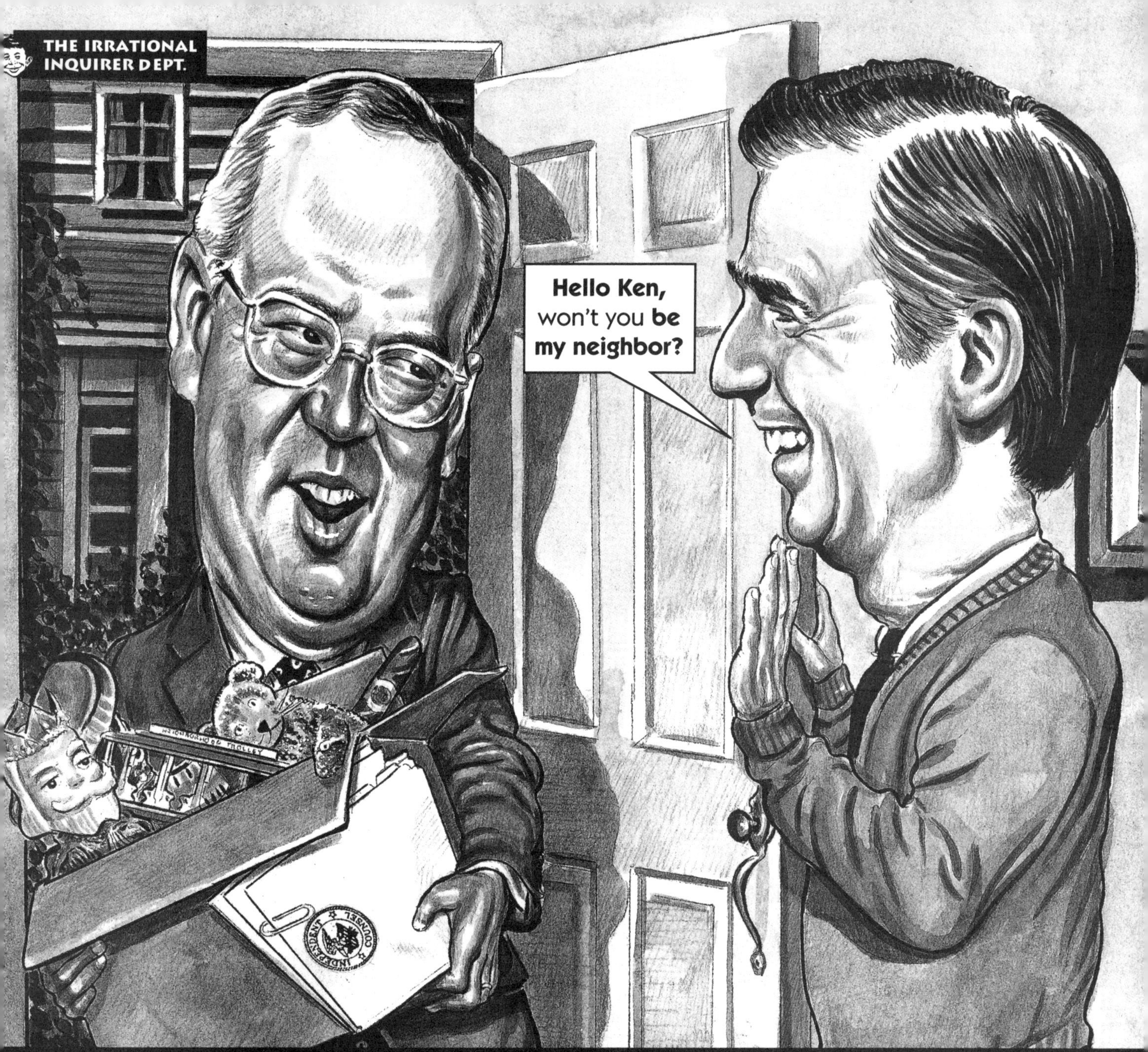
Hello Ken, won't you **be my neighbor?**

First, megalomaniac Ken Starr hounded the President, his staff, his friends, his former intern and just about everyone else in the Clinton White House, except Socks and Buddy! With that investigation in shambles, the overzealous prosecutor has turned his attention to others who, in his eyes, "threaten" the very foundation of our society! Here's a sneak peek of a confidential report sure to be illegally leaked by Starr and his thugs any day now...

THE SPECIAL PROSECUTOR'S OFFICIAL REPORT ON MISTER ROGERS

ARTIST: DREW FRIEDMAN
WRITER: DESMOND DEVLIN

INTRODUCTION:
THERE IS TROUBLE IN THE NEIGHBORHOOD

As required by United States Code Section PBS-13, Title 28, and brought to you by the letters "E" and "P," the Office of the Special Prosecutor hereby submits substantial and credible information that Fred "Mister Rogers" Rogers committed acts that may constitute grounds for immediate cancellation.

This investigation into Mister Rogers began in 1994, during the Special Prosecutor's look into President William J. Clinton and the Whitewater scandal. While no wrongdoing was discovered in Whitewater, facts from that case led to a study of the White House travel office and fundraising irregularities. Those inquiries were later closed without result, but not

before this office expanded its mission to include the Paula Jones lawsuit and the Lewinsky matter (AKA "Forni-Gate").

A remark by Lewinsky's dry cleaner indicated that President Clinton had watched part of the Ken Burns documentary on the Civil War before getting bored and switching over to the USA Network's *Silk Stalkings*. A $6 million dollar investigation into *TV Guide* subsequently revealed that the Civil War documentary had been shown on PBS television. This naturally led to a full inquiry into the entire PBS schedule. It was during this phase that the wrongdoing of Mister Rogers became virtually apparent.

This complex investigation into Mister Rogers' misdeeds cost $46 million dollars to complete, not counting free giveaway tote bags. This cost, naturally, must be paid by PBS. It is suggested that PBS make up the money by expanding their on-air pledge drive from 335 days per year to 363 days per year.

SECTION ONE:
INDIVIDUAL GROUNDS AND CHARGES

There is substantial and credible information that Mister Rogers committed acts that may constitute grounds for cancellation, depending on polls and how the FCC appointments turn out.

The information obtained reveals that Mister Rogers:

• **Lied** when he claimed that all his viewers were "special." The evidence will show that even while repeating these statements, Mister Rogers knew perfectly well that human life is cheap and that most of his viewers were in fact worthless lumps;

• **Misused** his position to teach 30 years' worth of children that it's okay to watch a grown man take off his clothes;

• **Conspired** to deprive jazz composers of their rightful royalties by having the invisible piano play random notes that only occasionally go near a melody;

• **Violated** Article 1, Section 9 of the U.S. Constitution by recognizing the royal sovereignty of King Friday XIII within United States borders;

• **Failed** to pay taxes on the teeny-tiny imaginary fares collected by the Magic Trolley;

• Has **never specifically disproved** his possible role in the mysterious death of *The Joy of Painting* host Bob Ross;

• **Inserted** his fist into numerous puppets.

SECTION TWO:
THE CONTENTS OF THE REFERRAL

Regrettably, this report contains some **sexually explicit material**, but usually not more than once or twice per paragraph. Sex, however, is only a small part of this investigation. This case is not about cheap, embarrassing quickies, but rather a **systemic betrayal of public trust**. Therefore, most sexual details, real or pretend, will be confined to a tiny, separate appendix. Following page 4 of this report, the sex appendix may be found on pages 5 through 3,528.

SECTION THREE:
THE NARRATIVE: JULY 22, 1998

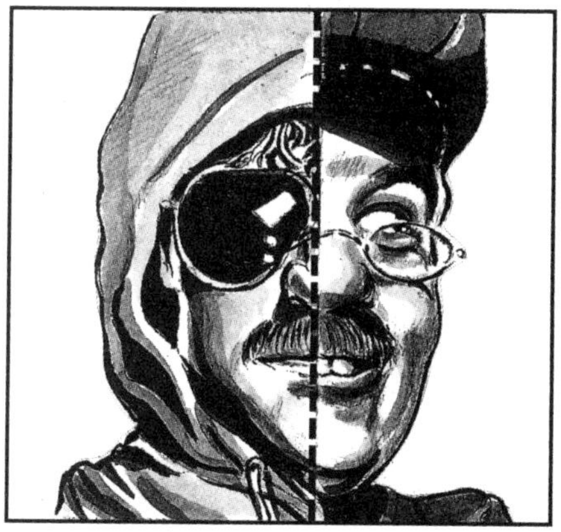

Mister Rogers entered his home at 10:30 a.m. (9:30 Central). He greeted his companion warmly. The companion, however, was not captured by the surveillance camera. After remarking how good it was to be alone again with the unnamed, unseen companion, Mister Rogers began to partially disrobe. Before he could undress fully, Mister Rogers' illicit encounter was interrupted by a knock on the door.

Mister Rogers feigned surprise, asking aloud, "My! Who can that be?" We characterize his reaction as false because there is a body of evidence showing that the last several hundred times there was a knock on the door, it was Mr. McFeely, and indeed it was once again Mr. McFeely. Mister Rogers' attitude of surprise was, in this office's opinion, a **clear attempt to mislead the public**.

It must not be forgotten that Mr. McFeely is a postman, the man who delivers the mail to the Neighborhood. These are the very same U.S. mails that have been used to **convey child pornography, narcotics and the very bombs that the Unabomber used** to maim and murder innocent victims. While Mr. McFeely may not have committed these acts himself, he **failed to prevent others from committing them**. As a uniformed postal worker, McFeely's inaction is, in our estimation, a **far greater crime**.

"I'm, only going to say this once. I... did... not... have sexual relations with that woman, Lady Elaine Fairchilde."

A Dangerous Game

Mr. McFeely was led inside the residence. McFeely had with him a package, perhaps brought in an attempt to buy influence. Mister Rogers smiled and said, **"My, what a big, thick package you have there!"** With two men alone in a house at the end of a dead-end street, this statement can be interpreted many ways. We pick the bad way.

The package contained an assortment of colorful building blocks. Mister Rogers and Mr. McFeely spent approximately two minutes stacking the blocks as high as they could until eventually the stack collapsed. No overt sexual incidents occurred during the block-stacking. Nonetheless, this incident raises troubling questions. "Raises troubling questions" is a phrase this office will use again and again in this investigation. In fact, it took this office four years to **raise troubling questions**; no way are we going to spend more time bothering to locate troubling answers.

SECTION FOUR:
MISTER ROGERS' ACCOMPLICES

Mister Rogers has surrounded himself with individuals who witness his illicit activities. This office succeeded in interviewing the fish, the trolley and the puppets out of Mister Rogers' presence, when Mister Rogers was not able to manipulate them and put words in their mouths. However, under repeated interrogations, these witnesses maintained their silence, refusing to provide any information at all. Clearly, they had been intimidated by Mister Rogers.

The following excerpts from the "Puppet-Gate" question-and-answer sessions indicates the level of silent denial:

SPECIAL PROSECUTOR: Queen Sarah, could you give more details about the shady land deal that allowed your family to take over The Land of Make-Believe?

QUEEN SARAH: *(no response)*

SPECIAL PROSECUTOR: Dr. Bill Platypus, isn't it true that according to your narrow definition, oral sex is not considered "sexual contact" among platypuses, because your comically flat bills are so long?

DR. BILL PLATYPUS: *(no response)*

SPECIAL PROSECUTOR: Trolley, weren't you in fact used to deliver unlawful communiqués and "talking points" to and from The Land of Make-Believe?

TROLLEY: Ding! Ding!

SPECIAL PROSECUTOR: X the Owl, isn't your name a transparent attempt by Mister Rogers to unethically curry favor among African-American viewers?

X THE OWL: *(no response)*

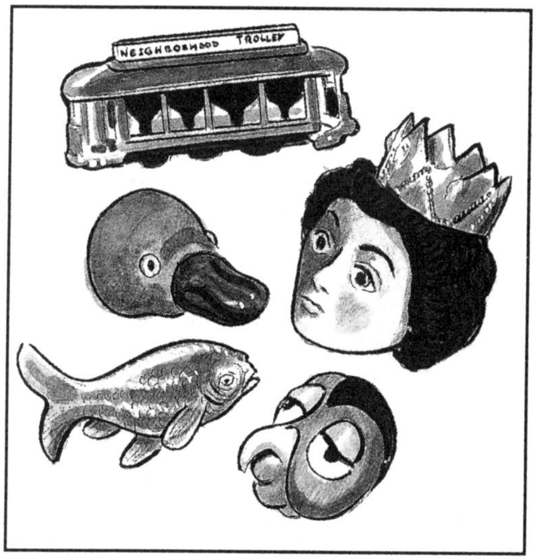
NEIGHBORHOOD TROLLEY

SPECIAL PROSECUTOR: Fish, from your vantage point in the kitchen, you are in close proximity to Mister Rogers' phone. Did you ever see him accept oral sex while making an important call?

THE FISH: Glurp blub glork.

SECTION FIVE:
THE NARRATIVE:
JULY 25, 1998

No surveillance of Mister Rogers could be done, because it was Saturday and they were showing a rerun of *This Old House* instead.

SECTION SIX:
EVIDENCE ESTABLISHING THE NATURE OF THE COVER-UP

DESTROYED PHYSICAL EVIDENCE

This office attempted to subpoena all images and visual content produced by Picture-Picture between the years of 1968 and 1997. Mister Rogers **illegally rejected the subpoena**, saying that Picture-Picture was magic, and that all of his pictures had long since vanished. "But memory is a kind of magic," added

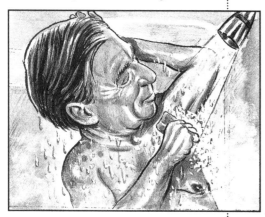

Mister Rogers. "You can get those pictures back any time you like, just by thinking about them." As the Mister Rogers inquiry has shown, however, the **memory is a slippery thing indeed**.

CODED MESSAGES

Several times, the Mister Rogers' Neighborhood program secretly sent hidden signals to the home viewers. When Mister Rogers was informed that **extensive evidence of signal-sending** was in the possession of this office, he

" Mr Rogers, you were quoted as saying, 'It's such a good feeling to know you're alive.' But that isn't the only good feeling, now is it?"

stated, "That's just an old traffic signal on my wall. Signaling is what it does best. I wonder what you like to do best." Unfortunately for Mister Rogers, this office is not the one under investigation. *And you will be crushed by me! You're going DOWN, you skinny little BASTARD! Oh, wait, did I include that or did I just think it?*

SECTION SEVEN:
THE NARRATIVE:
JULY 29, 1998

At approximately 10:38 a.m., Mister Rogers left his home to visit Chef Brockett. Mister Rogers' stated purpose was "to see how a birthday cake gets made." This office believes that Mister Rogers was actually preparing to conduct an **illegal fundraising visit**. Mister Rogers denies this, saying, "I don't talk about fundraising on my show. I try to talk about things that the children will be interested in. You know, I take showers and go to the bathroom, too, but you don't see that on my show either." (FBI surveillance photos captured Mister Rogers performing these acts.)

When Mister Rogers left his home, the camera suddenly showed aerial footage of cardboard streets and houses to indicate his journey to Chef Brockett's. It is uncertain how much **unseen illegal activity** took place during this 8-second interval.

SOMETHING'S COOKING

Mister Rogers arrived at Chef Brockett's kitchen at 10:39 a.m. Chef Brockett quickly showed Mister Rogers a **large quantity of white powder**. This office has not tested the powder, because just saying "large quantity of white powder" sounds worse. Chef Brockett and Mister Rogers broke four eggs and mixed them into the powder. "It's very messy, but I'll bet the cake will taste mighty good," remarked Mister Rogers. By **suggesting** that Chef Brockett would think the cake tasted good, Mister Rogers was boldly trying to **illegally influence and rehearse possible testimony**.

After the cake was finished, Mister Rogers asked Chef Brockett for the recipe. Chef Brockett replied, "It's all

up here," indicating his big floppy chef's hat. In other words, Chef Brockett kept his cooking knowledge in his brain with no notes. Mister Rogers had obviously urged his co-conspirators to **"never put anything down on paper."** Chef Brockett was called in to this office to answer questions but unfortunately, after several hours in custody, he called a lawyer, so this office couldn't do whatever it wanted to him.

" You may be the Special Prosecutor. But I happen to think any prosecutor is special."

SECTION EIGHT: STATEMENTS UNDER OATH

On August 12, 1998, Mister Rogers agreed to answer questions put to him before a Grand Jury. The following is part of his testimony:

SPECIAL PROSECUTOR: Do you like cigars, Mister Rogers?

MISTER ROGERS: Heavens, no. They're awfully smelly, aren't they?

SPECIAL PROSECUTOR: So you're testifying that you never smoke cigars?

MISTER ROGERS: That's right, I never have. No, I think tobacco plants should be allowed to grow and make beautiful gardens.

SPECIAL PROSECUTOR: Then what do you do with cigars, Mister Rogers?

MISTER ROGERS: Why, nothing at all.

SPECIAL PROSECUTOR: We'll let the American people judge your definition of "nothing at all." Isn't it true that if you don't smoke cigars, you obviously must use them for another purpose?

MISTER ROGERS: I'm sorry, but I don't have any cigars at all. I have some graham crackers if you'd like.

SPECIAL PROSECUTOR: No cigars left? Isn't it true that the reason you're "fresh out" of cigars is because you've used the entire box for your own perverse sexual gratification? Isn't it?

MISTER ROGERS: You have quite an imagination. You know, of all the nations on Earth, I think the very best one is imagination.

SPECIAL PROSECUTOR: Are you suggesting I use my imagination? That's disgusting, sir!

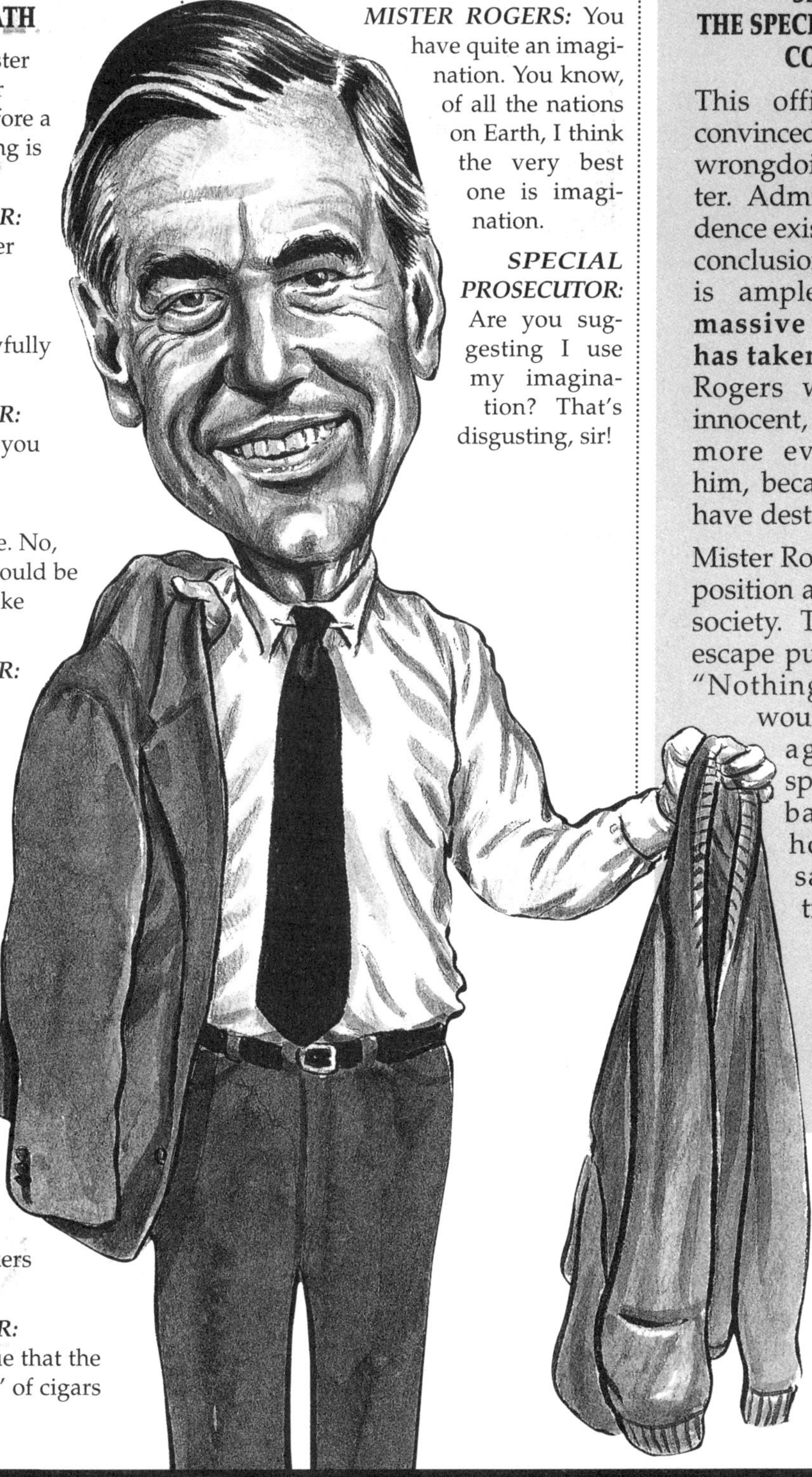

SECTION NINE: THE SPECIAL PROSECUTOR'S CONCLUSION

This office has become convinced of Mister Rogers' wrongdoing in some matter. Admittedly, little evidence exists to support this conclusion. However, that is ample proof of the **massive cover-up that has taken place.** If Mister Rogers were completely innocent, there would be more evidence against him, because he wouldn't have destroyed it all.

Mister Rogers holds a high position as a role model in society. To allow him to escape punishment in this "Nothing-Gate" matter would surely encourage other soft-spoken Pittsburgh-based television hosts to do the same. This country cannot afford such a crime wave. Can you say "Screw due process"? I knew you could.

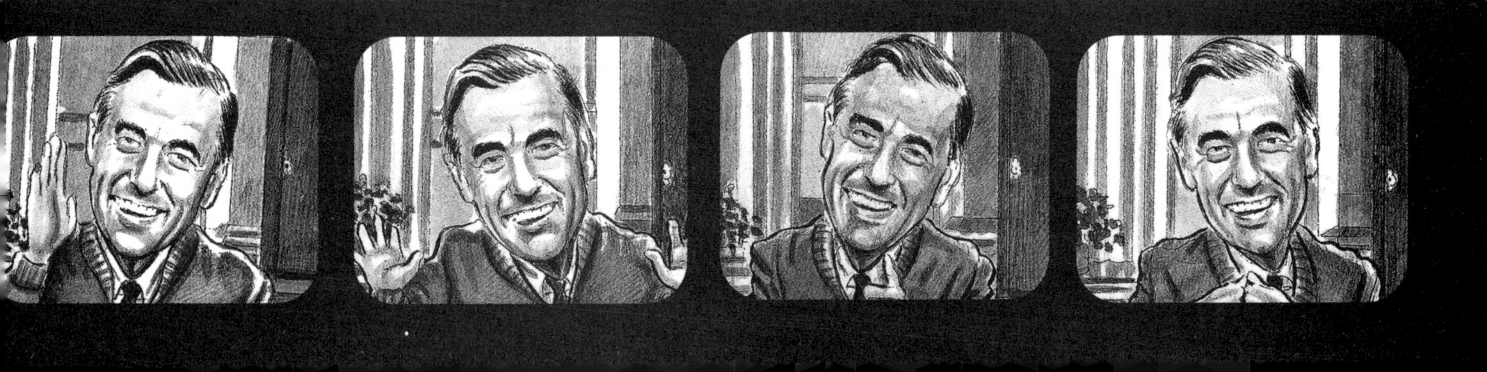

JERRY-MANDERING DEPT.

The handwriting is on the wall. NBC knows it's just a matter of time before the *Seinfeld* gang takes their millions and goes home. And when they do, there goes the network's lock on Thursday night. And when Thursday night goes, NBC's number one rating is sure to follow. Soon, stock in its parent company, General Electric, plummets. And when General Electric, which manufactures everything from light bulbs to nuclear weapons goes belly up, our country will be left dark and defenseless, vulnerable to hostile nations all over the world! We can only hope that somewhere, hidden in a vault in Burbank, some slimy TV exec has devised...

NBC's DESPERATE PLANS FOR *Seinfeld* SPINOFFS

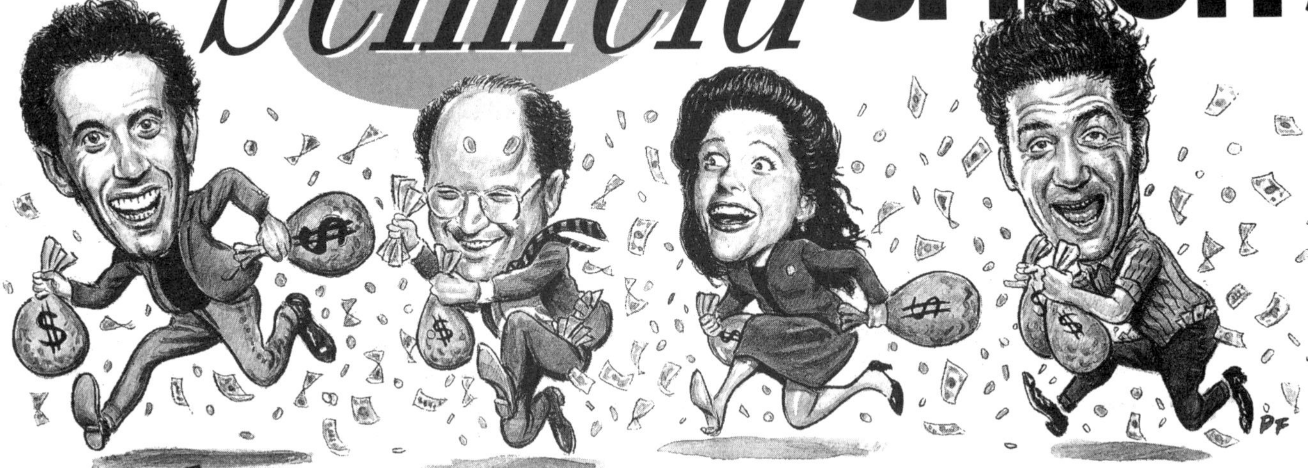

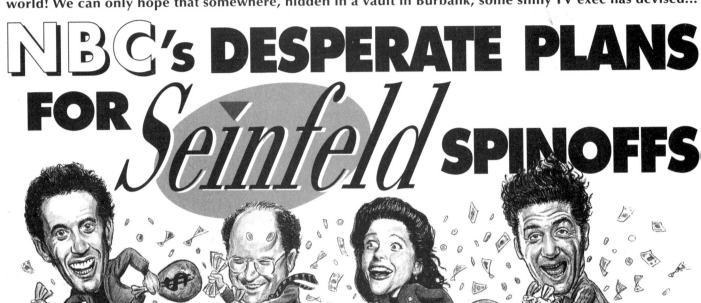

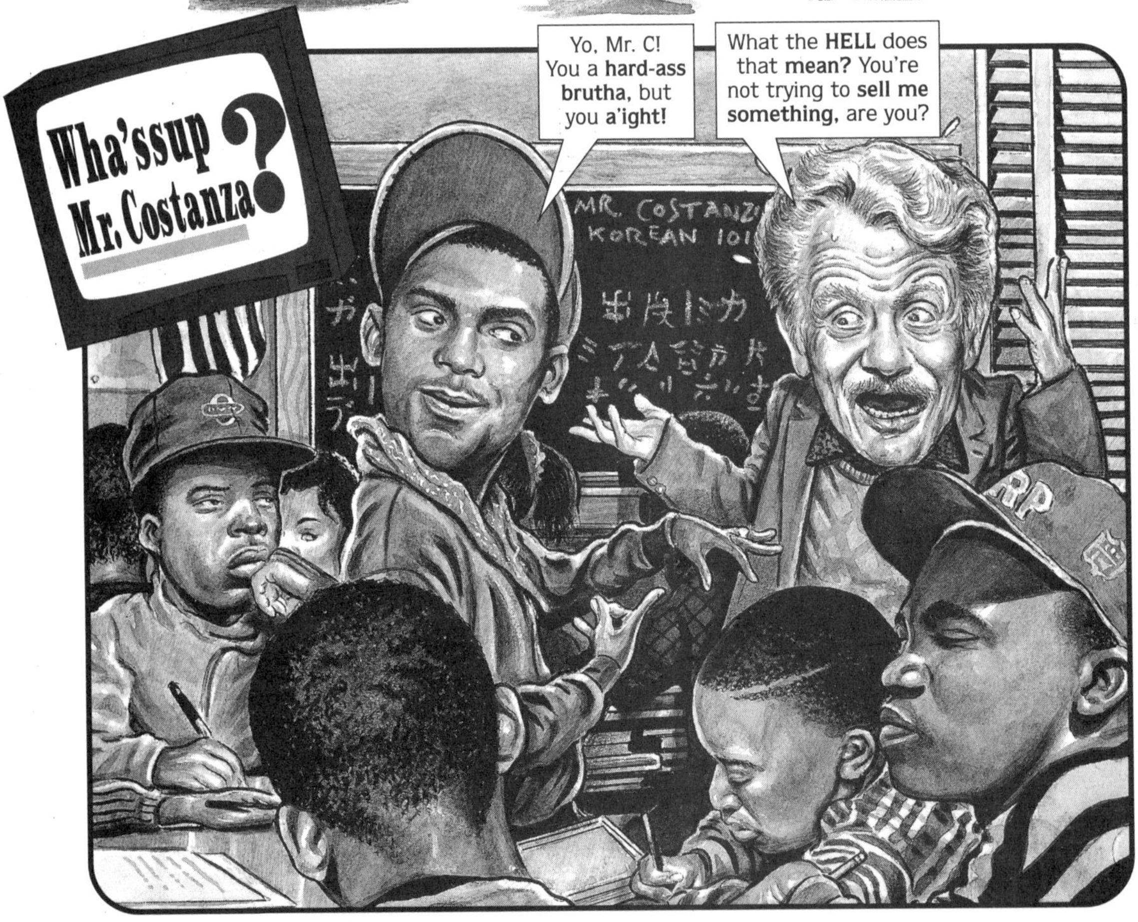
Wha'ssup Mr. Costanza?
Yo, Mr. C! You a **hard-ass brutha**, but you **a'ight!**
What the **HELL** does that **mean?** You're not trying to **sell me something**, are you?
MR. COSTANZ
KOREAN 101

In this show, targeted at the hip, urban audience, George Costanza's father (Jerry Stiller), leaves his wife moves to Los Angeles and takes a job teaching Korean at a rough South Central High School. At first, cultures clash when Mr. Costanza bans hip-hop music from the school dance in favor of Tony Bennett. But when he befriends the leader of the Crips (*French Prince of Bel Air's* Alfonso Ribeiro), the kids learn that he's funky fresh, phat, dope and down — even though he has no idea what that means!

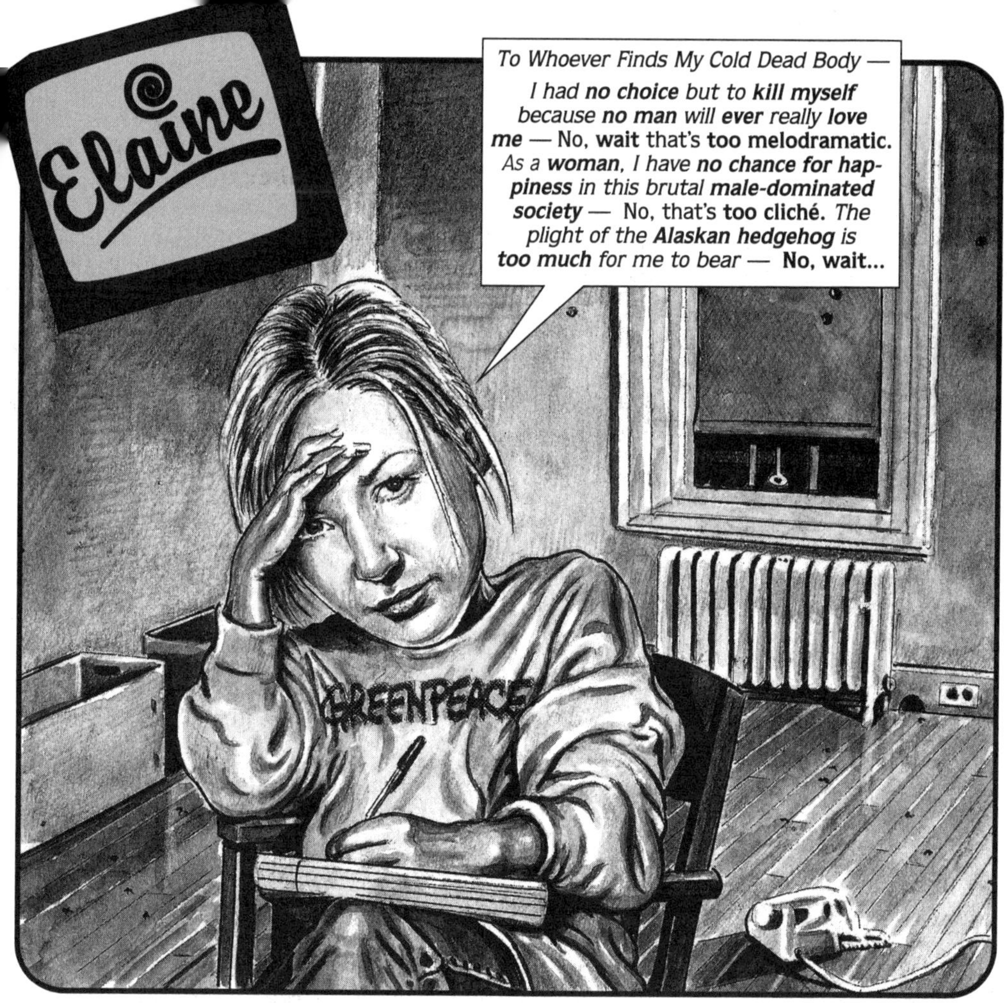
Elaine
To Whoever Finds My Cold Dead Body —
*I had **no choice** but to **kill myself** because **no man** will **ever** really **love me*** — No, **wait** that's **too melodramatic.** *As a **woman**, I have **no chance for happiness** in this brutal **male-dominated society*** — No, that's **too cliché.** *The plight of the **Alaskan hedgehog** is **too much** for me to bear* — **No, wait...**
GREENPEACE

With Julia Louis-Dreyfus demanding two million dollars an episode, plus a diamond-encrusted toilet in her dressing room, the Peacock Network makes a bold move and casts pop music sensation Jewel as the "new" Elaine Benes. To ensure that viewers will accept such a radically different looking Elaine, the show's catchy theme song tells the story of her gruesome car wreck, horrible disfigurement and successful reconstructive plastic surgery. Playing to Jewel's strengths, NBC also makes a few "minor changes" in her character. Due to the accident, the "new" Elaine is no longer witty, outgoing and fun to be with, but is now depressively needy, introspective and spends most of her time trying to perfect her suicide note.

ARTIST: DREW FRIEDMAN WRITERS: JOE RAIOLA & DAVID SHAYNE

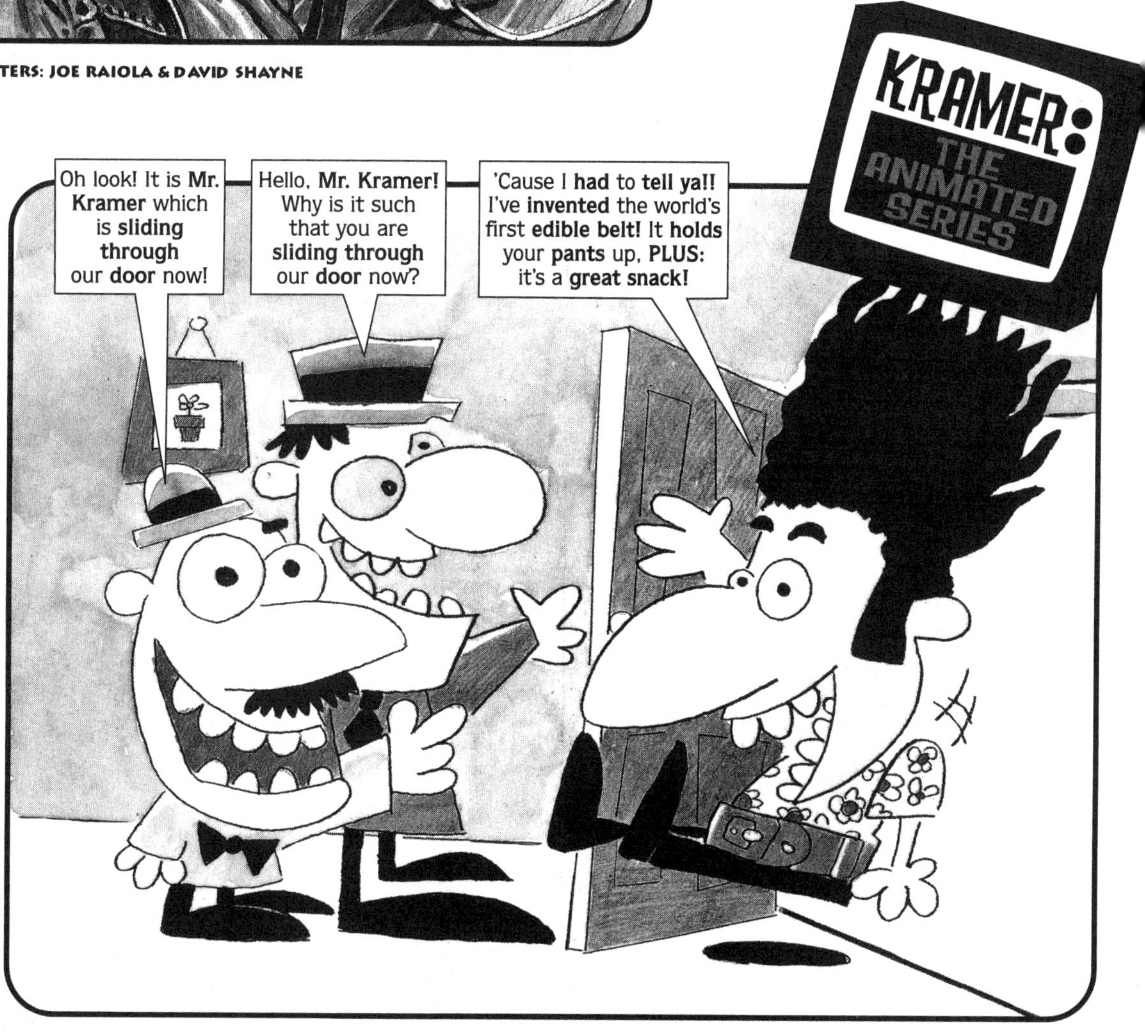
KRAMER: THE ANIMATED SERIES
Oh look! It is **Mr. Kramer** which is **sliding through** our **door** now!
Hello, **Mr. Kramer!** Why is it such that you are **sliding through** our **door** now?
'Cause I **had** to **tell ya!!** I've **invented** the world's first **edible belt!** It **holds** your **pants** up, **PLUS:** it's a **great snack!**

The good news is Michael Richards is back as the voice of Kramer in this new cartoon series in the subversive tradition of *The Simpsons*. The bad news is that due to his exorbitant salary, NBC must cut costs by having the show produced by a third-rate animation studio in Qandahar, Afghanistan. Rounding out the cast are international "stars" Ezekiel Shabidar, Achmel Barahahaha and Wendy Klein.

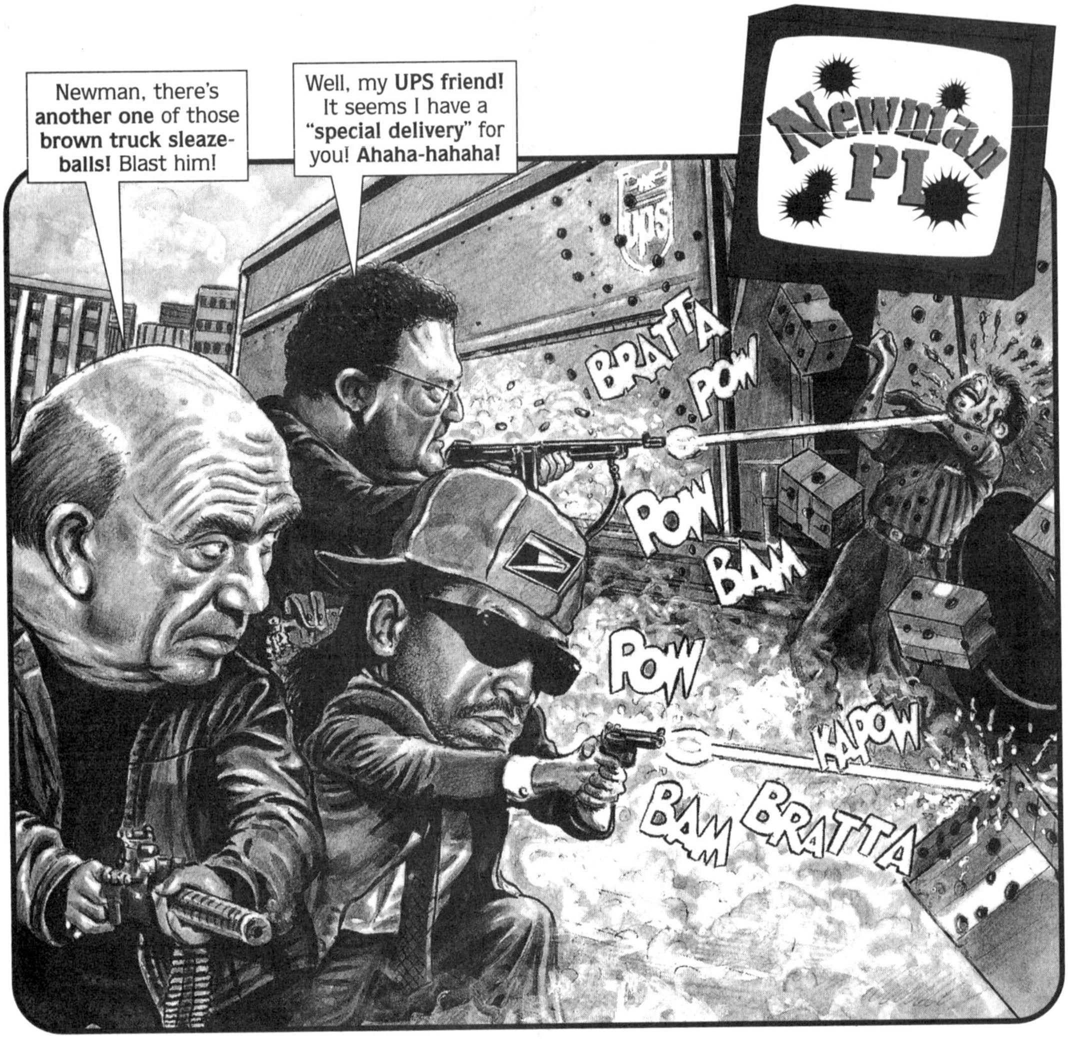
Newman PI
Newman, there's **another one** of those **brown truck sleaze-balls!** Blast him!
Well, my **UPS friend!** It seems I have a **"special delivery"** for you! **Ahaha-hahaha!**
UPS
BRATTA
POW
POW
BAM
POW
KAPOW
BAM
BRATTA

Wayne Knight reprises his role as the conniving and rotund Newman in television's first post office drama! In the series' two-hour pilot episode, Newman becomes a member of the ZIP Squad, an elite band of hard-nosed Postal Inspectors dedicated to "eliminating those damn efficient bastards at FedEx and UPS at any cost!" Costarring Ed Asner as "The Chief" and rapper Ice-T as "Jimmy-J," Newman's street-smart homeboy informant.

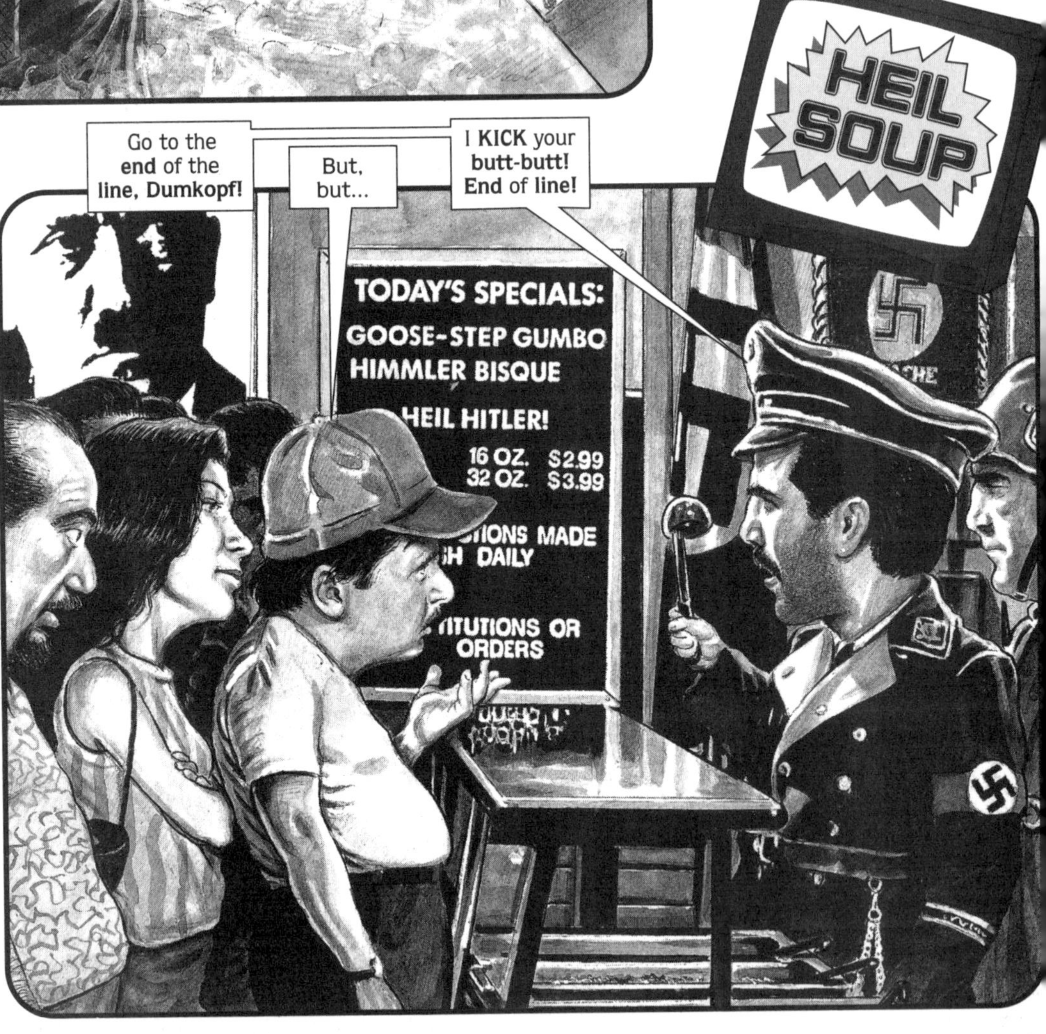
HEIL SOUP
Go to the **end** of the **line, Dumkopf!**
But, but...
I **KICK** your **butt-butt! End** of **line!**
TODAY'S SPECIALS:
GOOSE-STEP GUMBO
HIMMLER BISQUE
HEIL HITLER!
16 OZ. $2.99
32 OZ. $3.99

Seinfeld's most controversial guest character is back! In the pilot episode of this new sitcom, the obnoxious soup chef finally learns the terrible nickname everyone calls him behind his back — "The Soup Nazi." When his attempts to put an end to it fail, he decides to milk the Nazi label for everything it's worth! After studying up on the Third Reich and becoming an expert on the Fuhrer's favorite recipes, he changes the name of his shop to Heil Soup, and quadruples his already booming business by serving up Luftwaffe Lentil, Swastika Noodle Chowder and Gestapo Gazpacho.

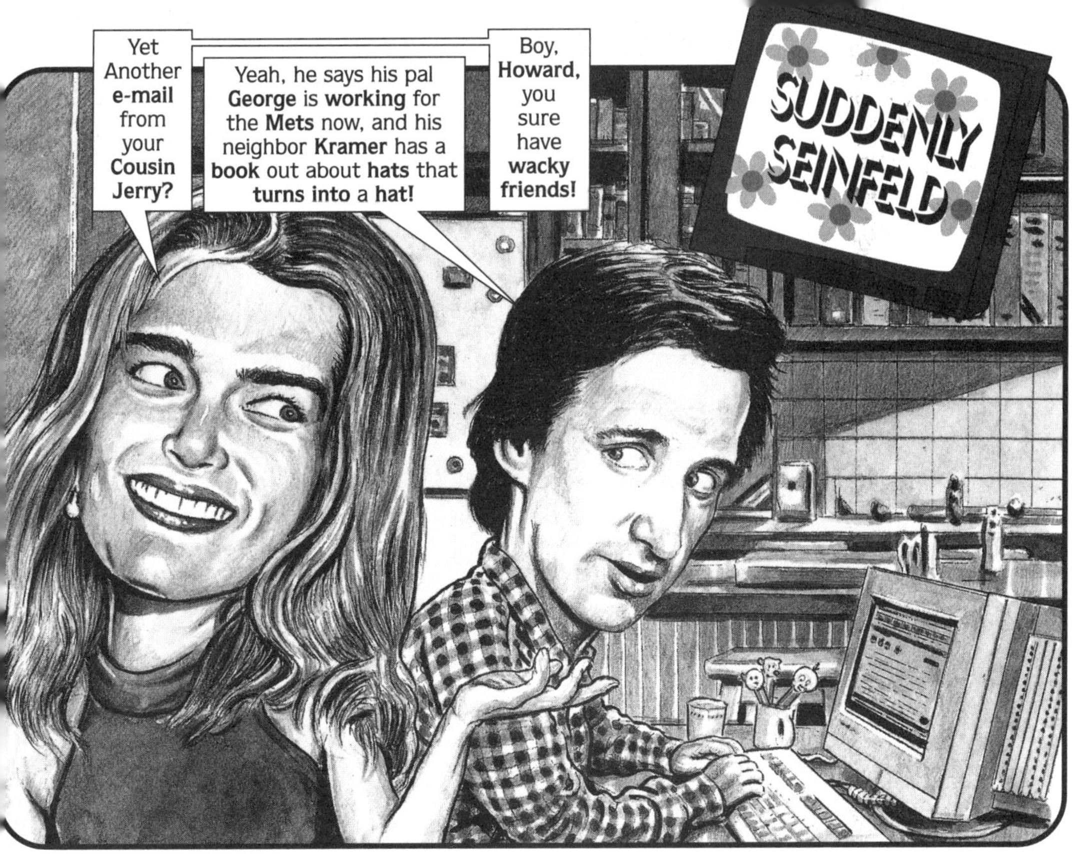

Yet Another e-mail from your Cousin Jerry?
Yeah, he says his pal George is working for the Mets now, and his neighbor Kramer has a book out about hats that turns into a hat!
Boy, Howard, you sure have wacky friends!
SUDDENLY SEINFELD

With NBC desperate for a show — any show — with the name "Seinfeld" in the title, the producers of Suddenly Susan rename their struggling sitcom. While technically not a *Seinfeld* spin-off, *Suddenly Seinfeld* at least has a character named Seinfeld — Jerry's third cousin and Susan's new husband, Howard Seinfeld (Bronson Pinchot). Viewers never actually see or even hear Jerry, but he and his wacky friends are constantly mentioned.

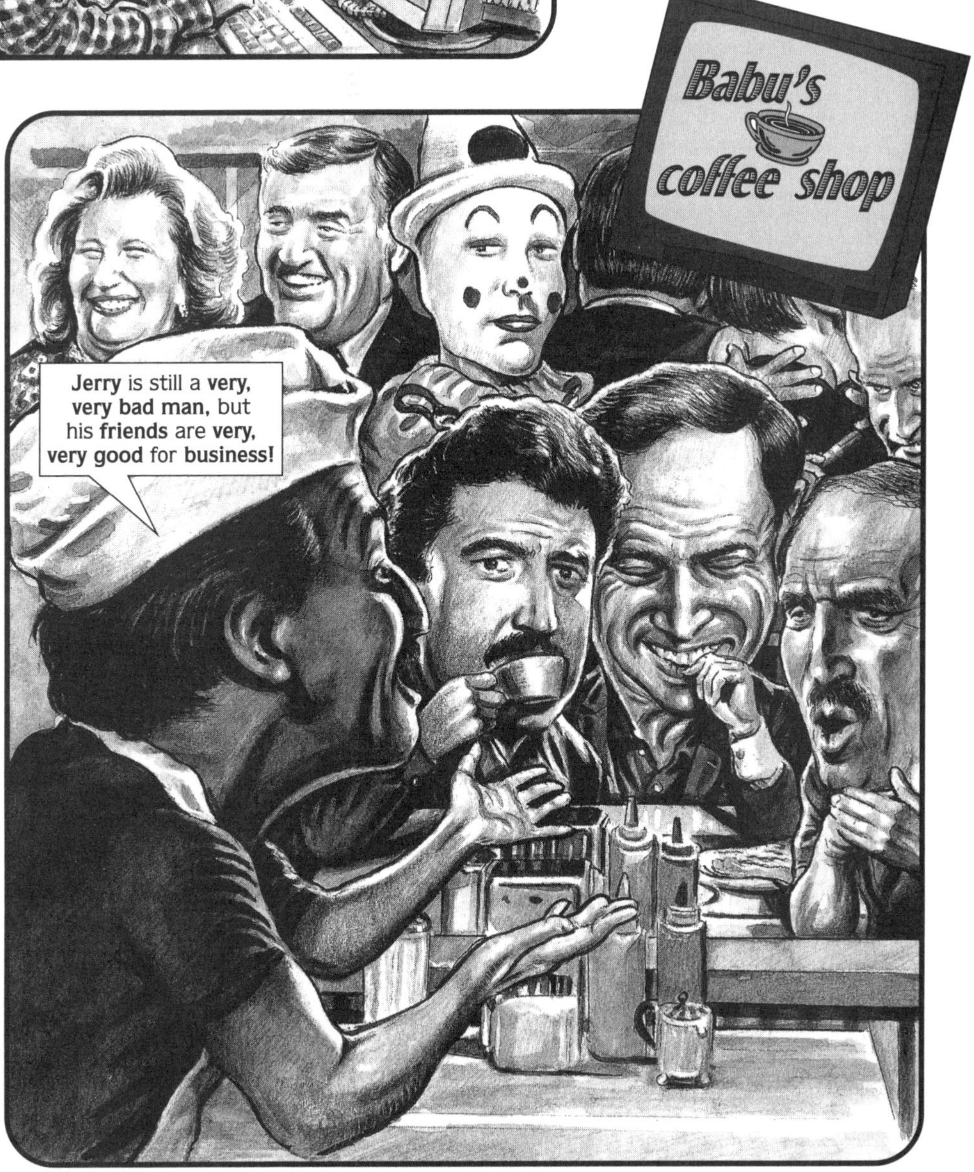

Babu's coffee shop
Jerry is still a very, very bad man, but his friends are very, very good for business!

For NBC it's cheap and easy: Assemble all of *Seinfeld's* recurring and one-shot characters and cram them into a leftover set from the original show. The legendary diner frequented by the old gang is bought out by Jerry's hapless immigrant ex-buddy, Babu. Among the story lines: Crazy Joe Davola stalks Uncle Leo! Poppie convinces George Steinbrenner (back view only) to hire him as the Yankees manager! The Woman With Man Hands accidentally feels up The Woman With Fabulous Breasts (Teri Hatcher)! Mulva marries The Boy In The Bubble! Milos The Tennis Pro and The Drake play Yahtzee with Jerry's parents! Comedian Kenny Bania and ex-big leaguer Keith Hernandez vie for the affection of The Woman Who Invented The Puffy Pirate Shirt! NBC also has plans for a "spin-off-spin-off" featuring every *Seinfeld* extra who ever had a non-speaking role or was seen briefly in the background.

PLANET OF THE GAPES DEPT.

Every morning NBC airs a little program called *The Today Show*. It's like a lot of other network morning programs, w
one exception — as part of its ground-floor studio, there's a giant window that looks out onto the streets of N
York! And outside that window is a collection of dweebs, geeks and yahoos so moronic, they make the cast of
Meets World look like the Nobel Prize selection committee! So, as a public service to our lazy, never-get-out-of-b
before-noon readers (i.e. you), we've gathered all these mouth-breathers together for a little feature we like to ca

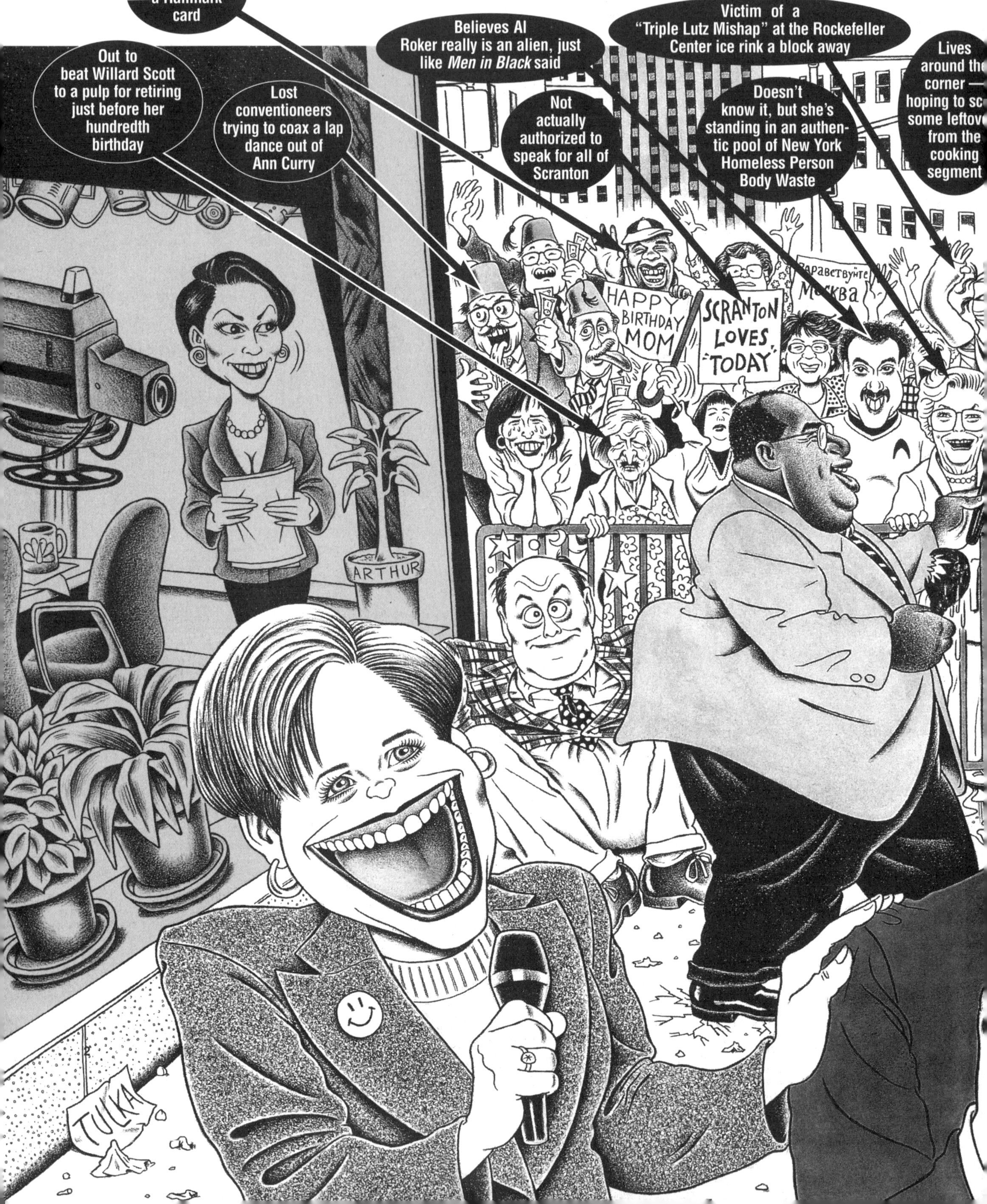

Too cheap to buy a Hallmark card
Out to beat Willard Scott to a pulp for retiring just before her hundredth birthday
Lost conventioneers trying to coax a lap dance out of Ann Curry
Believes Al Roker really is an alien, just like *Men in Black* said
Not actually authorized to speak for all of Scranton
Victim of a "Triple Lutz Mishap" at the Rockefeller Center ice rink a block away
Doesn't know it, but she's standing in an authentic pool of New York Homeless Person Body Waste
Lives around the corner — hoping to sc some leftov from the cooking segment
HAPPY BIRTHDAY MOM
SCRANTON LOVES TODAY
ARTHUR
TULKA

MAD'S GUIDE TO WHO'S WHO OUTSIDE THE TODAY SHOW WINDOW

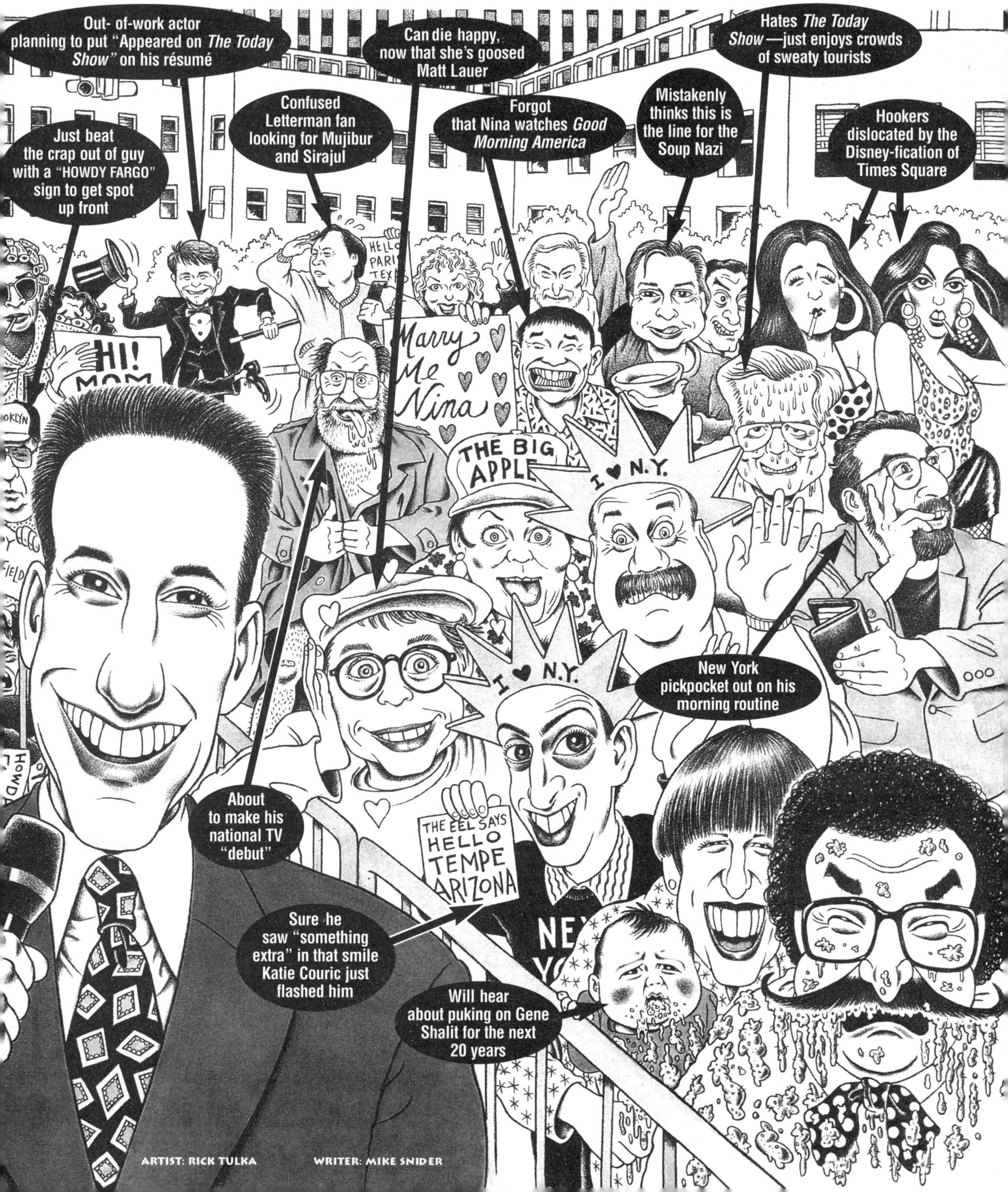
Out- of-work actor planning to put "Appeared on *The Today Show*" on his résumé
Can die happy, now that she's goosed Matt Lauer
Hates *The Today Show*—just enjoys crowds of sweaty tourists
Confused Letterman fan looking for Mujibur and Sirajul
Forgot that Nina watches *Good Morning America*
Mistakenly thinks this is the line for the Soup Nazi
Hookers dislocated by the Disney-fication of Times Square
Just beat the crap out of guy with a "HOWDY FARGO" sign to get spot up front
HI! MOM
Marry Me Nina
THE BIG APPLE
I ♥ N.Y.
I ♥ N.Y.
New York pickpocket out on his morning routine
About to make his national TV "debut"
THE EEL SAYS HELLO TEMPE ARIZONA
Sure he saw "something extra" in that smile Katie Couric just flashed him
Will hear about puking on Gene Shalit for the next 20 years

ARTIST: RICK TULKA WRITER: MIKE SNIDER

WHO GIVES A FLYING FLOCKHART DEPT.

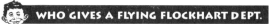

Ready for a spoof about TV's whiniest heroine? We're not either! But what the hell — we've g these five blank pages to fill, so we might as well fill them with a show that's hot! It's about neurotic Boston lawyer who has a tendency to muse and fantasize. As she does, we have a tende cy to doze and snore! Frankly, we don't get it! With a show this boring, there's no explanation for.

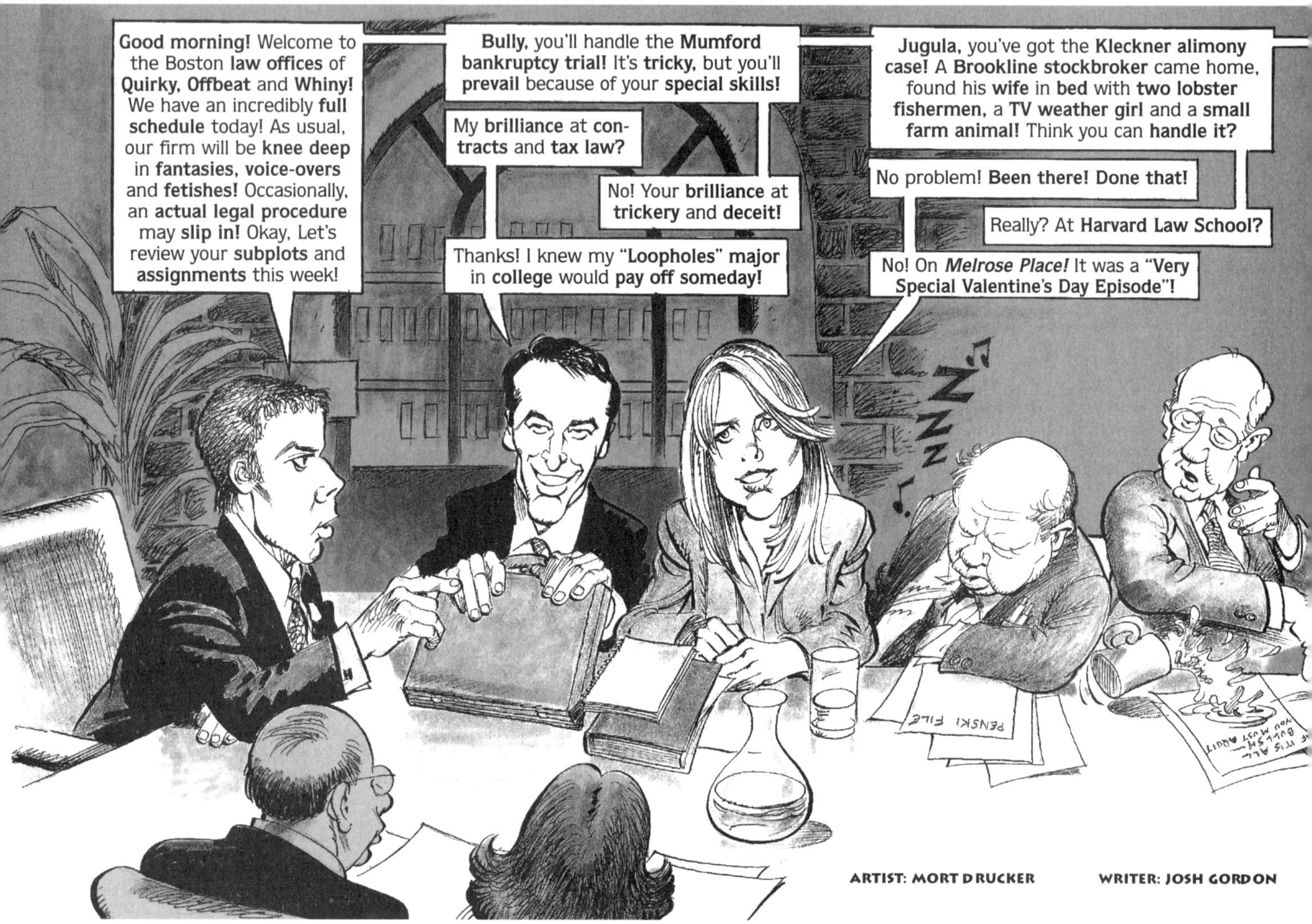

Good morning! Welcome to the Boston law offices of Quirky, Offbeat and Whiny! We have an incredibly full schedule today! As usual, our firm will be knee deep in fantasies, voice-overs and fetishes! Occasionally, an actual legal procedure may slip in! Okay, Let's review your subplots and assignments this week!
Bully, you'll handle the Mumford bankruptcy trial! It's tricky, but you'll prevail because of your special skills!
My brilliance at contracts and tax law?
No! Your brilliance at trickery and deceit!
Thanks! I knew my "Loopholes" major in college would pay off someday!
Jugula, you've got the Kleckner alimony case! A Brookline stockbroker came home, found his wife in bed with two lobster fishermen, a TV weather girl and a small farm animal! Think you can handle it?
No problem! Been there! Done that!
Really? At Harvard Law School?
No! On *Melrose Place!* It was a "Very Special Valentine's Day Episode"!
PENSKI FILE

ARTIST: MORT DRUCKER WRITER: JOSH GORDON

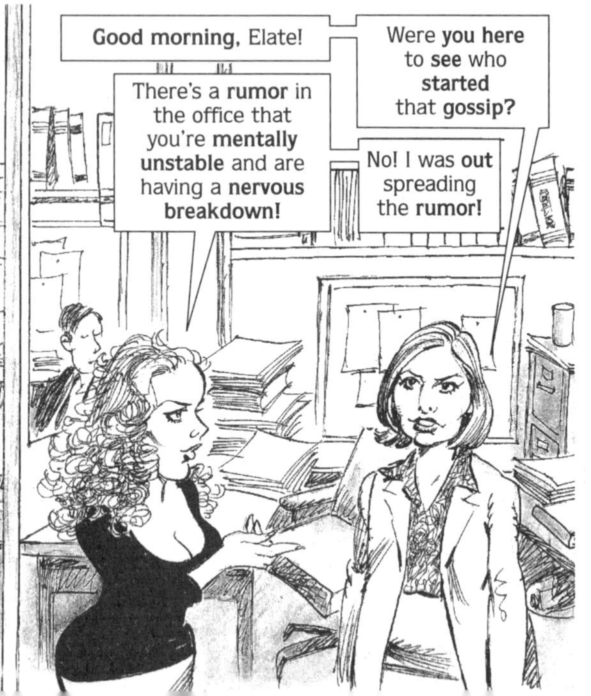

Good morning, Elate!
There's a rumor in the office that you're mentally unstable and are having a nervous breakdown!
Were you here to see who started that gossip?
No! I was out spreading the rumor!

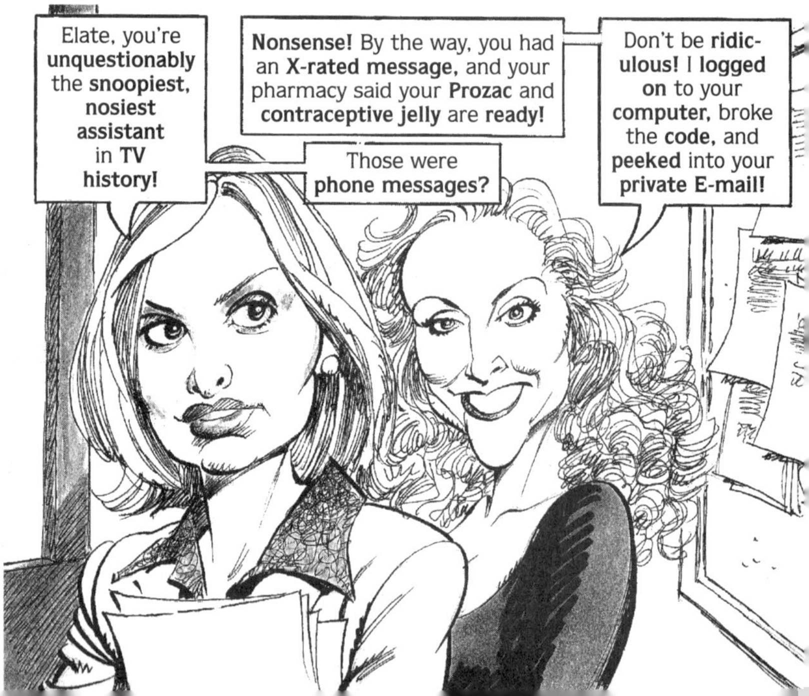

Elate, you're unquestionably the snoopiest, nosiest assistant in TV history!
Nonsense! By the way, you had an X-rated message, and your pharmacy said your Prozac and contraceptive jelly are ready!
Those were phone messages?
Don't be ridiculous! I logged on to your computer, broke the code, and peeked into your private E-mail!

Ally's Appeal

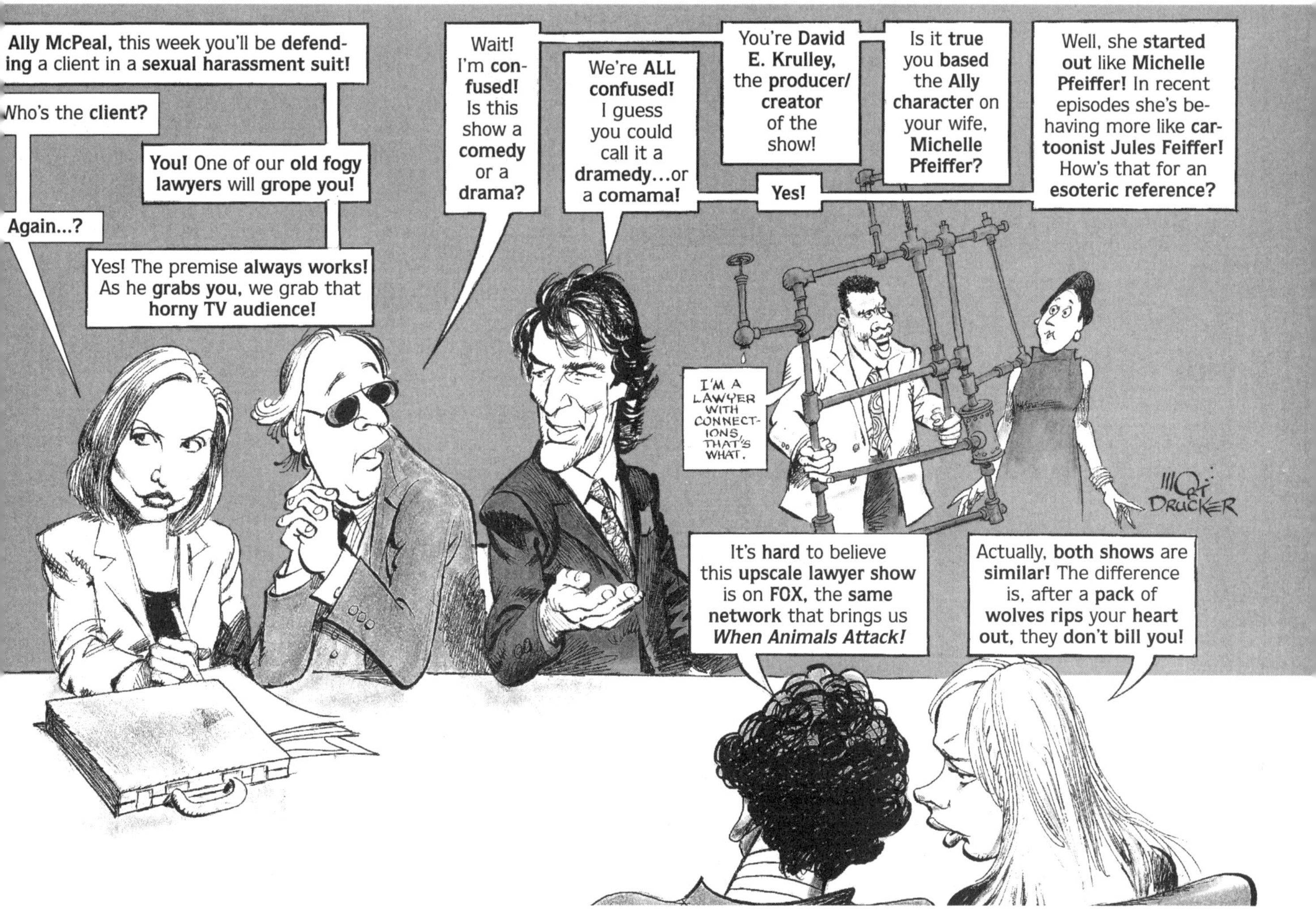

Ally McPeal, this week you'll be **defending** a client in a **sexual harassment suit!**
Who's the **client?**
You! One of our **old fogy lawyers** will **grope you!**
Again...?
Yes! The premise **always works!** As he **grabs you,** we grab that **horny TV audience!**
Wait! I'm **confused!** Is this show a **comedy** or a **drama?**
We're **ALL confused!** I guess you could call it a **dramedy**...or a **comama!**
You're **David E. Krulley,** the **producer/ creator** of the show!
Yes!
Is it **true** you **based** the **Ally character** on your wife, **Michelle Pfeiffer?**
Well, she **started out** like **Michelle Pfeiffer!** In recent episodes she's behaving more like **cartoonist Jules Feiffer!** How's that for an **esoteric reference?**
I'M A LAWYER WITH CONNECTIONS, THAT'S WHAT.
MORT DRUCKER
It's **hard** to believe this **upscale lawyer show** is on **FOX,** the **same network** that brings us ***When Animals Attack!***
Actually, **both shows** are **similar!** The difference is, after a **pack** of **wolves rips** your **heart out,** they **don't bill you!**

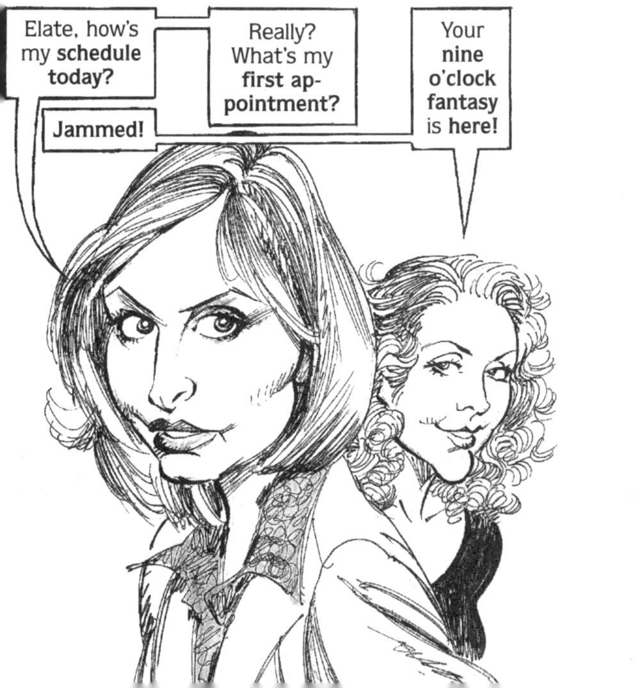

Elate, how's my **schedule today?**
Jammed!
Really? What's my **first appointment?**
Your **nine o'clock fantasy** is **here!**

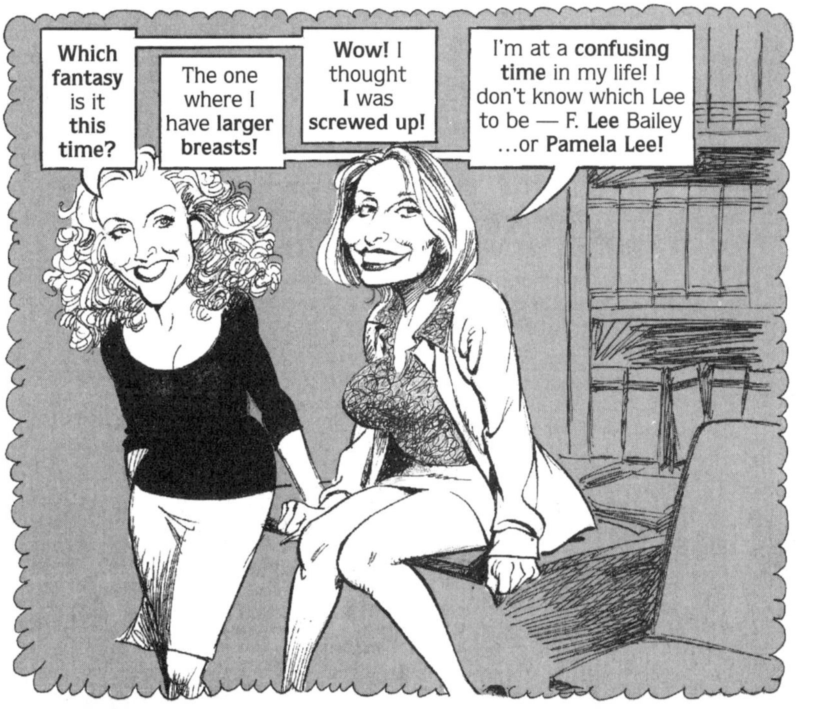

Which fantasy is it **this time?**
The one where I have **larger breasts!**
Wow! I thought **I was screwed up!**
I'm at a **confusing time** in my life! I don't know which Lee to be — F. **Lee** Bailey ...or **Pamela Lee!**

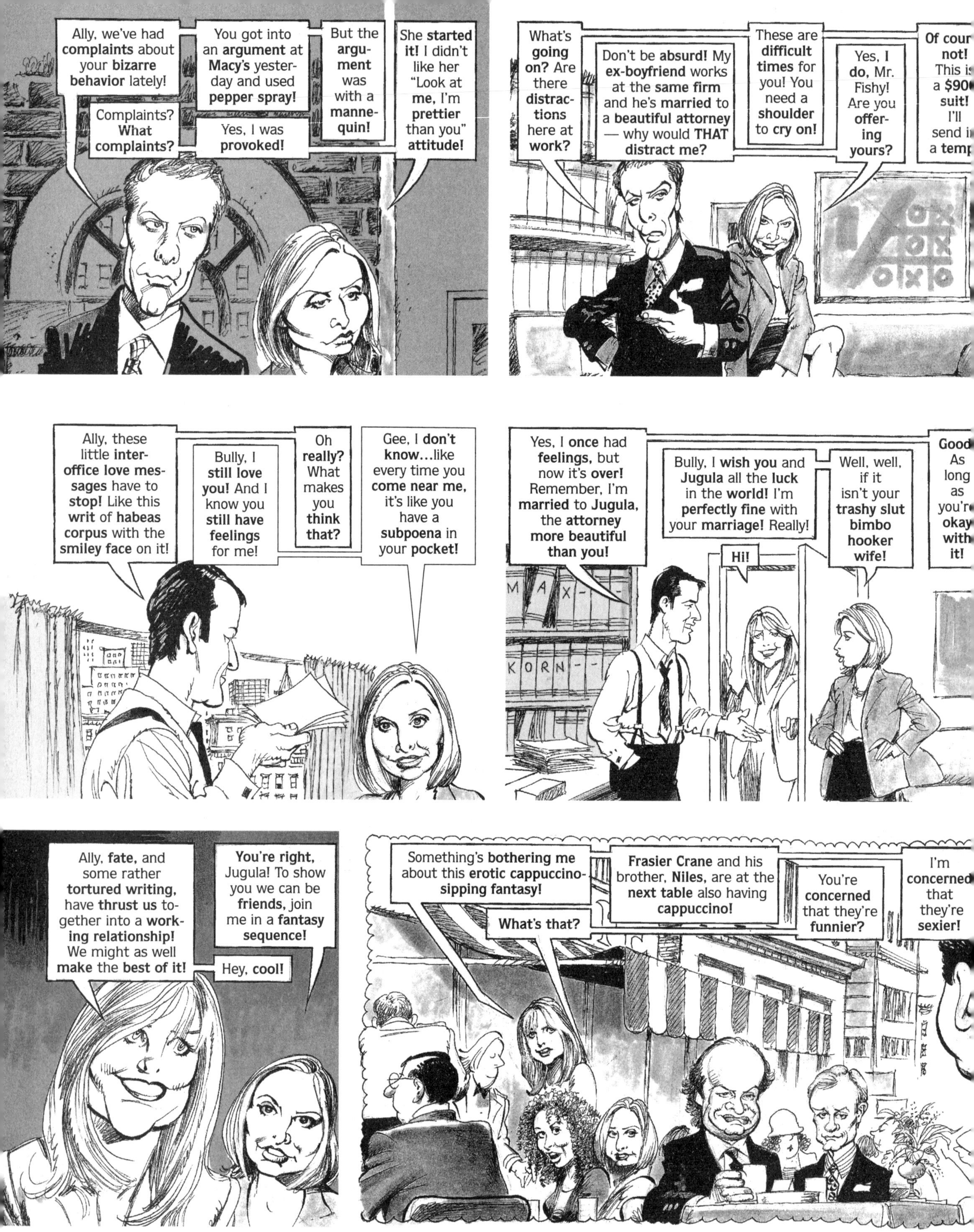
Ally, we've had complaints about your bizarre behavior lately!
Complaints? What complaints?
You got into an argument at Macy's yesterday and used pepper spray!
Yes, I was provoked!
But the argument was with a mannequin!
She started it! I didn't like her "Look at me, I'm prettier than you" attitude!
What's going on? Are there distractions here at work?
Don't be absurd! My ex-boyfriend works at the same firm and he's married to a beautiful attorney — why would THAT distract me?
These are difficult times for you! You need a shoulder to cry on!
Yes, I do, Mr. Fishy! Are you offering yours?
Of cour not! This i a $90 suit! I'll send i a temp
Ally, these little inter-office love messages have to stop! Like this writ of habeas corpus with the smiley face on it!
Bully, I still love you! And I know you still have feelings for me!
Oh really? What makes you think that?
Gee, I don't know…like every time you come near me, it's like you have a subpoena in your pocket!
Yes, I once had feelings, but now it's over! Remember, I'm married to Jugula, the attorney more beautiful than you!
Hi!
Bully, I wish you and Jugula all the luck in the world! I'm perfectly fine with your marriage! Really!
Well, well, if it isn't your trashy slut bimbo hooker wife!
Good! As long as you'r okay with it!
Ally, fate, and some rather tortured writing, have thrust us together into a working relationship! We might as well make the best of it!
You're right, Jugula! To show you we can be friends, join me in a fantasy sequence!
Hey, cool!
Something's bothering me about this erotic cappuccino-sipping fantasy!
What's that?
Frasier Crane and his brother, Niles, are at the next table also having cappuccino!
You're concerned that they're funnier?
I'm concerned that they're sexier!

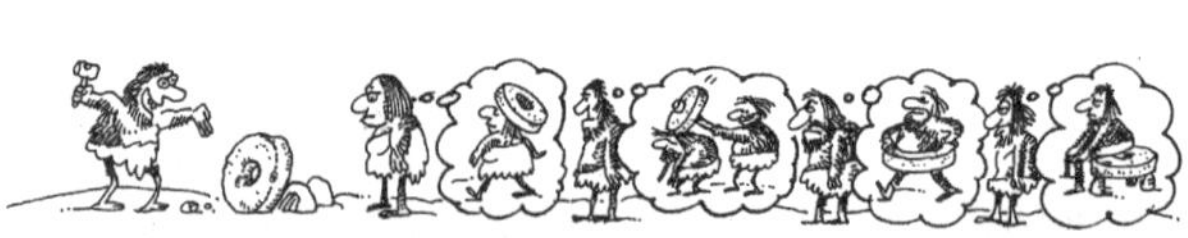

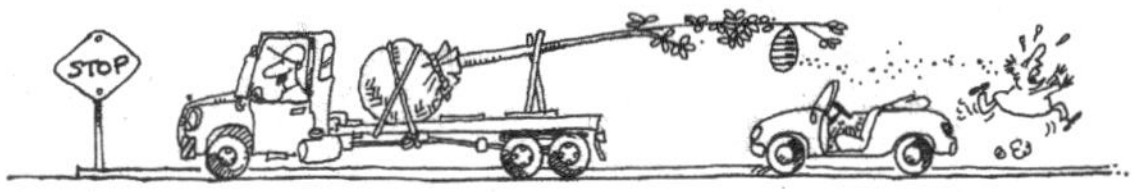
STOP

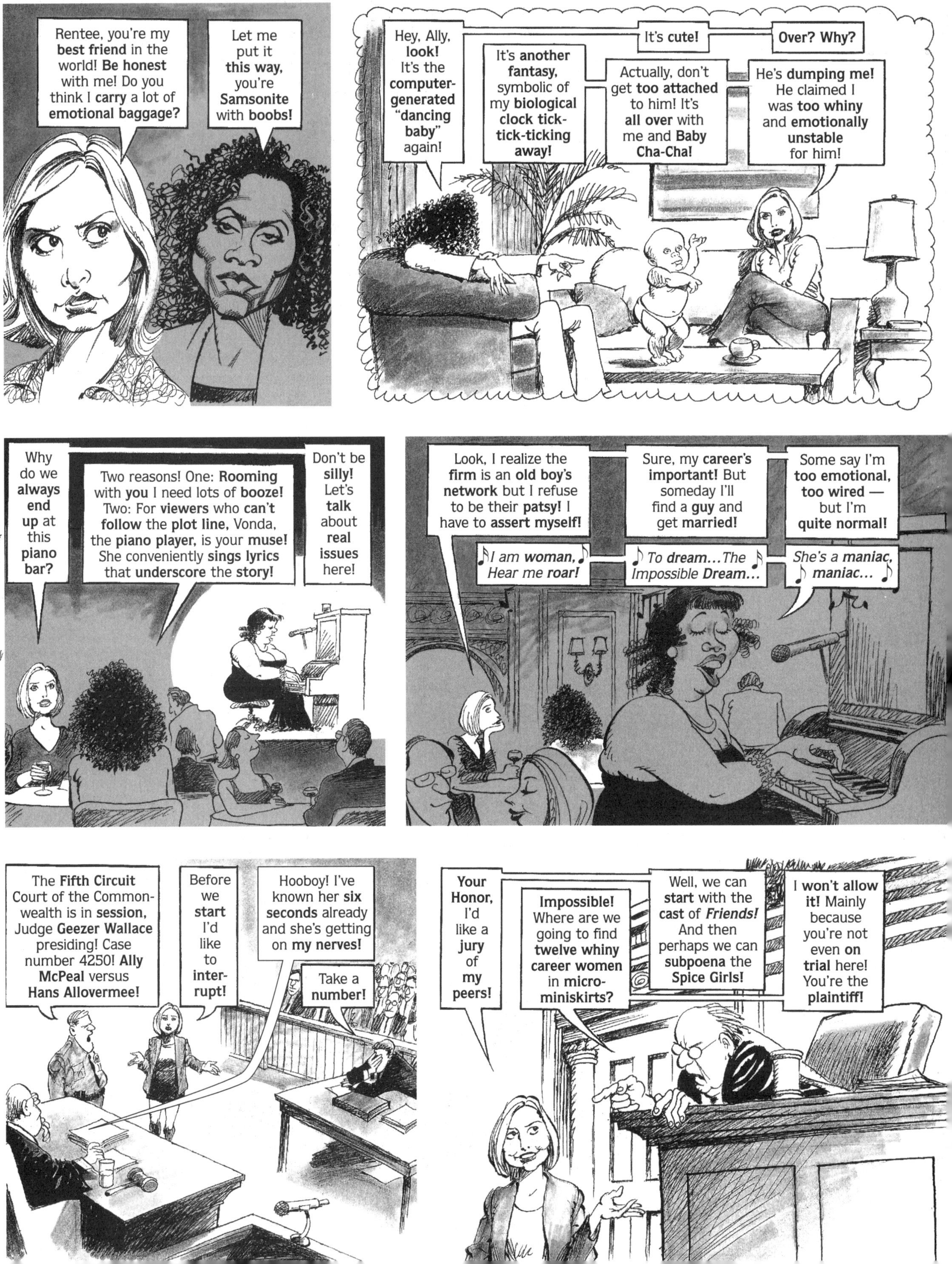
Rentee, you're my best friend in the world! Be honest with me! Do you think I carry a lot of emotional baggage?
Let me put it this way, you're Samsonite with boobs!
Hey, Ally, look! It's the computer-generated "dancing baby" again!
It's another fantasy, symbolic of my biological clock tick-tick-ticking away!
It's cute!
Actually, don't get too attached to him! It's all over with me and Baby Cha-Cha!
Over? Why?
He's dumping me! He claimed I was too whiny and emotionally unstable for him!
Why do we always end up at this piano bar?
Two reasons! One: Rooming with you I need lots of booze! Two: For viewers who can't follow the plot line, Vonda, the piano player, is your muse! She conveniently sings lyrics that underscore the story!
Don't be silly! Let's talk about real issues here!
Look, I realize the firm is an old boy's network but I refuse to be their patsy! I have to assert myself!
♪I am woman, ♪ Hear me roar!
Sure, my career's important! But someday I'll find a guy and get married!
♪ To dream…The ♪ Impossible Dream…
Some say I'm too emotional, too wired — but I'm quite normal!
She's a maniac, ♪ maniac… ♪
The Fifth Circuit Court of the Commonwealth is in session, Judge Geezer Wallace presiding! Case number 4250! Ally McPeal versus Hans Allovermee!
Before we start I'd like to interrupt!
Hooboy! I've known her six seconds already and she's getting on my nerves!
Take a number!
Your Honor, I'd like a jury of my peers!
Impossible! Where are we going to find twelve whiny career women in microminiskirts?
Well, we can start with the cast of *Friends!* And then perhaps we can subpoena the Spice Girls!
I won't allow it! Mainly because you're not even on trial here! You're the plaintiff!

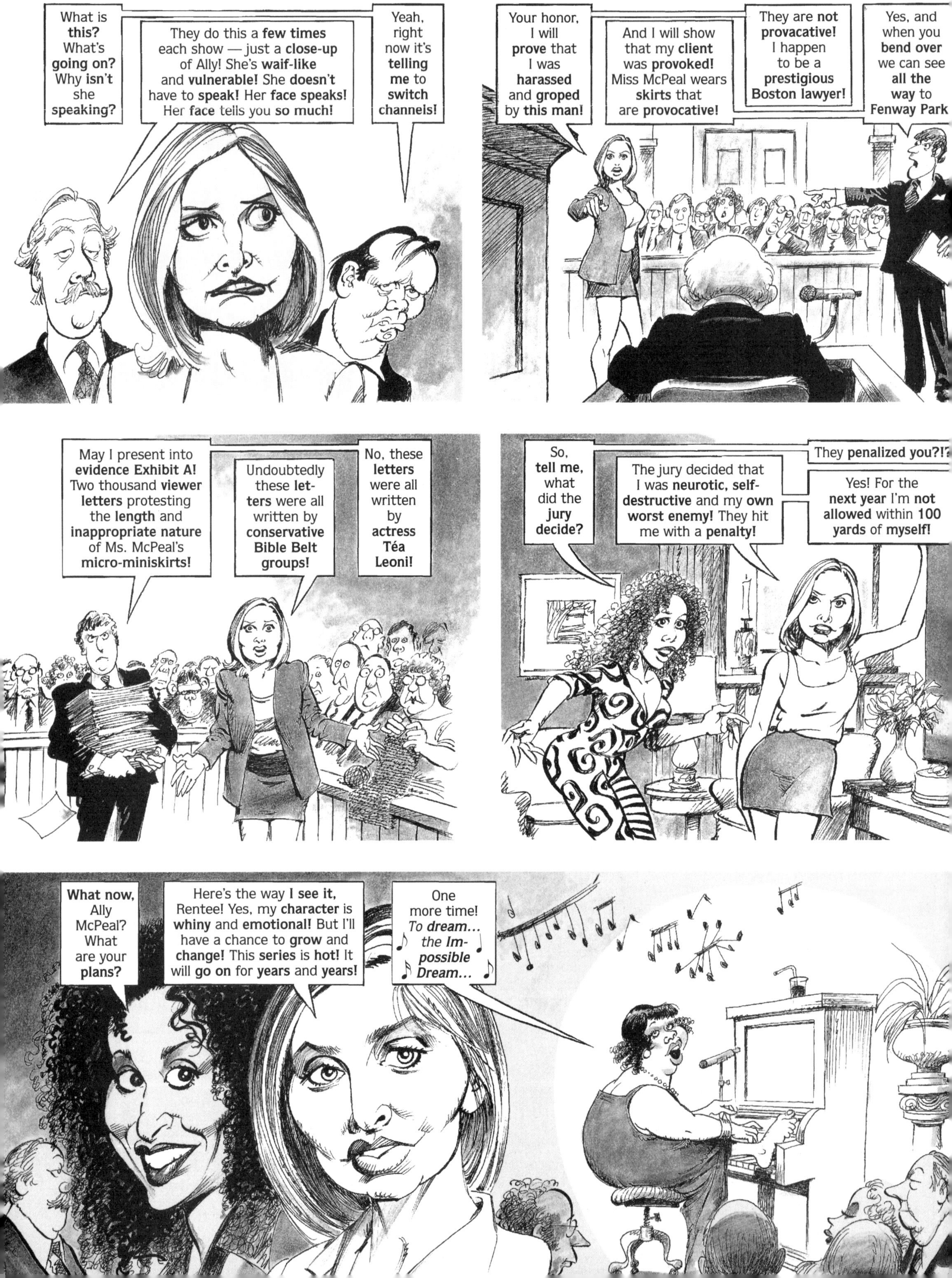

What is this? What's going on? Why isn't she speaking?
They do this a few times each show — just a close-up of Ally! She's waif-like and vulnerable! She doesn't have to speak! Her face speaks! Her face tells you so much!
Yeah, right now it's telling me to switch channels!
Your honor, I will prove that I was harassed and groped by this man!
And I will show that my client was provoked! Miss McPeal wears skirts that are provocative!
They are not provacative! I happen to be a prestigious Boston lawyer!
Yes, and when you bend over we can see all the way to Fenway Park
May I present into evidence Exhibit A! Two thousand viewer letters protesting the length and inappropriate nature of Ms. McPeal's micro-miniskirts!
Undoubtedly these letters were all written by conservative Bible Belt groups!
No, these letters were all written by actress Téa Leoni!
So, tell me, what did the jury decide?
The jury decided that I was neurotic, self-destructive and my own worst enemy! They hit me with a penalty!
They penalized you?!?
Yes! For the next year I'm not allowed within 100 yards of myself!
What now, Ally McPeal? What are your plans?
Here's the way I see it, Rentee! Yes, my character is whiny and emotional! But I'll have a chance to grow and change! This series is hot! It will go on for years and years!
One more time! To dream... the Impossible Dream...

APPRAISE THE THING DEPT.

PBS has this program where antique appraisers travel the country, and people bring them their family heirlooms, things they've dug out of the neighbor's trash, etc., to have them appraised. In case you haven't actually seen it, here are some...

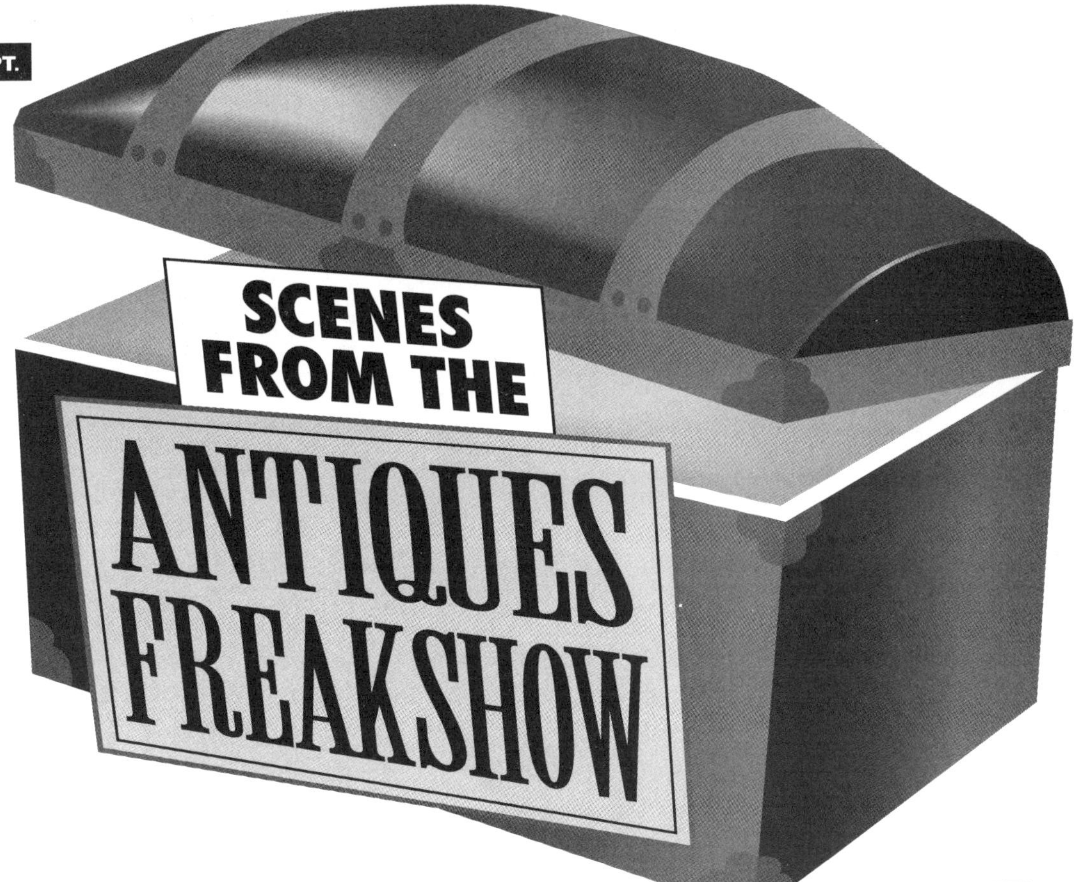

SCENES FROM THE
ANTIQUES FREAKSHOW

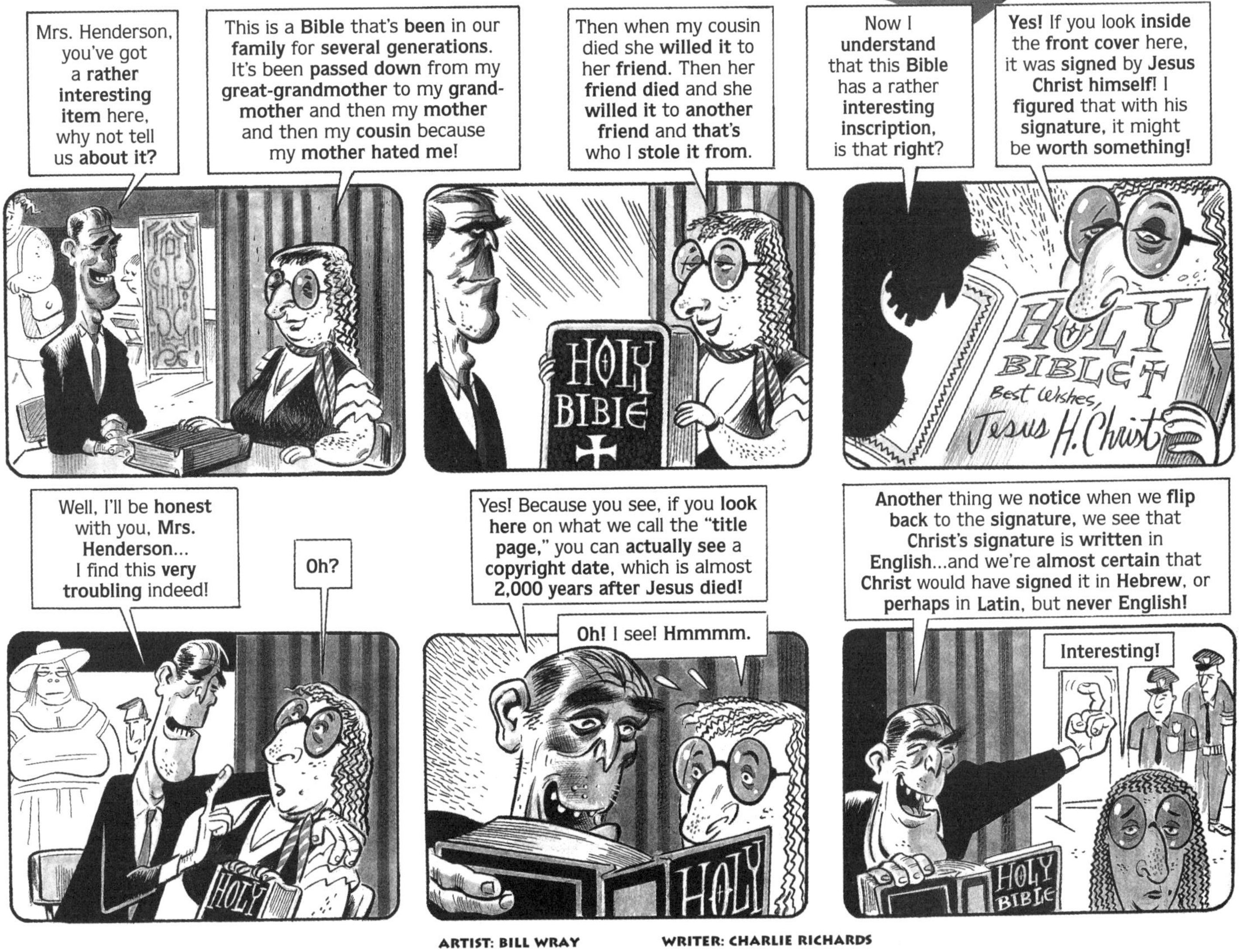

Mrs. Henderson, you've got a rather interesting item here, why not tell us about it?
This is a Bible that's been in our family for several generations. It's been passed down from my great-grandmother to my grand-mother and then my mother and then my cousin because my mother hated me!
Then when my cousin died she willed it to her friend. Then her friend died and she willed it to another friend and that's who I stole it from.
HOLY BIBLE
Now I understand that this Bible has a rather interesting inscription, is that right?
Yes! If you look inside the front cover here, it was signed by Jesus Christ himself! I figured that with his signature, it might be worth something!
HOLY BIBLE
Best Wishes,
Jesus H. Christ
Well, I'll be honest with you, Mrs. Henderson... I find this very troubling indeed!
Oh?
HOLY
Yes! Because you see, if you look here on what we call the "title page," you can actually see a copyright date, which is almost 2,000 years after Jesus died!
Oh! I see! Hmmmm.
HOLY
Another thing we notice when we flip back to the signature, we see that Christ's signature is written in English...and we're almost certain that Christ would have signed it in Hebrew, or perhaps in Latin, but never English!
Interesting!
HOLY BIBLE

ARTIST: BILL WRAY WRITER: CHARLIE RICHARDS

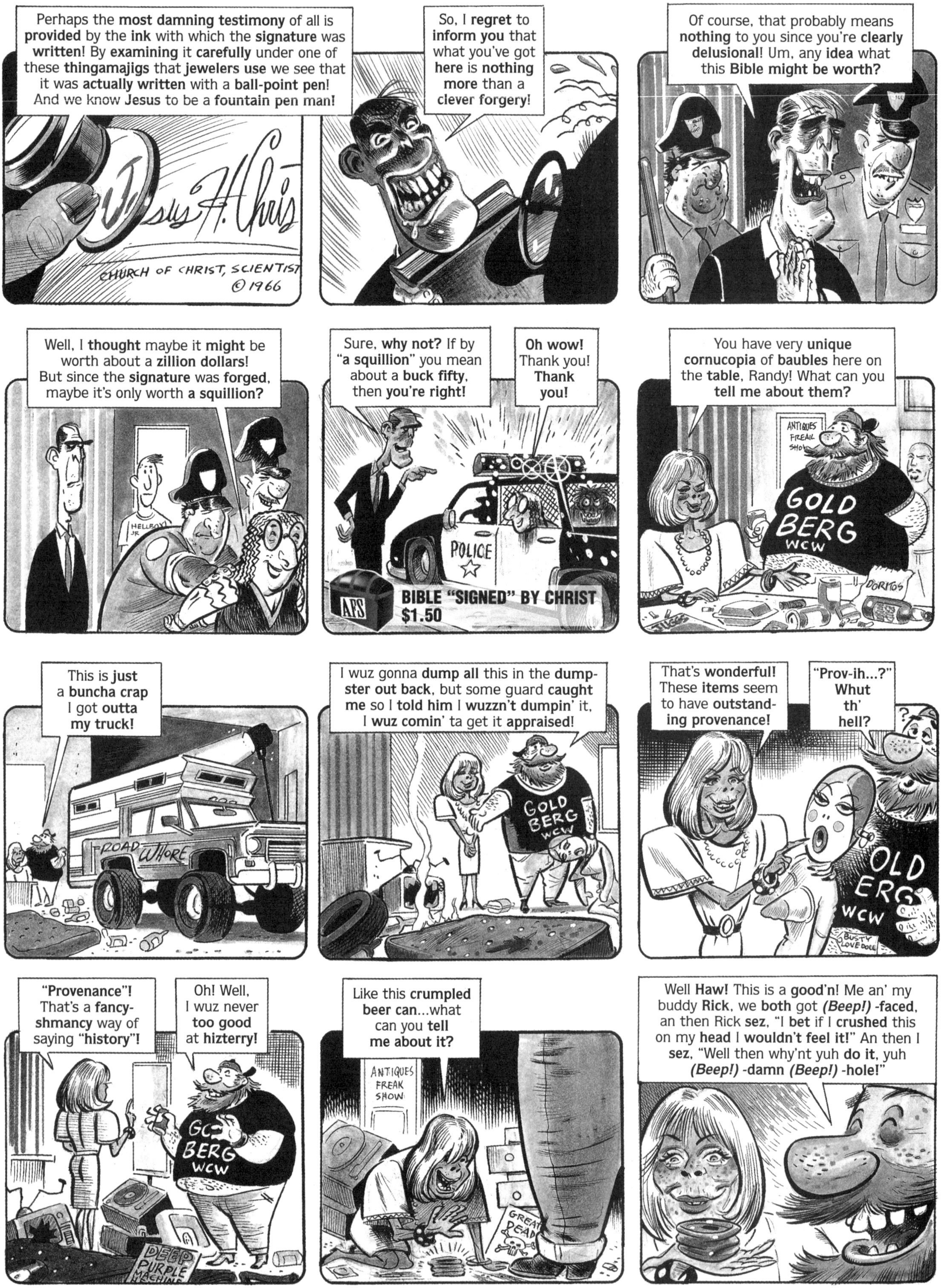

Perhaps the most damning testimony of all is provided by the ink with which the signature was written! By examining it carefully under one of these thingamajigs that jewelers use we see that it was actually written with a ball-point pen! And we know Jesus to be a fountain pen man!
CHURCH OF CHRIST, SCIENTIST © 1966
So, I regret to inform you that what you've got here is nothing more than a clever forgery!
Of course, that probably means nothing to you since you're clearly delusional! Um, any idea what this Bible might be worth?
Well, I thought maybe it might be worth about a zillion dollars! But since the signature was forged, maybe it's only worth a squillion?
HELLBOY JR
Sure, why not? If by "a squillion" you mean about a buck fifty, then you're right!
Oh wow! Thank you! Thank you!
POLICE
AFS
BIBLE "SIGNED" BY CHRIST $1.50
You have very unique cornucopia of baubles here on the table, Randy! What can you tell me about them?
ANTIQUES FREAK SHOW
GOLD BERG WCW
DORITOS
This is just a buncha crap I got outta my truck!
ROAD WHORE
I wuz gonna dump all this in the dumpster out back, but some guard caught me so I told him I wuzzn't dumpin' it, I wuz comin' ta get it appraised!
GOLD BERG WCW
That's wonderful! These items seem to have outstanding provenance!
"Prov-ih...?" Whut th' hell?
OLD ERG WCW
BUSTY LOVE DOLL
"Provenance"! That's a fancy-shmancy way of saying "history"!
Oh! Well, I wuz never too good at hizterry!
BERG WCW
DEEP PURPLE MACHINE
Like this crumpled beer can...what can you tell me about it?
ANTIQUES FREAK SHOW
GREAT DEAD
Well Haw! This is a good'n! Me an' my buddy Rick, we both got (Beep!) -faced, an then Rick sez, "I bet if I crushed this on my head I wouldn't feel it!" An then I sez, "Well then why'nt yuh do it, yuh (Beep!) -damn (Beep!) -hole!"

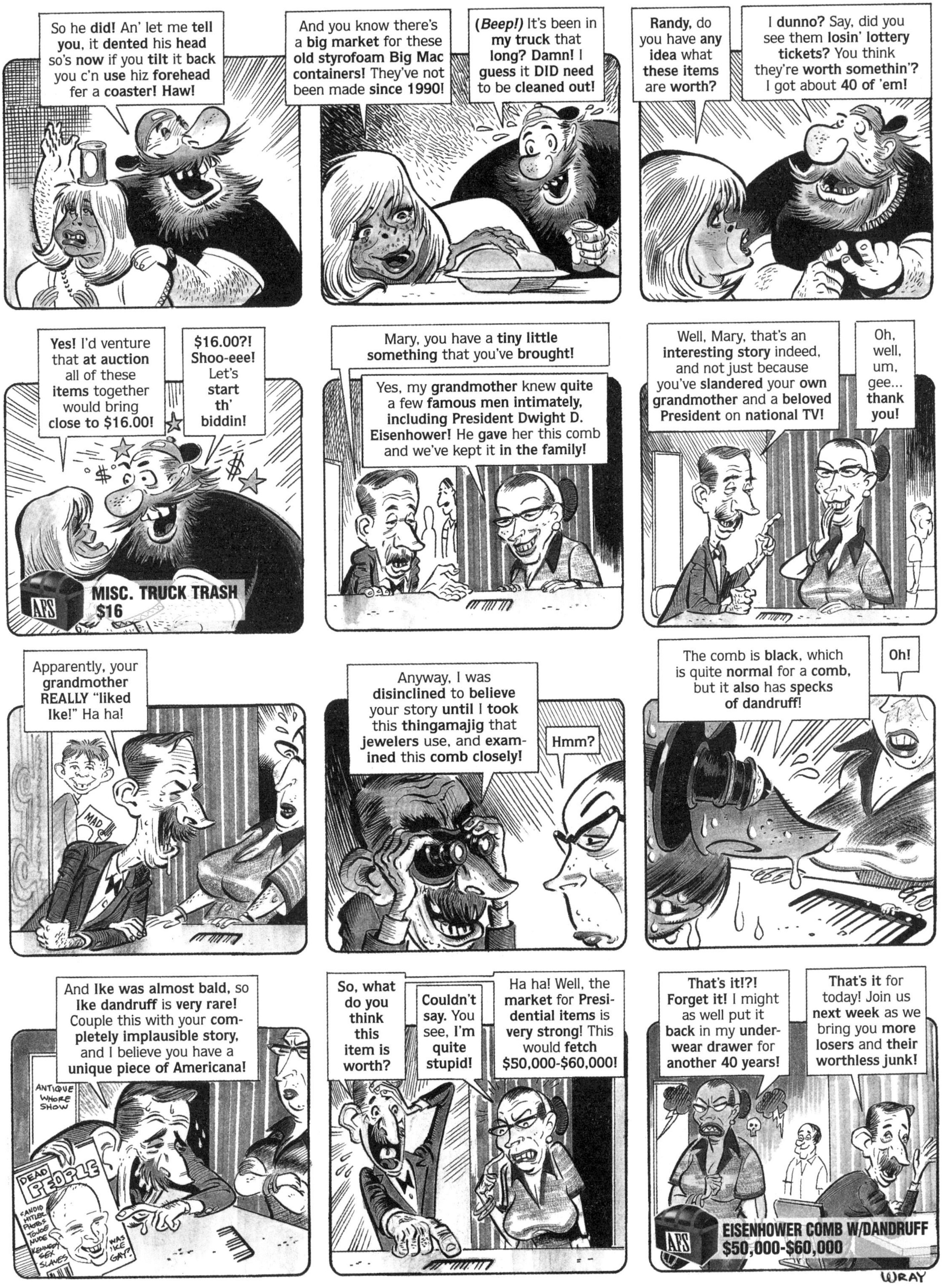

So he did! An' let me tell you, it dented his head so's now if you tilt it back you c'n use hiz forehead fer a coaster! Haw!
And you know there's a big market for these old styrofoam Big Mac containers! They've not been made since 1990!
(Beep!) It's been in my truck that long? Damn! I guess it DID need to be cleaned out!
Randy, do you have any idea what these items are worth?
I dunno? Say, did you see them losin' lottery tickets? You think they're worth somethin'? I got about 40 of 'em!
Yes! I'd venture that at auction all of these items together would bring close to $16.00!
$16.00?! Shoo-eee! Let's start th' biddin!
AFS
MISC. TRUCK TRASH
$16
Mary, you have a tiny little something that you've brought!
Yes, my grandmother knew quite a few famous men intimately, including President Dwight D. Eisenhower! He gave her this comb and we've kept it in the family!
Well, Mary, that's an interesting story indeed, and not just because you've slandered your own grandmother and a beloved President on national TV!
Oh, well, um, gee... thank you!
Apparently, your grandmother REALLY "liked Ike!" Ha ha!
MAD
Anyway, I was disinclined to believe your story until I took this thingamajig that jewelers use, and examined this comb closely!
Hmm?
The comb is black, which is quite normal for a comb, but it also has specks of dandruff!
Oh!
And Ike was almost bald, so Ike dandruff is very rare! Couple this with your completely implausible story, and I believe you have a unique piece of Americana!
ANTIQUE WHORE SHOW
DEAD PEOPLE
WAS IKE GAY?
So, what do you think this item is worth?
Couldn't say. You see, I'm quite stupid!
Ha ha! Well, the market for Presidential items is very strong! This would fetch $50,000-$60,000!
That's it!?! Forget it! I might as well put it back in my underwear drawer for another 40 years!
That's it for today! Join us next week as we bring you more losers and their worthless junk!
AFS
EISENHOWER COMB W/DANDRUFF
$50,000-$60,000
WRAY

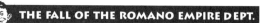

Both Jerry Seinfeld and Tim Allen took some of their stand-up routines and turned them into wildl successful sitcoms. Now, Ray Romano has taken some of his stand-up routines and woven ther into...well, let's put it this way: Good things don't necessarily come in threes! It's no wonder that.

Everybody Loathes Raymud

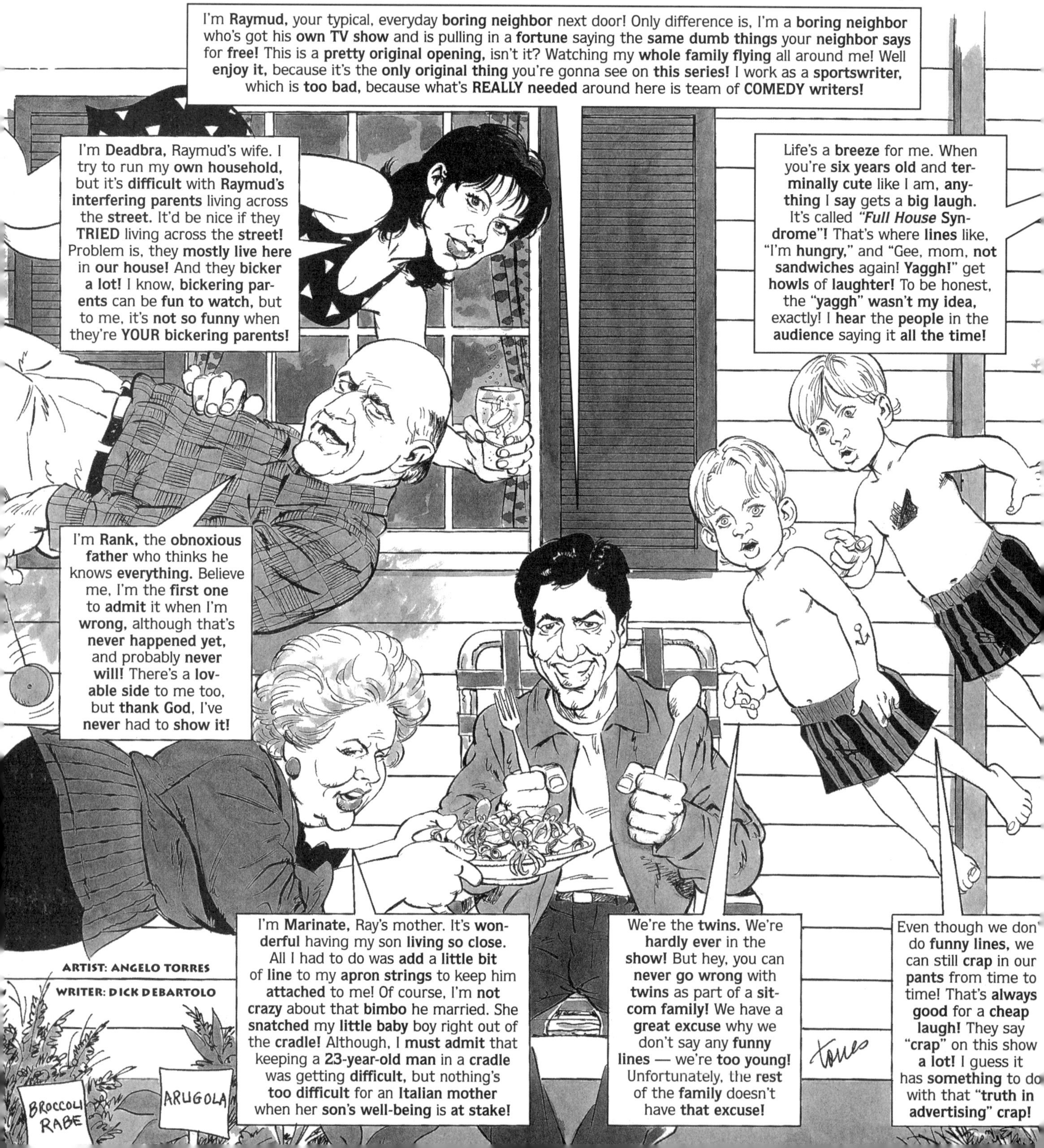
I'm Raymud, your typical, everyday boring neighbor next door! Only difference is, I'm a boring neighbor who's got his own TV show and is pulling in a fortune saying the same dumb things your neighbor says for free! This is a pretty original opening, isn't it? Watching my whole family flying all around me! Well enjoy it, because it's the only original thing you're gonna see on this series! I work as a sportswriter, which is too bad, because what's REALLY needed around here is team of COMEDY writers!
I'm Deadbra, Raymud's wife. I try to run my own household, but it's difficult with Raymud's interfering parents living across the street. It'd be nice if they TRIED living across the street! Problem is, they mostly live here in our house! And they bicker a lot! I know, bickering parents can be fun to watch, but to me, it's not so funny when they're YOUR bickering parents!
Life's a breeze for me. When you're six years old and terminally cute like I am, anything I say gets a big laugh. It's called "Full House Syndrome"! That's where lines like, "I'm hungry," and "Gee, mom, not sandwiches again! Yaggh!" get howls of laughter! To be honest, the "yaggh" wasn't my idea, exactly! I hear the people in the audience saying it all the time!
I'm Rank, the obnoxious father who thinks he knows everything. Believe me, I'm the first one to admit it when I'm wrong, although that's never happened yet, and probably never will! There's a lovable side to me too, but thank God, I've never had to show it!
I'm Marinate, Ray's mother. It's wonderful having my son living so close. All I had to do was add a little bit of line to my apron strings to keep him attached to me! Of course, I'm not crazy about that bimbo he married. She snatched my little baby boy right out of the cradle! Although, I must admit that keeping a 23-year-old man in a cradle was getting difficult, but nothing's too difficult for an Italian mother when her son's well-being is at stake!
We're the twins. We're hardly ever in the show! But hey, you can never go wrong with twins as part of a sitcom family! We have a great excuse why we don't say any funny lines — we're too young! Unfortunately, the rest of the family doesn't have that excuse!
Even though we don do funny lines, we can still crap in our pants from time to time! That's always good for a cheap laugh! They say "crap" on this show a lot! I guess it has something to do with that "truth in advertising" crap!
BROCCOLI RABE
ARUGOLA
Torres

ARTIST: ANGELO TORRES
WRITER: DICK DEBARTOLO

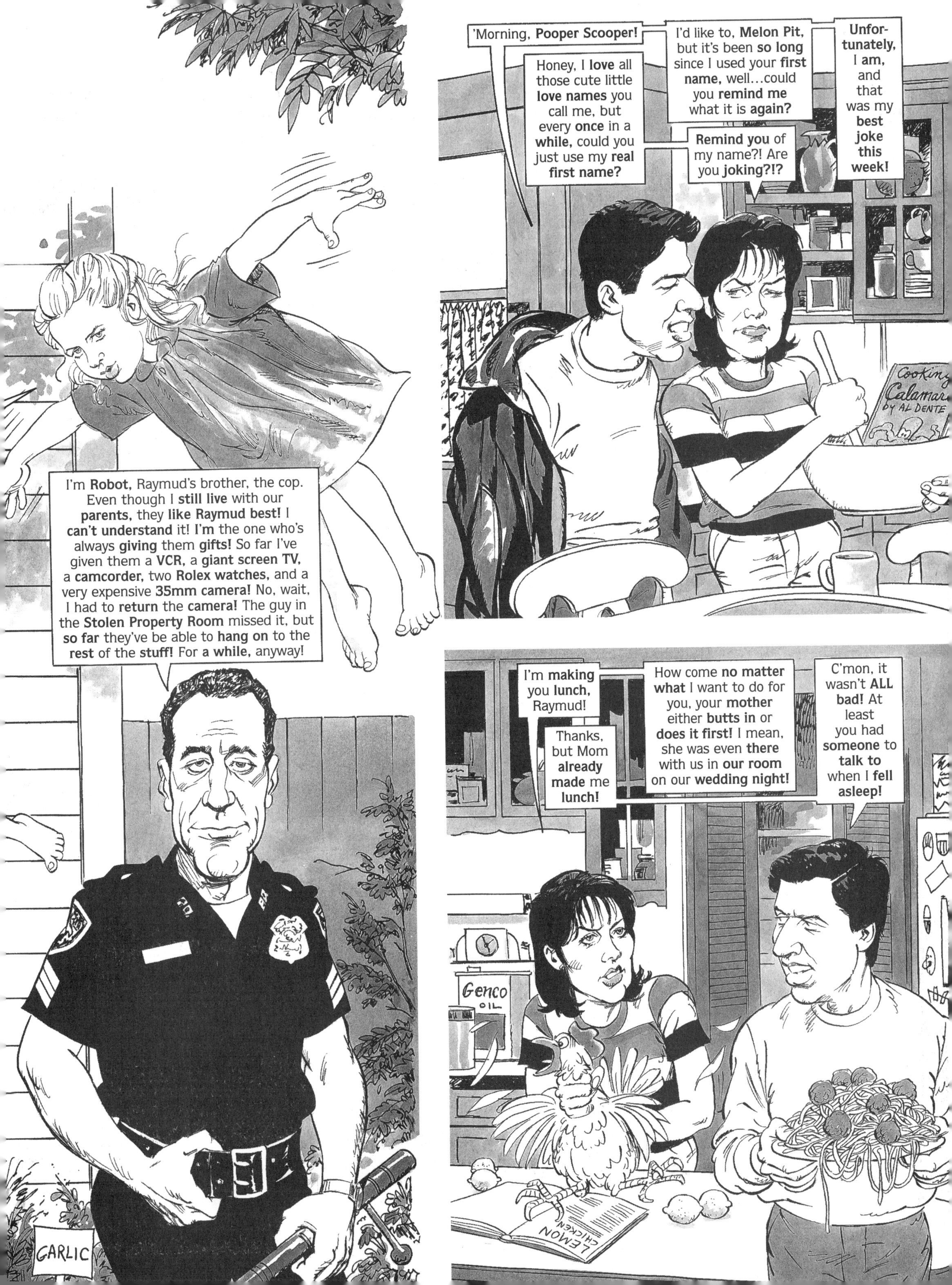
I'm Robot, Raymud's brother, the cop. Even though I still live with our parents, they like Raymud best! I can't understand it! I'm the one who's always giving them gifts! So far I've given them a VCR, a giant screen TV, a camcorder, two Rolex watches, and a very expensive 35mm camera! No, wait, I had to return the camera! The guy in the Stolen Property Room missed it, but so far they've be able to hang on to the rest of the stuff! For a while, anyway!
GARLIC
'Morning, Pooper Scooper!
Honey, I love all those cute little love names you call me, but every once in a while, could you just use my real first name?
I'd like to, Melon Pit, but it's been so long since I used your first name, well...could you remind me what it is again?
Remind you of my name?! Are you joking?!?
Unfortunately, I am, and that was my best joke this week!
Cooking Calamari BY AL DENTE
I'm making you lunch, Raymud!
Thanks, but Mom already made me lunch!
How come no matter what I want to do for you, your mother either butts in or does it first! I mean, she was even there with us in our room on our wedding night!
C'mon, it wasn't ALL bad! At least you had someone to talk to when I fell asleep!
Genco OIL
LEMON CHICKEN

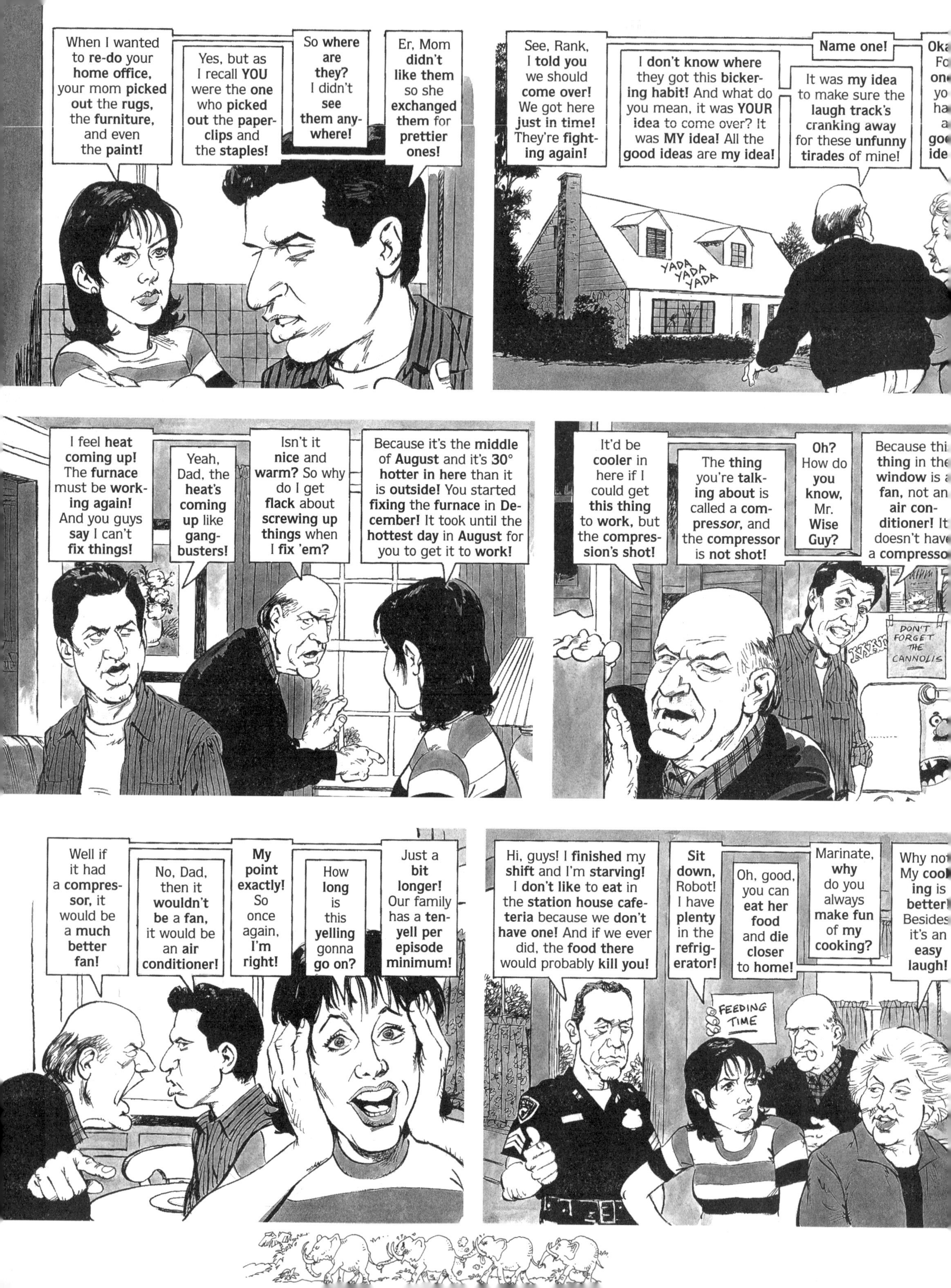

When I wanted to re-do your home office, your mom picked out the rugs, the furniture, and even the paint!
Yes, but as I recall YOU were the one who picked out the paper-clips and the staples!
So where are they? I didn't see them any-where!
Er, Mom didn't like them so she exchanged them for prettier ones!
See, Rank, I told you we should come over! We got here just in time! They're fight-ing again!
I don't know where they got this bicker-ing habit! And what do you mean, it was YOUR idea to come over? It was MY idea! All the good ideas are my idea!
Name one!
It was my idea to make sure the laugh track's cranking away for these unfunny tirades of mine!
Oka Fo one yo ha a goo ide
YADA YADA YADA
I feel heat coming up! The furnace must be work-ing again! And you guys say I can't fix things!
Yeah, Dad, the heat's coming up like gang-busters!
Isn't it nice and warm? So why do I get flack about screwing up things when I fix 'em?
Because it's the middle of August and it's 30° hotter in here than it is outside! You started fixing the furnace in De-cember! It took until the hottest day in August for you to get it to work!
It'd be cooler in here if I could get this thing to work, but the compres-sion's shot!
The thing you're talk-ing about is called a com-pressor, and the compressor is not shot!
Oh? How do you know, Mr. Wise Guy?
Because thi thing in the window is a fan, not an air con-ditioner! It doesn't have a compresso
DON'T FORGET THE CANNOLIS
Well if it had a compres-sor, it would be a much better fan!
No, Dad, then it wouldn't be a fan, it would be an air conditioner!
My point exactly! So once again, I'm right!
How long is this yelling gonna go on?
Just a bit longer! Our family has a ten-yell per episode minimum!
Hi, guys! I finished my shift and I'm starving! I don't like to eat in the station house cafe-teria because we don't have one! And if we ever did, the food there would probably kill you!
Sit down, Robot! I have plenty in the refrig-erator!
Oh, good, you can eat her food and die closer to home!
Marinate, why do you always make fun of my cooking?
Why no My coo ing is better Besides it's an easy laugh!
FEEDING TIME

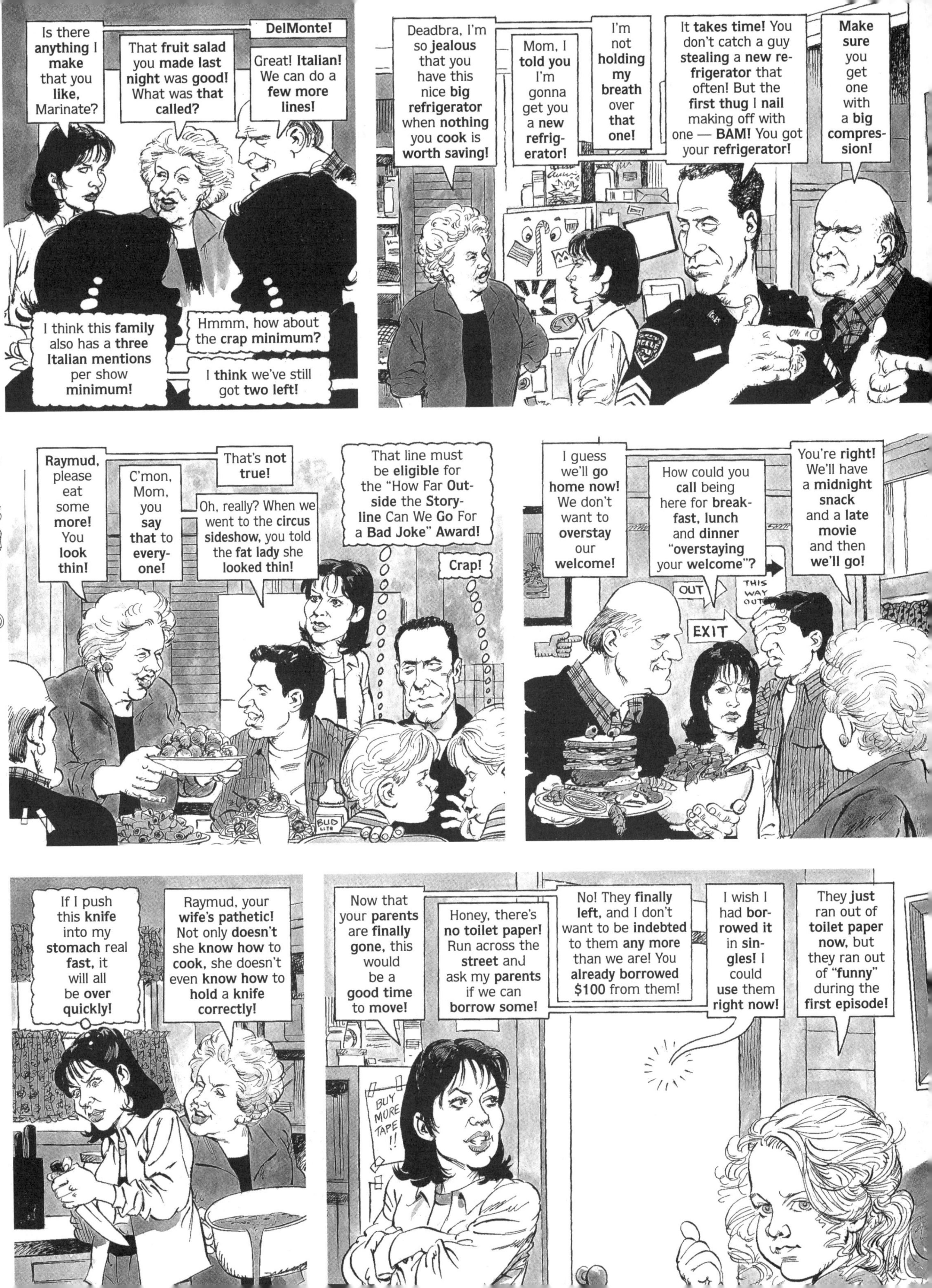

Is there anything I make that you like, Marinate?
That fruit salad you made last night was good! What was that called?
DelMonte!
Great! Italian! We can do a few more lines!
I think this family also has a three Italian mentions per show minimum!
Hmmm, how about the crap minimum?
I think we've still got two left!
Deadbra, I'm so jealous that you have this nice big refrigerator when nothing you cook is worth saving!
Mom, I told you I'm gonna get you a new refrigerator!
I'm not holding my breath over that one!
It takes time! You don't catch a guy stealing a new refrigerator that often! But the first thug I nail making off with one — BAM! You got your refrigerator!
Make sure you get one with a big compression!
Raymud, please eat some more! You look thin!
C'mon, Mom, you say that to everyone!
That's not true!
Oh, really? When we went to the circus sideshow, you told the fat lady she looked thin!
That line must be eligible for the "How Far Outside the Storyline Can We Go For a Bad Joke" Award!
Crap!
BUD LITE
I guess we'll go home now! We don't want to overstay our welcome!
How could you call being here for breakfast, lunch and dinner "overstaying your welcome"?
You're right! We'll have a midnight snack and a late movie and then we'll go!
OUT
THIS WAY OUT
EXIT
If I push this knife into my stomach real fast, it will all be over quickly!
Raymud, your wife's pathetic! Not only doesn't she know how to cook, she doesn't even know how to hold a knife correctly!
Now that your parents are finally gone, this would be a good time to move!
Honey, there's no toilet paper! Run across the street and ask my parents if we can borrow some!
No! They finally left, and I don't want to be indebted to them any more than we are! You already borrowed $100 from them!
I wish I had borrowed it in singles! I could use them right now!
They just ran out of toilet paper now, but they ran out of "funny" during the first episode!
BUY MORE TAPE !!

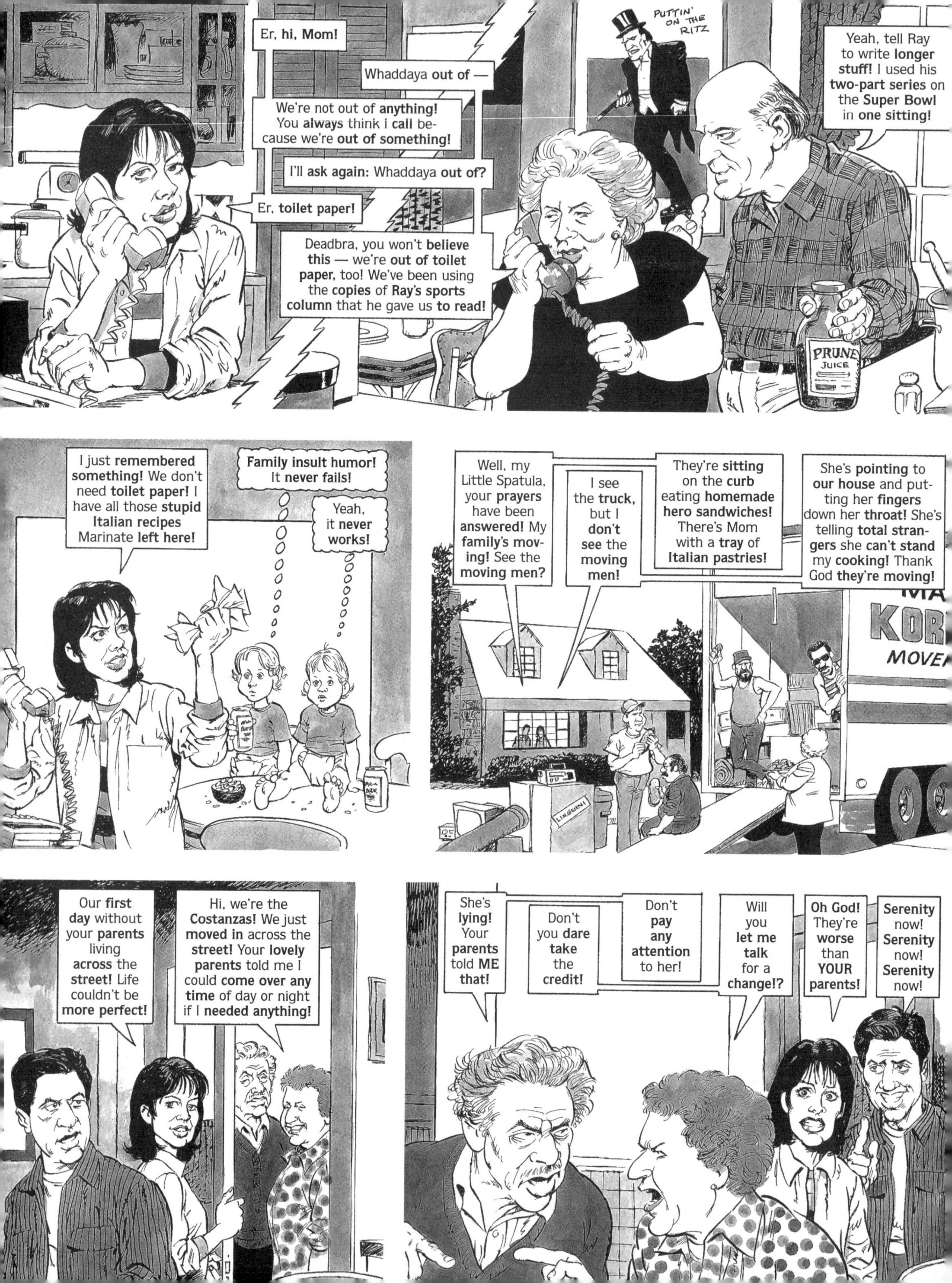
Er, hi, Mom!
Whaddaya out of —
We're not out of anything! You always think I call because we're out of something!
I'll ask again: Whaddaya out of?
Er, toilet paper!
Deadbra, you won't believe this — we're out of toilet paper, too! We've been using the copies of Ray's sports column that he gave us to read!
PUTTIN' ON THE RITZ
Yeah, tell Ray to write longer stuff! I used his two-part series on the Super Bowl in one sitting!
PRUNE JUICE
I just remembered something! We don't need toilet paper! I have all those stupid Italian recipes Marinate left here!
Family insult humor! It never fails!
Yeah, it never works!
Well, my Little Spatula, your prayers have been answered! My family's moving! See the moving men?
I see the truck, but I don't see the moving men!
They're sitting on the curb eating homemade hero sandwiches! There's Mom with a tray of Italian pastries!
She's pointing to our house and putting her fingers down her throat! She's telling total strangers she can't stand my cooking! Thank God they're moving!
LINGUINI
MOVE
Our first day without your parents living across the street! Life couldn't be more perfect!
Hi, we're the Costanzas! We just moved in across the street! Your lovely parents told me I could come over any time of day or night if I needed anything!
She's lying! Your parents told ME that!
Don't you dare take the credit!
Don't pay any attention to her!
Will you let me talk for a change!?
Oh God! They're worse than YOUR parents!
Serenity now! Serenity now! Serenity now!

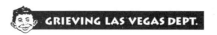

GRIEVING LAS VEGAS DEPT.

MAD's CELEBRITY CAUSE-OF-DEATH BETTING ODDS

Our team of crack oddsmakers gives you the latest Vegas line on how one of today's biggest stars is going to buy the cattle farm!

THIS MONTH'S BELOVED CADAVER TO BE:

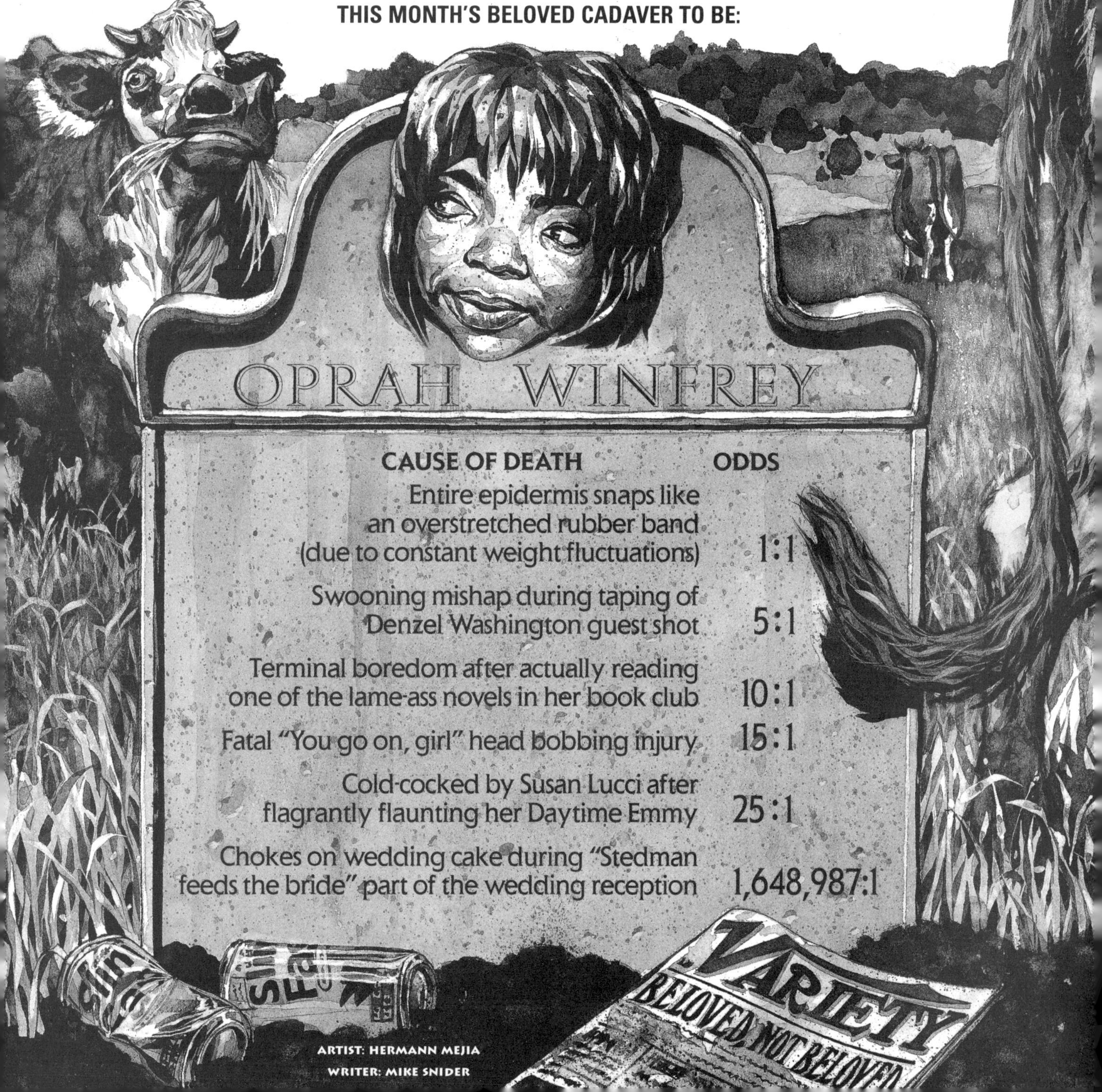

OPRAH WINFREY
CAUSE OF DEATH
ODDS
Entire epidermis snaps like an overstretched rubber band (due to constant weight fluctuations) 1:1
Swooning mishap during taping of Denzel Washington guest shot 5:1
Terminal boredom after actually reading one of the lame-ass novels in her book club 10:1
Fatal "You go on, girl" head bobbing injury 15:1
Cold-cocked by Susan Lucci after flagrantly flaunting her Daytime Emmy 25:1
Chokes on wedding cake during "Stedman feeds the bride" part of the wedding reception 1,648,987:1
VARIETY
BELOVED, NOT BELOVED

ARTIST: HERMANN MEJIA

WRITER: MIKE SNIDER

OH MY GOD — THEY ANALYZED KENNY DEPT.

IT TOOK THEM OVER A DECADE, BUT COMEDY CENTRAL HAS FINALLY HIT IT BIG! THEIR CRUDELY ANIMATED SQUIGGLEFEST, "DR. KATZ, PROFESSIONAL THERAPIST," HELPED PUT THE CHANNEL ON THE MAP, AND

DR. KATZ, PROFESSIONAL SOUTH

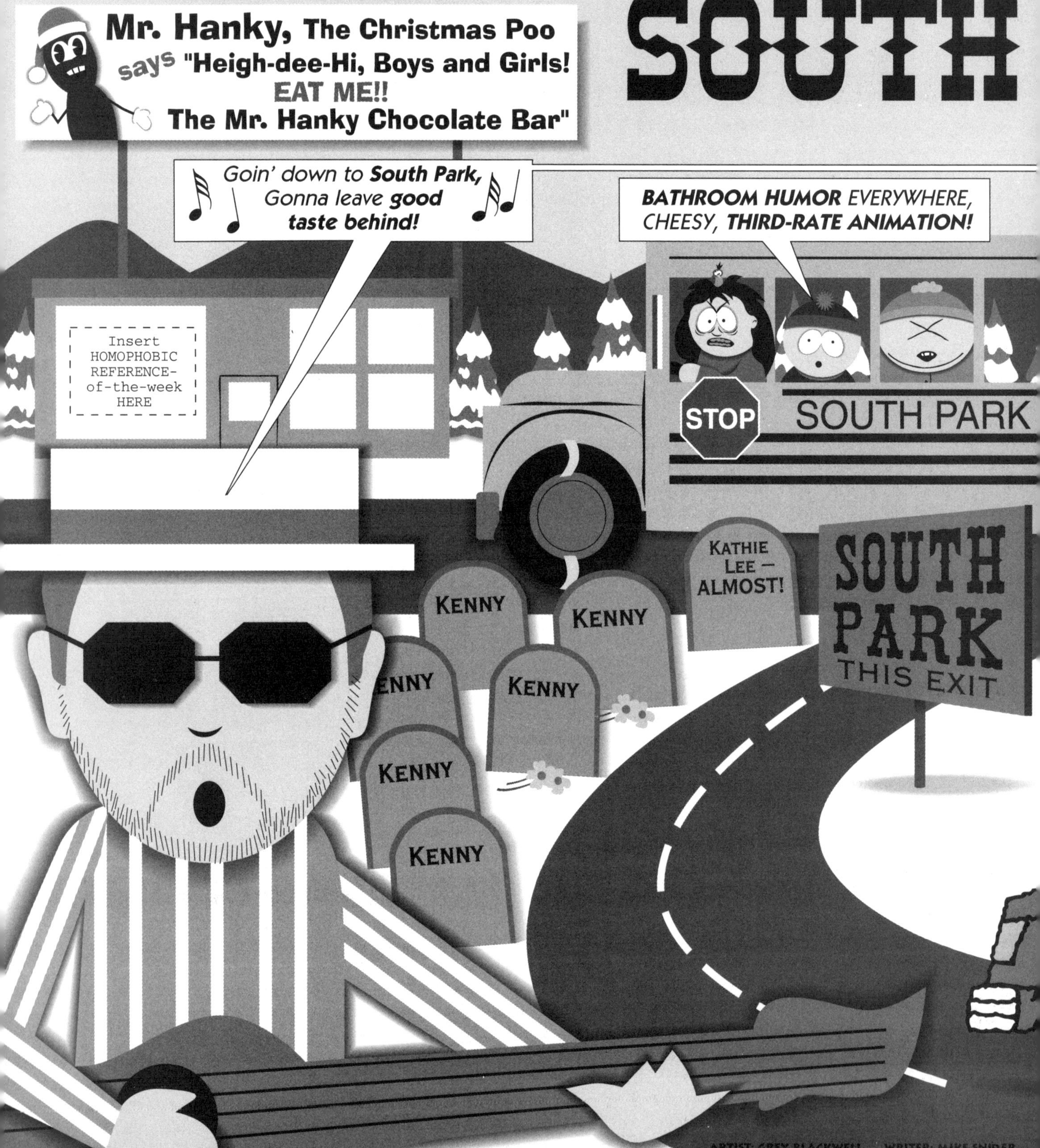

Mr. Hanky, The Christmas Poo says "Heigh-dee-Hi, Boys and Girls! EAT ME!! The Mr. Hanky Chocolate Bar"
Goin' down to South Park, Gonna leave good taste behind!
BATHROOM HUMOR EVERYWHERE, CHEESY, THIRD-RATE ANIMATION!
Insert HOMOPHOBIC REFERENCE-of-the-week HERE
STOP
SOUTH PARK
KATHIE LEE — ALMOST!
KENNY
KENNY
ENNY
KENNY
KENNY
KENNY
SOUTH PARK THIS EXIT

ARTIST: GREY BLACKWELL WRITER: MIKE SNIDER

THEIR EVEN MORE CRUDELY ANIMATED SWEARFEST, "SOUTH PARK," MADE IT FAMOUS! PROBLEM IS ALL THEIR OTHER SHOWS ARE TOTAL CRAP CAKES, WHICH IS WHY THEY SHOULD COMBINE THEIR TWO HITS TO CREATE...

THERAPIST MOVES TO...
PARK

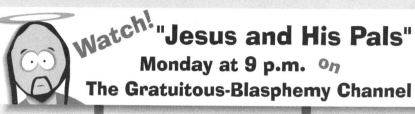

Watch! "Jesus and His Pals"
Monday at 9 p.m. on
The Gratuitous-Blasphemy Channel

Goin' down to **South Park**, even **ugly** to the **blind!**

RACIST JOKES AND **ETHNIC SLURS, KIDS** WHO **SWEAR** LIKE @#%!-ING **SAILORS!**

STARVIN' MARVIN's **Rib Joint**

ELEMENTARY R-1

Uh, **Dad,** tell me again **why** we're **moving** (gulp) **here!!?**

Ben, **South Park** is a **virtual mother lode** for a **psychologist.** There are more **mentally-unbalanced people** here, per capita, than **anywhere** else on **Earth,** except **possibly** a taping of **The Jerry Springer Show.**

Wow! But what about your **old practice** back **home?**

I believe my **job there** is **finished.**

You **mean** you **cured** all your **patients?**

No, I mean my **job is FINISHED.** My patients got **together** and **realized** they'd been **paying me** for **years** and I **hadn't helped** any of them **one bit.**

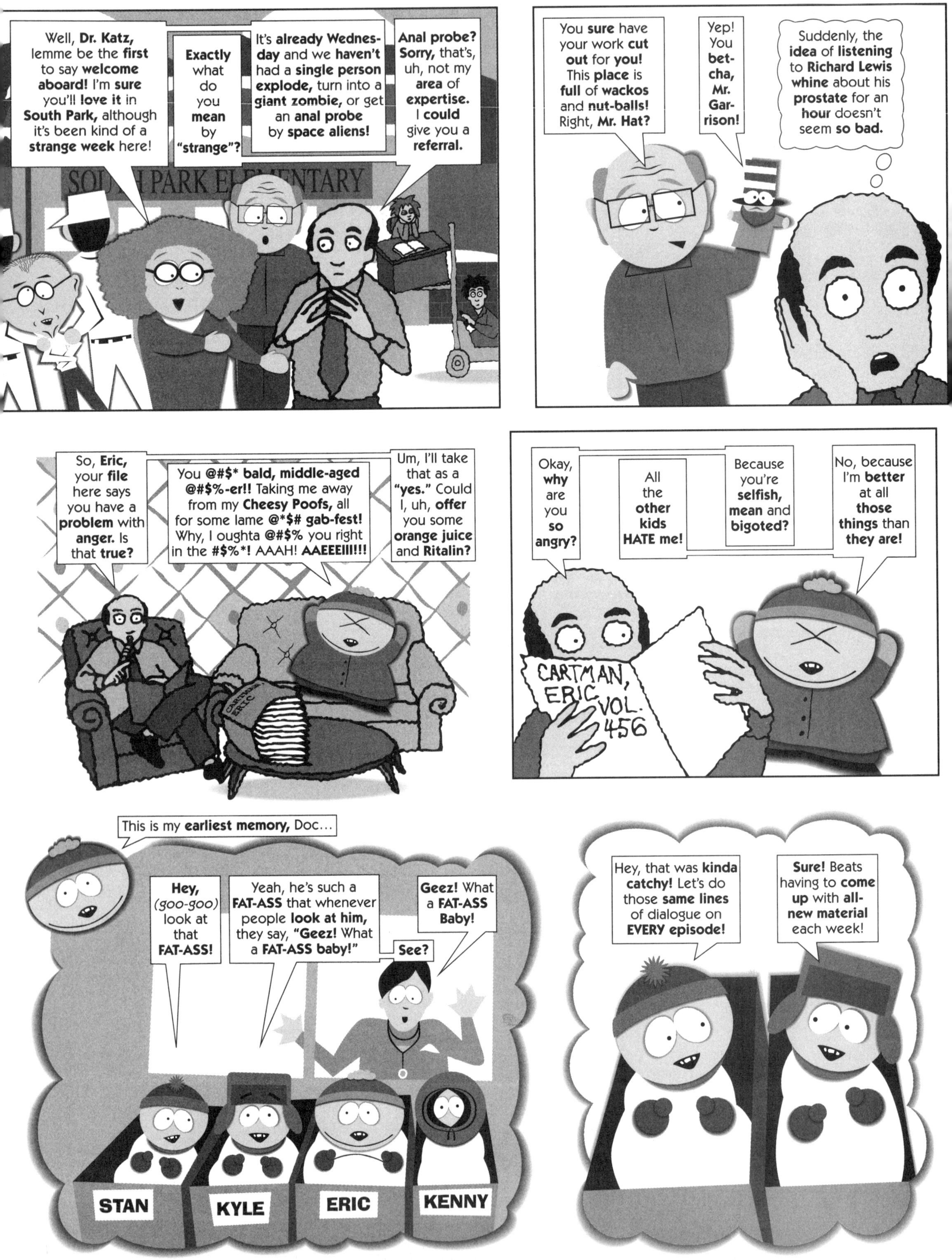
Well, Dr. Katz, lemme be the first to say welcome aboard! I'm sure you'll love it in South Park, although it's been kind of a strange week here!
Exactly what do you mean by "strange"?
It's already Wednesday and we haven't had a single person explode, turn into a giant zombie, or get an anal probe by space aliens!
Anal probe? Sorry, that's, uh, not my area of expertise. I could give you a referral.
SOUTH PARK ELEMENTARY
You sure have your work cut out for you! This place is full of wackos and nut-balls! Right, Mr. Hat?
Yep! You betcha, Mr. Garrison!
Suddenly, the idea of listening to Richard Lewis whine about his prostate for an hour doesn't seem so bad.
So, Eric, your file here says you have a problem with anger. Is that true?
You @#$* bald, middle-aged @#$%-er!! Taking me away from my Cheesy Poofs, all for some lame @*$# gab-fest! Why, I oughta @#$% you right in the #$%*! AAAH! AAEEEIII!!!
Um, I'll take that as a "yes." Could I, uh, offer you some orange juice and Ritalin?
CARTMAN, ERIC
Okay, why are you so angry?
All the other kids HATE me!
Because you're selfish, mean and bigoted?
No, because I'm better at all those things than they are!
CARTMAN, ERIC VOL. 456
This is my earliest memory, Doc…
Hey, (goo-goo) look at that FAT-ASS!
Yeah, he's such a FAT-ASS that whenever people look at him, they say, "Geez! What a FAT-ASS baby!"
See?
Geez! What a FAT-ASS Baby!
STAN
KYLE
ERIC
KENNY
Hey, that was kinda catchy! Let's do those same lines of dialogue on EVERY episode!
Sure! Beats having to come up with all-new material each week!

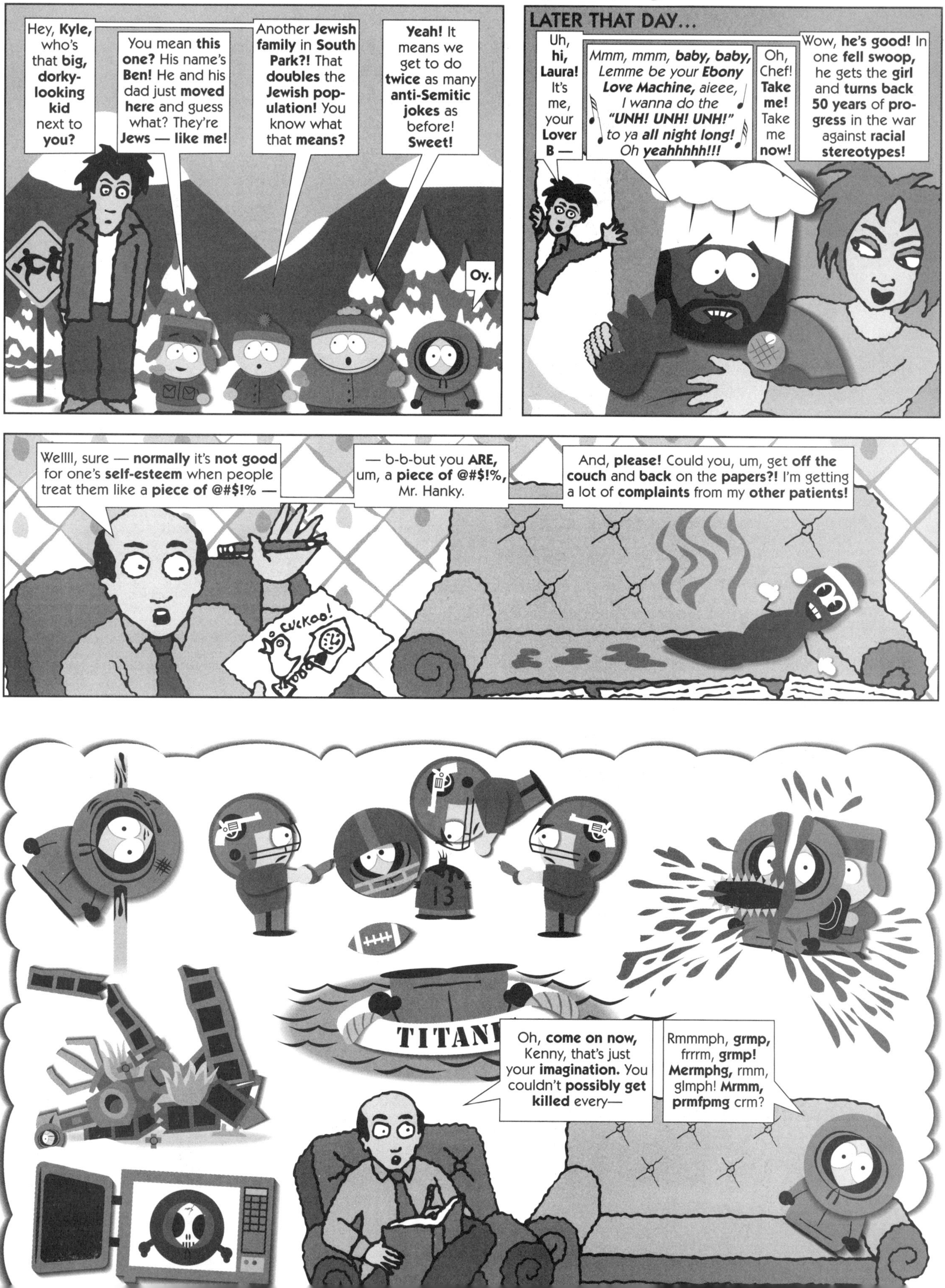
Hey, Kyle, who's that big, dorky-looking kid next to you?
You mean this one? His name's Ben! He and his dad just moved here and guess what? They're Jews — like me!
Another Jewish family in South Park?! That doubles the Jewish population! You know what that means?
Yeah! It means we get to do twice as many anti-Semitic jokes as before! Sweet!
Oy.
LATER THAT DAY...
Uh, hi, Laura! It's me, your Lover B —
Mmm, mmm, baby, baby, Lemme be your Ebony Love Machine, aieee, I wanna do the "UNH! UNH! UNH!" to ya all night long! Oh yeahhhhh!!!
Oh, Chef! Take me! Take me now!
Wow, he's good! In one fell swoop, he gets the girl and turns back 50 years of progress in the war against racial stereotypes!
Welll, sure — normally it's not good for one's self-esteem when people treat them like a piece of @#$!% —
— b-b-but you ARE, um, a piece of @#$!%, Mr. Hanky.
And, please! Could you, um, get off the couch and back on the papers?! I'm getting a lot of complaints from my other patients!
CUCKOO!
13
TITANI
Oh, come on now, Kenny, that's just your imagination. You couldn't possibly get killed every—
Rmmmph, grmp, frrrm, grmp! Mermphg, rmm, glmph! Mrmm, prmfpmg crm?

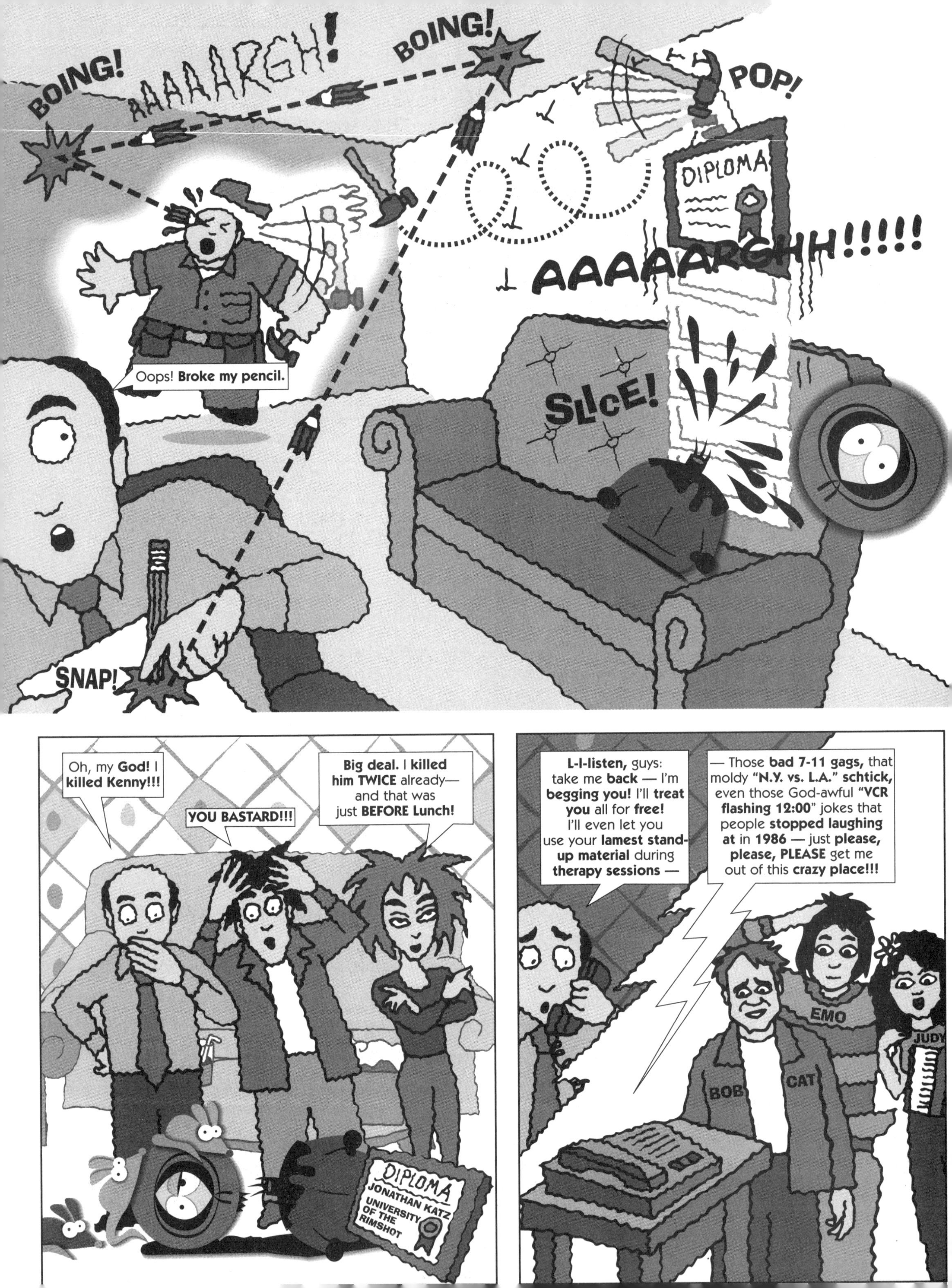
BOING!
AAAAARGH!
BOING!
POP!
DIPLOMA
AAAAARGHH!!!!!
Oops! Broke my pencil.
SLICE!
SNAP!
Oh, my God! I killed Kenny!!!
YOU BASTARD!!!
Big deal. I killed him TWICE already— and that was just BEFORE Lunch!
DIPLOMA
JONATHAN KATZ
UNIVERSITY OF THE RIMSHOT
L-l-listen, guys: take me back — I'm begging you! I'll treat you all for free! I'll even let you use your lamest stand-up material during therapy sessions —
— Those bad 7-11 gags, that moldy "N.Y. vs. L.A." schtick, even those God-awful "VCR flashing 12:00" jokes that people stopped laughing at in 1986 — just please, please, PLEASE get me out of this crazy place!!!
EMO
JUDY
BOB
CAT

STOP WORRYING ABOUT THE HIGH COST OF CABLE TV

And *Start* Worrying About The High Cost Of A Satellite Dish Antenna!

SLIMEDISH DIGITAL TELEVISION

WHAT A DEAL!

You'll receive all of the nation's top channels - unless you consider ABC, NBC, CBS or FOX "top channels"! Other super programming values include movie multi-channels like *Turnip Classic Movies, Greek HBO* and *Costner Movie Classics!* Call now to get more details from our Customer Service Representative — just as soon as we hire one.

So look to the leader in the industry for the best all-digital television value, but after you do, sign up with SlimeDish!

ONLY $39.95 PER MONTH!

Plus a convenient one-time installation fee of $12,449.

You Can't Get Any Lower Than This!*
*We're talking about program content, not price.

Sign Up Now And Get Two Free Months!*
*July 2079 and February 2102 only.

TURNIPCLASSICMOVIES

NICOTINE at NITE

ECCH!

COMMIE CENTRAL

FOX FAMINE CHANNEL

TLC THE LEANING CHANNEL

HeadlineNUDES

TB LAND

T'N'A

C-SPAM

C-SPAM2

m&m tv

AMC AMERICAN MOVIE CLINKERS

You'll Receive Unheard of Savings When You Subscribe to These Unheard of Cable Networks!

What if you have service problems after installation?

Just call our toll free number and we'll tell you about our exciting plans to create a service department!
(Note: toll free from Guam only)

30-Day Money Back Guarantee!

If for any reason we are not satisfied with you as a customer, we will return your money, no questions asked!

slimedish NETWORK

All prices, channel packages and programs subject to change without notice. Local, state and federal taxes you never heard of apply. There is an additional charge for extra services such as hooking your satellite dish to your converter box and your converter box to your TV set. Plugging it into the wall also costs more. There is also an additional charge if you want sound with your picture. Double that amount if you want stereo sound. Triple that amount if you want the sound to match the picture. WARNING: Some unscrupulous servicemen will illegally provide you with unauthorized satellite dish service. But there's no need to do business with them when you can deal with us directly!

A MAD AD PARODY

WRITER: DICK DEBARTOLO

THEY GET BY WITH A LITTLE HELP FROM THEIR FRANZ DEPT.

Back in MAD #329 we told you of a gritty, New York City police drama that was atop the ratings charts. Well, here it is several years later and this police drama is still on top of the charts. Proving once again that the American viewing public knows nothing about quality television! But wait! Something's changed! There are a lot of shiny new faces (not to mention saggy new asses). It's time for a another look at this fershlugginer show. It's time for...

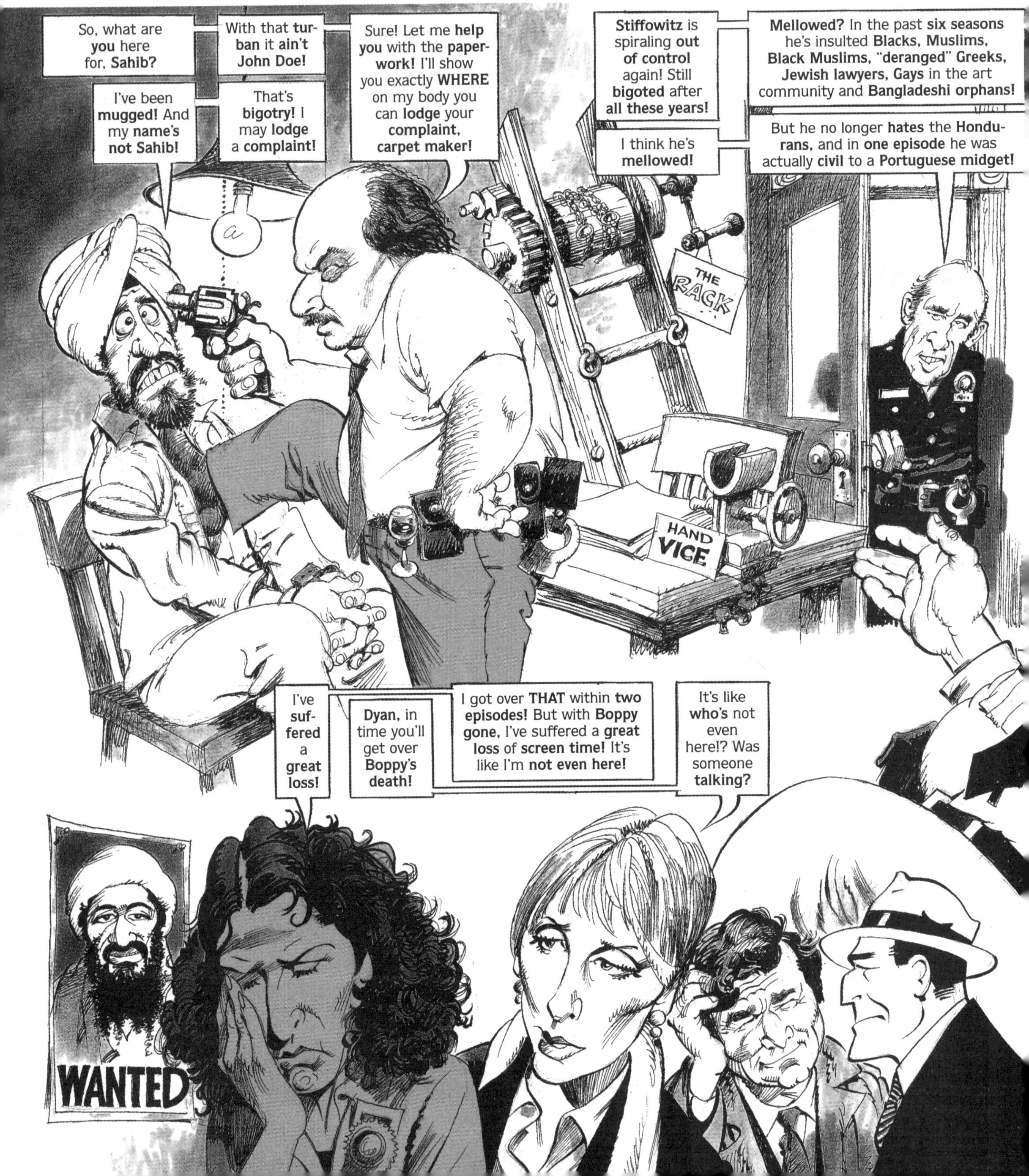

So, what are you here for, Sahib?
I've been mugged! And my name's not Sahib!
With that turban it ain't John Doe!
That's bigotry! I may lodge a complaint!
Sure! Let me help you with the paperwork! I'll show you exactly WHERE on my body you can lodge your complaint, carpet maker!
Stiffowitz is spiraling out of control again! Still bigoted after all these years!
I think he's mellowed!
Mellowed? In the past six seasons he's insulted Blacks, Muslims, Black Muslims, "deranged" Greeks, Jewish lawyers, Gays in the art community and Bangladeshi orphans!
But he no longer hates the Hondurans, and in one episode he was actually civil to a Portuguese midget!
THE RACK
HAND VICE
I've suffered a great loss!
Dyan, in time you'll get over Boppy's death!
I got over THAT within two episodes! But with Boppy gone, I've suffered a great loss of screen time! It's like I'm not even here!
It's like who's not even here!? Was someone talking?
WANTED

NYPD RE-DO

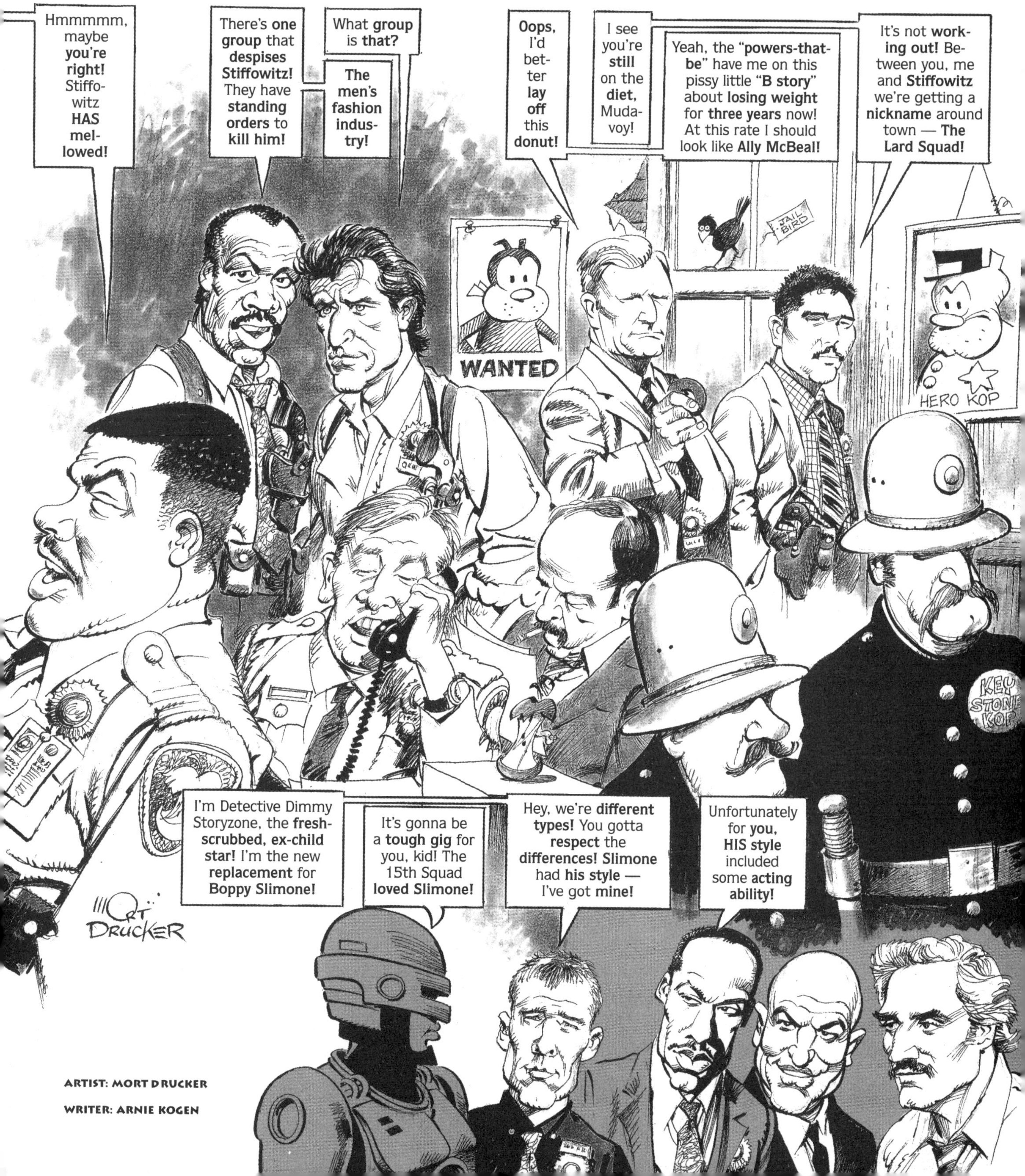

Hmmmmm, maybe you're right! Stiffowitz HAS mellowed!
There's one group that despises Stiffowitz! They have standing orders to kill him!
What group is that?
The men's fashion industry!
Oops, I'd better lay off this donut!
I see you're still on the diet, Mudavoy!
Yeah, the "powers-that-be" have me on this pissy little "B story" about losing weight for three years now! At this rate I should look like Ally McBeal!
It's not working out! Between you, me and Stiffowitz we're getting a nickname around town — The Lard Squad!
WANTED
JAIL BIRD
HERO KOP
KEY STONE KOP
I'm Detective Dimmy Storyzone, the fresh-scrubbed, ex-child star! I'm the new replacement for Boppy Slimone!
It's gonna be a tough gig for you, kid! The 15th Squad loved Slimone!
Hey, we're different types! You gotta respect the differences! Slimone had his style — I've got mine!
Unfortunately for you, HIS style included some acting ability!
MORT DRUCKER

ARTIST: MORT DRUCKER

WRITER: ARNIE KOGEN

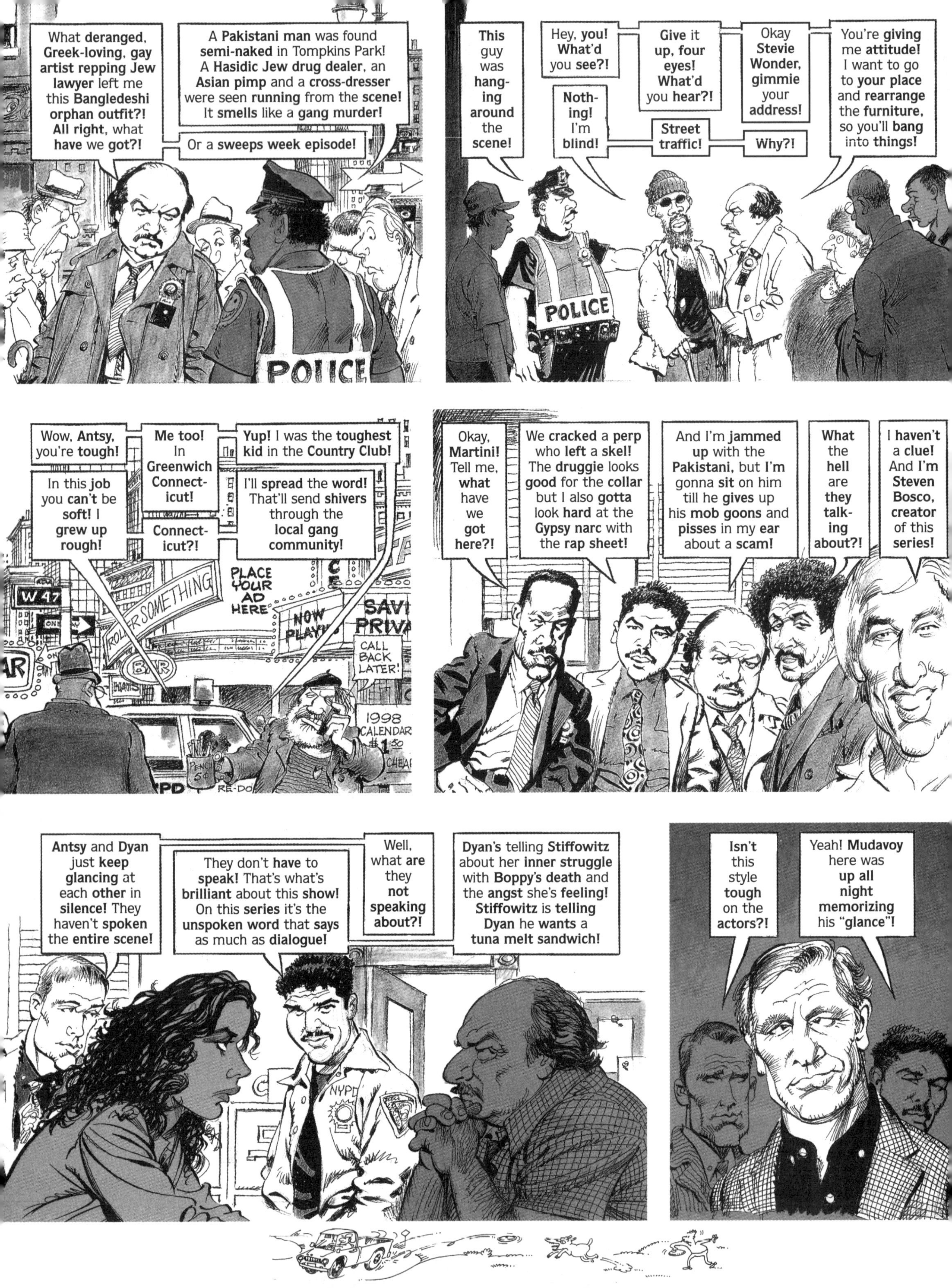
What deranged, Greek-loving, gay artist repping Jew lawyer left me this Bangledeshi orphan outfit?! All right, what have we got?!
A Pakistani man was found semi-naked in Tompkins Park! A Hasidic Jew drug dealer, an Asian pimp and a cross-dresser were seen running from the scene! It smells like a gang murder!
Or a sweeps week episode!
POLICE
This guy was hang-ing around the scene!
Hey, you! What'd you see?!
Noth-ing! I'm blind!
Give it up, four eyes! What'd you hear?!
Street traffic!
Okay Stevie Wonder, gimmie your address!
Why?!
You're giving me attitude! I want to go to your place and rearrange the furniture, so you'll bang into things!
POLICE
Wow, Antsy, you're tough!
Me too! In Greenwich Connect-icut!
Yup! I was the toughest kid in the Country Club!
In this job you can't be soft! I grew up rough!
Connect-icut?!
I'll spread the word! That'll send shivers through the local gang community!
W 47
PLACE YOUR AD HERE
CALL BACK LATER!
BAR
1998 CALENDAR $1.50
Okay, Martini! Tell me, what have we got here?!
We cracked a perp who left a skel! The druggie looks good for the collar but I also gotta look hard at the Gypsy narc with the rap sheet!
And I'm jammed up with the Pakistani, but I'm gonna sit on him till he gives up his mob goons and pisses in my ear about a scam!
What the hell are they talk-ing about?!
I haven't a clue! And I'm Steven Bosco, creator of this series!
Antsy and Dyan just keep glancing at each other in silence! They haven't spoken the entire scene!
They don't have to speak! That's what's brilliant about this show! On this series it's the unspoken word that says as much as dialogue!
Well, what are they not speaking about?!
Dyan's telling Stiffowitz about her inner struggle with Boppy's death and the angst she's feeling! Stiffowitz is telling Dyan he wants a tuna melt sandwich!
NYPD
Isn't this style tough on the actors?!
Yeah! Mudavoy here was up all night memorizing his "glance"!

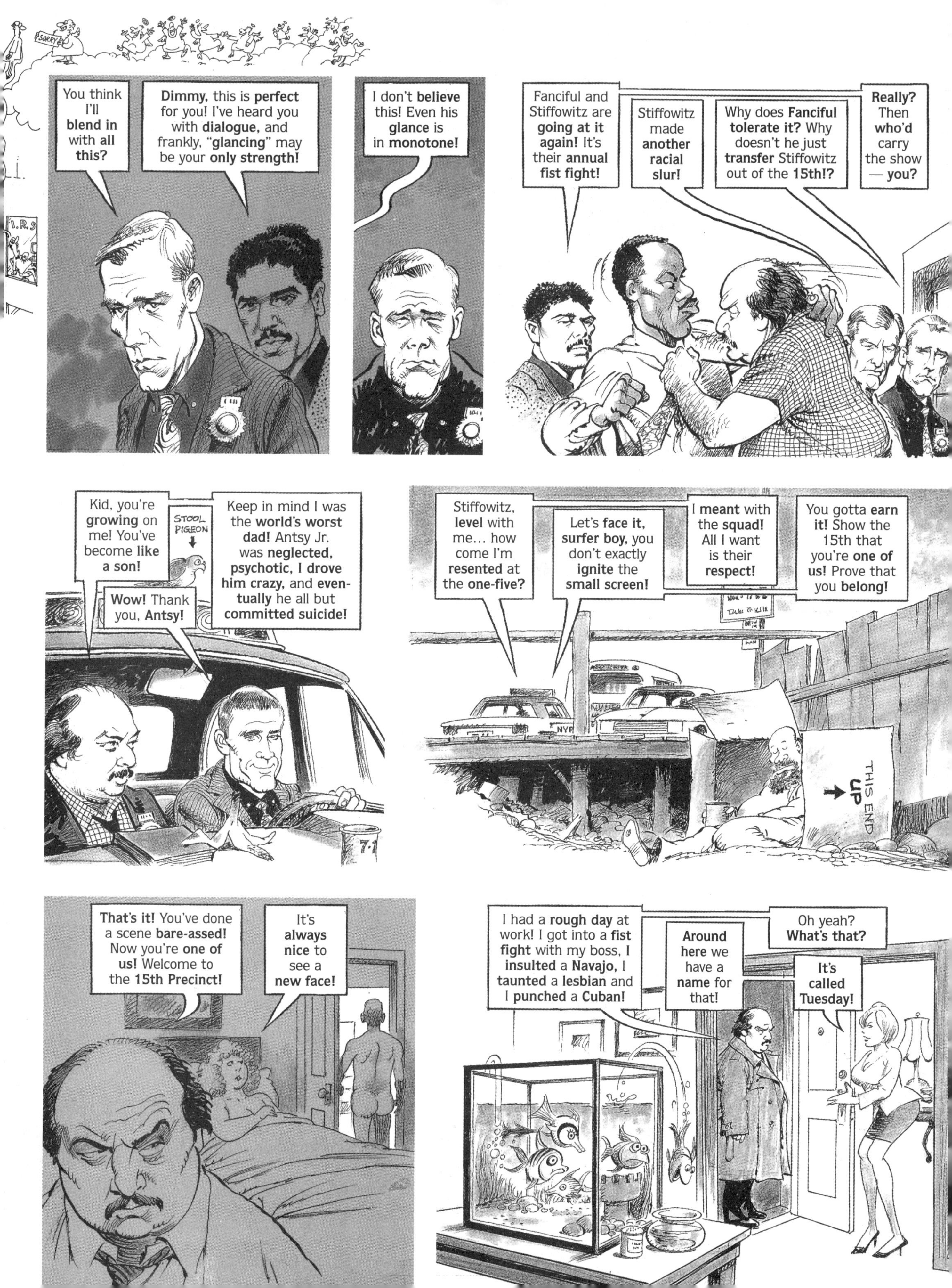
SORRY
You think I'll blend in with all this?
Dimmy, this is perfect for you! I've heard you with dialogue, and frankly, "glancing" may be your only strength!
I don't believe this! Even his glance is in monotone!
Fanciful and Stiffowitz are going at it again! It's their annual fist fight!
Stiffowitz made another racial slur!
Why does Fanciful tolerate it? Why doesn't he just transfer Stiffowitz out of the 15th!?
Really? Then who'd carry the show — you?
Kid, you're growing on me! You've become like a son!
STOOL PIGEON
Wow! Thank you, Antsy!
Keep in mind I was the world's worst dad! Antsy Jr. was neglected, psychotic, I drove him crazy, and eventually he all but committed suicide!
Stiffowitz, level with me... how come I'm resented at the one-five?
Let's face it, surfer boy, you don't exactly ignite the small screen!
I meant with the squad! All I want is their respect!
You gotta earn it! Show the 15th that you're one of us! Prove that you belong!
THIS END UP
That's it! You've done a scene bare-assed! Now you're one of us! Welcome to the 15th Precinct!
It's always nice to see a new face!
I had a rough day at work! I got into a fist fight with my boss, I insulted a Navajo, I taunted a lesbian and I punched a Cuban!
Oh yeah? What's that?
Around here we have a name for that!
It's called Tuesday!

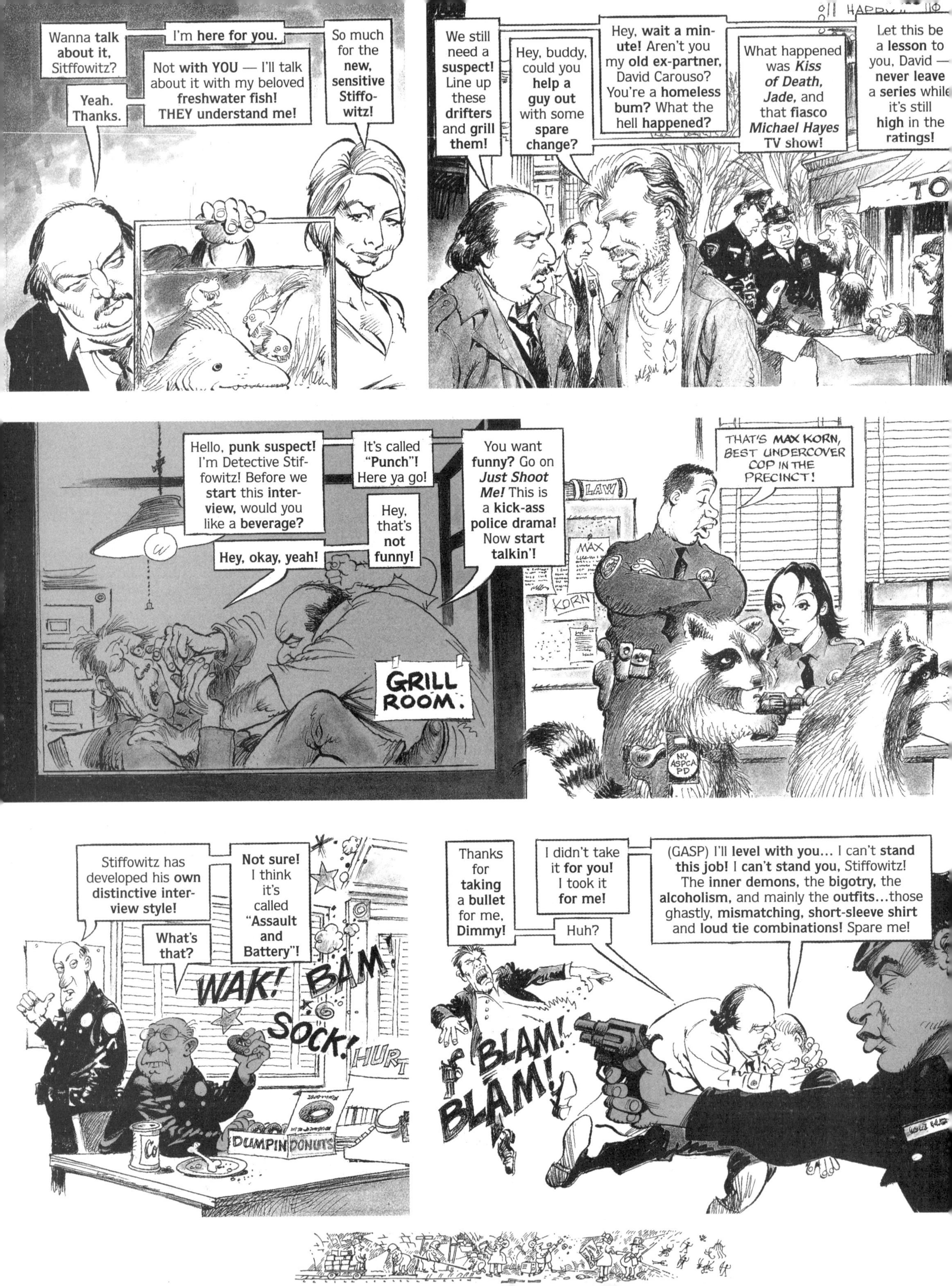

Wanna talk about it, Sitffowitz?
I'm here for you.
Yeah. Thanks.
Not with YOU — I'll talk about it with my beloved freshwater fish! THEY understand me!
So much for the new, sensitive Stiffowitz!
We still need a suspect! Line up these drifters and grill them!
Hey, buddy, could you help a guy out with some spare change?
Hey, wait a minute! Aren't you my old ex-partner, David Carouso? You're a homeless bum? What the hell happened?
What happened was Kiss of Death, Jade, and that fiasco Michael Hayes TV show!
Let this be a lesson to you, David — never leave a series while it's still high in the ratings!
Hello, punk suspect! I'm Detective Stiffowitz! Before we start this interview, would you like a beverage?
Hey, okay, yeah!
It's called "Punch"! Here ya go!
Hey, that's not funny!
You want funny? Go on Just Shoot Me! This is a kick-ass police drama! Now start talkin'!
GRILL ROOM
LAW
MAX
KORN
THAT'S MAX KORN, BEST UNDERCOVER COP IN THE PRECINCT!
NY ASPCA PD
Stiffowitz has developed his own distinctive interview style!
What's that?
Not sure! I think it's called "Assault and Battery"!
WAK! BAM! SOCK! HURT
DUMPIN DONUTS
Thanks for taking a bullet for me, Dimmy!
I didn't take it for you! I took it for me!
Huh?
(GASP) I'll level with you... I can't stand this job! I can't stand you, Stiffowitz! The inner demons, the bigotry, the alcoholism, and mainly the outfits...those ghastly, mismatching, short-sleeve shirt and loud tie combinations! Spare me!
BLAM! BLAM!

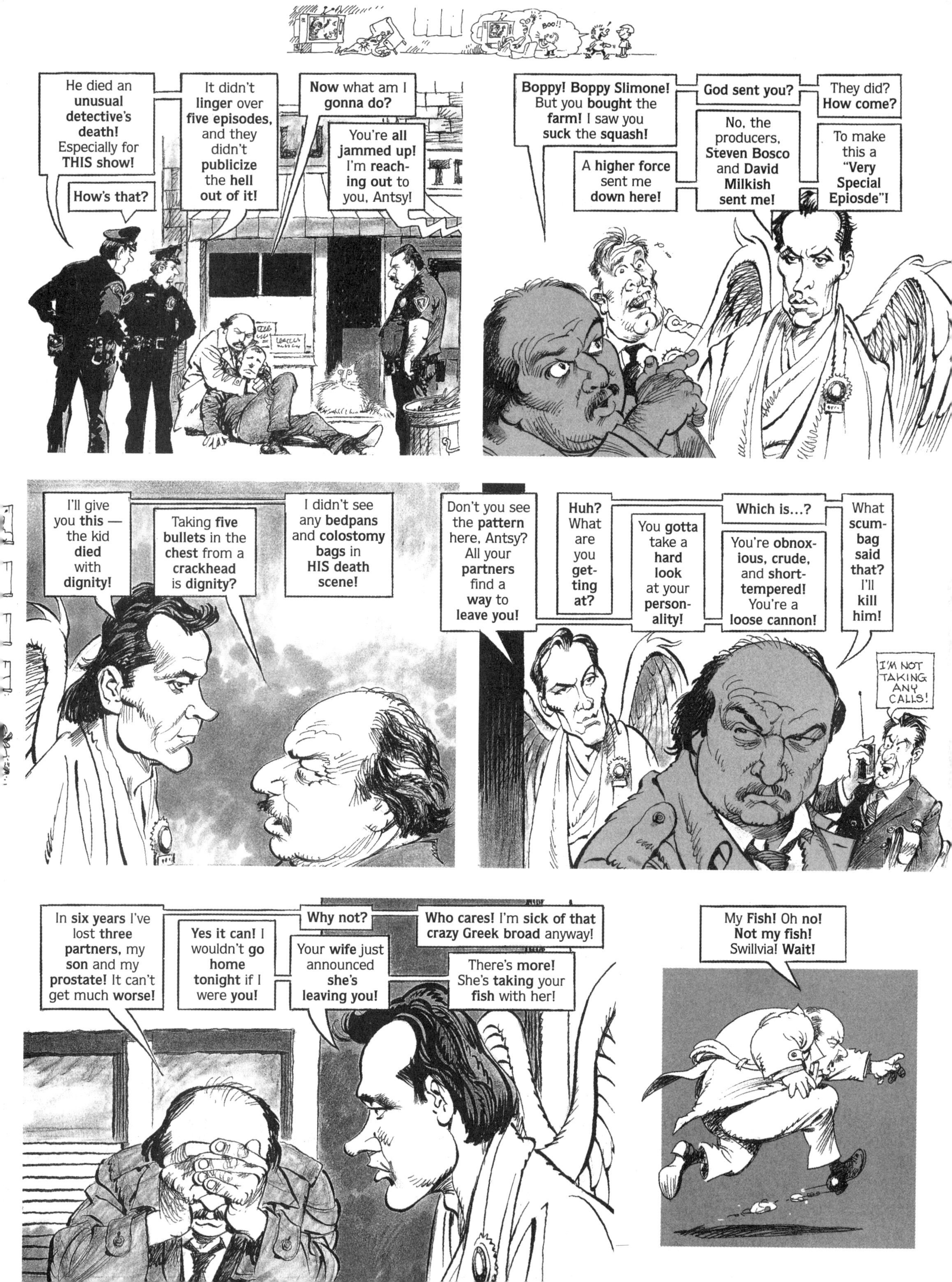
BOO!!
He died an unusual detective's death! Especially for THIS show!
How's that?
It didn't linger over five episodes, and they didn't publicize the hell out of it!
Now what am I gonna do?
You're all jammed up! I'm reaching out to you, Antsy!
Boppy! Boppy Slimone! But you bought the farm! I saw you suck the squash!
A higher force sent me down here!
God sent you?
No, the producers, Steven Bosco and David Milkish sent me!
They did? How come?
To make this a "Very Special Episode"!
I'll give you this — the kid died with dignity!
Taking five bullets in the chest from a crackhead is dignity?
I didn't see any bedpans and colostomy bags in HIS death scene!
Don't you see the pattern here, Antsy? All your partners find a way to leave you!
Huh? What are you getting at?
You gotta take a hard look at your personality!
Which is...?
You're obnoxious, crude, and short-tempered! You're a loose cannon!
What scumbag said that? I'll kill him!
I'M NOT TAKING ANY CALLS!
In six years I've lost three partners, my son and my prostate! It can't get much worse!
Yes it can! I wouldn't go home tonight if I were you!
Why not?
Your wife just announced she's leaving you!
Who cares! I'm sick of that crazy Greek broad anyway!
There's more! She's taking your fish with her!
My Fish! Oh no! Not my fish! Swillvia! Wait!

Each year, MTV brings a different group of seven strangers together and gives them a place to live in exchange for allowing their lives to be broadcast on national TV. Odd thing is, the group from one year pretty much looks like the group from any other year! Is it a coincidence? Divine intervention? Tainted Zima? Actually, they find their near-identical sets of twentysomething clones by making all applicants fill out...

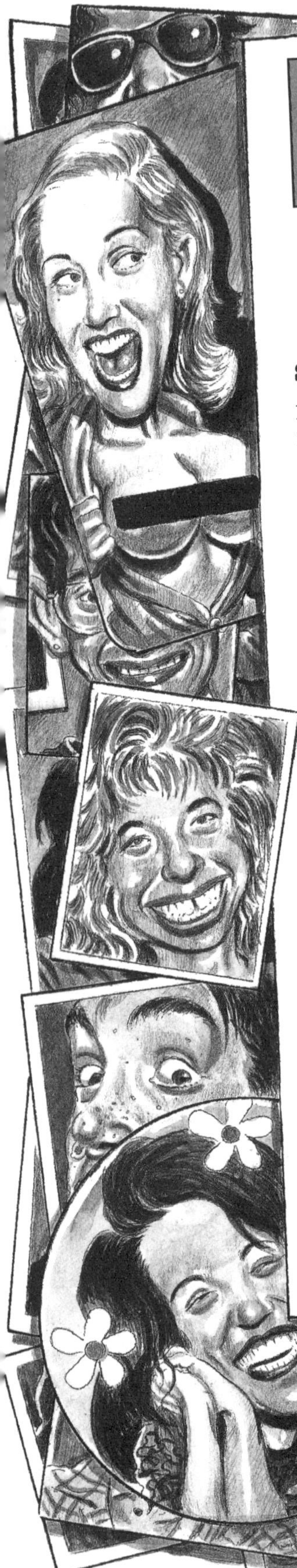
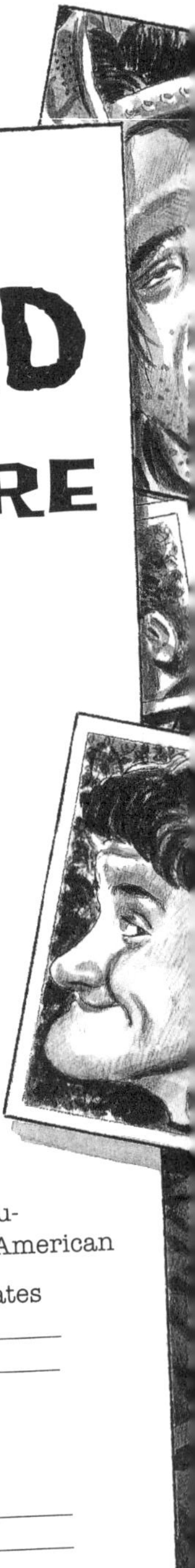

MTV'S REAL REAL WORLD CASTING QUESTIONNAIRE

SECTION I — PERSONAL INFORMATION

NAME: ______________________________

NICKNAME (that you think is cool but really just sounds stupid): ____________

ADDRESS OF PERSON YOU'RE CURRENTLY SPONGING OFF OF/CRASHING WITH:

CITY: __________ STATE: _____ ZIP: ________

NEAREST TELEPHONE WHERE
YOU CAN BE REACHED (that hasn't been turned off): ______________

AGE: ___ 18 ___ 19 ___ 20 ___ 21 ___ Over the Hill

SEX: ___ Male ___ Female ___ Whatever

SEXUAL IDENTITY:

___ Committed Virgin (but willing to give it up if it'll make a good scene!)
___ Committed Gay/Lesbian, with chip on shoulder
___ Committed Gay/Lesbian Virgin
___ Apologetic Heterosexual
___ Philosophical-Celibate (but non-stop flirt!)

ETHNIC GROUP:

___ White
___ Asian-American
___ Latino
___ Volatile African-American
___ Extremely Volatile African-American
___ Go-Ballistic-and-Call-You-a-Racist-if-You-Sneeze-at-Me-the-Wrong-Way-African-American

Do you have any bad habits? Specifically, something that might prompt your roommates to throw you out of the house, say, during Episode #7? ______________________

SECTION II — YOUR GEN-X QUALIFICATIONS

1. List all five jobs you've had and been fired from in the past year:
   1. ______________
   2. ______________
   3. ______________
   4. ______________
   5. ______________

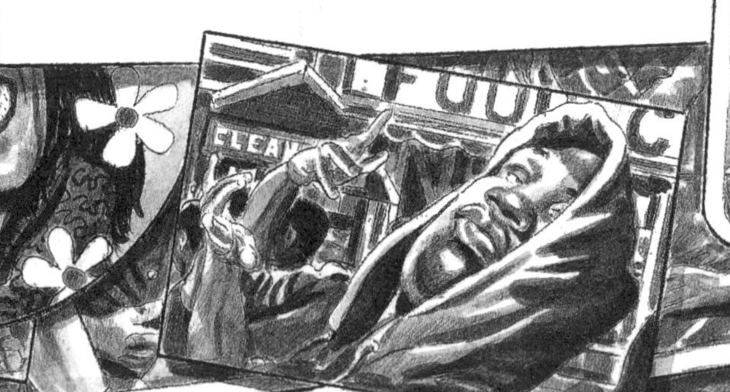
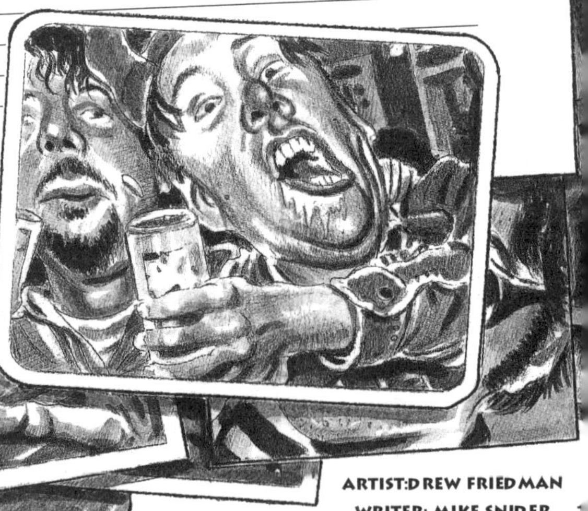

ARTIST: DREW FRIEDMAN
WRITER: MIKE SNIDER

MTV'S REAL WORLD
CASTING QUESTIONNAIRE

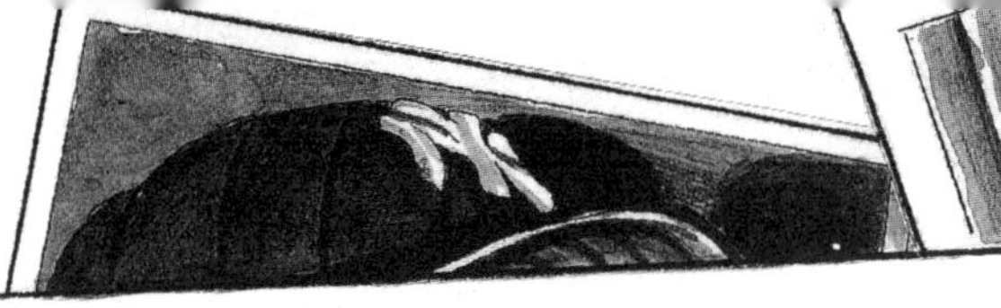

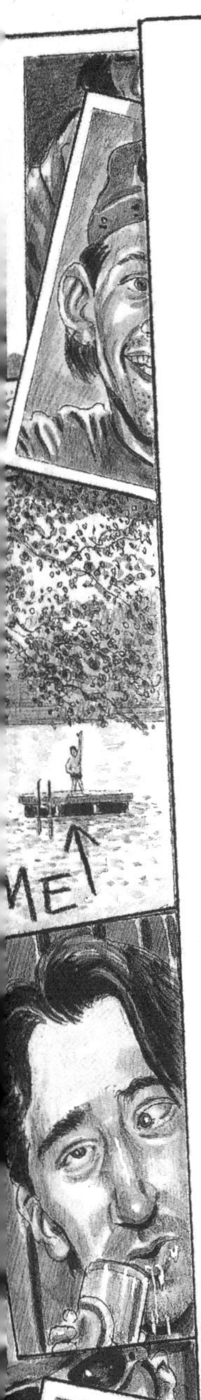
ME

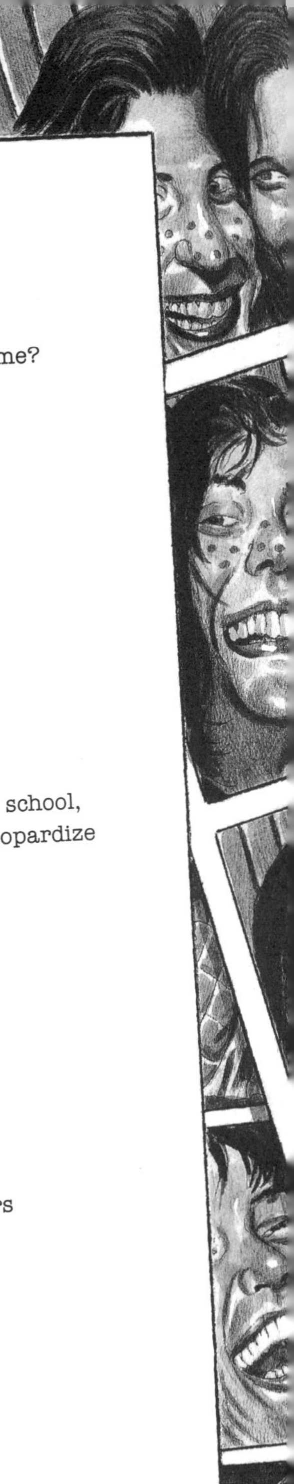

2. What is your long-term career goal (i.e. by this time next year):
   - ___ Independent Filmmaker
   - ___ Computer Billionaire
   - ___ Website Designer
   - ___ Hip-Hop Superstar
   - ___ Oscar-winning Actress
   - ___ Full-Time Slacker

3. Which of the following are essential elements to your idea of a quiet evening at home?
   - ___ Six other roommates wandering in and out
   - ___ 25,000-watts of stage lighting
   - ___ TV cameras and boom microphones everywhere
   - ___ A dozen bored crewmen milling around
   - ___ Millions of MTV viewers watching in later

4. Have you ever had a one-night stand with a roommate, then gone completely psycho on them the next day? Yes ___ No ___
   If no, would you like to? Yes ___ No ___

5. Which music group/artist do you love? ______________________

6. Which music group/artist do you hate?
   (so we can pair you up with a roommate who loves them!) ______________

7. If you're currently doing something important like going to medical school or law school, or are involved in a very serious romantic relationship, would you be willing to jeopardize all that by abruptly relocating to another city — just for a few months of fame?
   ___ Yes ___ Most definitely ___ Of course

8. Who is the Most Important Person in your life?
   ___ Me ___ Myself ___ I

9. In the World?
   ___ Me ___ Myself ___ I

10. Are you a vegetarian who considers people who eat meat to be murderers (and doesn't mind telling them!)

    OR

    Are you a meat-eater who considers vegetarians to be self-righteous tree-huggers (and doesn't mind telling them!)

    ___ The first one ___ The second one

11. Do you drink alcohol? If so, what kind of drunk are you?
    - ___ The funny kind
    - ___ The sad kind
    - ___ The kind who gets really nasty and starts slapping the female roommates around so badly you'd have to stop taping and call in the MTV lawyers!

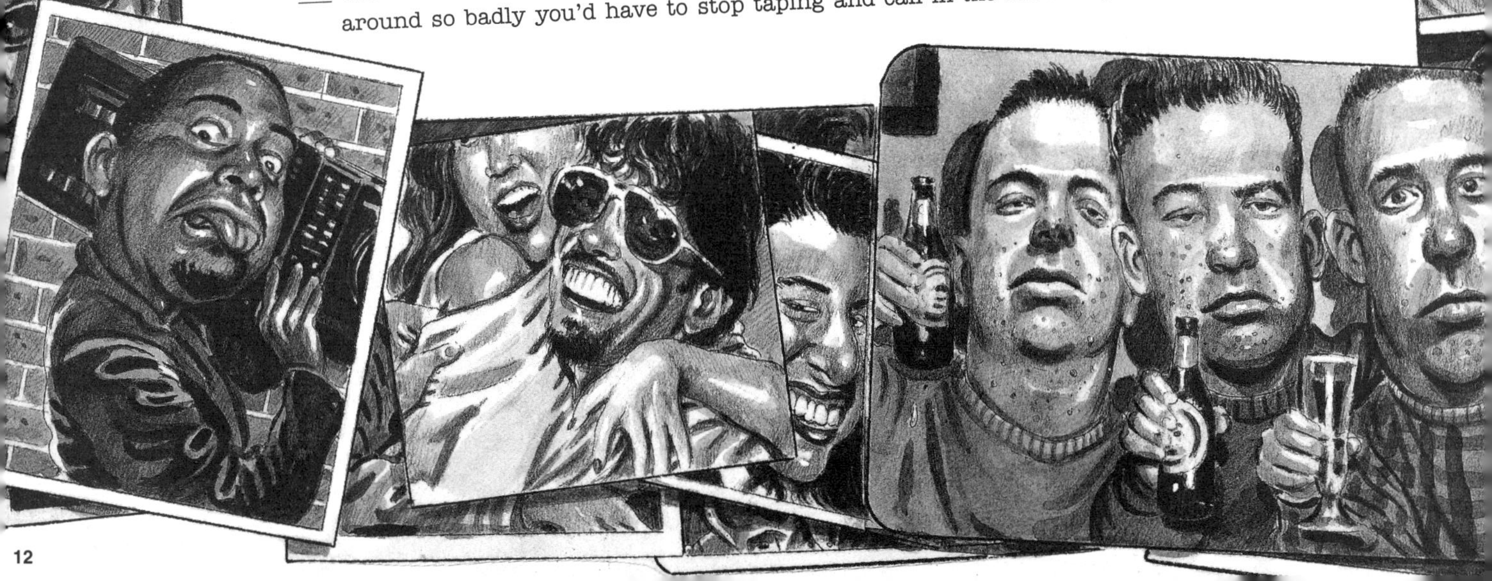

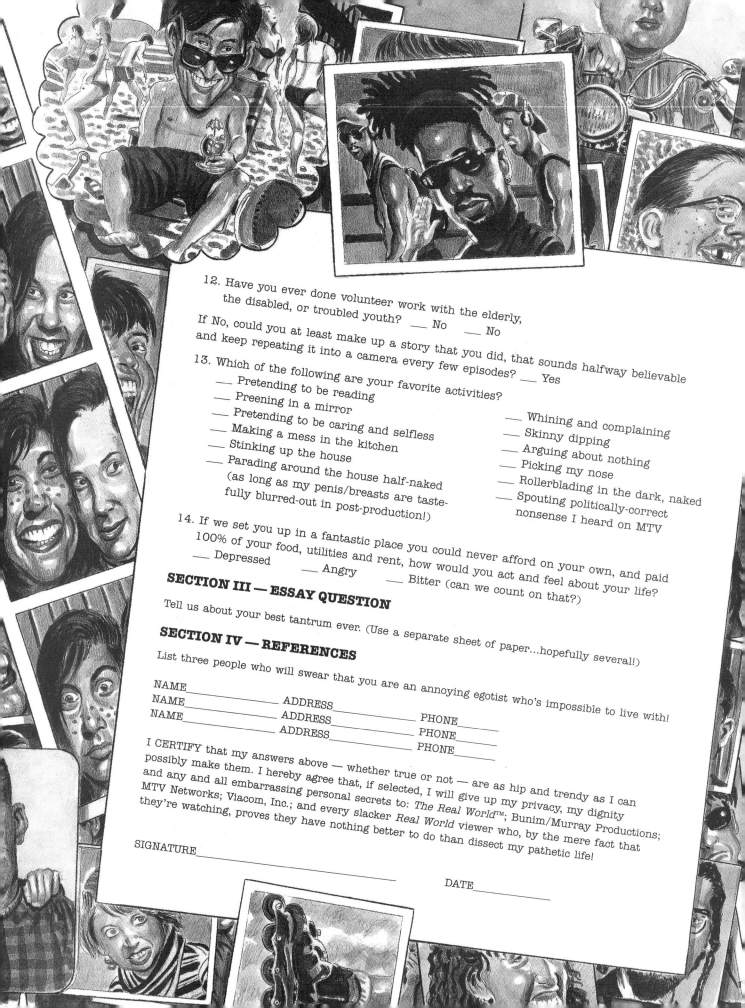

12. Have you ever done volunteer work with the elderly, the disabled, or troubled youth? ___ No ___ No

If No, could you at least make up a story that you did, that sounds halfway believable and keep repeating it into a camera every few episodes? ___ Yes

13. Which of the following are your favorite activities?
___ Pretending to be reading
___ Preening in a mirror
___ Pretending to be caring and selfless
___ Making a mess in the kitchen
___ Stinking up the house
___ Parading around the house half-naked (as long as my penis/breasts are tastefully blurred-out in post-production!)

___ Whining and complaining
___ Skinny dipping
___ Arguing about nothing
___ Picking my nose
___ Rollerblading in the dark, naked
___ Spouting politically-correct nonsense I heard on MTV

14. If we set you up in a fantastic place you could never afford on your own, and paid 100% of your food, utilities and rent, how would you act and feel about your life?
___ Depressed ___ Angry ___ Bitter (can we count on that?)

SECTION III — ESSAY QUESTION

Tell us about your best tantrum ever. (Use a separate sheet of paper...hopefully several!)

SECTION IV — REFERENCES

List three people who will swear that you are an annoying egotist who's impossible to live with!

NAME_____ ADDRESS_____ PHONE_____
NAME_____ ADDRESS_____ PHONE_____
NAME_____ ADDRESS_____ PHONE_____

I CERTIFY that my answers above — whether true or not — are as hip and trendy as I can possibly make them. I hereby agree that, if selected, I will give up my privacy, my dignity and any and all embarrassing personal secrets to: The Real World™; Bunim/Murray Productions; MTV Networks; Viacom, Inc.; and every slacker Real World viewer who, by the mere fact that they're watching, proves they have nothing better to do than dissect my pathetic life!

SIGNATURE_____

DATE_____